T0190412

Lecture Notes in Computer Science 12865

Founding Editors

Gerhard Goos
Karlsruhe Institute of Technology, Karlsruhe, Germany

Juris Hartmanis
Cornell University, Ithaca, NY, USA

Editorial Board Members

Elisa Bertino
Purdue University, West Lafayette, IN, USA

Wen Gao
Peking University, Beijing, China

Bernhard Steffen
TU Dortmund University, Dortmund, Germany

Gerhard Woeginger
RWTH Aachen, Aachen, Germany

Moti Yung
Columbia University, New York, NY, USA

More information about this subseries at http://www.springer.com/series/7407

François Boulier · Matthew England ·
Timur M. Sadykov · Evgenii V. Vorozhtsov (Eds.)

Computer Algebra in Scientific Computing

23rd International Workshop, CASC 2021
Sochi, Russia, September 13–17, 2021
Proceedings

 Springer

Editors
François Boulier ⓘ
Université de Lille
Villeneuve d'Ascq, France

Matthew England ⓘ
Coventry University
Coventry, UK

Timur M. Sadykov ⓘ
Plekhanov Russian University of Economics
Moscow, Russia

Evgenii V. Vorozhtsov ⓘ
Institute of Theoretical and Applied
Mechanics
Novosibirsk, Russia

ISSN 0302-9743   ISSN 1611-3349 (electronic)
Lecture Notes in Computer Science
ISBN 978-3-030-85164-4   ISBN 978-3-030-85165-1 (eBook)
https://doi.org/10.1007/978-3-030-85165-1

LNCS Sublibrary: SL1 – Theoretical Computer Science and General Issues

© Springer Nature Switzerland AG 2021
This work is subject to copyright. All rights are reserved by the Publisher, whether the whole or part of the material is concerned, specifically the rights of translation, reprinting, reuse of illustrations, recitation, broadcasting, reproduction on microfilms or in any other physical way, and transmission or information storage and retrieval, electronic adaptation, computer software, or by similar or dissimilar methodology now known or hereafter developed.
The use of general descriptive names, registered names, trademarks, service marks, etc. in this publication does not imply, even in the absence of a specific statement, that such names are exempt from the relevant protective laws and regulations and therefore free for general use.
The publisher, the authors and the editors are safe to assume that the advice and information in this book are believed to be true and accurate at the date of publication. Neither the publisher nor the authors or the editors give a warranty, expressed or implied, with respect to the material contained herein or for any errors or omissions that may have been made. The publisher remains neutral with regard to jurisdictional claims in published maps and institutional affiliations.

This Springer imprint is published by the registered company Springer Nature Switzerland AG
The registered company address is: Gewerbestrasse 11, 6330 Cham, Switzerland

Preface

The International Workshop on Computer Algebra in Scientific Computing (CASC) provides the opportunity both for researchers in theoretical computer algebra (CA) and engineers, as well as other allied professionals applying CA tools for solving problems in industry and in various branches of scientific computing, to present their results annually. CASC is the forum of excellence for the exploration of the frontiers in the field of computer algebra and its applications in scientific computing. It brings together scholars, engineers, and scientists from various disciplines that include computer algebra. This workshop provides a platform for the delegates to exchange new ideas and application experiences, share research results, and discuss existing issues and challenges.

Sirius Mathematics Center (SMC), located in the city of Sochi, Russian Federation, was established in 2019 by the "Talent and Success" Educational Foundation. This is an international institution for research and postgraduate training in mathematical sciences. Currently, the center uses the facilities of the Omega Sirius Hotel located between Sochi Olympic Park and the former Olympic Village near the Black Sea coast. The mission of the center is to support mathematical research in Russia as well as to promote personal and scientific contacts between mathematicians. The center strives to be a meeting point for scientists working in mathematical sciences, enabling them to exchange ideas, initiate new projects, meet, and train students and young scientists.

The SMC Scientific Board is responsible for establishing selection criteria for proposals of activities at the SMC, evaluating the proposals, and developing the scientific program of the center. The current members are Maria J. Esteban (CEREMADE, CNRS, and Université Paris-Dauphine, Paris), Sergey Lando (Higher School of Economics, Moscow and Skolkovo Institute of Science and Technology, Moscow), Ari Laptev (Imperial College, London), Alexey Shchuplev (SMC, Director), and August Tsikh (Siberian Federal University, Krasnoyarsk). In the autumn of 2020, the SMC administration offered the CASC workshop organizers significant financial support for arranging the CASC 2021 workshop on the SMC platform.

Therefore, it was decided, in the autumn of 2020, that the 23rd CASC International Workshop would be held at the Sirius Mathematics Center, Sochi, on September 13–17, 2021.

The organizing committee of the CASC 2021 International Workshop has been monitoring the developing COVID-19 pandemic. The safety and well-being of all conference participants have been our priority. Due to the current international situation, CASC 2021 was exceptionally held in the hybrid format: those able to travel to Sochi have attended in person while those prevented from coming by the restrictions on international travel were offered the opportunity to present their work remotely.

This year, the CASC International Workshop had two categories of participation: (1) talks with accompanying papers to appear in these proceedings, and (2) talks with accompanying extended abstracts for distribution locally at the conference only. The latter was for work either already published, or not yet ready for publication, but in either case still new and of interest to the CASC audience. The former was strictly for new and original research results, ready for publication.

All papers submitted for the LNCS proceedings received a minimum of three reviews. In addition, the whole Program Committee was invited to comment and debate on all papers. In total, this volume contains 23 papers and two invited talks. The paper by Ioannis Emiris presents an invited talk but went through the regular review process.

The invited talk by Alicia Dickenstein is devoted to the motivation and description of several algebraic-geometric computational techniques used for the study of families of polynomials that arise in the realm of biochemical reaction networks. The standard modelling of biochemical reaction networks gives rise to systems of ordinary polynomial differential equations depending on parameters. One is thus led to study families of polynomial ordinary differential equations, with a combinatorial structure that comes from the digraph of reactions. Attempts to explore the parameter space, in order to predict properties of the associated systems, challenge the standard current computational tools because, even for moderately small networks, there are many variables and many parameters. It is shown that different techniques can be strengthened and applied for systems with special structure even if the number of variables and parameters is arbitrarily large; in particular, for the systems defined by Alicia Dickenstein and Pérez Millán termed MESSI (Modifications of type Enzyme-Substrate or Swap with Intermediates), which are abundant among the enzymatic mechanisms.

The invited talk presented by Ioannis Emiris addresses one of the main problems in distance geometry: given a set of distances for some pairs of points, one must determine the unspecified distances. This is highly motivated by applications in molecular biology, robotics, civil engineering, sensor networks, and data science. A new method is proposed that introduces a combinatorial process in terms of directed graphs with constrained orientations, and manages to improve in all dimensions the existing bounds for roots count; this is achieved by employing the m-Bézout bound, thus arriving at tighter results than using the classic Bézout bound. The method readily leads to bounds on the m-Bézout number of a polynomial system, provided that the given system can be modelled by a graph whose vertices correspond to the variable subsets and whose edges correspond to the given equations.

Polynomial algebra, which is at the core of CA, is represented by contributions devoted to the use of comprehensive Gröbner bases for testing binomiality of chemical reaction networks, the parallel factorization of polynomials with multivariate power series coefficients, a new version of the root radii algorithm for finding the roots of a univariate polynomial, the use of subresultant chains for the solution of polynomial systems, the extension of Fulton's algorithm for determining the intersection multiplicity of two plane curves to the higher-dimensional case, the use of the resultants and of the computer algebra system (CAS) MAPLE in the investigation of the geometric properties of Fermat–Torricelli points on a sphere, and the derivation with the aid of Gröbner bases of new optimal symplectic fourth-order Runge–Kutta–Nyström methods for the numerical solution of molecular dynamics problems.

Four papers deal with ordinary and partial differential equations: the use of Weil algebras for the symbolic computation of univariate and multivariate higher-order partial derivatives, establishing the relationship between differential algebra and tropical differential algebra, applications of primitive recursive ordered fields to the computability and complexity of solution operators for some partial differential equations (PDEs), and the solution with guaranteed precision of the Cauchy problem for linear evolutionary systems of PDEs in the case of real analytic initial data.

Two papers are devoted to the applications of symbolic-numerical computations for computing orthonormal bases of the SU(3) group for orbital angular momentum implemented in the CAS MATHEMATICA and symbolic and numeric computations of the Frobenius norm real stability radius for some classes of matrices.

Applications of computer algebra systems in mechanics, physics, and chemistry are represented by the following themes: the derivation of first integrals and invariant manifolds in the generalized problem of the motion of a rigid body in a magnetic field with the aid of Gröbner bases and the CAS MATHEMATICA, and the detection of toricity of steady state varieties of chemical reaction networks with the aid of the CAS REDUCE.

The remaining topics include a new algorithm for decoupling multivariate fractions with the aid of trees, the simplification of nested real radicals in the CASs of a general kind, improved algorithms for approximate GCD in terms of robustness and distance, rational solutions of pseudo-linear systems, a new algorithm for testing the supersingularity of elliptic curves by using the Legendre form of elliptic curves, a new deterministic method for computing the Milnor number of an isolated complete intersection singularity, a new algorithm for computing the integer hull of a rational polyhedral set, and the construction of 8958 new nonisomorphic parallelisms of the three-dimensional projective space over the finite field $\mathbb{F}_5$.

Sadly, Vladimir P. Gerdt, who was one of the two co-founders (along with Prof. Dr. Ernst W. Mayr, Technical University of Munich) of the CASC International Workshops, passed away on January 5, 2021. In honor and memory of V.P. Gerdt, this volume contains an obituary which describes his contributions to different branches of computer algebra and to quantum computing. A special session dedicated to Gerdt's memory was held during this workshop.

The CASC 2021 workshop was supported financially by a generous grant from the Sirius Mathematics Center headed by Dr. Alexey Shchuplev. We appreciate that the SMC provided free accommodation for a number of participants. We also gratefully acknowledge support by the Ministry of Science and Higher Education of the Russian Federation, grant No. FSSW-2020-0008.

The local organizing committee of CASC 2021 at the Sirius Mathematics Center in Sochi provided excellent conference facilities, which enabled foreign participants to present their talks remotely.

Our particular thanks are due to the members of the CASC 2021 local organizing committee and staff at the SMC, i.e., Vitaly Krasikov (Chair), Alexey Shchuplev, Natalia Tokareva, Irina Klevtsova, Peter Karpov, Sergey Tikhomirov, and Timur Zhukov who ably handled all the local arrangements in Sochi.

Furthermore, we want to thank all the members of the Program Committee for their thorough work. We also thank the external referees who provided reviews.

We are grateful to the members of the group headed by Timur Sadykov for their technical help in the preparation of the camera-ready files for this volume. We are grateful to Dmitry Lyakhov (King Abdullah University of Science and Technology, Kingdom of Saudi Arabia) for the design of the conference poster. Finally, we are grateful to the CASC publicity chairs Hassan Errami and Dmitry Lyakhov for the management of the conference web page http://www.casc-conference.org/2021/.

July 2021   François Boulier
                                                             Matthew England
                                                             Timur M. Sadykov
                                                             Evgenii V. Vorozhtsov

Organization

CASC 2021 was hosted by Sirius Mathematics Center, Sochi, Russia.

Workshop General Chairs

François Boulier	Université de Lille, France
Timur M. Sadykov	Plekhanov Russian University of Economics, Russia

Program Committee Chairs

Matthew England	Research Centre for Computational Science & Mathematical Modelling, UK
Evgenii V. Vorozhtsov	Khristianovich Institute of Theoretical and Applied Mechanics, Russia

Program Committee

Changbo Chen	Key Laboratory of Automated Reasoning and Cognition Center, Chongqing Institute of Green and Intelligent Technology, Chinese Academy of Sciences, China
Jin-San Cheng	KLMM, Institute of Systems Science, AMSS, Chinese Academy of Sciences, China
Victor F. Edneral	Lomonosov Moscow State University, Russia
Matthew England	Research Centre for Computational Science & Mathematical Modelling, UK
Jaime Gutierrez	Universidad de Cantabria, Spain
Sergey A. Gutnik	MGIMO University, Russia
Amir Hashemi	Isfahan University of Technology, Iran
Hui Huang	Dalian University of Technology, China
François Lemaire	Centre de Recherche en Informatique, Signal et Automatique, France
Dominik L. Michels	KAUST, Saudi Arabia
Marc Moreno Maza	University of Western Ontario, Canada
Chenqi Mou	Beihang University, China
Gleb Pogudin	Institute Polytechnqiue de Paris, France
Alexander Prokopenya	Warsaw University of Life Sciences – SGGW, Poland
Hamid Rahkooy	Max Planck Institute for Informatics, Germany
Eugenio Roanes-Lozano	Universidad Complutense de Madrid, Spain
Timur M. Sadykov	Plekhanov Russian University of Economics, Russia
Doru Stefanescu (†)	University of Bucharest, Romania
Thomas Sturm	Lorraine Research Laboratory in Computer Science and its Applications, France
Akira Terui	University of Tsukuba, Japan
Elias Tsigaridas	Inria Paris, France
Jan Verschelde	University of Illinois at Chicago, USA

Local Organization

Vitaly Krasikov (Chair)	Plekhanov Russian University of Economics, Russia
Alexey Shchuplev	Sirius Mathematics Center, Russia
Peter Karpov	Plekhanov Russian University of Economics, Russia
Sergey Tikhomirov	Yaroslavl State Pedagogical University, Russia
Timur Zhukov	Plekhanov Russian University of Economics, Russia

Publicity Chairs

Hassan Errami	Universität Bonn, Germany
Dmitry Lyakhov	KAUST, Saudi Arabia

Advisory Board

Vladimir P. Gerdt (†)	Joint Institute for Nuclear Research, Russia
Wolfram Koepf	Universität Kassel, Germany
Ernst W. Mayr	Technische Universität München, Germany
Werner M. Seiler	Universität Kassel, Germany

Website

http://casc-conference.org/2021/
(Webmaster: Peter Karpov)

Memories on Vladimir Gerdt

Ernst W. Mayr[1], Werner M. Seiler[2], and Evgenii V. Vorozhtsov[3]

[1] Technical University of Munich, Dept. of Informatics, Chair of Efficient Algorithms, I14,
Boltzmannstrasse 3, 85748 Garching, Germany
[2] Institute for Mathematics, University of Kassel, 34109 Kassel, Germany
[3] Khristianovich Institute of Theoretical and Applied Mechanics of the Siberian Branch
of the Russian Academy of Sciences, Novosibirsk 630090, Russia
mayr@in.tum.de, seiler@mathematik.uni-kassel.de, vevg46@mail.ru

Prof. Vladimir P. Gerdt

It is our deepest regret to inform you that Vladimir Petrovich Gerdt, Professor, Head of
the Algebraic and Quantum Computing Group of the Scientific Department of Computational Physics of the Laboratory of Information Technologies (LIT) at the Joint Institute
of Nuclear Research (JINR) in Dubna, Oblast Moscow, Russia, died on January 5th, 2021
at the age of 73, following complications caused by COVID-19. Vladimir Gerdt was born
on January 21, 1947 in the town of Engels, Saratov region of the USSR. He began his
scientific career at JINR in November 1971, after graduating from the Physics Department of Saratov State University, first in the Department of Radiation Safety, and from
February 1977 on in the Laboratory of Computer Technology and Automation, which,
in the year 2000, was renamed to Laboratory of Information Technologies, where he was
engaged in the deployment of analytical computing software systems on the computers of the JINR Central Research Center, as well as their development and application
for solving physical problems. In 1983, he became the head of the Computer Algebra
Research Group (renamed in 2007 to Algebraic and Quantum Computing Group) at LIT.
In 1976, Vladimir Gerdt successfully defended his Ph.D. thesis (for *Kandidat nauk*) in
the field *Theoretical and Mathematical Physics*, and in 1992, his doctoral dissertation

(for *Doktor nauk*, D.Sc.) in the field *Application of Computer Technology, Mathematical Modeling, and Mathematical Methods for Scientific Research*. In 1997, he was awarded the academic title of Professor. In his long and distinguished research career, Vladimir Gerdt worked on many different topics. Even when he started to work on something new, he never forgot the old topics. Often, he also looked for, in a creative form, possible relationships between his various research questions exhibiting numerous interesting connections. In the following, we try to organize his research works into seven fields in which he was active and which we list roughly in chronological order according to his first publication in the respective field (and we also apologize for any omissions or errors due to our bias and the requirement to be succinct):

1. Physics: high energy physics, gauge theory and constrained dynamics
2. Differential equations: integrable systems, symmetry theory and completion questions
3. Lie algebra: representations and classifications
4. Commutative algebra: Gröbner and involutive bases, polynomial system solving
5. Differential and difference algebra: differential/difference ideal theory and non-commutative Gröbner and involutive bases
6. Quantum computing: quantum circuits and related algebraic problems, simulation of quantum algorithms, quantum error correction, mixed states
7. Numerical analysis: algebraic construction of finite difference methods, symbolic-numerical solution of quantum mechanical problems

In the sequel, we try to trace the main steps in Vladimir's scientific activities over his whole career spanning a period of almost 50 years. Of course, it is not possible to present everything he did, and our selection is certainly subjective and biased by our own research interest and, possibly, lack of knowledge. Nevertheless, we believe that this account is able to convey how broad his research interests were and how many important contributions he made. As, over the years, Vladimir collaborated with so many different people, we here omit the names of his cooperation partners in the various fields.

Vladimir began his career like many of the pioneers in computer algebra as a physicist. His first publications in the mid 1970s were concerned with phenomenological computations in high energy physics aiming at predicting the results of accelerator experiments. As such computations tend to be very demanding and time consuming, it was a natural thought to try to automatize them at least partially using computer algebra. Thus, his first publication with the words "computer algebra" in the title appeared in 1978 and was concerned with the computation of Feynman integrals (essentially the same problem that inspired a bit over a decade earlier Tony Hearn to develop Reduce, together with Macsyma the first general purpose computer algebra systems). At this time, for most physicists or mathematicians, computer algebra was still something rather exotic and a comprehensive list of articles describing such applications of computer algebra was rather short.

As many problems in physics boil down to the analysis of differential equations, it is not surprising that from the early 1980s on Vladimir got more and more involved in their theory. In the beginning, he was mainly interested in two topics: the explicit solution of ordinary differential equations and the theory of (completely) integrable systems. He developed for example a method to solve certain linear ordinary differential equations in terms of elliptic functions. Following ideas developed in the school of A.B. Shabat, he worked on computer algebra methods for the algorithmic classification of integrable systems in the form of evolution equations using symmetry methods (mainly generalized symmetries, often incorrectly called Lie-Bäcklund symmetries, although neither Lie nor Bäcklund ever worked on them). Again, in most cases, a symmetry analysis requires extensive computations and thus represents a natural application field for computer algebra. In fact, Vladimir never ceased to be interested in symmetry methods for differential equations. It was probably through these works that for the first time Vladimir also attracted the attention of a larger audience in the western computer algebra world, when he published no less than four articles in the proceedings of the EUROCAL '87 conference in Leipzig. His first paper in the Journal of Symbolic Computation, published in 1990, was also devoted to integrable systems.

The integrability analysis of evolution equations raises many interesting problems. In intermediate steps, one often has to solve large overdetermined systems of linear differential equations or one has to deal with polynomial systems. Symmetry reductions typically lead to ordinary differential equations, which one would like to solve analytically. The theory of Lie groups and algebras also features here prominently. Hence, in the early 1990s Vladimir started to work on these topics, independently from their direct application in the context of integrability analysis. He co-authored a computer algebra package for the analysis of polynomial systems using Gröbner basis techniques. In parallel, he began with the investigation of (super) Lie algebras — partially again using Gröbner bases. In the beginning, he was interested in automatically recognizing isomorphic Lie algebras. Later, he was more concerned with finitely presented Lie algebras and superalgebras. Here he developed in particular an algorithm for the construction of such (super)algebras out of a finite set of generators and relations.

The late 1990s represent a key phase in Vladimir's scientific oeuvre. From his research in Lie symmetry theory, he was familiar with the Janet-Riquier theory of differential equations, as it provides a popular approach to analyzing the large determining systems arising in the construction of Lie symmetry algebras. And, as just mentioned, he also was familiar with Gröbner bases from commutative algebra. From Janet's work on differential equations, he abstracted a general notion of what he called an involutive division and introduced, by combining it with concepts like normal forms and term orders, the notion of an involutive basis of a polynomial ideal as a Gröbner basis with additional combinatorial properties. For the rest of his life, involutive bases played a dominant role in Vladimir's research.

He was particularly interested in their algorithmic aspects. The basic involutive algorithm —rooted in Janet's work— can be seen as an optimization of the basic form of Buchberger's algorithm for the construction of Gröbner bases. Vladimir developed further optimizations specific to the involutive algorithm and adapted optimizations for the Buchberger algorithm to make them applicable also in the involutive setting. His group at JINR wrote the GINV package in C/C++ as a standalone program for (mainly) computing Janet bases and he participated in a Maple implementation of involutive bases.

Being a physicist, Vladimir recognized the possibilities offered by Gröbner or involutive bases in the context of mechanical systems with constraints. The famous Dirac procedure is essentially a differential completion procedure for the special case of Hamiltonian systems with constraints followed by a separation of the constraints into two different classes: first, constraints generating gauge symmetries, and second, constraints reducing the dimension of the phase space. While, in principle, the procedure is quite straightforward, it involves a notorious number of subtleties and pitfalls when applied to concrete systems. Vladimir showed that in the case of a polynomial Lagrangian most of these can be handled using Gröbner bases and provided a corresponding Maple package. Later, he co-authored a number of papers where these ideas were used to extend the classical Dirac procedure to light-cone Yang-Mills mechanics.

Rings of linear differential or difference operators may be considered as simple examples of non-commutative polynomial rings, and it is rather straightforward to adapt Gröbner or involutive bases to them. All implementations of involutive bases co-authored by Vladimir cover these two cases as well. For systems of linear differential or difference equations, such algorithms for instance allow for an effective completion to involutive or passive form, i.e., for the construction of all hidden integrability conditions, a fact relevant for analytic as well as numerical studies of the systems. In particular, it is crucial for determining the size of the solution space or consistent initial value problems.

The situation becomes much more complicated for non-linear systems. Around 2000, Vladimir started to look more deeply into differential algebra, in particular into differential ideal theory, and a bit later also into difference algebra. His key achievement here was the revival of the Thomas decomposition, an almost forgotten approach to both algebraic and differential ideal theory based on triangular sets and — in the differential case — Janet-Riquier theory. In a Thomas decomposition, an arbitrary system composed of equations and inequations is split into a disjoint union of so-called simple systems which are comparatively easy to analyze, because of their special properties. The disjointness of the resulting simple systems represents a specific feature of the Thomas decomposition, setting it apart from most other decompositions. Together with a group at RWTH in Aachen, Vladimir developed a fully algorithmic version of both the algebraic and the differential Thomas decomposition and co-authored implementations of them in Maple.

In effect, the Thomas decomposition was the second research topic which Vladimir studied intensively right until his death. He applied it in many different fields, ranging from the integrability analysis of fully non-linear systems of (partial) differential equations to an extension of the Dirac procedure to cases where the ranks of certain Jacobians are not constant (a case about which one can find nothing in the classical literature, but which is not uncommon in applications). His last significant and unfortunately unfinished project consisted of developing a difference version of it.

One reason for Vladimir's interest in difference algebra was the analysis and construction of numerical methods. So-called mimetic methods aim at setting up difference equations that have qualitative properties similar to the original differential equations. Such qualitative properties can be conserved quantities or more generally symmetries, but also certain structural features, in particular for equations which are not in Cauchy-Kovalevskaya form. Starting in the mid 2000s, Vladimir became interested in the effective construction of finite difference and finite volume methods preserving certain algebraic structures of the differential ideal generated by the given differential equations. A rigorous formulation of these ideas required parallel theories of differential and difference algebra. For linear differential equations, classical techniques from Gröbner and involutive bases were sufficient to effectively realize his approach; for a fully algorithmic treatment in the case of non-linear equations a difference Thomas decomposition would have been necessary. Vladimir treated a number of concrete non-linear examples, but the algebraic computations had to be done partially by hand. The numerical methods arising from this approach are quite non-standard, differing significantly from the usually applied methods, and the numerical experiments presented so far appear to indicate good performance. For the analysis of these methods, he introduced new notions of consistency and developed computer algebra methods for verifying the corresponding conditions.

In another line of work combining many of his research interests, Vladimir participated in projects for the symbolic-numerical solution of quantum mechanical problems, in particular in atomic physics, ranging from solving time-dependent Schrödinger equations to eigenvalue problems and on to the computation of matrix elements and boundary value problems for elliptic systems. The emphasis was on finite-dimensional quantum systems like atoms in external fields or quantum dots.

Also since the mid 2000s, Vladimir and his group was quite active in the field of quantum computing (in fact, to such an extent that his group at JINR was renamed to better reflect this additional research focus). He concentrated on related algebraic problems to which he applied e.g. involutive methods. In the beginning, the emphasis was on the circuit model of quantum computing. Vladimir developed algorithms for the construction of polynomial systems or unitary matrices describing such circuits and co-authored corresponding Mathematica and C# packages. He was also concerned with the simulation of quantum computations on classical computers and co-authored a Mathematica package for this task. After a brief study of quantum error correction, he moved on to investigating mixed states, mainly by group-theoretic means. Here the emphasis was on the effective construction of local invariants, since these facilitate checking whether a state is entangled or uncoupled. For this purpose, he showed how involutive bases can be used within computational invariant theory.

During his last years, Vladimir returned to the topic of Lie symmetry theory. He was interested in the algorithmic linearization of ordinary differential equations, i.e., in the construction of a point transformation reducing the given equation to a linear one. Lie already had shown for certain cases that one can decide whether a given non-linear ordinary differential equation can be linearized, based on its Lie symmetry group. Later, this topic was studied extensively by Bluman and his group. Vladimir derived fully algorithmic criteria for linearizability (in part based on the differential Thomas decomposition), a result for which he and his co-authors received the distinguished paper award at the ISSAC conference in 2017. He continued to work on improvements of this result, putting more emphasis on the symmetry algebra instead of the symmetry group, but, unfortunately, he died before this project was finished.

Altogether, Vladimir was the author or co-author of more than 240 scientific papers (a listing is available at his CV at JINR, and he was a leading expert in the field of symbolic and algebraic computation. He devoted a lot of effort and energy to train young researchers in these modern scientific areas. He was a professor at the Department of Distributed Information Computing Systems of Dubna State University, where, under his supervision, seven students successfully defended their Ph.D. thesis.

Vladimir also was the organizer of many international conferences on computer algebra. He was the (co-)chair of 29 conferences, a member of the organizing committee of 11 conferences, a member of the Program Committee for 27 conferences, and a member of the Scientific and Advisory Committee of 7 conferences: 74 conferences in total during the period from 1979 to 2020. Thus, Vladimir had, on average, organizational roles in almost two conferences each year, showing his inexhaustible energy.

In the context of this CASC conference (of 2021 in Sochi), it may be an opportunity (and even appropriate) to enlarge a bit on the history of CASC, the international workshop series *Computer Algebra in Scientific Computing*, in particular the events before its birth in St. Petersburg on April 20, 1998. The other co-founder of CASC (one of the present authors, referred to EWM in the text below), first became aware of Vladimir's scientific work in October of 1996 when he (EWM) was working together with his Ph.D. student Klaus Kühnle on an optimal worst-case space bound for algorithms to compute Gröbner bases. Since this bound (exponential space) is independent of the algorithm used, the news about involutive bases were very interesting. The year after, on June 5, EWM invited Vladimir to give a seminar talk about Involutive Gröbner Bases at TUM, which was very well received. During the after-session-get-together at the Parkcafe in Munich, the question was raised about the share of theoretical talks vs. the talks devoted to the numerous applications of the methods and algorithms of computer algebra in the natural sciences. EWM said that "I am a theoretician and trying to connect to applications", and Vladimir said "I am more applied but don't mind theory". The two of them also agreed that there were excellent scientists in the computer algebra field in Russia as well as in Germany. EWM also said that he admired the science that had been going on in certain parts of what was then the Commonwealth of Independent States (CIS) (like Tashkent) since his early study years, that he always had wanted to go there but never managed (since, among other things, he went to Stanford and the US for almost ten years). And suddenly the idea was "Why don't we have a joint (between Russia and Germany, or CIS and Germany) scientific workshop (with the title CASC, that was discussed there already)". Vladimir then right away persuaded Ph.D. Nikolay Vasiliev in St. Petersburg to organize the first instantiation), so this went very fast. For the following fifteen years, the team at EWM's chair at TUM could always rely on Vladimir and his excellent connections in Russia and CIS to persuade very competent colleagues at a number of very interesting places to locally organize CASC.

1990 (ISSAC)   **2019 (CASC)**

It also turned out that the Deutsche Forschungsgemeinschaft (DFG) was willing to support the CASC workshop in St. Petersburg as well as those in the series for about the following ten years. This support was very helpful in the beginning of CASC, since whenever CASC took place outside of CIS, the funds were used solely for supporting participants from CIS; for CASC workshops in CIS, the method was a bit more difficult and indirect, but with basically the same result. It is clear that in the beginning of CASC, when the financial situation was much more restricted than now, this support from DFG was invaluable. Of course, there was also some organizational work for the conference (in addition to the local organization; like designing and putting out the call for papers (including the conference poster), running the PC, organizing travel, –, putting together the proceedings, ...). As everybody handling the nitty-gritty of conferences knows this was considerable work, at times quite stressful (the less money you have the more stress), and performed by just a few people in EWM's group (in particular, his secretary A. Schmidt, his research assistant Dr. W. Meixner, his programmer Ernst Bayer, and his Russian-Bavarian coordinator Dr. Victor Ganzha). They also deserve a lot of thanks for their efforts and contributions.

Since 1998, the CASC workshops have been held annually (with one gap in 2008, because of political unrest in Georgia), alternating in principle between Russia and Germany, but also including other countries of CIS, in Western and Central Europe, and even in Japan and China. Giving evidence to its widespread attractiveness, the sequence of locations was: St. Petersburg, Herrsching (Munich), Samarkand, Konstanz, Big Yalta, Passau, St. Petersburg/Ladoga, Kalamata, Chisinau, Bonn, – , Kobe, Tsakhkadzor, Kassel, Maribor, Berlin, Warsaw, Aachen, Bucharest, Beijing, Lille, Moscow, Linz, Sochi (also see the CASC bibliography).

Vladimir was the co-chair of the CASC series from its foundation in 1998 onward until 2019. He also was very active in the *Applications of Computer Algebra* (ACA) conference series where he regularly organized sessions, in particular on differential and difference algebra.

He was a member of the editorial board of the *Journal of Symbolic Computation* (JSC), from its foundation on until 2020. Since 1991, he was a member of the largest international scientific and educational computing society *Association for Computing Machinery* (ACM) and the German special interest group for Computer Algebra.

During the period from 1981 to 2013, Vladimir presented 34 lecture courses for students and young scientists in various universities of the USSR/Russian Federation as well as in China, France, Sweden, and especially in Germany. As his family was partially of German origin, he felt very attached to Germany, where he had a number of relatives, whom he frequently visited. Since the late 1990s, he came to Germany almost every year. As a guest lecturer or visiting professor, he spent in total more than five years at German universities and applied universities in Greifswald, Ravensburg-Weingarten, Aachen and Kassel, teaching a wide variety of courses.

Vladimir was the winner of the first prize of JINR in 1986, the second prize of JINR in 2015 in the competition of scientific and methodological works. He was awarded the medal "In memory of the 850th anniversary of Moscow", the departmental badge of distinction in the field "Veteran of Nuclear Energy and Industry", and the "Certificate of Honor" of JINR. He was the founder of and a scientific leader at the School of Computer Algebra and Quantum Computing of JINR. As such, he largely defined the public perception of the Laboratory.

Optimism, openness, goodwill, and sincere interest in science always characterized Vladimir. He will be sadly missed by all who had the pleasure to collaborate and interact with him, and we would like to extend our sincere condolences to his colleagues and friends and, above all, his wife Evgeniya Almazova and his two sons, Anton and Peter.

Contents

Families of Polynomials in the Study of Biochemical Reaction Networks

Alicia Dickenstein[(✉)]

Department of Mathematics, FCEN, University of Buenos Aires and IMAS
(UBA-CONICET), C. Universitaria, Pab. I, C1428EGA Buenos Aires, Argentina
`alidick@dm.uba.ar`

Abstract. The standard mass-action kinetics modeling of the dynamics of biochemical reaction networks gives rise to systems of ordinary polynomial differential equations with (in general unknown) parameters. Attempts to explore the parameter space in order to predict properties of the associated systems challenge the standard current computational tools because even for moderately small networks we need to study families of polynomials with many variables and many parameters. These polynomials have a combinatorial structure that comes from the digraph of reactions. We show that different techniques can be strengthened and applied for biochemical networks with special structure.

1 Introduction

The basic definitions and properties of chemical reaction networks, together with the features of some important biochemical networks, can be found in the surveys [7–9] and Chap. 5 of the book [6], as well as in the book [12]. The starting information is a finite directed graph with r labeled edges that correspond to the reactions and nodes that correspond to complexes, given by nonnegative integer linear combinations of a set of s chemical species. The concentrations $x = (x_1, \ldots, x_s)$ of the chemical species are viewed as functions of time. Under mass-action kinetics, the labels of the edges are positive numbers called reaction rate constants and x is assumed to satisfy an autonomous system of ordinary differential equations $\frac{dx}{dt} = f(x)$. Here $f = (f_1, \ldots, f_s)$ is a vector of real polynomials that reflects the combinatorics of the graph.

The reaction rate constants are in general unknown or difficult to measure. Standard methods in other sciences involve exhaustive sampling. Instead, we think the vector κ of reaction rate constants as a vector of parameters. In general, there are further parameters involved in this setting. Linear relations describing the span S of the difference of the complexes on each side of a reaction give rise to linear conservation constants of the dynamics. This means that given a basis $\ell_1, \ldots, \ell_d$ of the orthogonal subspace $S^\perp$, any solution x defined in an interval satisfies linear constraints of the form $\ell_1(x) = T_1, \ldots, \ell_d(x) = T_d$. We say that $T = (T_1, \ldots, T_d)$ is a vector of total amounts and we consider (κ, T) as parameters.

© Springer Nature Switzerland AG 2021
F. Boulier et al. (Eds.): CASC 2021, LNCS 12865, pp. 1–5, 2021.
https://doi.org/10.1007/978-3-030-85165-1_1

The steady states of the the system $\frac{dx}{dt} = f(x)$ are the constant trajectories, that is the values of x^* for which $f(x^*) = 0$. If a trajectory converges, its limit is a steady state. Stable steady states attract nearby trajectories and unstable steady states also drive the dynamics. Multistationarity is a crucial property for chemical reaction networks modeling biological processes, since it allows for different "responses" of the cell. It corresponds to the existence of more than one *positive* steady state with the same total amounts, that is, to the existence of at least two positive zeros of the ideal $\langle f_1 \ldots, f_s, \ell_1 - T_1, \ldots, \ell_d - T_d \rangle$.

We look at these systems as special families of polynomial ordinary differential equations in s variables with $r + d$ parameters. Our aim is to explore the parameter space in order to predict properties of the systems associated to networks studied in systems biology, which usually have too many variables and too many parameters. There are many useful mathematical and computational tools, but we are forced to extend the mathematical results and to understand the structure of the networks to make the computations feasible.

In the following sections, I will very briefly summarize two of these recent advances. Besides consulting the references, the reader is invited to attend my lecture or to watch later the video for more information.

2   The ERK Pathway

As an example of more general results, we discuss the ERK pathway. It is an enzymatic network that consists of a cascade of phosphorylation of proteins in the cell that communicates a signal from a receptor on the outside membrane to the DNA inside the nucleus. It controlls different responses such as cell division [19]. It is known that the ERK pathway has the capacity for multistationarity and there are oscillatory solutions.

Deciding mulstistationarity is a question in real algebraic geometry that can be effectively decided in practice, but the associated family has 21 variables and $36 = 30 + 6$ parameters. So, how is it that we can study it with an algebro-geometric approach? This important signaling cascade, as most popular models in systems biology, has a *MESSI structure* [21]. There is a partition of the set of species and only certain type of reactions occur. Using this structure, we give combinatorial conditions on the network that ensure the following:

- There are no relevant boundary steady states. That is, there are no steady states (zeros of the polynomials $f_1, \ldots, f_{21}$) in the boundary of the nonnegative orthant which lie in the closure of the linear variety $S_T = \{\ell_1(x) = T_1, \ldots, \ell_d(x) = T_6\}$, for any choice of $\kappa \in \mathbb{R}^{30}_{>0}$ and T such that S_T intersects the positive orthant.
- The intersections $S_T \cap \mathbb{R}^{21}_{\geq 0}$ are compact and so the system is conservative.
- The system is *linearly binomial*, a concept introduced in [11], which implies that there is a system of binomial generators of the ideal $\langle f_1, \ldots, f_{21} \rangle$ obtained by linear algebra operations over $\mathbb{Q}(\kappa)$, involving rational functions whose denominators do not vanish over $\mathbb{R}^{30}_{>0}$.

– The positive points of the steady state variety $\{x \in \mathbb{R}^{21}_{>0} : f(x) = 0\}$ can be cut out by explicit binomials, and thus parametrized by explicit monomials with coefficients in $\mathbb{Q}(\kappa)$ as above.

One way to approximate the dynamics of biological models while dealing with less variables and parameters, is the elimination of the *intermediate complexes* [14]. Following [24], one could ask which are the minimal sets (with respect to inclusion) of intermediates that still give rise to multistationarity. These sets are termed *circuits of multistationarity*. We show in our forthcoming paper [10] that systems like the ERK pathway without intermediates cannot be multistationary and we use a computer algebra system to find all the corresponding circuits of multistationarity. We can also identify the circuits of multistationarity for phosphorylation networks with any number of species. The theoretical results are based on [5, 22].

3 Degenerations and Open Regions of Multistationarity

In the beautiful paper [3], regular subdivisions of the (convex hull of the) set of exponents of a polynomial system are used to get a lower bound on the number of positive solutions, with combinatorial arguments to get new lower bounds in terms of the number of variables and the difference between the cardinality of the support and the number of variables. This is based on classical results on degenerations that were used in [25] to study real roots of complete intersections. The idea is to add a parameter u raised to the different heights of a fixed lifting whose projection produces the given regular subdivision, thus giving a deformation of the coefficients of the system along a curve. For small positive values of u, one obtains a degeneration of the original system for which a lower bound on the number of positive roots can be given in terms of *decorated* simplices in the regular subdivision. Again, this is in general unfeasible in practice when there are many variables and many monomials.

On one side, we show how to replace a deformation using a single parameter with an open set defined in terms of the cone of all height functions that produce the regular subdivision. This way, we get an open region in parameter space where multistationarity occurs [2]. Even if deciding if simplices are part of a same regular subdivision is algorithmic, in order to do this when the dimension or the number of monomials is big, we use the simple idea that if two simplices share a facet, then this is always the case. Moreover, we heavily use results about the structure of *s-toric* MESSI systems from [21]. This allows us to find these open regions for cascades with any number of layers in [15], but the lower bound that we get is three. Regions of multistationarity with higher lower bounds are in general unknown, except for the case of sequential distributive phosphorylation networks [16]. There is also a degeneration approach with one parameter using arguments from geometric singular perturbation theory in [13].

4   Other Computational Approaches

There are several other computational approaches to study these systems. Of course, symbolic software using Gröbner bases and in particular real algebraic geometry libraries, as well as Cylindrical Algebraic Decomposition software. Also numerical methods in algebraic geometry can be used [17,18], as well as tropical tools to separate time scales [23]. Machine learning tools started to be used to improve both the symbolic and numeric calculations [1,4,20].

Acknowledgments. We acknowledge the support of ANPCyT PICT 2016-0398, UBACYT 20020170100048BA and CONICET PIP 11220150100473, Argentina.

References

1. Bernal, E., Hauenstein, J., Mehta, D, Regan, M., Tang, T.: Machine learning the discriminant locus. Preprint available at arXiv:2006.14078 (2020)
2. Bihan, F., Giaroli, M., Dickenstein, A.: Lower bounds for positive roots and regions of multistationarity in chemical reaction networks. J. Algebra **542**, 367–411 (2020)
3. Bihan, F., Santos, F., Spaenlehauer, P.-J.: A polyhedral method for sparse systems with many positive solutions. SIAM J. Appl. Algebra Geom. **2**(4), 620–645 (2018)
4. Böhm, J., Decker, W., Frühbis-Krüger, A., Pfreundt, F.-J., Rahn, M., Ristau, L.: Towards massively parallel computations in algebraic geometry. Found. Comput. Math. **21**(3), 767–806 (2020). https://doi.org/10.1007/s10208-020-09464-x
5. Conradi, C., Feliu, E., Mincheva, M., Wiuf, C.: Identifying parameter regions for multistationarity. PLoS Comput. Biol. **13**(10), e1005751 (2017)
6. Cox, D.A.: Applications of Polynomial Systems, with contributions by C. D'Andrea, A. Dickenstein, J. Hauenstein, H.Schenck, and J. Sidman. Co-publication of the AMS and CBMS (2020)
7. Dickenstein, A.: Biochemical reaction networks: an invitation for algebraic geometers. In: MCA 2013, Contemporary Mathematics, vol. 656, pp. 65–83 (2016)
8. Dickenstein, A.: Algebra and geometry in the study of enzymatic cascades. In: Araujo, C., Benkart, G., Praeger, C.E., Tanbay, B. (eds.) World Women in Mathematics 2018. AWMS, vol. 20, pp. 57–81. Springer, Cham (2019). https://doi.org/10.1007/978-3-030-21170-7_2
9. Dickenstein, A.: Algebraic geometry tools in systems biology. Notices Amer. Math. Soc. **67**(11), 1706–1715 (2020)
10. Dickenstein, A., Giaroli, M., Pérez Millán, M., Rischter, R.: Detecting the multistationarity structure in enzymatic networks. Manuscript (2021)
11. Dickenstein, A., Pérez Millán, M., Shiu, A., Tang, X.: Mutistationarity in structured reaction networks. Bull. Math. Biol. **81**, 1527–1581 (2019)
12. Feinberg, M.: Foundations of Chemical Reaction Network Theory. AMS, vol. 202. Springer, Cham (2019). https://doi.org/10.1007/978-3-030-03858-8
13. Feliu, E., Rendall, A., Wiuf, C.: A proof of unlimited multistability for phosphorylation cycles. Nonlinearity **33**(11), 5629 (2020)
14. Feliu, E., Wiuf, C.: Simplifying biochemical models with intermediate species. J. R. Soc. Interface **10**, 20130484 (2013)
15. Giaroli, M., Bihan, F., Dickenstein, A.: Regions of multistationarity in cascades of Goldbeter-Koshland loops. J. Math. Biol. **78**(4), 1115–1145 (2019)

16. Giaroli, M., Rischter, R., Pérez Millán, M., Dickenstein, A.: Parameter regions that give rise to $2\lfloor\frac{n}{2}\rfloor + 1$ positive steady states in the n-site phosphorylation system. Math. Biosci. Eng. **16**(6), 7589–7615 (2019)

17. Gross, E., Harrington, H.A., Rosen, Z., Sturmfels, B.: Algebraic systems biology: a case study for the Wnt pathway. Bull. Math. Biol. **78**(1), 21–51 (2015). https://doi.org/10.1007/s11538-015-0125-1

18. Nam, K., Gyori, B., Amethyst, S., Bates, D., Gunawardena, J.: Robustness and parameter geography in post-translational modification systems. PLoS Comput. Biol. **16**(5), e1007573 (2020)

19. Patel, A., Shvartsman, S.: Outstanding questions in developmental ERK signaling. Development **145**(14), dev143818 (2018)

20. Peifer, D., Stillman, M., Halpern-Leistner, D.: Learning selection strategies in Buchberger's algorithm. In: Proceedings of the 37th International Conference on Machine Learning, Online, PMLR 119, pp. 7575–7585 (2020)

21. Pérez Millán, M., Dickenstein, A.: The structure of MESSI biological systems. SIAM J. Appl. Dyn. Syst. **17**(2), 1650–1682 (2018)

22. Pérez Millán, M., Dickenstein, A., Shiu, A., Conradi, C.: Chemical reaction systems with toric steady states. Bull. Math. Biol. **74**(5), 1027–1065 (2012)

23. Radulescu, O.: Tropical geometry of biological systems (*Invited Talk*). In: Boulier, F., England, M., Sadykov, T.M., Vorozhtsov, E.V. (eds.) CASC 2020. LNCS, vol. 12291, pp. 1–13. Springer, Cham (2020). https://doi.org/10.1007/978-3-030-60026-6_1

24. Sadeghimanesh, A., Feliu, E.: The multistationarity structure of networks with intermediates and a binomial core network. Bull. Math. Biol. **81**, 2428–2462 (2019)

25. Sturmfels, B.: On the number of real roots of a sparse polynomial system. In: Hamiltonian and Gradient Flows, Algorithms and Control, Fields Inst. Commun., 3, Amer. Math. Soc., Providence, RI, pp. 137–143 (1994)

The m-Bézout Bound and Distance Geometry

Evangelos Bartzos[1,2](✉), Ioannis Z. Emiris[2,1], and Charalambos Tzamos[1]

[1] Department of Informatics and Telecommunications,
National and Kapodistrian University of Athens, 15784 Athens, Greece
{vbartzos,emiris,ctzamos}@di.uoa.gr
[2] "Athena" Research Center, 15125 Maroussi, Greece
emiris@athenarc.gr

Abstract. We offer a closed-form bound on the m-Bézout bound for multi-homogeneous systems whose equations include two variable subsets of the same degree. Our bound is expectedly not tight, since computation of the m-Bézout number is #P-hard by reduction to the permanent. On the upside, our bound is tighter than the existing closed-form bound derived from the permanent, which applies only to systems characterized by further structure.

Our work is inspired by the application of the m-Bézout bound to counting Euclidean embeddings of distance graphs. Distance geometry and rigidity theory study graphs with a finite number of configurations, up to rigid transformations, which are prescribed by the edge lengths. Counting embeddings is an algebraic question once one constructs a system whose solutions correspond to the different embeddings. Surprisingly, the best asymptotic bound on the number of embeddings had for decades been Bézout's, applied to the obvious system of quadratic equations expressing the length constraints. This is essentially 2^{dn}, for graphs of n vertices in d dimensions, and implies a bound of 4^n for the most famous case of Laman graphs in the plane. However, the best lower bound is about 2.5^n, which follows by numerically solving appropriate instances.

In [3], the authors leverage the m-Bézout bound and express it by the number of certain constrained orientations of simple graphs. A combinatorial process on these graphs has recently improved the bound on orientations and, therefore, has improved the bounds on the number of distance graph embeddings [4]. For Laman graphs the new bound is inferior to 3.8^n thus improving upon Bézout's bound for the first time. In this paper, we obtain a closed-form bound on the m-Bézout number of a class of multi-homogeneous systems that subsumes the systems encountered in distance graph embeddings.

Keywords: Graph embeddings · Graph orientations · Multi-homogeneous Bézout bound · Matrix permanent

EB was fully supported by project ARCADES which has received funding from the European Union's Horizon 2020 research and innovation programme under the Marie Skłodowska-Curie grant agreement No 675789. The authors are members of team ARO-MATH, joint between INRIA Sophia-Antipolis, France, and NKUA.

© Springer Nature Switzerland AG 2021
F. Boulier et al. (Eds.): CASC 2021, LNCS 12865, pp. 6–20, 2021.
https://doi.org/10.1007/978-3-030-85165-1_2

1   Introduction

Distance Geometry is the branch of mathematics studying configurations of sets of points, when only (some of) their distances are known. Given a set of distances for some pairs of points, one of the main problems in Distance Geometry is to determine the unspecified distances. This is highly motivated by applications in molecular biology [16], robotics [26], civil engineering [1,13], sensor network localization [27], data science [18], material theory [8,22].

Rigidity theory studies the properties of graphs that have rigid embeddings in Euclidean space for fixed edge weights that represent length between points. Rigidity is defined for a specific embedding space. Let $G = (V, E)$ be a simple undirected graph and $\mathbf{p} = \{p_1, \ldots, p_{|V|}\} \in \mathbb{R}^{d \cdot |V|}$ be a conformation of $|V|$ points in $\mathbb{R}^d$. The *framework* $G(\boldsymbol{p})$ is rigid if and only if there are only finite embeddings that satisfy the given edge lengths $\boldsymbol{\lambda} = (\|p_u - p_v\|)_{(u,v) \in E}$ induced by $\boldsymbol{p}$, where $p_v \in \mathbb{R}^d$ are the coordinates of vertex v. A graph is *generically rigid* if it is rigid for almost all conformations and this is a property of the underlying graph (and not of the specific embedding). In other words, genericity refers to the prescribed edge lengths of the graph.

A major open problem in rigidity theory is to find tight upper bounds on the number of realizations of minimally rigid graphs, e.g. [15]; we refer to this number as *embedding number*. A Euclidean embedding is related to the real solutions of a well-constrained system of algebraic equations. The complex solutions extend the notion of real to complex embeddings and allow one to leverage complex algebraic geometry. Direct application of Bézout's bound of the quadratic polynomial system that corresponds to the edge constraints yields a bound of $\mathcal{O}(2^{d \cdot |V|})$. In [7], they presented an upper bound that had been the best until recently, applying a theorem on the degree of determinantal varieties [14]. However, it does not improve asymptotically upon Bézout's. For $d = 2$, techniques using mixed volume have been introduced in [24], without managing to improve the bound. A recent result in algebraic frame theory establishes a bound on the degree of the projections of finite unit norm tight frames [5] using algebraic matroids.

Two recent publications dealing with that problem managed to improve the asymptotic bound based on the combinatorial properties of minimally rigid graphs. This is the approach on which the present work relies. In [3], outdegree-constrained orientations as well as matrix permanents are related to the m-Bézout bound of certain algebraic systems that compute the embedding number. This work resulted to improved asymptotic upper bounds for $d \geq 5$, using the Brégman-Minc permanent bound [9,21]. More importantly, this work led to the following combinatorial technique. In [4], the target is on a method that bounds the number of outdegree-constrained orientations. It managed to improve the bound on embeddings for all $d \geq 2$ (the case of $d = 1$ is trivial) and proved that the permanent bounds can be ameliorated in that case. For instance, in the case of $d = 2$, this approach results to an upper bound of $\mathcal{O}(3.77^n)$, while the Bézout bound is $\mathcal{O}(4^n)$.

It is well known that, applied to the same system, Bézout's bound is smaller or equal to the multi-homogeneous Bézout bound (m-Bézout) [23], which is smaller or equal to the BKK bound expressed by mixed volume [6]. The bounds coincide for dense systems, where all coefficients for a given total degree are nonzero, but differ as the system becomes sparser. Of course, each bound counts roots in a different ambient variety. These bounds are compared in [12], with emphasis on computing mixed volume, which coincides with the m-Bézout number for multi-homogeneous systems whose maximal monomials have nonzero coefficients. Formally, the latter condition requires that none of the monomials corresponding to vertices of the Newton polytopes vanishes.

Computing the m-Bézout number for a given variable partition is #P-hard by reduction to the permanent, which is the cornerstone #P-hard problem. The same hardness result holds for mixed volume, which coincides with the m-Bézout number for certain polynomial structures; when the system is sparse, in order words has certain zero coefficients, the mixed volume may be smaller. Moreover, it is known that mixed volume is APX-hard, in other words it is hard to deterministically approximate it within an error which is asymptotically smaller than exponential in the system's number of variables. Another problem is, given an algebraic system, to find the optimal variable partition so that the system is modeled as a multi-homogeneous one with minimum m-Bézout number, see Definition 2. This problem is not in APX, unless $P = NP$ [19].

Recently, other approaches came to our attention relating polynomial systems with graph theoretical concepts. More precisely, there are connections of the polynomial system with chordal graphs in order to enhance Cylindrical Algebraic Decomposition (CAD) [17] and Gröbner bases [10] algorithms.

Our Contribution. In this paper, we generalize the aforementioned approach to bounding the m-Bézout bound of a quite general class of multi-homogeneous polynomial systems, which subsumes the class of systems encountered in rigidity theory. We exploit the connection between the system's m-Bézout number and the number of constrained orientations of a simple graph that we specify for the systems under investigation, then bound the number of the graph's orientations. This procedure relies on the proofs in [3,4]. It offers the first closed-form bound on m-Bézout numbers; we hope this may prove useful in a fast estimation of the algebraic complexity of problems modeled by multi-homogeneous algebraic equations. Trivially, our closed-form upper bounds the mixed volume of these multi-homogeneous systems.

Our main result concerns any multi-homogeneous 0-dimensional polynomial system $P(x) = (P_1(x), P_2(x), \ldots, P_m(x))$ that cannot be split to smaller sub-systems: formally, there is no subset of equations P' including only a subset of variables that do not appear in $P \backslash P'$. The multi-homogeneous structure is manifest by partitioning the variables to subsets $(X_1, X_2, \ldots X_n)$ with $|X_i| = d_i$, $d_1 + \cdots + d_n = m$, so that each P_i is homogeneous in each X_j (see Definition 2 for more details).

Theorem 1. *Given multi-homogeneous system P as above, let us assume that*

- *every P_i contains at most two variable subsets,*
- *two polynomials P_i, P_j do not contain the same pair of variables, and*
- *the degree of each P_i, denoted by δ_i, is the same in both variable sets.*

Let $d = \max\limits_{1 \le i \le n} (d_i)$, $k = nd - m$, then the m-Bézout number of P is bounded by

$$\alpha_d^n \cdot \beta_d^{k-1} \cdot \prod_{i=1}^{m} \delta_i, \tag{1}$$

where

$$\alpha_d = \max_{p \ge d} \left(2^{p-d} \binom{p}{d}^{2d-3} \right)^{\frac{1}{2p-3}}, \quad \beta_d = \left(2\binom{p}{d}^{-2} \right)^{\frac{1}{2p-3}},$$

and $p \in \mathbb{N}$ appearing in β_d is the one which maximizes α_d.

Notice that $\beta_d < 1$, so α_d^n gives the asymptotic order of this bound. An asymptotic expression of α_d is given in [4]:

$$\alpha_d \simeq \sqrt{\frac{1}{2}\binom{2d}{d}} \left(1 + \mathcal{O}\left(\frac{\ln^2 d}{d}\right) \right).$$

Upper bounds on α_d^n are provided in Table 1.

Table 1. Upper bounds on α_d^n.

d	2	3	4	5	6	7	8	9
α_d^n	1.88^n	3.41^n	6.34^n	11.9^n	22.7^n	43.7^n	84.4^n	163.7^n

Paper Structure. The rest of the paper is organized as follows. In Sect. 2, we discuss established methods that relate the m-Bézout bound with the number of orientations of a graph, and methods that improve the upper bounds on the number of embeddings. In Sect. 3, we extend these methods to a class of multi-homogeneous systems, thus bounding their m-Bézout number. Finally, in Sect. 4 we present concluding remarks and present ideas of future work.

2 Bounds on the Embedding Number

In this section, we start by offering further background on rigid graphs. Then we present previous work, that relates the number of orientations of a graph to the m-Bézout, and methods that harness this relation to improve the asymptotic upper bounds on the embedding number.

A generically minimally rigid graph is a rigid graph that loses the rigidity property if any of its edges is removed. A fundamental theorem in graph rigidity due to Maxwell, gives a necessary condition for a graph and all its subgraphs to be rigid. In particular, if a graph G is minimally rigid in $\mathbb{R}^d$, then $|E| = d \cdot |V| - \binom{d+1}{2}$, and for every subgraph $G'(V', E') \subset G$ it holds that $|E'| \leq d \cdot |V'| - \binom{d+1}{2}$ [20]. Below this number of edge constraints shall become quite intuitive since it equals the number of unknown variables in the respective algebraic system.

In order to compute the embeddings of a rigid graph up to rigid motions, we use the following formulation used also in [11,24], which is called *sphere equations* in [2].

Definition 1 ([2]). *Let $G = (V, E)$ be a graph. We denote by $\boldsymbol{\lambda}$ the lengths of the edges on G and by $\tilde{X}_u = \{x_{u,1}, ..., x_{u,d}\}$ the d variables that correspond to the coordinates of a vertex u. The following system of equations gives the embedding number for G:*

$$||\tilde{X}_u||^2 = s_u, \quad \forall u \in V$$
$$s_u + s_v - 2\langle \tilde{X}_u, \tilde{X}_v \rangle = \lambda_{u,v}^2, \quad \forall (u,v) \in E \backslash E(K_d)$$

where $\langle \tilde{X}_u, \tilde{X}_v \rangle$ is the Euclidean inner product. The first set of equations shall be called magnitude equations, *while the second are the* edge equations.

This formulation is suitable for sparse elimination theory (see [3] for a general discussion on the algebraic system). In order to factor out rigid motions, if G possesses a complete subgraph in d vertices, the coordinates of these vertices shall be fixed.

Notice that, when we fix d vertices, the above algebraic system has $d \cdot n - d^2$ edge equations and $n - d$ magnitude equations. In [3] the variables are partitioned into subsets, such that each subset of variables contains these ones which correspond to the coordinates and the magnitude of a vertex $X_u = \tilde{X}_u \cup \{s_u\}$.

Let us formally define multi-homogeneous systems in general, thus subsuming the systems presented in the Introduction.

Definition 2. *Let $\boldsymbol{x}$ be a vector of m variables and $\boldsymbol{P}(\boldsymbol{x})$ be a system of m polynomial equations in $\mathbb{C}[\boldsymbol{x}]$. Let $X_1 = (x_{1,1}, x_{1,2}, \ldots, x_{1,d_1})$, $X_2 = (x_{2,1}, x_{2,2}, \ldots, x_{2,d_2})$, $\ldots$, $X_n = (x_{n,1}, x_{n,2}, \ldots, x_{n,d_n})$ be a partition of the affine variables, such that $|X_i| = d_i$, and $d_1 + \cdots + d_n = m$. The **degree** of a polynomial P_i in a variable set X_j is the same as the degree of this polynomial, if all variables $x_{j',k} \notin X_j$ were treated as coefficients and is denoted with $\delta_{i,j}$. Every P_i is homogeneous in each variable set X_j, with homogenizing variable $x_{i,0}$ and multidegree specified by vector $\boldsymbol{\delta_i} = (\delta_{i,1}, \delta_{i,2}, \ldots, \delta_{i,n})$. Then $\boldsymbol{P}$ is multi-homogeneous of type*

$$(d_1, \ldots, d_n; \boldsymbol{\delta_1}, \ldots, \boldsymbol{\delta_n}).$$

If all positive entries have the same value in a multidegree vector $\boldsymbol{\delta_i}$, then this value will be denoted with $mdeg(P_i)$.

Let us recall a classic theorem from algebraic geometry, see e.g. [23], defining the m-Bézout bound.

Theorem 2. *Consider the multi-homogeneous system $\boldsymbol{P}(\boldsymbol{x})$ defined above. The coefficient of the monomial $Y_1^{d_1} \cdots Y_n^{d_n}$ in the polynomial defined by the product*

$$\prod_{i=1}^{m} (\delta_{i,1} \cdot Y_1 + \cdots + \delta_{i,n} \cdot Y_n). \tag{2}$$

bounds the number of roots of $\boldsymbol{P}(\boldsymbol{x})$ in $\mathbb{P}^{d_1} \times \cdots \times \mathbb{P}^{d_n}$, where Y_i are new symbolic parameters, and $\mathbb{P}^j$ is the j-dimensional projective space over $\mathbb{C}$. The bound is tight for generic coefficients of $\boldsymbol{P}(\boldsymbol{x})$.

The most efficient method to compute the m-Bézout bound is by evaluating the permanent of a matrix capturing the polynomial structure, see [12]. Let this matrix be A for a multi-homogeneous system $\boldsymbol{P}$ as above, and let $per(A)$ denote the permanent of this matrix. Then the m-Bézout bound equals

$$\frac{1}{d_1! d_2! \cdots d_n!} \cdot per(A). \tag{3}$$

By applying Theorem 2, the following expansion is considered in the case of sphere equations (see Definition 1):

$$\prod_{u \in V'} 2 \cdot Y_u \prod_{(u,v) \in E'} (Y_u + Y_v) = 2^{n-d} \cdot \prod_{u \in V'} Y_u \prod_{(u,v) \in E'} (Y_u + Y_v),$$

where $G'(V', E') = G \backslash K_d$. Thus, it suffices to find the coefficient of $\prod_{u \in V'} Y_u^d$ in the expansion of the product:

$$\prod_{(u,v) \in E'} (Y_u + Y_v).$$

In [3], it is proven that this coefficient equals the cardinality of the set of those orientations of $G' = (V, E \backslash E(K_d))$ satisfying the conditions set in the following theorem.

Theorem 3 ([3]). *Let $G = (V, E)$ be a minimally rigid graph that contains at least one complete subgraph on d vertices, denoted by $K_d = (v_1, \ldots, v_d)$. Let $\mathcal{B}(G, K_d)$, stand for the number of outdegree-constrained orientations of $G' = (V, E \backslash E(K_d))$, such that:*

- *the outdegree of $v_1, \ldots, v_d$ is 0.*
- *the outdegree of every vertex in $V \backslash \{v_1, ..., v_d\}$ is d.*

The orientations that satisfy these constraints are called valid. *Then the number of embeddings of G in $\mathbb{C}^d$, does not exceed*

$$2^{|V|-d} \cdot \mathcal{B}(G, K_d).$$

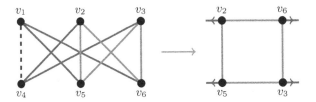

Fig. 1. Left: Graph $K_{3,3}$ where v_1, v_2 are chosen as fixed vertices ($d = 2$). Right: the resulting pseudograph, after removing the fixed vertices. (Color figure online)

The theorem extends to the case where a fixed K_d does not exist [4].

In [4], this method yields the current record upper bounds on the number of embeddings. To achieve this, the valid orientations of Theorem 3 are associated to a graphical structure in which the vertices that have fixed outdegree 0 are omitted. This graphical structure is called *pseudograph* [4], and extends the notion of a standard graph by allowing *hanging edges*, which have a single endpoint; hanging edges are always oriented outwards from its incident vertex. In correspondence with Theorem 3, the hanging edges represent edges incident to the missing vertices in the original graph. It is thus a collection $\mathcal{G} = (V, E, H)$, where V denotes the vertices, E the edges with two endpoints and H the hanging edges.

An elimination process that applies to a pseudograph bounds the number of orientations. At each step, one or more vertices (see Fig. 2) are removed from the pseudograph and their incident edges are either removed or become hanging edges in a smaller graph. The number of possible outcomes in every step multiplies the current count until a terminal condition is reached; the overall product bounds the number of valid orientations.

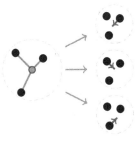

Fig. 2. Excerpt from [4]. Left: a (blue) vertex with 3 neighbours and no hanging edges. Right: 3 possible cases for the orientation, after the removal of the blue vertex, when $d = 2$. The number of possible cases is multiplied in every elimination step, which eventually bounds the number of valid orientations. (Color figure online)

We remark that from an algebraic point of view, the hanging edges correspond to variables that can be eliminated linearly using the edge equations from Definition 1. In other words, they represent a reduction in the cardinality of the variables set of the specific vertex (see Fig. 1).

Theorem 4 ([4]). *Let $B_d(n,k)$ denote the maximal number of orientations with outdegree d for a connected pseudograph with n vertices and k hanging edges. Then it holds that:*

$$B_d(n,k) \leq \alpha_d^n \cdot \beta_d^{k-1},$$

where α_d and β_d are defined as in Theorem 1.

For $d = 2, \ldots, 9$, the formula yields improved bounds on the number of orientations which are expressed by a_d^n, see Table 1, since $\beta_d < 1$. Due to Theorem 3, these quantities multiplied by 2^n, bound the number of embeddings in the d-dimensional complex space. In the case of $d = 2$ and $d = 3$, this improved the asymptotic bound on the embedding number to $\mathcal{O}(3.77^n)$ and $\mathcal{O}(6.82^n)$ respectively.

3   Algebraic Systems Modeled by Simple Graphs

In this section we exploit the methods described above to bound the m-Bézout number of a class of multi-homogeneous algebraic systems that shall be modeled via a simple graph.

Recall the polynomial systems described in Theorem 1: For every polynomial P_i containing variable sets X_u, X_v, it holds for the degree $mdeg(P_i) = \delta_{i,j}$ only for $j \in \{u,v\}$, whereas $\delta_{i,j} = 0$, for all $j \notin \{u,v\}$. We also require that the polynomial system cannot be split into smaller subsystems with disjoint variables, and that two different polynomials cannot contain the same pair of variable sets.

We call such systems *simple graph polynomial systems* since they define a simple connected graph $G(\boldsymbol{P}) = (V, E)$ as follows: The vertices of G correspond to the n variable subsets, while each polynomial yields an edge whose endpoints are the respective vertices. There are no loops, because no polynomial contains a single variable set. Since the pair of variable sets is unique for each polynomial, there can be only one edge with the same endpoints, hence no multiple edges appear. Furthermore, if the graph was disconnected, every connected component would contain vertices corresponding to sets of variables that do not appear in the other connected components, which has been excluded. All these conditions indicate that the graph is simple and connected.

The main observation here is that we can relate the m-Bézout bound in the cases of simple graph polynomial systems with valid orientations, as described in Sect. 2, but we can relax those conditions since it is not necessary to restrain these constraints to outdegree d and outdegree 0 cases (see Theorem 3).

Theorem 5. *Let* P *be a simple graph polynomial system with* m *equations for a partition of variables* $X_1, X_2, \ldots, X_n$ *and let* $G(P) = (V, E)$ *be the associated simple graph. Let* $|X_j| = d_j$, $d = (d_1, d_2, \ldots d_n)$ *and* $mdeg(P_{(u,v)}) = \delta_{(u,v)}$, *where* (u, v) *is the edge associated with the polynomial containing* X_u, X_v. *We denote by* $\mathcal{B}(G(P), d)$ *the number of orientations of* $G(P)$, *constrained so that each vertex* u *representing* X_u *has outdegree* d_u. *Then, the* m-*Bézout number for* P *under this variable partition is exactly*

$$\mathcal{B}(G(P), d) \cdot \prod_{(u,v) \in E} \delta_{(u,v)}.$$

Proof. The m-Bézout bound is the coefficient of the term $Y = Y_1^{d_1} \cdots Y_2^{d_2} \cdot Y_n^{d_n}$ in the polynomial $\prod_{(u,v) \in E} (\delta_{(u,v)} \cdot Y_u + \delta_{(u,v)} \cdot Y_v)$, where every Y_k is a new symbolic parameter. Clearly the latter is equal with

$$\left(\prod_{(u,v) \in E} \delta_{(u,v)} \right) \cdot \prod_{(u,v) \in E} (Y_u + Y_v).$$

Using a similar argument to that in the proof of Theorem 3 in [3], the monomial Y appears only if each term Y_u is selected exactly d_u times in the expansion of this product. Since each set of variables represents a vertex and each polynomial represents an edge in $G(P)$, this can be connected to d_u edges directed outwards from u in a graph orientation.   □

Now, we can derive general upper bounds on the m-Bézout number using the pseudograph formulation. Combining Theorem 5 and Theorem 4 leads to the following proof of Theorem 1.

Proof (of Theorem 1). Let $d = \max(d)$, for a system P, with d as defined above. Let $\mathcal{G} = (V, E, H)$ be a pseudograph, such that V, E are the vertices and the edges of $G(P)$, respectively, H are the hanging edges, where a vertex v has exactly $d - d_v$ hanging edges as specified in Sect. 2. Now, if a vertex v has no hanging edges, then all of its $d_v = d$ edges should be directed outwards from it. On the other hand, for a vertex v that has $k_v = d - d_v$ hanging edges, then d_v edges in E should be out-directed, which correspond to d_v edges directed outwards in $G(P)$. These cases capture exactly all valid orientations of $G(P)$. The latter orientations are used to compute the m-Bézout bound of a simple graph polynomial in Theorem 5.

Now, it suffices to bound the number of valid orientations of this pseudograph, by extending the techniques of [4]. The bound on valid orientations with fixed outdegree d for all pseudographs with $|V| = n$ vertices and $|H| = k$ hanging edges is given by Theorem 4, thus establishing that Equation (1) bounds the m-Bézout bound.   □

Let us present two examples of simple graph polynomial systems, by computing the m-Bézout number, and by deriving the bound in Theorem 1 that concerns all systems whose graph has the same vertices and hanging edges.

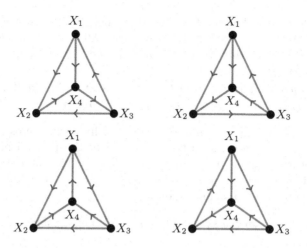

Fig. 3. The 4 outdegree-constrained orientations of $G(\boldsymbol{P})$ in Example 1. Since $|X_1| = |X_3| = 2, |X_2| = |X_4| = 1$, the outdegree of X_1, X_3 is 2, while that of X_2, X_4 is 1. (Color figure online)

Example 1. *The following system $\boldsymbol{P}$ is a simple graph polynomial system:*

$$P_{(X_1,X_2)} = x_{1,1}x_{2,1} + 5x_{1,2}x_{2,1} + 2x_{1,2} + 3$$
$$P_{(X_1,X_3)} = 2x_{1,1}^2x_{3,1}^2 + 2x_{1,1}^2x_{3,2}^2 + 2x_{1,2}^2x_{3,2}^2 + x_{1,1}x_{1,2}x_{3,1}x_{3,2} + 2x_{1,2} - 13$$
$$P_{(X_1,X_4)} = x_{1,1}x_{1,2}x_{4,1}^2 - x_{1,1}^2x_{4,1}^2 + x_{1,2}x_{4,1}$$
$$P_{(X_2,X_3)} = 4x_{2,1}^3x_{3,1}^2x_{3,2} + x_{2,1}x_{3,1}^2x_{3,2} + 2x_{3,2} + 7$$
$$P_{(X_2,X_4)} = 2x_{2,1}x_{4,1} + 3x_{2,1} + 5x_{4,1} - 9$$
$$P_{(X_3,X_4)} = 4x_{3,1}x_{4,1} + 5x_{3,2}x_{4,1} + 7x_{3,1} + 2x_{4,1}$$

for the partition of variables $X_1 = \{x_{1,1}, x_{1,2}\}$, $X_2 = \{x_{2,1}\}$, $X_3 = \{x_{3,1}, x_{3,2}\}$, $X_4 = \{x_{4,1}\}$. Of course, it is sparse in the sense that not all expected terms appear with nonzero coefficient; hence, one would expect its mixed volume to be inferior to its m-Bézout number. The vertices of $G(\boldsymbol{P})$ are labeled by these subsets; the cardinalities are $|X_1| = |X_3| = 2$ and $|X_2| = |X_4| = 1$, hence $\boldsymbol{d} = (2, 1, 2, 1)$. The edge set is:

$$E = \{(X_1, X_2), (X_1, X_3), (X_1, X_4), (X_2, X_3), (X_2, X_4), (X_3, X_4)\}.$$

The multi-homogeneous degrees are $\delta_{(X_1,X_2)} = 1$, $\delta_{(X_1,X_3)} = 2$, $\delta_{(X_1,X_4)} = 2$, $\delta_{(X_2,X_3)} = 3$, $\delta_{(X_2,X_4)} = 1$, $\delta_{(X_3,X_4)} = 1$.

We compute the m-Bézout bound by Theorem 5. Since $d_1 = d_3 = 2$, $d_2 = d_4 = 1$ the outdegree of vertices X_1, X_3 should be 2, while that of X_2, X_4 should be 1 for a valid orientation. There are 4 such orientations (Fig. 3). Therefore the m-Bézout bound is $12 \cdot 4 = 48$. The BKK bound gives a tighter bound by exploiting sparseness: using $\mathtt{phcpy}$ [25], we found a mixed volume of 44, which is the actual number of complex roots.

In order to apply Theorem 1, we set $d = \max(\boldsymbol{d}) = 2$, so $\alpha_2 = 24^{1/5}$ and $\beta_2 = 18^{-1/5}$. Since the number of vertices of $G(\boldsymbol{P})$ is $n = 4$ and the number of equations $m = 6$, we have $k = nd - m = 2$, and $\prod_E \delta_{(X_i, X_j)} = 12$, then the bound is $\lfloor 12 \cdot 24^{4/5} \cdot 18^{-1/5} \rfloor = 85$.

Let us compare this estimate to the Bézout bound. The total degrees of the equations are $2, 4, 6, 2, 4, 2$; the Bézout bound is therefore 768.

In the second example the multidegree vector has either zeros or ones. This means that we can relate the m-Bézout bound to the permanent of a $(0, 1)$-matrix A capturing the polynomial structure. For this kind of matrices, there is a permanent bound, better known as the *Brègman-Minc bound* [9, 21]. Therefore, we shall also compare this bound to ours.

Example 2. *The following system $\boldsymbol{Q}$ is a simple graph polynomial system:*

$$Q_{(X_1, X_2)} = x_{1,1}x_{2,1} + 2x_{1,1} + 3x_{2,1}$$
$$Q_{(X_1, X_3)} = 2x_{1,1}x_{3,1} + x_{1,1}x_{3,2} + x_{3,1} + x_{3,2} + 2x_{1,1}$$
$$Q_{(X_1, X_5)} = 5x_{1,1}x_{5,1} + 2x_{1,1}x_{5,2} + x_{5,1} + x_{5,2} + x_{1,1}$$
$$Q_{(X_2, X_4)} = 9x_{2,1}x_{4,1} + x_{2,1}x_{4,2} + x_{4,1} + x_{4,2} + x_{2,1}$$
$$Q_{(X_2, X_5)} = 9x_{2,1}x_{5,1} + x_{2,1}x_{5,2} + x_{5,1} + x_{5,2} + x_{2,1}$$
$$Q_{(X_3, X_4)} = 4x_{3,2}x_{4,1} + 2x_{3,2}x_{4,2} + 5x_{3,1}x_{4,1} + 9x_{3,1}x_{4,2} + x_{3,1} + x_{3,2} + x_{4,1}$$
$$Q_{(X_3, X_5)} = 3x_{3,2}x_{5,1} + 4x_{3,2}x_{5,2} + x_{3,1}x_{5,1} + 7x_{3,1}x_{5,2} + x_{3,1} + x_{3,2} + 2x_{5,1}$$
$$Q_{(X_4, X_5)} = x_{4,2}x_{5,1} + 9x_{4,2}x_{5,2} + 3x_{4,1}x_{5,1} + 4x_{4,1}x_{5,2} + 2x_{4,1} + x_{4,2} + 14x_{5,1}$$

for the partition of variables $X_1 = \{x_{1,1}\}$, $X_2 = \{x_{2,1}\}$, $X_3 = \{x_{3,1}, x_{3,2}\}$, $X_4 = \{x_{4,1}, x_{4,2}\}, X_5 = \{x_{5,1}, x_{5,2}\}$; the cardinalities of the subsets are $|X_1| = |X_2| = 1$, $|X_3| = |X_4| = |X_5| = 2$, indicating that $\boldsymbol{d} = (1, 1, 2, 2, 2)$. The multi-homogeneous degree is $\delta_{(X_i, X_j)} = 1$ for all $(X_i, X_j) \in E$ but, of course, there are some terms missing due to vanishing coefficients.

The vertices of $G(\boldsymbol{Q})$ are labeled by these subsets. The edge set E is:

$$\{(X_1, X_2), (X_1, X_3), (X_1, X_5), (X_2, X_4), (X_2, X_5), (X_3, X_4), (X_3, X_5), (X_4, X_5)\}.$$

We count orientations such that the outdegrees of X_1, X_2 is $d_1 = d_2 = 1$, while that of X_3, X_4, X_5 is $d_3 = d_4 = d_5 = 2$. Thus the m-Bézout number is the same as the number of the orientations namely 6 (See Fig. 4). In that case this bound is exact, since the number of roots is also 6, and so is the BKK bound.

We have $d = 2$, so $\alpha_2 = 24^{1/5}$ and $\beta_2 = 18^{-1/5}$. We have $n = 5$ and $k = 2$, indicating that the bound from Theorem 1 is $\lfloor 24 \cdot 18^{-1/5} \rfloor = 13$.

In order to use the Brègman-Minc bound, one constructs a matrix with rows representing the variables and columns representing the equations (see [12] for details). The entry (i', j) equals $\delta_{i,j}$ for all $x_{i'} \in X_i$. The matrix is:

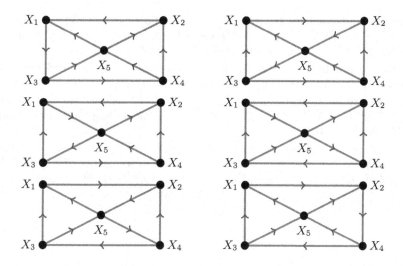

Fig. 4. The 6 valid orientations of the graph in Example 2. (Color figure online)

	$Q_{(X_1,X_2)}$	$Q_{(X_1,X_3)}$	$Q_{(X_1,X_5)}$	$Q_{(X_2,X_4)}$	$Q_{(X_2,X_5)}$	$Q_{(X_3,X_4)}$	$Q_{(X_3,X_5)}$	$Q_{(X_4,X_5)}$
$x_{1,1}$	1	1	1	0	0	0	0	0
$x_{2,1}$	1	0	0	1	1	0	0	0
$x_{3,1}$	0	1	0	0	0	1	1	0
$x_{3,2}$	0	1	0	0	0	1	1	0
$x_{4,1}$	0	0	0	1	0	1	0	1
$x_{4,2}$	0	0	0	1	0	1	0	1
$x_{5,1}$	0	0	1	0	1	0	1	1
$x_{5,2}$	0	0	1	0	1	0	1	1

The Brègman-Minc bound for $(0,1)$-matrices is $\prod_i (r_i!)^{1/r_i}$, where r_i is the sum of entries in row i. Thus the permanent is bounded by $6^2 \cdot 24^{1/2}$. Based on Equation (3) one divides by $\prod_{i=1}^{n} d_i! = 8$ and obtains a bound of $\lfloor 9\sqrt{6} \rfloor = 22$ on the m-Bézout number, which is looser than our method's.

The Bézout bound is 256, since all total degrees are 2.

In both examples above, the maximum outdegree d for a vertex in the associated graphs was 2. To conclude let us give some brief examples for the computation of the bound using the closed-formula of Theorem 1 for larger d, given the same graph with different cardinalities for the sets of variables. In all cases we will consider $\delta_i = 1$.

The graph that will be analyzed has 6 vertices and 13 edges. The edge set is the following (see Fig. 5): $(X_1, X_2), (X_1, X_3), (X_1, X_4), (X_1, X_5), (X_2, X_3), (X_2, X_4), (X_2, X_5), (X_3, X_4), (X_4, X_5), (X_5, X_6)$.

We will first consider the case that the cardinalities are $|X_1| = |X_3| = 1$, $|X_4| = 2, |X_2| = |X5| = |X_6| = 3$. We have $d = 3$, so $\alpha_3 = 40^{1/3}$, $\beta_3 = 200^{-1/9}$, while $k = 5$. All these lead to $\lfloor 40^2 \cdot 200^{-4/9} \rfloor = 151$ as a bound.

If the cardinalities change so do the constraints on the outdegrees. For example for the following case $|X_6| = |X_3| = 1, |X_4| = |X_5| = 2, |X_1| = 3, |X_2| = 4$ we have clearly that $d = 4$, so $k = 11$. This means that we shall use $\alpha_4 = 2^{9/13} \cdot 35^{5/13}$, $\beta_4 = 2^{-1/13} \cdot 35^{-2/13}$, concluding that the bound is $\lfloor 2^{43/13} \cdot 35^{8/13} \rfloor = 160$.

Finally, let us present the case that $|X_1| = 5, |X_2| = 3, |X_3| = 2, |X_4| = |X_5| = |X_6| = 1$. Now $d = 5, k = 17$ and also $\alpha_5 = 2^{19/17} \cdot 63^{7/17}$, $\beta_5 = 2^{-3/17} \cdot 63^{-2/17}$. The bound in that case is $\lfloor 2^{66/17} \cdot 63^{10/17} \rfloor = 168$.

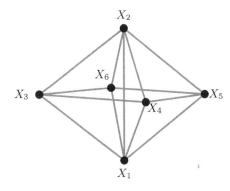

Fig. 5. An example graph on 6 vertices and 13 edges. The bound for simple graph polynomial systems with different variable set cardinalities is analyzed in the text.

4   Conclusion

In this paper, we studied methods that use the multi-homogeneous Bézout to improve the upper bounds on the number of embeddings of minimally rigid graphs. We generalized these methods to polynomial systems which represent simple graphs, and not only minimally rigid graphs. An open question is to further understand the algebraic implications of our results. The graph elimination process that yields the closed-form bound on the number of orientations can be paralleled to algebraic variable elimination. The main open question is whether our approach may be extended to a wider class of well-constrained algebraic systems. This would require extending the proof that bounds the number of graph orientations to the graph corresponding to the more general class of algebraic systems.

Another open question is to obtain tight upper bound on the number of orientations of graphs. A result on this would immediately improve the upper bound on the m-Bézout number. This is actually our current work. A more theoretical question would be to estimate the error of our approximation.

References

1. Baglivo, J., Graver, J.: Incidence and Symmetry in Design and Architecture. No. 7 in Cambridge Urban and Architectural Studies, Cambridge University Press (1983)
2. Bartzos, E., Emiris, I., Legerský, J., Tsigaridas, E.: On the maximal number of real embeddings of minimally rigid graphs in $\mathbb{R}^2$, $\mathbb{R}^3$ and S^2. J. Symbol. Comput. **102**, 189–208 (2021). https://doi.org/10.1016/j.jsc.2019.10.015
3. Bartzos, E., Emiris, I., Schicho, J.: On the multihomogeneous Bézout bound on the number of embeddings of minimally rigid graphs. J. Appl. Algebra Eng. Commun. Comput. **31** (2020). https://doi.org/10.1007/s00200-020-00447-7
4. Bartzos, E., Emiris, I., Vidunas, R.: New upper bounds for the number of embeddings of minimally rigid graphs. arXiv:2010.10578 [math.CO] (2020)
5. Bernstein, D., Farnsworth, C., Rodriguez, J.: The algebraic matroid of the finite unit norm tight frame (FUNTF) variety. J. Pure Appl. Algebra **224**(8) (2020). https://doi.org/10.1016/j.jpaa.2020.106351
6. Bernstein, D.: The number of roots of a system of equations. Func. Anal. Appl. **9**(3), 183–185 (1975). https://doi.org/10.1007/BF01075595
7. Borcea, C., Streinu, I.: The number of embeddings of minimally rigid graphs. Discret. Comput. Geomet. **31**(2), 287–303 (2004). https://doi.org/10.1007/s00454-003-2902-0
8. Borcea, C., Streinu, I.: Periodic tilings and auxetic deployments. Math. Mech. Solids **26**(2), 199–216 (2021). https://doi.org/10.1177/1081286520948116
9. Brègman, L.: Some properties of nonnegative matrices and their permanents. Dokl. Akad. Nauk SSSR **211**(1), 27–30 (1973)
10. Cifuentes, D., Parrilo, P.: Exploiting chordal structure in polynomial ideals: a Gröbner bases approach. SIAM J. Discret. Math. **30**(3), 1534–1570 (2016). https://doi.org/10.1137/151002666
11. Emiris, I., Tsigaridas, E., Varvitsiotis, A.: Mixed volume and distance geometry techniques for counting Euclidean embeddings of rigid graphs. In: Mucherino, A., Lavor, C., Liberti, L., Maculan, N. (eds.) Distance Geometry: Theory, Methods and Applications, pp. 23–45. Springer, New York (2013). https://doi.org/10.1007/978-1-4614-5128-0_2
12. Emiris, I., Vidunas, R.: Root ounts of semi-mixed systems, and an application to counting Nash equilibria. In: Proceedings of ACM International Symposium Symbolic & Algebraic Computation, pp. 154–161. ISSAC, ACM (2014). https://doi.org/10.1145/2608628.2608679
13. Emmerich, D.: Structures Tendues et Autotendantes. Ecole d'Architecture de Paris, La Villette, France (1988)
14. Harris, J., Tu, L.: On symmetric and skew-symmetric determinantal varieties. Topology **23**, 71–84 (1984)
15. Jackson, W., Owen, J.: Equivalent realisations of a rigid graph. Discrete Appl. Math. **256**, 42–58 (2019). https://doi.org/10.1016/j.dam.2017.12.009. Special Issue on Distance Geometry: Theory & Applications'16
16. Lavor, C., et al.: Minimal NMR distance information for rigidity of protein graphs. Discrete Appl. Math. **256**, 91–104 (2019). www.sciencedirect.com/science/article/pii/S0166218X18301793. Special Issue on Distance Geometry Theory & Applications'16

17. Li, H., Xia, B., Zhang, H., Zheng, T.: Choosing the variable ordering for cylindrical algebraic decomposition via exploiting chordal structure. In: Proceedings of International Symposium on Symbolic and Algebraic Computation, ISSAC 2021. ACM (2021)
18. Liberti, L.: Distance geometry and data science. TOP **28**, 271–339 (2020)
19. Malajovich, G., Meer, K.: Computing minimal multi-homogeneous Bezout numbers is Hard. Theory Comput. Syst. **40**(4), 553–570 (2007). https://doi.org/10.1007/s00224-006-1322-y
20. Maxwell, J.: On the calculation of the equilibrium and stiffness of frames. Philos. Mag. **39**(12) (1864)
21. Minc, H.: Upper bounds for permanents of $(0, 1)$-matrices. Bull. AMS **69**, 789–791 (1963). https://doi.org/10.1090/S0002-9904-1963-11031-9
22. Rocklin, D., Zhou, S., Sun, K., Mao, X.: Transformable topological mechanical metamaterials. Nat. Commun. **8** (2017). https://doi.org/10.1038/ncomms14201
23. Shafarevich, I.: Intersection Numbers, pp. 233–283. Springer, Heidelberg (2013). https://doi.org/10.1007/978-3-642-37956-7_4
24. Steffens, R., Theobald, T.: Mixed volume techniques for embeddings of Laman graphs. Comput. Geom. **43**, 84–93 (2010)
25. Verschelde, J.: Modernizing PHCpack through phcpy. In: Proceedings of the 6th European Conference on Python in Science (EuroSciPy 2013), pp. 71–76 (2014)
26. Zelazo, D., Franchi, A., Allgöwer, F., Bülthoff, H.H., Giordano, P.: Rigidity maintenance control for multi-robot systems. In: Proceedings of Robotics: Science & Systems, Sydney, Australia (2012)
27. Zhu, Z., So, A.C., Ye, Y.: Universal rigidity and edge sparsification for sensor network localization. SIAM J. Optim. **20**(6), 3059–3081 (2010)

Computational Schemes for Subresultant Chains

Mohammadali Asadi$^{(\boxtimes)}$, Alexander Brandt, and Marc Moreno Maza

Department of Computer Science, University of Western Ontario, London, Canada
{masadi4,abrandt5}@uwo.ca, moreno@csd.uwo.ca

Abstract. Subresultants are one of the most fundamental tools in computer algebra. They are at the core of numerous algorithms including, but not limited to, polynomial GCD computations, polynomial system solving, and symbolic integration. When the subresultant chain of two polynomials is involved in a client procedure, not all polynomials of the chain, or not all coefficients of a given subresultant, may be needed. Based on that observation, this paper discusses different practical schemes, and their implementation, for efficiently computing subresultants. Extensive experimentation supports our findings.

Keywords: Resultant · Subresultant chain · Modular arithmetic · Polynomial system solving · GCDs

1 Introduction

The goal of this paper is to investigate how several optimization techniques for subresultant chain computations benefit polynomial system solving in practice. These optimizations rely on ideas which have appeared in previous works, but without the support of successful experimental studies. Therefore, this paper aims at filling this gap.

The first of these optimizations takes advantage of the *Half-GCD* algorithm for computing GCDs of univariate polynomials over a field **k**. For input polynomials of degree (at most) n, this algorithm runs within $O(\mathrm{M}(n)\log n)$ operations in **k**, where $\mathrm{M}(n)$ is a polynomial multiplication time, as defined in [12, Chapter 8]. The *Half-GCD* algorithm originated in the ideas of [16,18] and [26], while a robust implementation was a challenge for many years. One of the earliest correct designs was introduced in [28].

The idea of speeding up subresultant chain computations by means of the *Half-GCD* algorithm takes various forms in the literature. In [25], Reischert proposes a fraction-free adaptation of the *Half-GCD* algorithm, which can be executed over an effective integral domain $\mathbb{B}$, within $O(\mathrm{M}(n)\log n)$ operations in $\mathbb{B}$. We are not aware of any implementation of Reischert's algorithm.

In [20], Lickteig and Roy propose a "divide and conquer" algorithm for computing subresultant chains, the objective of which is to control coefficient growth

© Springer Nature Switzerland AG 2021
F. Boulier et al. (Eds.): CASC 2021, LNCS 12865, pp. 21–41, 2021.
https://doi.org/10.1007/978-3-030-85165-1_3

in defective cases. Lecerf in [17] introduces extensions and a complexity analysis of the algorithm of Lickteig and Roy, with a particular focus on bivariate polynomials. When run over an effective ring endowed with the partially defined division routine, the algorithm yields a running time estimate similar to that of Reischert's. Lecerf realized an implementation of that algorithm, but observed that computations of subresultant chains based on Ducos' algorithm [10], or on evaluation-interpolation strategies, were faster in practice.

In [12, Chapter 11], von zur Gathen and Gerhard show how the nominal leading coefficients (see Sect. 2 for this term) of the subresultant chain of two univariate polynomials a, b over a field can be computed within $O(\mathrm{M}(n) \log n)$ operations in $\mathbf{k}$, by means of an adaptation of the Half-GCD algorithm. In this paper, we extend their approach to compute any pair of consecutive non-zero subresultants of a, b within the same time bound. The details are presented in Sect. 3.

Our next optimization for subresultant chain computations relies on the observation that not all non-zero subresultants of a given subresultant chain may be needed. To illustrate this fact, consider two commutative rings $\mathbb{A}$ and $\mathbb{B}$, two non-constant univariate polynomials a, b in $\mathbb{A}[y]$ and a ring homomorphism Ψ from $\mathbb{A}$ to $\mathbb{B}$ so that $\Psi(\mathrm{lc}(a)) \neq 0$ and $\Psi(\mathrm{lc}(b)) \neq 0$ both hold. Then, the specialization property of subresultants (see the precise statement in Sect. 2) tells us that the subresultant chain of $\Psi(a), \Psi(b)$ is the image of the subresultant chain of a, b via Ψ.

This property has at least two important practical applications. When $\mathbb{B}$ is polynomial ring over a field, say $\mathbb{B}$ is $\mathbb{Z}/p\mathbb{Z}[x]$ and $\mathbb{A}$ is $\mathbb{Z}/p\mathbb{Z}$, then one can compute a GCD of $\Psi(a), \Psi(b)$ via evaluation and interpolation techniques. Similarly, say $\mathbb{B}$ is $\mathbb{Q}[x]/\langle m(x)\rangle$, where $m(x)$ is a square-free polynomial, then $\mathbb{B}$ is a product of fields then, letting $\mathbb{A}$ be $\mathbb{Q}[x]$, one can compute a GCD of $\Psi(a), \Psi(b)$ using the celebrated D5 Principle [8]. More generally, if $\mathbb{B}$ is $\mathbb{Q}[x_1, \ldots, x_n]/\langle T\rangle$, where $T = (t_1(x_1), \ldots, t_n(x_1, \ldots, x_n))$ is a zero-dimensional regular chain (generating a radical ideal), and $\mathbb{A}$ is $\mathbb{Q}[x_1, \ldots, x_n]$, then one can compute a so-called regular GCD of a and b modulo $\langle T\rangle$, see [5]. The principle of that calculation generalizes the D5 Principle as follows:

1. if the resultant of a, b is invertible modulo $\langle T\rangle$ then 1 is a regular GCD of a and b modulo $\langle T\rangle$;
2. if, for some k, the nominal leading coefficients $s_0, \ldots, s_{k-1}$ are all zero modulo $\langle T\rangle$, and s_k is invertible modulo $\langle T\rangle$, then the subresultant S_k of index k of a, b is a regular GCD of a and b modulo $\langle T\rangle$; and
3. one can always reduce to one of the above two cases by splitting T, when a zero-divisor of $\mathbb{B}$ is encountered.

In practice, in the above procedure, k is often zero, which can be seen as a consequence of the celebrated *Shape Lemma* [4]. This suggests to compute the subresultant chain of a, b in $\mathbb{A}[y]$ speculatively. To be precise, and taking advantage of the Half-GCD algorithm, it is desirable to compute the subresultants of index 0 and 1, delaying the computation of subresultants of higher index until proven necessary.

We discuss that idea of computing subresultants speculatively in Sect. 3. Making that approach successful, in comparison to non-speculative approaches, requires to overcome several obstacles:

1. computing efficiently the subresultants S_0 and S_1, via the Half-GCD; and
2. developing an effective "recovery" strategy in case of "misprediction", that is, when subresultants of index higher than 1 turn out to be needed.

To address the first obstacle, our implementation combines various schemes for the Half-GCD, inspired by the work done in NTL [27]. To address the second obstacle, when we compute the subresultants of index 0 and 1 via the Half-GCD, we record or *cache* the sequence of quotients (associated with the Euclidean remainders) so as to easily obtain subresultants of index higher than 1, if needed.

There are subresultant algorithms in almost all computer algebra software. Most notably, the *RegularChains* library [19] in MAPLE provides three different algorithms to compute the entire chain based on Ducos' optimization [9], Bézout matrix [1], or evaluation-interpolation based on FFT. Each one is well-suited for a particular type of input polynomials w.r.t the number of variables and the coefficients ring; see the MAPLE help page for SubresultantChain command. Similarly, the ALGEBRAMIX library in MATHEMAGIX [14] implements different subresultant algorithms, including routines based on evaluation-interpolation, Ducos' algorithm, and an enhanced version of Lickteig-Roy' s algorithm [17].

The extensive experimentation results in Sect. 5 indicate that the performance of our univariate polynomials over finite fields (based on FFT) are closely comparable with their counterparts in NTL. In addition, we have aggressively tuned our subresultant schemes based on evaluation-interpolation techniques. Our modular subresultant chain algorithms are up to $10\times$ and $400\times$ faster than non-modular counterparts (mainly Ducos' subresultant chain algorithm) in $\mathbb{Z}[y]$ and $\mathbb{Z}[x, y]$, respectively. Further, utilizing the Half-GCD algorithm to compute subresultants yields an additional speed-up factor of $7\times$ and $2\times$ for polynomials in $\mathbb{Z}[y]$ and $\mathbb{Z}[x, y]$, respectively.

Further still, we present a third optimization for subresultant chain computations through a simple improvement of Ducos' subresultant chain algorithm. In particular, we consider memory usage and data locality to improve practical performance; see Sect. 4. We have implemented both the original Ducos algorithm [10] and our optimized version over arbitrary-precision integers. For univariate polynomials of degree as large as 2000, the optimized algorithm uses $3.2\times$ and $11.7\times$ less memory, respectively, than our implementation of the original Ducos' algorithm and the implementation of Ducos' algorithm in MAPLE.

All of our code, providing also univariate and multivariate polynomial arithmetic, is open source and part of the Basic Polynomial Algebra Subprograms (BPAS) library available at www.bpaslib.org. Our many subresultant schemes have been integrated, tested, and utilized in the multithreaded BPAS polynomial system solver [3].

This paper is organized as follows. Section 2 presents a review of subresultant theory following the presentations of [9] and [15]. Our modular method to compute subresultants speculatively via Half-GCD is discussed in Sect. 3. Section 4 examines practical memory optimizations for Ducos' subresultant chain algorithm. Lastly, implementation details and experimental results are presented in Sect. 5.

2   Review of Subresultant Theory

In this review of subresultant theory, we follow the presentations of [9] and [15]. Let $\mathbb{B}$ be a commutative ring with identity and let $m \leq n$ be positive integers. Let M be a $m \times n$ matrix with coefficients in $\mathbb{B}$. Let M_i be the square submatrix of M consisting of the first $m - 1$ columns of M and the i-th column of M, for $m \leq i \leq n$; let $\det(M_i)$ be the determinant of M_i. The *determinantal polynomial* of M denoted by $\mathrm{dpol}(M)$ is a polynomial in $\mathbb{B}[y]$, given by

$$\mathrm{dpol}(M) = \det(M_m)y^{n-m} + \det(M_{m+1})y^{n-m-1} + \cdots + \det(M_n).$$

Note that, if $\mathrm{dpol}(M)$ is not zero, then its degree is at most $n - m$. Let $f_1, \ldots, f_m$ be polynomials of $\mathbb{B}[y]$ of degree less than n. We denote by $\mathrm{mat}(f_1, \ldots, f_m)$ the $m \times n$ matrix whose i-th row contains the coefficients of f_i, sorted in order of decreasing degree, and such that f_i is treated as a polynomial of degree $n - 1$. We denote by $\mathrm{dpol}(f_1, \ldots, f_m)$ the determinantal polynomial of $\mathrm{mat}(f_1, \ldots, f_m)$.

Let $a, b \in \mathbb{B}[y]$ be non-constant polynomials of respective degrees $m = \deg(a)$, $n = \deg(b)$ with $m \geq n$. The leading coefficient of a w.r.t. y is denoted by $\mathrm{lc}(a)$. Let k be an integer with $0 \leq k < n$. Then, the k-th *subresultant* of a and b (also known as the *subresultant of index k* of a and b), denoted by $S_k(a, b)$, is

$$S_k(a, b) = \mathrm{dpol}(y^{n-k-1}a, y^{n-k-2}a, \ldots, a, y^{m-k-1}b, \ldots, b).$$

This is a polynomial which belongs to the ideal generated by a and b in $\mathbb{B}[y]$. In particular, $S_0(a, b)$ is the resultant of a and b denoted by $\mathrm{res}(a, b)$. Observe that if $S_k(a, b)$ is not zero then its degree is at most k. If $S_k(a, b)$ has degree k, then $S_k(a, b)$ is said to be *non-defective* or *regular*; if $S_k(a, b) \neq 0$ and $\deg(S_k(a, b)) < k$, then $S_k(a, b)$ is said to be *defective*. We call k-th *nominal leading coefficient*, demoted by s_k, the coefficient of $S_k(a, b)$ in y^k. Observe that if $S_k(a, b)$ is defective, then we have $s_k = 0$. For convenience, we extend the definition to the n-th subresultant as follows:

$$S_n(a, b) = \begin{cases} \gamma(b)b, & \text{if } m > n \text{ or } \mathrm{lc}(b) \in \mathbb{B} \text{ is regular} \\ \text{undefined}, & otherwise \end{cases},$$

where $\gamma(b) = \mathrm{lc}(b)^{m-n-1}$. In the above, *regular* means *not a zero-divisor*. Note that when m equals n and $\mathrm{lc}(b)$ is a regular element in $\mathbb{B}$, then $S_n(a, b) = \mathrm{lc}(b)^{-1}b$ is in fact a polynomial over the total fraction ring of $\mathbb{B}$. We call *specialization property of subresultants* the following property. Let $\mathbb{A}$ be another commutative ring with identity and Ψ a ring homomorphism from $\mathbb{B}$ to $\mathbb{A}$ such that we have $\Psi(\mathrm{lc}(a)) \neq 0$ and $\Psi(\mathrm{lc}(b)) \neq 0$. Then, for $0 \leq k \leq n$, we have $S_k(\Psi(a), \Psi(b)) = \Psi(S_k(a, b))$.

From now on, we assume that the ring $\mathbb{B}$ is an integral domain. Writing $\delta = \deg(a) - \deg(b)$, there exists a unique pair (q, r) of polynomials in $\mathbb{B}[y]$ satisfying $ha = qb + r$, where $h = \mathrm{lc}(b)^{\delta+1}$, and either $r = 0$ or $\deg(r) < \deg(b)$;

the polynomials q and r, denoted respectively pquo(a, b) and prem(a, b), are the *pseudo-quotient* and *pseudo-reminder* of a by b. The *subresultant chain* of a and b, defined as subres$(a, b) = (S_n(a, b), S_{n-1}(a, b), S_{n-2}(a, b), \ldots, S_0(a, b))$, satisfies relations which induce a Euclidean-like algorithm for computing the entire subresultant chain: subres(a, b). This algorithm runs within $O(n^2)$ operations in $\mathbb{B}$, when $m = n$, see [9]. For convenience, we simply write S_k instead of $S_k(a, b)$ for each k. We write $a \sim b$, for $a, b \in \mathbb{B}[y]$, whenever a, b are associate elements in frac$(\mathbb{B})[y]$, the field of fractions of $\mathbb{B}$. Then for $1 \le k < n$, we have:

(i) $S_{n-1} = \text{prem}(a, -b)$; if S_{n-1} is non-zero, defining $e := \deg(S_{n-1})$, then we have:

$$S_{e-1} = \frac{\text{prem}(b, -S_{n-1})}{\text{lc}(b)^{(m-n)(n-e)+1}},$$

(ii) if $S_{k-1} \neq 0$, defining $e := \deg(S_{k-1})$ and assuming $e < k-1$ (thus assuming S_{k-1} defective), then we have:
  (a) $\deg(S_k) = k$, thus S_k is non-defective,
  (b) $S_{k-1} \sim S_e$ and $\text{lc}(S_{k-1})^{k-e-1} S_{k-1} = s_k^{k-e-1} S_e$, thus S_e is non-defective,
  (c) $S_{k-2} = S_{k-3} = \cdots = S_{e+1} = 0$,

(iii) if both S_k and S_{k-1} are non-zero, with respective degrees k and e then we have:

$$S_{e-1} = \frac{\text{prem}(S_k, -S_{k-1})}{\text{lc}(S_k)^{k-e+1}}.$$

Algorithm 1. SUBRESULTANT (a, b, y)

Input: $a, b \in \mathbb{B}[y]$ with $m = \deg(a) \ge n = \deg(b)$ and $\mathbb{B}$ is an integral domain
Output: the non-zero subresultants from $(S_n, S_{n-1}, S_{n-2}, \ldots, S_0)$
1: **if** $m > n$ **then**
2:      $S := (\text{lc}(b)^{m-n-1} b)$
3: **else** $S := ()$
4: $s := \text{lc}(b)^{m-n}$
5: $A := b;\ B := \text{prem}(a, -b)$
6: **while** true **do**
7:      $d := \deg(A);\ e := \deg(B)$
8:      **if** $B = 0$ **then return** S
9:      $S := (B) \cup S;\ \delta := d - e$
10:      **if** $\delta > 1$ **then**
11:          $C := \frac{\text{lc}(B)^{\delta-1} B}{s^{\delta-1}}$
12:          $S := (C) \cup S$
13:      **else** $C := B$
14:      **if** $e = 0$ **then return** S
15:      $B := \frac{\text{prem}(A, -B)}{s^\delta \text{lc}(A)}$
16:      $A := C;\ s := \text{lc}(A)$
17: **end while**

Algorithm 1 from [10] is a known version of this procedure that computes all non-zero subresultants $a, b \in \mathbb{B}[y]$. Note that the core of this algorithm is the while-loop in which the computation of the subresultants S_e and S_{e-1}, with the notations of the above points (ii) and (iii), are carried out.

3   Computing Subresultant Chains Speculatively

As discussed in the introduction, when the ring $\mathbb{B}$ is a field $\mathbf{k}$, the computation of the subresultant chain of the polynomials $a, b \in \mathbb{B}[y]$ can take advantage of asymptotically fast algorithms for computing $\gcd(a, b)$. After recalling its specifications, we explain how we take advantage of the Half-GCD algorithm in order to compute the subresultants in $\mathrm{subres}(a, b)$ speculatively.

Consider two non-zero univariate polynomials $a, b \in \mathbf{k}[y]$ with $n_0 := \deg(a)$, $n_1 := \deg(b)$ with $n_0 \geq n_1$. The extended Euclidean algorithm (EEA) computes the successive remainders $(r_0 := a, r_1 := b, r_2, \ldots, r_\ell = \gcd(a, b))$ with degree sequence $(n_0, n_1, n_2 := \deg(r_2) \ldots, n_\ell := \deg(r_\ell))$ and the corresponding quotients $(q_1, q_2, \ldots, q_\ell)$ defined by $r_{i+1} = \mathrm{rem}(r_i, r_{i-1}) = r_{i-1} - q_i r_i$, for $1 \leq i \leq \ell$, $q_i = \mathrm{quo}(r_i, r_{i-1})$ for $1 \leq i \leq \ell$, $n_{i+1} < n_i$, for $1 \leq i < \ell$, and $r_{\ell+1} = 0$ with $\deg(r_{l+1}) = -\infty$. This computation requires $O(n^2)$ operations in $\mathbf{k}$. We denote by Q_i, the *quotient matrices*, defined, for $1 \leq i \leq \ell$, by $Q_i = \begin{bmatrix} 0 & 1 \\ 1 & -q_i \end{bmatrix}$, so that, for $1 \leq i < \ell$, we have

$$\begin{bmatrix} r_i \\ r_{i+1} \end{bmatrix} = Q_i \begin{bmatrix} r_{i-1} \\ r_i \end{bmatrix} = Q_i \ldots Q_1 \begin{bmatrix} r_0 \\ r_1 \end{bmatrix}. \tag{1}$$

We define $m_i := \deg(q_i)$, so that we have $m_i = n_{i-1} - n_i$ for $1 \leq i \leq \ell$. The degree sequence $(n_0, \ldots, n_l)$ is said to be *normal* if $n_{i+1} = n_i - 1$ holds, for $1 \leq i < \ell$, or, equivalently if $\deg(q_i) = 1$ holds, for $1 \leq i \leq \ell$.

Using the remainder and degree sequences of non-zero polynomials $a, b \in \mathbf{k}[y]$, Proposition 1, known as the *fundamental theorem on subresultants*, introduces a procedure to compute the nominal leading coefficients of polynomials in the subresultant chain.

Proposition 1. *For $k = 0, \ldots, n_1$, the nominal leading coefficient of the k-th subresultant of (a, b) is either 0 or s_k if there exists $i \leq \ell$ such that $k = \deg(r_i)$,*

$$s_k = (-1)^{\tau_i} \prod_{1 \leq j < i} \mathrm{lc}(r_j)^{n_{j-1} - n_{j+1}} \mathrm{lc}(r_i)^{n_{i-1} - n_i},$$

where $\tau_i = \sum_{1 \leq j < i} (n_{j-1} - n_i)(n_j - n_i)$ [12, Theorem 11.16].

The *Half-GCD*, also known as the *fast extended Euclidean algorithm*, is a divide and conquer algorithm for computing a single row of the EEA, say the last one. This can be interpreted as the computation of a 2×2 matrix Q over $\mathbf{k}[y]$ so that we have:

$$\begin{bmatrix} \gcd(a, b) \\ 0 \end{bmatrix} = Q \begin{bmatrix} a \\ b \end{bmatrix}.$$

The major difference between the classical EEA and the Half-GCD algorithm is that, while the EEA computes all the remainders $r_0, r_1, \ldots, r_\ell = \gcd(r_0, r_1)$, the Half-GCD computes only two consecutive remainders, which are derived from the Q_i quotient matrices, which in turn are obtained from a sequence of "truncated remainders", instead of the original r_i remainders.

Here, we take advantage of the Half-GCD algorithm presented in [12, Chapter 11]. For a non-negative $k \leq n_0$, this algorithm computes the quotients $q_1, \ldots, q_{h_k}$ where h_k is defined as

$$h_k = \max\left\{0 \leq j \leq \ell \mid \sum_{i=1}^{j} m_i \leq k\right\}, \tag{2}$$

the maximum $j \in \mathbb{N}$ so that $\sum_{1 \leq i \leq j} \deg(q_i) \leq k$. This is done within $(22\mathrm{M}(k) + O(k)) \log k$ operations in $\mathbf{k}$. From Eq. 2, $h_k \leq \min(k, \ell)$, and

$$\sum_{i=1}^{h_k} m_i = \sum_{i=1}^{h_k}(n_{i-1} - n_i) = n_0 - n_{h_k} \leq k < \sum_{i=1}^{h_k+1} m_i = n_0 - n_{h_k+1}. \tag{3}$$

Thus, $n_{h_k+1} < n_0 - k \leq n_{h_k}$, and so h_k can be uniquely determined; see Algorithm 11.6 in [12] for more details.

Due to the deep relation between subresultants and the remainders of the EEA, the Half-GCD technique can support computing subresultants. This approach is studied in [12]. The Half-GCD algorithm is used to compute the nominal leading coefficient of subresultants up to s_ρ for $\rho = n_{h_k}$ by computing the quotients $q_1, \ldots, q_{h_k}$, calculating the $\mathrm{lc}(r_i) = \mathrm{lc}(r_{i-1})/\mathrm{lc}(q_i)$ from $\mathrm{lc}(r_0)$ for $1 \leq i \leq h_k$, and applying Proposition 1. The resulting procedure runs within the same complexity as the Half-GCD algorithm.

However, for the purpose of computing two successive subresultants $S_{n_v}, S_{n_{v+1}}$ given $0 \leq \rho < n_1$, for $0 \leq v < \ell$ so that $n_{v+1} \leq \rho < n_v$, we need to compute quotients $q_1, \ldots, q_{h_\rho}$ where h_ρ is defined as

$$h_\rho = \max\left\{0 \leq j < \ell \mid n_j > \rho\right\}, \tag{4}$$

using Half-GCD. Let $k = n_0 - \rho$, Eqs. 3 and 4 deduce $n_{h_\rho+1} \leq n_0 - k < n_{h_\rho}$, and $h_\rho \leq h_k$. So, to compute the array of quotients $q_1, \ldots, q_{h_\rho}$, we can utilize an adaptation of the Half-GCD algorithm of [12]. Algorithm 2 is this adaptation and runs within the same complexity as the algorithm of [12].

Algorithm 2 receives as input two polynomials $r_0 := a, r_1 := b$ in $\mathbf{k}[y]$, with $n_0 \geq n_1$, $0 \leq k \in \mathbb{N}$, $\rho \leq n_0$ where ρ, by default, is $n_0 - k$, and the array $\mathcal{A}$ of the leading coefficients of the remainders that have been computed so far. This array should be initialized to size $n_0 + 1$ with $\mathcal{A}[n_0] = \mathrm{lc}(r_0)$ and $\mathcal{A}[i] = 0$ for $0 \leq i < n_0$. $\mathcal{A}$ is updated in-place as necessary. The algorithm returns the array of quotients $\mathcal{Q} := (q_1, \ldots, q_{h_\rho})$ and matrix $M := Q_{h_\rho} \cdots Q_1$.

Algorithm 2 and *the fundamental theorem on subresultants* yield Algorithm 3. This algorithm is a *speculative* subresultant algorithm based on Half-GCD to

---

Algorithm 2. ADAPTEDHGCD$(r_0, r_1, k, \rho, \mathcal{A})$

Input: $r_0, r_1 \in \mathbf{k}[y]$ with $n_0 = \deg(r_0) \geq n_1 = \deg(r_1)$, $0 \leq k \leq n_0$, $0 \leq \rho \leq n_0$ is an upper bound for the degree of the last computed remainder that, by default, is $n_0 - k$ and is fixed in recursive calls (See Algorithm 3), the array $\mathcal{A}$ of the leading coefficients of the remainders (in the Euclidean sequence) which have been computed so far

Output: $h_\rho \in \mathbb{N}$ so that $h_\rho = \max\{j \mid n_j > \rho\}$, the array $\mathcal{Q} := (q_1, \ldots, q_{h_\rho})$ of the first h_ρ quotients associated with remainders in the Euclidean sequence and the matrix $M := Q_{h_\rho} \cdots Q_1$; the array $\mathcal{A}$ of leading coefficients is updated in-place

1: **if** $r_1 = 0$ or $\rho \geq n_1$ **then return** $\left(0, (), \begin{bmatrix} 1 & 0 \\ 0 & 1 \end{bmatrix}\right)$

2: **if** $k = 0$ and $n_0 = n_1$ **then**

3:     **return** $\left(1, (\mathrm{lc}(r_0)/\mathrm{lc}(r_1)), \begin{bmatrix} 0 & 1 \\ 1 & -\mathrm{lc}(r_0)/\mathrm{lc}(r_1) \end{bmatrix}\right)$

4: $m_1 := \lceil \frac{k}{2} \rceil$; $\delta_1 := \max(\deg(r_0) - 2\,(m_1 - 1), 0)$; $\lambda := \max(\deg(r_0) - 2k, 0)$

5: $\left(h', (q_1, \ldots, q_{h'}), R\right) := $ ADAPTEDHGCD$(\mathrm{quo}(r_0, y^{\delta_1}), \mathrm{quo}(r_1, y^{\delta_1}), m_1 - 1, \rho, \mathcal{A})$

6: $\begin{bmatrix} c \\ d \end{bmatrix} := R \begin{bmatrix} \mathrm{quo}(r_0, y^\lambda) \\ \mathrm{quo}(r_1, y^\lambda) \end{bmatrix}$ where $R := \begin{bmatrix} R_{00} & R_{01} \\ R_{10} & R_{11} \end{bmatrix}$

7: $m_2 := \deg(c) + \deg(R_{11}) - k$

8: **if** $d = 0$ or $m_2 > \deg(d)$ **then return** $\left(h', (q_1, \ldots, q_{h'}), R\right)$

9: $r := \mathrm{rem}(c, d)$; $q := \mathrm{quo}(c, d)$; $Q := \begin{bmatrix} 0 & 1 \\ 1 & -q \end{bmatrix}$

10: $n_{h'+1} := n_{h'} - \deg(q)$

11: **if** $n_{h'+1} \leq \rho$ **then return** $\left(h', (q_1, \ldots, q_{h'}, q), R\right)$

12: $\mathcal{A}[n_{h'+1}] := \mathcal{A}[n_{h'}]/\mathrm{lc}(q)$

13: $\delta_2 := \max(2m_2 - \deg(d), 0)$

14: $\left(h^*, (q_{h'+2}, \ldots, q_{h'+h^*+1}), S\right) :=$
    ADAPTEDHGCD$(\mathrm{quo}(d, y^{\delta_2}), \mathrm{quo}(r, y^{\delta_2}), \deg(d) - m_2, \rho, \mathcal{A})$

15: **return** $\left(h_\rho := h' + h^* + 1, \mathcal{Q} := (q_1, \ldots, q_{h_\rho}), M := SQR\right)$

---

calculate two successive subresultants without computing others in the chain. Moreover, this algorithm returns intermediate data that has been computed by the Half-GCD algorithm—the array $\mathcal{R}$ of the remainders, the array $\mathcal{Q}$ of the quotients and the array $\mathcal{A}$ of the leading coefficients of the remainders in the Euclidean sequence—to later calculate higher subresultants in the chain without calling Half-GCD again. This *caching* scheme is shown in Algorithm 4.

Let us explain this technique with an example. For non-zero polynomials $a, b \in \mathbf{k}[y]$ with $n_0 = \deg(a), n_1 = \deg(b)$, so that we have $n_0 \geq n_1$. The subresultant call SUBRESULTANT$(a, b, 0)$ returns $S_0(a, b), S_1(a, b)$ speculatively without computing $(S_{n_1}, S_{n_1-1}, S_{n_1-2}, \ldots, S_2)$, arrays $\mathcal{Q} = (q_1, \ldots, q_\ell)$, $\mathcal{R} = (r_\ell, r_{\ell-1})$, and $\mathcal{A}$. Therefore, any attempt to compute subresultants with higher indices can be addressed by utilizing the arrays $\mathcal{Q}, \mathcal{R}, \mathcal{A}$ instead of calling Half-GCD again. In the *Triangularize* algorithm for solving systems of polynomial

---

Algorithm 3. SUBRESULTANT(a, b, ρ)

Input: $a, b \in \mathbf{k}[x] \setminus \{0\}$ with $n_0 = \deg(a) \geq n_1 = \deg(b)$, $0 \leq \rho \leq n_0$

Output: Subresultants $S_{n_v}(a, b)$, $S_{n_{v+1}}(a, b)$ for such $0 \leq v < \ell$ so that $n_{v+1} \leq \rho < n_v$, the array $\mathcal{Q}$ of the quotients, the array $\mathcal{R}$ of the remainders, and the array $\mathcal{A}$ of the leading coefficients of the remainders (in the Euclidean sequence) that have been computed so far

1: $\mathcal{A} := (0, \ldots, 0, \mathrm{lc}(a))$ where $\mathcal{A}[n_0] = \mathrm{lc}(a)$ and $\mathcal{A}[i] = 0$ for $0 \leq i < n_0$

2: **if** $\rho \geq n_1$ **then**

3: $\quad \mathcal{A}[n_1] = \mathrm{lc}(b)$

4: $\quad$ **return** $\left((a, \mathrm{lc}(b)^{m-n-1} b), (), (), \mathcal{A} \right)$

5: $(v, \mathcal{Q}, M) := \mathrm{ADAPTEDHGCD}(a, b, n_0 - \rho, \rho, \mathcal{A})$

6: *deduce* $\left(n_0 = \deg(a), n_1 = \deg(b), \ldots, n_v = \deg(r_v) \right)$ *from* a, b *and* $\mathcal{Q}$.

7: $\begin{bmatrix} r_v \\ r_{v+1} \end{bmatrix} := M \begin{bmatrix} a \\ b \end{bmatrix}$; $\mathcal{R} := (r_v, r_{v+1})$; $n_{v+1} := \deg(r_{v+1})$

8: $\tau_v := 0$; $\tau_{v+1} := 0$; $\alpha := 1$

9: **for** j **from** 1 **to** $v - 1$ **do**

10: $\quad \tau_v := \tau_v + (n_{j-1} - n_v)(n_j - n_v)$

11: $\quad \tau_{v+1} := \tau_{v+1} + (n_{j-1} - n_{v+1})(n_j - n_{v+1})$

12: $\quad \alpha := \alpha \, \mathcal{A}[n_j]^{n_{j-1} - n_{j+1}}$

13: $\tau_{v+1} := \tau_{v+1} + (n_{v-1} - n_{v+1})(n_v - n_{v+1})$

14: $S_{n_v} := (-1)^{\tau_v} \alpha \, r_v$

15: $S_{n_{v+1}} := (-1)^{\tau_{v+1}} \alpha \, \mathcal{A}[n_v]^{n_{v-1} - n_{v+1} + 1} \, r_{v+1}$

16: **return** $\left((S_{n_v}, S_{n_{v+1}}), \mathcal{Q}, \mathcal{R}, \mathcal{A} \right)$

---

equations by triangular decomposition, the *RegularGCD* subroutine relies on this technique for improved performance; see [3,5] for more details and algorithms.

For polynomials $a, b \in \mathbb{Z}[y]$ with integer coefficients, a modular algorithm can be achieved by utilizing the *Chinese remainder theorem* (CRT). In this approach, we use Algorithms 2 and 3 for a prime field $\mathbf{k}$. We define $\mathbb{Z}_p[y]$ as the ring of univariate polynomials with coefficients in $\mathbb{Z}/p\mathbb{Z}$, for some prime p. Further, we use an iterative and probabilistic approach to CRT from [22]. We iteratively calculate subresultants modulo different primes $p_0, p_1, \ldots$, continuing to add modular images to the CRT direct product $\mathbb{Z}_{p_0} \otimes \cdots \otimes \mathbb{Z}_{p_i}$ for $i \in \mathbb{N}$ until the reconstruction *stabilizes*. That is to say, the reconstruction does not change from $\mathbb{Z}_{p_0} \otimes \cdots \otimes \mathbb{Z}_{p_{i-1}}$ to $\mathbb{Z}_{p_0} \otimes \cdots \otimes \mathbb{Z}_{p_i}$.

We further exploit this technique to compute subresultants of bivariate polynomials over prime fields and the integers. Let $a, b \in \mathbb{B}[y]$ be polynomials with coefficients in $\mathbb{B} = \mathbb{Z}_p[x]$, thus $\mathbb{B}[y] = \mathbb{Z}_p[x, y]$, where the main variable is y and $p \in \mathbb{N}$ is an odd prime. A desirable subresultant algorithm then uses an evaluation-interpolation scheme and the aforementioned univariate routines to compute subresultants of univariate images of a, b over $\mathbb{Z}_p[y]$ and then interpolates back to obtain subresultants over $\mathbb{Z}_p[x, y]$. This approach is well-studied in [22] to compute the resultant of bivariate polynomials. We can use the same

---

Algorithm 4. SUBRESULTANT$(a, b, \rho, \mathcal{Q}, \mathcal{R}, \mathcal{A})$

Input: $a, b \in \mathbf{k}[x] \setminus \{0\}$ with $n_0 = \deg(a) \geq n_1 = \deg(b)$, $0 \leq \rho \leq n_0$, the list $\mathcal{Q}$ of all the quotients in the Euclidean sequence, the list $\mathcal{R}$ of the remainders that have been computed so far; we assume that $\mathcal{R}$ contains at least $r_\mu, \ldots r_{\ell-1}, r_\ell$ with $0 \leq \mu \leq \ell - 1$, and the list $\mathcal{A}$ of the leading coefficients of the remainders in the Euclidean sequence

Output: Subresultants $S_{n_v}(a, b)$, $S_{n_{v+1}}(a, b)$ for such $0 \leq v < \ell$ so that $n_{v+1} \leq \rho < n_v$; the list $\mathcal{R}$ of the remainders is updated in-place

1: *deduce* $\left(n_0 = \deg(a), n_1 = \deg(b), \ldots, n_\ell = \deg(r_\ell) \right)$ *from* a, b *and* $\mathcal{Q}$
2: **if** $n_\ell \leq \rho$ **then** $v := \ell$
3: **else** *find* $0 \leq v < \ell$ *such that* $n_{v+1} \leq \rho < n_v$.
4: **if** $v = 0$ **then**
5:     **return** $\left(a, \mathrm{lc}(b)^{m-n-1} b \right)$
6: **for** i **from** $\max(v, \mu + 1)$ **down to** v **do**
7:     $r_i := r_{i+1} q_{i+1} + r_{i+2}$; $\mathcal{R} := \mathcal{R} \cup (r_i)$
8: *compute* $S_{n_v}, S_{n_{v+1}}$ *using Proposition 1 from* r_v, r_{v+1}
9: **return** $\left(S_{n_v}, S_{n_{v+1}} \right)$

---

technique to compute the entire subresultant chain, or even particular subresultants speculatively through Algorithms 2 and 3.

We begin with choosing a set of evaluation points of size $N \in \mathbb{N}$ and evaluate each coefficient of $a, b \in \mathbb{Z}_p[x, y]$ with respect to the main variable (y). Then, we call the subresultant algorithm to compute subresultants images over $\mathbb{Z}_p[y]$. Finally, we can retrieve the bivariate subresultants by interpolating each coefficient of each subresultant from the images. The number of evaluation points is determined from an upper-bound on the degree of subresultants and resultants with respect to x. From [12], the following inequality holds: $N \geq \deg(b, y) \deg(a, x) + \deg(a, y) \deg(b, x) + 1$.

For bivariate polynomials with integer coefficients, we can use the CRT algorithm in a similar manner to that which has already been reviewed for univariate polynomials over $\mathbb{Z}$. Figure 1 demonstrates this procedure for two polynomials $a, b \in \mathbb{Z}[x, y]$. In this commutative diagram, $\bar{a}, \bar{b}$ represent the modular images of the polynomials a, b modulo prime p_i for $0 \leq i \leq e$.

In practice, as the number of variables increases, the use of dense evaluation-interpolation schemes become less effective, since degree bound estimates become less sharp. In fact, sparse evaluation-interpolation schemes become more attractive [23, 29], and we will consider them in future works.

4 Optimized Ducos' Subresultant Chain

In [10], Ducos proposes two optimizations for Algorithm 1. The first one, attributed to Lazard, deals with the potentially expensive exponentiations and division at Line 11 of Algorithm 1. The second optimizations considers the potentially expensive exact division (of a pseudo-remainder by an element from the

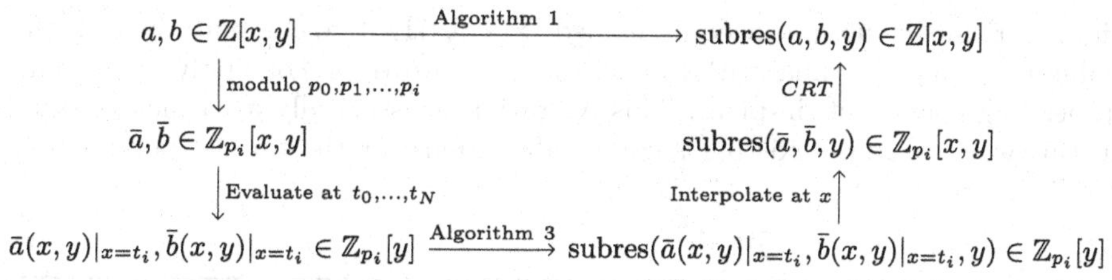

$$a, b \in \mathbb{Z}[x, y] \xrightarrow{\quad\text{Algorithm 1}\quad} \text{subres}(a, b, y) \in \mathbb{Z}[x, y]$$

$\Big\downarrow$ modulo $p_0, p_1, \ldots, p_i$ $\qquad\qquad\qquad\qquad$ $CRT \Big\uparrow$

$$\bar{a}, \bar{b} \in \mathbb{Z}_{p_i}[x, y] \qquad\qquad\qquad\qquad \text{subres}(\bar{a}, \bar{b}, y) \in \mathbb{Z}_{p_i}[x, y]$$

$\Big\downarrow$ Evaluate at $t_0, \ldots, t_N$ $\qquad\qquad\qquad$ Interpolate at x $\Big\uparrow$

$$\bar{a}(x, y)|_{x=t_i}, \bar{b}(x, y)|_{x=t_i} \in \mathbb{Z}_{p_i}[y] \xrightarrow{\text{Algorithm 3}} \text{subres}(\bar{a}(x, y)|_{x=t_i}, \bar{b}(x, y)|_{x=t_i}, y) \in \mathbb{Z}_{p_i}[y]$$

Fig. 1. Computing the subresultant chain of $a, b \in \mathbb{Z}[x, y]$ using modular arithmetic, evaluation-interpolation and CRT algorithms where $(t_0, \ldots, t_N)$ is the list of evaluation points, $(p_0, \ldots, p_i,)$ is the list of distinct primes, $\bar{a} = a \bmod p_i$, and $\bar{b} = b \bmod p_i$

coefficient ring) at Line 15 of this algorithm. Applying both improvements to Algorithm 1 yields an efficient subresultant chain procedure that is known as Ducos' algorithm.

Algorithm 5. Ducos Optimization (S_d, S_{d-1}, S_e, s_d)

Input: Given $S_d, S_{d-1}, S_e \in \mathbb{B}[y]$ and $s_d \in \mathbb{B}$
Output: S_{e-1}, the next subresultant in the subresultant chain of subres(a, b)
1: $(d, e) := (\deg(S_d), \deg(S_{d-1}))$
2: $(c_{d-1}, s_e) := (\text{lc}(S_{d-1}), \text{lc}(S_e))$
3: **for** $j = 0, \ldots, e - 1$ **do**
4: $\quad H_j := s_e y^j$
5: $H_e := s_e y^e - S_e$
6: **for** $j = e + 1, \ldots, d - 1$ **do**
7: $\quad H_j := y H_{j-1} - \dfrac{\text{coeff}(y H_{j-1}, e) S_{d-1}}{c_{d-1}}$
8: $D := \dfrac{\sum\limits_{j=0}^{d-1} \text{coeff}(S_d, j) H_j}{\text{lc}(S_d)}$
9: **return** $(-1)^{d-e+1} \dfrac{c_{d-1}(y H_{d-1} + D) - \text{coeff}(y H_{d-1}, e) S_{d-1}}{s_d}$

The Ducos optimization that is presented in Algorithm 5, and borrowed from [10], is a well-known improvement of Algorithm 1 to compute the subresultant S_{e-1} (Line 15). This optimization provides a faster procedure to compute the pseudo-division of two successive subresultants, namely $S_d, S_{d-1} \in \mathbb{B}[y]$, and a division by a power of $\text{lc}(S_d)$. The main part of this algorithm is for-loops to compute:

$$D := \frac{\sum\limits_{j=0}^{d-1} \text{coeff}(S_d, j) H_j}{\text{lc}(S_d)},$$

where $\text{coeff}(S_d, j)$ is the coefficient of S_d in y^j.

We now introduce a new optimization for this algorithm to make better use of memory resources through in-place arithmetic. This is shown in Algorithm 6. In this algorithm we use a procedure named INPLACETAIL to compute the tail (the reductum of a polynomial with respect to its main variable) of a polynomial, and its leading coefficient, in-place. This operation is essentially a coefficient shift. In this way, we reuse existing memory allocations for the tails of polynomials S_d, S_{d-1}, and S_e.

Algorithm 6. *memory-efficient* **Ducos Optimization** (S_d, S_{d-1}, S_e, s_d)

Input: $S_d, S_{d-1}, S_e \in \mathbb{B}[y]$ and $s_d \in \mathbb{B}$
Output: S_{e-1}, the next subresultant in the subresultant chain of subres(a, b)
1: $(p, c_d) := $ INPLACETAIL(S_d)
2: $(q, c_{d-1}) := $ INPLACETAIL(S_{d-1})
3: $(h, s_e) := $ INPLACETAIL(S_e)
4: *Convert* p to a recursive representation format in-place
5: $h := -h; \ a := \text{coeff}(p, e) \ h$
6: **for** $i = e + 1, \ldots, d - 1$ **do**
7:     **if** $\deg(h) = e - 1$ **then**
8:         $h := y \ \text{tail}(h) - $ EXACTQUOTIENT$(\text{lc}(h) \ q, c_{d-1})$
9:     **else** $h := y \ \text{tail}(h)$
10:     $a := a + \text{lc}(\text{coeff}(p, i)) \ h$
11: $a := a + s_e \ \sum_{i=0}^{e-1} \text{coeff}(p, i) y^i$
12: $a := $ EXACTQUOTIENT(a, c_d)
13: **if** $\deg(h) = e - 1$ **then**
14:     $a := c_{d-1} \ (y \ \text{tail}(h) + a) - \text{lc}(h) \ q$
15: **else** $a := c_{d-1} \ (y \ h + a)$
16: **return** $(-1)^{d-e+1} $ EXACTQUOTIENT(a, s_d)

Furthermore, we reduce the cost of calculating $\sum_{j=e}^{d-1} \text{coeff}(S_d, j) H_j$ with computing the summation iteratively and in-place in the same for-loop that is used to update polynomial h (lines 6–10 in Algorithm 6). This greatly improves data locality. We also update the value of h depending on its degree with respect to y as $\deg(h) \leq e - 1$ for all $e + 1 \leq i < d$. We utilize an optimized exact division algorithm denoted by EXACTQUOTIENT to compute quotients rather a classical Euclidean algorithm.

5   Implementation and Experimentation

In this section, we discuss the implementation and performance of our various subresultant algorithms and their underlying core routines. Our methods are implemented as part of the Basic Polynomial Algebra Subprograms (BPAS) library [2] and we compare their performance against the NTL library [27] and MAPLE 2020 [21]. Throughout this section, our benchmarks were collected on a machine running Ubuntu 18.04.4, BPAS v1.791, GMP 6.1.2, and NTL 11.4.3, with an Intel Xeon X5650 processor running at 2.67 GHz, with 12×4GB DDR3 memory at 1.33 GHz.

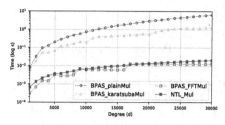

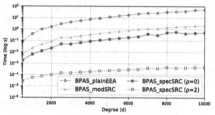

Fig. 2. Comparing plain, Karatsuba, and FFT-based multiplication in BPAS with the wrapper `mul` method in NTL to compute ab for polynomials $a, b \in \mathbb{Z}_p[y]$ with $\deg(a) = \deg(b) + 1 = d$

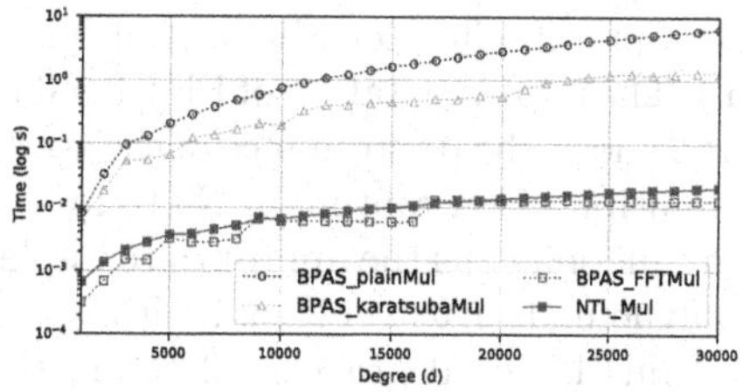

Fig. 3. Comparing Euclidean and fast division algorithms in BPAS with the division method in NTL to compute $\mathrm{rem}(a, b)$ and $\mathrm{quo}(a, b)$ for polynomials $a, b \in \mathbb{Z}_p[y]$ with $\deg(a) = 2(\deg(b) - 1) = d$

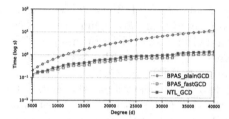

Fig. 4. Comparing Euclidean-based GCD and Half-GCD-based GCD algorithms in BPAS with the GCD algorithm in NTL to compute $\gcd(a, b) = 1$ for polynomials $a, b \in \mathbb{Z}_p[y]$ with $\deg(a) = \deg(b) + 1 = d$

Fig. 5. Comparing EEA, modular subresultant, and Half-GCD-based subresultant (`BPAS_specSRC`, $\rho = 0, 2$), in BPAS for dense polynomials $a, b \in \mathbb{Z}_p[y]$ with $\deg(a) = \deg(b) + 1 = d$

5.1 Routines over $\mathbb{Z}_p[y]$

We begin with foundational routines for arithmetic in finite fields and polynomials over finite fields. For basic arithmetic over a prime field $\mathbb{Z}_p$ where p is an odd prime, Montgomery multiplication, originally presented in [24], is used to speed up multiplication. This method avoids division by the modulus without any effect on the performance of addition, and so, yields faster modular inverse and division algorithms.

We have developed a dense representation of univariate polynomials which take advantage of Montgomery arithmetic (following the implementation in [6]) for prime fields with $p < 2^{64}$. Throughout this section we examine the performance of each operation for two randomly generated dense polynomials $a, b \in \mathbb{Z}_p$ with a 64-bit prime $p = 4179340454199820289$. Figures 2, 3, 4 and 5 examine, respectively, multiplication, division, GCD, and subresultant chain operations. These plots compare the various implementations within BPAS against NTL.

Our multiplication over $\mathbb{Z}_p[y]$ dynamically chooses the appropriate algorithm based on the input polynomials: plain or Karatsuba algorithms (following the routines in [12, Chapter 8]), or multiplication based on fast Fourier transform (FFT). The implementation of FFT itself follows that which was introduced in [7]. Figure 2 shows the performance of these routines in BPAS against a similar "wrapper" multiplication routine in NTL. From empirical data, our wrapper multiplication function calls the appropriate implementation of multiplication as follows. For polynomials a, b over $\mathbb{Z}_p[y]$, with $p < 2^{63}$, the plain algorithm is called when $s := \min\left(\deg(a), \deg(b)\right) < 200$ and the Karatsuba algorithm is called when $s \geq 200$. For 64-bit primes $(p > 2^{63})$, plain and Karatsuba algorithms are called when $s < 10$ and $s < 40$, respectively, otherwise FFT-based multiplication is performed.

The division operation is again a wrapper function, dynamically choosing between Euclidean (plain) and fast division algorithms. The fast algorithm is an optimized power series inversion procedure that is firstly implemented in Aldor [11] using the so-called middle-product trick. Figure 3 shows the performance of these two algorithms in comparison with the NTL division over $\mathbb{Z}_p[y]$. For polynomials a, b over $\mathbb{Z}_p[y]$, b the divisor, empirical data again guides the choice of appropriate implementation. Plain division is called for primes $p < 2^{63}$ and $\deg(b) < 1000$. However, for 64-bit primes, the plain algorithm is used when $\deg(b) < 100$, otherwise fast division supported by FFT is used.

Our GCD operation over $\mathbb{Z}_p[y]$ had two implementations: the classical extended Euclidean algorithm (EEA) and the Half-GCD (fast EEA) algorithm, respectively following the pseudo-codes in [12, Chapter 11] and the implementation in the NTL library [27]. Figure 4 shows the performance of these two approaches named BPAS_plainGCD and BPAS_fastGCD, respectively, in comparison with the NTL GCD algorithm for polynomials $a, b \in \mathbb{Z}_p[y]$ where $\gcd(a, b) = 1$.

To analyze the performance of our subresultant schemes, we compare the naïve EEA algorithm with the modular subresultant chain and the speculative subresultant algorithm for $\rho = 0, 2$ in Fig. 5. As this figure shows, using the Half-GCD algorithm to compute two successive subresultants S_1, S_0 for $\rho = 0$ is approximately $5\times$ faster than computing the entire chain, while calculating other subresultants, e.g. S_3, S_2 for $\rho = 2$ with taking advantage of the *cached* information from the first call (for $\rho = 0$), is nearly instantaneous.

5.2   Subresultants over $\mathbb{Z}[y]$ and $\mathbb{Z}[x, y]$

We have developed a dense representation of univariate and bivariate polynomials over arbitrary-precision integers, using low-level procedures of the GNU Multiple Precision Arithmetic library (GMP) [13]. Basic dense arithmetic operations, like addition, multiplication, and division, follows [12]. The representation of a dense bivariate polynomial $a \in \mathbb{Z}[x, y]$ (or $\mathbb{Z}_p[x, y]$ for a prime p) is stored as a dense array of coefficients (polynomials in $\mathbb{Z}[x]$), possibly including zeros.

Following our previous discussion of various schemes for subresultants, we have implemented several subresultant algorithms over $\mathbb{Z}[y]$ and $\mathbb{Z}[x, y]$. We have four families of implementations:

(i) BPAS_modSRC, that computes the entire subresultant chain using Proposition 1 and the CRT algorithm (and evaluation-interpolation over $\mathbb{Z}[x, y]$);

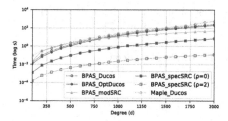

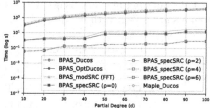

Fig. 6. Comparing (optimized) Ducos' subresultant chain algorithm, modular subresultant chain, and speculative subresultant for $\rho = 0, 2$, algorithms in BPAS with Ducos' subresultant chain algorithm in MAPLE for polynomials $a, b \in \mathbb{Z}[y]$ with $\deg(a) = \deg(b)+1 = d$

Fig. 7. Comparing (optimized) Ducos' subresultant chain, modular subresultant chain, and speculative subresultant for $\rho = 0, 2, 4, 6$, in BPAS with Ducos' algorithm in MAPLE for dense polynomials $a, b \in \mathbb{Z}[x < y]$ with $\deg(a, y) = \deg(b, y) + 1 = 50$ and $\deg(a, x) = \deg(b, x) + 1 = d$

(ii) BPAS_specSRC, that refers to Algorithms 3 and 4 to compute two successive subresultants using Half-GCD and caching techniques;

(iii) BPAS_Ducos, for Ducos' algorithm, based on Algorithm 5; and

(iv) BPAS_OptDucos, for Ducos' algorithm based on Algorithm 6.

Figure 6 compares the running time of those subresultant schemes over $\mathbb{Z}[y]$ in the BPAS library and MAPLE. The modular approach is up to $5\times$ faster than the optimized Ducos' algorithm. Using speculative algorithms to compute only two successive subresultants yields a speedup factor of 7 for $d = 2000$. Figure 7 provides a favourable comparison between the family of subresultant schemes in BPAS and the subresultant algorithm in MAPLE for dense bivariate polynomials $a, b \in \mathbb{Z}[x, y]$ where the main degree is fixed to 50, i.e. $\deg(a, y) = \deg(b, y) + 1 = 50$, and $\deg(a, x) = \deg(b, x) + 1 = d$ for $d \in \{10, 20, \ldots, 100\}$. Note that the BPAS_specSRC algorithm for $\rho = 0, 2, 4, 6$ is caching the information for the next call with taking advantage of Algorithm 4.

We further compare our routines with the Ducos subresultant chain algorithm in MAPLE, which is implemented as part of the *RegularChains* library [19]. Table 1 shows the memory usage for computing the entire subresultant chain of polynomials $a, b \in \mathbb{Z}[y]$, with $\deg(a) = \deg(b) + 1 = d$. The table presents BPAS_Ducos, BPAS_OptDucos, and Maple_Ducos. For $d = 2000$, Table 1 shows that the optimized algorithm uses approximately $3\times$ and $11\times$ less memory than our original implementation and the Ducos' algorithm in MAPLE, respectively.

We next compare more closely the two main ways of computing an entire subresultant chain: the direct approach following Algorithm 1, and a modular approach using evaluation-interpolation and CRT (see Fig. 1). Figure 8 shows the performance of the direct approach (the top surface), calling our memory-optimized Ducos' algorithm BPAS_OptDucos, in comparison with the modular approach (the bottom surface), calling BPAS_modSRC. Note that, in this figure, interpolation may be based on Lagrange interpolation or FFT algorithms depending on the degrees of the input polynomials.

Table 1. Comparing memory usage (GB) of Ducos' subresultant chain algorithms for polynomials $a, b \in \mathbb{Z}[y]$ with $\deg(a) = \deg(b) + 1 = d$ in Fig. 6 over $\mathbb{Z}[y]$

Degree	BPAS_Ducos	BPAS_OptDucos	Maple_Ducos
1000	1.088	0.320	3.762
1100	1.450	0.430	5.080
1200	1.888	0.563	6.597
1300	2.398	0.717	8.541
1400	2.968	0.902	10.645
1500	3.655	1.121	12.997
1600	4.443	1.364	15.924
1700	5.341	1.645	19.188
1800	6.325	1.958	23.041
1900	7.474	2.332	27.353
2000	8.752	2.721	31.793

Next, Fig. 9 highlights the benefit of our speculative approach to compute the resultant and subresultant of index 1 compared to computing the entire. The FFT-based modular algorithm is presented as the top surface, while the speculative subresultant algorithm based on the Half-GCD is the bottom surface.

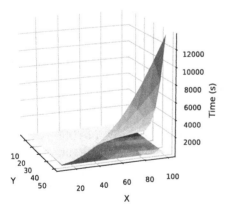
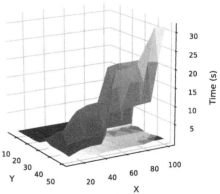

Fig. 8. Comparing Opt. Ducos' algorithm (the top surface) and modular subresultant chain (the bottom surface) to compute the entire chain for polynomials $a, b \in \mathbb{Z}[x < y]$ with $\deg(a, y) = \deg(b, y) + 1 = Y$ and $\deg(a, x) = \deg(b, x) + 1 = X$

Fig. 9. Comparing modular subresultant chain with using FFT (the top surface), and speculative subresultant ($\rho = 0$) (the bottom surface) for polynomials $a, b \in \mathbb{Z}[x < y]$ with $\deg(a, y) = \deg(b, y) + 1 = Y$ and $\deg(a, x) = \deg(b, x) + 1 = X$

Table 2. Comparing the execution time (in seconds) of subresultant schemes on the BPAS *Triangularize* solver for well-known bivariate systems in the literature. We call optimized Ducos' subresultant chain algorithm in the OptDucos mode, modular subresultant chain algorithms (FFT and Lagrange) in the ModSRC mode, and Half-GCD based subresultant algorithms in the SpecSRCnaive and SpecSRCcached modes. We do cache subresultant information for further calls in the ModSRC and SpecSRCcached modes; deg(src[idx]) shows a list of minimum main degrees of the computed subresultants in each subresultant call and Indexes indicates a list of requested subresultant indexes.

SysName	ModSRC	SpecSRCnaive	SpecSRCcached	OptDucos	deg(src[idx])	Indexes
13_sings_9	3.416	3.465	3.408	3.417	(1)	(0)
compact_surf	11.257	26.702	10.26	10.258	(0, 2, 4, 6)	(0, 3, 5, 6)
curve24	4.992	4.924	4.911	4.912	(0, 0, 1)	(0, 0, 0)
curve_issac	2.554	2.541	2.531	2.528	(0, 0, 1)	(0, 0, 0)
cusps_and_flexes	4.656	8.374	4.656	4.488	(0, ..., 2)	(0, ..., 2)
degree_6_surf	81.887	224.215	79.394	344.564	(0, 2, 4, 4)	(0, 2, 4, 4)
hard_one	48.359	197.283	47.213	175.847	(0, ..., 2)	(0, ..., 2)
huge_cusp	23.406	33.501	23.41	23.406	(0, 2, 2)	(0, 2, 2)
L6_circles	32.906	721.49	33.422	32.347	(0, ..., 6)	(0, ..., 6)
large_curves	65.353	64.07	63.018	366.432	(0, 0, 1, 1)	(0, 0, 0, 0)
mignotte_xy	348.406	288.214	287.248	462.432	(1)	(0)
SA_2_4_eps	4.141	37.937	4.122	4.123	(0, ..., 6)	(0, ..., 6)
SA_4_4_eps	222.825	584.318	216.065	197.816	(0, ..., 3)	(0, ..., 6)
spider	293.701	294.121	295.198	293.543	(0, 0, 1, 1)	(0, 0, 0, 0)
spiral29_24	647.469	643.88	644.379	643.414	(1)	(0)
ten_circles	3.255	56.655	2.862	2.116	(0, ..., 4)	(0, ..., 4)
tryme	3728.085	4038.539	2415.28	4893.04	(0, 2)	(0, 2)
vert_lines	1.217	24.956	1.02	1.021	(0, ..., 6)	(0, ..., 6)

Lastly, we investigate the effects of different subresultant algorithms on the performance of the BPAS polynomial system solved based on triangular decomposition and regular chains; see [3,5]. Subresultants play a crucial role in computing regular GCDs (see Sect. 1) and thus in solving systems via triangular decomposition. Tables 2, 3, and 4 investigate the performance of BPAS_modSRC, and BPAS_specSRC and the caching technique, for system solving.

Table 2 shows the running time of well-known and challenging bivariate systems, where we have forced the solver to use only one particular subresultant scheme. In SpecSRCnaive, BPAS_specSRC does not cache data and thus does not reuse the sequence of quotients computed from previous calls. Among those systems, the caching ratio (SpecSRCnaive/SpecSRCcached) of vert_lines, L6_circles, ten_circles, and SA_2_4_eps are 24.5, 21.6, 19.8, 9.2, respectively, while the speculative ratio (ModSRC/SpecSRCcached) of tryme, mignotte_xy, and vert_lines are 1.5, 1.2, and 1.2, respectively.

Tables 3 and 4 examine the performance of the polynomial system solver on constructed systems which aim to exploit the maximum speed-up of these new schemes. Listing 1.1 and 1.2 in Appendix A provide the MAPLE code to construct these input systems. For those systems created by Listing 1.1, we get 3× speed-up through caching the intermediate speculative data rather than repeatedly calling the Half-GCD algorithm for each subresultant call. Using BPAS_specSRC provides a 1.5× speed-up over using the BPAS_modSRC algorithm. Another family of constructed examples created by Listing 1.2 is evaluated in Table 4. Here, we get up to 3× speed-up with the use of cached data, and up to 2× speed-up over the modular method.

Table 3. Comparing the execution time (in seconds) of subresultant schemes on the BPAS *Triangularize* system solver for constructed bivariate systems in Listing 1.1 to exploit the speculative scheme. Column headings follow Table 2, and FFTBlockSize is block size used in the FFT-based evaluation and interpolation algorithms.

n	ModSRC	SpecSRC$_\text{naive}$	SpecSRC$_\text{cached}$	deg(src[idx])	Indexes	FFTBlockSize
50	9.382	25.025	6.295	(0, 25, 50, 75)	(0, 26, 51, 75)	512
60	22.807	82.668	23.380	(0, 30, 60, 90)	(0, 31, 61, 90)	1024
70	23.593	105.253	30.477	(0, 35, 70, 105)	(0, 36, 71, 105)	1024
80	36.658	156.008	47.008	(0, 40, 80, 120)	(0,41,81,120)	1024
100	171.213	272.939	83.966	(0, 50, 100, 150)	(0, 51, 101, 150)	1024
110	280.952	370.628	117.106	(0, 55, 110, 165)	(0, 56, 111, 165)	1024
120	491.853	1035.810	331.601	(0, 60, 120, 180)	(0, 61, 121, 180)	2048
130	542.905	1119.720	362.631	(0, 65, 130, 195)	(0, 66, 131, 195)	2048
140	804.982	1445.000	470.649	(0, 70, 140, 210)	(0, 71, 141, 210)	2048
150	1250.700	1963.920	639.031	(0, 75, 150, 225)	(0, 76, 151, 225)	2048

Table 4. Comparing the execution time (in seconds) of subresultant schemes on the BPAS *Triangularize* system solver for constructed bivariate systems in Listing 1.2 to exploit the speculative scheme. Column headings follow Table 3.

n	ModSRC	SpecSRC$_\text{naive}$	SpecSRC$_\text{cached}$	deg(src[idx])	Indexes	FFTBlockSize
100	894.139	1467.510	474.241	(0, 2, 2)	(0, 2, 2)	512
110	1259.850	2076.920	675.806	(0, 2, 2)	(0, 2, 2)	512
120	1807.060	2757.390	963.547	(0, 2, 2)	(0, 2, 2)	512
130	2897.150	4311.990	1505.080	(0, 2, 2)	(0, 2, 2)	1024
140	4314.300	5881.640	2134.190	(0, 2, 2)	(0, 2, 2)	1024
150	5177.410	7869.700	2609.170	(0, 2, 2)	(0, 2, 2)	1024

Acknowledgments. The authors would like to thank Robert H. C. Moir and NSERC of Canada (award CGSD3-535362-2019).

A   MAPLE code for Polynomial Systems

```
1   SystemGenerator1 := proc(n)
2   local R := PolynomialRing([x,y]);
3   local J := PolynomialIdeals:-Intersect(<x^2+1,xy+2>,
4   <x^2+3,xy^floor(n/2)+floor(n/2)+1>);
5   J := PolynomialIdeals:-Intersect(J, <x^2+3,xy^n+n+1>);
6   local dec := Triangularize(Generators(J),R);
7   dec := map(NormalizeRegularChain,dec,R);
8   dec := EquiprojectableDecomposition([%[1][1],%[2][1]],R);
9   return map(expand, Equations(op(dec),R));
10  end proc:
```

Listing 1.1. MAPLE code of constructed polynomials in Table 3.

```
1   SystemGenerator2 := proc(n)
2   local R := PolynomialRing([x,y]);
3   local f := randpoly([x],dense,coeffs=rand(-1..1),degree=n);
4   local J := <f,xy+2>;
5   J :=PolynomialIdeals:-Intersect(J,<x^2+2,(x^2+3x+1)y^2+3>);
6   local dec := Triangularize(Generators(J),R);
7   dec := map(NormalizeRegularChain,dec,R);
8   dec := EquiprojectableDecomposition([%[1][1],%[2][1]],R);
9   return map(expand,Equations(op(dec),R));
10  end proc:
```

Listing 1.2. MAPLE code of constructed polynomials in Table 4.

References

1. Abdeljaoued, J., Diaz-Toca, G.M., González-Vega, L.: Bezout matrices, subresultant polynomials and parameters. Appl. Math. Comput. **214**(2), 588–594 (2009)
2. Asadi, M., et al.: Basic Polynomial Algebra Subprograms (BPAS) (version 1.791) (2021). http://www.bpaslib.org
3. Asadi, M., Brandt, A., Moir, R.H.C., Moreno Maza, M., Xie, Y.: Parallelization of triangular decompositions: techniques and implementation. J. Symb. Comput. (2021, to appear)
4. Becker, E., Mora, T., Grazia Marinari, M., Traverso, C.: The shape of the shape lemma. In: Proceedings of ISSAC 1994, pp. 129–133. ACM (1994)
5. Chen, C., Moreno Maza, M.: Algorithms for computing triangular decomposition of polynomial systems. J. Symb. Comput. **47**(6), 610–642 (2012)
6. Covanov, S., Mohajerani, D., Moreno Maza, M., Wang, L.: Big prime field FFT on multi-core processors. In: Proceedings of the 2019 International Symposium on Symbolic and Algebraic Computation (ISSAC), pp. 106–113. ACM (2019)
7. Covanov, S., Moreno Maza, M.: Putting Fürer algorithm into practice. Technical report (2014). http://www.csd.uwo.ca/~moreno//Publications/Svyatoslav-Covanov-Rapport-de-Stage-Recherche-2014.pdf

8. Della Dora, J., Dicrescenzo, C., Duval, D.: About a new method for computing in algebraic number fields. In: Caviness, B.F. (ed.) EUROCAL 1985. LNCS, vol. 204, pp. 289–290. Springer, Heidelberg (1985). https://doi.org/10.1007/3-540-15984-3_279

9. Ducos, L.: Algorithme de Bareiss, algorithme des sous-résultants. Informatique Théorique et Applications **30**(4), 319–347 (1996)

10. Ducos, L.: Optimizations of the subresultant algorithm. J. Pure Appl. Algebra **145**(2), 149–163 (2000)

11. Filatei, A., Li, X., Moreno Maza, M., Schost, E.: Implementation techniques for fast polynomial arithmetic in a high-level programming environment. In: Proceedings of ISSAC, pp. 93–100 (2006)

12. von zur Gathen, J., Gerhard, J.: Modern Computer Algebra, 3rd edn. Cambridge University Press, Cambridge (2013)

13. Granlund, T.: The GMP Development Team: GNU MP: the GNU multiple precision arithmetic library (version 6.1.2) (2020). http://gmplib.org

14. van der Hoeven, J., Lecerf, G., Mourrain, B.: Mathemagix (from 2002). http://www.mathemagix.org

15. Kahoui, M.E.: An elementary approach to subresultants theory. J. Symb. Comput. **35**(3), 281–292 (2003)

16. Knuth, D.E.: The analysis of algorithms. Actes du congres international des Mathématiciens **3**, 269–274 (1970)

17. Lecerf, G.: On the complexity of the Lickteig-Roy subresultant algorithm. J. Symb. Comput. **92**, 243–268 (2019)

18. Lehmer, D.H.: Euclid's algorithm for large numbers. Am. Math. Mon. **45**(4), 227–233 (1938)

19. Lemaire, F., Moreno Maza, M., Xie, Y.: The RegularChains library in MAPLE. In: Maple Conference, vol. 5, pp. 355–368 (2005)

20. Lickteig, T., Roy, M.F.: Semi-algebraic complexity of quotients and sign determination of remainders. J. Complex. **12**(4), 545–571 (1996)

21. Maplesoft, a division of Waterloo Maple Inc.: Maple (2020). www.maplesoft.com

22. Monagan, M.: Probabilistic algorithms for computing resultants. In: Proceedings of ISSAC 2005, pp. 245–252. ACM (2005)

23. Monagan, M., Tuncer, B.: Factoring multivariate polynomials with many factors and huge coefficients. In: Gerdt, V.P., Koepf, W., Seiler, W.M., Vorozhtsov, E.V. (eds.) CASC 2018. LNCS, vol. 11077, pp. 319–334. Springer, Cham (2018). https://doi.org/10.1007/978-3-319-99639-4_22

24. Montgomery, P.L.: Modular multiplication without trial division. Math. Comput. **44**(170), 519–521 (1985)

25. Reischert, D.: Asymptotically fast computation of subresultants. In: Proceedings of ISSAC 1997, pp. 233–240. ACM (1997)

26. Schönhage, A.: Schnelle Berechnung von Kettenbruchentwicklungen. Acta Informatica **1**, 139–144 (1971)

27. Shoup, V., et al.: NTL: a library for doing number theory (version 11.4.3) (2021). www.shoup.net/ntl

28. Thull, K., Yap, C.: A unified approach to HGCD algorithms for polynomials and integers. Manuscript (1990)
29. Zippel, R.: Probabilistic algorithms for sparse polynomials. In: Ng, E.W. (ed.) Symbolic and Algebraic Computation. LNCS, vol. 72, pp. 216–226. Springer, Heidelberg (1979). https://doi.org/10.1007/3-540-09519-5_73

On Rational Solutions of Pseudo-linear Systems

Moulay A. Barkatou, Thomas Cluzeau$^{(\boxtimes)}$, and Ali El Hajj

University of Limoges, CNRS, XLIM UMR 7252, 123 Avenue Albert Thomas,
87060 Limoges Cedex, France
{moulay.barkatou,thomas.cluzeau,ali.el-hajj}@unilim.fr

Abstract. We develop a new algorithm for computing rational solutions of partial pseudo-linear systems. The algorithm uses a recursive process based on the computation of rational solutions for a sole pseudo-linear system. Using the general setting of pseudo-linear algebra, we revisit the computation of rational solutions for a pseudo-linear system. In particular, we provide a unified and efficient approach for computing a universal denominator. All the algorithms are implemented in Maple.

1 Introduction

Let C be a field of characteristic zero and $K = C(x_1, \ldots, x_m)$ the field of rational functions in m independent variables $x_1, \ldots, x_m$ with coefficients in C. In the present paper, the object of study is a *partial pseudo-linear system* of the form:

$$\begin{cases} \delta_1(\mathbf{y}) - M_1\,\phi_1(\mathbf{y}) = 0, \\ \quad \vdots \\ \delta_m(\mathbf{y}) - M_m\,\phi_m(\mathbf{y}) = 0, \end{cases} \tag{1}$$

where $\mathbf{y}$ is a vector of n unknown functions of $x_1, \ldots, x_m$, for all $i = 1, \ldots, m$, $M_i \in \mathbb{M}_n(K)$, ϕ_i is a C-automorphism of K, and δ_i is a ϕ_i-derivation such that for all $j \neq i$, x_j is a constant with respect to ϕ_i and δ_i, i.e., $\phi_i(x_j) = x_j$ and $\delta_i(x_j) = 0$. One underlying motivation for considering such partial pseudo-linear systems is that many special functions are solutions of such systems. For instance, one can think of Hermite or Legendre polynomials. We assume that System (1) satisfies the *integrability conditions*: $[L_i, L_j] := L_i \circ L_j - L_j \circ L_i = 0$, for all $i, j = 1, \ldots, m$, where $L_i := I_n\,\delta_i - M_i\,\phi_i$ denotes the matrix operator associated to the ith equation of System (1). A *rational solution* of System (1) is a vector $\mathbf{y} \in K^n$ that satisfies $L_i(\mathbf{y}) = 0$, for all $i = 1, \ldots, m$. In this paper we are interested in computing rational solutions of an integrable system of the form (1). The integrability conditions assure that the space of rational solutions of such a system is of finite dimension over C (at most n). This implies, in particular, that there exists a (not necessarily unique) polynomial (called *universal denominator*) $U \in C[x_1, \ldots, x_m]$ such that for any rational solution $\mathbf{y}$ of (1), $U\mathbf{y}$ is a vector of polynomials. The concept of universal denominators was introduced first in [3].

© Springer Nature Switzerland AG 2021
F. Boulier et al. (Eds.): CASC 2021, LNCS 12865, pp. 42–61, 2021.
https://doi.org/10.1007/978-3-030-85165-1_4

Note that, the existence of a universal denominator is not always guaranteed if one considers other kinds of linear partial differential (or difference) systems or equations. For instance, it was shown in [37,38] that there is no algorithm for testing the existence of a universal denominator for rational solutions of linear partial differential or difference equations with rational function coefficients. One can also consult [32,33] where it was shown that for some scalar linear partial difference equations (such as $y(x_1+1, x_2) - y(x_1, x_2+1) = 0$), there is no universal denominator for all rational solutions.

The computation of rational solutions and other kind of closed form (as polynomial, hypergeometric,...) solutions of linear functional systems has been widely studied in the particular cases of differential and (q-)difference systems: see, for instance, [4,5,7,8,10,27,39,40]. Moreover, algorithms to compute rational and hyperexponential solutions of integrable connections (i.e., the case of System (1) with m differential systems) have been developed in [17]. Also, in [24,28,34,35,41], the authors study different issues concerning partial pseudo-linear systems.

The main contribution of the present paper is a new efficient algorithm for computing rational solutions of System (1). To the authors' knowledge, there exist no algorithm performing such a task, except in the purely differential case [17]. The basic ideas of our algorithm were already given in our previous work [18] for a partial pseudo-linear system composed of one pure differential system and one pure difference system. The recursive method, described in details in Sect. 4.1, uses the same strategy as in [17]. In particular, it requires, for $i = 1, \ldots, m$, an algorithm for computing rational solutions of a sole pseudo-linear system of the form $\delta_i(\mathbf{y}) - N \phi_i(\mathbf{y}) = 0$, where $N \in \mathbb{M}_s(C(p_1, \ldots, p_r)(x_i))$, $1 \le s \le n$ and $p_1, \ldots, p_r$ are parameters which are constants with respect to ϕ_i and δ_i.

Therefore, before considering the case of a partial pseudo-linear system, we first concentrate on the case of a single pseudo-linear system, (i.e., $m = 1$ in System (1)). The setting of pseudo-linear algebra used in the present paper has been introduced in [30] (see also [13,25,26]). It allows to have a unified setting for handling many classes of linear functional systems including differential and (q-)difference systems. In this spirit, the next contribution of our paper is to provide a unified algorithm for computing a universal denominator for rational solutions of all difference systems of the form

$$\phi(\mathbf{y}) = B\,\mathbf{y}, \tag{2}$$

where $B \in \mathrm{GL}_n(C(x))$ and $\phi(f(x)) = f(qx + r)$ for all $f \in C(x)$. Here $r \in C$ and $q \in C^*$ is not a root of unity, but if $r \ne 0$ then q is allowed to be equal to 1. We will refer to a system of the form (2) as a ϕ-system. Such a system can be written (in various ways) as a pseudo-linear system $\delta(\mathbf{y}) = M \phi(\mathbf{y})$ (see Sect. 2). Systems of the form (2) include pure difference ($q = 1$ and $r \ne 0$) and pure q-difference ($r = 0$) systems for which algorithms for computing a universal denominator and rational solutions have been respectively developed in [11] and [4]. Generalizing the methods in [4,11] to more general values for r and $q \ne 1$, we write a universal denominator for System (2) under the form

$(x-\frac{r}{1-q})^{\alpha} U(x)$, where the polynomial $U(x)$ is not divisible by $x-\frac{r}{1-q}$ and $\alpha \in \mathbb{N}$. On one hand, we obtain a bound for α by computing a simple form (see [18] and references therein) of our system at the ϕ-*fixed singularity* $x_{\phi} = \frac{r}{1-q}$. On the other hand, following the ideas of [36] (see also [6,31]), we propose an efficient algorithm for computing $U(x)$.

Another important aspect of our contribution is that the different algorithms developed in the present paper are fully implemented in the Maple package PseudoLinearSystems [19]. In order to speed up the computation of rational solutions of System (1), our implementation takes into account two aspects. First, some necessary conditions for an irreducible polynomial to appear in the denominator of a rational solution are obtained by inspecting the irreducible factors of the denominators of all the matrices M_i (see Sect. 4.2). Moreover, in the recursive process, as the m pseudo-linear systems in (1) can be considered in an arbitrary order, we tried to see (through examples) if there are some orders better than others from the computational point of view. The timings obtained from our experiments (see Sect. 4.3) indicate that the best strategy seems to be to consider first the non-differential systems (i.e., $\phi_i \neq \mathrm{id}$) and then the differential systems.

The rest of the paper is organised as follows. The next section recalls useful notions on pseudo-linear systems. Section 3 concerns the case of a sole pseudo-linear system for which we provide a unified efficient approach for computing a universal denominator for rational solutions. In Sect. 4, we present our recursive algorithm for computing rational solutions of partial pseudo-linear systems. Finally, we provide some explanations concerning our implementation. This includes necessary conditions for an irreducible polynomial to appear in the denominator of a rational solution and this also includes timings comparing different strategies.

2   Pseudo-linear Systems

Let K be a commutative field of characteristic zero, ϕ an automorphism of K, and δ a ϕ-derivation that is a map from K to K satisfying $\delta(a+b) = \delta(a) + \delta(b)$ and $\delta(ab) = \phi(a)\delta(b) + \delta(a)b$ (Leibniz rule), for all $a, b \in K$.

If $\phi = \mathrm{id}_K$, then δ is a usual derivation. Otherwise, i.e. when $\phi \neq \mathrm{id}_K$, it is known (see, e.g., [25]) that δ is necessarily of the form $\gamma(\mathrm{id}_K - \phi)$ for some $\gamma \in K^*$. The subfield $C_K \subset K$ containing all elements c in K that satisfy $\phi(c) = c$ and $\delta(c) = 0$ is called the *field of constants* of K.

A first order *pseudo-linear system* of size n over K is a system of the form

$$\delta(\mathbf{y}) = M \phi(\mathbf{y}), \tag{3}$$

where $\mathbf{y}$ is a vector of n unknown functions and $M \in \mathbb{M}_n(K)$. A solution of System (3) over K is a vector $\mathbf{y} \in K^n$ such that $\delta(\mathbf{y}) = M \phi(\mathbf{y})$. The set of solutions of System (3) over K is a vector space over C_K of dimension at most n (see [12]).

When $K = C(x)$ and $\phi \neq \mathrm{id}_K$, one often prefer to write a pseudo-linear system (3) in the form of a ϕ-system (2). On one hand, every ϕ-system can be easily converted into a pseudo-linear system of the form (3) (see [13, Appendix A.1]).

On the other hand, if we note $\delta = \gamma \,(\mathrm{id}_K - \phi)$ for some $\gamma \in K^*$, then System (3) is either equivalent to the ϕ-system $\tilde{\phi}(\mathbf{y}) = B\mathbf{y}$ with $\tilde{\phi} = \phi^{-1}$ and $B = \tilde{\phi}(\gamma^{-1} M + I_n)$ or to $\phi(\mathbf{y}) = B\mathbf{y}$ with $B = (\gamma^{-1} M + I_n)^{-1}$ provided that this inverse exists. This is the reason why, in the following of the paper, when we consider a pseudo-linear system (3) with $\phi \neq \mathrm{id}_K$ and $\delta = \gamma \,(\mathrm{id}_K - \phi)$ for some $\gamma \in K^*$, we will always assume that the matrix $M + \gamma I_n$ is invertible. In this case, System (3) is called *fully integrable*. Note that for a ϕ-system (2), being fully integrable means that B is invertible.

Remark 1. Considering solutions over a suitable field extension F of K, every fully integrable system admits a solution space of dimension n over $C_F = C_K$. We refer to [35] for a notion of Picard-Vessiot extensions in the present setting. Moreover, from [14, Proposition 2], every ϕ-system can be effectively reduced to a ϕ-system of smaller size with either B invertible (i.e., we have an equivalent fully integrable system) or $B = 0$. For instance, the system

$$\delta(\mathbf{y}) = \begin{pmatrix} -1 & 1 & \cdots & 1 \\ 0 & \ddots & \ddots & \vdots \\ \vdots & \ddots & \ddots & 1 \\ 0 & \cdots & 0 & -1 \end{pmatrix} \phi(\mathbf{y}), \quad \phi \neq \mathrm{id}_K, \quad \delta = \mathrm{id}_K - \phi,$$

is not fully integrable. It can be reduced to the scalar pseudo-linear equation $\delta(y) = -\phi(y)$ which is equivalent to $y = 0$.

In Sect. 3, we shall consider the case of $m = 1$ pseudo-linear system of the form (3) and more particularly, we will show how to handle ϕ-systems of the form (2) in a unified manner. Then, in Sect. 4, we consider the general case of a partial pseudo-linear system of the form (1). In the latter general case, in addition to the assumption that each ϕ-system is fully integrable (i.e., for all $i = 1, \ldots, m$ with $\phi_i \neq \mathrm{id}_K$ and $\delta_i = \gamma_i \,(\mathrm{id}_K - \phi_i)$ with $\gamma_i \in K^*$, the matrix $M_i + \gamma_i I_n$ is invertible), in which case we shall say that System (1) is fully integrable, we suppose that System (1) satisfies the *integrability conditions*: namely, if for $i = 1, \ldots, m$, $L_i := I_n \delta_i - M_i \phi_i$ denotes the matrix operator associated to the ith equation of System (1), then we assume that $[L_i, L_j] := L_i \circ L_j - L_j \circ L_i = 0$, for all $i, j = 1, \ldots, m$.

3 Universal Denominators of Rational Solutions of a Single Pseudo-linear System

The computation of rational solutions for differential, difference, and q-difference systems has been studied respectively in [10,11], and [4]. In the latter works, the algorithms developed share a common strategy for computing rational solutions. They first compute a *universal denominator*, namely, a polynomial that is a multiple of the denominator of any rational solution. Then a suitable change of dependent variables reduces the problem to computing polynomial solutions of a system of the same type. In the present section, we focus on the computation of a universal denominator for a pseudo-linear system. Polynomial solutions can then be computed using, for instance, the monomial-by-monomial approach developed in [13].

In the general setting of pseudo-linear algebra with $K = C(x)$, two cases can be distinguished:

1. The case $\phi = \mathrm{id}_K$ corresponds to differential systems.
2. The case $\phi \neq \mathrm{id}_K$ corresponds to ϕ-systems of the form (2) which includes the pure difference and q-difference cases.

In the differential case $\phi = \mathrm{id}_K$, assuming that $\delta = \frac{d}{dx}$ is the usual derivation of $K = C(x)$, we have a linear differential system of the form $\mathbf{y}' = A\mathbf{y}$, with $' := \frac{d}{dx}$ and $A \in \mathbb{M}_n(K)$. Here, the poles of any rational solution are among the poles of the matrix A. Consequently, the denominator of any rational solution has the form $\prod_{i=1}^{s} p_i^{\alpha_i}$, where $p_1, \ldots, p_s$ are the irreducible factors of the denominator $\mathrm{den}(A)$ of the matrix A and, for $i = 1, \ldots, s$, α_i is a *local exponent* at p_i (see, for instance, [10]). A universal denominator can thus be deduced from the knowledge of the local exponents at each p_i which can be computed using either *super-reduction* algorithms [9,13,23,26,29] or by computing a *simple form* of the differential system at p_i. The interested reader can consult [10,18,20] for details about simple forms and their computations.

Concerning the case $\phi \neq \mathrm{id}_K$, algorithms for computing a universal denominator have been developed only for the pure difference [11] and q-difference [4] cases. In Sect. 3.2, we shall develop a unified and efficient method for computing a universal denominator of a ϕ-system (2) in the case where the automorphism ϕ of $K = C(x)$ is given by $\phi(f(x)) = f(qx + r)$ for all $f \in C(x)$, with $r \in C$ and $q \in C^*$ is not a root of unity, but if $r \neq 0$ then q is allowed to be equal to 1. Note that this restriction on the automorphism ϕ of $C(x)$ is natural as, for the purposes of the present paper, one needs ϕ to send polynomials to polynomials. From the denominators of the matrix $B \in \mathrm{GL}_n(C(x))$ of System (2) and its inverse, we define the following two polynomials in the variable x:

$$a := \phi^{-1}(\mathrm{den}(B)), \quad b := \mathrm{den}(B^{-1}). \tag{4}$$

The *dispersion set* $E_\phi(a, b)$ of the polynomials a and b is defined as:

$$E_\phi(a, b) := \{s \in \mathbb{N}\,;\, \deg\left(\gcd(a, \phi^s(b))\right) > 0\}, \tag{5}$$

and plays an important role in the following. Note that the notion of the dispersion set was firstly introduced in [2]. Except in the pure difference case ($r \neq 0$ and $q = 1$) which is considered in Sect. 3.1 below, a universal denominator for rational solutions of System (2) is decomposed into two distinct parts, i.e., two polynomial factors, that are treated separately and with different methods. One part is called the ϕ-*fixed part* as it corresponds to the ϕ-fixed singularity $x_\phi := \frac{r}{1-q}$ (see Proposition 2 below) and the other part is called the non ϕ-*fixed part*. On one hand, the computation of the ϕ-fixed part can be tackled by computing a simple form (see [18] and references therein) at x_ϕ to get the local exponents at x_ϕ (it is similar to the computation of the part of a universal denominator corresponding to a given p_i in the differential case considered above). On the other hand, the non ϕ-fixed part can be computed from the dispersion set $E_\phi(a, b)$ of a and b. The computation of the non ϕ-fixed part is the purpose of the rest of this section. Before developing our unified and efficient approach (see Sect. 3.2) to compute this non ϕ-fixed part, we briefly recall how one proceeds in the known cases of pure difference and q-difference systems.

3.1 Existing Methods for Pure Difference and q-Difference Systems

Let us consider a pure difference system of the form $\phi(\mathbf{y}) = B\,\mathbf{y}$, where, for all $f \in C(x)$, $\phi(f(x)) = f(x+1)$, i.e., $q = r = 1$, and $B \in \mathrm{GL}_n(C(x))$. From [11, Proposition 1], we know that the irreducible factors of a universal denominator are among the irreducible factors of a and b defined by (4) or their shifts. We have the following result:

Proposition 1 ([11], Theorem 1). *If $E_\phi(a, b) = \emptyset$, then $U(x) = 1$ is a universal denominator, i.e., all rational solutions are polynomials. Otherwise, a universal denominator is given by:*

$$U(x) = \gcd\left(\prod_{i=0}^{N} \phi^{-i}(a(x)), \prod_{j=0}^{N} \phi^{j}(b(x))\right), \quad N := \max(E_\phi(a, b)). \quad (6)$$

We refer to [11] for more details. From a computational point of view, the result in [11, Proposition 3] (see also [5, Section 3.1]) allows to compute a universal denominator without expanding the products in Formula (6).

Let us now consider a pure q-difference system of the form $\phi(\mathbf{y}) = B\,\mathbf{y}$, where, for all $f \in C(x)$, $\phi(f(x)) = f(q\,x)$, q is not a root of unity, and $B \in \mathrm{GL}_n(C(x))$. The computation of rational solutions of q-difference systems is studied in [4]. A universal denominator is written under the form $x^\alpha\,U(x)$, where $\alpha \in \mathbb{N}$ and $U(x) \in C[x]$ is not divisible by x. Note that, here, x is the only monic irreducible polynomial that is fixed by ϕ in the sense that x and $\phi(x)$ divide each other (see also Proposition 2 below for $r = 0$). The factor x^α of a universal denominator is thus what we call the ϕ-fixed part. A bound for α can be obtained from the local exponents at the ϕ-fixed singularity $x_\phi = 0$ which can be computed either using the technique of *EG-eliminations* (see [1, Section 2.2]) or by computing a simple form at 0 (see [18, Section 5]). The other factor $U(x)$ of a universal denominator is what we call the non ϕ-fixed part. It can be computed as in the pure difference case using the formula (6) in Proposition 1 above. The reader can consult [1,4] for additional details concerning universal denominators and rational solutions of q-difference systems.

3.2   A Unified and Efficient Approach for Pseudo-linear Systems

We consider a ϕ-system (2), where the automorphism ϕ of $K = C(x)$ is given by $\phi(f(x)) = f(q\,x + r)$ for all $f \in C(x)$, with $r \in C$ and $q \in C^*$ is not a root of unity, but if $r \neq 0$ then q is allowed to be equal to 1.

Let us first remark that in the case $r \neq 0$ and $q \neq 1$ is not a root of unity, performing the change of independent variable $x = z - \frac{r}{1-q}$, we are reduced to a pure q-difference system. In other words, after performing (if necessary) a change of independent variables, the computation of a universal denominator for the class of ϕ-systems considered here can always be done using one of the algorithms recalled in Sect. 3.1 for the pure difference and q-difference cases. However, in the following, we prefer to develop a unified approach treating directly all the ϕ-systems.

As for pure q-difference systems, we shall decompose a universal denominator as a product of two factors: the ϕ-fixed part and the non ϕ-fixed part. To achieve this, we first need to determine the polynomials that are fixed by ϕ. We say that two polynomials p_1 and p_2 in $C[x]$ are *associated*, and we write $p_1 \sim p_2$, if they divide each other. We introduce the set

$$F_\phi := \{p \in C[x]\backslash\{0\} \; ; \; \deg(p) \geq 1, \exists s \in \mathbb{N}^*, p \sim \phi^s(p)\},$$

where $\phi^s(p(x)) = p(\phi^s(x))$. We remark that

$$\forall s \in \mathbb{N}, \quad \phi^s(x) = q^s\,x + r\,[s]_q, \quad [s]_q := \begin{cases} \dfrac{q^s - 1}{q - 1} & ; \quad q \neq 1, \\[2mm] s & ; \quad q = 1. \end{cases} \tag{7}$$

Proposition 2. *With the previous notation, we have the following:*

1. *If $q = 1$, then $F_\phi = \emptyset$.*
2. *Otherwise, $F_\phi = \left\{c\left(x - \frac{r}{1-q}\right)^s \; ; \; c \in C^*, s \in \mathbb{N}^*\right\}$.*

Proof. If $q = 1$, then $p \sim \phi^j(p)$ for some $j \neq 0$ if and only if p is a constant and we are done. Now let $q \neq 1$. From (7), we have that, for all $j \in \mathbb{N}^*$, $\phi^j(x) = q^j\,x + r\frac{q^j-1}{q-1} = \tilde{q}\,x + \tilde{r}$ has the same form as $\phi(x) = q\,x + r$ so that it suffices to look for non constant polynomials p such that $p \sim \phi(p)$. Let us write $p(x) = \sum_{i=0}^s p_i\,x^{s-i}$ with $p_0 = 1$ and $s \geq 1$. Then $p \sim \phi(p)$ means that there exists $\alpha \in C^*$ such that $\phi(p) = \alpha\,p$ which yields

$$(q\,x + r)^s + p_1\,(q\,x + r)^{s-1} + \cdots + p_s = \alpha\,(x^s + p_1\,x^{s-1} + \cdots + p_s).$$

By expanding the lefthand side of the latter equality and equating the coefficients of each x^i, $i = 0, \ldots, s$, we get

$$q^s = \alpha, \quad \forall i = 1, \ldots, s, \; (q^i - 1)\,p_i = \sum_{j=0}^{i-1} \binom{s-j}{s-i} r^{i-j}\,p_j.$$

Solving the latter linear system successively for $p_1, p_2, \ldots, p_s$, we obtain

$$\forall i = 1, \ldots, s, \quad p_i = \binom{s}{i} \left(\frac{r}{q-1} \right)^i,$$

which yields $p(x) = \left(x - \frac{r}{1-q} \right)^s$ and ends the proof.

From Proposition 2, for $q = 1$ and $r \neq 0$, the set F_ϕ is empty which justifies why in the pure difference case, one does not have to consider a ϕ-fixed part in a universal denominator. Moreover, for the pure q-difference case $q \neq 1$ and $r = 0$, Proposition 2 implies that the only monic irreducible element in F_ϕ is x, meaning that the only ϕ-fixed singularity is $x_\phi = 0$. In the general case with $q \neq 1$, the only monic irreducible element in F_ϕ is $x - \frac{r}{1-q}$ and we thus write a universal denominator as a product

$$\left(x - \frac{r}{1-q} \right)^\alpha U(x), \tag{8}$$

where $\alpha \in \mathbb{N}$ and the polynomial $U(x)$ is not divisible by $x - \frac{r}{1-q}$. Here, $\left(x - \frac{r}{1-q} \right)^\alpha$ is the ϕ-fixed part and $U(x)$ is the non ϕ-fixed part. In order to construct a universal denominator, one needs to determine both a bound for α and a multiple of the polynomial $U(x)$ in (8). On one hand, an upper bound for α can be obtained from a simple form at the ϕ- fixed singularity $x_\phi = \frac{r}{1-q}$. We refer to [18] for a unified algorithm computing simple of pseudo-linear systems. On the other hand, a multiple of the non ϕ-fixed part $U(x)$ can be obtained using Proposition 1. As we have already noticed, the result developed in [11, Proposition 3] (see also [5, Section 3.1], [4, Section 2.1]) allows to compute $U(x)$ with the formula (6) of Proposition 1 without expanding the products. To achieve this, one first needs to compute the dispersion set $E_\phi(a, b)$, which is usually done by a resultant computation, and then, for each $m \in E_\phi(a, b)$, several gcd's are computed in order to get $U(x)$. However, in [36] (see also [6,31]), the authors remark that if we first compute a factorization of the polynomials a and b, then $E_\phi(a, b)$ can be computed without computing resultants, which is often more efficient in practice. Note that [36] also includes a complexity analysis confirming the timings observed in practice. In the next section, we give a unified version of the latter efficient approach for all ϕ-systems.

3.3   Computing the Dispersion Set and the Non ϕ-Fixed Part

Let us consider a ϕ-system (2). The dispersion set $E_\phi(a, b)$ defined by (5) is usually computed as follows. One first compute the resultant $\mathrm{Res}_x(a, \phi^m(b))$. This resultant is a polynomial in $[m]_q$ defined in (7) and the elements of $E_\phi(a, b)$ are computed from the roots in C of this polynomial. In this section, we extend the ideas of [36] to compute the dispersion set $E_\phi(a, b)$ for any ϕ defined by $\phi(f(x)) = f(qx + r)$ for all $f \in C(x)$, with $r \in C$ and $q \in C^*$ is not a root of unity, but if $r \neq 0$ then q is allowed to be equal to 1. The approach relies on a factorization into irreducible factors of the polynomials a and b given in (4).

First note that there exists $s \in \mathbb{N}$ such that $\deg(\gcd(a, \phi^s(b))) > 0$ if and only if there exist an irreducible factor f of a and an irreducible factor g of b such that $f \sim \phi^s(g)$. Then, we have the following result:

Proposition 3. *Let us consider two monic irreducible polynomials f and g of the same degree d and write $f(x) = \sum_{i=0}^{d} f_i x^{d-i}$, $f_0 = 1$, $g(x) = \sum_{i=0}^{d} g_i x^{d-i}$, $g_0 = 1$. If $f \sim \phi^s(g)$, then we have the following explicit formulas for s:*

1. *If $q = 1$, then $s = \frac{f_1 - g_1}{d\,r}$ (see [36]).*

2. *Otherwise, if f and g are both different from $x - \frac{r}{1-q}$, then if k denotes the smallest positive integer such that $(q-1)^k f_k - \binom{d}{k} r^k \neq 0$, we have*

$$s = \frac{\log(A_k)}{k \log(q)}, \quad A_k := 1 + \frac{(q-1)^k (g_k - f_k)}{(q-1)^k f_k - \binom{d}{k} r^k}. \tag{9}$$

Proof. If $f \sim \phi^s(g)$, then necessarily $\phi^s(g) = q^{d\,s} f$. Now, a direct calculation shows that

$$\phi^s(g) = \sum_{k=0}^{d} \sum_{i=d-k}^{d} q^{s\,(d-k)} \binom{i}{d-k} g_{d-i}\, r^{i-d+k}\, [s]_q^{i-d+k}\, x^{d-k}.$$

Therefore, equating the coefficients of x^{d-k} in the equality $\phi^s(g) = q^{d\,s} f$, for $k \in \{1, \ldots, d\}$, yields an equation of degree k in $[s]_q$ which can be written as:

$$f_k - g_k + \sum_{i=1}^{k} \left(f_k \binom{k}{i} (q-1)^i - \binom{d-k+i}{i} r^i g_{k-i} \right) [s]_q^i = 0. \tag{10}$$

For $k = 1$, Eq. (10) implies

$$\left((q-1) f_1 - d\,r \right) [s]_q + f_1 - g_1 = 0. \tag{11}$$

If $q = 1$, then (11) yields $[s]_q = s = \frac{f_1 - g_1}{d\,r}$ which was also the result obtained in [36]. Otherwise, when $q \neq 1$, it may happen (namely, when $f_1(q-1) - d\,r = 0$) that the coefficient of $[s]_q$ in (11) vanishes which implies $g_1 = f_1$ and in this case Eq. (10) for $k = 1$ will not provide any formula for $[s]_q$.

Let k be the smallest positive integer such that $f_k (q-1)^k - \binom{d}{k} r^k \neq 0$. Such a k always exists as, by hypothesis, $f(x) \neq x - \frac{r}{q-1} \notin F_\phi$. From Eq. (10), we then have that, for all $i = 1, \ldots, k$, $g_{k-i} = f_{k-i} = \frac{\binom{d}{k-i} r^{k-i}}{(q-1)^{k-i}}$. Moreover, Eq. (10) has then exactly degree k in $[s]_q$ and can be simplified to get:

$$f_k - g_k + \left(f_k - \frac{\binom{d}{k} r^k}{(q-1)^k} \right) \left((1 + (q-1) [s]_q)^k - 1 \right) = 0.$$

Finally, using the definition (7) of $[s]_q$, we obtain $q^{s\,k} = A_k$ where A_k is defined in the statement of the proposition. This ends the proof.

Proposition 3 leads to an efficient unified algorithm for computing the dispersion set. Note also that, for our purpose, an important advantage of this approach, compared to resultant based algorithms that still need gcd's calculations, is that it also provides directly the factors of a multiple of the non ϕ-fixed part of a universal denominator of the rational solutions of a ϕ-system. This is summarized in the following scheme:

Input: A system of the form (2).
Output: The dispersion set $E_\phi(a,b)$ of a and b defined by (4) and a multiple of the non ϕ-fixed part of a universal denominator for rational solutions of (2).

1. Set $E_\phi(a,b) = \emptyset$ and $U = 1$.
2. Factor a and b defined by (4) as products of powers of distinct monic irreducible polynomials called respectively u_j's and v_l's.
3. **For** each pair (u_j, v_l) such that $\deg(v_l) = \deg(u_j) = d$
   (we write $u_j(x) = \sum_{i=0}^d f_i\, x^{d-i}$, $v_l(x) = \sum_{i=0}^d g_i\, x^{d-i}$ - see Proposition 3)
   - **If** $q = 1$, then $s = \frac{f_1 - g_1}{d\, r}$.
     Else let k be the smallest positive integer such that
     $f_k\,(q-1)^k - \binom{d}{k} r^k \neq 0$ and s be as in (9).
     End If
   - **If** $s \in \mathbb{N}$ and $u_j \sim \phi^s(v_l)$, then we set $E_\phi(a,b) = E_\phi(a,b) \cup \{s\}$ and
     $U = U \prod_{i=0}^s \phi^{-i}(u_j)$.
     End If
   End For
4. **Return** $E_\phi(a,b)$ and U.

Example 1. Let us consider the ϕ-system (2) with $q = 3$, $r = 2$ and

$$
B := \begin{bmatrix} \frac{3\,x+2}{9x} & 0 \\[2mm] \frac{2(x+1)^3(13\,x+2)}{3(3\,x+2)(3\,x+1)x} & \frac{(x-1)(x-2)}{3(3\,x+2)(3\,x+1)} \end{bmatrix}.
$$

The only ϕ-fixed singularity is $x_\phi = -1$ and we thus write a universal denominator under the form $(x+1)^\alpha\, U(x)$, where $U(x)$ is not divisible by $x+1$. Using the algorithm of [18] for computing a simple form at $x_\phi = -1$, we get the local exponents at $x_\phi = -1$ and the bound 2 for α. The factorizations of the polynomials a and b defined in (4) are given by:

$$
a(x) = x\,(x-1)\,(x-2), \quad b(x) = (x-1)\,(x-2)\left(x + \frac{2}{3}\right).
$$

Here, by directly inspecting the pairs of irreducible factors of a and b, we easily check that:

$$
x \sim \phi^1(x-2), \quad x-1 \sim \phi^0(x-1), \quad x-2 \sim \phi^0(x-2)
$$

are the only possible associations. The dispersion set is thus $E_\phi(a,b) = \{0,1\}$ and the multiple of $U(x)$ obtained is $\phi^0(x)\,\phi^{-1}(x)\,\phi^0(x-1)\,\phi^0(x-2) = x\,(x-1)$

$(x-2)^2$ because $\phi^{-1}(x) = \frac{1}{3}(x-2)$. Finally a universal denominator is given by $(x+1)^2\, x\, (x-1)\, (x-2)^2$ which agrees with the fact that a basis of the rational solutions of the ϕ-system is given by:

$$\mathbf{y}_1(x) = \begin{bmatrix} \frac{x}{(x+1)^2} \\ 1 \end{bmatrix}, \quad \mathbf{y}_2(x) = \begin{bmatrix} 0 \\ \frac{1}{x(x-1)(x-2)} \end{bmatrix}.$$

4   Rational Solutions of Partial Pseudo-linear Systems

In this section, we present a new algorithm for computing rational solutions of a partial pseudo-linear system (1) which is fully integrable and satisfies the integrability conditions (see Sect. 2). We extend the ideas developed in [17] for integrable connections (i.e., the case where all the systems are differential systems). For $i = 1, \ldots, m$, the pseudo-linear system $L_i(\mathbf{y}) = 0$ is viewed as a pseudo-linear system with respect to one independent variable x_i as, by assumptions, the other variables x_j, $j \neq i$ are constants with respect to ϕ_i and δ_i and can thus be considered as constant parameters.

Definition 1. *Let $K = C(x_1, \ldots, x_m)$. A rational solution of System (1) is a vector $\mathbf{y} \in K^n$ that satisfies $L_i(\mathbf{y}) = 0$, for all $i = 1, \ldots, m$.*

Example 2. Let $K = C(x_1, x_2)$ and consider the partial pseudo-linear system $\{\delta_1(\mathbf{y}) = (x_2/x_1)\,\phi_1(\mathbf{y}), \delta_2(\mathbf{y}) = (x_1 - 1)\,\phi_2(\mathbf{y})\}$, where $\phi_1 = \mathrm{id}_K$, $\delta_1 = \frac{\partial}{\partial x_1}$, $\phi_2 : (x_1, x_2) \mapsto (x_1, x_2 - 1)$, and $\delta_2 = \mathrm{id}_K - \phi_2$. One can check that the function $y(x_1, x_2) = x_1^{x_2}$ is a solution of the system but it is not a rational solution in the sense of Definition 1.

4.1   A Recursive Approach

Our method proceeds by recursion and relies on an algorithm for computing rational solutions of each pseudo-linear system $\delta_i(\mathbf{y}) = M_i\,\phi_i(\mathbf{y})$, $i = 1, \ldots, m$. Such an algorithm has been described in Sect. 3 both for differential systems ($\phi_i = \mathrm{id}_K$) and for ϕ-systems such that $\phi(f(x)) = f(q\,x + r)$ for all $f \in C(x)$, with $r \in C$ and $q \in C^*$ is not a root of unity, but if $r \neq 0$ then q is allowed to be equal to 1. Consequently, for all $i = 1, \ldots, m$ such that $\phi_i \neq \mathrm{id}_K$, we assume that ϕ_i satisfies the above conditions.

Let us now give the details of our recursive approach. We first consider the pseudo-linear system $L_1(\mathbf{y}) = 0$ (see also Sect. 4.3) over $K = C(x_2, \ldots, x_m)$ (x_1). We compute a basis $\mathbf{u}_1, \ldots, \mathbf{u}_s \in K^n$ ($0 \leq s \leq n$) of rational solutions of $L_1(\mathbf{y}) = 0$ (see Sect. 3). If we do not find any nonzero rational solution, then we stop as (1) does not admit any nonzero rational solution. Otherwise, denote by $U \in \mathbb{M}_{n \times s}(K)$ the matrix whose columns are the $\mathbf{u}_i$'s. We complete $\mathbf{u}_1, \ldots, \mathbf{u}_s$ into a basis $\mathbf{u}_1, \ldots, \mathbf{u}_n$ of K^n and define $P = (U \quad V) \in \mathrm{GL}_n(K)$, where $V \in \mathbb{M}_{n \times (n-s)}(K)$ has $\mathbf{u}_{s+1}, \ldots, \mathbf{u}_n$ as columns. Performing the change of dependent variables $\mathbf{y} = P\mathbf{z}$ in System (1), we obtain the equivalent system

$$\begin{cases} \widetilde{L_1}(\mathbf{z}) := \delta_1(\mathbf{z}) - N_1 \, \phi_1(\mathbf{z}) = 0, \\ \quad \vdots \\ \widetilde{L_m}(\mathbf{z}) := \delta_m(\mathbf{z}) - N_m \, \phi_m(\mathbf{z}) = 0, \end{cases} \tag{12}$$

where $N_i := P^{-1} \left[M_i \, \phi_i(P) - \delta_i(P) \right]$, $i = 1, \ldots, m$.

Lemma 1. *With the above notations, let us decompose the matrices N_i's of System (12) by blocks as*

$$N_i = \left[\begin{array}{c|c} N_i^{11} & N_i^{12} \\ \hline N_i^{21} & N_i^{22} \end{array} \right],$$

where $N_i^{11} \in \mathbb{M}_s(K)$. Then, for all $i = 1, \ldots, m$, $N_i^{11} \in \mathbb{M}_s(C(x_2, \ldots, x_m))$ does not depend on x_1. Moreover it can be computed as the unique solution of the matrix linear system $U \, N_i^{11} = -L_i(U)$, and, in particular $N_1^{11} = 0$. Finally, for all $i = 1, \ldots, m$, $N_i^{21} = 0$.

Proof. The equation $P \, N_i = M_i \, \phi_i(P) - \delta_i(P)$ yields $U \, N_i^{11} + V \, N_i^{21} = -L_i(U)$. From the integrability conditions $L_i \circ L_j - L_j \circ L_i = 0$, for all $1 \leq i, j \leq m$, we get that, for all $i = 1, \ldots, m$, $L_i(U)$ is a rational solution of the system $L_1(\mathbf{y}) = 0$ so that there exists a unique constant matrix $W \in \mathbb{M}_s(C(x_2, \ldots, x_m))$, i.e., not depending on x_1, such that $L_i(U) = U W$. We then obtain, for all $i = 1, \ldots, m$, $U (N_i^{11} + W) + V \, N_i^{21} = 0$ which ends the proof as the columns of $P = (U \quad V)$ form a basis of K^n. ∎

From Lemma 1, we deduce the following result justifying the correctness of our iterative algorithm for computing rational solutions of System (1).

Theorem 1. *Let $U \in \mathbb{M}_{n \times s}(K)$ be a matrix whose columns form a basis of the rational solutions of $L_1(\mathbf{y}) = 0$. For $i = 2, \ldots, m$, let $N_i^{11} \in \mathbb{M}_s(C(x_2, \ldots, x_m))$ be the unique solution of the matrix linear system $U \, N_i^{11} = -L_i(U)$. Suppose that $Z \in \mathbb{M}_{s \times r}(C(x_2, \ldots, x_m))$ is a matrix whose columns form a basis of the rational solutions of the partial pseudo-linear system of size s over $C(x_2, \ldots, x_m)$*

$$\begin{cases} \delta_2(\mathbf{y}) - N_2^{11} \, \phi_2(\mathbf{y}) = 0, \\ \quad \vdots \\ \delta_m(\mathbf{y}) - N_m^{11} \, \phi_m(\mathbf{y}) = 0, \end{cases} \tag{13}$$

then the columns of the matrix $UZ \in \mathbb{M}_{n \times r}(K)$ form a basis of all rational solutions of (1).

Proof. Let $Z \in \mathbb{M}_{s \times r}(C(x_2, \ldots, x_m))$ be a matrix whose columns form a basis of all rational solutions of (13) and let us consider $Y = UZ$. We have $L_1(Y) = \delta_1(U)\phi_1(Z) + U\delta_1(Z) - M_1\phi_1(U)\phi_1(Z) = \delta_1(U)Z - M_1\phi_1(U)Z = 0$. Now for $i = 2, \ldots, m$, by definition of N_i^{11}, we have $L_i(Y) = \delta_i(U)\phi_i(Z) + U\delta_i(Z) -$

$M_i \phi_i(U) \phi_i(Z) = [\delta_i(U) + U N_i^{11} - M_i \phi_i(U)] \phi_i(Z) = 0$. This ends the first part of the proof. Now let Y be a solution of (1). In particular, Y is a rational solution of $L_1(\mathbf{y}) = 0$ so that there exists $Z \in \mathbb{M}_s(C(x_2, \ldots, x_m))$ such that $Y = UZ = (U \quad V)(Z^T \quad 0^T)^T$. Thus, for $i = 2, \ldots, m$, Y is a solution of $L_i(\mathbf{y}) = 0$ if and only if $(Z^T \quad 0^T)^T$ is a solution of the system (12). This is equivalent to Z being a solution to system (13) and yields the desired result.

Theorem 1 shows that rational solutions of (1) can be computed recursively. Indeed, we have reduced the problem of computing rational solutions of System (1) of size n in m variables to that of computing rational solutions of System (13) of size $s \leq n$ in $m - 1$ variables. This leads to the following iterative algorithm for computing a basis of rational solutions of System (1). It proceeds as follows:

Algorithm **RationalSolutions_PLS**

Input: A system of the form (1).
Output: A matrix whose columns form a basis of rational solutions of (1) or 0_n (the zero vector of dimension n) if no non-trivial rational solution exists.

1. Compute a basis of rational solutions of $L_1(\mathbf{y}) = 0$ (see Section 3).
2. If there are no non-trivial rational solutions of $L_1(\mathbf{y}) = 0$, then **Return** 0_n and **Stop**.
3. Let $U \in \mathbb{M}_{n \times s}(K)$ be a matrix whose columns form a basis of the rational solutions of $L_1(\mathbf{y}) = 0$.
4. If $m = 1$, then **Return** U and **Stop**.
5. For $i = 2, \ldots, m$, compute the unique solution $N_i^{11} \in \mathbb{M}_s(C(x_2, \ldots, x_m))$ of the matrix linear system $U N_i^{11} = -L_i(U)$.
6. **Return** U multiplied by the result of applying the algorithm to System (13).

Let us illustrate our algorithm on the following example.

Example 3. We consider a partial pseudo-linear system composed of one pure difference system, one pure q-difference system and one pure differential system defined as follows:

$$\begin{cases} \mathbf{y}(x_1 + 1, x_2, x_3) = A_1(x_1, x_2, x_3)\, \mathbf{y}(x_1, x_2, x_3), \\ \mathbf{y}(x_1, qx_2, x_3) = A_2(x_1, x_2, x_3)\, \mathbf{y}(x_1, x_2, x_3), \\ \frac{\partial}{\partial x_3}\mathbf{y}(x_1, x_2, x_3) = A_3(x_1, x_2, x_3)\mathbf{y}(x_1, x_2, x_3), \end{cases} \tag{14}$$

where $q \in \mathbb{Q}^*$ is not a root of unity. Let $K = \mathbb{Q}(q)(x_1, x_2, x_3)$. The matrices $A_1, A_2 \in \mathrm{GL}_2(K)$ and $A_3 \in \mathbb{M}_2(K)$ are given by:

$$A_1 = \begin{bmatrix} \frac{x_1+1}{x_1} & \frac{-qx_3(x_3+x_1)}{x_2^2 x_1} \\ 0 & \frac{x_3+x_1}{x_3+x_1+1} \end{bmatrix}, \quad A_2 = \begin{bmatrix} 1 & \frac{-x_3(x_3+x_1)(q-1)}{x_2^2} \\ 0 & q \end{bmatrix}, \quad A_3 = \begin{bmatrix} 0 & \frac{q(x_3+x_1)}{x_2^2} \\ 0 & \frac{-1}{x_1+x_3} \end{bmatrix}.$$

Rewriting the three ϕ-systems as pseudo-linear systems (see Sect. 2 for more details), System (14) can be transformed into the form (1) with

$$\begin{cases} L_1(\mathbf{y}) := \delta_1(\mathbf{y}) - M_1\,\phi_1(\mathbf{y}), & M_1 = \phi_1(A_1) - I_2, \\ L_2(\mathbf{y}) := \delta_2(\mathbf{y}) - M_2\,\phi_2(\mathbf{y}), & M_2 = \phi_2(A_2) - I_2, \\ L_3(\mathbf{y}) := \delta_3(\mathbf{y}) - M_3\,\phi_3(\mathbf{y}), & M_3 = A_3, \end{cases} \tag{15}$$

where the ϕ_i's are the automorphisms defined by:

$$\phi_1 : (x_1, x_2, x_3) \mapsto (x_1 - 1, x_2, x_3), \quad \phi_2 : (x_1, x_2, x_3) \mapsto (x_1, x_2/q, x_3), \quad \phi_3 = \mathrm{id}_K,$$

and the δ_i's are the ϕ_i-derivations defined by:

$$\delta_1 = \mathrm{id}_K - \phi_1, \quad \delta_2 = \mathrm{id}_K - \phi_2, \quad \delta_3 = \partial/\partial x_3.$$

Let us describe our iterative process for computing rational solutions of System (15). Computing rational solutions of the pure difference system $L_1(\mathbf{y}) = 0$, we get two linearly independent rational solutions given by the columns of

$$U_1 = \begin{bmatrix} \frac{x_1 - x_3}{x_2^4} & \frac{1}{x_2^4} \\ \frac{-1}{q\,x_2^2\,(x_3 + x_1)} & \frac{1}{q\,x_2^2\,x_3\,(x_3 + x_1)} \end{bmatrix}.$$

Solving the linear systems $U_1\,N_2^{11} = -L_2(U_1)$ and $U_1\,N_3^{11} = -L_3(U_1)$ we get:

$$N_2^{11} = \begin{bmatrix} -q^4 + 1 & 0 \\ -q^3\,(q-1)\,x_3 & -q^3 + 1 \end{bmatrix}, \quad N_3^{11} = \begin{bmatrix} 0 & 0 \\ 0 & -1 \end{bmatrix}.$$

We are then reduced to solving the partial pseudo-linear system

$$\begin{cases} \widetilde{L_2}(\mathbf{y}) := \delta_2(\mathbf{y}) - N_2^{11}\,\phi_2(\mathbf{y}) = 0, \\ \widetilde{L_3}(\mathbf{y}) := \delta_3(\mathbf{y}) - N_3^{11}\,\phi_3(\mathbf{y}) = 0. \end{cases}$$

The rational solutions of the pure q-difference system $\widetilde{L_2}(\mathbf{y}) = 0$ are given by the columns of the matrix

$$U_2 = \begin{bmatrix} x_2^4 & 0 \\ x_2^4\,x_3 & x_2^3 \end{bmatrix}.$$

Now, solving the linear system $U_2\,\widehat{N_3}^{11} = -\widetilde{L_3}(U_2)$, we get

$$\widehat{N_3}^{11} = \begin{bmatrix} 0 & 0 \\ 0 & -1 \end{bmatrix}.$$

We are next reduced to computing rational solutions of the pure differential system $\delta_3(\mathbf{y}) - \widehat{N_3}^{11}\,\phi_3(\mathbf{y}) = 0$. We find that they are given by the columns of the matrix

$$U_3 = \begin{bmatrix} 0 & 1 \\ x_3 & 0 \end{bmatrix}.$$

Finally, a basis of rational solutions of (14) is spanned by the columns of

$$U_1\,U_2\,U_3 = \begin{bmatrix} \frac{x_3}{x_2} & x_1 \\ \frac{x_2}{(x_3+x_1)q} & 0 \end{bmatrix}.$$

4.2   Necessary Conditions for Denominators

A rational solution of the partial pseudo-linear system (1) is, in particular, a rational solution of each pseudo-linear system $\delta_i(\mathbf{y}) = M_i\,\phi(\mathbf{y})$, $i = 1, \ldots, m$. This necessarily imposes some necessary conditions on the irreducible factors of the denominator of a rational solution of System (1) (see [17, Proposition 8] in the integrable connection case). In some cases, taking into account these necessary conditions can significantly speed up the timings of Algorithm **RationalSolutions_PLS** as it allows to not consider some irreducible factors when computing universal denominators.

For a pure differential system ($\phi_i = \mathrm{id}_K$ and $\delta_i = \partial/\partial x_i$), we know that an irreducible factor of the denominator of a rational solution must divide the denominator of the matrix M_i. For the case of a ϕ-system we have the following consequence of Proposition 1. This result can be found in [11] for the pure difference case and can be adapted directly for any ϕ-system considered here.

Proposition 4 ([11], Proposition 2). *With the notations of Sect. 3, assume that $E_\phi(a,b) \neq \emptyset$ and let $N := \max(E_\phi(a,b))$. Let $p \neq x - \frac{r}{1-q} \in C[x]$ be an irreducible polynomial. If p divides the denominator of a non-zero rational solution of System (2), then there exist $1 \leq i \leq N+1$ and $0 \leq j \leq N$ such that $i + j \in E_\phi(a,b)$ and p divides both $\phi^{-i}(\mathrm{den}(B))$ and $\phi^j(\mathrm{den}(B^{-1}))$.*

For the sake of clarity, before giving a result in the general case, we first consider the case of a partial pseudo-linear system with only $m = 2$ pseudo-linear systems being written either as a pure differential system or a ϕ-system. We obtain the following result as a consequence of the discussion above and Proposition 4.

Necessary Condition 1. *Let $K = C(x_1, x_2)$ and consider a partial pseudo-linear system*

$$L_1(\mathbf{y}) = 0, \quad L_2(\mathbf{y}) = 0. \tag{16}$$

Let A_1 denote the matrix of the system $L_1(\mathbf{y}) = 0$ and $p \in C[x_1, x_2]$ be an irreducible factor of $\mathrm{den}(A_1)$ which involves the variable x_2. Then we have the following result depending on the type of each pseudo-linear system:

1. *If for $i = 1, 2$, $L_i = I_n \frac{\partial}{\partial x_i} - A_i$ then if p appears in the denominator of a rational solution of (16), then $p \mid \mathrm{den}(A_2)$ (see [17, Proposition 8]).*
2. *If $L_1 = I_n \frac{\partial}{\partial x_1} - A_1$, $L_2 = I_n\,\phi_2 - A_2$, then if p appears in the denominator of a rational solution of (16), there exists $i \in \mathbb{N}^*$ such that $p \mid \phi_2^{-i}(\mathrm{den}(A_2))$.*
3. *If $L_1 = I_n\,\phi_1 - A_1$, $L_2 = I_n \frac{\partial}{\partial x_2} - A_2$, then if p appears in the denominator of a rational solution of (16), there exists $i \in \mathbb{N}^*$ such that $p \mid \phi_1^i(\mathrm{den}(A_2))$.*

4. If for $i = 1, 2$, $L_i = I_n \phi_i - A_i$, then if p appears in the denominator of a rational solution of (16), there exists $i, j \in \mathbb{N}^*$ such that $p \mid \phi_1^i(\phi_2^{-j}(\text{den}(A_2)))$.

Let us illustrate the latter necessary condition on an example.

Example 4. Consider a partial pseudo linear system of the form

$$\frac{\partial \mathbf{y}}{\partial x}(x, k) = A(x, k)\mathbf{y}(x, k), \quad \mathbf{y}(x, k + 1) = B(x, k)\mathbf{y}(x, k),$$

where the matrices A and B are given by:

$$A(x, k) = \begin{bmatrix} \frac{-1}{(x+k)} & \frac{-k(k-x)(x+2\,k)}{(x+k)x^3\left(k^2-kx+x\right)} \\ 0 & \frac{k}{(k-x)\left(k^2-kx+x\right)} \end{bmatrix}, \quad B(x, k) = \begin{bmatrix} \frac{x+k}{x+k+1} & \frac{(k-x)(2\,k+x+1)}{(x+k+1)x^2\left(k^2-kx+x\right)} \\ 0 & \frac{\left(k^2-kx+2\,k+1\right)(k-x)}{(k+1-x)\left(k^2-kx+x\right)} \end{bmatrix}.$$

The factorizations of the denominators of the matrices A and B are given respectively by:

$$\text{den}(A)(x, k) = (x + k)\, x^3 \left(k^2 - kx + x\right)(k - x),$$

$$\text{den}(B)(x, k) = (x + k + 1)\, x^2 \left(k^2 - kx + x\right)(k + 1 - x).$$

The irreducible factor $p(x, k) = k^2 - kx + x$ of den(A) clearly satisfies that, for all $i \in \mathbb{N}^*$, $p \nmid \text{den}(B)(x, k - i)$. Therefore, from Case 2 of Necessary Condition 1, p can not appear in the denominator of any rational solution of the system. However, the latter necessary condition does not allow to draw any conclusion concerning the factors $x+k$ and $k-x$ of den(A) (the factor x does not involve the variable k so that it can not be considered in our result). We can indeed check the previous observations as the rational solutions of the system are given by:

$$\mathbf{y}_1(x) = \begin{bmatrix} \frac{1}{(x+k)} \\ 0 \end{bmatrix}, \quad \mathbf{y}_2(x) = \begin{bmatrix} \frac{k}{x^2} \\ k + \frac{x}{k-x} \end{bmatrix}.$$

The gain for our algorithm is that when computing a universal denominator for the differential system $\frac{\partial \mathbf{y}}{\partial x}(x, k) = A(x, k)\mathbf{y}(x, k)$, there is no need to compute a simple form at $p(x) = k^2 - kx + x$ (see Sect. 3).

We now give a generalization of the latter necessary condition in the case of a partial pseudo-linear system (1) composed of m pseudo-linear systems. We distinguish the case when the first system is a differential system (Necessary Condition 2) from that where it is a ϕ-system (Necessary Condition 3). Note that for $\phi_i \neq \text{id}_K$, the systems are written here under the form of a pseudo-linear system $\delta_i(\mathbf{y}) = M_i\, \phi_i(\mathbf{y})$ and not of a ϕ-system $\phi_i(\mathbf{y}) = B_i\, \mathbf{y}$. This is the reason why matrices $\gamma_i^{-1} M_i + I_n$ appear in the following results (see Sect. 2).

Necessary Condition 2. *Let $K = C(x_1, \ldots, x_m)$. Consider a system of the form (1) and suppose that $L_1(\mathbf{y}) = 0$ is a pure differential system, i.e., $\phi_1 = \text{id}_K$ and $\delta_1 = \frac{\partial}{\partial x_1}$. Let $p \in C[x_1, \ldots, x_m]$ be an irreducible factor of den(M_1) such that p involves the variable x_i for some $i \in \{2, \ldots, m\}$. Moreover, suppose that one of the following two conditions holds:*

1. $(\phi_i, \delta_i) = (\mathrm{id}_K, \frac{\partial}{\partial x_i})$ and $p \nmid \mathrm{den}(M_i)$.
2. $\phi_i \neq \mathrm{id}_K$ (i.e., $\delta_i = \gamma_i (\mathrm{id}_K - \phi_i)$ for some $\gamma_i \in K^*$) and

$$\forall j \in \mathbb{N}^*, \quad \phi_i^j(p) \nmid \mathrm{den}((\gamma_i^{-1} M_i + I_n)^{-1}).$$

Then p cannot appear in the denominator of a rational solution of (1).

Necessary Condition 3. *Let $K = C(x_1, \ldots, x_m)$. Consider a system of the form (1) and suppose that $\phi_1 \neq \mathrm{id}_K$ (i.e., $\delta_1 = \gamma_1 (\mathrm{id}_K - \phi_1)$ for some $\gamma_1 \in K^*$). Let $p \in C[x_1, \ldots, x_m]$ be an irreducible factor of $\mathrm{den}((\gamma_1^{-1} M_1 + I_n)^{-1})$ such that p involves the variable x_i for some $i \in \{2, \ldots, m\}$. Moreover, suppose that one of the following two conditions holds:*

1. $(\phi_i, \delta_i) = (\mathrm{id}_K, \frac{\partial}{\partial x_i})$ and, for all $j \in \mathbb{N}^*$, $p \nmid \phi_i^j(\mathrm{den}(M_i))$.
2. $\phi_i \neq \mathrm{id}_K$ (i.e., $\delta_i = \gamma_i (\mathrm{id}_K - \phi_i)$ for some $\gamma_i \in K^*$) and

$$\forall j, k \in \mathbb{N}^*, \quad p \nmid \phi_1^j(\phi_i^{-k}(\mathrm{den}((\gamma_i^{-1} M_i + I_n)^{-1}))).$$

Then p cannot appear in the denominator of a rational solution of (1).

4.3   Implementation and Comparison of Different Strategies

Algorithm **RationalSolutions_PLS** has been implemented in Maple in our `PseudoLinearSystems` package [19]. It includes an implementation of the unified and efficient algorithm developed in Sect. 3.3 for computing a multiple of the non ϕ-fixed part of a universal denominator of ϕ-systems. For the ϕ-fixed part and for computing a universal denominator of differential systems, we use our generic implementation of the simple form algorithm developed in [18]. Moreover our implementation includes part of the necessary conditions given in Sect. 4.2.

In the recursive process of Algorithm **RationalSolutions_PLS**, the pseudo-linear systems in (1) can be considered in an arbitrary order. We have thus tried to see (through examples) if there are some orders better than others from the computational point of view. Let us give some timings of one of our experiments in the case of $m = 2$ pseudo-linear systems where one system is a pure differential system (with independent variable x and usual derivation $\frac{\partial}{\partial x}$) and the other is a pure difference system (with independent variable k, $\phi : (x, k) \mapsto (x, k - 1)$ and $\delta = \mathrm{id}_K - \phi$). In this experiment the matrices of the systems are generated from a randomly chosen fundamental matrix of rational solutions but whose denominator denoted by U is fixed as a product of some of the following three polynomials:

$$U_1(x, k) = (x + k)(x - k)^2 (-k^2 + x)(-k^3 + x^2 + 3),$$

$$U_2(x, k) =$$
$$-77 k^8 x^6 + 51 k^2 x^{12} - 31 k^5 x^8 + 10 k^4 x^9 - 68 x^{13} - 91 x^{12} + 81 k^{10} - 40 k^4 x^6 + 47 k^2 x^5 + 49 kx,$$

$$U_3(x, k) =$$
$$k (6 k^{10} x + 5 kx^9 + 6 k^2 x^7 + 3 k^7 + 2 k^6 x - 4 x^7 + 4 k^4 x^2 + k^4 x - 3 x^4 - 5 k).$$

We compare two strategies:

1. Strategy 1: we start with the differential system.
2. Strategy 2: we start with the difference system.

The following table gives the timings (in seconds) obtained for computing the fundamental matrix of rational solutions with each strategy, for different dimensions n of the systems, and for different fixed denominators U of the rational solutions.

	$U = U_1$			$U = U_1 U_2$			$U = U_1 U_2 U_3$		
	$n = 3$	$n = 6$	$n = 9$	$n = 3$	$n = 6$	$n = 9$	$n = 3$	$n = 6$	$n = 9$
Strategy 1	0.483	2.295	9.012	22.928	187.556	574.839	249.924	912.906	1703.79
Strategy 2	0.399	2.831	16.463	0.354	2.162	12.222	0.948	3.398	15.171

The table seems to indicate that Strategy 2, i.e., starting with the difference system, gives, in general, better timings. We do not have yet a complete complexity analysis justifying the latter observation but we have made several experimentations which confirm it. In particular, the difference between the distinct timings seems to be particularly significant when the denominator includes *large* irreducible factors as U_2 and U_3. In the case $U = U_1$, we do not have large singularities in the denominator and Strategy 1 behaves well. Going deeper into the analysis of these timings for each step of the algorithm, we can see that, in Strategy 1, most of the time is spent in computing simple forms which can be quite involved for singularities as the ones given by U_2 and U_3. In Strategy 2, we have no simple form computations to get a universal denominator of the first system (as it is a difference system) and then, the large factors U_2 and U_3 disappear as the differential system to be considered next only involves the variable x. For instance, in Example 3, if we start with the differential system with matrix $M_3 = A_3$, we must compute a simple form at the singularity given by the irreducible factor $x_1 + x_3$ of den(A_3). But if we treat first the difference and the q-difference systems as it is done in Example 3, we can see that at the end of the process, the differential system to be considered is $\delta_3(\mathbf{y}) - \widehat{N_3}^{11} \phi_3(\mathbf{y}) = 0$, where $\widehat{N_3}^{11}$ has no finite singularities, and therefore no simple form computations are needed to get a universal denominator of the differential system.

From these observations (and other comparisons that we have performed), we make the choice to treat the ϕ-systems ($\phi_i \neq \mathrm{id}_K$) first and to consider the differential systems at the end of the iterative process, where the systems involve fewer independent variables and may also be of smaller size.

References

1. Abramov, S.: EG-eliminations. J. Differ. Equations Appl. **5**(4–5), 393–433 (1999)
2. Abramov, S.: On the summation of rational functions. USSR Comput. Math. Math. Phys. **11**(4), 324–330 (1971)

3. Abramov, S.: Rational solutions of linear differential and difference equations with polynomial coefficients. USSR Comput. Math. Math. Phys. **29**(6), 7–12 (1989)
4. Abramov, S.: A direct algorithm to compute rational solutions of first order linear q-difference systems. Discret. Math. **246**, 3–12 (2002)
5. Abramov, S., Barkatou, M.A.: Rational solutions of first order linear difference systems. In: Proceedings of ISSAC 1998, pp. 124–131 (1998)
6. Abramov, S.A., Gheffar, A., Khmelnov, D.E.: Factorization of polynomials and GCD computations for finding universal denominators. In: Gerdt, V.P., Koepf, W., Mayr, E.W., Vorozhtsov, E.V. (eds.) CASC 2010. LNCS, vol. 6244, pp. 4–18. Springer, Heidelberg (2010). https://doi.org/10.1007/978-3-642-15274-0_2
7. Abramov, S., Paule, P., Petkovsek, M.: q-hypergeometric solutions of q-difference equations. Discret. Math. **180**, 3–22 (1998)
8. Abramov, S.A., Petkovšek, M., Ryabenko, A.A.: Hypergeometric solutions of first-order linear difference systems with rational-function coefficients. In: Gerdt, V.P., Koepf, W., Seiler, W.M., Vorozhtsov, E.V. (eds.) CASC 2015. LNCS, vol. 9301, pp. 1–14. Springer, Cham (2015). https://doi.org/10.1007/978-3-319-24021-3_1
9. Barkatou, M.A.: Contribution à l'étude des équations différentielles et aux différences dans le champ complexe. Ph.D. Thesis, Institut Nat. Polytech. Grenoble (1989)
10. Barkatou, M.A.: On rational solutions of systems of linear differential equations. J. Symb. Comput. **28**, 547–567 (1999)
11. Barkatou, M.A.: Rational solutions of matrix difference equations: the problem of equivalence and factorization. In: Proceedings of ISSAC 1999, pp. 277–282 (1999)
12. Barkatou, M.A.: Factoring Systems of Linear Functional Systems Using Eigenrings. Computer algebra 2006, 22–42, World Sci. Publ., Hackensack, NJ (2007)
13. Barkatou, M.A., Broughton, G., Pflügel, E.: A monomial-by-monomial method for computing regular solutions of systems of pseudo-linear equations. Math. Comp. Sci. **4**(2–3), 267–288 (2010)
14. Barkatou, M.A., Chen, G.: Some formal invariants of linear difference systems and their computations. Crelle's J. **1–23**, 2001 (2001)
15. Barkatou, M.A., Cluzeau, T., El Bacha, C.: Simple forms of higher-order linear differential systems and their applications in computing regular solutions. J. Symb. Comput. **46**(6), 633–658 (2011)
16. Barkatou, M.A., Cluzeau, T., El Bacha, C.: On the computation of simple forms and regular solutions of linear difference systems. In: Schneider, C., Zima, E. (eds.) WWCA 2016. SPMS, vol. 226, pp. 19–49. Springer, Cham (2018). https://doi.org/10.1007/978-3-319-73232-9_2
17. Barkatou, M.A., Cluzeau, T., El Bacha, C., Weil, J.A.: Computing closed form solutions of integrable connections. In: Proceedings of ISSAC 2012, pp. 43–50 (2012)
18. Barkatou, M.A., Cluzeau, T., El Hajj, A.: Simple forms and rational solutions of pseudo-linear systems. In: Proceedings of ISSAC 2019, pp. 26–33 (2019)
19. Barkatou, M.A., Cluzeau, T., El Hajj, A.: PseudoLinearSystems - a maple package for studying systems of pseudo-linear equations. Maple Math. Educ. Res. 327–329. http://www.unilim.fr/pages_perso/ali.el-hajj/PseudoLinearSystems.html
20. Barkatou, M.A., El Bacha, C.: On k-simple forms of first-order linear differential systems and their computation. J. Symb. Comput. **54**, 36–58 (2013)
21. Barkatou, M.A., El Bacha, C., Pflügel, E.: An algorithm computing the regular formal solutions of a system of linear differential equations. In: Proceedings of ISSAC 2010, pp. 45–52 (2010)
22. Barkatou, M.A., Pflügel, E.: Simultaneously row- and column-reduced higher-order linear differential systems. J. Symb. Comput. **28**(4–5), 569–587 (1999)

23. Barkatou, M.A., Pflügel, E.: On the Moser- and super-reduction algorithms of systems of linear differential equations and their complexity. J. Symb. Comput. **44**(8), 1017–1036 (2009)
24. Bronstein, M., Li, Z., Wu, M.: Picard-Vessiot extensions for linear functional systems. In: Proceedings of ISSAC 2005, pp. 68–75 (2005)
25. Bronstein, M., Petkovsek, M.: An introduction to pseudo-linear algebra. Theor. Comput. Sci. **157**, 3–33 (1996)
26. Broughton, G.: Symbolic algorithms for the local analysis of systems of pseudo-linear equations. Ph.D. Thesis, Kingston University (2013)
27. Cluzeau, T., van Hoeij, M.: Computing hypergeometric solutions of linear difference equations. Appl. Algebra Eng. Commun. Comput. **17**, 83–115 (2006). https://doi.org/10.1007/s00200-005-0192-x
28. Feng, R., Singer, M.F., Wu, M.: An algorithm to compute Liouvillian solutions of prime order linear difference-differential equations. J. Symb. Comput. **45**(3), 306–323 (2010)
29. Hilali, A., Wazner, A.: Formes super-irréductibles des systèmes différentiels linéaires. Numer. Math. **50**, 429–449 (1987)
30. Jacobson, N.: Pseudo-linear transformations. Annals Math. **38**(2), 484–507 (1937). Second series
31. Khmelnov, D.E.: Improved algorithms for solving difference and q-difference equations. Program. Comput. Softw. **26**(2), 107–115 (2000). (translated from Programmirovanie No. 2)
32. Kauers, M., Schneider, C.: Partial denominator bounds for partial linear difference equations. In: Proceedings of ISSAC 2010, pp. 211–218 (2010)
33. Kauers, M., Schneider, C.: A refined denominator bounding algorithm for multivariate linear difference equations. In: Proceedings of ISSAC 2011, pp. 201–208 (2011)
34. Li, Z., Singer, M.F., Wu, M., Zheng, D.: A recursive method for determining the one-dimensional submodules of Laurent-Ore modules. In: Proceedings of ISSAC 2006, pp. 200–208 (2006)
35. Li, Z., Wu, M.: On solutions of linear systems and factorization of Laurent-Ore modules. Computer algebra 2006, 109–136, World Sci. Publ., Hackensack, NJ (2007)
36. Man, Y.K., Write, F.J: Fast polynomial dispersion computation and its application to indefnite summation. In: Proceedings of ISSAC 1994, pp. 175–180 (1994)
37. Paramonov, S.V.: On rational solutions of linear partial differential or difference equations. Program Comput. Soft **39**, 57–60 (2013)
38. Paramonov, S.V.: Checking existence of solutions of partial differential equations in the fields of Laurent series. Program Comput. Soft. **40**, 58–62 (2014)
39. Pflügel, E.: An algorithm for computing exponential solutions of first order linear differential systems. In: Proceedings of ISSAC 1997, pp. 146–171 (1997)
40. Singer, M.F.: Liouvillian solutions of linear differential equations with Liouvillian coefficients. In: Kaltofen, E., Watt, S.M. (eds.) Computers and Mathematics, pp. 182–191. Springer, New York (1989)
41. Wu, M.: On solutions of linear functional systems and factorization of modules over Laurent-Ore algebras. Ph.D. Thesis, Univ. of Nice-Sophia Antipolis (2005)

On the Relationship Between Differential Algebra and Tropical Differential Algebraic Geometry

François Boulier[1]($\boxtimes$), Sebastian Falkensteiner[2], Marc Paul Noordman[3], and Omar León Sánchez[4]

[1] Univ. Lille, CNRS, Centrale Lille, Inria, UMR 9189 - CRIStAL - Centre de Recherche en Informatique Signal et Automatique de Lille, 59000 Lille, France
francois.boulier@univ-lille.fr
[2] Research Institute for Symbolic Computation (RISC), Johannes Kepler University Linz, Linz, Austria
[3] Bernoulli Institute, University of Groningen, Groningen, The Netherlands
[4] Department of Mathematics, University of Manchester, Manchester, UK
omar.sanchez@manchester.ac.uk
https://pro.univ-lille.fr/francois-boulier,
https://risc.jku.at/m/sebastian-falkensteiner,
https://www.rug.nl/staff/m.p.noordman

Abstract. This paper presents the relationship between differential algebra and tropical differential algebraic geometry, mostly focusing on the existence problem of formal power series solutions for systems of polynomial ODE and PDE. Moreover, it improves an approximation theorem involved in the proof of the fundamental theorem of tropical differential algebraic geometry which permits to improve this latter by dropping the base field uncountability hypothesis used in the original version.

1 Introduction

Differential algebra is an algebraic theory for systems of ordinary or partial polynomial differential equations. It was founded by Ritt in the first half of the former century [13,14] and developed by Kolchin [10]. Tropical differential algebraic geometry is a much more recent theory, founded by Grigoriev [8] aiming at applying the concepts of tropical algebra (aka min-plus algebra) to the study of formal power series solutions of systems of ODE. Tropical differential algebra obtained an important impulse by the proof of the fundamental theorem of tropical differential algebraic geometry [1] which was recently extended to the partial case in [7]. The common topic of both theories is the existence problem of formal power series solutions of polynomial differential equations on which an important paper [6] by Denef and Lipshitz was published in 1984.

In both [1] and [7], the fundamental theorem applies to a polynomial differential system Σ with coefficients in formal power series rings $\mathscr{F}[[x]]$ (ordinary case) or $\mathscr{F}[[x_1, \ldots, x_m]]$ (partial case) where $\mathscr{F}$ is a characteristic zero differential field of constants which is both algebraically closed and uncountable. In this paper,

© Springer Nature Switzerland AG 2021
F. Boulier et al. (Eds.): CASC 2021, LNCS 12865, pp. 62–77, 2021.
https://doi.org/10.1007/978-3-030-85165-1_5

we prove that the uncountability hypothesis can be dropped. Indeed, we prove that the fundamental theorem holds provided that $\mathscr{F}$ is algebraically closed and has countable[1] transcendence degree over some field of definition $\mathscr{F}_0$ of Σ. This improvement of the fundamental theorem is achieved by generalizing the proof of a key proposition, which is an approximation theorem. This generalization is achieved in our Theorem 1, which is the main result of our paper. The new versions of the fundamental theorem, which follow, are stated in Theorem 2 and Theorem 3.

For the sake of simplicity, the introductory part of our paper focuses on the ordinary case. For completeness, the partial case is covered as well in the more technical sections. The paper is structured as follows. We recall in Sect. 2 the basic ideas underlying formal power series solutions of ODE and point out issues and known results, from the differential algebra literature. We state and explain the fundamental theorem of tropical differential algebra in Sect. 3. We provide our new approximation theorem in Sect. 5 (covering the partial differential case) and show how it is obtained by adapting the corresponding proposition given in [7]. The new version of the fundamental theorem, in the ordinary case, is provided in Sect. 6. In the final Sect. 7, we give an overview on the generalizations to the partial case, including the partial version of the fundamental theorem.

2   Formal Power Series Solutions of ODE

Let us start with a single autonomous ODE (i.e. an ODE the coefficients of which do not depend of the independent variable x) in a single differential indeterminate y (standing for the unknown function $y(x)$):

$$\dot{y}^2 + 8\,y^3 - 1 = 0\,.$$

Differentiate it many different times.

$$2\,\dot{y}\,\ddot{y} + 24\,y^2\,\dot{y}\,,$$
$$2\,\dot{y}\,y^{(3)} + 2\,\ddot{y}^2 + 24\,y^2\,\ddot{y} + 48\,y\,\dot{y}^2\,,$$
$$\vdots$$

Rename each derivative $y^{(k)}$ as v_k. Solve the obtained polynomial system (observe there are infinitely many solutions). The result is a truncated arc $\underline{v}$

$$(v_0, v_1, v_2, v_3, v_4, v_5, v_6, v_7, \ldots) = (0, 1, 0, 0, -24, 0, 0, 2880, \ldots)\,.$$

Substitute the arc in the generic formula

$$\Psi(\underline{v}) = \sum \frac{v_i}{i\,!}\,x^i\,.$$

---

[1] In this paper, "countable" stands for "countably infinite".

One obtains a formal power series solution centered at the origin. Since the ODE is autonomous, the same arc, substituted in the following generic formula

$$\Psi_\alpha(\underline{v}) = \sum \frac{v_i}{i\,!}\,(x - \alpha)^i \tag{1}$$

provides a formal power series solution centered at any expansion point $x = \alpha$.

If the ODE is not autonomous, the arc depends on the expansion point. The process is thus a variant. Consider some non-autonomous ODE

$$x\,\dot{y}^2 + 8\,x\,y^3 - 1 = 0\,.$$

Differentiate the ODE many different times.

$$2\,x\,\dot{y}\,\ddot{y} + \dot{y}^2 + 24\,x\,y^2\,\dot{y} + 8\,y^3\,,$$
$$\vdots$$

Then fix an expansion point α and evaluate the independent variable at $x = \alpha$. Solve the obtained polynomial system. The result is a truncated arc. Substitute it in (1) (for the chosen value of α). One gets a formal power series solution centered at $x = \alpha$.

In the above processes, the only issue lies in the polynomial solving step. Indeed, each differentiated equation introduces a new leading derivative. These leading derivatives admit as leading coefficients the initial or the separant of the ODE. If these two polynomials do not vanish at the expansion point and the already secured coordinates of the truncated arc (the initial values, somehow, of the initial value problem), then the formal power series solution exists, is unique and straightforward to compute up to any term. However, if these polynomials vanish, the formal power series solution may fail to exist or be unique.

A device borrowed from [6, page 236] illustrates the issue. It shows how to build an ODE p with coefficients in $\mathbb{Q}[x]$ from a polynomial $f(z)$ in $\mathbb{Q}[z]$. The ODE admits a formal power series solution centered at the origin if and only if the polynomial $f(z)$ has no positive integer solution. In the ordinary case, this device permits to build interesting examples. The approach generalizes to the partial case. It permits to relate the existence problem of formal power series solutions centered at the origin for PDE systems to Hilbert's Tenth Problem and Matiiassevich undecidability result [6, Theorem 4.11]. For more details see [3, Sect 1.6].

It is interesting also to observe that any non-autonomous ODE can be viewed as an autonomous one by performing a change of independent variable and introducing an extra ODE. Indeed, call ξ the new independent variable. View the former independent variable x as a new differential indeterminate (i.e. as an unknown function $x(\xi)$) and introduce the extra ODE $\dot{x} = 1$. This reduction method only applies to ODE with *polynomial* coefficients in x. However, if $x = \alpha$ was a problematic expansion point before the reduction then $x(0) = \alpha$ becomes a problematic initial value (hence arc coordinate) after reduction. For more details see [3, Sect 1.4.2].

In his books [13,14], Ritt implicitly considers autonomous systems (the "autonomous" qualifier does not belong to differential algebra) and we may assume he had in mind the above reduction trick. Though Taylor expansions of solutions are discussed at different places (mostly in a chapter dedicated to PDE), Ritt does not explicitly address the existence problem of formal power series solutions. However, he pioneered differential elimination methods by means of his theory of characteristic sets (which was much developed afterwards, leading to the theories of regular chains and differential regular chains). This elimination theory solves in particular the following decision problem: given any finite system Σ of ordinary or partial differential polynomial, does $1 \in [\Sigma]$ where $[\Sigma]$ denotes the differential ideal generated by Σ? This problem is equivalent to the following one, which is thus seen to be decidable: does there exist initial values for which Σ has formal power series solutions[2]?

In the case of systems of non-autonomous ODE, thanks to the reduction method to the autonomous case, we can then conclude that the following problem is decidable: given any system Σ, do expansion point and initial values exist for which Σ has formal power series solutions?

3   The Fundamental Theorem of Tropical Differential Algebraic Geometry

In the tropical differential case, the systems under consideration belong to some differential polynomial ring $\mathscr{F}[[x]]\{y_1, \ldots, y_n\}$ where $\mathscr{F}$ is a characteristic zero field of constants. Differential polynomials have formal power series coefficients. Thus the reduction trick to the autonomous case does not apply and formal power series solutions are only sought at a fixed expansion point: the origin. More precisely, formal power series solutions are sought in the coefficient ring $\mathscr{F}[[x]]$ of the equations.

The existence problem of such formal power series solutions is much more difficult. An important related paper is [6]. Indeed, [6, Theorem 3.1] claims that, in the case of systems with coefficients in $\mathbb{Q}[x]$, the existence problem of formal power series solutions (with coefficients in $\mathbb{C}$, $\mathbb{R}$ or $\mathbb{Q}_p$) is decidable. It is however important to note that, in the same setting, the existence problem of nonzero formal power series solutions is undecidable. See [6, Proposition 3.3] which refers to [16].

In this context, the fundamental theorem of tropical differential geometry does not solve any problem left open in [6]. It only states the following equivalence

$$\operatorname{supp}(\operatorname{sol}(\Sigma)) = \operatorname{sol}(\operatorname{trop}(\Sigma)), \tag{2}$$

---

[2] Indeed, the *characteristic sets* or *regular differential chains* computed by differential elimination methods can be viewed as differential systems sufficiently simplified to generalize, for systems of differential equations, the basic methods sketched at the top of the section for computing formal power series solutions.

where Σ is a differential ideal and the base field $\mathscr{F}$ is both algebraically closed and uncountable (we relinquish this last condition in this paper).

Before entering sophisticated issues, let us clarify the notations used in (2). The support[3] $\mathrm{supp}(\varphi)$ of the formal power series (3) is the set $\{i \in \mathbb{N} \mid a_i \neq 0\}$.

$$\varphi = \sum a_i\, x^i \tag{3}$$

Since Σ depends on n differential indeterminates $y_1, \ldots, y_n$, its formal power series solutions actually are tuples of n formal power series. One then extends the above definition to tuples of formal power series: the support of a tuple

$$\varphi = (\varphi_1, \ldots, \varphi_n) \tag{4}$$

is defined as the tuple $\mathrm{supp}(\varphi) = (\mathrm{supp}(\varphi_1), \ldots, \mathrm{supp}(\varphi_n))$.

On the left hand side of (2), $\mathrm{sol}(\Sigma)$ denotes the set of formal power series solutions of Σ with coefficients in $\mathscr{F}$. Hence, the left hand side of (2) is a set of tuples of the supports of all the formal power series solutions of Σ.

Let us address now the right hand side of (2). The valuation of a formal power series (3) is defined as ∞ if $\varphi = 0$ and as the smallest $i \in \mathbb{N}$ such that $a_i \neq 0$ otherwise.

$$\mathscr{F}[[x]] \xrightarrow{\ \mathrm{supp}\ } \mathcal{P}(\mathbb{N})$$
$$\searrow_{\text{valuation}} \qquad \downarrow^{\min}$$
$$\mathbb{N}$$

Let us now define the tropicalization of the differential monomial (the coefficient $c \in \mathscr{F}[[x]]$ and the term t is a power product of derivatives $v_1, \ldots, v_r$ of the n differential indeterminates $y_1, \ldots, y_n$)

$$m = c\,t = c\,v_1^{d_1} \cdots v_r^{d_r} \tag{5}$$

at a tuple of supports

$$S = (S_1, \ldots, S_n). \tag{6}$$

Consider any tuple of formal power series (4) whose support is S. Since m is a monomial, the support of the formal power series $m(\varphi)$ is uniquely defined by S: it does not depend on the actual coefficients of φ. We are led to the following definition[4].

The *tropicalization* of a differential monomial m at S is defined as the valuation of $m(\varphi)$ where φ is any tuple of formal power series whose support is S. The table below gives a few examples.

monomial m	support S	trop(m) at S
$x^2 y$	$\{0, 1, 2\}$	2
$x^2 y$	$\{2\}$	4
$\dot{y}^3$	$\{0, 3\}$	6
$\dot{y}^3$	$\{0, 1\}$	∞

---

[3] In [1,8], the notation trop(φ) is used instead of supp(φ) but may be misleading in some cases.

[4] This is not the definition given in [1, sect. 4] but both definitions are equivalent.

Let us now consider a nonzero differential polynomial, expanded as a sum of monomials of the form (5) with pairwise distinct terms:

$$p = m_1 + m_2 + \cdots + m_q. \tag{7}$$

The *tropicalization* of p at S is defined as

$$\mathrm{trop}(p) = \min_{i=1}^{q} \mathrm{trop}(m_i). \tag{8}$$

The tropicalization of the zero polynomial is defined as ∞.

As an example, let us consider the differential polynomial

$$p = \dot{y}^2 - 4y \tag{9}$$

whose solutions are $\varphi = 0$ (support $S = \varnothing$) and $\varphi = (x+c)^2$ where c is an arbitrary constant (supports $S = \{0,1,2\}$ and $\{2\}$). The first and second derivatives of p are

$$\dot{p} = 2\dot{y}\ddot{y} - 4\dot{y}, \tag{10}$$
$$\ddot{p} = 2\dot{y}y^{(3)} + 2\ddot{y}^2 - 4\ddot{y}. \tag{11}$$

In the next table, all the considered supports are supports of solutions of the differential polynomials. In the last column, the list of the $\mathrm{trop}(m_i)$ is provided, rather than their minimum. The first row indicates that both monomials of p vanish at $\varphi = 0$. The second row indicates that the two monomials do not vanish but may possibly cancel each other at $\varphi = a_2 x^2$, for some $a_2 \neq 0$ (indeed, they vanish but only for $a_2 = 1$). The third row indicates that, among the three monomials of $\ddot{p}$, the first one vanishes at any $\varphi = a_2 x^2$ while the two last ones may cancel each other for some $a_2 \neq 0$.

polynomial	support S	list $\mathrm{trop}(m_i)$ at S
p	$\varnothing$	$[\infty, \infty]$
p	$\{2\}$	$[2, 2]$
$\ddot{p}$	$\{2\}$	$[\infty, 0, 0]$

In the next table, the considered support $S = \{0,1\}$ is not the support of any solution of p, since p has no solution of the form $\varphi = a_0 + a_1 x$ with $a_0, a_1 \neq 0$. This fact is not observed on the first row, which considers p itself. It is however observed on the second row, which considers the first derivative of p: one of the two monomials vanishes while the second one evaluates to some nonzero formal power series.

polynomial	support S	list $\mathrm{trop}(m_i)$ at S
p	$\{0,1\}$	$[0,0]$
$\dot{p}$	$\{0,1\}$	$[\infty, 0]$

The observed phenomena suggest the following definition, which permits to understand the right hand side of (2).

Let p be a polynomial of the form (7). View trop(p) as a function of n unknown supports. Then $(S_1, \ldots, S_n)$ is said to be a *solution* of trop(p) if either

1. each trop(m_i) = ∞ or

2. there exists m_i, m_j $(i \neq j)$ such that $\text{trop}(m_i) = \text{trop}(m_j) = \min_{k=1}^{q}(\text{trop}(m_k))$.

Let us conclude this section by a few remarks. In the fundamental theorem of tropical differential algebraic geometry, the inclusion supp(sol(Σ)) $\subset$ sol(trop(Σ)) is easy. The difficult part is the converse inclusion. It requires Σ to be a differential ideal because one may need to consider arbitrary high derivatives of the elements of Σ in order to observe that a given support is not a solution. See the example above or even simpler, consider $p = \dot{y} - y$ and $S = \{0, \ldots, n\}$ with $n \in \mathbb{N}$: it is necessary to differentiate n times the differential polynomial p in order to observe that it has no solution with support S. Moreover, the base field $\mathscr{F}$ is required to be algebraically closed because of the polynomial system solving step and the fact that solutions are sought in $\mathscr{F}[[x]]$.

Last, the proof of the converse inclusion relies on an approximation theorem. The two versions of this approximation theorem given in [1, Proposition 7.3] and [7, Proposition 6.3] assume $\mathscr{F}$ to be uncountable. Our new version (Theorem 1) relies on weaker hypotheses.

4   Fields of Definition and Countability

We are concerned with a differential ideal Σ [10, I, sect. 2] in a characteristic zero partial differential polynomial ring $\mathscr{F}[[x_1, \ldots, x_m]]\{y_1, \ldots, y_n\}$ where $\mathscr{F}$ is an algebraically closed field of constants, the m derivation operators $\delta_1, \ldots, \delta_m$ act as $\partial/\partial x_1, \ldots, \partial/\partial x_m$ and $y_1, \ldots, y_n$ are n differential indeterminates.

Thanks to the Ritt-Raudenbush Basis Theorem (see [4] for details), the differential ideal Σ can be presented by finitely many differential polynomials $g_1, \ldots, g_s \in \mathscr{F}[[x_1, \ldots, x_m]]\{y_1, \ldots, y_n\}$ in the sense that the perfect [10, 0, sect. 5] differential ideals $\{\Sigma\}$ and $\{g_1, \ldots, g_s\}$ are equal.

A *field of definition*[5] of Σ is any subfield $\mathscr{F}_0 \subset \mathscr{F}$ such that there exist $g_1, \ldots, g_s \in \Sigma \cap \mathscr{F}_0[[x_1, \ldots, x_m]]\{y_1, \ldots, y_n\}$ with $\Sigma \subseteq \{g_1, \ldots, g_s\}$ (the perfect differential ideal generated by $g_1, \ldots, g_s$).

Proposition 1. *Any differential ideal Σ has a countable algebraically closed field of definition $\mathscr{F}_0$. Moreover, if $\mathscr{F}$ has countable transcendence degree over $\mathscr{F}_0$ then $\mathscr{F}$ also is countable.*

Proof. Let S be the family of the coefficients of the formal power series coefficients of any basis of Σ which are transcendental over the field $\mathbb{Q}$ of the rational numbers. The family S is countable. An algebraically closed field of definition $\mathscr{F}_0$ can be defined as the algebraic closure of $\mathbb{Q}(S)$.

---

[5] This definition is adapted from [10, I, sect. 5].

Now, the field $\mathbb{Q}$ is countable. If $\mathscr{L}$ is a countable field and S is a countable family of transcendental elements over $\mathscr{L}$ then $\mathscr{L}(S)$ is countable. Moreover, if $\mathscr{L}$ is countable then its algebraic closure is countable [9, Theorem 65].

The last statement of the proposition follows using the same arguments.

In the sequel, $\mathscr{F}_0$ denotes an algebraically closed field of definition of Σ.

5   The Approximation Theorem

Denote by Θ the commutative semigroup of the derivative operators generated by the derivation operators i.e. $\Theta = \{\delta_1^{a_1} \cdots \delta_m^{a_m} \mid a_1, \ldots, a_m \in \mathbb{N}\}$.

Define a one-to-one correspondence between the set of all pairs $(i, \theta) \in [1, n] \times \Theta$ and the set $\mathbb{N}$ of nonnegative integers. This correspondence permits us to enumerate all derivatives θy_i of the differential indeterminates. Fix a correspondence which defines an orderly ranking (derivatives are enumerated by increasing order) [10, chap. I, sect. 8]. The derivatives of the y are denoted $v_0, v_1, v_2, \ldots$

As in Sect. 4, let Σ be a differential ideal included in the perfect differential ideal $\{g_1, \ldots, g_s\}$ generated by $g_1, \ldots, g_s \in \Sigma$ with field of definition equal to $\mathscr{F}_0$. Define another one-to-one correspondence between the set of all pairs $(i, \theta) \in [1, s] \times \Theta$ and $\mathbb{N}$. This correspondence permits us to enumerate all derivatives $\theta\, g_i$. Again, fix a correspondence which defines an orderly ranking on the derivatives of the g (viewing them as s differential indeterminates). The derivatives of the g, evaluated at $x_1 = \cdots = x_m = 0$, are denoted $f_0, f_1, f_2, \ldots$ The polynomials f thus belong to $\mathscr{F}_0\{y_1, \ldots, y_n\}$.

Let k be a positive integer. Denote

$$\Sigma_k = \{f_i \mid 0 \le i \le k\},$$
$$\Sigma_\infty = \{f_i \mid i \in \mathbb{N}\}.$$

Define $\kappa(k) = \kappa$ as the smallest integer such that $\Sigma_k \subset \mathscr{F}_0[v_0, \ldots, v_\kappa]$. The index κ exists because the ranking is orderly. Define

$$A_k = \{a \in \mathscr{F}_0^{\kappa+1} \mid f_0(a) = \cdots = f_k(a) = 0\}.$$

Let now S be any subset of $\mathbb{N}$. Define $A_{k,S}$ as the set of zeros of A_k which are *compatible with S*:

$$A_{k,S} = \{a \in A_k \mid a_i \ne 0 \text{ if and only if } i \in S \cap [0, \kappa]\}.$$

Indeed, thanks to the fixed one-to-one correspondence between the derivatives of the differential indeterminates and the set $\mathbb{N}$, any such set S encodes a tuple of n supports of formal power series. Given any field extension $\mathscr{E}$ of $\mathscr{F}_0$, define

$$A_\infty(\mathscr{E}) = \{a \in \mathscr{E}^{\mathbb{N}} \mid f_i(a) = 0 \text{ for each } i \in \mathbb{N}\},$$
$$A_{\infty,S}(\mathscr{E}) = \{a \in A_\infty(\mathscr{E}) \mid a_i \ne 0 \text{ if and only if } i \in S\}.$$

The elements of $A_\infty(\mathscr{F})$ give exactly the formal power series solutions of Σ. The elements of $A_{\infty,S}(\mathscr{F})$ give the formal power series solutions whose supports are encoded by S.

Theorem 1. *Assume $\mathscr{F}$ has countable transcendence degree over $\mathscr{F}_0$ and is algebraically closed. Let S be any subset of $\mathbb{N}$. If $A_{k,S} \neq \varnothing$ for each $k \in \mathbb{N}$ then $A_{\infty,S}(\mathscr{F}) \neq \varnothing$.*

There are many proofs which have the following sketch in common:

1. one first proves that Σ_∞ admits a solution compatible with S in some (big) field extension $\mathscr{E}$ of $\mathscr{F}_0$. This solution is an arc $a = (a_i)$ with coordinates $a_i \in \mathscr{E}$ for $i \in \mathbb{N}$. With other words, $A_{\infty,S}(\mathscr{E}) \neq \varnothing$;
2. the arc a can be mapped to another arc $\phi(a)$ with coordinates in $\mathscr{F}$ which is also a solution of Σ_∞ compatible with S. Thus $A_{\infty,S}(\mathscr{F}) \neq \varnothing$ and Theorem 1 is proved.

There are actually many different ways to prove Step 1 above. The next sections provide three different variants.

5.1 Proof of Step 1 by Ultraproducts

The idea of this proof is mostly due do Marc Paul Noordman. It is inspired by techniques used in [6]. A minimal introduction of ultraproducts for casual readers is provided in Sect. A.

Proof. Let $\mathscr{R}$ be the ring obtained by inversion of all derivatives with indices in S and quotient by the ideal equal to the sum of the ideal generated by Σ_∞ and the ideal generated by the derivatives with indices not in S, i.e.

$$\mathscr{R} = \mathscr{F}_0[v_i, v_j^{-1} \mid i \in \mathbb{N}, j \in S]/(f_i, v_j \mid i \in \mathbb{N}, j \notin S). \tag{12}$$

By Lemma 1 (below), this ring is not the null ring. By Krull's Theorem, it contains a maximal ideal $\mathfrak{m}$. A suitable field extension $\mathscr{E}$ of $\mathscr{F}_0$ is given by $\mathscr{R}/\mathfrak{m}$. The coordinates of the arc (a_i) are the images of the derivatives v_i by the natural $\mathscr{F}_0$-algebra homomorphism $\mathscr{R} \to \mathscr{R}/\mathfrak{m}$.

Lemma 1. *The ring $\mathscr{R}$ defined in (12) is not the null ring.*

Proof. We prove the lemma by showing that Σ_∞ admits a solution in some field $\mathscr{F}_0^*$ (which turns out to be an ultrafield - see Sect. A) and constructing a map $\mathscr{F}_0\{y_1, \ldots, y_n\} \to \mathscr{F}_0^*$ which factors as $\mathscr{F}_0\{y_1, \ldots, y_n\} \to \mathscr{R} \to \mathscr{F}_0^*$.

To each $k \in \mathbb{N}$ associate an element $a^k \in A_{k,S}$. We have

$$a^k = (a_0^k, a_1^k, \ldots, a_\kappa^k) \in \mathscr{F}_0^\kappa.$$

Fix any non principal ultrafilter $\mathscr{D}$ on $\mathbb{N}$ and consider the ultrafield $\mathscr{F}_0^* = (\prod_{i \in \mathbb{N}} \mathscr{F}_0)/\mathscr{D}$. For each $i \in \mathbb{N}$ define $u_i \in \mathscr{F}_0^*$ by

$$u_0 = (a_0^0,\ a_0^1,\ a_0^2,\ \ldots,\ a_0^k,\ \ldots),$$
$$u_1 = (a_1^0,\ a_1^1,\ a_1^2,\ \ldots,\ a_1^k,\ \ldots),$$
$$\vdots$$
$$u_i = (a_i^0,\ a_i^1,\ a_i^2,\ \ldots,\ a_i^k,\ \ldots),$$
$$\vdots$$

On each column k of the above "array", the elements a_i^k such that $i > \kappa$ are not defined. Set them to zero. Observe that on each row, there are only finitely many such elements.

We have thus defined a map $v_i \mapsto u_i$.

Let now $i \in \mathbb{N}$ be the index of some polynomial $f_i = f$. Evaluate f to an element of $\mathscr{F}_0^*$ by substituting u_j to v_j for each $j \in \mathbb{N}$. Ultrafield operations are performed componentwise and the zeros of the f appear on the columns in the above array. Thus, f evaluates to zero over the kth coordinate of $\mathscr{F}_0^*$ for all sufficiently large values of k. This set of values of k is cofinite and hence, f evaluates to zero in $\mathscr{F}_0^*$.

Let now $i \in \mathbb{N}$ be the index of some derivative v_i. By definition of $A_{k,S}$, if $i \notin S$ then all the coordinates of u_i are zero so that u_i is zero in $\mathscr{F}_0^*$; if $i \in S$ then the coordinates a_i^k of u_i are nonzero for all sufficiently large values of k and u_i is nonzero in $\mathscr{F}_0^*$.

The mapping $v_i \mapsto u_i$ thus defines a zero of Σ_∞ which is compatible with S and with coordinates in $\mathscr{F}_0^*$.

5.2 Proof of Step 1 by a Model Theoretic Argument

The idea of this proof is due to Omar León Sánchez.

Proof. Define

$$\Omega(v) = \{f_i = 0 \mid i \in \mathbb{N}\} \cup \{v_i = 0 \mid i \notin S\} \cup \{v_i \neq 0 \mid i \in S\}.$$

For any subcollection $\Omega_0(v)$ of $\Omega(v)$, there is a large enough $k \in \mathbb{N}$ such that if $a \in A_{k,S}$ then a is a solution of $\Omega_0(v)$. Hence the assumption that $A_{k,S} \neq \varnothing$, for all $k \in \mathbb{N}$, yields that $\Omega(v)$ is *finitely satisfiable*.

By the compactness theorem in first-order logic (see for instance [12, Chapter 3]) applied in the context of fields, the fact that $\Omega(v)$ is finitely satisfiable implies that there is a field extension $\mathscr{E}$ of $\mathscr{F}_0$ and an arc $a = (a_i)$ with coordinates in $\mathscr{E}$ solving $\Omega(v)$.

Remark 1. We note that Theorem 1 should not be too surprising to a model-theorist; as it can be seen as an application of general results on strongly minimal theories (for instance, the fact that in a strongly minimal theory there is a unique non-algebraic complete 1-type over any set of parameters). Here the theory in mind is algebraically closed fields and the slightly more general result is as follows: Let $x = (x_i)_{i \in I}$ be a tuple of variables and L/K a field extension of transcendence degree at least $|I|$ with L algebraically closed. Suppose $T(x)$ is a collection of polynomial equations and in-equations over K. If $T(x)$ is finitely satisfiable, then there is a solution of $T(x)$ in L.

5.3 Proof of Step 1 by Lang's Infinite Nullstellensatz

The idea of this proof was suggested by an anonymous reviewer.

Proof. Enlarge the set of derivatives (v_i) with another infinite set of derivatives (w_i) where $i \in \mathbb{N}$. Define

$$\Omega_\infty = \Sigma_\infty \cup \{v_i \mid i \notin S\} \cup \{v_i w_i - 1 \mid i \in S\}.$$

Any solution of Ω_∞ provides a solution of Σ_∞ which is compatible with S. The set of variables v, w is indexed by $\mathbb{N}$. Let $\mathcal{E}$ be any uncountable field. Note that the ideal generated by Ω_∞ in the polynomial ring $\mathcal{E}[v, w]$ is proper; otherwise, 1 could be written as a linear combination (over $\mathcal{E}[v, w]$) of finitely many of the elements of Ω_∞, but this implies $A_{k,S} = \varnothing$ for some large enough $k \in \mathbb{N}$ (contradicting our hypothesis). Then, by [11, Theorem, conditions (ii) and S2], the system Ω_∞ has a solution in $\mathcal{E}$. Thus $A_{\infty,S}(\mathcal{E}) \neq \varnothing$.

5.4   Proof of Step 2

In Step 1, we have proved that there exists a field extension $\mathcal{E}$ of $\mathcal{F}_0$ such that $A_{\infty,S}(\mathcal{E}) \neq \varnothing$. Let us prove that $A_{\infty,S}(\mathcal{F}) \neq \varnothing$.

Proof. Consider some $a \in A_{\infty,S}(\mathcal{E})$. Let $J \subset \mathbb{N}$ be such that $(a_j)_{j \in J}$ is a transcendence basis of $\mathcal{F}_0(a)$ over $\mathcal{F}_0$. Denote $\mathcal{F}_1$ the algebraic closure of $\mathcal{F}_0(a_j)_{j \in J}$. Then the full arc a has coordinates in $\mathcal{F}_1$. Since $\mathcal{F}$ has countable transcendence degree over $\mathcal{F}_0$ we have $\mathrm{trdeg}(\mathcal{F}/\mathcal{F}_0) \geq \mathrm{trdeg}(\mathcal{F}_1/\mathcal{F}_0) = |J|$. Moreover, since $\mathcal{F}$ is algebraically closed, there exists a $\mathcal{F}_0$-algebra homomorphism $\phi : \mathcal{F}_1 \to \mathcal{F}$ such that $\phi(a)$ is a solution of Σ_∞ compatible with S. Thus $A_{\infty,S}(\mathcal{F}) \neq \varnothing$.

6   The New Version of the Fundamental Theorem

For completeness, we provide the part of the proof of the fundamental theorem which makes use of our Theorem 1. The proof is the same as that of [1, Theorem 8]. We start with an easy Lemma [1, Remark 4.1].

Lemma 2. *Let $S = (S_1, \ldots, S_n)$ be a tuple of n supports and $m = c\, v_1^{d_1} \cdots v_r^{d_r}$ be a monomial. Then $\mathrm{trop}(m) = 0$ at S if and only if the valuation of c is zero and each factor $v^d = (y_j^{(k)})^d$ of m is such that $k \in S_j$.*

Before stating the fundamental theorem, let us stress that the fields $\mathcal{F}_0$ and $\mathcal{F}$ mentioned in Theorem 2 can be assumed to be countable, by Proposition 1.

Theorem 2 (Fundamental Theorem for ODE). *Let Σ be a differential ideal of $\mathcal{F}[[x]]\{y_1, \ldots, y_n\}$ where $\mathcal{F}$ is an algebraically closed field of constants and $\mathcal{F}_0$ be an algebraically closed field of definition of Σ. If $\mathcal{F}$ has countable transcendence degree over $\mathcal{F}_0$ then*

$$\mathrm{supp}(\mathrm{sol}(\Sigma)) = \mathrm{sol}(\mathrm{trop}(\Sigma)). \tag{13}$$

Proof. Let us first address a few particular cases.

Case 1: there exists some nonzero $c \in \Sigma \cap \mathscr{F}[[x]]$. Differentiating c sufficiently many times, we see that $1 \in \Sigma$. Then, on the one hand, $\text{supp}(\text{sol}(\Sigma)) = \varnothing$. On the other hand, $\text{sol}(\text{trop}(1)) = \varnothing$. Thus the theorem holds in Case 1.

Case 2: $\Sigma = (0)$. Then, on the one hand $\text{supp}(\text{sol}(\Sigma))$ contains all supports. On the other hand, $\text{sol}(\text{trop}(0))$ contains all supports too. Thus the theorem holds in Case 2.

Let us now address the general case. The inclusion $\subset$ is easy. We prove the converse one. We assume that S is not the support of any solution of Σ and we show that S is not a solution of $\text{trop}(\Sigma)$.

For this, we are going to build a differential polynomial $h \in \Sigma$, expanding to a sum of monomials

$$h = m_1 + m_2 + \cdots + m_r, \tag{14}$$

such that $\text{trop}(m_1) = 0$ and $\text{trop}(m_i) > 0$ for $2 \leq i \leq r$.

By the Ritt-Raudenbush Basis Theorem (see [4] for details), there exists a finite set $g_1, \ldots, g_s$ of differential polynomials of Σ such that the solution set of Σ is the solution set of the differential ideal $[g_1, \ldots, g_s]$ generated by the g.

From now on, we use the notations introduced in Sect. 5. Since $[g_1, \ldots, g_s]$ has no solution with support S we have $A_{\infty,S}(\mathscr{F}) = \varnothing$ whence, by Theorem 1, there exists some index k such that $A_{k,S} = \varnothing$. Recall that $A_{k,S}$ is a subset of the algebraic variety of some polynomial system obtained by prolonging, and evaluating at $x = 0$, the system of the g up to some order and that the prolonged system belongs to some polynomial ring $\mathscr{F}_0[v_1, \ldots, v_\kappa]$.

Claim: there exists a differential polynomial

$$\hat{h} = \hat{m}_1^d + \hat{m}_2 + \cdots + \hat{m}_{\hat{r}} \tag{15}$$

in the ideal $(f_0, \ldots, f_k)$ of the Noetherian polynomial ring $\mathscr{F}_0[v_1, \ldots, v_\kappa]$ such that $\text{trop}(\hat{m}_1) = 0$ and $\text{trop}(\hat{m}_i) > 0$ for $2 \leq i \leq \hat{r}$.

The ideal $(f_0, \ldots, f_k)$ has no solution compatible with S. This means that (the right hand side of the first line holds only for a non-empty support S but the one of the second line holds in general):

$$[f_0 = \cdots = f_k = 0 \text{ and } v_j = 0 \text{ for all } v_j \text{ s.t. } j \notin S] \Rightarrow v_\ell = 0 \text{ for some } \ell \in S$$

$$\Rightarrow \underbrace{\prod_{\ell \in S, \ell \leq \kappa} v_\ell}_{\hat{m}_1} = 0.$$

By Lemma 2 we have $\text{trop}(\hat{m}_1) = 0$ at S. By Hilbert's Nullstellensatz, we have

$$\hat{m}_1 \in \sqrt{(f_0, \ldots, f_k, (v_j)_{j \notin S})}.$$

Thus there exists a positive integer d and monomials $\hat{m}_2, \ldots, \hat{m}_{\hat{r}}$ defining the polynomial $\hat{h}$ as in (15). We have $\hat{h} \in (f_0, \ldots, f_k)$ and for each $2 \leq i \leq \hat{r}$, there exists some $j \notin S$ for which $\deg(\hat{m}_i, v_j) > 0$. By Lemma 2, we thus have $\mathrm{trop}(\hat{m}_i) > 0$ at S for each $2 \le i \le \hat{r}$. The claim is thus proved.

Now, since $\hat{h} \in (f_0, \ldots, f_k)$ we see that $\hat{h}$ can also be obtained by evaluating at $x = 0$ some polynomial $h \in \Sigma$. Consider any monomial m of h, of the form (5). If the evaluation at $x = 0$ maps m to zero then the valuation of the coefficient c of m is positive. In such a case, $\mathrm{trop}(m) > 0$ by Lemma 2. If it maps m to some nonzero monomial $\hat{m}$ then the valuation of c is nonzero, both m and $\hat{m}$ share the same term and $\mathrm{trop}(m) = \mathrm{trop}(\hat{m})$. Thus the polynomial h has the form (14) and the theorem is proved.

7   The Partial Differential Case

In this section we give an overview on the generalization to the case of partial differential equations.

We seek for solutions of systems $\Sigma \subset \mathscr{F}[[x_1, \ldots, x_m]]\{y_1, \ldots, y_m\}$ in the ring of multivariate formal power series $\mathscr{F}[[x_1, \ldots, x_m]]$.

In this case, the algorithmic problems are even worse than in the ordinary case. According to [6, Theorem 4.11], there even cannot be an algorithm for deciding solvability of linear systems, a subclass of algebraic differential equations as we consider. Instead of actually computing the solutions of Σ, we again present an equivalent description of the solutions in the form of (2).

As in the ordinary case $(m = 1)$, the support of a formal power series

$$\varphi = \sum a_I \, x^I = \sum a_{(i_1, \ldots, i_m)} \, x_1^{i_1} \cdots x_m^{i_m}$$

is the set $\{I \in \mathbb{N}^m \mid a_I \ne 0\}$. Hence, the left hand side of (2) is defined also for $m > 1$.

For the tropicalization of Σ, the generalization cannot be done straightforward, since there is no well-defined minimum of elements in $\mathbb{N}^m$. In [7] is used instead a very specific partial order induced by vertex sets, which we briefly describe here.

Let $X \subset \mathbb{N}^m$. The *Newton polytope* $\mathcal{N}(X) \subseteq \mathbb{R}_{\ge 0}^m$ of X is defined as the convex hull of $X + \mathbb{N}^m = \{x + n \mid x \in X, n \in \mathbb{N}^m\}$. Moreover, $x \in X$ is called a *vertex* if $x \notin \mathcal{N}(X \setminus \{x\})$, and vert is the set of vertices of X. It follows that $\mathrm{vert}(X)$ is the minimal set in $\mathbb{N}^m$ (with respect to the relation "$\subset$") generating $\mathcal{N}(X)$. Let us denote all vertex sets as $\mathbb{T}_m = \{\mathrm{vert} \mid X \subset \mathbb{N}^m\}$. Then, the composition of taking the support and then its vertex set of the formal power series defines a *non-degenerate valuation* such that some ideas of [1] can be recovered.

$$\mathscr{F}[[x_1, \ldots, x_m]] \xrightarrow{\mathrm{supp}} \mathcal{P}(\mathbb{N}^m)$$

$$\mathrm{non-deg.\,valuation} \searrow \quad \downarrow \mathrm{vert}$$

$$\mathbb{T}_m$$

The tropicalization of a differential monomial $m = cv_1^{d_1} \cdots v_r^{d_r}$ at a tuple of supports $S = (S_1, \ldots, S_n) \subset (\mathbb{N}^m)^n$ is defined as the non-degenerate valuation of $m(\varphi)$ from above with $\mathrm{supp}(\varphi) = S$. Let us illustrate this.

monomial m	support S	trop(m) at S
$x_1 x_2 y$	$\{(1,0),(0,1)\}$	$\{(2,0),(0,2)\}$
$(\frac{\partial y}{\partial x_1})^2$	$\{(2,0),(0,2)\}$	$\{(2,0)\}$
$(\frac{\partial^2 y}{\partial x_1 \partial x_2})^2$	$\{(2,0),(0,2)\}$	$\varnothing$

The tropicalization of a differential polynomial p of the form (5) at S is defined as

$$\mathrm{trop}(p) = \mathrm{vert}(\bigcup_{i=1}^{q} \mathrm{trop}(m_i)). \tag{16}$$

Let us consider the polynomial

$$p = \frac{\partial y}{\partial x_1} \cdot \frac{\partial y}{\partial x_2} + (-x_1^2 + x_2^2)\frac{\partial^2 y}{\partial x_1 \partial x_2}. \tag{17}$$

polynomial	support S	list trop(m_i) at S
p	$\{(2,0),(0,2)\}$	$[\{(1,1)\}, \varnothing]$
p	$\{(2,0),(1,1),(0,2)\}$	$[\{(2,0),(1,1),(0,2)\},\{(2,0),(0,2)\}]$

Considering trop(p) as a function of n unknown supports, $(S_1, \ldots, S_n)$ is said to be a *solution* of trop(p) if for every vertex $J \in \mathrm{trop}(p)$ there exists m_i, m_j $(i \neq j)$ such that $J \in \mathrm{trop}(m_i) \cap \mathrm{trop}(m_j)$. In the example above, we see that there cannot be a solution of p with support equals $\{(2,0),(0,2)\}$, but $\varphi = x_1^2 + 2x_1 x_2 - x_2^2$ is indeed a solution.

For more illustrations of the tropicalization of (partial) differential polynomials, see [5].

As in the ordinary case, the inclusion $\mathrm{supp}(\mathrm{sol}(\Sigma)) \subset \mathrm{sol}(\mathrm{trop}(\Sigma))$ in the fundamental theorem is relatively easy [7, Proposition 5.7]. The converse inclusion can be shown exactly as in [7, Section 6], except that we replace Proposition 6.3 by the Approximation Theorem 1.

For consistency let us recall the main result here.

Theorem 3 (Fundamental Theorem for PDE). *Let Σ be a differential ideal of $\mathscr{F}[[x_1, \ldots, x_m]]\{y_1, \ldots, y_n\}$ where $\mathscr{F}$ is an algebraically closed field of constants and $\mathscr{F}_0$ be an algebraically closed field of definition of Σ. If $\mathscr{F}$ has countable transcendence degree over $\mathscr{F}_0$ then*

$$\mathrm{supp}(\mathrm{sol}(\Sigma)) = \mathrm{sol}(\mathrm{trop}(\Sigma)). \tag{18}$$

Acknowledgments. The authors would like to thank Zoé Chatzidakis and Mercedes Haiech for their help and their comments. The first author would like to acknowledge the support of the bilateral project ANR-17-CE40-0036 DFG-391322026 SYMBIONT. The second author was supported by the AustrianScience Fund (FWF): P 31327-N32.

A   Basic Notions on Ultraproducts

This appendix is much inspired by [15, chap. 2] with the notations of [2]. It is only provided for the convenience of casual readers.

The set $\mathbb{N}$ is used as an index set on which we fix a (so called) *non-principal ultrafilter* $\mathscr{D}$. It is by definition a collection of infinite subsets of $\mathbb{N}$ closed under finite intersection, with the property that for any subset $E \subset \mathbb{N}$ either E or its complement $\mathbb{N} \setminus E$ belongs to $\mathscr{D}$. In particular, the empty set does not belong to $\mathscr{D}$ and, if $E \in \mathscr{D}$ and F is an arbitrary set containing E then also $F \in \mathscr{D}$. Otherwise, $\mathbb{N} \setminus F \in \mathscr{D}$ and therefore, $\varnothing = E \cap (\mathbb{N} \setminus F) \in \mathscr{D}$: a contradiction. Since every set in $\mathscr{D}$ must be infinite, it follows that every set whose complement is finite (such a set is called *cofinite*) belongs to $\mathscr{D}$.

Let $\mathscr{R}_i$ ($i \in \mathbb{N}$) be a collection of rings. We form the ultraproduct $\mathscr{R}^* = (\prod_{i \in \mathbb{N}} \mathscr{R}_i)/\mathscr{D}$ (or the ultrapower $\mathscr{R}^{\mathbb{N}}/\mathscr{D}$ if all rings $\mathscr{R}_i$ are the same ring $\mathscr{R}$) as follows. On the Cartesian product $\prod_{i \in \mathbb{N}} \mathscr{R}_i$ we define the equivalence relation: $a \equiv b$ if and only if the set of indices i such that $a_i = b_i$ belongs to the ultrafilter $\mathscr{D}$.

We are going to use the following facts.

Consider an element $a \in \mathscr{R}^*$ which has no nonzero coordinates. The set of indices such that $a_i = 0$ is empty. Since the empty set does not belong to the ultrafilter, $a \neq 0$ in $\mathscr{R}^*$.

Consider an element $a \in \mathscr{R}^*$ which has only finitely many nonzero coordinates. The set of indices such that $a_i = 0$ is cofinite. Thus it belongs to $\mathscr{D}$. Thus $a = 0$ in $\mathscr{R}^*$.

An ultraproduct of rings is a ring: addition and multiplication are performed componentwise. Let us prove that an ultraproduct of fields is a field (called an *ultrafield*). Consider some $a \neq 0$ in $\mathscr{R}^*$. Then the set $E = \{i \in \mathbb{N} \mid a_i = 0\}$ does not belong to $\mathscr{D}$. Thus its complement $F = \mathbb{N} \setminus E$ belongs to $\mathscr{D}$. Define $\bar{a}$ as follows: for each $i \in \mathbb{N}$, if $a_i = 0$ take $\bar{a}_i = 0$ else take $\bar{a}_i = a_i^{-1}$. Let $u = a\,\bar{a}$. The set of indices such that $u_i = 1$ is F, which belongs to $\mathscr{D}$. Thus a admits an inverse and $\mathscr{R}^*$ is a field.

References

1. Aroca, F., Garay, C., Toghani, Z.: The fundamental theorem of tropical differential algebraic geometry. Pacific J. Math. **283**(2), 257–270 (2016)
2. Becker, J., Denef, J., Lipshitz, L., van den Dries, L.: Ultraproducts and approximation in local rings I. Invent. Math. **51**, 189–203 (1979)
3. Boulier, F.: A differential algebra introduction for tropical differential geometry. In: Lecture Notes for the Workshop on Tropical Differential Geometry, Queen Mary College of the University of London, 2–7 December. Available at https://hal.archives-ouvertes.fr/hal-02378197
4. Boulier, F., Haiech, M.: The Ritt-Raudenbush Theorem and Tropical Differential Geometry (2019). https://hal.archives-ouvertes.fr/hal-02403365
5. Cotterill, E., Garay, C., Luviano, J.: Exploring tropical differential equations. Preprint available at http://arxiv.org/abs/2012.14067 (2020)

6. Denef, J., Lipshitz, L.: Power series solutions of algebraic differential equations. Math. Ann. **267**, 213–238 (1984)
7. Falkensteiner, S., Garay-López, C., Haiech, M., Noordman, M.P., Toghani, Z., Boulier, F.: The Fundamental Theorem of Tropical Partial Differential Algebraic Geometry. In: Proceedings of ISSAC 2020, Kalamata, Greece, pp. 178–185 (2020)
8. Grigoriev, D.: Tropical differential equations. Adv. Appl. Math. **82**, 120–128 (2017)
9. Kaplansky, I.: Fields and Rings, 2nd edn. The University of Chicago, Chicago (1972)
10. Kolchin, E.R.: Differential Algebra and Algebraic Groups. Academic Press, New York (1973)
11. Lang, S.: Hilbert's Nullstellensatz in infinite-dimensional space. Proc. Am. Math. Soc. **3**(3), 407–410 (1952)
12. Marker, D.: Model Theory: An Introduction, vol. 217. Springer, New York (2006). https://doi.org/10.1007/b98860
13. Ritt, J.F.: Differential Equations from the Algebraic Standpoint. American Mathematical Society Colloquium Publications, vol. 14. American Mathematical Society, New York (1932)
14. Ritt, J.F.: Differential Algebra, American Mathematical Society Colloquium Publications, vol. 33. American Mathematical Society, New York (1950)
15. Schoutens, H.: The Use of Ultraproducts in Commutative Algebra. LNCS, Springer, Heidelberg (2010). https://doi.org/10.1007/978-3-642-13368-8
16. Singer, M.: The model theory of ordered differential fields. J. Symb. Log. **43**(1), 82–91 (1978)

On the Complexity and Parallel Implementation of Hensel's Lemma and Weierstrass Preparation

Alexander Brandt[(✉)] and Marc Moreno Maza

Department of Computer Science, The University of Western Ontario,
London, Canada
abrandt5@uwo.ca, moreno@csd.uwo.ca

Abstract. Hensel's lemma, combined with repeated applications of Weierstrass preparation theorem, allows for the factorization of polynomials with multivariate power series coefficients. We present a complexity analysis for this method and leverage those results to guide the load-balancing of a parallel implementation to concurrently update all factors. In particular, the factorization creates a *pipeline* where the terms of degree k of the first factor are computed simultaneously with the terms of degree $k-1$ of the second factor, etc. An implementation challenge is the inherent irregularity of computational work between factors, as our complexity analysis reveals. Additional resource utilization and load-balancing is achieved through the parallelization of Weierstrass preparation. Experimental results show the efficacy of this mixed parallel scheme, achieving up to 9× parallel speedup on a 12-core machine.

Keywords: Formal power series · Weierstrass preparation · Hensel's lemma · Hensel factorization · Parallel processing · Parallel pipeline

1 Introduction

Factorization via Hensel's lemma, or simply Hensel factorization, provides a mechanism for factorizing univariate polynomials with multivariate power series coefficients. In particular, for a multivariate polynomial in $(X_1, \ldots, X_n, Y)$, monic and square-free as a polynomial in Y, one can compute its roots with respect to Y as power series in $(X_1, \ldots, X_n)$. For a bivariate polynomial in (X_1, Y), the classical Newton–Puiseux method is known to compute the polynomial's roots with respect to Y as univariate Puiseux series in X_1. The transition from power series to Puiseux series arises from handling the non-monic case.

The *Hensel–Sasaki Construction* or *Extended Hensel Construction* (EHC) was proposed in [24] as an efficient alternative to the Newton–Puiseux method for the case of univariate coefficients. In the same paper, an extension of the Hensel–Sasaki construction for multivariate coefficients was proposed, and then later extended, see e.g., [17,25]. In [1], EHC was improved in terms of algebraic complexity and practical implementation.

© Springer Nature Switzerland AG 2021
F. Boulier et al. (Eds.): CASC 2021, LNCS 12865, pp. 78–99, 2021.
https://doi.org/10.1007/978-3-030-85165-1_6

In this paper, we present a parallel algorithm and its implementation for Hensel factorization based on repeated applications of Weierstrass preparation theorem. Our method uses a *lazy evaluation* scheme, meaning that more terms can be computed on demand without having to restart the computation. This contrasts with a *truncated* implementation where only terms up to a pre-determined degree are computed. Unfortunately, such a degree often cannot be determined before calculations start, or later may be found to not go far enough. This scenario occurs, for instance, when computing limits of real rational functions [1].

Lazy evaluation is not new, having previously been employed in sparse polynomial arithmetic [22] and *univariate* power series arithmetic [9, 15]. Our previous work in [8] is, to the best of our knowledge, the first lazy multivariate power series implementation. Our implementation of lazy and parallel power series supports an arbitrary number of variables. However, the complexity estimates of our proposed methods are measured in the bivariate case; see Sect. 4. This allows us to obtain sharp complexity estimates, giving the number of operations required to update each factor of a Hensel factorization individually. This information helps guide and load-balance our parallel implementation. Further, limiting to the bivariate case allows for comparison with existing works.

Denote by $M(n)$ a polynomial multiplication time [12, Ch. 8] (the cost sufficient to multiply two polynomials of degree n), Let $\mathbb{K}$ be algebraically closed and $f \in \mathbb{K}[[X_1]][Y]$ have degree d_Y in Y and total degree d. Our Hensel factorization computes the first k terms of all factors of f within $\mathcal{O}(d_Y^3 k + d_Y^2 k^2)$ operations in $\mathbb{K}$. We conjecture in Sect. 4 that we can achieve $\mathcal{O}(d_Y^3 k + d_Y^2 M(k) \log k)$ using relaxed algorithms [15]. The EHC of [1] computes the first k terms of all factors in $\mathcal{O}(d^3 M(d) + k^2 dM(d))$. Kung and Traub show that, over the complex numbers $\mathbb{C}$, the Newton–Puiseux method can do the same in $\mathcal{O}(d^2 kM(k))$ (resp. $\mathcal{O}(d^2 M(k))$) operations in $\mathbb{C}$ using a linear lifting (resp. quadratic lifting) scheme [18]. This complexity is lowered to $\mathcal{O}(d^2 k)$ by Chudnovsky and Chudnovsky in [10]. Berthomieu, Lecerf, and Quintin in [7] also present an algorithm and implementation based on Hensel lifting which performs in $\mathcal{O}(M(d_Y) \log(d_Y) kM(k))$; this is better than previous methods with respect to d (or d_Y), but worse with respect to k.

However, these estimates ignore an initial root finding step. Denote by $R(n)$ the cost of finding the roots in $\mathbb{K}$ of a degree n polynomial (e.g. [12, Th. 14.18]). Our method then performs in $\mathcal{O}(d_Y^3 k + d_Y^2 k^2 + R(d_Y))$. Note that the $R(d_Y)$ term does not depend on k, and is thus ignored henceforth. For comparison, however, Neiger, Rosenkilde, and Schost in [23] present an algorithm based on Hensel lifting which, *ignoring polylogarithmic factors*, performs in $\mathcal{O}(d_Y k + kR(d_Y))$.

Nonetheless, despite a higher asymptotic complexity, the formulation of EHC in [1] is shown to be practically much more efficient than that of Kung and Traub. Our serial implementation of lazy Hensel factorization (using plain, quadratic arithmetic) has already been shown in [8] to be orders of magnitude faster than that implementation of EHC. Similarly, in [8], we show that our serial lazy power series is orders of magnitude faster than the truncated implementations of MAPLE's [19] `mtaylor` and SAGEMATH's [28] `PowerSeriesRing`. This highlights that a lazy scheme using suboptimal routines—but a careful implementation—can still be practically efficient despite higher asymptotic complexity.

Further still, it is often the case that asymptotically fast algorithms are much more difficult to parallelize, and have high parallel overheads, e.g. polynomial multiplication based on FFT. Hence, in this work, we look to improve the practical performance (i.e. when $k \gg d$) of our previous lazy implementation through the use of parallel processing rather than by reducing asymptotic bounds.

In Hensel factorization, computing power series terms of each factor relies on the computed terms of the previous factor. In particular, the output of one Weierstrass preparation becomes the input to another. These successive dependencies naturally lead to a parallel *pipeline* or chain of *producer-consumer* pairs. Within numerical linear algebra, pipelines have already been employed in parallel implementations of singular value decomposition [14], LU decomposition, and Gaussian elimination [21]. Meanwhile, to the best of our knowledge, the only use of parallel pipeline in symbolic computation is [5], which examines a parallel implementation of triangular decomposition of polynomial systems.

However, in our case, work reduces with each pipeline stage, limiting throughput. To overcome this challenge, we first make use of our complexity estimates to dynamically estimate the work required to update each factor. Second, we compose parallel schemes by applying the celebrated map-reduce pattern within Weierstrass preparation, and thus within a stage of the pipeline. Assigning multiple threads to a single pipeline stage improves load-balance and increases throughput. Experimental results show this composition is effective, with a parallel speedup of up to $9\times$ on a 12-core machine.

The remainder of this paper is organized as follows. Section 2 reviews mathematical background and notations. Further background on our lazy power series of [8] is presented in Sect. 3. Algorithms and complexity analyses of Weierstrass preparation and Hensel factorization are given in Sect. 4. Section 5 presents our parallel variations, where our complexity estimates are used for dynamic scheduling. Finally, Sect. 6 discusses experimental data.

2   Background

We take this section to present basic concepts and notation of multivariate power series and univariate polynomials over power series (UPoPS). Further, we present constructive proofs for the theorems of Weierstrass preparation and Hensel's lemma for UPoPS, from which algorithms are adapted; see Sects. 4.1 and 4.2. Further introductory details may be found in the book of G. Fischer [11].

2.1   Power Series and Univariate Polynomials over Power Series

Let $\mathbb{K}$ be an algebraically closed field. We denote by $\mathbb{K}[[X_1, \ldots, X_n]]$ the ring of formal power series with coefficients in $\mathbb{K}$ and with variables $X_1, \ldots, X_n$.

Let $f = \sum_{e \in \mathbb{N}^n} a_e X^e$ be a formal power series, where $a_e \in \mathbb{K}$, $X^e = X_1^{e_1} \cdots X_n^{e_n}$, $e = (e_1, \ldots, e_n) \in \mathbb{N}^n$, and $|e| = e_1 + \cdots + e_n$. Let k be a non-negative integer. The *homogeneous part* of f in degree k, denoted $f_{(k)}$, is defined by $f_{(k)} = \sum_{|e|=k} a_e X^e$. The *order* of f, denoted $\text{ord}(f)$, is defined as $\min\{i \mid f_{(i)} \neq 0\}$, if $f \neq 0$, and as ∞ otherwise.

Recall several properties regarding power series. First, $\mathbb{K}[[X_1, \ldots, X_n]]$ is an integral domain. Second, the set $\mathcal{M} = \{f \in \mathbb{K}[[X_1, \ldots, X_n]] \mid \mathrm{ord}(f) \geq 1\}$ is the only maximal ideal of $\mathbb{K}[[X_1, \ldots, X_n]]$. Third, for all $k \in \mathbb{N}$, we have $\mathcal{M}^k = \{f \in \mathbb{K}[[X_1, \ldots, X_n]] \mid \mathrm{ord}(f) \geq k\}$. Note that for $n = 0$ we have $\mathcal{M} = \langle 0 \rangle$. Further, note that $f_{(k)} \in \mathcal{M}^k \setminus \mathcal{M}^{k+1}$ and $f_{(0)} \in \mathbb{K}$. Fourth, a unit $u \in \mathbb{K}[[X_1, \ldots, X_n]]$ has $\mathrm{ord}(u) = 0$ or, equivalently, $u \notin \mathcal{M}$.

Let $f, g, h, p \in \mathbb{K}[[X_1, \ldots, X_n]]$. The *sum* and *difference* $f = g \pm h$ is given by $\sum_{k \in \mathbb{N}} (g_{(k)} \pm h_{(k)})$. The product $p = g\,h$ is given by $\sum_{k \in \mathbb{N}} \left(\Sigma_{i+j=k}\, g_{(i)} h_{(j)} \right)$. Notice that the these formulas naturally suggest a *lazy evaluation* scheme, where the result of an arithmetic operation can be incrementally computed for increasing *precision*. A power series f is said to be known to precision $k \in \mathbb{N}$, when $f_{(i)}$ is known for all $0 \leq i \leq k$. Such an update function, parameterized by k, for addition or subtraction is simply $f_{(k)} = g_{(k)} \pm h_{(k)}$; an update function for multiplication is $p_{(k)} = \sum_{i=0}^{k} g_{(i)} h_{(k-i)}$. Lazy evaluation is discussed further in Sect. 3. From these update formulas, the following observation follows.

Observation 2.1 (power series arithmetic). *Let $f, g, h, p \in \mathbb{K}[[X_1]]$ with $f = g \pm h$ and $p = g\,h$. $f_{(k)} = g_{(k)} \pm h_{(k)}$ can be computed in 1 operation in $\mathbb{K}$. $p_{(k)} = \sum_{i=0}^{k} g_{(i)} h_{(k-i)}$ can be computed in $2k - 1$ operations in $\mathbb{K}$.*

Now, let $f, g \in \mathbb{A}[Y]$ be univariate polynomials over power series where $\mathbb{A} = \mathbb{K}[[X_1, \ldots, X_n]]$. Writing $f = \sum_{i=0}^{d} a_i Y^i$, for $a_i \in \mathbb{A}$ and $a_d \neq 0$, we have that the degree of f (denoted $\deg(f, Y)$ or simply $\deg(f)$) is d. Note that arithmetic operations for UPoPS are easily derived from the arithmetic of its power series coefficients. A UPoPS is said to be known up to precision k if each of its power series coefficients are known up to precision k. A UPoPS f is said to be *general (in Y) of order j* if $f \bmod \mathcal{M}[Y]$ has order j when viewed as a power series in Y. Thus, for $f \notin \mathcal{M}[Y]$, writing $f = \sum_{i=0}^{d} a_i Y^i$, we have $a_i \in \mathcal{M}$ for $0 \leq i < j$ and $a_j \notin \mathcal{M}$.

2.2 Weierstrass Preparation Theorem and Hensel Factorization

The Weierstrass Preparation Theorem (WPT) is fundamentally a theorem regarding factorization. In the context of analytic functions, WPT implies that any analytic function resembles a polynomial in the neighbourhood of the origin. Generally, WPT can be stated for power series over power series, i.e. $\mathbb{A}[[Y]]$. This can be used to prove that $\mathbb{A}$ is both a unique factorization domain and a Noetherian ring. See [8] for such a proof of WPT. Here, it is sufficient to state the theorem for UPoPS. First, we begin with a simple lemma.

Lemma 2.2. *Let $f, g, h \in \mathbb{K}[[X_1, \ldots, X_n]]$ such that $f = gh$. Let $f_i = f_{(i)}, g_i = g_{(i)}, h_i = h_{(i)}$. If $f_0 = 0$ and $h_0 \neq 0$, then g_k is uniquely determined by $f_1, \ldots, f_k$ and $h_0, \ldots, h_{k-1}$*

PROOF. We proceed by induction on k. Since $f_0 = g_0 h_0 = 0$ and $h_0 \neq 0$ both hold, the statement holds for $k = 0$. Now let $k > 0$, assuming the hypothesis

holds for $k - 1$. To determine g_k it is sufficient to expand $f = gh$ modulo $\mathcal{M}^{k+1}$:
$$f_1 + f_2 + \cdots + f_k = g_1 h_0 + (g_1 h_1 + g_2 h_0) + \cdots + (g_1 h_{k-1} + \cdots + g_{k-1} h_1 + g_k h_0);$$
and, recalling $h_0 \in \mathbb{K} \backslash \{0\}$, we have $g_k = {}^1\!/\!_{h_0} (f_k - g_1 h_{k-1} - \cdots - g_{k-1} h_1)$. $\quad\square$

Theorem 2.3 (Weierstrass Preparation Theorem). *Let f be a polynomial of $\mathbb{K}[[X_1, \ldots, X_n]][Y]$ so that $f \not\equiv 0 \mod \mathcal{M}[Y]$ holds. Write $f = \sum_{i=0}^{d+m} a_i Y^i$, with $a_i \in \mathbb{K}[[X_1, \ldots, X_n]]$, where $d \geq 0$ is the smallest integer such that $a_d \notin \mathcal{M}$ and m is a non-negative integer. Assume $f \not\equiv 0 \mod \mathcal{M}[Y]$. Then, there exists a unique pair p, α satisfying the following:*

(i) $f = p\alpha$,
(ii) α is an invertible element of $\mathbb{K}[[X_1, \ldots, X_n]][[Y]]$,
(iii) p is a monic polynomial of degree d,
(iv) writing $p = Y^d + b_{d-1} Y^{d-1} + \cdots b_1 Y + b_0$, we have $b_{d-1}, \ldots, b_0 \in \mathcal{M}$.

PROOF. If $n = 0$, writing $f = \alpha Y^d$ with $\alpha = \sum_{i=0}^m a_{i+d} Y^i$ proves the existence of the decomposition. Now, assume $n \geq 1$. Write $\alpha = \sum_{i=0}^m c_i Y^i$, with $c_i \in \mathbb{K}[[X_1, \ldots, X_n]]$. We will determine $b_0, \ldots, b_{d-1}, c_0, \ldots, c_m$ modulo successive powers of $\mathcal{M}$. Since we require α to be a unit, $c_0 \notin \mathcal{M}$ by definition. $a_0, \ldots, a_{d-1}$ are all $0 \mod \mathcal{M}$. Then, equating coefficients in $f = p\alpha$ we have:

$$
\begin{aligned}
a_0 &= b_0 c_0 \\
a_1 &= b_0 c_1 + b_1 c_0 \\
&\;\;\vdots \\
a_{d-1} &= b_0 c_{d-1} + b_1 c_{d-2} + \cdots + b_{d-2} c_1 + b_{d-1} c_0 \\
a_d &= b_0 c_d + b_1 c_{d-1} + \cdots + b_{d-1} c_1 + c_0 \\
&\;\;\vdots \\
a_{d+m-1} &= b_{d-1} c_m + c_{m-1} \\
a_{d+m} &= c_m
\end{aligned}
\tag{1}
$$

and thus $b_0, \ldots, b_{d-1}$ are all $0 \mod \mathcal{M}$. Then, $c_i \equiv a_{d+i} \mod \mathcal{M}$ for all $0 \leq i \leq m$. All coefficients have thus been determined $\mod \mathcal{M}$. Let $k \in \mathbb{Z}^+$. Assume inductively that all $b_0, \ldots, b_{d-1}, c_0, \ldots, c_m$ have been determined $\mod \mathcal{M}^k$.

It follows from Lemma 2.2 that b_0 can be determined $\mod \mathcal{M}^{k+1}$ from the equation $a_0 = b_0 c_0$. Consider now the second equation. Since b_0 is known $\mod \mathcal{M}^{k+1}$, and $b_0 \in \mathcal{M}$, the product $b_0 c_1$ is also known $\mod \mathcal{M}^{k+1}$. Then, we can determine b_1 using Lemma 2.2 and the formula $a_1 - b_0 c_1 = b_1 c_0$. This procedure follows for $b_2, \ldots, b_{d-1}$. With $b_0, \ldots, b_{d-1}$ known $\mod \mathcal{M}^{k+1}$ each $c_0, \ldots, c_m$ can be determined $\mod \mathcal{M}^{k+1}$ from the last $m + 1$ equations. $\quad\square$

One requirement of WPT is that $f \not\equiv 0 \mod \mathcal{M}[Y]$. That is to say, f cannot vanish at $(X_1, \ldots, X_n) = (0, \ldots, 0)$ and, specifically, f is general of order $d = \deg(p)$. A suitable linear change in coordinates can always be applied to meet this requirement; see Algorithm 2 in Sect. 4. Since Weierstrass preparation provides a mechanism to factor a UPoPS into two factors, suitable changes in coordinates and several applications of WPT can fully factorize a UPoPS. The existence of such a factorization is given by Hensel's lemma for UPoPS.

Theorem 2.4 (Hensel's Lemma). *Let* $f = Y^d + \sum_{i=0}^{d-1} a_i Y^i$ *be a monic polynomial with* $a_i \in \mathbb{K}[[X_1, \ldots, X_n]]$. *Let* $\bar{f} = f(0, \ldots, 0, Y) = (Y - c_1)^{d_1}(Y - c_2)^{d_2} \cdots (Y - c_r)^{d_r}$ *for* $c_1, \ldots, c_r \in \mathbb{K}$ *and positive integers* $d_1, \ldots, d_r$. *Then, there exists* $f_1, \ldots, f_r \in \mathbb{K}[[X_1, \ldots, X_n]][Y]$, *all monic in* Y, *such that:*

(i) $f = f_1 \cdots f_r$,
(ii) $\deg(f_i, Y) = d_i$ *for* $1 \leq i \leq r$, *and*
(iii) $\bar{f}_i = (Y - c_i)^{d_i}$ *for* $1 \leq i \leq r$.

PROOF. We proceed by induction on r. For $r = 1$, $d_1 = d$ and we have $f_1 = f$, where f_1 has all the required properties. Now assume $r > 1$. A change of coordinates in Y, sends c_r to 0. Define $g(X_1, \ldots, X_n, Y) = f(X_1, \ldots, X_n, Y + c_r) = (Y + c_r)^d + a_{d-1}(Y + c_r)^{d-1} + \cdots + a_0$. By construction, g is general of order d_r and WPT can be applied to obtain $g = p\alpha$ with p being of degree d_r and $\bar{p} = Y^{d_r}$. Reversing the change of coordinates we set $f_r = p(Y - c_r)$ and $f^* = \alpha(Y - c_r)$, and we have $f = f^* f_r$. f_r is a monic polynomial of degree d_r in Y with $\bar{f}_r = (Y - c_r)^{d_r}$. Moreover, we have $\bar{f}^* = (Y - c_1)^{d_1}(Y - c_2)^{d_2} \cdots (Y - c_{r-1})^{d_{r-1}}$. The inductive hypothesis applied to f^* implies the existence of $f_1, \ldots, f_{r-1}$. □

2.3 Parallel Patterns

We are concerned with *thread-level parallelism*, where multiple threads of execution within a single process enable concurrent processing. Our parallel implementation employs several so-called *parallel patterns*—algorithmic structures and organizations for efficient parallel processing. We review a few patterns: *map*, *producer-consumer*, and *pipeline*. See [20] for a detailed discussion.

Map. The map pattern applies a function to each item in a collection, simultaneously executing the function on each independent data item. Often, the application of a map produces a new collection with the same shape as the input collection. Alternatively, the map pattern may modify each data item in place or, when combined with the *reduce* pattern, produce a single data item. The reduce pattern combines data items pair-wise using some *combiner* function.

When data items to be processed outnumber available threads, the map pattern can be applied block-wise, where the data collection is (evenly) partitioned and each thread assigned a partition rather than a single data item.

Where a **for** loop has independent iterations, the map pattern is easily applied to execute each iteration of the loop concurrently. Due to this ubiquity, the map pattern is often implicit with such parallel for loops simply being labelled **parallel_for**. In this way, the number of threads to use and the partitioning of the data collection can be a dynamic property of the algorithm.

Producer-Consumer and Asynchronous Generators. The producer-consumer pattern describes two functions connected by a queue. The producer creates data items, pushing them to the queue, meanwhile the consumer processes data items, pulling them from the queue. Where both the creation of data and its processing requires substantial work, producer and consumer may operate concurrently, with the queue providing inter-thread communication.

A *generator* or *iterator* is a special kind of co-routine function which **yields** data elements one at a time, rather than many together as a collection; see, e.g. [26, Ch. 8]. Combining the producer-consumer pattern with generators allows for an *asynchronous generator*, where the generator function is the producer and the calling function is the consumer. The intermediary queue allows the generator to produce items meanwhile the calling function processes them.

Pipeline. The pipeline pattern is a sequence of stages, where the output of one stage is used as the input to another. Two consecutive stages form a producer-consumer pair, with internal stages being both a consumer and a producer. Concurrency arises where each stage of the pipeline may be executed in parallel. Moreover, the pipeline pattern allows for earlier data items to flow from one stage to the next without waiting for later items to become available.

In terms of the latency of processing a single data item, a pipeline does not improve upon its serial counterpart. Rather, a parallel pipeline improves throughput, the amount of data that can be processed in a given amount of time. Throughput is limited by the slowest stage of a pipeline, and thus special care must be given to ensure each stage of the pipeline runs in nearly equal time.

A pipeline may be implicitly and dynamically created where an asynchronous generator consumes data from another asynchronous generator. The number of asynchronous generator calls, and thus the number of stages in the pipeline, can be dynamic to fit the needs of the application at runtime.

3   Lazy Power Series

As we have seen in Sect. 2.1, certain arithmetic operations on power series naturally lead to a lazy evaluation scheme. In this scheme, homogeneous parts of a power series are computed one at a time for increasing degree, as requested. Our serial implementation of lazy power series is detailed in [8]. The underlying implementation of (sparse multivariate) polynomial arithmetic is that of [4] (indeed, dense multivariate arithmetic could prove beneficial, but that is left to future work). For the remainder of this paper, it is sufficient to understand that lazy power series rely on the following three principles:

  (i) an update function to compute the homogeneous part of a given degree;
 (ii) capturing of parameters required for that update function; and
(iii) storage of previously computed homogeneous parts.

Where a power series is constructed from arithmetic operations on other power series, the latter may be called the *ancestors* of the former. For example, the power series $f = g\,h$ has ancestors g and h and an update function $f_{(k)} = \sum_{i=0}^{k} g_{(i)} h_{(k-i)}$. In implementation, and in the algorithms which follow in this paper, we can thus augment a power series with: (i) its current precision; (ii) references to its ancestors, if any; and (iii) a reference to its update function.

Under this scheme, we make three remarks. Firstly, a power series can be lazily constructed using essentially no work. Indeed, the initialization of a lazy power series only requires specifying the appropriate update function and storing references to its ancestors. Secondly, specifying an update function and the ancestors of a power series is sufficient for defining and computing that power series. Thirdly, when updating a particular power series, its ancestors can automatically and recursively be updated as necessary using their own update functions.

Hence, it is sufficient to simply define the update function of a power series. For example, Algorithm 1 simultaneously updates p and α as produced from a Weierstrass preparation. Further, operations on power series should be understood to be only the initialization of a power series, with no terms of the power series yet computed; e.g., Algorithm 3 for Hensel factorization.

4 Algorithms and Complexity

In this section we present algorithms for Weierstrass preparation and Hensel factorization adapted from their constructive proofs; see Sect. 2. For each algorithm we analyze its complexity. The algorithms—and eventual parallel variations and implementations, see Sects. 5–6—are presented for the general multivariate case, with only the complexity estimates limited to the bivariate case. These results culminate as Theorem 4.3 and Corollary 4.8, which respectively give the overall complexity of our algorithms for WPT and Hensel factorization. Meanwhile, Observation 4.2, Corollary 4.4, and Theorem 4.6 more closely analyze the distribution of work to guide and load-balance our parallel algorithms.

4.1 Weierstrass Preparation

From the proof of Weierstrass preparation (Theorem 2.3), we derive WEIERSTRASSUPDATE (Algorithm 1). That proof proceeds modulo increasing powers of the maximal ideal $\mathcal{M}$, which is equivalent to computing homogeneous parts of increasing degree, just as required for our lazy power series. For an application of Weierstrass preparation producing p and α, this WEIERSTRASSUPDATE acts as the update function for p and α, updating both simultaneously.

By rearranging the first d equations of (1) and applying Lemma 2.2 we obtain "phase 1" of WEIERSTRASSUPDATE, where each coefficient of p is updated. By rearranging the next $m + 1$ equations of (1) we obtain "phase 2" of WEIERSTRASSUPDATE, where each coefficient of α is updated. From Algorithm 1, it is then routine to show the following two observations, which lead to Theorem 4.3.

Observation 4.1 (Weierstrass phase 1 complexity). *For* WEIERSTRASSUPDATE *over* $\mathbb{K}[[X_1]][Y]$, *computing* $b_{i(k)}$, *for* $0 \le i < d$, *requires* $2ki + 2k - 1$ *operations in* $\mathbb{K}$ *if* $i \le m$, *or* $2km + 2k - 1$ *operations in* $\mathbb{K}$ *if* $i > m$.

Observation 4.2 (Weierstrass phase 2 complexity). *For* WEIERSTRASSUPDATE *over* $\mathbb{K}[[X_1]][Y]$, *computing* $c_{m-i(k)}$, *for* $0 \le i < m$, *requires* $2ki$ *operations in* $\mathbb{K}$ *if* $i \le d$, *or* $2kd$ *operations in* $\mathbb{K}$ *if* $i > d$.

Theorem 4.3 (Weierstrass preparation complexity). *Weierstrass preparation producing* $f = p\alpha$, *with* $f, p, \alpha \in \mathbb{K}[[X_1]][Y]$, $\deg(p) = d$, $\deg(\alpha) = m$, *requires* $dmk^2 + dk^2 + dmk$ *operations in* $\mathbb{K}$ *to compute* p *and* α *to precision* k.

Algorithm 1. WEIERSTRASSUPDATE(k, f, p, α)

Input: $f = \sum_{i=0}^{d+m} a_i Y^i$, $p = Y^d + \sum_{i=0}^{d-1} b_i Y^i$, $\alpha = \sum_{i=0}^{m} c_i Y^i$, $a_i, b_i, c_i \in \mathbb{K}[[X_1, \ldots, X_n]]$ satisfying Theorem 2.3, with $b_0, \ldots, b_{d-1}, c_0, \ldots, c_m$ known modulo $\mathcal{M}^k$, $\mathcal{M}$ the maximal ideal of $\mathbb{K}[[X_1, \ldots, X_n]]$.

Output: $b_0, \ldots, b_{d-1}, c_0, \ldots, c_m$ known modulo $\mathcal{M}^{k+1}$, updated in-place.

1: **for** $i := 0$ to $d - 1$ **do**   ▷ phase 1
2: $\quad$ $F_{i(k)} := a_{i(k)}$
3: $\quad$ **if** $i \leq m$ **then**
4: $\quad\quad$ **for** $j := 0$ to $i - 1$ **do**
5: $\quad\quad$ $\quad$ $F_{i(k)} := F_{i(k)} - (b_j c_{i-j})_{(k)}$
6: $\quad$ **else**
7: $\quad\quad$ **for** $j := 0$ to $m - 1$ **do**
8: $\quad\quad$ $\quad$ $F_{i(k)} := F_{i(k)} - (b_{i+j-m} c_{m-j})_{(k)}$
9: $\quad$ $s := 0$
10: $\quad$ **for** $j := 1$ to $k - 1$ **do**
11: $\quad\quad$ $s := s + b_{i(k-j)} \times c_{0(j)}$
12: $\quad$ $b_{i(k)} := \left(F_{i(k)} - s \right) / c_{0(0)}$

13: $c_{m(k)} := a_{d+m(k)}$ ▷ phase 2
14: **for** $i := 1$ to m **do**
15: $\quad$ **if** $i \leq d$ **then**
16: $\quad\quad$ $c_{m-i(k)} := a_{d+m-i(k)} - \sum_{j=1}^{i} \left(b_{d-j} c_{m-i+j} \right)_{(k)}$
17: $\quad$ **else**
18: $\quad\quad$ $c_{m-i(k)} := a_{d+m-i(k)} - \sum_{j=1}^{d} \left(b_{d-j} c_{m-i+j} \right)_{(k)}$

PROOF. Let i be the index of a coefficient of p or α. Consider the cost of computing the homogeneous part of degree k of each coefficient of p and α. First consider $i < t = \min(d, m)$. From Observations 4.1 and 4.2, computing the kth homogeneous part of each b_i and c_i respectively requires $2ki + 2k - 1$ and $2ki$ operations in $\mathbb{K}$. For $0 \leq i < t$, this yields a total of $2kt^2 + 2kt - t$. Next, we have three cases: (a) $t = d = m$, (b) $m = t < i < d$, or (c) $d = t < i < m$. In case (a) there is no additional work. In case (b), phase 1 contributes an additional $(d - m)(2km + 2k - 1)$ operations. In case (c), phase 2 contributes an additional $(m - d)(2kd)$ operations. In all cases, the total number of operations to update p and α from precision $k - 1$ to precision k is $2dmk + 2dk - d$. Finally, to compute p and α up to precision k requires $dmk^2 + dk^2 + dmk$ operations in $\mathbb{K}$.   □

A useful consideration is when the input to Weierstrass preparation is monic; this arises for each application of WPT in Hensel factorization. Then, α is necessarily monic, and the overall complexity of Weierstrass preparation is reduced. In particular, we save computing $(b_{i-m} c_m)_{(k)}$ for the update of b_i, $i \geq m$ (Algorithm 1, Line 8), and save computing $(b_{d-i} c_m)_{(k)}$ for the update of each c_{m-i}, $i \leq d$ (Algorithm 1, Line 16). The following corollary states this result.

Corollary 4.4 (Weierstrass preparation complexity for monic input). *Weierstrass preparation producing $f = p\alpha$ with $f, p, \alpha \in \mathbb{K}[[X_1]][Y]$, f monic*

Algorithm 2. TAYLORSHIFTUPDATE(k, f, $\mathbf{S}$, i)

Input: For $f = \sum_{j=0}^{d} a_j Y^j$, $g = f(Y + c) = \sum_{j=0}^{d} b_j Y^j$, obtain the homogeneous part
of degree k for b_i. $\mathbf{S} \in \mathbb{K}^{(d+1)\times(d+1)}$ is a lower triangular matrix of coefficients of
$(Y + c)^j$ for $j = 0, \ldots, d$,
Output: $b_{i(k)}$, the homogeneous part of degree k of b_i.
1: $b_{i(k)} := 0$
2: **for** $\ell := i$ to d **do**
3: $\quad | \quad j := \ell + 1 - i$
4: $\quad | \quad b_{i(k)} := b_{i(k)} + S_{\ell+1,j} \times a_{\ell(k)}$
5: **return** $b_{i(k)}$

Algorithm 3. HENSELFACTORIZATION(f)

Input: $f = Y^d + \sum_{i=0}^{d-1} a_i Y^i, a_i \in \mathbb{K}[[X_1, \ldots, X_n]]$.
Output: $f_1, \ldots, f_r$ satisfying Theorem 2.4.
1: $\bar{f} = f(0, \ldots, 0, Y)$
2: $(c_1, \ldots, c_r), (d_1, \ldots, d_r) :=$ roots and their multiplicities of $\bar{f}$
3: $c_1, \ldots, c_r :=$ SORT($[c_1, \ldots, c_r]$) by increasing multiplicity $\qquad \triangleright$ see Theorem 4.6
4: $\widehat{f}_1 := f$
5: **for** $i := 1$ to $r - 1$ **do**
6: $\quad | \quad g_i := \widehat{f}_i(Y + c_i)$
7: $\quad | \quad p_i, \alpha_i :=$ WEIERSTRASSPREPARATION(g)
8: $\quad | \quad f_i := p_i(Y - c_i)$
9: $\quad | \quad \widehat{f}_{i+1} := \alpha_i(Y - c_i)$
10: $f_r := \widehat{f}_r$
11: **return** $f_1, \ldots, f_r$

$$
\begin{array}{ccccccccc}
& p_1 \xrightarrow{-c_1} f_1 & & & p_2 \xrightarrow{-c_2} f_2 & & & p_3 \xrightarrow{-c_3} f_3 & \\
& \nearrow & & & \nearrow & & & \nearrow & \\
f \xrightarrow{+c_1} g_1 \longrightarrow \alpha_1 \xrightarrow{-c_1} \widehat{f}_2 \xrightarrow{+c_2} g_2 \longrightarrow \alpha_2 \xrightarrow{-c_2} \widehat{f}_3 \xrightarrow{+c_3} g_3 \longrightarrow \alpha_3 \xrightarrow{-c_3} f_4
\end{array}
$$

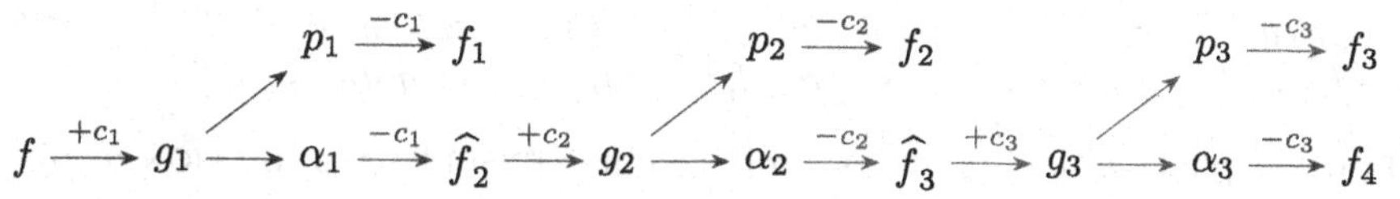

Fig. 1. The ancestor chain for the Hensel factorization $f = f_1 f_2 f_3 f_4$. Updating f_1
requires updating g_1, p_1, α_1; then updating f_2 requires updating $\widehat{f}_2, g_2, p_2, \alpha_2$; then
updating f_3 requires updating $\widehat{f}_3, g_3, p_3, \alpha_3$; then updating f_4 requires only its own
Taylor shift. These groupings form the eventual stages of the Hensel pipeline (Algorithm 8).

in Y, $\deg(p) = d$ and $\deg(\alpha) = m$, requires $dmk^2 + dmk$ operations in $\mathbb{K}$ to
compute p and α up to precision k.

4.2 Hensel Factorization

Before we begin Hensel factorization, we will first see how to perform a translation, or Taylor shift, by lazy evaluation. For $f = \sum_{i=0}^{d} a_i Y^i \in \mathbb{K}[[X_1, \ldots, X_n]][Y]$

and $c \in \mathbb{K}$, computing $f(Y + c)$ begins by pre-computing the coefficients of the binomial expansions $(Y + c)^j$ for $0 \leq j \leq d$. These coefficients are stored in a matrix $\mathbf{S}$. Then, each coefficient of $f(Y + c) = \sum_{i=0}^{d} b_i Y^i$ is a linear combination of the coefficients of f scaled by the appropriate elements of $\mathbf{S}$. Since those elements of $\mathbf{S}$ are only elements of $\mathbb{K}$, this linear combination does not change the degree and, for some integer k, $b_{i(k)}$ relies only on $a_{\ell(k)}$ for $i \leq \ell \leq d$. This method is described in Algorithm 2; and its complexity is easily stated as Observation 4.5.

Observation 4.5 (Taylor shift complexity). *For a UPoPS $f = \sum_{i=0}^{d} a_i Y^i \in \mathbb{K}[[X_1]][Y]$, computing the homogeneous part of degree k for all coefficients of the shifted UPoPS $f(Y + c)$ requires $d^2 + 2d + 1$ operations in $\mathbb{K}$.*

Having specified the update functions for WPT and Taylor shift, lazy Hensel factorization is immediate, requiring only the appropriate chain of ancestors. Algorithm 3 shows this initialization through repeated applications of Taylor shift and Weierstrass preparation. Note that factors are sorted by increasing degree to enable better load-balance in the eventual parallel algorithm. Figure 1 shows the chain of ancestors created by $f = f_1 f_2 f_3 f_4$ and the grouping of ancestors required to update each factor; the complexity of which is shown in Theorem 4.6. Corollary 4.7 follows immediately and Corollary 4.8 gives the total complexity of Hensel factorization. Here, we ignore the initial cost of factorizing $\bar{f}$.

Theorem 4.6 (Hensel factorization complexity per factor). *Let $\widehat{d}_i$ be the degree of $\widehat{f}_i$ during HENSELFACTORIZATION applied to $f \in \mathbb{K}[[X_1]][Y]$, $\deg(f) = d$. To update f_1, $\deg(f_1) = d_1$ to precision k requires $d_1 \widehat{d}_2 k^2 + d^2 k + d_1 dk + 2d_1 k + 2dk + 2k$ operations in $\mathbb{K}$. To update f_i, $\deg(f_i) = d_i$, for $1 < i < r$, to precision k requires $d_i \widehat{d}_{i+1} k^2 + 2\widehat{d}_i^2 k + d_i \widehat{d}_i k + 2d_i k + 4\widehat{d}_i k + 3k$ operations in $\mathbb{K}$. To update f_r, $\deg(f_r) = d_r$, to precision k requires $d_r^2 k + 2d_r k + k$ operations in $\mathbb{K}$.*

PROOF. Updating the first factor produced by HENSELFACTORIZATION requires one Taylor shift of degree d, one Weierstrass preparation producing p_1 and α_1 of degree d_1 and $\widehat{d}_2 = d - d_1$, and one Taylor shift of degree d_1 to obtain f_1 from p. From Observation 4.5 and Corollary 4.4 we have that the Taylor shifts require $k(d^2 + 2d + 1) + k(d_1^2 + 2d_1 + 1)$ operations in $\mathbb{K}$ and the Weierstrass preparation requires $d_1(d - d_1)k^2 + d_1(d - d_1)k$ operations in $\mathbb{K}$. The total cost counted as operations in $\mathbb{K}$ is thus $d_1 \widehat{d}_2 k^2 + d^2 k + d_1 dk + 2d_1 k + 2dk + 2k$.

Updating each following factor, besides the last, requires one Taylor shift of degree $\widehat{d}_i$ to update $\widehat{f}_i$ from α_{i-1}, one Taylor shift of degree $\widehat{d}_i$ to update g_i from $\widehat{f}_i$, one Weierstrass preparation to obtain p_i and α_i of degree d_i and $\widehat{d}_{i+1} = \widehat{d}_i - d_i$, and one Taylor shift of degree d_i to obtain f_i from p_i. The Taylor shifts require $2k(\widehat{d}_i^2 + 2\widehat{d}_i + 1) + k(d_i^2 + 2d_i + 1)$ operations in $\mathbb{K}$. The Weierstrass preparation requires $d_i(\widehat{d}_i - d_i)k^2 + d_i(\widehat{d}_i - d_i)k$ operations in $\mathbb{K}$. The total cost counted as operations in $\mathbb{K}$ is thus $d_i \widehat{d}_{i+1} k^2 + 2\widehat{d}_i^2 k + d_i \widehat{d}_i k + 2d_i k + 4\widehat{d}_i k + 3k$.

Finally, updating the last factor to precision k requires a single Taylor shift of degree d_r costing $d_r^2 k + 2d_r k + k$ operations in $\mathbb{K}$. $\qquad\square$

Corollary 4.7 (Hensel factorization complexity per iteration). *Let $\widehat{d}_i$ be the degree of $\widehat{f}_i$ during the* HENSELFACTORIZATION *algorithm applied to $f \in \mathbb{K}[[X_1]][Y]$, $\deg(f) = d$. Computing the kth homogeneous part of f_1, $\deg(f_1) = d_1$, requires $2d_1\widehat{d}_2k + d_1^2 + d^2 + 2d_1 + 2d + 2$ operations in $\mathbb{K}$. Computing the kth homogeneous part of f_i, $\deg(f_i) = d_i$, $1 < i < r$, requires $2d_i\widehat{d}_{i+1}k + d_i^2 + 2\widehat{d}_i^2 + 4\widehat{d}_i + 2d_i + 3$ operations in $\mathbb{K}$. Computing the kth homogeneous part of f_r, $\deg(f_r) = d_r$, requires $d_r^2 + 2d_r + 1$ operations in $\mathbb{K}$.*

Corollary 4.8 (Hensel factorization complexity). HENSELFACTORIZA-TION *producing $f = f_1 \cdots f_r$, with $f \in \mathbb{K}[[X_1]][Y]$, $\deg(f) = d$, requires $\mathcal{O}(d^3k + d^2k^2)$ operations in $\mathbb{K}$ to update all factors to precision k.*

PROOF. Let $f_1, \ldots, f_r$ have respective degrees $d_1, \ldots, d_r$. Let $\widehat{d}_i = \sum_{j=i}^r d_j$ (thus $\widehat{d}_1 = d$ and $\widehat{d}_r = d_r$). From Theorem 4.6, each f_i, $1 \leq i < r$ requires $\mathcal{O}(d_i\widehat{d}_{i+1}k^2 + \widehat{d}_i^2 k)$ operations in $\mathbb{K}$ to be updated to precision k (or $\mathcal{O}(d_r^2k)$ for f_r). We have $\sum_{i=1}^{r-1} d_i\widehat{d}_{i+1} \leq \sum_{i=1}^{r-1} d_i d < d^2$ and $\sum_{i=1}^r \widehat{d}_i^2 \leq \sum_{i=1}^r d^2 = rd^2 \leq d^3$. Hence, all factors can be updated to precision k within $\mathcal{O}(d^3k + d^2k^2)$ operations in $\mathbb{K}$. □

Corollary 4.8 shows that the two dominant terms in the cost of computing a Hensel factorization of a UPoPS of degree d, up to precision k, are d^3k and d^2k^2. From the proof of Theorem 4.6, the former term arises from the cost of the Taylor shifts in Y, meanwhile, the latter term arises from the (polynomial) multiplication of homogeneous parts in Weierstrass preparation. This observation then leads to the following conjecture. Recall that $M(n)$ denotes a polynomial multiplication time [12, Ch. 8]. From [15], relaxed algorithms, which improve the performance of lazy evaluation schemes, can be used to compute a power series product in $\mathbb{K}[[X_1]]$ up to precision k in at most $\mathcal{O}(M(k)\log k)$ operations in $\mathbb{K}$ (or less, in view of the improved relaxed multiplication of [16]).

Conjecture 4.9. *Let $f \in \mathbb{K}[[X_1]][Y]$ factorize as $f_1 \cdots f_r$ using* HENSELFAC-TORIZATION. *Let $\deg(f) = d$. Updating the factors $f_1, \ldots, f_r$ to precision k using relaxed algorithms requires at most $\mathcal{O}(d^3k + d^2M(k)\log k)$ operations in $\mathbb{K}$.*

Comparatively, the Hensel–Sasaki Construction requires at most $\mathcal{O}(d^3M(d) + dM(d)k^2)$ operations in $\mathbb{K}$ to compute the first k terms of all factors of $f \in \mathbb{K}[X_1, Y]$, where f has total degree d [1]. The method of Kung and Traub [18], requires $\mathcal{O}(d^2M(k))$. Already, Corollary 4.8—where $d = \deg(f, Y)$—shows that our Hensel factorization is an improvement on Hensel–Sasaki (d^2k^2 versus $dM(d)k^2$). If Conjecture 4.9 is true, then Hensel factorization can be within a factor of $\log k$ of Kung and Traub's method. Nonetheless, this conjecture is highly encouraging where $k \gg d$, particularly where we have already seen that our current, suboptimal, method performs better in practice than Hensel–Sasaki and the method of Kung and Traub [8]. Proving this conjecture is left to future work.

Algorithm 4. UPDATETODEGPARALLEL(k, f, t)

Input: A positive integer k, $f \in \mathbb{K}[[X_1, \ldots, X_n]]$ known to at least precision $k - 1$. If f has ancestors, it is the result of a binary operation. A positive integer t for the number of threads to use.

Output: f is updated to precision k, in place.

1: **if** $f_{(k)}$ already computed **then**
2: | **return**
3: g, h := FIRSTANCESTOR(f), SECONDANCESTOR(f)
4: UPDATETODEGPARALLEL(k, g, t);
5: UPDATETODEGPARALLEL(k, h, t);
6: **if** f is a product **then**
7: | $\mathcal{V} := [0, \ldots, 0]$ ▷ 0-indexed list of size t
8: | **parallel_for** $j := 0$ to $t - 1$
9: | | **for** $i := {}^{jk}/_t$ to $^{(j+1)k}/_t - 1$ **while** $i \leq k$ **do**
10: | | | $\mathcal{V}[j] := \mathcal{V}[j] + g_{(i)}h_{(k-i)}$
11: | $f_{(k)} := \sum_{j=0}^{t-1} \mathcal{V}[j]$ ▷ reduce
12: **else if** f is a p from a Weierstrass preparation **then**
13: | WEIERSTRASSPHASE1PARALLEL(k,g,f,h,WEIERSTRASSDATA(f),t)
14: **else if** f is an α from a Weierstrass preparation **then**
15: | WEIERSTRASSPHASE2PARALLEL(k, g, h, f, t)
16: **else**
17: | UPDATETODEG(k, f)

---

5   Parallel Algorithms

Section 4 presented lazy algorithms for Weierstrass preparation, Taylor shift, and Hensel factorization. It also presented complexity estimates for those algorithms. Those estimates will soon be used to help dynamically distribute hardware resources (threads) in a parallel variation of Hensel factorization; in particular, a Hensel factorization pipeline where each pipeline stage updates one or more factors, see Algorithms 7–9. But first, we will examine parallel processing techniques for Weierstrass preparation.

5.1   Parallel Algorithms for Weierstrass Preparation

Algorithm 1 shows that p and α from a Weierstrass preparation can be updated in two phases: p in phase 1, and α in phase 2. Ultimately, these updates rely on the computation of the homogeneous part of some power series product. Algorithm 4 presents a simple map-reduce pattern (see Sect. 2.3) for computing such a homogeneous part. Moreover, this algorithm is designed such that, recursively, all ancestors of a power series product are also updated using parallelism. Note that UPDATETODEGPARALLEL called on a UPoPS simply recurses on each of its coefficients.

Using the notation of Algorithm 1, recall that, e.g., $F_i := a_i - \sum_{j=0}^{i-1}(b_j c_{i-j})$, for $i \leq m$. Using lazy power series arithmetic, this entire formula can be encoded by a chain of ancestors, and one simply needs to update F_i to trigger a cascade of

---

Algorithm 5. LEMMAFORWEIERSTRASS(k, f, g, h, t)

Input: $f, g, h \in \mathbb{K}[[X_1, \ldots, X_n]]$ such that $f = gh$, $f_{(0)} = 0$, $h_{(0)} \neq 0$, f known to precision k, and g, h known to precision $k - 1$. $t \geq 1$ the number of threads to use.

Output: $g_{(k)}$.

1: $\mathcal{V} := [0, \ldots, 0]$ ▷ 0-indexed list of size t
2: **parallel_for** $j := 0$ to $t - 1$
3:    **for** $i := {}^{jk}/_t + 1$ to ${}^{(j+1)k}/_t$ **while** $i < k$ **do**
4:      $\mathcal{V}[j] := \mathcal{V}[j] + g_{(k-i)} h_{(i)}$
5: **end for**
6: **return** $\left(f_{(k)} - \sum_{j=0}^{t-1} \mathcal{V}[j] \right) / h_{(0)}$

---

updates through its ancestors. In particular, using Algorithm 4, the homogeneous part of each product $b_j c_{i-j}$ is recursively computed using map-reduce. Similarly, Lemma 2.2 can be implemented using map-reduce (see Algorithm 5) to replace Lines 9–12 of Algorithm 1. Phase 1 of Weierstrass, say WEIERSTRASSPHASE1-PARALLEL, thus reduces to a loop over i from 0 to $d - 1$, calling Algorithm 4 to update F_i to precision k, and calling Algorithm 5 to compute $b_{i(k)}$.

Algorithm 4 uses several simple subroutines: FIRSTANCESTOR and SECONDANCESTOR gets the first and second ancestor of a power series, WEIERSTRASSDATA gets a reference to the list of F_i's, and UPDATETODEG calls the serial update function of a lazy power series to ensure its precision is at least k; see Sect. 3.

Now consider phase 2 of WEIERSTRASSUPDATE. Notice that computing the homogeneous part of degree k for c_{m-i}, $0 \leq i \leq m$ only requires each c_{m-i} to be known up to precision $k - 1$, since each $b_j \in \mathcal{M}$ for $0 \leq j < d$. This implies that the phase 2 **for** loop of WEIERSTRASSUPDATE has independent iterations. We thus apply the map pattern directly to this loop itself, rather than relying on the map-reduce pattern of UPDATETODEGPARALLEL. However, consider the following two facts: the cost of computing each c_{m-i} is different (Observation 4.2 and Corollary 4.4), and, for a certain number of available threads t, it may be impossible to partition the iterations of the loop into t partitions of equal work. Yet, partitioning the loop itself is preferred for greater parallelism.

Hence, for phase 2, a dynamic decision is made to either apply the map pattern to the loop over c_{m-i}, or to apply the map pattern within UPDATE-TODEGPARALLEL for each c_{m-i}, or both. This decision process is detailed in Algorithm 6, where t partitions of equal work try to be found to apply the map pattern to only the loop itself. If unsuccessful, $t/2$ partitions of equal work try to be found, with 2 threads to be used within UPDATETODEGPARALLEL of each partition. If that, too, is unsuccessful, then each c_{m-i} is updated one at a time using the total number of threads t within UPDATETODEGPARALLEL.

5.2 Parallel Algorithms for Hensel Factorization

Let $f = f_1 \cdots f_r$ be a Hensel factorization where the factors have respective degrees $d_1, \ldots, d_r$. From Algorithm 3 and Fig. 1, we have already seen that the

---

Algorithm 6. WEIERSTRASSPHASE2PARALLEL(k, f, p, α, t)

Input: $f = \sum_{i=0}^{d+m} a_i Y^i$, $p = Y^d + \sum_{i=0}^{d-1} b_i Y^i$, $\alpha = \sum_{i=0}^{m} c_i Y^i$, $a_i, b_i, c_i \in \mathbb{K}[[X_1, \ldots, X_n]]$ satisfying Theorem 2.3. $b_0, \ldots, b_{d-1}$ known modulo $\mathcal{M}^{k+1}$, $c_0, \ldots, c_m$ known modulo $\mathcal{M}^k$, for $\mathcal{M}$ the maximal ideal of $\mathbb{K}[[X_1, \ldots, X_n]]$. $t \geq 1$ for the number of threads to use.

Output: $c_0, \ldots, c_m$ known modulo $\mathcal{M}^{k+1}$, updated in-place.

1: $work := 0$
2: **for** $i := 1$ to m **do**   ▷ estimate work using Observation 4.2, Corollary 4.4
3:   | **if** $i \leq d$ **then** $work := work + i - (a_{d+m} = 0)$ ▷ eval. Boolean as an integer
4:   | **else** $work := work + d$
5: $t' := 1$; $targ := work / t$
6: $work := 0$; $j := 1$
7: $\mathcal{I} := [-1, 0, \ldots, 0]$ ▷ 0-indexed list of size $t + 1$
8: **for** $i := 1$ to m **do**
9:   | **if** $i \leq d$ **then** $work := work + i - (a_{d+m} = 0)$
10:   | **else** $work := work + d$
11:   | **if** $work \geq targ$ **then**
12:   | | $\mathcal{I}[j] := i$; $work := 0$; $j := j + 1$
13: **if** $j \leq t$ **and** $t' < 2$ **then** ▷ work did not distribute evenly; try again with $t = {}^t/_2$
14:   | $t := t / 2$; $t' := 2$
15:   | **goto** Line 6
16: **else if** $j \leq t$ **then**   ▷ still not even, use all threads in UPDATETODEGPARALLEL
17:   | $\mathcal{I}[1] := m$; $t' := 2t$; $t := 1$
18: **parallel_for** $\ell := 1$ to t
19:   | **for** $i := \mathcal{I}[\ell - 1] + 1$ to $\mathcal{I}[\ell]$ **do**
20:   | | UPDATETODEGPARALLEL(k, c_{m-i}, t')

---

repeated applications of Taylor shift and Weierstrass preparation naturally form a chain of ancestors, and thus a pipeline. Using the notation of Algorithm 3, updating f_1 requires updating g_1, p_1, α_1. Then, updating f_2 requires updating f_2, g_2, p_2, α_2, and so on. These groups easily form stages of a pipeline, where updating f_1 to degree $k - 1$ is a prerequisite for updating f_2 to degree $k - 1$. Moreover, meanwhile f_2 is being updated to degree $k - 1$, f_1 can simultaneously be updated to degree k. Such a pattern holds for all successive factors.

Algorithms 7 and 8 show how the factors of a Hensel factorization can all be simultaneously updated to degree k using asynchronous generators, denoted by the constructor ASYNCGENERATOR, forming the so-called *Hensel pipeline*. Algorithm 7 shows a single pipeline stage as an asynchronous generator, which itself consumes data from another asynchronous generator—just as expected from the pipeline pattern. Algorithm 8 shows the creation, and joining in sequence, of those generators. The key feature of these algorithms is that a generator (say, stage i) produces a sequence of integers (j) which signals to the consumer (stage $i+1$) that the previous factor has been computed up to precision j and thus the required data is available to update its own factor to precision j.

Notice that Algorithm 8 still follows our lazy evaluation scheme. Indeed, the factors are updated all at once up to precision k, starting from their current

---

Algorithm 7. HENSELPIPELINESTAGE(k, f_i, t, GEN)

Input: A positive integer k, $f_i = Y^{d_i} + \sum_{i=0}^{d_i-1} a_i Y^i, a_i \in \mathbb{K}[[X_1, \ldots, X_n]]$. A positive integer t the number of threads to use within this stage. GEN a generator for the previous pipeline stage.

Output: a sequence of integers j signalling f_i is known to precision j. This sequence ends with k.

1: $p := $ PRECISION(f_i)   ▷ get the current precision of f_i
2: **do**
3: $\quad$ $k' := $ GEN()   ▷ A blocking function call until GEN yields
4: $\quad$ **for** $j := p$ to k' **do**
5: $\quad\quad$ UPDATETODEGPARALLEL(j, f_i, t)
6: $\quad\quad$ **yield** j
7: $\quad$ $p := k'$
8: **while** $k' < k$

Algorithm 8. HENSELFACTORIZATIONPIPELINE(k, $\mathcal{F}$, $\mathcal{T}$)

Input: A positive integer k, $\mathcal{F} = \{f_1, \ldots, f_r\}$, the output of HENSELFACTORIZATION. $\mathcal{T} \in \mathbb{Z}^r$ a 0-indexed list of the number of threads to use in each stage, $\mathcal{T}[r-1] > 0$.

Output: $f_1, \ldots, f_r$ updated in-place to precision k.

1: GEN := ( ) $\rightarrow$ {**yield** k}   ▷ An anonymous function asynchronous generator
2: **for** $i := 0$ to $r-1$ **do**
3: $\quad$ **if** $\mathcal{T}[i] > 0$ **then**
$\quad\quad\quad$ ▷ Capture HENSELPIPELINESTAGE(k, f_{i+1}, $\mathcal{T}[i]$, GEN) as a
$\quad\quad\quad$ function object, passing the previous GEN as input
4: $\quad\quad$ GEN := ASYNCGENERATOR(HENSELPIPELINESTAGE, k, f_{i+1}, $\mathcal{T}[i]$, GEN)
5: **do**
6: $\quad$ $k' := $ GEN()   ▷ ensure last stage completes before returning
7: **while** $k' < k$

---

precision. However, for optimal performance, the updates should be applied for large increases in precision, rather than repeatedly increasing precision by one.

Further considering performance, Theorem 4.6 showed that the cost for updating each factor of a Hensel factorization is different. In particular, for $\hat{d}_i := \sum_{j=i}^r d_j$, updating factor f_i scales as $d_i \hat{d}_{i+1} k^2$. The work for each stage of the proposed pipeline is unequal and the pipeline is unlikely to achieve good parallel speedup. However, Corollary 4.7 shows that the work ratios between stages do not change for increasing k, and thus a static scheduling scheme is sufficient.

Notice that Algorithm 7 takes a parameter t for the number of threads to use internally. As we have seen in Sect. 5.1, the Weierstrass update can be performed in parallel. Consequently, each stage of the Hensel pipeline uses t threads to exploit such parallelism. We have thus composed the two parallel schemes, applying map-reduce within each stage of the parallel pipeline. This composition serves to load-balance the pipeline. For example, the first stage may be given t_1 threads and the second stage given t_2 threads, with $t_1 > t_2$, so that the two stages may execute in nearly equal time.

Algorithm 9. DISTRIBUTERESOURCESHENSEL($\mathcal{F}$, t_{tot})

Input: $\mathcal{F} = \{f_1, \ldots, f_r\}$ the output of HENSELFACTORIZATION. $t_{tot} > 1$ the total number of threads.

Output: $\mathcal{T}$, a list of size r, where $\mathcal{T}[i]$ is the number of threads to use for updating f_{i+1}. The number of positive entries in $\mathcal{T}$ determines the number of pipeline stages. $\mathcal{T}[i] = 0$ encodes that f_{i+1} should be computed within the same stage as f_{i+2}.

1: $\mathcal{T} := [0, \ldots, 0, 1]$; $t := t_{tot} - 1$ ▷ $\mathcal{T}[r-1] = 1$ ensures last factor gets updated
2: $d := \sum_{i=1}^{r} \deg(f_i)$
3: $\mathcal{W} := [0, \ldots, 0]$ ▷ A 0-indexed list of size r
4: **for** $i := 1$ to $r - 1$ **do**
5:    | $\mathcal{W}[i-1] := \deg(f_i)(d - \deg(f_i))$ ▷ Estimate work by Theorem 4.6, $d_i \widehat{d}_{i+1}$
6:    | $d := d - \deg(f_i)$
7: $totalWork := \sum_{i=0}^{r-1} \mathcal{W}[i]$
8: $ratio := 0$; $targ := 1 / t$
9: **for** $i := 0$ to r **do**
10:   | $ratio := ratio + (\mathcal{W}[i] / totalWork)$
11:   | **if** $ratio \geq targ$ **then**
12:   | | $\mathcal{T}[i] := $ ROUND$(ratio \cdot t)$; $ratio := 0$
13: $t := t_{tot} - \sum_{i=0}^{r-1} \mathcal{T}[i]$ ▷ Give any excess threads to the earlier stages
14: **for** $i := 0$ to $r - 1$ **while** $t > 0$ **do**
15:   | $\mathcal{T}[i] := \mathcal{T}[i] + 1$; $t := t - 1$
16: **return** $\mathcal{T}$

To further encourage load-balancing, each stage of the pipeline need not update a single factor, but rather a group of successive factors. Algorithm 9 applies Theorem 4.6 to attempt to load-balance each stage s of the pipeline by assigning a certain number of threads t_s and a certain group of factors $f_{s_1}, \ldots, f_{s_2}$ to it. The goal is for $\sum_{i=s_1}^{s_2} d_i \widehat{d}_{i+1} / t_s$ to be roughly equal for each stage.

6   Experimentation and Discussion

The previous section introduced parallel schemes for Weierstrass preparation and Hensel factorization based on the composition of the map-reduce and pipeline parallel patterns. Our lazy power series and parallel schemes have been implemented in C/C++ as part of the Basic Polynomial Algebra Subprograms (BPAS) library [2]. These parallel algorithms are implemented using generic support for task parallelism, thread pools, and asynchronous generators, also provided in the BPAS library. The details of this parallel support are discussed in [5] and [6].

Our experimentation was collected on a machine running Ubuntu 18.04.4 with two Intel Xeon X5650 processors, each with 6 cores (12 cores total) at 2.67 GHz, and a 12×4 GB DDR3 memory configuration at 1.33 GHz. All data shown is an average of 3 trials. BPAS was compiled using GMP 6.1.2 [13]. We work over $\mathbb{Q}$ as these examples do not require algebraic numbers to factor into linear factors. We thus borrow univariate integer polynomial factorization from NTL 11.4.3 [27]. Where algebraic numbers are required, the `MultivariatePowerSeries` package of MAPLE [3], an extension of our work in [8], is available.

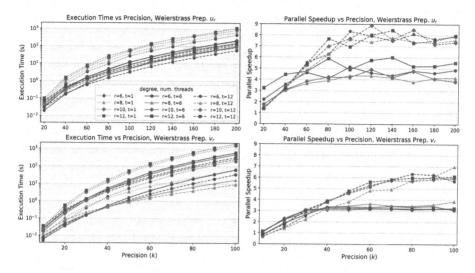

Fig. 2. Comparing Weierstrass preparation of u_r and v_r for $r \in \{6, 8, 10, 12\}$ and number of threads $t \in \{1, 6, 12\}$. First column: execution time of u_r and v_r; second column: parallel speedup of u_r and v_r. Profiling of v_6 shows that its exceptional relative performance is attributed to remarkably good branch prediction.

We begin by evaluating Weierstrass preparation for two families of examples:

(i) $u_r = \sum_{i=2}^{r}(X_1^2 + X_2 + i)Y^i + (X_1^2 + X_2)Y + X_1^2 + X_1 X_2 + X_2^2$,

(ii) $v_r = \sum_{i=\lceil r/2 \rceil}^{r}(X_1^2 + X_2 + i)Y^i + \sum_{i=1}^{\lceil r/2 \rceil - 1}(X_1^2 + X_2)Y^i + X_1^2 + X_1 X_2 + X_2^2$.

Applying Weierstrass preparation to u_r results in p with degree 2. Applying Weierstrass preparation to v_r results in p with degree $\lceil r/2 \rceil$. Figure 2 summarizes the resulting execution times and parallel speedups. Generally, speedup increases with increasing degree in Y and increasing precision computed.

Recall that parallelism arises in two ways: computing summations of products of homogeneous parts (the **parallel_for** loops in Algorithms 4 and 5), and the **parallel_for** loop over updating c_{m-i} in Algorithm 6. The former has an inherent limitation: computing a multivariate product with one operand of low degree and one of high degree is much easier than computing one where both operands are of moderate degree. Evenly partitioning the iterations of the loop does not result in even work per thread. This is evident in comparing the parallel speedup between u_r and v_r; the former, with higher degree in α, relies less on parallelism coming from those products. Better partitioning is needed and is left to future work.

We evaluate our parallel Hensel factorization using three families of problems:

(i) $x_r = \prod_{i=1}^{r}(Y - i) + X_1(Y^3 + Y)$,

(ii) $y_r = \prod_{i=1}^{r}(Y - i)^i + X_1(Y^3 + Y)$,

(iii) $z_r = \prod_{i=1}^{r}(Y + X_1 + X_2 - i) + X_1 X_2(Y^3 + Y)$.

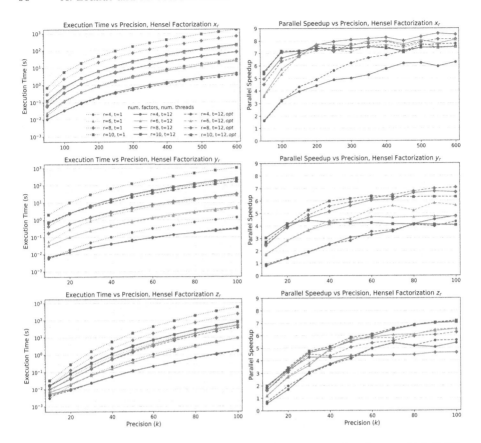

Fig. 3. Comparing parallel Hensel factorization for x_r, y_r, and z_r for $r \in \{4, 6, 8, 10\}$. First column: execution time; second column: parallel speedup. For number of threads $t = 12$ resource distribution is determined by Algorithm 9; for $t = 12$, opt serial execution time replaces complexity measures as work estimates in Algorithm 9, Lines 4–6.

These families represent three distinct computational configurations: (i) factors of equal degree, (ii) factors of distinct degrees, and (iii) multivariate factors. The comparison between x_r and y_r is of interest in view of Theorem 4.6.

Despite the inherent challenges of irregular parallelism arising from stages with unequal work, the composition of parallel patterns allows for load-balancing between stages and the overall pipeline to achieve relatively good parallel speedup. Figure 3 summarizes these results while Table 1 presents the execution time per factor (or stage, in parallel). Generally speaking, potential parallelism increases with increasing degree and increasing precision.

The distribution of a discrete number of threads to a discrete number of pipeline stages is a challenge; a perfect distribution requires a fractional number of threads per stage. Nonetheless, in addition to the distribution technique presented in Algorithm 9, we can examine hand-chosen assignments of threads

Table 1. Times for updating each factor within the Hensel pipeline, where f_i is the factor with i as the root of $\bar{f}_i$, for various numbers of threads per stage. Complexity-estimated threads use complexity estimates to estimate work within Algorithm 9; time-estimated threads use the serial execution time to estimate work and distribute threads.

	factor	serial time (s)	shift time (s)	Complexity-Est. threads	parallel time (s)	wait time (s)	Time-est. parallel threads	time (s)	wait time (s)
x_4 $k = 600$	f_1	18.1989	0.0012	6	4.5380	0.0000	7	3.5941	0.0000
	f_2	6.6681	0.0666	4	4.5566	0.8530	3	3.6105	0.6163
	f_3	3.4335	0.0274	1	4.5748	1.0855	0	-	-
	f_4	0.0009	0.0009	1	4.5750	4.5707	2	3.6257	1.4170
totals		28.3014	0.0961	12	4.5750	6.5092	12	3.6257	2.0333
y_4 $k = 100$	f_1	0.4216	0.0003	3	0.1846	0.0000	4	0.1819	0.0000
	f_2	0.5122	0.0427	5	0.2759	0.0003	4	0.3080	0.0001
	f_3	0.4586	0.0315	3	0.2842	0.0183	0	-	-
	f_4	0.0049	0.0048	1	0.2844	0.2780	4	0.3144	0.0154
totals		1.3973	0.0793	12	0.2844	0.2963	12	0.3144	0.0155
z_4 $k = 100$	f_1	5.2455	0.0018	6	1.5263	0.0000	7	1.3376	0.0000
	f_2	2.5414	0.0300	4	1.5865	0.2061	3	1.4854	0.0005
	f_3	1.2525	0.0151	1	1.6504	0.1893	0	-	-
	f_4	0.0018	0.0018	1	1.6506	1.6473	2	1.5208	0.7155
totals		9.0412	0.0487	12	1.6506	2.0427	12	1.5208	0.7160

to stages. One can first determine the time required to update each factor in serial, say for some small k, and then use that time as the work estimates in Algorithm 9, rather than using the complexity estimates. This latter technique is depicted in Fig. 3 as *opt* and in Table 1 as Time-est. threads. This is still not perfect, again because of the discrete nature of threads, and the imperfect parallelization of computing summations of products of homogeneous parts.

In future, we must consider several important factors to improve performance. Relaxed algorithms should give better complexity and performance. For parallelism, better partitioning schemes for the map-reduce pattern within Weierstrass preparation should be considered. Finally, for the Hensel pipeline, more analysis is needed to optimize the scheduling and resource distribution, particularly considering coefficient sizes and the multivariate case.

Acknowledgments. The authors would like to thank the reviewers for their helpful comments and NSERC of Canada (award CGSD3-535362-2019).

References

1. Alvandi, P., Ataei, M., Kazemi, M., Moreno Maza, M.: On the extended Hensel construction and its application to the computation of real limit points. J. Symb. Comput. **98**, 120–162 (2020)
2. Asadi, M., et al.: Basic Polynomial Algebra Subprograms (BPAS) (version 1.791) (2021). http://www.bpaslib.org
3. Asadi, M., Brandt, A., Kazemi, M., Moreno Maza, M., Postma, E.: Multivariate power series in Maple. In: Proceedings of MC 2020 (2021, to appear)

4. Asadi, M., Brandt, A., Moir, R.H.C., Moreno Maza, M.: Algorithms and data structures for sparse polynomial arithmetic. Mathematics **7**(5), 441 (2019)
5. Asadi, M., Brandt, A., Moir, R.H.C., Moreno Maza, M., Xie, Y.: On the parallelization of triangular decompositions. In: Proceedings of ISSAC 2020, pp. 22–29. ACM (2020)
6. Asadi, M., Brandt, A., Moir, R.H.C., Moreno Maza, M., Xie, Y.: Parallelization of triangular decompositions: techniques and implementation. J. Symb. Comput. (2021, to appear)
7. Berthomieu, J., Lecerf, G., Quintin, G.: Polynomial root finding over local rings and application to error correcting codes. Appl. Algebra Eng. Commun. Comput. **24**(6), 413–443 (2013)
8. Brandt, A., Kazemi, M., Moreno-Maza, M.: Power series arithmetic with the BPAS library. In: Boulier, F., England, M., Sadykov, T.M., Vorozhtsov, E.V. (eds.) CASC 2020. LNCS, vol. 12291, pp. 108–128. Springer, Cham (2020). https://doi.org/10.1007/978-3-030-60026-6_7
9. Burge, W.H., Watt, S.M.: Infinite structures in scratchpad II. In: Davenport, J.H. (ed.) EUROCAL 1987. LNCS, vol. 378, pp. 138–148. Springer, Heidelberg (1989). https://doi.org/10.1007/3-540-51517-8_103
10. Chudnovsky, D.V., Chudnovsky, G.V.: On expansion of algebraic functions in power and Puiseux series I. J. Complex. **2**(4), 271–294 (1986)
11. Fischer, G.: Plane Algebraic Curves. AMS (2001)
12. von zur Gathen, J., Gerhard, J.: Modern Computer Algebra, 2nd edn. Cambridge University Press, New York (2003)
13. Granlund, T.: The GMP development team: GNU MP: The GNU Multiple Precision Arithmetic Library (version 6.1.2) (2020). http://gmplib.org
14. Haidar, A., Kurzak, J., Luszczek, P.: An improved parallel singular value algorithm and its implementation for multicore hardware. In: Proceedings of SC 2013. ACM (2013)
15. van der Hoeven, J.: Relax, but don't be too lazy. J. Symb. Comput. **34**(6), 479–542 (2002)
16. van der Hoeven, J.: Faster relaxed multiplication. In: Proceedings of ISSAC 2014, pp. 405–412. ACM (2014)
17. Iwami, M.: Analytic factorization of the multivariate polynomial. In: Proceedings of CASC 2003, pp. 213–225 (2003)
18. Kung, H.T., Traub, J.F.: All algebraic functions can be computed fast. J. ACM **25**(2), 245–260 (1978)
19. Maplesoft, a division of Waterloo Maple Inc.: Maple (2020). www.maplesoft.com/
20. McCool, M., Reinders, J., Robison, A.: Structured Parallel Programming: Patterns for Efficient Computation. Elsevier, Amsterdam (2012)
21. Michailidis, P.D., Margaritis, K.G.: Parallel direct methods for solving the system of linear equations with pipelining on a multicore using OpenMP. J. Comput. Appl. Math. **236**(3), 326–341 (2011)
22. Monagan, M., Vrbik, P.: Lazy and forgetful polynomial arithmetic and applications. In: Gerdt, V.P., Mayr, E.W., Vorozhtsov, E.V. (eds.) CASC 2009. LNCS, vol. 5743, pp. 226–239. Springer, Heidelberg (2009). https://doi.org/10.1007/978-3-642-04103-7_20
23. Neiger, V., Rosenkilde, J., Schost, É.: Fast computation of the roots of polynomials over the ring of power series. In: Proceedings of ISSAC 2017, pp. 349–356. ACM (2017)
24. Sasaki, T., Kako, F.: Solving multivariate algebraic equation by Hensel construction. Japan J. Indust. Appl. Math. **16**(2), 257–285 (1999)

25. Sasaki, T., Inaba, D.: Enhancing the extended Hensel construction by using Gröbner bases. In: Gerdt, V.P., Koepf, W., Seiler, W.M., Vorozhtsov, E.V. (eds.) CASC 2016. LNCS, vol. 9890, pp. 457–472. Springer, Cham (2016). https://doi.org/10.1007/978-3-319-45641-6_29

26. Scott, M.L.: Programming Language Pragmatics, 3rd edn. Academic Press, New York (2009)

27. Shoup, V., et al.: NTL: A library for doing number theory (version 11.4.3) (2020). www.shoup.net/ntl/

28. The Sage Developers: SageMath, the Sage Mathematics Software System (version 9.1) (2020). https://www.sagemath.org

Symbolic-Numeric Algorithms for Computing Orthonormal Bases of SU(3) Group for Orbital Angular Momentum

Algirdas Deveikis[1], Alexander Gusev[2(✉)], Sergue Vinitsky[2,3], Andrzej Góźdź[4], Aleksandra Pędrak[5], Čestmir Burdik[6], and George Pogosyan[7]

[1] Vytautas Magnus University, Kaunas, Lithuania
[2] Joint Institute for Nuclear Research, Dubna, Russia
gooseff@jinr.ru
[3] RUDN University, 6 Miklukho-Maklaya, 117198 Moscow, Russia
[4] Institute of Physics, Maria Curie-Skłodowska University, Lublin, Poland
[5] National Centre for Nuclear Research, Warsaw, Poland
[6] Czech Technical University, Prague, Czech Republic
[7] Yerevan State University, Yerevan, Armenia

Abstract. We have developed symbolic-numeric algorithms implemented in the Wolfram Mathematica to compute the orthonormal canonical Gel'fand–Tseitlin (G-T), non-canonical Bargmann-Moshinsky (B-M) and Elliott (E) bases of irreducible representations $SU(3) \supset SO(3) \supset SO(2)$ group for a given orbital of angular momentum. The algorithms resolve the missing label problem by solving eigenvalue problem for the "labeling" B-M operator $X^{(3)}$. The effective numeric algorithm for construction of the G-T basis provides a unique capability to perform large scale calculations even with 8 byte real numbers. The algorithms for the construction of B-M and E bases implemented very fast modified Gramm–Schmidt orthonormalization procedure. In B-M basis, a very effective formula for calculation of the matrix $X^{(3)}$ is derived by graphical method. The implemented algorithm for construction of the B-M basis makes it possible to perform large scale exact as well as arbitrary precision calculations. The algorithm for the construction of the E basis resolves the missing label problem by calculation of the matrix $X^{(3)}$ in an orthogonal basis from this matrix previously built in non-orthogonal basis. The implementation of this algorithm provides large scale calculations with arbitrary precision.

Keywords: Orthonormal non-canonical basis · $SU(3) \supset SO(3) \supset SO(2)$ · Irreducible representations · Missing label problem · Gram–Schmidt orthonormalization · Gel'fand–Tseitlin basis · Bargmann–Moshinsky basis · Elliott basis

1 Introduction

One of the main tools for shell type of nuclear models calculations are non-orthogonal bases of irreducible representations (irrs.) of the non-canonical group

© Springer Nature Switzerland AG 2021
F. Boulier et al. (Eds.): CASC 2021, LNCS 12865, pp. 100–120, 2021.
https://doi.org/10.1007/978-3-030-85165-1_7

chain of SU(3)⊃SO(3)⊃SO(2) [20]. In spite of a long history of application of the non-orthogonal Elliot (E) basis [1, 3–5, 10–15, 17, 27, 30], there are still no sufficiently efficient and cost effective algorithms and programs for constructing the required orthogonal non-canonical bases and calculating tensor operators using a computer algebra system [25] as it can be done in the canonical orthogonal Gel'fand–Tseitlin (G-T) basis [16, 19, 23, 26]. First steps to construct the appropriate algorithms and programs which can be implemented in the Wolfram Mathematica [22] with the non-canonical and non-orthogonal Bargmann–Moshinsky (B-M) basis [2, 6, 24] have been presented in [7–9, 31].

These bases are characterized by the following quantum numbers: the angular momentum L and its projection M on the Z axis of the laboratory frame, a missing label which determines a degeneracy of the basis with respect to L and M at fixed integers λ and μ. The latter are determined by the relations $m_{13} = \lambda + \mu$ and $m_{23} = \lambda$ or $m_{23} = \mu$ in the conjugate and $m_{13} = 2m_{23}$ ($\lambda = \mu$) in the self-conjugate representations of SU(3) group characterized by a set of integers $m_{13} \geq m_{23} \geq m_{33}$ at $m_{33} = 0$ describing the canonical G-T basis [19, 24]. The first set of algorithms resolves the missing label problem with *non-integer eigenvalues* x. It is done by solving the eigenvalue problem for the labeling operator $\boldsymbol{X}^{(3)}$ proposed by Bargmann–Moshinsky (B-M), which belongs to the SU(3) enveloping algebra [6, 24]. The construction is performed in the G-T canonical orthonormal basis and the non-canonical non-orthogonal B-M and E bases as well as in the non-canonical orthogonal B-M and E bases calculated with the help of the second set of algorithms. The second set of algorithms implements the Gramm–Schmidt (G-S) procedure and resolves the missing label problem with *integer quantum numbers* α or K. It calculates the elements of orthogonalized matrices of the non-canonical nonorthogonal B-M or E bases using some overlap integrals of Ref. [2] or Refs. [4, 27], respectively.

The known program for resolving the missing "label" problem by solving the eigenvalue problem for the "labeling" B-M operator $\boldsymbol{X}^{(3)}$ in the G-T basis [23] is capable to produce calculations only for rather moderate scale calculations up to SU(3) representation ($m_{13} = 18, m_{23} = 9, m_{33} = 0$). In view of the importance of this basis in nuclear and particle physics it is necessary to elaborate the efficient algorithms for large scale calculations, i.e., one needs to have at least 10 times larger labels of the SU(3) representations in G-T basis. The calculations in G-T basis may serve as a complementary tool for calculations in non-canonical bases.

Application of algebraic methods in nuclear calculations often rely on arbitrary precision or even exact arithmetics. In this context, the B-M basis plays a distinct role because of its well determined algebraic structure. However, due to the complex nature of the formulae for the overlap integrals in this basis [2], very effective orthonormalization algorithms as well as formulas with minimal number of summations for the calculation of operators matrix elements should be elaborated. The implementation of these algorithms for computation of the matrix $\boldsymbol{X}^{(3)}$ may provide an opportunity to perform the large scale symbolic calculations in nuclear physics.

The application of widely used in nuclear physics E basis is related to even more problems than the problems inherent in the B-M basis. First, the values of the E basis overlap integrals have significantly more complex root rational fractional form and second, the negative values of additional quantum number should be taken into account when calculating the matrix elements of operators [4,27]. There is a number of formulas of the overlap integrals in the E basis [4,27] which efficiency still needs to be investigated. It is well known that there are no effective implementations of algorithms for calculation of the matrix $\boldsymbol{X}^{(3)}$ in the orthogonal E basis. So a very promising solution may be the calculation of this matrix from its significantly more simple counterpart in the non-orthogonal basis in the case if any effective basis orthonormalization algorithm is provided. Because of universal character of the developed orthonormalization algorithm the large scale calculations of the matrix $\boldsymbol{X}^{(3)}$ may be performed.

In this paper, we have developed symbolic-numeric algorithms and programs implemented in the Wolfram Mathematica [22] to compute the orthonormal canonical G-T basis [16], and the non-canonical B-M [6,24] and Elliot(E) bases [15] of symmetric irrs. of the SU(3)⊃SO(3)⊃SO(2) group for given orbital angular momenta. We also calculate required tensor operators. We present benchmark calculations of the eigenvalue problem for the labeling operator $\boldsymbol{X}^{(3)}$ in the canonical orthogonal G-T basis and use it like a guarantee of correctness of algorithms and codes elaborated for calculations of matrix elements of tensor operators in the non-canonical B-M and E bases. In particular, to check the correctness of calculations of the eigenvalues x having the same absolute values with opposite signs in conjugate and self-conjugate representations and sufficiency of the main set of eigenvectors in E basis using our algorithms and code without an additional extra set eigenvectors at $L>\lambda$ for $\lambda>\mu$ or at $L>\mu$ for $\mu>\lambda$ that is needed in an alternative procedure for solving Eqs. (129)–(131) of Ref. [27]).

The structure of the paper is following. In Sect. 2, the algorithm for calculating the eigenvalues and eigenvectors of labeling the B-M operator $\boldsymbol{X}^{(3)}$ in the orthonormal G-T basis labeled by eigenvalues of two scalars of SO(3) group is presented. In Sects. 3 and 4, the algorithm of construction of the orthonormal B-M and E bases and the operator $\boldsymbol{X}^{(3)}$ and benchmark calculations of orthogonalization matrices and eigenvalues and eigenvectors of labeling the B-M operator $\boldsymbol{X}^{(3)}$ are presented. In Sect. 5, the summary of main results and conclusions is given. The CPU times of the benchmark calculations give needed estimations for choosing the appropriate versions of the presented symbolic-numeric algorithms and programs discussed in Conclusions. The computations were performed with Wolfram Mathematica 10.1 on a PC with a 2.40 GHz Intel i7-36030QM CPU, 8 GB of RAM, and 64-bit Windows 8 OS.

2   Algorithm of Calculating $\boldsymbol{X}^{(3)}$-Orthonormal G-T Basis

The generators of Lie algebra corresponding to the group chain U(3) ⊃ SU(2) × U(1) fulfil the commutation relations [16]

$$[\boldsymbol{E}_{ik}, \boldsymbol{E}_{jl}] = \delta_{kj}\boldsymbol{E}_{il} - \delta_{il}\boldsymbol{E}_{jk}. \tag{1}$$

The Casimir operators of the second and third orders $C_2(SU(3))$ and $C_3(SU(3))$ are given by

$$C_2(SU(3)) = \sum_{ik} E_{ik}E_{ki}, \quad C_3(SU(3)) = \sum_{ijk} E_{ij}E_{jk}E_{ki}. \qquad (2)$$

We are using generators of this Lie algebra that transform under the group SO(3) as spherical tensors of the rank 1 and 2, respectively. The spherical components of the angular momentum operator $L \equiv L^{(1)}$ (the superscript indicates the rank) are defined as in [23]

$$L_1 = -E_{12} - E_{23}, \ L_0 = E_{11} - E_{33}, \ L_{-1} = E_{21} + E_{32}, \qquad (3)$$

and the spherical components of the quadrupole momentum operator $Q \equiv Q^{(2)}$ are defined as in [23], but with the factor $3^{1/2}$

$$Q_2 = 6^{\frac{1}{2}}E_{13}, \ Q_1 = 3^{\frac{1}{2}}(E_{23} - E_{12}), \ Q_0 = E_{11} + E_{33} - 2E_{22},$$
$$Q_{-1} = 3^{\frac{1}{2}}(E_{21} - E_{32}), \ Q_{-2} = 6^{\frac{1}{2}}E_{31}. \qquad (4)$$

Using (1), (3), and (4) at $k, n = -1, 0, +1$ and $m = -2, -1, 0, +1, +2$ we obtain the following commutator relations $[L_0, L_{\pm 1}] = \pm L_{\pm 1}, [L_1, L_{-1}] = -L_0$:

$$[L_m, L_n] = -\sqrt{2}C^{1\,m+n}_{1m1n}L_{m+n}, [L_0, Q_m] = mQ_m, \qquad (5)$$
$$[L_m, Q_n] = -\sqrt{6}C^{2\,m+n}_{1m2n}Q_{m+n}, \quad [Q_m, Q_n] = 3\sqrt{10}C^{1\,m+n}_{2m2n}L_{m+n}. \qquad (6)$$

Remark 1. If one interchanges indices 1 and 2 of the operators a_i, a_i^+ and correspondingly of E_{ij} for $i, j = 1, 2, 3$ in Eqs. (8)–(15) of Ref. [27], then one has the following correspondence of such reordered operators with respect to the ones determined in Eqs. (3) and (4). The vector operator of the angular momentum $L = L^{(1)}$ in Eq. (3) is denoted as $Q^{(1)}$ in Eq.(13) of Ref. [27], i.e., $L_{+1} = Q^{(1)}_1$, $L_{-1} = Q^{(1)}_{-1}$ and $L_0 = Q^{(1)}_0$. The quadrupole operator Q in Eq. (4) coincides up to the factor $\sqrt{6}$ with $Q^{(2)}$ in Eq.(14) of Ref. [27], i.e., $Q = \sqrt{6}Q^{(2)}$.

The construction of the complete orthonormal G-T basis with well defined angular momentum quantum numbers L and $-L \leq M \leq L$, where M is a projection of L on the Z-axis of a laboratory frame may be performed by means of two commuting SO(3) scalars.

$$L^2 = \sum_{m=-1}^{1}(-1)^m L_m L_{-m} \qquad (7)$$

and the second one is the labeling operator $X^{(3)}$

$$X^{(3)} = -\sqrt{\frac{5}{6}} \sum_{m_1=-1}^{1} \sum_{m_2=-2}^{2} C^{1m_1+m_2}_{1m_12m_2} C^{00}_{1m_1+m_21\,-m_1-m_2} L_{m_1}Q_{m_2}L_{-m_1-m_2}, (8)$$

where C^{**}_{****} are Clebsch–Gordan coefficients of the group SO(3) [29]. The numerical factor for the operator $X^{(3)}$ may be chosen arbitrarily. Here, its value $-\sqrt{5/6}$

Table 1. *Algorithm* for calculating eigenvectors V and eigenvalues x of the matrix of the operator $X^{(3)}$ with definite values L through eigenvalues $L(L+1)$ of matrices for square of the orbital angular momentum $(L \cdot L)$ in the G-T basis.

Input:	U(3) representation m_{13}, m_{23}, m_{33}
Output:	The eigenvalues x and eigenvectors V of the matrix of the operator $X^{(3)}$
1	Calculation of the matrix of the operator $X^{(3)}$ with respect to the Gel'fand–Tseitlin patterns for a given U(3) representation
2	Computation of eigenvalues x and eigenvectors V of matrix $X^{(3)}$
3	Calculation of the matrix W of the operator $(L \cdot L)$ with respect to the Gel'fand-Tseitlin patterns for a given U(3) representation
4	Computation of the matrix multiplication of the matrices $Y = V \times W$
5	Determination of L values corresponding to the x and V:
5.1	For every row of the matrix Y calculate the sum S_1 of the absolute values of its entries
5.2	For every row of the matrix V calculate the sum S_2 of the absolute values of its entries
5.3	For every row of these matrices calculate the $L = \texttt{Floor}\left(\sqrt{\frac{S_1}{S_2}}\right)$
6	Reorder the sequence of the obtained L values in the descending order and correspondingly reorder the rows of x and V matrices

is chosen to get the same eigenvalues of this operator as the eigenvalues calculated in other bases considered in this article. In order to get the same eigenvalues of the operator $X^{(3)}$ presented in [23] the coefficient $3\sqrt{5/6}$ is required. Usually this factor is taken differently by different authors. The matrix elements of the operators L^2 and $X^{(3)}$ may be expressed in terms of matrix elements of the generators E_{ij} calculated within the $|GTP\rangle$ vectors

$$\left| \begin{matrix} m_{13} \ m_{23} \ m_{33} \\ L \ M \ x \end{matrix} \right\rangle = \sum_{m_{12}m_{22}m_{11}} V^{LMx}_{m_{12}m_{22}m_{11}} \left| \begin{matrix} m_{13} \ m_{23} \ m_{33} \\ m_{12} \ m_{22} \\ m_{11} \end{matrix} \right\rangle, \qquad (9)$$

where $m_{i,k+1} \geq m_{i,k} \geq m_{i+1,k}$ at integer $m_{i,k}$. We use the known action of generators E_{ij} on the G-T basis [16,26] that modify labels of only last two rows of the G-T pattern ($|GTP\rangle$) at a given U(3) representation. After the reduction of U(3) to SU(3) assuming $m_{33} = 0$ the action of $L_0 = E_{11} - E_{33}$ on the vectors $|GTP\rangle$ gives the required values of $M = m_{11} + m_{12} + m_{22} - m_{13} - m_{23} - m_{33}$. Since $X^{(3)}$ does not connect patterns with different M, so we can take $M = 0$. Then, the irreducible representations are conventionally labeled by indices $\lambda = m_{13} - m_{23}$ and $\mu = m_{23} - m_{33}$, i.e., $\mu = m_{23}$ and $\lambda \geq \mu$, or $\mu = m_{13} - m_{23}$ and $\lambda = m_{23} - m_{33}$, i.e., $\lambda = m_{23}$ and $\mu \geq \lambda$. Both bases, i.e., B-M and E bases are, in addition, labeled by the quantum numbers L, M and missing label which is an *integer number* α or K, or *noninteger number* represented by eigenvalues x of the labeling operator $X^{(3)}$, as it is explained below. Algorithm given in Table 1 calculates the matrices for square of the orbital angular momentum $(L \cdot L)$ and the labeling operator $X^{(3)}$ in the G-T basis of any arbitrary U(3) irreducible

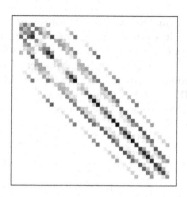 

Fig. 1. The gray scale output of the matrices of the operators $X^{(3)}$ (left) and $(L \cdot L)$ (right) with respect to the G-T patterns for U(3) representation $m_{13} = 16$, $m_{23} = 6$, $m_{33} = 0$. The values of elements of the matrix are shown in a discrete array of squares. The values with larger absolute value are represented by a darker square (zero values are displayed by white color).

Table 2. Eigenvalues $x = x_{nL}$ of the matrix $X^{(3)}$ with respect to the G-T patterns for U(3) representation $m_{13} = 16, m_{23} = 6, m_{33} = 0$. The columns of this table are formed by eigenvalues E_{nL} corresponding to a definite value of angular momentum L, the eigenvalues are numbered by their sequence number No. ($\equiv n$) as well.

No., L	0	2	3	4	5	6	7	8
1	0.000000	−31.3847	0.000000	137.0156	93.00000	320.3878	256.2905	−506.4812
2		31.38471		−122.7053	−93.00000	−281.7338	−240.3314	−204.1943
3				−14.31030		−84.20615	−15.95906	185.7775
4						45.55215		−55.10207

No., L	9	10	11	12	13	14	15	16
1	−447.4137	−796.0580	−714.8744	−633.5932	−554.7808	−483.5491	−418.0000	−396.6667
2	−155.1731	−389.3111	−332.4611	−295.7156	−230.5525	−264.4509		
3	109.5868	−160.5985	−54.66451	−124.6912				
4		31.30092						

representation. It computes their eigenvalues $L(L+1)$ and x respectively, solving the eigenvalue problem $X^{(3)}V = Vx$, e.g. $V^{-1}X^{(3)}V = x$, to find the common eigenvectors V. It should be noted that the eigenvalues of the matrix $X^{(3)}$ will change their sign under substitution $E_{ik} \rightarrow -E_{ki}$ in Eqs. (3) and (4). Also the eigenvalues of the matrix $X^{(3)}$ of a pair of conjugate states differ only in their signs. The pair of conjugate (contragradient) states are defined to have the same label $m_{13} = \lambda + \mu$, but if one of states in the pair is characterized by $m_{23} = \mu, (\lambda > \mu)$ the other state has $m_{23} = \lambda, (\mu > \lambda)$. The self-conjugate (self-contragredient) case when $\lambda = \mu$, i.e., $m_{13} = 2\mu$ and $m_{23} = \mu$ have completely different eigenvalues of the matrix $X^{(3)}$ from the previous case. In this case, the eigenvalues for the same L join in pairs and have the same absolute values, but differ in sign. However, if the number of eigenvalues with the same L is uneven (odd) then at least one of these eigenvalues has to be equal to 0.

Table 3. The example of calculations of the matrix $\boldsymbol{X}^{(3)}$ with respect to the G-T patterns for a number of μ and fixed $\lambda = 125$. The columns of the table are formed by μ, the maximum value of the angular momentum $L_{\max}$ for a given U(3) representation with corresponding μ and λ (the number $L_{\min} = 1$ and the number of different L is equal to the $L_{\max}$), the dimension of the corresponding matrix $\boldsymbol{X}^{(3)}$, the maximal dimension of the matrix $\boldsymbol{X}^{(3)}$ for given μ and λ of SU(3)$\supset$ SO(3) (the minimum dimension of this matrix is equal to 1), the CPU time for calculations of the matrix $\boldsymbol{X}^{(3)}$ for a given U(3) representation with corresponding μ and λ.

μ	$L_{\max}$	dim $\boldsymbol{X}^{(3)}$	max dim $\boldsymbol{X}^{(3)}$	CPU time
10	135	693	6	47.78 s
20	145	1323	11	1.97 min
40	165	2583	21	5.62 min
60	185	3843	31	10.91 min
80	205	5103	41	18.03 min
100	225	6363	51	26.78 min
120	245	7623	61	37.12 min

Remark 2. At $M = m_{11} + m_{12} + m_{22} - 3m_{23} = 0$, the corrected formula corresponding to Eq. (55) in [19] has the following form

$$\sum \left\langle \begin{matrix} m_{12}m_{22} \\ m_{11} \end{matrix} \left| X^{(3)} \right| \begin{matrix} m'_{12}m'_{22} \\ m'_{11} \end{matrix} \right\rangle = 0. \tag{10}$$

with summation over $m_{11}+m_{12}+m_{22} = m_{13}+m_{23}, m'_{11}+m'_{12}+m'_{22} = m_{13}+m_{23}$.

In Table 2, we present the eigenvalues x_{nL} of the $\boldsymbol{X}^{(3)}$ matrix in the G-T basis for U(3) representation $m_{13} = 16, m_{23} = 6, m_{33} = 0$ labeled by the definite value of the angular momentum L and n which is the sequence number of eigenvalues and it is introduced here for the convenience only. The dimension of the $\boldsymbol{X}^{(3)}$ matrix in the G-T basis, i.e., the number of patterns that exist for a given irreducible U(3) representation, is 39 (see Fig. 1).

In Table 3, we present an example of the CPU time of calculations of the matrix $\boldsymbol{X}^{(3)}$ with respect to the G-T patterns for a number of μ and fixed $\lambda = 125$. It should be stressed that the presented procedure is very effective and could be applied for large scale calculations since the quantum numbers managed significantly outperform the considered as "...very large values, e.g., $\lambda \sim 100$ and $\mu \sim 10$." [25].

3   Algorithm and Calculations in Orthonormal B-M Basis

The B-M basis is constructed by making use of two SO(3) spherical boson vector operators $\boldsymbol{\xi}$ and $\boldsymbol{\eta}$ [29,31] which belong to two fundamental irrs. SU(3):

$$\xi_{\pm} = \mp \frac{1}{\sqrt{2}}(\xi_x \pm \imath \xi_y), \quad \xi_0 = \xi_z, \quad \eta_{\pm} = \mp \frac{1}{\sqrt{2}}(\eta_x \pm \imath \eta_y), \quad \eta_0 = \eta_z. \tag{11}$$

The B-M states are polynomials constructed from these operators which act on the vacuum state denoted by $|0\rangle$. The pairs of creation ξ_m and η_m, and annihilation ξ_m^+ and η_m^+ vector-boson operators are defined by the relations

$$\xi_m^+|0\rangle = \eta_m^+|0\rangle = 0, \quad [\xi_m^+, \xi_n] = [\eta_m^+, \eta_n] = (-1)^m \delta_{-m,n}. \tag{12}$$

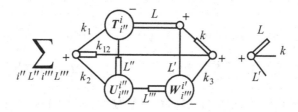

Fig. 2. The graphical representation of the matrix elements of the general tensor product of three operators corresponding to the Eq. (14) is derived by the graphical method [18].

With the help of ξ and η one can construct the additional, helpful, irreducible tensor operators $F_M^L = \sum_{\mu\nu} C_{1\mu1\nu}^{LM}(\xi_\mu\xi_\nu^+ + \eta_\mu\eta_\nu^+)$. The vectors ξ^+ and η^+ can be chosen in the form $\xi_\nu^+ = (-1)^\nu \partial/\partial\xi_{-\nu}$, $\eta_\nu^+ = (-1)^\nu \partial/\partial\eta_{-\nu}$, i.e. the vectors ξ, η and ξ^+, η^+ are considered as creation and annihilation operators of two distinct kinds of vector bosons in the Fock representation. The tensor operators satisfy the following commutation relations

$$[F_{M_1}^{L_1}, F_{M_2}^{L_2}] = B_{L_1,L_2}\sum_L[(-1)^L - (-1)^{L_1+L_2}]C_{L_1M_1L_2M_2}^{LM_1+M_2}\begin{Bmatrix} L_1 & L_2 & L \\ 1 & 1 & 1 \end{Bmatrix} F_{M_1+M_2}^L, \tag{13}$$

where $B_{L_1,L_2} = \sqrt{(2L_1+1)(2L_2+1)}$ and $\{{}^{***}_{***}\}$ is 6j Symbol of SO(3) [29].

One can see that for $L_m = \sqrt{2}F_m^1$, $Q_k = \sqrt{6}F_k^2$, the operators $L_m(m = 0, \pm1)$ and $Q_k(k = 0, \pm1, \pm2)$ satisfy the standard commutation relations of the group SU(3) given by Eqs. (5)–(6) defined in G–T basis and the second-order Casimir operator $C_2(SU(3)) = Q \cdot Q + 3L \cdot L = 4(\lambda^2 + \mu^2 + \lambda\mu + 3\lambda + 3\mu)$ was described in [2] and implemented as a symbolic algorithm in [7,8]. It is evident (from the above commutation relations) that the operators L_m, where $m = 0, \pm1$ define the algebra of the angular momentum SO(3) and the operators Q_k, $k = 0, \pm1, \pm2$, extend this algebra to the SU(3) algebra. The dimension of any SU(3) irrep for a given λ, μ can be calculated by using the following formula: $D_{\lambda\mu} = \frac{1}{2}(\lambda+1)(\mu+1)$ $(\lambda + \mu + 2)$. Definition of the corresponding labeling operator $X^{(3)}$ [4] is given by $X^{(3)} = \left([L^{(1)} \otimes L^{(1)}]^{(2)} \cdot Q^{(2)}\right)$. The tensor product $X^{(3)}$ of three angular momentum operators is expressed as

$$\langle iLM | \left[[T^{(k_1)} \otimes U^{(k_2)}]^{(k_{12})} \otimes W^{(k_3)}\right]_q^{(k)} | i'L'M'\rangle$$

$$= \sum_{i''L''M''q_1,q_2}\sum_{i'''L'''M'''q_{12},q_3}(k_1q_1\,k_2q_2|k_{12}q_{12})(k_{12}q_{12}\,k_3q_3|kq) \tag{14}$$

$$\times\langle iLM | T_{q_1}^{(k_1)} | i''L''M''\rangle\langle i''L''M'' | U_{q_2}^{(k_2)} | i'''L'''M'''\rangle\langle i'''L'''M''' | W_{q_3}^{(k_3)} | i'L'M'\rangle.$$

The effective expression for matrix elements of the three operators tensor products may be derived by the graphical method [18]. Firstly, the general tensor product of three operators can be expressed in the graphical form as in Fig. 2. The great advantage of usually this graphical method is that it can significantly simplify the momentum recoupling coefficients that are inherently presented in formulas of this type. Secondly, using the graphical methods Eq. (14) may be simplified

$$\left\langle iLM \,\middle|\, \left[[\boldsymbol{T}^{(k_1)} \otimes \boldsymbol{U}^{(k_2)}]^{(k_{12})} \otimes \boldsymbol{W}^{(k_3)}\right]_q^{(k)} \,\middle|\, i'L'M' \right\rangle$$

$$= (L'M' \, kq | LM) \sum_{i'' L'' i''' L'''} [(2L+1)(2L''+1)(2L'''+1)]^{-1/2} \tag{15}$$

$$\times \left\langle iL \,\|\, \boldsymbol{T}^{(k_1)} \,\|\, i''L'' \right\rangle \left\langle i''L'' \,\|\, \boldsymbol{U}^{(k_2)} \,\|\, i'''L''' \right\rangle \left\langle i'''L''' \,\|\, \boldsymbol{W}^{(k_3)} \,\|\, i'L' \right\rangle$$

$$\times \langle (L', ((k_1,k_2)k_{12},k_3)k)L | (((L',k_3)L''',k_2)L'',k_1)L\rangle,$$

where $\langle y\|A\|y'\rangle$ are reduced matrix elements with respect to the SO(3) group [29]. Finally, the angular momentum recoupling the coefficients appearing in Eq. (15) can be simplified significantly by the graphical method. In this way, a simple formula for matrix elements of the operator $\boldsymbol{X}^{(3)}$ is derived

$$\left\langle \begin{matrix} (\lambda\mu) \\ j, L', M' \end{matrix} \,\middle|\, \boldsymbol{X}^{(3)} \,\middle|\, \begin{matrix} (\lambda\mu) \\ i, L, M \end{matrix} \right\rangle = \frac{1}{6}(L+1)(2L+3)\, q_{ij0}^{(\lambda\mu)}(L)\, \delta_{LL'}\, \delta_{MM'}. \tag{16}$$

The q-coefficients required in the orthonormalization scheme use the non-normalized overlap integrals and they are defined as

$$q_{ijk}^{(\lambda\mu)}(L) = \sum_{\alpha=0}^{\alpha_{\max}} \sum_{s=0,\pm 1} \mathcal{A}_{i,\alpha}^{(\lambda\mu)}(L) a_s^{(k)} (\mathcal{A}^{-1})_{(\alpha+s),j}^{(\lambda\mu)}(L+k), \tag{17}$$

where the coefficients $a_s^{(k)}$ are given in Ref. [9,31] and they read as

$$a_0^{(2)} = \frac{6(\lambda+\mu-L-2\alpha-\beta)}{[(L+2)(2L+3)]^{1/2}}, \quad a_{-1}^{(2)} = \frac{12\alpha}{[(L+2)(2L+3)]^{1/2}}, \quad a_{-1}^{(2)} = 0,$$

$$a_0^{(1)} = -6\frac{2\alpha\beta(L+2\alpha-\mu+1)+(\lambda+\mu-L-2\alpha-\beta)(\mu-2\alpha-\beta)}{(L+2)(L+1)^{1/2}} - \frac{6\beta}{(L+1)^{1/2}},$$

$$a_{-1}^{(1)} = \frac{12\alpha(\lambda-\mu+2\alpha)}{(L+2)(L+1)^{1/2}}, \quad a_1^{(1)} = \frac{6\beta(\lambda+\mu-L-2\alpha-\beta)}{(L+2)(L+1)^{1/2}},$$

$$a_0^{(0)} = 4\alpha\frac{L(L+1)-3(L+2\alpha-\mu+\beta)^2}{(L+1)(2L+3)} - 2(\lambda+\mu-L-\beta-2\alpha)\frac{L(L+1)-3(\mu-2\alpha)^2}{(L+1)(2L+3)}$$

$$-(L-\mu+4\alpha+\beta)\left(1+\frac{3\beta}{L+1}\right),$$

$$a_{-1}^{(0)} = \frac{6(\lambda+\mu-L-2\alpha-\beta)(L-\mu+2\alpha)(L-\mu+2\alpha-1)}{(L+1)(2L+3)},$$

$$a_1^{(0)} = -\frac{6(\lambda+\mu-L-2\alpha-\beta)(\mu-2\alpha-\beta)(\mu-2\alpha-\beta-1)}{(L+1)(2L+3)},$$

$$\beta = \begin{cases} 0, & \lambda+\mu-L \text{ even}, \\ 1, & \lambda+\mu-L \text{ odd}. \end{cases}$$

The q-coefficients in the orthonormalization scheme that uses the normalized overlap integrals (defined below and denoted for some formulas simplification by the same symbol $q_{ijk}^{(\lambda\mu)}(L)$ as in (17)) are calculated as

$$q_{ijk}^{(\lambda\mu)}(L) = \sum_{\substack{\alpha=0,\ldots,\alpha_{\max} \\ s=0,\pm1}} \mathcal{A}_{i,\alpha}^{(\lambda\mu)}(L)\sqrt{\frac{\langle u_{\alpha+s}|u_{\alpha+s}\rangle_{L+k}}{\langle u_\alpha|u_\alpha\rangle_L}} a_s^{(k)}(\mathcal{A}^{-1})_{(\alpha+s),j}^{(\lambda\mu)}(L+k), \qquad (18)$$

where $\langle u_\alpha|u_{\alpha'}\rangle_L$ denotes the non-normalized overlap integrals.

In this section, we use the following form of the formula for the overlap integral of the non-canonical B-M states presented in [2]

$$\langle u_\alpha|u_{\alpha'}\rangle_L \equiv \left\langle \begin{matrix}(\lambda,\mu)_B \\ \alpha,L,L\end{matrix} \middle| \begin{matrix}(\lambda,\mu)_B \\ \alpha',L,L\end{matrix} \right\rangle = C_1(\lambda,L,\Delta)(\lambda+2)^\beta(L-\mu+2\alpha)!$$
$$\times(\lambda-L+\mu-2\alpha'-\beta)!!(\mu-2\alpha'-\beta+\Delta-1)!!$$
$$\times\sum_{l,z}\binom{\alpha'}{1/2(l-\beta-\Delta)}(-1)^{(\mu+2\alpha-\Delta-\beta)/2+z}\binom{\frac{1}{2}(\mu-2\alpha-\Delta-\beta)}{z}$$
$$\times\frac{(\mu-l)!!}{(\mu-l-2z)!!}\frac{(\mu+\beta+\Delta)!!}{(\mu-2\alpha'+l)!!}(l-\Delta+\beta-1)!!(\mu-\Delta-\beta-2z)!!$$
$$\times\frac{(\lambda-L+\mu-2\alpha-\beta)!!}{(\lambda-L+\Delta+2z)!!}\frac{(\lambda+L-\Delta+2)!!}{(\lambda+L-\mu+2\alpha+\beta+2z+2)!!}\frac{(L+l)!}{L!}$$
$$\times\frac{(\lambda+\mu+L+\beta+2)!!}{(\lambda+L+l+\beta+2z+2)!!}\frac{(\lambda+\beta+2z+1)!}{(\lambda+\beta+1)!}\frac{(\lambda+\mu-l-L+\Delta)!!}{(\lambda-L+\mu-2\alpha'-\beta)!!}$$
$$\times C_2(\lambda,L,\Delta,z). \qquad (19)$$

Here $\alpha \geq \alpha'$ and we use the following notations

$$\beta = \begin{cases}0, & \lambda+\mu-L \text{ even,} \\ 1, & \lambda+\mu-L \text{ odd,}\end{cases} \quad \Delta = \begin{cases}0, & \lambda-L \text{ even,} \\ 1, & \lambda-L \text{ odd,}\end{cases} \quad \binom{m}{n} = \frac{m!}{n!(m-n)!},$$

$$C_1(\lambda,L,\Delta) = \begin{cases}1, & L>\lambda+\Delta, \\ \frac{(\lambda+L+\Delta+1)!!}{(2L+1)!!}, & L\leq\lambda+\Delta,\end{cases} \quad C_2(\lambda,L,\Delta,z) = \begin{cases}\frac{(\lambda+L+\Delta+1+2z)!!}{(2L+1)!!}, & L>\lambda+\Delta, \\ \frac{(\lambda+L+\Delta+1+2z)!!}{(\lambda+L+\Delta+1)!!}, & L\leq\lambda+\Delta.\end{cases}$$

It should be emphasized that the calculation of the matrix $\mathbf{X}^{(3)}$ in both cases with the non-normalized and normalized overlap integrals is performed by using the same Eq. (16). The only difference is that in the Eq. (16) for calculations with the non-normalized overlap integrals, the q-coefficients defined in Eq. (17) should be applied and for the calculations with the normalized overlap integrals, the q-coefficients Eq. (18) should be used. It is to be noted that the states (2.3) from paper [2] differ from the states (3.8) from paper [24] in the definition of the number α and coincide up to phase factor $(-1)^\alpha$.

3.1   Calculations in the B-M Basis

The transformation from the non-orthogonal basis $|u_\alpha\rangle$ to the orthogonal $|\phi_i\rangle$ basis is given by the left upper triangle matrix $\mathcal{A}$:

$$|\phi_i\rangle = \sum_\alpha \mathcal{A}_{i\alpha}|u_\alpha\rangle, \quad \mathcal{A}_{i\alpha} = 0; \quad i > \alpha, \quad \mathcal{U} = \langle u|u'\rangle = \mathcal{A}^{-1}(\mathcal{A}^T)^{-1}.$$

Table 4. Computation of $\mathcal{A}$ matrix for $\lambda = 125$ and $L = 120$ (precision $= 300$).

μ	CPU time exact	CPU time numerical
40	7.48 s	2.33 s
60	36.27 s	11.47 s
80	2.10 min	34.23 s
100	5.94 min	1.46 min
120	15.03 min	3.01 min

Then we have the following relations:

$$\langle \phi_i | \phi_j \rangle = \sum_{\alpha\alpha'} \langle u_\alpha | \mathcal{A}^T_{\alpha i} \mathcal{A}_{j\alpha'} | u_{\alpha'} \rangle = \sum_{\alpha\alpha'} \mathcal{A}_{i\alpha} \langle u_\alpha | u_{\alpha'} \rangle (\mathcal{A}^T)_{\alpha' j} = \delta_{ij}.$$

The diagonalization example of the matrix $\boldsymbol{X}^{(3)}$ defined by Eq. (16) with $\mu = 6$, $\lambda = 10$ and $L = 6$ in the B-M orthonormal basis with use of the Alisauskas formula Eq. (19) for the overlap integrals is presented. The entries of the matrix $\mathcal{U}$ are the overlap integrals $\langle u_\alpha | u_{\alpha'} \rangle$, Eq. (19)

$$\mathcal{U} = \begin{pmatrix} 7.420552446 & 1.265307137 & 0.7182987559 & 0.5360438477 \\ 1.265307137 & 1.202208278 & 0.8437655038 & 0.6732710727 \\ 0.7182987559 & 0.8437655038 & 1.042308835 & 0.9930943247 \\ 0.5360438477 & 0.6732710727 & 0.9930943247 & 2.782445237 \end{pmatrix} \times 10^{16}. \tag{20}$$

The matrix $\mathcal{A}$ contains the B-M basis orthonormalization coefficients

$$\mathcal{A} = \begin{pmatrix} -0.4074172336 & 0.5379900162 & -0.1598566047 & 0.005366888407 \\ 0 & -1.400458233 & 1.228635203 & -0.09964711136 \\ 0 & 0 & -1.205730325 & 0.4303423216 \\ 0 & 0 & 0 & 0.5994965488 \end{pmatrix} \times 10^{-8}. \tag{21}$$

Comparison of computation times of exact and numerical orthonormalisation of B-M basis is shown in Table 4.

$$\boldsymbol{X}^{(3)}(\lambda\mu L) = \begin{pmatrix} 319.7180436 & 13.74962194 & 0 & 0 \\ 13.74962194 & 34.17110415 & 41.32579910 & 0 \\ 0 & 41.32579910 & -125.1337108 & -89.49710939 \\ 0 & 0 & -89.49710939 & -228.7554369 \end{pmatrix}. \tag{22}$$

Numerical eigenvalues $\boldsymbol{x} \equiv \boldsymbol{x}^{\lambda\mu}(L)$ of the matrix $\boldsymbol{X}^{(3)}(\lambda\mu L)$:

$$\boldsymbol{x}^{\lambda\mu}(L) = \begin{pmatrix} 320.3878386 & 0 & 0 & 0 \\ 0 & -281.7338447 & 0 & 0 \\ 0 & 0 & -84.20614615 & 0 \\ 0 & 0 & 0 & 45.55215226 \end{pmatrix}, \tag{23}$$

coincide with the eigenvalues calculated in the G-T basis presented in Table 2. The eigenvectors $\mathcal{V}$ of the $\boldsymbol{X}^{(3)}(\lambda\mu L)$ matrix are of the form

$$
\mathcal{V} = \begin{pmatrix}
0.9988044336 & 0.001521525127 & -0.009720865112 & -0.047884164096 \\
-0.04865546258 & -0.06655631440 & 0.2855709474 & 0.9548047638 \\
0.004665953573 & 0.5082672123 & -0.8147802593 & 0.2788831277 \\
-0.0007604378964 & 0.8586223750 & 0.5044679057 & -0.09098994985
\end{pmatrix}. \tag{24}
$$

Since the $\boldsymbol{X}^{(3)}(\lambda\mu L)$ matrix is symmetric, these vectors $\mathcal{V}$ are orthonormalized.

The calculation of the matrix $\boldsymbol{X}^{(3)}$ was performed in the B-M orthonormal basis calculated with the normalized Alisauskas formula (19) for the overlap integrals as well. For comparison, we use here the same parameters $\mu = 6$, $\lambda = 10$ and $L = 6$ as in the calculations without overlap integrals.

$$
\mathcal{U} = \begin{pmatrix}
1.000000000 & 0.4236312421 & 0.2582788150 & 0.1179692678 \\
0.4236312421 & 1.000000000 & 0.7537610627 & 0.3681177725 \\
0.2582788150 & 0.7537610627 & 1.000000000 & 0.5831482514 \\
0.1179692678 & 0.3681177725 & 0.5831482514 & 1.000000000
\end{pmatrix}, \tag{25}
$$

$$
\mathcal{A} = \begin{pmatrix}
-1.109832696 & 0.5898805458 & -0.1632032466 & 0.008952325776 \\
0 & -1.535536055 & 1.254357019 & -0.1662179900 \\
0 & 0 & -1.230972621 & 0.7178395313 \\
0 & 0 & 0 & 1.000000000
\end{pmatrix}. \tag{26}
$$

The matrix $\boldsymbol{X}^{(3)}(\lambda\mu L)$ calculated in the normalized B-M basis has the same entries as in the non-normalized case (22). The matrix $\boldsymbol{X}^{(3)}(\lambda\mu L)$ has the same eigenvalues from (23) and eigenvectors (24) as in the case of calculations with non-normalized overlaps.

3.2   Calculations of $\boldsymbol{X}^{(3)}$ with Summation in the B-M Basis

The reduced matrix element of the quadrupole operator is given by

$$
\left\langle \begin{matrix} (\lambda\mu) \\ j, L+k \end{matrix} \middle\| Q^{(2)} \middle\| \begin{matrix} (\lambda\mu) \\ i, L \end{matrix} \right\rangle = (-1)^k \frac{\sqrt{2L+1}}{(L+k, L, 20|LL)} q_{i,j,k}^{(\lambda,\mu)}(L), \tag{27}
$$

where the q-coefficients are defined by (17). The matrix elements of the quadrupole operator components can be obtained from the reduced matrix elements (27) by the Wigner–Eckart theorem:

$$
\left\langle \begin{matrix} (\lambda\mu) \\ jL'M' \end{matrix} \middle| Q_p^{(2)} \middle| \begin{matrix} (\lambda\mu) \\ iLM \end{matrix} \right\rangle = \frac{(LM\,2p|L',M')}{\sqrt{2L'+1}} \left\langle \begin{matrix} (\lambda\mu) \\ j, L' \end{matrix} \middle\| Q^{(2)} \middle\| \begin{matrix} (\lambda\mu) \\ i, L \end{matrix} \right\rangle. \tag{28}
$$

Direct summation in the formula (14) gives

$$
\left\langle \begin{matrix} (\lambda\mu) \\ j, L', L' \end{matrix} \middle| X^{(3)} \middle| \begin{matrix} (\lambda\mu) \\ i, L, L \end{matrix} \right\rangle = \sqrt{\frac{5}{6}} \delta_{LL'} \sum_{m_1=-1}^{1} \sum_{m_4=-2}^{2} (1\,m_1\,1-m_1|00)
$$

$$
\times (1\,m_1-m_4\,2m_4|1\,m_1) \left\langle \begin{matrix} (\lambda\mu) \\ j, L, L \end{matrix} \middle| L_{m_1-m_4}^{(1)} \middle| \begin{matrix} (\lambda\mu) \\ j, L, L-m_1+m_4 \end{matrix} \right\rangle \tag{29}
$$

$$
\times \left\langle \begin{matrix} (\lambda\mu) \\ j, L, L-m_1+m_4 \end{matrix} \middle| Q_{m_4}^{(2)} \middle| \begin{matrix} (\lambda\mu) \\ i, L, L-m_1 \end{matrix} \right\rangle \left\langle \begin{matrix} (\lambda\mu) \\ j, L, L-m_1 \end{matrix} \middle| L_{-m_1}^{(1)} \middle| \begin{matrix} (\lambda\mu) \\ j, L, L \end{matrix} \right\rangle.
$$

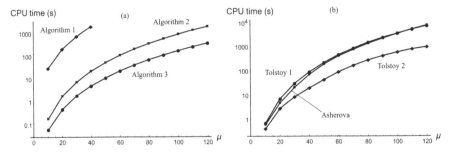

Fig. 3. (a) The CPU time versus parameter μ in the interval $\mu = 10\ldots120$ for calculations of the matrix $\boldsymbol{X}^{(3)}$ in the B-M basis with $\lambda = 125$ and $L = 120$ using the different computation Algorithms. Algorithm 1 represents the calculations with non-normalized overlaps, Algorithm 2 with normalized overlaps, and Algorithm 3 with direct summation formula. The computations were performed with 300 decimal digits of precision. (b) The CPU time versus the parameter μ in the interval $\mu = 10\ldots120$ for calculations of the matrix $\bar{\boldsymbol{X}}^{(3)}$ in the orthonormal Elliott basis Eq. (39) with $\lambda = 125$ and $L = 120$ using the different computation procedures. The computations were performed with 300-digit precision.

The dimension of the quadrupole and angular momentum operator matrices is $D_{\lambda\mu}$ determined above. The matrix $\boldsymbol{X}^{(3)}(\lambda\mu L)$ calculated with direct summation formula has the same entries, eigenvalues, and eigenvectors as in the case with the non-normalized and normalized overlaps presented in Subsect. 3.1. The efficiency of the developed algorithms is presented in Fig. 3a. The CPU time versus parameter μ in the interval $\mu = 10\ldots120$ for calculations of the $\boldsymbol{X}^{(3)}$ matrix in the Bargmann–Moshinsky basis with $\lambda = 125$ and $L = 120$ using the different algorithms determined by Eqs. (17), (18) and (29) are presented. The computations were performed with 300 decimal digits of precision (DDP).[1]

Remark 3. In the Mathematica language, a matrix of eigenvectors is the matrix presented by rows but in Maple it is the matrix presented by columns which is a standard accepted in literature. Below we use a transposed matrix of eigenvectors calculated in Mathematica.

---

[1] *Question*: How to decide what accuracy is sufficient? Why 300-DDP? *Answer*: Calculations are carried out, with very large numbers produced by the presence of factorials in expressions. Computational accuracy should ensure the accuracy of calculations, which is estimated by the product of normalization tests, eigenvalues, and equation of eigenvalues. In these calculations, computational accuracy 300-DDP was taken to ensure that the absolute accuracy of each matrix element of the test result is not worse than 10^{-50}. It should be noted that when calculating with large quantum numbers ($\mu = 120$, $\lambda = 125$, $L = 120$), low computational accuracy (200-DDP) makes the calculations themselves impossible, leading to a division error by zero, and insufficient computational accuracy (250-DDP) although it already allows you to calculate the matrix $X^{(3)}$ but not accurately enough, therefore, it is not yet ensured that its eigenvalues and vectors are found.

4   Algorithm of Construction and Calculations of the E Basis

The first overlap $\langle(\lambda\mu)(K')L'M'|(\lambda\mu)(K)LM\rangle = \delta_{LL'}\delta_{MM'}\mathcal{U}^{(\lambda\mu)}(K'LK)$ where $\mathcal{U}^{(\lambda\mu)}(K'LK) = \langle\Phi_K\,|\,P_{KK'}^L\,|\,\Phi_{K'}\rangle$ is given by formula (2.14) of Asherova [4]

$$
\langle\Phi_K\,|\,P_{KK'}^L\,|\,\Phi_{K'}\rangle = \left[\frac{(L+K)!(L-K)!(L+K')!\,(\frac{1}{2}(\mu-K))!\,(\frac{1}{2}(\mu-K'))!}{(L-K')!\,(\frac{1}{2}(\mu+K))!\,(\frac{1}{2}(\mu+K'))!}\right]^{\frac{1}{2}}
$$

$$
\times\frac{(-1)^{\frac{1}{2}(K'-K)}}{L!(2L-1)!!}\sum_{x,s}\frac{(-1)^s(2x-1)!!\,(\frac{1}{2}(2\lambda+\mu-K')+x-s)!}{2^{x+K'}s!(2x-s)!\,(x+\frac{1}{2}(K'-K))!\,(\frac{1}{2}(\mu-K')-x)!}
$$

$$
\times\frac{(\frac{1}{2}(\mu+K')+x)!}{(\frac{1}{2}(2\lambda+\mu+K')-L+x-s)!}
$$

$$
\times{}_2F_1\left(-\left(\frac{1}{2}(2\lambda+\mu+K')-L+x-s\right),L-K+1;2L+2;2\right). \tag{30}
$$

The second overlap integral of the non-orthonormalized E basis is given by the first formula (43) of the Tolstoy paper [27]

$$
\mathcal{U}^{(\lambda\mu)}(K'LK) = (-1)^{L-\frac{1}{2}(K+K')}(2L+1)
$$

$$
\times\sqrt{\frac{(L+K)!\,(L+K')!\,(\frac{1}{2}(\mu-K))!\,(\frac{1}{2}(\mu-K'))!}{(L-K)!\,(L-K')!\,(\frac{1}{2}(\mu+K))!\,(\frac{1}{2}(\mu+K'))!}}
$$

$$
\times\sum_{rt_z'}\frac{(-2)^{L+r-2t_z'}\,(L-K+r)!\,(L-K'+r)!}{r!\,(2L+1+r)!\,(\lambda+\frac{1}{2}\mu-L-r+t_z')!\,(L+r-2t_z')!}
$$

$$
\times\frac{(\lambda+\frac{1}{2}\mu-t_z')!\,(\frac{1}{2}\mu+t_z')!}{(t_z'-\frac{1}{2}K)!\,(t_z'-\frac{1}{2}K')!\,(\frac{1}{2}\mu-t_z')!}. \tag{31}
$$

The third overlap integral of the non-orthonormalized E basis is given by the second formula (49) of the Tolstoy paper [27]

$$
\mathcal{U}^{(\lambda\mu)}(K'LK) = (-1)^{L-\frac{1}{2}(K+K')}(2L+1)
$$

$$
\times\sqrt{\frac{(L+K)!\,(L+K')!\,(\frac{1}{2}(\mu-K))!\,(\frac{1}{2}(\mu-K'))!}{(L-K)!\,(L-K')!\,(\frac{1}{2}(\mu+K))!\,(\frac{1}{2}(\mu+K'))!}}
$$

$$
\times\sum_{t_z'}\frac{(-2)^{\lambda+\frac{1}{2}\mu-t_z'}\,(\lambda+\frac{1}{2}\mu-K+t_z')!\,(\lambda+\frac{1}{2}\mu-K'+t_z')!}{(\lambda+\frac{1}{2}\mu+L+t_z'+1)!\,(\lambda+\frac{1}{2}\mu-L+t_z')!}
$$

$$
\times\frac{(\frac{1}{2}\mu+t_z')!}{(t_z'-\frac{1}{2}K)!\,(t_z'-\frac{1}{2}K')!\,(\frac{1}{2}\mu-t_z')!}
$$

$$
\times{}_3F_2\left(\begin{array}{c}-\lambda-\frac{1}{2}\mu-L-t_z'-1,\,-\lambda-\frac{1}{2}\mu+L-t_z',\,-\lambda-\frac{1}{2}\mu+t_z'\\-\lambda-\frac{1}{2}\mu+K-t_z',\,-\lambda-\frac{1}{2}\mu+K'-t_z'\end{array}\bigg|\frac{1}{2}\right). \tag{32}
$$

It should be noted that for conjugate basis $|(\lambda\mu)(K)LM\rangle_{\mathcal{L}}$ at $\mu>\lambda$ overlap $A_{\mathcal{L}}^{\lambda\mu}(K'LK) = (-1)^{\lambda-1/2(K+K')}A_{\mathcal{L}}^{\mu\lambda}(K'LK)$ from Eq. (80) of Ref. [27]. It should

Table 5. Computation of $\boldsymbol{A}$ matrix for $\lambda = 125$ and $L = 120$ (precision $= 300$)

μ	Asherova (30)	Tolstoy1 (31)	Tolstoy2 (32)
40	2.174 s	3.06 s	0.81 s
60	10.81 s	13.31 s	2.19 s
80	39.78 s	39.80 s	5.38 s
100	1.70 min	1.57 min	11.48 s
120	3.40 min	3.22 min	21.53 s

be stressed that all these formulas for overlap integrals give the same numerical values but their efficiency is quite different. An example of the orthonormalization of the E basis calculated with non-normalized overlap integrals for $\mu = 6$, $\lambda = 10$ and $L = 6$ (here $K_{\min} = 0$, $K_{\max} = 6$, $\Delta K = 2$) is shown below

$$\mathcal{U}^{\lambda\mu}(L) = \begin{pmatrix} \frac{221059}{572033} & -\frac{2405}{52003\sqrt{11}} & \frac{67}{52003}\sqrt{\frac{3}{11}} & -\frac{1}{7429}\sqrt{\frac{15}{77}} \\ -\frac{2405}{52003\sqrt{11}} & \frac{317467}{1716099} & -\frac{2963}{81719\sqrt{3}} & \frac{181}{81719}\sqrt{\frac{15}{7}} \\ \frac{67}{52003}\sqrt{\frac{3}{11}} & -\frac{2963}{81719\sqrt{3}} & \frac{204329}{1716099} & -\frac{4129}{81719}\sqrt{\frac{5}{7}} \\ -\frac{1}{7429}\sqrt{\frac{15}{77}} & \frac{181}{81719}\sqrt{\frac{15}{7}} & -\frac{4129}{81719}\sqrt{\frac{5}{7}} & \frac{16415}{81719} \end{pmatrix},$$

$$\mathcal{A}^{\lambda\mu}(L) = \begin{pmatrix} -\frac{5}{64}\sqrt{\frac{38687}{91}} & -\frac{11121}{160\sqrt{320047}} & -\frac{1353}{320}\sqrt{\frac{3}{320047}} & -\frac{11}{32}\sqrt{\frac{3}{228605}} \\ 0 & -\frac{1}{80}\sqrt{\frac{124210581}{3517}} & -\frac{15789}{20}\sqrt{\frac{209}{696728251}} & -\frac{9333}{16}\sqrt{\frac{209}{24385488785}} \\ 0 & 0 & -\frac{7}{2}\sqrt{\frac{294063}{396206}} & -\frac{4129}{14}\sqrt{\frac{627}{132729010}} \\ 0 & 0 & 0 & \frac{1}{7}\sqrt{\frac{81719}{335}} \end{pmatrix},$$

where $\mathcal{U}^{\lambda\mu}(L)$ is the matrix of the overlap integrals $\mathcal{U}^{(\lambda\mu)}(K'LK)$.

A comparison of CPU time of computation of the matrix $\boldsymbol{A}$ with overlaps in the E basis given by Eqs. (30), (31) and (32) is presented in Table 5.

4.1 Calculations of $X^{(3)}$ in Non-orthogonal E Basis

The normalized E basis calculated with Asherova and Tolstoy formulas (30), (31) and (32) ($\lambda \geq \mu$, $\lambda \leq \mu$) are given by:

$$U^{(\lambda\mu)}(KLK') = \left\langle \begin{matrix} (\lambda,\mu)_E \\ K,L,L \end{matrix} \middle| \begin{matrix} (\lambda,\mu)_E \\ K',L,L \end{matrix} \right\rangle = \frac{1}{u(LK)u(LK')}\mathcal{U}^{(\lambda\mu)}(KLK'), \quad (33)$$

where $u^2(LK) = \mathcal{U}^{(\lambda\mu)}(KLK)$. An expansion of eigenvectors of the $X^{(3)}(\mu\lambda L)$ matrix in terms of the non-orthogonal E basis is

$$\left| \begin{matrix} (\lambda,\mu)_E \\ x,L,L \end{matrix} \right\rangle = \sum_{K=K_{\min}}^{K_{\max}} C_{xK} \left| \begin{matrix} (\lambda,\mu)_E \\ K,L,L \end{matrix} \right\rangle. \quad (34)$$

Here x denotes the eigenvalues of the $X^{(3)}(\lambda\mu L)$ matrix. *It should be stressed that eigenvalues of the matrix $X^{(3)}$ have the same numerical values independently of a basis.*

The eigenvalues and eigenvectors of the $\boldsymbol{X}^{(3)}(\lambda\mu L)$ matrix can be obtained by solving the appropriate generalized eigenvalue problem:

$$\sum_{K=K_{\min}}^{K_{\max}} C_{xK} \left(\left\langle \begin{matrix} (\lambda\mu)_E \\ KLL \end{matrix} \middle| X^{(3)} \middle| \begin{matrix} (\lambda\mu)_E \\ K'L'L \end{matrix} \right\rangle - x \left\langle \begin{matrix} (\lambda,\mu)_E \\ K,L,L \end{matrix} \middle| \begin{matrix} (\lambda,\mu)_E \\ K',L,L \end{matrix} \right\rangle \right) = 0. \quad (35)$$

Matrix elements of the matrix $\boldsymbol{X}^{(3)}(\lambda\mu L)$ in the non-orthogonal E basis read as

$$\left\langle \begin{matrix} (\lambda\mu)_E \\ KLL \end{matrix} \middle| X^{(3)} \middle| \begin{matrix} (\lambda\mu)_E \\ K'L'L \end{matrix} \right\rangle$$
$$= -\frac{1}{2}\left(1 + \frac{1}{3}(2\lambda + \mu)\right)(L(L+1) - 3K^2)\left\langle \begin{matrix} (\lambda,\mu)_E \\ K,L,L \end{matrix} \middle| \begin{matrix} (\lambda,\mu)_E \\ K',L,L \end{matrix} \right\rangle$$
$$-\frac{1}{4}\sqrt{(\mu+K)(\mu-K+2)(L+K)(L-K+1)(L+K-1)(L-K+2)}$$
$$\times \frac{u(LK-2)}{u(LK)}\left\langle \begin{matrix} (\lambda,\mu)_E \\ K-2,L,L \end{matrix} \middle| \begin{matrix} (\lambda,\mu)_E \\ K',L,L \end{matrix} \right\rangle \qquad (36)$$
$$-\frac{1}{4}\sqrt{(\mu-K)(\mu+K+2)(L-K)(L+K+1)(L-K-1)(L+K+2)}$$
$$\times \frac{u(LK+2)}{u(LK)}\left\langle \begin{matrix} (\lambda,\mu)_E \\ K+2,L,L \end{matrix} \middle| \begin{matrix} (\lambda,\mu)_E \\ K',L,L \end{matrix} \right\rangle.$$

Below we present the solution of the generalized eigenvalue problem for the matrix $\boldsymbol{X}^{(3)} = \left([\boldsymbol{L}^{(1)}\otimes\boldsymbol{L}^{(1)}]^{(2)}\cdot\boldsymbol{Q}^{(2)}\right)$ with $\mu = 6$, $\lambda = 10$ and $L = 6$ in the non-orthogonal E basis. The matrix $\boldsymbol{X}^{(3)}(\lambda\mu L)$ defined by Eq. (36) in the non-orthogonal E basis reads:

$$\boldsymbol{X}^{(3)}(\lambda\mu L) = \begin{pmatrix} 319.7180436 & -30.40475773 & 2.942648053 & -0.2996013406 \\ -30.40475773 & 36.37991665 & -45.86740146 & 12.00462530 \\ 2.942648053 & -45.86740146 & -110.4027084 & -53.26181618 \\ -0.2996013406 & 12.00462530 & -53.26181618 & -172.8154127 \end{pmatrix}.$$

The matrix $\boldsymbol{U}^{\mu\lambda}(L)$ of the normalized overlap integrals defined by Eqs. (33) of the non-orthogonal E basis is the following:

$$U^{\lambda\mu}(L) = \begin{pmatrix} 1.000000000 & -0.05215172237 & 0.003136702244 & -0.0002132393883 \\ -0.05215172237 & 1.000000000 & -0.1410509515 & 0.01681957796 \\ 0.003136702244 & -0.1410509515 & 1.000000000 & -0.2761245773 \\ -0.0002132393883 & 0.01681957796 & -0.2761245773 & 1.000000000 \end{pmatrix}. \quad (37)$$

Numerical eigenvalues $x \equiv x^{\lambda\mu}(L)$ of the matrix $\boldsymbol{X}^{(3)}(\lambda\mu L)$ obtained by solving the generalized eigenvalue problem defined by Eq. (35) coincide with those from (23). The same eigenvalues will be obtained for the matrix $\boldsymbol{X}^{(3)}(\lambda\mu L)$ calculated not by normalized overlap integrals $U^{(\lambda\mu)}(KLK')$ Eq. (33), but by non-normalized overlap integrals Eqs. (30), (31), (32) as well. Of course the entries of $\boldsymbol{X}^{(3)}(\lambda\mu L)$ and $\boldsymbol{U}^{\lambda\mu}(L)$ are completely different in this case.

Table 6. Computation of the matrix $X^{(3)}$ in the non-orthogonal E basis Eq. (36) for $\lambda = 125$ and $L = 120$ (precision $= 300$)

μ	Asherova (30)	Tolstoy1 (31)	Tolstoy2 (32)
40	1.17 min	1.5 min	24.84 s
60	6.13 min	7.05 min	1.43 min
80	20.05 min	22.43 min	4.08 min
100	53.71 min	53.97 min	8.69 min
120	1.92 h	1.82 h	14.27 min

Remark 4. For checking our results the matrix $X^{(3)}(\lambda\mu L)$ was also calculated by using Eqs. (129)–(131) of Tolstoy paper [27]. The eigenvalues of this matrix are equal to the eigenvalues of the $X^{(3)}(\mu\lambda L)$ matrix calculated by Eq. (36).

The eigenvectors C of eigenvalue problem $X^{(3)}C - UCx = 0$ have the form

$$(C_1, ..., C_4) = \begin{pmatrix} 0.998827 & -0.100335 & -0.029577 & -0.006434 \\ -0.048196 & -0.953926 & -0.414649 & -0.134402 \\ 0.004503 & 0.265111 & -0.718457 & -0.643440 \\ -0.000793 & -0.098353 & 0.557682 & -0.753576 \end{pmatrix}.$$

Comparison of the CPU time for computing the matrix $X^{(3)}$ in the non-orthogonal E basis with overlaps Eqs. (30), (31), (32) is presented in Table 6.

4.2   Calculations of $X^{(3)}$ in Orthogonal E Basis

Now we solve the same eigenvalue problem in the orthogonal basis $|\phi\rangle = |u\rangle A^T$. In the orthogonal basis, Eqs. (35) are expressed in terms of the operator $X^{(3)}$ calculated in the non-orthogonal basis in the following form

$$AX^{(3)}A^T B - Bx = 0. \tag{38}$$

The expression for labeling operator $\bar{X}^{(3)}$ in the orthonormal E basis reads as

$$\bar{X}^{(3)} = AX^{(3)}A^T. \tag{39}$$

For the example with $\mu = 6$, $\lambda = 10$ and $L = 6$ the matrix A in the E basis is

$$A = \begin{pmatrix} -1.001371945 & -0.05284392928 & -0.004466788619 & -0.0005581094723 \\ 0 & -1.010371879 & -0.1491969336 & -0.02420291165 \\ 0 & 0 & -1.040450798 & -0.2872940369 \\ 0 & 0 & 0 & 1.000000000 \end{pmatrix}. \tag{40}$$

Here the tridiagonal matrix $\bar{X}^{(3)}$ Eq. (39) in the orthogonal basis reads as

$$\bar{X}^{(3)} = \begin{pmatrix} 317.482 & -29.02009 & -2.1 \times 10(-10) & -9.7 \times 10(-11) \\ -29.02009 & 20.9536 & -66.6970 & -3.6 \times 10(-9) \\ -2.1 \times 10(-10) & -66.697 & -165.620 & 105.065 \\ -9.7 \times 10(-11) & -3.6 \times 10(-9) & 105.0651 & -172.815 \end{pmatrix}. \tag{41}$$

The eigenvalues of the matrix $\bar{X}^{(3)}$ are the same ones as in (23) and the eigenvectors normalized by the scalar product $B^T B = I$ have the following form

$$(B_1, ..., B_4) = \begin{pmatrix} 0.994918 & -0.096471 & -0.027807 & -0.007620 \\ -0.099615 & -0.903976 & -0.384899 & -0.157341 \\ 0.014330 & 0.375369 & -0.594764 & -0.710737 \\ 0.003052 & 0.180604 & -0.705219 & 0.685593 \end{pmatrix}. \tag{42}$$

There is a relation between eigenvector matrices B and C:

$$B = D\mathcal{D}\mathcal{B}. \tag{43}$$

Here $D = (A^T)^{-1}C$, $\mathcal{D}$ is the diagonal matrix with diagonal elements equal to the reciprocals of diagonal elements of the matrix D and $\mathcal{B}$ is a diagonal matrix with diagonal elements of the matrix B on its diagonal.

The CPU times versus parameter μ in the interval $\mu = 10 \ldots 120$ for calculations of the matrix $\bar{X}^{(3)}$ in the orthonormal Elliott basis with $\lambda = 125$ and $L = 120$ using different computation procedures with the overlaps given by Eqs. (30), (31) and (32) are presented in Fig. 3b. The computations were performed with 300-digit precision.

Remark 5. In the limit of large λ or μ, the overlap in the Elliot basis tends to a diagonal matrix. In this limit, the matrix of the operator $X^{(3)}$ and its eigenvalues and eigenvectors tend to those known for an asymmetric top [4, 21, 28].

5   Results and Conclusions

In this paper we have developed the symbolic-numeric and fast computation procedures for calculation of the matrix $X^{(3)}(\lambda\mu L)$ in the Gel'fand–Tseitlin (G-T), Bargmann–Moshinsky (B-M) and Elliott (E) bases that could be applied to a very large quantum numbers.

The advantages of the G-T basis from the computational point of view are: its original orthonormality, the simplicity of expressions for matrix elements of physically significant operators, and a possibility to construct their matrices with symbolic calculations. However, one needs to take into account that required calculations of the matrix $X^{(3)}(\lambda\mu L)$ for all L have to be performed in one run that destroys fast performance. This disadvantage of the G-T basis is related to a necessity to perform the calculations for all L at the same time. So, the dimension of matrices is significantly larger than in the B-M and E bases. For example, even if in the B-M and E bases, the dimension of the matrix $X^{(3)}(\lambda\mu L)$ for some particular L is one, the dimension of the corresponding eigenvector column G-T basis is the sum of dimensions of the matrices $X^{(3)}(\lambda\mu L)$ for all L. In the considered example with $\mu = 6$ and $\lambda = 10$, this dimension is 39. For comparison, in this example, the maximum possible dimension of the matrix $X^{(3)}(\lambda\mu L)$ in the B-M and E bases is only 4. It should be noted that due to the simplicity of the matrix elements of the generators E_{ij} (due to the absence of factorials in the expressions for the GT basis) calculated within the G-T vectors the machine precision of Mathematica (18 decimal digits of precision (DDP)) is sufficient for large scale numerical calculations. This computational accuracy ensures absolute accuracy of each matrix element of the test result not less than 10^{-12}. This advantage of G-T basis greatly increase the number of various computation systems that could be applied for this kind of calculations.

The notable advantages of the B-M basis are its inherent specification by angular momentum L and integer values of overlap integrals. The disadvantages of the B-M basis are its non-orthogonality and complicated formula for calculating the overlap integrals. In the present paper, we have elaborated new efficient symbolic-numeric algorithms for the calculation of the matrix $\boldsymbol{X}^{(3)}(\lambda\mu L)$ in the B-M basis. The distinct advantage of these algorithms is that they do not involve any square root operation on the expressions coming from the previous steps for the computation of the orthonormalization coefficients for this basis. This makes the proposed method very suitable for symbolic calculations and calculations with an arbitrary precision as well. The effectiveness of the developed algorithms derived by graphical methods is demonstrated by their 100–1000 times superiority in CPU time over computations using the direct summation in the $\boldsymbol{X}^{(3)}(\lambda\mu L)$ definition formula.

The E basis is well known for its widespread use in nuclear calculations. The disadvantages of the E basis are its non-orthogonality, complicated formula for the calculation of overlap integrals and root rational fraction form of some their values. The calculation of the matrix $\boldsymbol{X}^{(3)}(\lambda\mu L)$ in the E basis was implemented by the formulas of Asherova (30) and Tolstoy: (31) and (32). The fastest formula for the overlap integrals is the Tolstoy formula (32). It significantly outperforms all other formulas for the overlap integrals in both the E as well as B-M basis. This is due to the fact of transferring of the large part of computations, in this case, to very efficient internal Wolfram Mathematica hypergeometric functions. However, since the overlap integrals in the E basis have the root rational fraction form the scale of exact calculations in this basis is rather limited comparing with the computations in the B-M basis. For example, for considered cases of $\lambda = 125$ and $L = 120$, Mathematica is able to perform exact computations only up to $\mu = 9$. At the same time, since in the B-M basis, the overlap integrals are just integer numbers, there are no restrictions for exact calculations in this basis. Nevertheless in the case of numerical computations, the calculations in the E basis compete with analogous calculations in the B-M basis.

In the present paper, we have elaborated new efficient symbolic-numeric algorithms and procedures implemented in the Wolfram Mathematica for computing the matrix $\boldsymbol{X}^{(3)}(\lambda\mu L)$ in the G-T, B-M and E bases. The developed code XGTBME solves the non-canonical group chain of SU(3)⊃SO(3)⊃ SO(2) labeling problem for large-scale calculations in these bases. The program XGTBME is already prepared and will be published in JINR Program Library.

Acknowledgments. Čestmir Burdik thanks Prof. V.N. Tolstoy for fruitful discussion. The work was partially supported by the RFBR and MECSS, project number 20-51-44001, the Bogoliubov–Infeld program, the Blochintsev–Votruba program, by the RUDN University Strategic Academic Leadership Program and grant of Plenipotentiary of the Republic of Kazakhstan in JINR.

References

1. Akiyama, Y., Draayer, J.P.: A user's guide to Fortran programs for Wigner and Racah coefficients of SU$_3$. Comput. Phys. Commun. **5**, 405–415 (1973)
2. Alisauskas, S., Raychev, P., Roussev, R.: Analytical form of the orthonormal basis of the decomposition $SU(3) \supset O(3) \supset O(2)$ for some (λ, μ) multiplets. J. Phys. G: Nucl. Phys. **7**, 1213–1226 (1981)
3. Asherova, R.M., Smirnov, Y.F.: New expansions of the projecting operator in Elliot's SU$_3$ scheme. Nucl. Phys. A **144**, 116–128 (1970)
4. Asherova, R.M., Smirnov, Y.F.: On asymptotic properties of a quantum number Ω in a system with SU(3) symmetry. Reports Math. Phys. **4**, 83–95 (1973)
5. Bargmann, V., Moshinsky, M.: Group theory of harmonic oscillators (I). Nucl. Phys. **18**, 697–712 (1960)
6. Bargmann, V., Moshinsky, M.: Group theory of harmonic oscillators (II). Nucl. Phys. **23**, 177–199 (1961)
7. Deveikis, A., Gusev, A.A., Gerdt, V.P., Vinitsky, S.I., Góźdź, A., Pędrak, A.: Symbolic algorithm for generating the orthonormal Bargmann–Moshinsky basis for SU(3) group. In: Gerdt, V.P., Koepf, W., Seiler, W.M., Vorozhtsov, E.V. (eds.) CASC 2018. LNCS, vol. 11077, pp. 131–145. Springer, Cham (2018). https://doi.org/10.1007/978-3-319-99639-4_9
8. Deveikis, A., et al.: Symbolic-numeric algorithm for computing orthonormal basis of O(5) × SU(1,1) group. In: Boulier, F., England, M., Sadykov, T.M., Vorozhtsov, E.V. (eds.) CASC 2020. LNCS, vol. 12291, pp. 206–227. Springer, Cham (2020). https://doi.org/10.1007/978-3-030-60026-6_12
9. Deveikis, A., et al.: On calculation of quadrupole operator in orthogonal Bargmann-Moshinsky basis of SU(3) group. J. Phys. Conf. Ser. **1416**, 012010 (2019)
10. Draayer, J.P., Pursey, D.L., Williams, S.A.: Elliott angular momentum states projected from the Gel'fand U(3) Basis. Nuclear Phys. A **ll9**, 577–590 (1968)
11. Draayer, J.P., Williams, S.A.: Coupling coefficients and matrix elements of arbitrary tensors in the Elliott projected angular momentum basis. Nucl. Phys. A **129**, 647–665 (1969)
12. Draayer, J.P.: Akiyama, Y: Wigner and Racah coefficients for SU$_3$. J. Math. Phys. **14**, 1904–1912 (1973)
13. Bahri, C., Rowe, D.J., Draayer, J.P.: Programs for generating Clebsch-Gordan coefficients of $SU(3)$ in $SU(2)$ and $SO(3)$ bases. Comput. Phys. Commun. **159**, 121–143 (2004)
14. Elliott, J.P.: Collective motion in the nuclear shell model I. Classification schemes for states of mixed configurations. Proc. R. Soc. London **245**, 128–145 (1958)
15. Elliott, J.P.: Collective motion in the nuclear shell model II. The introduction of intrinsic wave-functions. Proc. R. Soc. London **245**, 568–581 (1958)
16. Gel'fand, I.M., Tseitlin, M.L.: Finite-dimensional representations of the group of unimodular matrices. Dokl. Akad. Nauk SSSR (N.S.) **71**, 825–828 (1950). (in Russian)

17. Harvey, M.: The nuclear SU_3 model. In: Baranger, M., Vogt, E. (eds.) Advances in Nuclear Physics, vol. 1, pp. 67–182. Springer, Boston (1968). https://doi.org/10.1007/978-1-4757-0103-6_2
18. Jucys, A., Bandzaitis, A.: Theory of angular momentum in quantum mechanics. Mokslas, Vilnius (1997)
19. Judd, B.R., Miller, W., Patera, J., Winternitz, P.: Complete sets of commuting operators and O(3) scalars in the enveloping algebra of SU(3). J. Math. Phys. **15**, 1787–1799 (1974)
20. Kota, V.K.B.: SU(3) Symmetry in Atomic Nuclei. Springer, Singapore (2020). https://doi.org/10.1007/978-981-15-3603-8
21. Landau, L.D., Lifshitz, E.M.: Quantum Mechanics: Non-relativistic Theory. Pergamon press, N.Y. (1977)
22. MathWorld - A Wolfram Web Resource. http://mathworld.wolfram.com
23. McKay, W., Patera, J., Sharp, R.T.: Eigenstates and eigenvalues of labelling operators for O(3) bases of U(3) representations. Comput. Phys. Commun. **10**, 1–10 (1975)
24. Moshinsky, M., Patera, J., Sharp, R.T., Winternitz, P.: Everything you always wanted to know about SU(3) ⊃ O(3). Ann. Phys. **95**, 139–169 (1975). F. Gursey (ed.) Gordon and Breach, New York (1964)
25. Pan, F., Yuan, S., Launey, K.D., Draayer, J.P.: A new procedure for constructing basis vectors of $SU(3) \supset SO(3)$. Nucl. Phys. A **743**, 70–99 (2016)
26. Patera, J.: The Nagel-Moshinsky operators for $U(p,1) \supset U(P)$. J. Math. Phys. **14**, 279–284 (1973)
27. Tolstoy, V.N.: SU(3) Symmetry for orbital angular momentum and method of extremal projection operators. Phys. Atomic Nuclei **69**(6), 1058–1084 (2006)
28. Ui, H.: Quantum mechanical rigid rotator with an arbitrary deformation. I. Progr. Theor. Phys. **44**(1), 153–171 (1970)
29. Varshalovitch, D.A., Moskalev, A.N., Hersonsky, V.K.: Quantum Theory of Angular Momentum. Nauka, Leningrad (1975). (also World Scientific, Singapore (1988))
30. Vergados, J.D.: SU (3)⊃ R (3) Wigner coefficients in the 2s-1d shell. Nucl. Phys. A **111**, 681–754 (1968)
31. Vinitsky, S., et al.: On generation of the Bargmann-Moshinsky basis of SU(3) group. J. Phys. Conf. Ser. **1194**, 012109 (2019)

Improved Supersingularity Testing of Elliptic Curves Using Legendre Form

Yuji Hashimoto[1,2(✉)] and Koji Nuida[2,3]

[1] Graduate School of Information Science and Technology, The University of Tokyo, 7-3-1 Hongo, Bunkyo-ku, Tokyo 113-8654, Japan
hashimoto-yuji715ewwwd@g.ecc.u-tokyo.ac.jp
[2] National Institute of Advanced Industrial Science and Technology, 2-3-26 Aomi, Koto-ku, Tokyo 135-0064, Japan
nuida@imi.kyushu-u.ac.jp
[3] Institute of Mathematics for Industry (IMI), Kyushu University, 744 Motooka, Nishi-ku, Fukuoka 819-0395, Japan

Abstract. There are two types of elliptic curves, ordinary elliptic curves and supersingular elliptic curves. In 2012, Sutherland proposed an efficient and almost deterministic algorithm for determining whether a given curve is ordinary or supersingular. Sutherland's algorithm is based on sequences of isogenies started from the input curve, and computation of each isogeny requires square root computations, which is the dominant cost of the algorithm. In this paper, we reduce this dominant cost of Sutherland's algorithm to approximately a half of the original. In contrast to Sutherland's algorithm using j-invariants and modular polynomials, our proposed algorithm is based on Legendre form of elliptic curves, which simplifies the expression of each isogeny. Moreover, by carefully selecting the type of isogenies to be computed, we succeeded in gathering square root computations at two consecutive steps of Sutherland's algorithm into just a single fourth root computation (with experimentally almost the same cost as a single square root computation). The results of our experiments using Magma are supporting our argument; for cases of characteristic p of 768-bit to 1024-bit lengths, our algorithm runs 43.6% to 55.7% faster than Sutherland's algorithm.

Keywords: Isogenies · Supersingular elliptic curves · Isogeny graphs · Legendre form

1 Introduction

There are two types of elliptic curves, ordinary elliptic curves and supersingular elliptic curves. Several supersingularity testing algorithms to determine whether a given curve is ordinary or supersingular have been proposed (see Sect. 1.3). Among them, Sutherland's algorithm [18] is both efficient (of order $\tilde{O}((\log_2 p)^3)$ where p is the finite characteristic of the coefficient field) and almost deterministic (i.e., it becomes fully deterministic once a quadratic non-residue and a cubic

© Springer Nature Switzerland AG 2021
F. Boulier et al. (Eds.): CASC 2021, LNCS 12865, pp. 121–135, 2021.
https://doi.org/10.1007/978-3-030-85165-1_8

non-residue over $\mathbb{F}_{p^2}$ are given as auxiliary inputs). To the best of our knowledge, this is the fastest algorithm in the literature achieving the two properties simultaneously.

Besides purely mathematical interests, supersingularity testing algorithms also have potential importance in cryptography. Currently, there are elliptic curve cryptosystems [10,12] and isogeny-based cryptosystems [3,6] as typical examples of cryptosystems using elliptic curves. Usually, the former uses ordinary curves, while the latter uses supersingular curves. For parameter settings in isogeny-based cryptosystems to select supersingular curves, recently a method to generate a supersingular curve in a way that nobody can know explicitly how the curve is generated is proposed as an application of secure multiparty computation [14]. In such a case, unless the protocol implementation is fully trustable, a supersingularity testing algorithm is needed for a user to be sure that the generated curve is indeed supersingular. An efficient supersingularity testing algorithm will be worthy in real-time use of such cryptographic applications.

1.1   Supersingularity Testing Algorithms Based on Isogeny Graphs

The 2-isogeny graph is a graph where the vertices consist of isomorphism classes of elliptic curves and the edges correspond to isogenies of degree 2. In 2012, Sutherland proposed an efficient supersingularity testing algorithm based on isogeny graphs [18]. Isogeny graphs based on ordinary elliptic curves have a graph structure called volcano graph [7,11,19] and isogeny graphs based on supersingular elliptic curves have a graph structure called Ramanujan graph [4,15]. Sutherland's algorithm can be implemented as a deterministic algorithm when quadratic and cubic non-residues over $\mathbb{F}_{p^2}$ are given as auxiliary inputs. This algorithm draws a graph by iteratively performing isogeny computations using a modular polynomial, and determines supersingularity based on whether the isogeny graph is a volcano graph or a Ramanujan graph. When the input curve is supersingular, Sutherland's algorithm must run $O(n)$ square root computations over $\mathbb{F}_{p^2}$ where $n = \log_2 p$. The computational complexity of square root computation over $\mathbb{F}_{p^2}$ is $O(n^2(\log_2 n)^2)$. Thus, the total computational complexity of Sutherland's algorithm is $O(n^3(\log_2 n)^2)$. For the above reasons, the square root computation over $\mathbb{F}_{p^2}$ is dominant in Sutherland's algorithm. Therefore, reducing the number of square root computations is important for improving the efficiency of this supersingularity testing algorithm. For related work, Hashimoto and Takashima proposed an improved supersingularity testing algorithm [9] by applying an efficient computation technique in 2-isogeny sequence computation (proposed by Yoshida and Takashima [20]) to Sutherland's algorithm. In iterated computation step dominating the computational time, Sutherland's algorithm requires 9 multiplications, 3 square root computations, and 15 constant multiplications, whereas Hashimoto–Takashima algorithm requires 3 multiplications, 3 square root computations, and 0 constant multiplication.

1.2   Contributions

In this paper, we propose a supersingularity testing algorithm that is more efficient than Sutherland's algorithm. In detail, for $n = \log_2 p$, in $\lfloor n \rfloor + 1$ iterated isogeny computation steps dominating the computational time, Sutherland's algorithm requires 3 square root computations on $\mathbb{F}_{p^2}$ per step whereas our proposed algorithm requires $3/2$ fourth root computations on $\mathbb{F}_{p^2}$ per step. Our proposed algorithm can be computed more efficiently than Sutherland's algorithm since the computational costs of square root and fourth root computations are almost equal (see our experimental result in Sect. 9). We note that our proposed algorithm is applicable for any prime $p \geq 5$.

The computational cost of our proposed algorithm depends on the isogeny computations between Legendre form. In detail, whereas Sutherland's algorithm uses the j-invariant of the elliptic curve as a tool for determining supersingularity, our proposed algorithm makes it possible to determine supersingularity by iteratively computing the x-coordinate λ of a 2-torsion point of the Legendre form for each curve. Therefore, it is important to efficiently obtain the values of λ. In order to improve the efficiency, we wanted to utilize the simplest kind of isogenies at every step, which would enable us to efficiently gather the sequential isogeny computations. However, our argument in Sect. 4 shows that the simplest known isogeny in the literature cannot be used consecutively, as it causes backtracking on the graph. For avoiding the obstacle, we prove a key result named λ-switching theorem (see Sect. 5), which is about efficient composition of the original isogeny with some isomorphism to obtain a new isogeny. This enabled us to use a relatively simple isogeny in every iterative step and, therefore, to improve the average cost for the iterative steps. See Sect. 7 for the description of our proposed algorithm. We also give theoretical and experimental comparisons with Sutherland's algorithm in Sects. 8 and 9, respectively. The results of our experiments are supporting our theoretical argument; for cases of characteristic p of 768-bit to 1024-bit lengths, our algorithm runs 43.6% to 55.7% faster than Sutherland's algorithm.

1.3   Related Work

The requirement that an elliptic curve E over a finite field $\mathbb{F}_q$ of characteristic p is supersingular is equivalent to the condition $\sharp E(\mathbb{F}_q) \equiv 1 \bmod p$. Then, practically, we can verify the condition by checking that the order of a random point $P \in E(\mathbb{F}_q)$ is given by $p + 1$ or $p - 1$. (Refer to [5,18] for details.) Since the check consists of scalar multiplications, the computational complexity is $\tilde{O}(n^2)$. Here, since it can erroneously misidentify ordinary curves (as supersingular one) like the Miller–Rabin primality testing, we should use multiple random points P for reducing the error probability [18]. However, the improvement cannot lead to a deterministic algorithm by using a polynomial number of random points similarly to the Miller–Rabin. To obtain polynomial time deterministic algorithms, we can use the Schoof algorithm, i.e., compute orders $\sharp E(\mathbb{F}_q)$, and then determine the supersingularity, whose cost is $O(n^5)$. Moreover, by using mod ℓ decomposition properties of modular polynomials (for $\ell \neq p$) that is the core of the Schoof–Elkies–Atkin (SEA) algorithm, we can reduce the complexity to $O(n^4)$ [18]. However, those algorithms are less efficient than the Sutherland's algorithm with complexity $\tilde{O}(n^3)$.

2 Preliminaries

In this section, we explain some properties of elliptic curves in Weierstrass form and Legendre form. By using these properties, we improve supersingularity testing algorithm. Hereafter, let p be a prime with $p \geq 5$. $\mathbb{F}_q$ denotes a finite field of characteristic p and $\bar{\mathbb{F}}_p$ denotes an algebraic closure of $\mathbb{F}_q$. For any $\alpha \in \mathbb{F}_q$, let $\sqrt{\alpha}$ and $\sqrt[4]{\alpha}$ denote a square root and a fourth root of α (possibly in a larger extension field), respectively. For simplicity, an expression like $\sqrt{A^2}$ will be regarded as A instead of $-A$. A similar remark also applies to $\sqrt[4]{A}$.

2.1 Weierstrass Curves

In this subsection, we explain elliptic curves (see [16, Chapter 3] for details). Every elliptic curve E over $\mathbb{F}_q$ is given by the following short Weierstrass form such that $4A^3 + 27B^2 \neq 0$:

$$E : y^2 = x^3 + Ax + B \ (A, B \in \mathbb{F}_q).$$

$\mathcal{O}_E$ denotes the point at infinity of E. There exists an invariant of elliptic curves. This invariant is called j-invariant and the j-invariant in Weierstrass form is given as $j(A, B) = 1728 \frac{4A^3}{4A^3 + 27B^2}$. For two elliptic curves over $\mathbb{F}_q$, their j-invariants are equal if and only if these curves are isomorphic over $\bar{\mathbb{F}}_p$. The $\mathbb{F}_q$-rational points of E over $\mathbb{F}_q$ are denoted by

$$E(\mathbb{F}_q) = \{(x, y) \in \mathbb{F}_q \mid y^2 = x^3 + Ax + B\} \cup \{\mathcal{O}_E\}.$$

Let ℓ be a prime with $\ell \neq p$. The group of ℓ-torsion points of an elliptic curve E over $\mathbb{F}_q$ is defined by

$$E[\ell] = \{P \in E(\bar{\mathbb{F}}_p) \mid \ell P = \mathcal{O}_E\}.$$

It holds that $E[\ell] \cong \mathbb{Z}/\ell\mathbb{Z} \times \mathbb{Z}/\ell\mathbb{Z}$. Then there exist $(\ell^2 - 1)/(\ell - 1) = \ell + 1$ subgroups of order ℓ in $E[\ell]$. $E[p]$ is isomorphic to $\{0\}$ or $\mathbb{Z}/p\mathbb{Z}$. An elliptic curve E over $\mathbb{F}_q$ is called supersingular if $E[p] \cong \{0\}$ and ordinary if $E[p] \cong \mathbb{Z}/p\mathbb{Z}$.

2.2 Legendre Form

In this subsection, we explain basic concepts of Legendre form of elliptic curves and how to transform from Weierstrass form to Legendre form (see [2,16] for the details). If $p \neq 2$, any elliptic curve can be transformed to Legendre form.

Proposition 1 ([16, Section 3.1]). *Every elliptic curve over $\bar{\mathbb{F}}_p$ is isomorphic to an elliptic curve of Legendre form.*

$$E_{(-(\lambda+1),\lambda)} : \quad y^2 = x(x-1)(x-\lambda) \ (\lambda \in \bar{\mathbb{F}}_p, \lambda \neq 0, 1)$$

The j-invariant of $E_{(-(\lambda+1),\lambda)}$ is defined by

$$j(E_{(-(\lambda+1),\lambda)}) = \frac{256 \left(\lambda^2 - \lambda + 1\right)^3}{\lambda^2(\lambda-1)^2}.$$

We call λ Legendre parameter of this elliptic curve. Next, we explain how to transform from Weierstrass form to Legendre form.

Proposition 2 ([16, Section 3.1]). *Let the short Weierstrass form of an elliptic curve E be factored as $y^2 = (x - e_1)(x - e_2)(x - e_3)$ (where $e_1, e_2, e_3 \in \bar{\mathbb{F}}_p$ are different from each other). Then, for $\lambda = \frac{e_3 - e_1}{e_2 - e_1}$, E is isomorphic to $E_{(-(\lambda+1),\lambda)}$.*

In the above proposition, by taking into account the order of e_1, e_2, e_3 there exist 6 choices of λ (denoted here by $\hat{\lambda}$):

$$\hat{\lambda} \in [\lambda] = \left\{ \frac{e_3 - e_1}{e_2 - e_1}, \frac{e_2 - e_1}{e_3 - e_1}, \frac{e_3 - e_2}{e_1 - e_2}, \frac{e_1 - e_2}{e_3 - e_2}, \frac{e_1 - e_3}{e_2 - e_3}, \frac{e_2 - e_3}{e_1 - e_3} \right\}$$

$$= \left\{ \lambda, \frac{1}{\lambda}, 1 - \lambda, \frac{1}{1-\lambda}, \frac{\lambda}{\lambda-1}, \frac{\lambda-1}{\lambda} \right\}.$$

The following is a known important property of the Legendre form.

Corollary 1 ([16, Section 3.1]). *Let $E : y^2 = (x - e_1)(x - e_2)(x - e_3)$ $(e_1, e_2, e_3 \in \bar{\mathbb{F}}_p)$ be an elliptic curve. The transformation from E to Legendre form $E_{(-(\lambda+1),\lambda)}$ is unique up to isomorphism without depending on the order of e_1, e_2, e_3.*

The following proposition can be used as a condition for determining whether an elliptic curve is ordinary or supersingular in our proposed algorithm.

Proposition 3 ([1]). *If $E_{(-(\lambda+1),\lambda)}$ is a supersingular elliptic curve then λ is in $\mathbb{F}_{p^2}$.*

2.3 Isogenies

In this subsection, we explain isogenies. For the details, refer to [8]. For two elliptic curves E, E' over $\mathbb{F}_q$, a homomorphism $\phi : E \to E'$ which is given by rational functions (and sends $\mathcal{O}_E$ to $\mathcal{O}_{E'}$) is called an isogeny. In this paper, only non-zero ϕ is considered. Let $\phi^* : \mathbb{F}_q(E') \to \mathbb{F}_q(E)$ be the injective homomorphism between the corresponding function fields induced by ϕ. We call the isogeny ϕ separable when the field extension $\mathbb{F}_q(E)/\phi^*(\mathbb{F}_q(E'))$ is a separable extension. For an integer $\ell \geq 1$ with $p \nmid \ell$, a separable isogeny is called ℓ-isogeny if the kernel $\text{Ker}\,\phi$ is isomorphic to the cyclic group $\mathbb{Z}/\ell\mathbb{Z}$. For an ℓ-isogeny ϕ, there exists an isogeny $\hat{\phi} : E' \to E$ such that $\hat{\phi} \circ \phi = [\ell]$ (ℓ-multiplication on E). This isogeny $\hat{\phi}$ is called the dual isogeny of ϕ.

The following proposition is used in isogeny computations between Legendre curves in the proposed algorithm.

Proposition 4 ([13], [16, **Section 3.4**]). *Let a, b be elements in $\mathbb{F}_q$ such that $b \neq 0, a^2 - 4b \neq 0$. Let $E_{(a,b)}$ be an elliptic curve represented by*

$$E_{(a,b)} : y^2 = x^3 + ax^2 + bx$$

such that 2-torsion points of the elliptic curve $E_{(a,b)}$ are $P_0 = (0,0), P_\gamma = (\gamma, 0), P_\delta = (\delta, 0)$. Then, there exists the following 2-isogeny $\phi_{P_0} : E_{(a,b)} \to E_{(a,b)}/\langle P_0 \rangle$:

$$\phi_{P_0} : (x, y) \mapsto \left(\frac{y^2}{x^2}, \frac{y(b - x^2)}{x^2} \right).$$

$E_{(a,b)}/\langle P_0 \rangle$ is represented as follows:

$$E_{(a,b)}/\langle P_0 \rangle : y^2 = x^3 - 2ax^2 + (a^2 - 4b)x.$$

Let $\phi_{P_\gamma} : E_{(a,b)} \to E_{(a,b)}/\langle P_\gamma \rangle$ and $\phi_{P_\delta} : E_{(a,b)} \to E_{(a,b)}/\langle P_\delta \rangle$ be 2-isogenies. Then, $\phi_{P_\gamma}(E_{(a,b)})$ is equal to $\phi_{P_0}(E_{(2\gamma-\delta, \gamma(\gamma-\delta))})$ and $\phi_{P_\delta}(E_{(a,b)})$ is equal to $\phi_{P_0}(E_{(2\delta-\gamma, \delta(\delta-\gamma))})$.

We examine $\phi_{P_0}(E_{(2\gamma-\delta, \gamma(\gamma-\delta))}), \phi_{P_0}(E_{(2\delta-\gamma, \delta(\delta-\gamma))})$ in detail. The elliptic curve $E_{(2\gamma-\delta, \gamma(\gamma-\delta))}$ is represented by

$$E_{(2\gamma-\delta, \gamma(\gamma-\delta))} : y^2 = x^3 + (2\gamma - \delta)x^2 + \gamma(\gamma - \delta)x.$$

Thus, the elliptic curve $\phi_{P_\gamma}(E_{(a,b)})$ is represented as follows:

$$\phi_{P_\gamma}(E_{(a,b)}) = E_{(a,b)}/\langle P_\gamma \rangle : y^2 = x^3 - 2(2\gamma - \delta)x^2 + ((2\gamma - \delta)^2 - 4\gamma(\gamma - \delta))x.$$

By using $(2\gamma - \delta)^2 - 4\gamma(\gamma - \delta) = \delta^2$, we obtain the following elliptic curve:

$$E_{(a,b)}/\langle P_\gamma \rangle : y^2 = x^3 - 2(2\gamma - \delta)x^2 + \delta^2 x.$$

The right-hand side of $E_{(a,b)}/\langle P_\gamma \rangle$ is factored as follows:

$$x^3 - 2(2\gamma - \delta)x^2 + \delta^2 x = x(x + \delta - 2\gamma + 2\sqrt{\gamma^2 - \gamma\delta})(x + \delta - 2\gamma - 2\sqrt{\gamma^2 - \gamma\delta}).$$

Thus, for $\lambda' = \frac{2\gamma - \delta + 2\sqrt{\gamma^2 - \gamma\delta}}{2\gamma - \delta - 2\sqrt{\gamma^2 - \gamma\delta}}$, $E_{(a,b)}/\langle P_\gamma \rangle$ is isomorphic to $y^2 = x(x-1)(x-\lambda')$.

Let $\gamma = 1, \delta = \lambda$ be the x-coordinates of 2-torsion points in Legendre curve $E_{(-(\lambda+1), \lambda)}$. We can also compute $\phi_{P_1} : E_{(-(\lambda+1), \lambda)} \to E_{(-(\lambda+1), \lambda)}/\langle P_1 \rangle$ as above. Let φ_{P_1} be a map from Legendre parameter of $E_{(-(\lambda+1), \lambda)}$ to Legendre parameter of the Legendre form of $E_{(-(\lambda+1), \lambda)}/\langle P_1 \rangle$. Then,

$$\varphi_{P_1}(\lambda) = \frac{2 - \lambda + 2\sqrt{1 - \lambda}}{2 - \lambda - 2\sqrt{1 - \lambda}} = \left(\frac{\sqrt{1 - \lambda} + 1}{\sqrt{1 - \lambda} - 1} \right)^2.$$

Similarly, let $\gamma = \lambda, \delta = 1$ be the x-coordinates of 2-torsion points in Legendre curve $E_{(-(\lambda+1),\lambda)}$. Let φ_{P_λ} be a map from Legendre parameter of $E_{(-(\lambda+1),\lambda)}$ to Legendre parameter of the Legendre form of $E_{(-(\lambda+1),\lambda)}/\langle P_\lambda \rangle$. Then,

$$\varphi_{P_\lambda}(\lambda) = \frac{2\lambda - 1 + 2\sqrt{\lambda^2 - \lambda}}{2\lambda - 1 - 2\sqrt{\lambda^2 - \lambda}} = \left(\frac{\sqrt{\lambda - 1} + \sqrt{\lambda}}{\sqrt{\lambda - 1} - \sqrt{\lambda}} \right)^2.$$

We also explain the Legendre form of $E_{(-(\lambda+1),\lambda)}/\langle P_0 \rangle$ obtained by using $\phi_{P_0} : E_{(-(\lambda+1),\lambda)} \to E_{(-(\lambda+1),\lambda)}/\langle P_0 \rangle$. $E_{(-(\lambda+1),\lambda)}/\langle P_0 \rangle$ is represented by

$$y^2 = x^3 + 2(\lambda + 1)x^2 + (\lambda - 1)^2 x = x(x + (\sqrt{\lambda} + 1)^2)(x + (\sqrt{\lambda} - 1)^2).$$

Let φ_{P_0} be a map from Legendre parameter of $E_{(-(\lambda+1),\lambda)}$ to the Legendre parameter of the Legendre form of $E_{(-(\lambda+1),\lambda)}/\langle P_0 \rangle$. Then,

$$\varphi_{P_0}(\lambda) = \left(\frac{\sqrt{\lambda} + 1}{\sqrt{\lambda} - 1} \right)^2.$$

We call $\varphi_{P_0}, \varphi_{P_1}, \varphi_{P_\lambda}$ fundamental Legendre map (see Sect. 4 for detail).

3   Isogeny Volcano Graphs of Ordinary Curves

In this section, we explain isogeny graphs. For the details, refer to [19]. For ℓ with $p \nmid \ell$, the ℓ-isogeny graph $G_\ell(\mathbb{F}_{p^2})$ is the graph in which the vertices consist of $\mathbb{F}_{p^2}$-isomorphism classes of elliptic curves over $\mathbb{F}_{p^2}$ and the edges correspond to ℓ-isogenies defined over $\mathbb{F}_{p^2}$. We denote by $G_\ell(E/\mathbb{F}_{p^2})$ the connected component of $G_\ell(\mathbb{F}_{p^2})$ containing an elliptic curve E defined over $\mathbb{F}_{p^2}$. We note that the vertex set of a connected component of $G_\ell(\mathbb{F}_{p^2})$ consists of either ordinary curves only or supersingular curves only. It is known that the connected component $G_\ell(E/\mathbb{F}_{p^2})$ of an isogeny graph at an ordinary elliptic curve E forms an ℓ-volcano graph of height h for some h, defined as follows (see Fig. 1 for an example of volcano graphs).

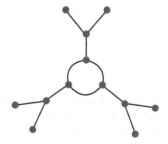

Fig. 1. An example of 2-volcano graphs of height 2

Definition 1 (Def. 1 in [17]). *A connected, undirected, and simple graph V is an ℓ-volcano graph of height h if there exist $h + 1$ disjoint subgraphs $V_0, \ldots, V_h$ (called level graphs) such that any vertex of V belongs to some of $V_0, \ldots, V_h$ and the following conditions hold.*

1. *The degree of vertices except for V_h is $\ell + 1$ and the degree of vertices in V_h is 1 when $h > 0$ and at most 2 when $h = 0$ (the degree in this case depends on the form of V_0).*
2. *The V_0 is one of the following; a cycle (of at least three vertices), a single edge (with two vertices), or a single vertex. Moreover, if $h > 0$, then all the other outgoing edges from a vertex in V_0 are joined to vertices in V_1.*
3. *In the case of $h > i > 0$, each vertex in the level i graph V_i is adjacent to only one vertex in the level $i - 1$ graph V_{i-1} and all the other outgoing edges are joined to vertices in V_{i+1}.*
4. *If $h > 0$, then each vertex of V_h has only one outgoing edge and it is joined to a vertex in V_{h-1}.*

The graph $G_\ell(\mathbb{F}_{p^2})$ has a connected component of all the supersingular curves over $\bar{\mathbb{F}}_p$ [11]. Therefore, other connected components in $G_\ell(\mathbb{F}_{p^2})$ consist of ordinary curves. For the connected components of ordinary curves, Sutherland obtained the following result about the upper bound of the height of the ℓ-volcano.

Proposition 5 ([19]). *Heights of ℓ-volcano connected components of $G_\ell(\mathbb{F}_{p^2})$ are less than or equal to $\log_\ell(2p)$.*

4 Composition of Fundamental Legendre Maps

In this section, we investigate the compositions of fundamental Legendre maps and some properties of those compositions. By using fundamental Legendre maps, it becomes possible to efficiently compute isogenies between Legendre form. However, it is not possible to draw isogeny graphs using only the fundamental Legendre maps without any modification (see Sect. 5 for detail).

We explain $\varphi_{P_0}(\varphi_{P_0}(\lambda)), \varphi_{P_0}(\varphi_{P_1}(\lambda)), \varphi_{P_0}(\varphi_{P_\lambda}(\lambda))$. Those compositions of fundamental Legendre maps are backtracking map. In other words, $\varphi_{P_0}(\varphi_{P_0}(\lambda))$, $\varphi_{P_0}(\varphi_{P_1}(\lambda)), \varphi_{P_0}(\varphi_{P_\lambda}(\lambda)) \in [\lambda]$. In detail,

$$\varphi_{P_0}(\varphi_{P_0}(\lambda)) = \lambda, \varphi_{P_0}(\varphi_{P_1}(\lambda)) = 1 - \lambda, \varphi_{P_0}(\varphi_{P_\lambda}(\lambda)) = \frac{\lambda - 1}{\lambda}.$$

From the point of view of isogeny graphs, after moving through an edge corresponding to any of the three inner fundamental Legendre maps, the outer map φ_{P_0} lets us backtrack the same edge to the original vertex.

Next, we explain the compositions of the other six pairs of two fundamental Legendre maps. In detail,

$$\varphi_{P_1}(\varphi_{P_0}(\lambda)) = \left(\frac{\sqrt[4]{\lambda}+\sqrt{-1}}{\sqrt[4]{\lambda}-\sqrt{-1}}\right)^4, \qquad \varphi_{P_\lambda}(\varphi_{P_0}(\lambda)) = \left(\frac{\sqrt[4]{\lambda}+1}{\sqrt[4]{\lambda}-1}\right)^4,$$

$$\varphi_{P_1}(\varphi_{P_1}(\lambda)) = \left(\frac{\sqrt[4]{1-\lambda}+\sqrt{-1}}{\sqrt[4]{1-\lambda}-\sqrt{-1}}\right)^4, \qquad \varphi_{P_\lambda}(\varphi_{P_1}(\lambda)) = \left(\frac{\sqrt[4]{1-\lambda}+1}{\sqrt[4]{1-\lambda}-1}\right)^4,$$

$$\varphi_{P_1}(\varphi_{P_\lambda}(\lambda)) = \left(\frac{\sqrt[4]{\lambda-1}+\sqrt{-1}\sqrt[4]{\lambda}}{\sqrt[4]{\lambda-1}-\sqrt{-1}\sqrt[4]{\lambda}}\right)^4, \quad \varphi_{P_\lambda}(\varphi_{P_\lambda}(\lambda)) = \left(\frac{\sqrt[4]{\lambda-1}+\sqrt[4]{\lambda}}{\sqrt[4]{\lambda-1}-\sqrt[4]{\lambda}}\right)^4.$$

Among the six compositions, the first two involving the map φ_{P_0} have simpler expressions, so we want to use them in our proposed algorithm. However, now the issue of backtracking occurs again: not any of these compositions can be selected in any step because they also are dual of the previous.

From the above, in order to compute the isogenies between Legendre form, it is necessary to devise so that these fundamental Legendre maps do not backtrack.

5 λ-switching Theorem

In this section, we introduce and prove λ-switching theorem. By using λ-switching theorem, we can iteratively compute the isogenies between Legendre form without backtracking. Note that since $1-\varphi_P(\lambda)$ in $[\lambda]$, the isogenous curve $\varphi_P(\lambda)$ can be taken as $1 - \varphi_P(\lambda)$.

Theorem 1 (λ-switching). *Let P be P_0, P_1, or P_λ, and P' be P_0 or P_λ. Then we have $1 - \varphi_{P_1}(1 - \varphi_P(\lambda)) \in [\lambda]$. Moreover, if the Legendre curve $E_{(-(\lambda+1),\lambda)}$ is ordinary, then we have $1 - \varphi_{P'}(1 - \varphi_P(\lambda)) \notin [\lambda]$.*

Proof. First, we have

$$\varphi_{P_1}(1 - \varphi_P(\lambda)) = \left(\frac{\sqrt{1 - (1 - \varphi_P(\lambda))}+1}{\sqrt{1 - (1 - \varphi_P(\lambda))}-1}\right)^2$$

$$= \left(\frac{\sqrt{\varphi_P(\lambda)}+1}{\sqrt{\varphi_P(\lambda)}-1}\right)^2 = \varphi_{P_0}(\varphi_P(\lambda)) .$$

Hence we have $\varphi_{P_1}(1-\varphi_P(\lambda)) = \varphi_{P_0}(\varphi_P(\lambda)) \in [\lambda]$ as shown in Sect. 4, therefore, $1 - \varphi_{P_1}(1 - \varphi_P(\lambda)) \in [\lambda]$.

Secondly, when $E_{(-(\lambda+1),\lambda)}$ is ordinary, by the structure of the connected component of the 2-isogeny graph being a 2-volcano graph, if a map φ_{P_1} applied to a vertex lets us backtrack, then the other two maps φ_{P_0} and φ_{P_λ} do not let us backtrack. This and the result above imply that $\varphi_{P'}(1 - \varphi_P(\lambda)) \notin [\lambda]$, therefore, $1 - \varphi_{P'}(1 - \varphi_P(\lambda)) \notin [\lambda]$.   □

In detail, we have

$$1 - \varphi_{P_0}(1 - \varphi_{P_0}(\lambda)) = -\frac{8\sqrt{-1}\sqrt[4]{\lambda}(\sqrt{\lambda}-1)}{(\sqrt[4]{\lambda}-\sqrt{-1})^4},$$

$$1 - \varphi_{P_\lambda}(1 - \varphi_{P_0}(\lambda)) = -\frac{8\sqrt[4]{\lambda}(\sqrt{\lambda}+1)}{(\sqrt[4]{\lambda}-1)^4},$$

$$1 - \varphi_{P_0}(1 - \varphi_{P_1}(\lambda)) = -\frac{8\sqrt{-1}\sqrt[4]{1-\lambda}(\sqrt{1-\lambda}-1)}{(\sqrt[4]{1-\lambda}-\sqrt{-1})^4},$$

$$1 - \varphi_{P_\lambda}(1 - \varphi_{P_1}(\lambda)) = -\frac{8\sqrt[4]{1-\lambda}(\sqrt{1-\lambda}+1)}{(\sqrt[4]{1-\lambda}-1)^4},$$

$$1 - \varphi_{P_0}(1 - \varphi_{P_\lambda}(\lambda)) = -\frac{8\sqrt{-1}\sqrt[4]{\lambda(\lambda-1)}(\sqrt{\lambda-1}-\sqrt{\lambda})}{(\sqrt[4]{\lambda-1}-\sqrt{-1}\sqrt[4]{\lambda})^4},$$

$$1 - \varphi_{P_\lambda}(1 - \varphi_{P_\lambda}(\lambda)) = -\frac{8\sqrt[4]{\lambda(\lambda-1)}(\sqrt{\lambda-1}+\sqrt{\lambda})}{(\sqrt[4]{\lambda-1}-\sqrt[4]{\lambda})^4}.$$

By using λ-switching theorem, we can use the fundamental Legendre maps $1 - \varphi_{P'}(1 - \varphi_P)$ twice in a row. In other wards, $1 - \varphi_{P'}(1 - \varphi_P)(\lambda)$ is a 2^2-isogenious curve of $E_{-(\lambda+1),\lambda}$.

6   Sutherland's Supersingularity Testing Algorithm

In this section, we describe the Sutherland's algorithm [18]. In Sutherland's algorithm [18], modular polynomials $\Phi_\ell(X,Y) \in \mathbb{Z}[X,Y]$ [19] (of 2 variables X,Y with integral coefficients) play an important role. They are symmetric with respect to X and Y, and of degree $\ell+1$. In particular, when ℓ is prime the condition that E_1 and E_2 are ℓ-isogenous is equivalent to $\Phi_\ell(j(E_1), j(E_2)) = 0$. From the above relation between the roots of modular polynomials and j-invariants of isogenous curves, the graph $G_\ell(\mathbb{F}_{p^2})$ can be identified with the (directed, non-simple) graph on vertex set $\mathbb{F}_{p^2}$ in which $(j_1, j_2) \in (\mathbb{F}_{p^2})^2$ is an edge if and only if $\Phi_\ell(j_1, j_2) = 0$.

Sutherland's algorithm outputs $\mathtt{true}$ if and only if the input is supersingular. Precisely, the input is an elliptic curve E over $\mathbb{F}_{p^2}$ of characteristic p (≥ 5) and the algorithm is given below.

1. If the cubic polynomial $\Phi_2(j(E), X)$ with respect to X does not have three roots in $\mathbb{F}_{p^2}$, then output $\mathtt{false}$. Otherwise, let the roots be $j_0, j_1, j_2 (\in \mathbb{F}_{p^2})$.
2. For $\mu = 0, 1, 2$, set $j'_\mu \leftarrow j(E)$.
3. Let $m := \lfloor \log_2 p \rfloor + 1$, and iterate the following from $i = 1$ to m: For $\mu = 0, 1, 2$:
   (a) Calculate the quadratic polynomial

$$f_\mu(X) \leftarrow \Phi_2(j_\mu, X)/(X - j'_\mu),$$

   and set $j'_\mu \leftarrow j_\mu$.

(b) If $f_\mu(X)$ has no root in $\mathbb{F}_{p^2}$, output **false**. Otherwise, let j_μ be one of the two roots.

4. (If **false** is not outputted in the above,) output **true**.

If E is ordinary, the 2-isogeny graph is of 2-volcano. In Step 3, we construct three non-backtracking paths whose initial points are j_0, j_1, j_2 in Step 1, respectively. Therefore, at least one of the paths is descending on the volcano. Moreover, the descending path cannot have length $m + 1 \geq \log_2(2p) + 1$ by Proposition 5, and the algorithm outputs **false** in Step 3 if E is ordinary.

Sutherland gives the following time estimate in [18]. Let $n = \log_2(p)$ from now on.

Proposition 6 (Prop. 5 in [18]). *Sutherland's algorithm can be implemented as a deterministic algorithm with running-time $\tilde{O}(n^3)$ and space complexity $O(n)$ when quadratic and cubic non-residues are given as auxiliary inputs.*

7 Our Proposed Algorithm

In this section, we explain our proposed supersingularity testing algorithm. Given the short Weierstrass form $E: y^2 = f(x)$ of an elliptic curve E over $\mathbb{F}_{p^2}$, our proposed algorithm is run as follows.

1. If the cubic polynomial $f(x)$ does not have three different roots in $\mathbb{F}_{p^2}$, then output **false**. Otherwise, let the roots be $e_1, e_2, e_3 (\in \mathbb{F}_{p^2})$.
2. By using Proposition 2, for $\lambda = \frac{e_3 - e_1}{e_2 - e_1}$ compute Legendre form $E_{(-(\lambda+1),\lambda)}$: $y^2 = x(x - 1)(x - \lambda)$ of the input curve E.
3. Let $\lambda_{1,1} := \lambda, \lambda_{1,2} := \lambda, \lambda_{1,3} := \lambda$.
4. The following computations are run.
   (a) Compute $A = \sqrt[4]{\lambda_{1,1}}$ and $\lambda_{2,1} = 1 - \varphi_{P_0}(\lambda_{1,1}) = -\frac{4A^2}{(A^2-1)^2}$. Then, output **false** if $\lambda_{2,1} \notin \mathbb{F}_{p^2}$.
   (b) By using A in Step (a), compute $\lambda_{3,1} = 1 - \varphi_{P_0}(\lambda_{2,1}) = -\frac{8\sqrt{-1}A(A^2-1)}{(A-\sqrt{-1})^4}$. Then, output **false** if $\lambda_{3,1} \notin \mathbb{F}_{p^2}$.
   (c) Compute $B = \sqrt[4]{1 - \lambda_{1,2}}$ and $\lambda_{2,2} = 1 - \varphi_{P_1}(\lambda_{1,2}) = -\frac{4B^2}{(B^2-1)^2}$. Then, output **false** if $\lambda_{2,2} \notin \mathbb{F}_{p^2}$.
   (d) By using B in Step (c), compute $\lambda_{3,2} = 1 - \varphi_{P_0}(\lambda_{2,2}) = -\frac{8\sqrt{-1}B(B^2-1)}{(B-\sqrt{-1})^4}$. Then, output **false** if $\lambda_{3,2} \notin \mathbb{F}_{p^2}$.
   (e) Compute $C_1 = \sqrt[4]{\lambda_{1,3}}$, $C_2 = \sqrt[4]{\lambda_{1,3} - 1}$ and $\lambda_{2,3} = 1 - \varphi_{P_\lambda}(\lambda_{1,3}) = -\frac{4C_1^2 C_2^2}{(C_2^2 - C_1^2)^2}$. Then, output **false** if $\lambda_{2,3} \notin \mathbb{F}_{p^2}$.
   (f) By using C_1 and C_2 in Step (e), compute $\lambda_{3,3} = 1 - \varphi_{P_0}(\lambda_{2,3}) = -\frac{8\sqrt{-1}C_1 C_2(C_2^2 - C_1^2)}{(C_2 - \sqrt{-1}C_1)^4}$. Then, output **false** if $\lambda_{3,3} \notin \mathbb{F}_{p^2}$.
5. Let $m := \lfloor \log_2 p \rfloor + 1$ and iterate the following from $i = 3$ to m. For $\mu = 1, 2, 3$, execute the following part (a) when i is odd, and the following part (b) when i is even.

(a) Compute $d_{i,\mu} = \sqrt[4]{\lambda_{i,\mu}}$ and

$$\lambda_{i+1,\mu} = 1 - \varphi_{P_0}(\lambda_{i,\mu}) = -\frac{4d_{i,\mu}^2}{(d_{i,\mu}^2 - 1)^2} \quad .$$

Then, output `false` if $\lambda_{i+1,\mu} \notin \mathbb{F}_{p^2}$.

(b) By using $d_{i-1,\mu}$ in the previous Step (a), compute

$$\lambda_{i+1,\mu} = 1 - \varphi_{P_0}(\lambda_{i,\mu}) = -\frac{8\sqrt{-1}d_{i-1,\mu}(d_{i-1,\mu}^2 - 1)}{(d_{i-1,\mu} - \sqrt{-1})^4} \quad .$$

Then, output `false` if $\lambda_{i+1,\mu} \notin \mathbb{F}_{p^2}$.

6. Output `true` if `false` is not output in the above.

8   Comparison

We compare Sutherland's algorithm [18] in Sect. 6 and our algorithm proposed in Sect. 7. For both algorithms, the most time-consuming step, i.e., Step 3 of Sutherland's algorithm and Step 5 of our proposed algorithm, iterates computation step including square root or fourth root computation $m := \lfloor \log_2 p \rfloor + 1$ times. We call this the fundamental step, and summarize the average numbers of $\mathbb{F}_{p^2}$ operations needed in the fundamental step in Table 1. Here we do not distinguish the numbers of square root computations and fourth root computations, since our experiment in Sect. 9 below shows that the computation times of these two operations are similar.

Our proposed algorithm reduced the number of square/fourth root computations by half, which is the dominant cost of supersingularity testing algorithms based on isogeny graphs. The main reason of this efficiency improvement is that, in contrast to Sutherland's algorithm where square root computation is needed in every iterative step, in our proposed algorithm, fourth root computation is needed only for the steps with odd index i and is not needed when i is even.

Table 1. Average numbers of $\mathbb{F}_{p^2}$ operations in the fundamental step (here "Root" means square or fourth root computation, "Inv" means multiplicative inverse, "Mult" means multiplication, and "Const. Mult" means multiplication by constant)

$\mathbb{F}_{p^2}$ operations	Root	Inv	Mult	Const. Mult
Sutherland [18]	3	0	9	15
Our algorithm	3/2	3	9	3

9   Experimental Results

In this section, by using Magma computational algebra system, we compare the computational time of square root with the computational time of fourth root over $\mathbb{F}_{p^2}$. We also compare the performance of our proposed algorithm with the performance of Sutherland's algorithm.

All tests were run on the following platform: Magma V2.23-10 on 2.10 GHz Intel Xeon Skylake Gold 6130 Processor. In experiment of Sutherland's algorithm, we used Magma code provided by Sutherland himself.

9.1   Computational Time in Square Root and Fourth Root

We investigate the computational time of square root computation and the computational time of fourth root computation of Legendre parameter λ of 1024-bit length. We randomly selected ten 1024-bit prime numbers p. For each prime p, we generated ten Legendre parameters λ and investigated those computational times. Table 2 gives the average execution times. The result in this table suggests that the time for fourth root computation is almost the same as the time for square root computation.

Table 2. Average execution time of square root and fourth root

	CPU time, ms
Square Root	40
Fourth Root	41

9.2   Computational Time in Supersingularity Testing Algorithm

We investigate the performance of Sutherland's algorithm and the performance of our proposed algorithm. We denote by b the bit-length of p. For each value b of bit-length in Table 3, we randomly selected ten b-bit prime numbers p. For each prime p, we generated a supersingular elliptic curves over $\mathbb{F}_{p^2}$.

Here we only used supersingular curves because we wanted to evaluate the computational time for the case where the maximum number of iteration steps are executed. Table 3 gives the average execution times and the percentages of the execution times for our proposed algorithm relative to that for Sutherland's algorithm. This table shows that the ratio of the computational times for the two algorithms is almost the same as the ratio of the numbers of square/fourth root computations in these algorithms, and our improvement of the algorithm indeed reduces the running time significantly.

Table 3. Average execution times of the two algorithms

b	(CPU times in milliseconds)		Percentage
	Sutherland's algorithm	Our algorithm	
768	48178	20996	43.6
832	50533	24354	48.2
896	87331	39071	44.7
960	89885	43289	48.2
1024	110947	61837	55.7

Acknowledgments. We thank Andrew V. Sutherland for kindly sending us the Magma code of Sutherland's algorithm. We thank Momonari Kudo for his helpful comments. This work was supported by JSPS KAKENHI Grant Number JP19J23395.

References

1. Auer, R., Top, J.: Legendre elliptic curves over finite fields. J. Number Theory **95**(2), 303–312 (2002)
2. Brillhart, J., Morton, P.: Class numbers of quadratic fields, Hasse invariants of elliptic curves, and the supersingular polynomial. J. Number Theory **106**, 79–111 (2004)
3. Castryck, W., Lange, T., Martindale, C., Panny, L., Renes, J.: CSIDH: an efficient post-quantum commutative group action. In: Peyrin, T., Galbraith, S. (eds.) ASI-ACRYPT 2018. LNCS, vol. 11274, pp. 395–427. Springer, Cham (2018). https://doi.org/10.1007/978-3-030-03332-3_15
4. Charles, D.X., Lauter, K.E., Goren, E.Z.: Cryptographic hash functions from expander graphs. J. Cryptol. **22**(1), 93–113 (2009)
5. Costello, C., Longa, P., Naehrig, M.: Efficient algorithms for supersingular isogeny Diffie-Hellman. In: Robshaw, M., Katz, J. (eds.) CRYPTO 2016. LNCS, vol. 9814, pp. 572–601. Springer, Heidelberg (2016). https://doi.org/10.1007/978-3-662-53018-4_21
6. De Feo, L., Jao, D., Plût, J.: Towards quantum-resistant cryptosystems from super-singular elliptic curve isogenies. J. Math. Cryptol. **8**(3), 209–247 (2014)
7. Fouquet, M., Morain, F.: Isogeny volcanoes and the SEA algorithm. In: Fieker, C., Kohel, D.R. (eds.) ANTS 2002. LNCS, vol. 2369, pp. 276–291. Springer, Heidelberg (2002). https://doi.org/10.1007/3-540-45455-1_23
8. Galbraith, S.: Mathematics of Public Key Cryptography. Cambridge University Press, Cambridge (2012)
9. Hashimoto, Y., Takashima, K.: Improved supersingularity testing of elliptic curves. JSIAM Lett. **13**, 29–32 (2021)
10. Koblitz, K.: Elliptic curve cryptosystems. Math. Comput. **48**, 203–209 (1987)
11. Kohel, D.: Endomorphism rings of elliptic curves over finite fields. Ph.D. thesis, University of California, Berkeley (1996)
12. Miller, V.S.: Use of elliptic curves in cryptography. In: Williams, H.C. (ed.) CRYPTO 1985. LNCS, vol. 218, pp. 417–426. Springer, Heidelberg (1986). https://doi.org/10.1007/3-540-39799-X_31

13. Miret, J.M., Moreno, R., Sadornil, D., Tena, J., Valls, M.: An algorithm to compute volcanoes of 2-isogenies of elliptic curves over finite fields. Appl. Math. Comput. **176**, 739–750 (2006)

14. Moriya, T., Takashima, K., Takagi, T.: Group key exchange from CSIDH and its application to trusted setup in supersingular isogeny cryptosystems. In: Liu, Z., Yung, M. (eds.) Inscrypt 2019. LNCS, vol. 12020, pp. 86–98. Springer, Cham (2020). https://doi.org/10.1007/978-3-030-42921-8_5

15. Pizer, A.: Ramanujan graphs and Hecke operators. Bull. AMS **23**(1), 127–137 (1990)

16. Silverman, J.H.: The Arithmetic of Elliptic Curves. GTM, vol. 106. Springer, Heidelberg (1986). https://doi.org/10.1007/978-1-4757-1920-8

17. Sutherland, A.V.: Computing Hilbert class polynomials with the Chinese remainder theorem. Math. Comput. **80**(273), 501–538 (2011). https://doi.org/10.1090/S0025-5718-2010-02373-7

18. Sutherland, A.: Identifying supersingular elliptic curves. LMS J. Comput. Math. **15**, 317–325 (2012)

19. Sutherland, A.: Isogeny volcanoes. In: Howe, E.W., Kedlaya, K. (eds.) ANTS X. The Open Book Series, vol. 1, no. 1, pp. 507–530. Mathematical Sciences Publishers, Berkeley (2013)

20. Yoshida, R., Takashima, K.: Computing a sequence of 2-isogenies on supersingular elliptic curves. IEICE Trans. Fundam. **96-A**(1), 158–165 (2013)

Root Radii and Subdivision
for Polynomial Root-Finding

Rémi Imbach[1]($\boxtimes$) and Victor Y. Pan[2]

[1] Courant Institute of Mathematical Sciences, New York University, New York, USA
remi.imbach@nyu.edu
[2] Lehman College and Graduate Center of City University of New York,
New York, USA
victor.pan@lehman.cuny.edu

Abstract. We depart from our approximation of 2000 of all root radii of a polynomial, which has readily extended Schönhage's efficient algorithm of 1982 for a single root radius. We revisit this extension, advance it, based on our simple but novel idea, and yield significant practical acceleration of the known near optimal subdivision algorithms for complex and real root-finding of user's choice. We achieve this by means of significant saving of exclusion tests and Taylor's shifts, which are the bottleneck of subdivision root-finders. This saving relies on our novel recipes for the initialization of root-finding iterations of independent interest. We demonstrate our practical progress with numerical tests, provide extensive analysis of the resulting algorithms, and show that, like the preceding subdivision root-finders, they support near optimal Boolean complexity bounds.

Keywords: Real root isolation · Complex root clustering · Root radii algorithm · Subdivision iterations

1 Introduction

Overview. The recent subdivision iterations for univariate polynomial Complex Root Clustering (CRC) and Real Root Isolation (RRI) approximate all roots in a fixed Region of Interest (RoI) and, like the algorithm of Pan (1995, 2002), achieve near optimal bit complexity for the so called benchmark problem. Furthermore they allow robust implementations, one of which is currently the user's choice for solving the RRI problem, including the task of the approximation of all real roots. Another implementation, for the CRC problem, is slower by several orders of magnitude than the package MPSolve (the user's choice) for the task of finding all complex roots. However it outperforms MPSolve for solving the CRC problem where the RoI contains only a small number of roots. We significantly accelerate these highly efficient root-finding iterations by applying our novel

Victor's work is supported by NSF Grants CCF 1563942 and CCF 1733834 and PSC CUNY Award 63677 00 51.

© Springer Nature Switzerland AG 2021
F. Boulier et al. (Eds.): CASC 2021, LNCS 12865, pp. 136–156, 2021.
https://doi.org/10.1007/978-3-030-85165-1_9

techniques for their initialization. Next we specify the background and outline our contributions.

Polynomial Roots and Root Radii. For a polynomial P of degree d in $\mathbb{Z}[z]$ and a Gaussian integer $c \in \mathbb{G} := \{a + \mathbf{i}b \mid a \in \mathbb{Z}, b \in \mathbb{Z}\}$, let $\alpha_1(P, c), \ldots, \alpha_d(P, c)$ be the d non-necessarily distinct roots of P such that

$$|\alpha_1(P,c) - c| \geq |\alpha_2(P,c) - c| \geq \ldots \geq |\alpha_{d-1}(P,c) - c| \geq |\alpha_d(P,c) - c|. \quad (1)$$

For all $1 \leq i \leq d$, write $r_i(P, c) := |\alpha_i(P, c) - c|$, $\alpha_i(P) := \alpha_i(P, 0)$ and $r_i(P) := r_i(P, 0)$, so that

$$r_1(P, c) \geq r_2(P, c) \geq \ldots \geq r_{d-1}(P, c) \geq r_d(P, c). \quad (2)$$

Then

Root Radii Covering (RRC) Problem
Given: a polynomial $P \in \mathbb{Z}[z]$ of degree d, a Gaussian integer $c \in \mathbb{G}$, a real number $\delta > 0$
Output: d positive numbers $\rho_{c,1}, \ldots, \rho_{c,d}$ satisfying

$$\forall s = 1, \ldots, d, \quad \frac{\rho_{c,s}}{1+\delta} \leq r_s(P, c) \leq (1+\delta)\rho_{c,s}. \quad (3)$$

$\rho_{c,1}, \ldots, \rho_{c,d}$ of Eq. (3) for fixed $c \in \mathbb{G}$ and $\delta > 0$ define d possibly overlaping concentric annuli. The connected components of their union form a set $\mathcal{A}_c$ of $d_c \leq d$ disjoint concentric annuli centered at c. They cover all roots of P and are said to be an *annuli cover* of the roots of P. We are going to use them in subdivision root-finding iterations.

Two Root-Finding Problems. We count roots with multiplicity and consider discs $D(c, r) := \{z \mid |z - c| \leq r\}$ on the complex plane. For a positive δ let $\delta\Delta$ and δB denote the concentric δ-dilation of a disc Δ and a real line segment (*i.e.* interval) B. Then

---
Complex Root Clustering (CRC) Problem
Given: a polynomial $P \in \mathbb{Z}[z]$ of degree d, $\varepsilon > 0$
Output: $\ell \leq d$ couples $(\Delta^1, m^1), \ldots, (\Delta^\ell, m^\ell)$ satisfying:

 – the Δ^j's are pairwise disjoint discs of radii $\leq \varepsilon$,
 – Δ^j and $3\Delta^j$ contain $m^j > 0$ roots,
 – each complex root of P is in a Δ^j.

Real Root Isolation (RRI) Problem
Given: a polynomial $P \in \mathbb{Z}[z]$ of degree d
Output: $\ell \leq d$ couples $(B^1, m^1), \ldots, (B^\ell, m^\ell)$ satisfying:

 – the B^i's are disjoint real line segments,
 – each B^i contains a unique real root of multiplicity m^j,
 – each real root of P is in a B^i.

Table 1. Runs of `Risolate`, `RisolateR`, `Ccluster` and `CclusterR` on two polynomials. `Ccluster` and `CclusterR` are called with input $\varepsilon = 2^{-53}$.

			Risolate		RisolateR			Ccluster		CclusterR		
d	τ	$d_{\mathbb{R}}$	t	n	t	n	t'	t	n	t	n	t'
					Bernoulli polynomial							
512	2590	124	6.15	672	0.38	17	0.25	136	13940	50.7	4922	7.59
					Mignotte polynomial							
512	256	4	1.57	49	1.67	14	0.27	88.8	10112	28.3	2680	3.05

It is quite common to pre-process $P \in \mathbb{Z}[z]$ in order to make it square-free, with $m^j = 1$ for all j, but we do not use this option. We can state both CRC and RRI problems for P with rational coefficients and readily reduce them to the above versions with integer coefficients by scaling.

Write $\|P\| := \|P\|_{\infty}$ and call the value $\log_2 \|P\|$ the *bit-size* of P.

The Benchmark Problem. For the bit-complexity of the so called *benchmark* root-finding problem of the isolation of all roots of a square-free $P \in \mathbb{Z}[z]$ of degree d and bit-size τ the record bound of 1995 [13] is $\widetilde{O}(d^2(d + \tau))$, near optimal for $\tau > d$ and based on a divide and conquer approach. It was reached again in 2016 [1,2], based on subdivision iterations and implemented in [8].

Our Contributions. We first present and analyze an algorithm `SolveRRC` that solves the RRC problem for polynomials with integer coefficients and any fixed center $c \in \mathbb{G}$. Our algorithm is adapted from work [12] (which has extended Schönhage's highly efficient approximation of a single root radius in [15]) to simultaneous approximation of all d root radii. Our specialization of this root radii algorithm to the case of integer polynomials and our analysis of its bit-complexity are novel. We use `SolveRRC` for $\delta \in d^{-O(1)}$ and $|c| \in O(1)$; under such assumptions, it solves the RRC problem with a bit-complexity in $\widetilde{O}(d^2(d + \tau))$.

We then improve solvers for the RRI and the CRC problems based on subdivision with annuli covers that we compute by applying `SolveRRC`. The complexity of subdivision root-finders is dominated at its bottleneck stages of root-counting and particularly exclusion tests, at which costly *Taylor's shifts*, aka the shifts of the variable, are applied. We significantly accelerate the root-finders for both RRI and CRC problems by means of using fewer exclusion tests and calls for root-counting and hence fewer Taylor's shifts. We achieve this by limiting complex root-finding to the intersection of three annuli covers of the roots centered in 0, 1 and $\mathbf{i}$ and by limiting real root-finding to the intersection of a single annuli cover centered in 0 with the real line.

Our improvements are implemented within the C library `Ccluster`[1] which provides an eponymous solver for the CRC problem and a solver for the RRI problem called `Risolate`. Our novel solvers are called below `CclusterR` and `RisolateR`, and in Table 1 we overview how those two solvers perform against `Ccluster` and `Risolate` on a Bernoulli and a Mignotte polynomial. For each test polynomial we show its degree d, its bit-size τ, and the number $d_{\mathbb{R}}$ of real roots. For each solver, t denotes the sequential running time in seconds on an `Intel(R) Core(TM) i7-8700 CPU @ 3.20 GHz` machine with Linux and n denotes the total number of Taylor's shift required in the subdivision process. For `CclusterR` and `RisolateR`, t' is the time spent on solving the RRC problem with `SolveRRC`.

We compute the annuli covers in a pre-processing step by applying algorithm `SolveRRC` for input relative width $\delta = 1/d^2$. This choice of δ is empiric, and in this sense our improvement of subdivision is heuristic. From a theoretical point of view, this allows our algorithms for solving the RRI and the CRC problems to support a near optimal bit-complexity. From a practical point of view, this allows us to significantly reduce the running time of solvers based on subdivision by using fewer Taylor's shifts in exclusion and root-counting tests, as we highlighted in Table 1 (see the columns t and n).

The distance between roots of a polynomial of degree d and bit-size τ can be way less than $1/d^2$ (see for instance [11]); thus by computing with `SolveRRC` intervals that contain the root radii of relative width $\delta = 1/d^2$, we do not intend to separate the roots of input polynomials, and our improvement has no effect in the cases where distances between some roots are less than δ. We illustrate this in Table 1 for a Mignotte polynomial that has four real roots among which two roots have a pairwise distance that is close to the theoretical separation bound. Most of the computational effort in a subdivision solver for real roots isolation is spent on the separation of the close roots, and this remains true where we use annuli covers with relative width larger than the roots separation.

We compare our implementation with `ANewDsc` (see [10], implementing [14]) and `MPSolve` (see [3], implementing Ehrlich's iterations), which are the current user's choices for solving the RRI and the CRC problems, respectively.

Related Work. We departed from the subdivision polynomial root-finding for the CRC and RRI problems in [1] and [14], resp., and from the algorithms for the RRC problem in [15] (see [15][Cor. 14.3], and [5][Algorithm 2]) and [12]. We achieved practical progress by complementing these advanced works with our novel techniques for efficient computation of $O(1)$ annuli covers of the roots. We rely on the customary framework for the analysis of root-finding algorithms and cite throughout the relevant sources of our auxiliary techniques.

Organization of the Paper. In Sect. 2 we describe an algorithm for solving the RRC problem. In Sects. 3 and 4 we present our algorithms for solving the

---

[1] https://github.com/rimbach/Ccluster.

RRI and CRC problem, respectively. In Subsect. 1.1 we introduce definitions. In Subsect. 1.2 we briefly describe the subdivision algorithm for the CRC problem of [1] and its adaptation to the solution of the RRI problem.

1.1   Definitions

Write $P := P(z) := P_d \prod_{i=1}^{d}(z - \alpha_i(P)) = \sum_{j=0}^{d} P_j z^j$.

Root Squaring Iterations. For a positive integer ℓ write

$$P^{[\ell]} := (P_d)^{2^\ell} \prod_{i=1}^{d}(z - \alpha_i(P)^{2^\ell}) \tag{4}$$

and so $P^{[0]} = P$, $P^{[\ell]} = (P^{[\ell-1]})^{[1]}$ for $\ell \geq 1$, and

$$|\alpha_1(P^{[\ell]})| \geq |\alpha_2(P^{[\ell]})| \geq \ldots \geq |\alpha_{d-1}(P^{[\ell]})| \geq |\alpha_d(P^{[\ell]})|. \tag{5}$$

$P^{[\ell]}$ is called the ℓ-th root squaring iteration of P, aka the ℓ-th Dandelin-Lobachevsky-Gräffe (DLG) iteration of P.

Write $P^{[\ell-1]} = \sum_{j=0}^{d}(P^{[\ell-1]})_j z^j$, $P_e^{[\ell-1]} = \sum_{j=0}^{\lfloor \frac{d}{2} \rfloor}(P^{[\ell-1]})_{2j} z^j$ and $P_o^{[\ell-1]} = \sum_{j=0}^{\lfloor \frac{d-1}{2} \rfloor}(P^{[\ell-1]})_{2j+1} z^j$. $P^{[\ell]}$ can be computed iteratively based on the formula:

$$P^{[\ell]} = (-1)^d \left[(P_e^{[\ell-1]})^2 - z(P_o^{[\ell-1]})^2 \right]. \tag{6}$$

The j-th coefficient $(P^{[\ell]})_j$ of $P^{[\ell]}$ is related to the coefficients of $P^{[\ell-1]}$ by:

$$(P^{[\ell]})_j = (-1)^{d-j}(P^{[\ell-1]})_j^2 + 2 \sum_{k=\max(0,2j-d)}^{j-1} (-1)^{d-j}(P^{[\ell-1]})_k (P^{[\ell-1]})_{2j-k} \tag{7}$$

L-bit Approximations. For any number $c \in \mathbb{C}$, we say that $\tilde{c} \in \mathbb{C}$ is an L-bit approximation of c if $\|\tilde{c} - c\| \leq 2^{-L}$. For a polynomial $P \in \mathbb{C}[z]$, we say that $\tilde{P} \in \mathbb{C}$ is an L-bit approximation of P if $\|\tilde{P} - P\| \leq 2^{-L}$, or equivalently if $\|\widetilde{P_j} - P_j\| \leq 2^{-L}$ for all j.

Boxes, Quadri-Section, Line Segments, Bi-section. $[a - w/2, a + w/2] + \mathbf{i}[b - w/2, b + w/2]$ is the box B of width w centered at $c = a + \mathbf{i}b$. The disc $\Delta(B) := D(c, \frac{3}{4}w)$ is a *cover* of B.

Partition B into four congruent boxes (children of B), of width $w/2$ and centered at $(a \pm \frac{w}{4}) + \mathbf{i}(b \pm \frac{w}{4})$.

$\Delta(B) := D(c, w/2)$ is the minimal disc that covers a real line segment $B := [c - w/2, c + w/2]$ of width w centered at $c \in \mathbb{R}$.

Partition the segment B into two segments (children of B) of width $w/2$ centered at $(c \pm \frac{w}{4}))$.

Let $\mathcal{C}$ be a connected component of boxes (resp. real line segments); $B_\mathcal{C}$ is the minimal box (resp. real line segment) covering $\mathcal{C}$.

1.2   Subdivision Approach to Root-Finding

The work [1] describes an algorithm for solving a local version of the CRC problem: for an initial RoI B_0 (a box) it finds clusters of roots with pairwise distance less than ε in a small inflation of B_0. Since our CRC problem is for input polynomials in $\mathbb{Z}[z]$, one can define a RoI containing all the roots by using, for instance, the Fujiwara bound (see [4]).

Subdivision Iterations. The algorithm in [1] uses subdivision iterations or Quad-tree algorithms (inherited from [7], see also [12]), which constructs a tree rooted in the RoI B_0 whose nodes are sub-boxes of B_0. A node B is *included* only if $2B$ contains a root, *excluded* only if it contains no root. A node is *active* if it is neither included nor excluded. At the beginning of a subdivision iteration, each active node B is tested for exclusion. Then active boxes are grouped into connected components, and for each connected component $\mathcal{C}$ such that $4\Delta(B_{\mathcal{C}})$ intersect no other connected component, a root-counter is applied to $2\Delta(B_{\mathcal{C}})$. If $2\Delta(B_{\mathcal{C}})$ contains $m > 0$ roots and $\Delta(B_{\mathcal{C}})$ has radius less than ε, then $(\Delta(B_{\mathcal{C}}), m)$ is returned as a solution and the boxes of $\mathcal{C}$ are marked as included. Each remaining active node is quadrisected into its four active children, to which a new subdivision iteration is applied. Incorporation of Newton's iterations enables quadratic convergence toward clusters of radii ε.

Solving the RRI Problem. Using a root separation lower bound (e.g., of [11]), one can derive from [1] a solution of the RRI problem based on the symmetry of roots of $P \in \mathbb{Z}[z]$ along the real axis. Let disc $D(c, r)$ with $c \in \mathbb{R}$ contain m roots of P. For $m = 1$ the root in $D(c, r)$ is real. If $m \geq 1$ and $r \leq \mathrm{sep}(P)$, then $D(c, r)$ contains a real root of multiplicity m, where $\mathrm{sep}(P)$ is a root separation lower bound for P. For the RRI problem, the RoI B_0 is a line segment, and the subdivision tree of B_0 is built by means of segment bisection.

The T^0 and T^* Tests. In the algorithm of [1], the exclusion test and root counter are based on Pellet's theorem (see [2]). For a disc $\Delta = D(c, r)$, the counting test $T^*(\Delta, P)$ returns an integer $k \in \{-1, 0, \dots, d\}$ such that $k \geq 0$ only if P has k roots in Δ. A result $k = -1$ accounts for a failure and holds when some roots of P are close to the boundary of Δ. For a given disc Δ, the exclusion test $T^0(\Delta, P)$ returns 0 if $T^*(\Delta, P)$ returns 0 and returns -1 if $T^*(\Delta, P)$ returns a non-zero integer. The T^* of [2] takes as an input an L-bit approximation of P and with working absolute precision L performs about $\log \log d$ DLG iterations of the Taylor's shift $P(c+rz)$ of P. Write $L(\Delta, P)$ for the precision L required to carry out the T^*-test. Based on Pellet's theorem we obtain the following results.

Proposition 1 (see [2], Lemmas 4 and 5). *Let B be the box (or real line segment) centered in c with width w. The total cost in bit operations for carrying out $T^*(\Delta(B), P)$ or $T^0(\Delta(B), P)$ is bounded by*

$$\widetilde{O}(d(\log \|P\| + d \log \max(1, |c|, w) + L(\Delta, P))). \tag{8}$$

$T^*(\Delta(B), P)$ *returns an integer* $k \in \{-1, 0, \ldots, d\}$; *if* $k \geq 0$ *then* $\Delta(B)$ *contains k roots; if* $k = -1$ *then* P *has a root in* $2B \setminus (1/2)B$. $T^0(\Delta(B), P)$ *returns an integer* $k \in \{-1, 0\}$; *if* $k = 0$ *then* P *has no root in* $\Delta(B)$; *if* $k = -1$ *then* P *has a root in* $2B$.

Bit Complexity. Proposition 1 enables one to bound the Boolean cost of exclusion tests and root-counting as well as the size of the subdivision tree and hence the cost of solving the benchmark problem in [1].

By applying subdivision iterations with an exclusion test and a root counter satisfying Proposition 1 one yields an algorithm with the same bit-complexity as the algorithm of [1], namely, $\widetilde{O}(d^2(d + \tau))$ for the benchmark problem.

Implementations. A modified version of [1] for the CRC problem has been implemented and made public within the library `Ccluster`. An implementation of the modified algorithm of [1] solving the RRI problem, called `Risolate`, is also available within `Ccluster`.

2   Root Radii Computation

We describe and analyse an algorithm for solving the RRC problem for a $P \in \mathbb{G}[z]$. Let $c \in \mathbb{G}$ and $Pc(z) := P(c+z)$, so that $r_s(P, c) = r_s(Pc)$ for all $1 \leq s \leq d$. Hence the RRC problem for a $c \neq 0$ reduces to the RRC problem for $c = 0$ at the cost of shifting the variable.

The next remark reduces the RRC problem for $c = 0$ and any $\delta > 0$ to the RRC problem for $1 + \delta = 4d$ by means of DLG iterations:

Remark 2. *Let* $g = \lceil \log \dfrac{\log(4d)}{\log(1 + \delta)} \rceil$, *let* $\rho' > 0$ *such that there exist an s with:*

$$\frac{\rho'}{4d} < r_s(Pc^{[g]}) < (4d)\rho'. \tag{9}$$

Define $\rho = (\rho')^{\frac{1}{2^g}}$ *and recall that* $r_s(Pc^{[g]}) = r_s(P, c)^{2^g}$. *Then*

$$\frac{\rho}{1+\delta} < r_s(P, c) < (1+\delta)\rho. \tag{10}$$

g *is in* $O(\log d)$ *if* δ *is in* $d^{-O(1)}$ *(for instance,* $\delta \geq d^{-1}$ *or* $\delta \geq d^{-2}$).

Now define the RRC* problem as the RRC problem for $1 + \delta = 4d$ and $c = 0$:

RRC* problem
Given: a polynomial $P \in \mathbb{G}[z]$ of degree d, satisfying $P(0) \neq 0$
Output: d positive real numbers $\rho'_1, \ldots, \rho'_d$ satisfying

$$\forall s = 1, \ldots, d, \quad \frac{\rho'_s}{4d} < r_s(P) < (4d)\rho'_s. \tag{11}$$

In this setting, we assume that 0 is not a root of P and thus $P_0 \neq 0$. When 0 is a root of multiplicity m, then $r_d(P) = \ldots = r_{d-m+1}(P) = 0$ and $P_0 = \ldots = P_{m-1} = 0$, which is easily detected (since $P \in \mathbb{G}[z]$) and treated accordingly.

In Subsect. 2.1 we recall an algorithm SolveRRC* satisfying:

Proposition 3. *Algorithm* SolveRRC* *in Algorithm 1 solves the RRC* problem by involving $O(d \log \|P\|)$ bit operations.*

In Subsect. 2.2 we prove this proposition. In Subsect. 2.3 we present an algorithm SolveRRC satisfying:

Theorem 4. *The algorithm* SolveRRC *of Subsect. 2.3 solves the RRC problem for $\delta = d^{-2}$ at a Boolean cost in*

$$\widetilde{O}(d^2(d \log(|c| + 1) + \log \|P\|)). \tag{12}$$

This bound turns into $\widetilde{O}(d^2(d + \log \|P\|))$ for $|c| \in O(1)$ and into $\widetilde{O}(d^2 \log \|P\|)$ for $|c| = 0$.

Below we will use root radii computation as a pre-processing step for Complex Root Clustering and Real Root Isolation. For Real Root Isolation, we use SolveRRC to compute an annuli cover centered at 0. For Complex Root Clustering, we use SolveRRC to compute three annuli covers with the three centers $0, 1, \mathbf{i}$. According to our analysis of the RRC problem, the cost of its solution for $O(1)$ centers c such that $|c| \in O(1)$ is dominated by a near optimal bit-complexity of root-finding.

For $c = 0$, our algorithm has a larger bit complexity than the algorithm of [15] (see [15][Cor. 14.3] and [5][Algorithm 2]), which is in $\widetilde{O}(d^2 \log^2 d)$ when $\log \|P\| \in O(d)$. Our algorithm, however, computes d root radii at once where Schönhage's algorithm computes only a single root radius. It is not clear whether the latter algorithm can be extended to an algorithm that would solve the RRC problem within the same bit-complexity bound.

2.1   Solving the RRC* Problem

Recall that $P = \sum_{i=0}^{d} P_i z^i$ and define, for $i = 0, \ldots, d$,

$$p_i = \begin{cases} \log |P_i| & \text{if } P_i \neq 0, \\ -\infty & \text{otherwise.} \end{cases} \tag{13}$$

According to the following result, adapted from Proposition 4.2 and its proof in [12], one can solve the RRC* problem by computing the upper part of the convex hull of the set of points $\{(i, p_i)|i = 0, \ldots, d\}$ and assuming that the points $(i, -\infty)$ lie below any line in the plane.

Proposition 5. *Given an integer s, let t' and h' be integers s.t.*

(i') $t' < d + 1 - s \leq t' + h' \leq d$, and
(ii') $\forall 0 \leq i \leq d$, the point (i, p_i) lies below the line $((t', p_{t'}), (t' + h', p_{t'+h'}))$.

Then $\rho'_s = \left| \dfrac{P_{t'}}{P_{t'+h'}} \right|^{\frac{1}{h'}}$ satisfies: $\dfrac{\rho'_s}{2d} < r_s(P) < (2d)\rho'_s$.

Call CH the upper part of the convex hull of the points $\{(i, p_i)|i = 0, \ldots, d\}$, and remark that for a given integer s, the integers t' and $t'+h'$ satisfying (i') and (ii') in Proposition 5 are the abscissæ of the endpoints of the segment of CH above (s, p_s). CH can be computed exactly (the P_i's are Gaussian integers). However for solving the RRC* problem, it is sufficient to compute the upper part of the convex hull of M-bit approximations of the p_i's with $M \geq 1$. For $i = 0, \ldots, d$, define

$$\widetilde{p}_i := \begin{cases} M\text{-bit approximation of } p_i & \text{if } |P_i| > 1, \\ 0 & \text{if } |P_i| = 1, \\ -\infty & \text{otherwise.} \end{cases} \quad (14)$$

Let $\widetilde{CH}$ be the upper part of the convex hull of $\{(i, \widetilde{p}_i)|i = 0, \ldots, d\}$ and let points $(i, -\infty)$ lie below any line in the plane. Given an index s, the following proposition bounds the slope of the edge of CH above $d + 1 - s$ in terms of the slope of the edge of $\widetilde{CH}$ above $d + 1 - s$ and M.

Proposition 6. *Given an integer s, let t, h, t', and h' be integers such that*

(i) $t < d + 1 - s \leq t + h \leq d$,
(ii) $\forall 0 \leq i \leq d$, the point $(i, \widetilde{p}_i)$ lies below the line $((t, \widetilde{p}_t), (t + h, \widetilde{p_{t+h}}))$,
(i') $t' < d + 1 - s \leq t' + h' \leq d$, and
(ii') $\forall 0 \leq i \leq d$, the points (i, p_i) lie below the line $((t', p_{t'}), (t' + h', p_{t'+h'}))$.

Then

$$\frac{\widetilde{p_{t+h}} - \widetilde{p}_t}{h} - 2^{-M+1} \leq \frac{p_{t'+h'} - p_{t'}}{h'} \leq \frac{\widetilde{p_{t+h}} - \widetilde{p}_t}{h} + 2^{-M+1}. \quad (15)$$

For a given integer s, the existence of integers t, h, t', h' satisfying (i), (ii), (i'), (ii') follows from the existence of the convex hulls CH and $\widetilde{CH}$. We postpone the proof of Proposition 6. Remark that $2^{2^{-L}} \leq 1 + 2^{-L}$ for $L \geq 0$, apply Proposition 5, and obtain:

Corollary 7 (of Proposition 6). *Let s, t, h be as in Proposition 6. Define $\widetilde{\rho}_s'$ as $\left| \dfrac{P_t}{P_{t+h}} \right|^{\frac{1}{h}}$. Then*

$$\frac{\widetilde{\rho}_s'}{(2d)(1 + 2^{-M+1})} < r_s(P) < (2d)(1 + 2^{-M+1})\widetilde{\rho}_s'. \quad (16)$$

We are ready to describe our Algorithm 1, which solves the RRC* problem. In steps 1–2, 1-bit approximations $\widetilde{p}_i$ of $p_i = \log |P_i|$ are computed from P_i, for $i = 0, \ldots, d$. This requires $O(d \log \|P\|)$ bit operations. In step 3 we compute the convex hull $\widetilde{CH}$ of a polygon with $d + 1$ vertices $(0, \widetilde{p}_0), \ldots, (d, \widetilde{p}_d)$ ordered with respect to their ordinates. Using Graham's algorithm of [6], we only need

---

Algorithm 1. SolveRRC*(P)

Input: $P \in \mathbb{G}[z]$ of degree d s.t. $P(0) \neq 0$.
Output: d positive real numbers $\tilde{\rho}_1', \ldots, \tilde{\rho}_d'$.
1: **for** $i = 0, \ldots, d$ **do**
2:     Compute $\tilde{p}_i$, a 1-bit approximation of p_i, as defined in Eq. (14).
3: $\widetilde{CH} \leftarrow \{(i_k, \widetilde{p_{i_k}})|k = 0, \ldots, \ell\}$, the upper part of the convex hull of $\{(i, \tilde{p}_i)|i = 0, \ldots, d\}$
4: **for** $k = 1, \ldots, \ell$ **do**
5:     **for** $s = d + 1 - i_k, \ldots, d + 1 - i_{k-1}$ **do**
6:         $\tilde{\rho}_s' \leftarrow |\frac{P_{i_{k-1}}}{P_{i_k}}|^{\frac{1}{i_k - i_{k-1}}}$ //double precision floating point
7: **return** $\tilde{\rho}_1', \ldots, \tilde{\rho}_d'$

$O(d)$ arithmetic operations (additions) with numbers of magnitude $O(\log \|P\|)$. In steps 4,5,6, the $\tilde{\rho}_s'$'s for $s = 0, \ldots, d$ are computed as in Corollary 7. This task is performed with rounding to double precision arithmetic and requires $O(d)$ bit operations. Finally, $(1 + 2^{-M+1}) \leq 2$ if $M \geq 1$; thus the $\tilde{\rho}_s'$'s in the output satisfy $\forall s = 1, \ldots, d, \quad \frac{\tilde{\rho}_s'}{4d} < r_s(P) < (4d)\tilde{\rho}_s'$, and Proposition 3 follows.

2.2   Proof of Proposition 6

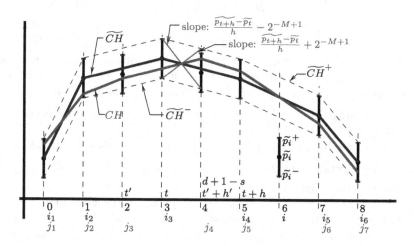

Fig. 1. The convex hulls CH and $\widetilde{CH}$ (Color figure online)

For $i = 0, \ldots, d$, define $\tilde{p}_i^+$ and $\tilde{p}_i^-$ as

$$\tilde{p}_i^+ = \begin{cases} \tilde{p}_i + 2^{-M} & \text{if } |\tilde{p}_i| > -\infty, \\ -\infty & \text{otherwise} \end{cases}, \text{ and } \tilde{p}_i^- = \begin{cases} \tilde{p}_i - 2^{-M} & \text{if } |\tilde{p}_i| > -\infty, \\ -\infty & \text{otherwise} \end{cases}. \quad (17)$$

$\widetilde{CH}$ is the upper part of the convex hull of $\{(i, \widetilde{p_i})|i = 0, \ldots, d\}$. Suppose that it is the poly-line passing through $\{(i_k, \widetilde{p_{i_k}})|k = 0, \ldots, \ell\}$. It defines two poly-lines:

– $\widetilde{CH}^+$, the poly-line with vertices $\{(i_k, \widetilde{p_{i_k}}^+|k = 0, \ldots, \ell\}$, and
– $\widetilde{CH}^-$, the poly-line with vertices $\{(i_k, \widetilde{p_{i_k}}^-)|k = 0, \ldots, \ell\}$.

CH is the upper part of the convex hull of $\{(i, p_i)|i = 0, \ldots, d\}$, and suppose it is the poly-line with vertices $\{(j_k, p_{j_k})|k = 0, \ldots, \ell'\}$. For demonstration see Fig. 1 where $d = 8$, the $\widetilde{p_i}$'s are drawn with black circles, the intervals $[\widetilde{p_i}^-, \widetilde{p_i}^+]$ with bold vertical bars, $\widetilde{CH}$ with a bold blue poly-line, $\widetilde{CH}^+$ and $\widetilde{CH}^-$ with dashed blue poly-lines, and CH with a bold red line. One has:

Proposition 8. *The poly-line CH lies below the poly-line $\widetilde{CH}^+$ and above the poly-line $\widetilde{CH}^-$.*

Proof of Proposition 8: In order to prove that CH lies below $\widetilde{CH}^+$, we show that if $j_t, i_k, i_{k'}$ is a triple of integers such that (j_t, p_{j_t}) is a vertex of CH and $[(i_k, \widetilde{p_{i_k}}^+), (i_{k'}, \widetilde{p_{i_{k'}}}^+)]$ is an edge of $\widetilde{CH}^+$, then (j_t, p_{j_t}) lies on or below the line $((i_k, \widetilde{p_{i_k}}^+), (i_{k'}, \widetilde{p_{i_{k'}}}^+))$. Suppose this is not the case, *i.e.* the point (j_t, p_{j_t}) lies strictly above the line $((i_k, \widetilde{p_{i_k}}^+), (i_{k'}, \widetilde{p_{i_{k'}}}^+))$. Since $p_{j_t} \leq \widetilde{p_{j_t}}^+$, $\widetilde{p_{j_t}}^+$ lies strictly above $((i_k, \widetilde{p_{i_k}}^+), (i_{k'}, \widetilde{p_{i_{k'}}}^+))$, thus $\widetilde{p_{j_t}}$ lies strictly above $((i_k, \widetilde{p_{i_k}}), (i_{k'}, \widetilde{p_{i_{k'}}}))$ and $\widetilde{CH}$ is not the convex hull of $\{(i, \widetilde{p_i})|i = 0, \ldots, d\}$, which is a contradiction.

In order to show that $\widetilde{CH}^-$ lies below CH, we show that for a given triple of integers $i_t, j_k, j_{k'}$ such that $(i_t, \widetilde{p_{i_t}}^-)$ is a vertex of $\widetilde{CH}^-$ and $[(j_k, p_{j_k}), (j_{k'}, p_{j_{k'}})]$ is an edge of CH, the point $(i_t, \widetilde{p_{i_t}}^-)$ lies on or below the line $((j_k, p_{j_k}), (j_{k'}, p_{j_{k'}}))$. Suppose it is not the case. Since $p_{i_t} \geq \widetilde{p_{i_t}}^-$, the point p_{i_t} lies strictly above the line passing through $((j_k, p_{j_k}), (j_{k'}, p_{j_{k'}}))$ and CH is not the convex hull of $\{(i, p_i)|i = 0, \ldots, d\}$, which is a contradiction. □

Proof of Proposition 6: Given the integer s, let t, h, t', h' be integers such that conditions $(i), (ii), (i')$ and (ii') hold.

By virtue of (i') and (ii'), $](t', p_{t'}), (t' + h', p_{t'+h'})]$ is the edge of CH whose orthogonal projection onto the abscissa axis contains $d + 1 - s$, and $\dfrac{p_{t'+h'} - p_{t'}}{h'}$ is the slope of that edge.

By virtue of (i) and (ii), $](t, \widetilde{p_t}), (t + h, \widetilde{p_{t+h}})]$ is the edge of $\widetilde{CH}$ whose orthogonal projection onto the abscissa axis contains $d + 1 - s$. Consider the two segments $](t, \widetilde{p_t}^-), (t + h, \widetilde{p_{t+h}}^-)]$ and $](t, \widetilde{p_t}^+), (t + h, \widetilde{p_{t+h}}^+)]$ that are the edges of $\widetilde{CH}^-$ and $\widetilde{CH}^+$, respectively, whose orthogonal projections onto the abscissa axis also contain $d + 1 - s$.

From Proposition 8 CH is a poly-line enclosed by $\widetilde{CH}^-$ and $\widetilde{CH}^+$ and since the first coordinates of its vertices are integers, its slope $\dfrac{p_{t'+h'} - p_{t'}}{h'}$ above $d + 1 - s$ is bounded below by $\dfrac{\widetilde{p_{t+h}} - \widetilde{p_t}}{h} - 2^{-M+1}$ and above by $\dfrac{\widetilde{p_{t+h}} - \widetilde{p_t}}{h} + 2^{-M+1}$, which proves Proposition 6. See Fig. 1 for an illustration. □

Algorithm 2. SolveRRC(P, c, δ)

Input: $P \in \mathbb{Z}[z]$ of degree d, a center $c \in \mathbb{G}$ and a relative precision $\delta > 0$.
Output: d positive real numbers $\rho_{c,s}, \ldots, \rho_{c,d}$ solving task S.

1: $g \leftarrow \lceil \log \dfrac{\log(4d)}{\log(1+\delta)} \rceil$
2: compute $Pc^{[g]}$
3: $\rho'_1, \ldots, \rho'_d \leftarrow$ SolveRRC$^*(Pc^{[g]})$
4: **for** $s = 0, \ldots, d$ **do**
5:     $\rho_{c,s} \leftarrow (\rho'_s)^{1/2^g}$
6: **return** $\rho_{c,1}, \ldots, \rho_{c,d}$

2.3   Solving the RRC Problem

Using Remark 2, we define in Algorithm 2 the algorithm SolveRRC. To estimate the cost at steps 2 and 3, let $\mathcal{M} : \mathbb{N} \to \mathbb{N}$ be such that two polynomials of degree at most d and bit-size at most τ can be multiplied by using $O(\mathcal{M}(d\tau))$ bit operations. Recall the following:

1. computing Pc requires $O(\mathcal{M}(d^2 \log d + d^2 \log(|c| + 1) + d \log \|P\|))$ bit operations,
2. $\|Pc\| \leq \|P\|(|c| + 1)^d$,
3. computing $\|Pc^{[i]}\|$ from $\|Pc^{[i-1]}\|$ requires $O(\mathcal{M}(d \log \|Pc^{[i-1]}\|))$ bit operations,
4. $\|Pc^{[i]}\| \leq (d+1)(\|Pc^{[i-1]}\|)^2 \leq \ldots \leq (d+1)^{2^i}(\|Pc\|)^{2^i}$.

For 1 and 2, see for instance [16][Theorem 2.4] and [16][Lemma 2.1]). 3 and 4 are derived from Eqs. (6) and (7), respectively. From 2, 4 and $g \in O(\log d)$ one obtains

$$\log \|Pc^{[g]}\| \in O(d \log(d+1) + d \log \|P\| + d^2 \log(|c| + 1)), \tag{18}$$

thus performing g DLG iterations for Pc involves

$$O(g\mathcal{M}(d \log \|Pc^{[g]}\|)) = O(\log d \mathcal{M}(d(d \log(d+1) + d \log \|P\| + d^2 \log(|c| + 1)))) \tag{19}$$

bit operations; this dominates the cost of step 2. Due to Schönhage-Strassen or Harvey-van der Hoeven multiplication, $\mathcal{M}(n) \in \widetilde{O}(n)$, and so step 2 involves

$$\widetilde{O}(d^2 \log \|P\| + d^3 \log(|c| + 1)) \tag{20}$$

bit operations. Step 3 involves $O(d \log \|Pc^{[g]}\|)$ bit operations, the cost of the **for** loop in steps 4–5 is dominated by the cost of step 2, and we complete the proof of Theorem 4.

2.4   Implementation Details

The exact computation of $Pc^{[g]}$ can involve numbers of very large bit-size (see Eq. (18)), and the key point for the practical efficiency of our implementation of Algorithm 2 is to avoid this. Instead, we use *ball arithmetic*, *i.e.* arbitrary precision floating point arithmetic with absolute error bounds, implemented for instance in the C library `arb` (see [9]).

3   Real Root Isolation

In this section, we approximate the root distances to 0 in order to improve in practice subdivision approaches to real root isolation, and in particular the one described in Subsect. 1.2. Let us define the notion of annuli cover of the roots of $P \in \mathbb{Z}[z]$.

Definition 1. *A set $\mathcal{A}_c$ of disjoint concentric annuli centered in c is an* annuli cover *of the roots of P of degree d if*

1. $\forall A \in \mathcal{A}_c$, there are integers $t(A)$ and $h(A)$ such that

$$\alpha_{t(A)}(P, c), \alpha_{t(A)+1}(P, c), \ldots, \alpha_{t(A)+h(A)}(P, c) \in A, \qquad (21)$$

2. $\forall i \in \{1, \ldots, d\}$, there is an $A \in \mathcal{A}_c$ such that $\alpha_i(P, c) \in A$.

For an annulus $A \in \mathcal{A}_c$, $\underline{r}(A)$ and $\overline{r}(A)$ are the interior and exterior radii of A, respectively. Write $s_+(A) := P(c + \underline{r}(A))P(c + \overline{r}(A))$ and $s_-(A) := P(c - \underline{r}(A))P(c - \overline{r}(A))$.

Given an annuli cover $\mathcal{A}_0$ centered at 0, we can skip many calls for exclusion and root-counting based on the following:

Remark 9. *Let $A \in \mathcal{A}_0$ such that $\underline{r}(A) > 0$.*

1. If $h(A) = 0$ and $s_+(A) > 0$ (resp. $s_-(A) > 0$), $A \cap \mathbb{R}_+$ (resp. $A \cap \mathbb{R}_-$) contains no real root of P.
2. If $h(A) = 0$ and $s_+(A) < 0$ (resp. $s_-(A) < 0$), $A \cap \mathbb{R}_+$ (resp. $A \cap \mathbb{R}_-$) contains one real root of P.
3. If $h(A) > 0$ and $s_+(A) < 0$ (resp. $s_-(A) < 0$), $A \cap \mathbb{R}_+$ (resp. $A \cap \mathbb{R}_-$) contains at least one real root of P.

In Subsects. 3.1 and 3.2 we describe our exclusion test and root counter based on Remark 9. In Subsect. 3.3 we describe our algorithm solving the RRI problem. In Subsect. 3.4 we present the results of our numerical tests.

3.1   Annuli Cover and Exclusion Test

Let B be a real line segment that does not contain 0, let $\mathcal{A}$ be an annuli cover centered in 0, and let $A \in \mathcal{A}$. Define that:

- s_B, the sign of B, is -1 (resp. 1) if $B < 0$ (resp. $B > 0$),
- $\mathbb{R}s_B(A)$ is $A \cap \mathbb{R}_-$ if $s_B < 0$, and is $A \cap \mathbb{R}_+$ otherwise,
- $ss_B(A)$ is $s_-(A)$ if $s_B < 0$, and is $s_+(A)$ otherwise,
- $n(\mathcal{A}, B)$ is the number of annuli $A \in \mathcal{A}$ s.t. $A \cap B \neq \emptyset$,

---

Algorithm 3. $C_{\mathbb{R}}^0(B, P, \mathcal{A})$

Input: A polynomial $P \in \mathbb{Z}[z]$ of degree d, a segment B of $\mathbb{R}$, an annuli cover $\mathcal{A}$ of the roots of P centered in 0. Assume $0 \notin B$.
Output: an integer in $\{-1, 0\}$; if 0 then P has no real root in B; if -1 then there is a root in $2B$.
1: Compute $n(\mathcal{A}, B)$, $n_0(\mathcal{A}, B)$ and $n_{\geq 1}(\mathcal{A}, B)$
2: **if** $n(\mathcal{A}, B) = n_0(\mathcal{A}, B)$ **then**
3:     **return** 0
4: **if** $n_{\geq 1}(\mathcal{A}, B) >= 1$ **then**
5:     **return** -1
6: **return** $T^0(\Delta(B), P)$

– $n_0(\mathcal{A}, B)$ is the number of annuli $A \in \mathcal{A}$ s.t.

$$(A \cap B \neq \emptyset) \wedge (h(A) = 0) \wedge ss_B(A) > 0, \tag{22}$$

– $n_{\geq 1}(\mathcal{A}, B)$: the number of annuli $A \in \mathcal{A}$ s.t.

$$(A \cap B \neq \emptyset) \wedge (h(A) \geq 0) \wedge ss_B(A) < 0 \wedge \mathbb{R}s_B(A) \subseteq 2B. \tag{23}$$

By virtue of Remark 9, if $n(\mathcal{A}, B) = n_0(\mathcal{A}, B)$, then all the annuli intersecting B contain no root, thus B contains no root. If $n_{\geq 1}(\mathcal{A}, B) \geq 1$ then $2B$ contains at least one real root.

Our exclusion test $C_{\mathbb{R}}^0$ is described in Algorithm 3. For computing $n(\mathcal{A}, B)$, $n_0(\mathcal{A}, B)$ and $n_{\geq 1}(\mathcal{A}, B)$ in Step 1, we use double precision interval arithmetic, hence Step 1 involves $O(d)$ bit operations. This implies

Proposition 10. *Let B be a real line segment with $0 \notin B$, and let $\mathcal{A}$ be an annuli cover of the roots of P centered in 0. The cost of carrying out $C_{\mathbb{R}}^0(B, P, \mathcal{A})$ is bounded by the cost of carrying out $T^0(\Delta(B), P)$.*

$C_{\mathbb{R}}^0(B, P, \mathcal{A})$ *returns an integer k in $\{-1, 0\}$. If $k = 0$, then P has no real roots in B. If $k = -1$, then P has a root in $2B$.*

3.2 Annuli Cover and Root Counter

In order to describe our root counter, we define:

– $n_1(\mathcal{A}, B)$: the number of annuli $A \in \mathcal{A}$ s.t. :

$$(A \cap B \neq \emptyset) \wedge (h(A) = 0) \wedge (ss_B(A) < 0) \wedge (\mathbb{R}s_B(A) \subseteq B), \tag{24}$$

– $n_{\geq 1}'(\mathcal{A}, B)$: the number of annuli $A \in \mathcal{A}$ s.t.:

$$(A \cap B \neq \emptyset) \wedge (h(A) \geq 0) \wedge ss_B(A) < 0 \wedge (\mathbb{R}s_B(A) \subseteq 2B \setminus (1/2)B). \tag{25}$$

By virtue of Remark 9, if $n(\mathcal{A}, B) = n_0(\mathcal{A}, B) + n_1(\mathcal{A}, B)$, B contains exactly $n_1(\mathcal{A}, B)$ real roots. If $n_{\geq 1}'(\mathcal{A}, B) \geq 1$ then P has at least one real root in $2B \setminus (1/2)B$.

Our root counter is described in Algorithm 4. We use double precision interval arithmetic for computing $n(\mathcal{A}, B)$, $n_0(\mathcal{A}, B)$, $n_1(\mathcal{A}, B)$ and $n_{\geq 1}'(\mathcal{A}, B)$ in Step 1, thus Step 1 involves $O(d)$ bit operations.

Algorithm 4. $C_{\mathbb{R}}^*(B, P, \mathcal{A})$

Input: A polynomial $P \in \mathbb{Z}[z]$ of degree d, a segment B of $\mathbb{R}$, an annuli cover $\mathcal{A}$ of the roots of P centered in 0. Assume $0 \notin 2B$.

Output: an integer k in $\{-1, 0, 1, \ldots, d\}$; if $k \geq 0$ then P has k roots in B; if -1 then there is a root in $2B \setminus (1/2)B$.

1: Compute $n(\mathcal{A}, B)$, $n_0(\mathcal{A}, B)$, $n_1(\mathcal{A}, B)$ and $n'_{\geq 1}(\mathcal{A}, B)$
2: **if** $n(\mathcal{A}, B) = n_0(\mathcal{A}, B) + n_1(\mathcal{A}, B)$ **then**
3:      **return** $n_1(\mathcal{A}, B)$
4: **if** $n'_{\geq 1}(\mathcal{A}, B) \geq 1$ **then**
5:      **return** -1
6: **return** $T^*(\Delta(B), P)$

Proposition 11. *Let B be a real line segment with $0 \notin B$ and let $\mathcal{A}$ be an annuli cover of the roots of P centered in 0. The cost of carrying out $C_{\mathbb{R}}^*(B, P, \mathcal{A})$ is bounded by the cost of carrying out $T^*(\Delta(B), P)$.*

$C_{\mathbb{R}}^*(B, P, \mathcal{A})$ returns an integer k in $\{-1, 0, \ldots, d\}$. If $k \geq 0$, then P has k roots in $\Delta(B)$. If $k = -1$, then P has a root in $2B \setminus (1/2)B$.

3.3 Annuli Cover and the RRI Problem

Consider the following procedure.

Stage 1: Compute $\mathcal{A}_0$ by calling `SolveRRC`$(P, 0, d^{-2})$.
Stage 2: Apply the subdivision procedure of Subsect. 1.2 while using $C_{\mathbb{R}}^0(B, P, \mathcal{A}_0)$ (resp. $C_{\mathbb{R}}^*(B, P, \mathcal{A}_0)$) as an exclusion test (resp. root counter) for real line segment B of the subdivision tree. In the verification step of Newton iterations, use the T^*-test of [2].

At Stage 1, we obtain $\mathcal{A}_0$ by computing the connected components made up of the concentric annuli defined by the output of `SolveRRC`$(P, 0, d^{-2})$.

By virtue of Theorem 4 and Propositions 10 and 11, this procedure solves the RRI problem, and its bit-complexity is bounded by the bit-complexity of the algorithm described in [1], thus it is near optimal for the benchmark problem.

3.4 Experimental Results

The procedure given in Subsect. 3.3 has been implemented within the library `Ccluster`; we call this implementation `RisolateR`. Comparison of `RisolateR` with `Risolate` reveals practical improvement due to using our root radii algorithms in subdivision process. We also compare `RisolateR` with the subdivision algorithm of [14] whose implementation `ANewDsc` is described in [10] and is currently the user's choice for real root isolation.

Test Polynomials. We consider the following polynomials.

The Bernoulli polynomial of degree d is $B_d(z) = \sum_{k=0}^{d} \binom{d}{k} b_{d-k} z^k$ where the b_i's are the Bernoulli numbers.

The Wilkinson polynomial of degree d is $W_d(z) = \prod_{i=1}^{d}(z - i)$.

For integers $n > 0$, we define polynomials with $(2n + 1) \times (2n + 1)$ roots on the nodes of a regular grid centered at 0 as

$$P_{(2n+1) \times (2n+1)}(z) = \prod_{-n \leq a,b \leq n} (z - a + ib). \tag{26}$$

The Mignotte polynomial of degree d and bitsize τ is $M_{d,\tau}(z) = z^d - 2(2^{\frac{\tau}{2}-1}z - 1)^2$.

We also consider dense polynomials of degree d with coefficients randomly chosen within $[-2^{\tau-1}, 2^{\tau-1}]$ (under the uniform distribution).

Results. In our test polynomials with several degrees/bit-sizes, we used Risolate, RisolateR and ANewDsc to solve the RRI problem. Our non-random examples have only simple roots and for those examples ANewDsc is called with option -S 1 to avoid testing input polynomial for being square-free.

Times are sequential times in seconds on a Intel(R) Core(TM) i7-8700 CPU @ 3.20 GHz machine with Linux. We report in Table 2:

- d, τ and $d_{\mathbb{R}}$, that is, the degree, the bit-size and the number of real roots, respectively,
- t_1 (resp. t_2), the running time of Risolate (resp. RisolateR),
- n_1 (resp. n_2), the number of T^0-tests in Risolate (resp. RisolateR),
- n_1' (resp. n_2'), the number of T^*-tests in Risolate (resp. RisolateR),
- t_3, the time required to compute the annuli cover in RisolateR,
- t_4, the running time in second of ANewDsc.

For random polynomials, we display averages over 10 examples of those values. We also display σ_1, σ_2, and σ_4, the standard deviation of running time of Risolate, RisolateR and ANewDsc, respectively.

Compare columns n_1, n_1' and n_2, n_2' in Table 2: using the annuli cover both in exclusion tests and root counter reduces dramatically the number of Pellet's tests performed in the subdivision process, and significantly decreases the running time (see column t_2/t_1). In the cases where the ratio τ/d is low RisolateR spent most of the time on solving the RRC problem (see column t_3/t_2). Finally, ANewDsc remains faster than RisolateR for polynomials having a few real roots or a low bit-size, whereas this trend seems to reverse when the ratios of the number of real roots and/or bit-size over the degree increase (see columns t_2 and t_4). Mignotte polynomials of even degree have four real roots among which two are separated by a distance way less than the relative size of d^{-2}, the relative size of annuli in the computed annuli cover. In such cases, the knowledge of root radii enables no significant improvement because subdivision solvers spend most of their running time on performing Newton's iterations that converge to the cluster of two close roots, and then on separating the two roots.

Table 2. Runs of `Risolate`, `RisolateR` and `ANewDsc` on our test polynomials

			Risolate		RisolateR				ANewDsc
d	τ	$d_{\mathbb{R}}$	$t_1\ (\sigma_1)$	n_1, n_1'	$t_2\ (\sigma_2)$	n_2, n_2'	$t_3/t_2\ (\%)$	$t_2/t_1\ (\%)$	$t_4\ (\sigma_4)$
				10 monic random dense polynomials per degree/bit-size					
256	8192	6.00	3.02 (1.13)	128.,80.2	.374 (.080)	4.40,25.3	16.3	12.3	.784 (1.73)
256	16384	7.80	5.09 (1.99)	183.,122.	.499 (.132)	2.60,22.9	22.2	9.80	2.76 (5.19)
256	32768	7.40	7.59 (3.20)	172.,125.	.442 (.174)	4.40,27.4	16.3	5.82	1.18 (.600)
256	65536	7.00	10.7 (6.33)	170.,140.	.480 (.160)	4.30,25.4	10.4	4.46	1.91 (1.18)
391	8192	7.20	8.87 (2.99)	157.,107.	1.12 (.310)	4.60,26.0	15.0	12.6	3.29 (5.42)
391	16384	8.40	10.1 (4.12)	186.,116.	1.39 (.575)	6.20,28.9	15.3	13.7	10.2 (19.8)
391	32768	8.60	18.6 (6.98)	202.,155.	1.38 (.528)	4.00,29.0	14.5	7.41	1.67 (.750)
391	65536	7.60	23.9 (13.9)	178.,137.	1.88 (1.17)	3.90,33.6	18.5	7.86	13.9 (18.9)
512	8192	6.60	31.1 (18.5)	158.,104.	3.68 (4.72)	6.00,25.9	12.4	11.8	1.26 (1.03)
512	16384	5.20	41.1 (20.1)	152.,106.	5.00 (4.63)	6.50,25.8	5.37	12.1	1.70 (2.17)
512	32768	6.00	56.7 (28.1)	167.,122.	2.00 (.596)	4.40,28.4	18.1	3.53	5.95 (7.61)
512	65536	6.60	86.5 (34.2)	180.,137.	4.84 (3.67)	5.90,32.7	5.19	5.60	60.1 (118.)
				Bernoulli polynomials					
256	1056	64	1.13	292, 82	0.08	12, 3	54.2	7.77	0.20
391	1809	95	2.66	460, 145	0.30	12, 2	76.1	11.2	1.09
512	2590	124	6.15	528, 144	0.38	14, 3	65.9	6.30	1.58
791	4434	187	16.3	892, 264	2.39	20, 1	85.0	14.6	9.92
1024	6138	244	56.3	1048, 283	2.42	12, 3	76.5	4.30	14.9
				Wilkinson polynomials					
256	1690	256	3.63	1030, 283	0.17	0, 10	41.1	4.90	1.57
391	2815	391	17.6	1802, 541	0.68	0, 10	51.7	3.88	5.69
512	3882	512	25.9	2058, 533	1.04	0, 11	46.9	4.01	27.1
791	6488	791	165.	3698, 1110	7.04	0, 11	57.1	4.26	158.
1024	8777	1024	265.	4114, 1049	8.38	0, 12	51.2	3.15	309.
				Polynomials with roots on a regular grid					
289	741	17	0.40	86, 30	0.13	0, 16	81.7	34.4	0.09
441	1264	21	0.91	106, 36	0.21	0, 20	77.3	23.4	0.39
625	1948	25	1.59	118, 39	0.92	0, 24	89.1	58.0	0.80
841	2800	29	3.30	154, 51	1.67	0, 28	87.4	50.7	2.56
1089	3828	33	8.06	166, 55	2.20	0, 32	76.4	27.3	4.49
				Mignotte polynomials					
512	256	4	1.57	34, 15	1.67	2, 12	16.5	106.	0.76
512	512	4	3.07	34, 15	4.81	2, 14	5.70	156.	1.90
512	1024	4	5.91	34, 15	5.96	2, 10	4.13	100.	5.28
512	2048	4	13.8	34, 15	13.2	2, 9	2.42	95.3	14.1
512	4096	4	29.7	50, 17	30.8	2, 6	.753	103.	36.0

4   Complex Root Clustering

In this section, by approximating the root distances from three centers, namely 0, 1 and i we improve practical performance of subdivision algorithms for complex root clustering.

Using three annuli covers $\mathcal{A}_0, \mathcal{A}_1$ and $\mathcal{A}_i$ of the roots of P, one can compute a set $\mathcal{D}$ of $O(d^2)$ complex discs containing all the roots of P, and then skip expensive Pellet-based exclusion tests of the boxes that do not intersect the union of these discs.

In Subsect. 4.1 we describe an exclusion test using the set $\mathcal{D}$ of discs containing the roots of P, and in Subsect. 4.2 we present a procedure solving the CRC with near optimal bit complexity. In Subsect. 4.3 we show experimental results.

4.1   Annuli Cover and Exclusion Test

Let $\mathcal{D}$ be a set of $O(d^2)$ complex discs covering all the roots of P, *i.e.* any root of P is in at least one disc in $\mathcal{D}$. A box B such that $B \cap \mathcal{D} = \emptyset$ cannot contain a root of P.

We define an exclusion test based on the above consideration, called $C_{\mathbb{C}}^0$-test and described in Algorithm 5. For a box B having a nonempty intersection with the real line, the number $n_{\geq 1}(\mathcal{A}_0, B)$ of annuli intersecting B and containing at least one real root in $B \cap \mathbb{R}$ is used to save some T^0-tests.

Algorithm 5. $C_{\mathbb{C}}^0(B, P, \mathcal{D}, \mathcal{A}_0)$

Input: A polynomial $P \in \mathbb{Z}[z]$ of degree d, a box B of $\mathbb{C}$, a set $\mathcal{D}$ of $O(d^2)$ complex discs covering all the roots of P, an annuli cover $\mathcal{A}_0$ centered in 0

Output: an integer in $\{-1, 0\}$; if 0 then P has no real root in B; if -1 then there is a root in $2B$.

1: Compute the number n of discs in $\mathcal{D}$ having nonempty intersection with B.
2: **if** $n = 0$ **then**
3:     **return** 0
4: **if** $B \cap \mathbb{R} \neq \emptyset$ **then**
5:     Compute $n_{\geq 1}(\mathcal{A}_0, B)$
6:     **if** $n_{\geq 1}(\mathcal{A}_0, B) >= 1$ **then**
7:         **return** -1
8: **return** $T^0(\Delta(B), P)$

Proposition 12. *Let $\mathcal{D}$ contain $O(d^2)$ discs covering the roots of P and let $\mathcal{A}_0$ be an annuli cover of the roots of P centered in 0. The cost of performing $C_{\mathbb{C}}^0(B, P, \mathcal{D}, \mathcal{A}_0)$ is bounded by the cost of performing $T^0(\Delta(B), P)$.*

$C_{\mathbb{C}}^0(B, P, \mathcal{D}, \mathcal{A}_0)$ returns an integer k in $\{-1, 0\}$. If $k = 0$, then P has no root in B. If $k = -1$, then P has a root in $2B$.

4.2   Annuli Cover and the CRC Problem

Consider the following procedure.

Stage 1: For $c = 0, 1, \mathbf{i}$, compute $\mathcal{A}_c$ by calling `SolveRRC`(P, c, d^{-2}).
Stage 2: Use $\mathcal{A}_0$, $\mathcal{A}_1$ and $\mathcal{A}_{\mathbf{i}}$ to compute a set $\mathcal{D}$ of at most $2d^2$ discs covering all roots of P.
Stage 3: Apply the Complex Root Clustering Algorithm of Subsect. 1.2 but let it apply $C_{\mathbb{C}}^0(B, P, \mathcal{D}, \mathcal{A}_0)$ instead of $T^0(\Delta(B), P)$ as the exclusion test for

boxes B of the subdivision tree. In the verification step of Newton iterations, use the T^*-test of [2].

In Stage 1, for $c = 0, 1, i$, $\mathcal{A}_c$ is obtained by computing the connected components of the concentric annnuli defined by the output of SolveRRC(P, c, d^{-2}). According to Theorem 4, Stage 1 involves $\widetilde{O}(d^2(d + \log \|P\|_\infty))$ bit operations.

In Stage 2, $\mathcal{D}$ is computed as follows: using double precision floating point arithmetic with correct rounding, first compute complex discs containing all possible intersections of an annulus in $\mathcal{A}_0$ with an annulus in $\mathcal{A}_1$, and obtain a set $\mathcal{D}$ of at most $2d^2$ complex discs containing all roots of P. Then, for each disc Δ in $\mathcal{D}$ check if Δ and its complex conjugate $\overline{\Delta}$ have a nonempty intersection with at least one annulus of $\mathcal{A}_i$, and remove Δ from $\mathcal{D}$ if it does not. This step has cost in $O(d^3)$.

By virtue of Proposition 12, the cost of performing Stage 3 is bounded by the cost of performing the algorithm described in Subsect. 1.2. This procedure solves the CRC problem and supports near optimal complexity for the benchmark problem.

4.3   Experimental Results

The procedure of Subsect. 4.2 is implemented within Ccluster; below we call this implementation CclusterR and present experimental results that highlight practical improvement due to using our root radii algorithm in subdivision.

We used Ccluster and CclusterR with input value $\varepsilon = 2^{-53}$ to find clusters of size at most ε. We also used MPSolve-3.2.1, with options -as -Ga -o16 -j1 to find approximations with 16 correct digits of the roots.

For our test polynomials (see 3.4) we report in Table 3:

- d and τ denoting the degree and the bit-size, respectively,
- t_1 (resp. t_2), the running time of Ccluster (resp. CclusterR),
- n_1 (resp. n_2), the number of T^0-tests in Ccluster (resp. CclusterR),
- t_3, the time for computing the three annuli covers in CclusterR, - t_4, the running time of MPSolve in seconds.

For random polynomials, we show averages over 10 examples of those values. We also show σ_1, σ_2, and σ_4, the standard deviations of the running times of Ccluster, CclusterR and MPSolve. For the real root isolator presented in Sect. 3, using root radii enables significant saving of Pellet-based exclusion tests in the subdivision process (compare columns n_1 and n_2) and yields a speed-up factor about 3 for our examples (see column t_2/t_1). This speed-up increases as the number of real roots increases (see, e.g., Wilkinson polynomials) because some exclusion tests for boxes B containing the real line are avoided when $2B$ contains at least one root which we can see from the number $n_{\geq 1}(\mathcal{A}_0, B)$ computed in the $C_{\mathbb{C}}^0$ test. The time spent for computing the three annuli covers remains low compared to the running time of CclusterR (see column t_3/t_2). MPSolve remains the user's choice for approximating all complex roots.

Table 3. Runs of Ccluster, CclusterR and MPSolve on our test polynomials

d	τ	$t_1\ (\sigma_1)$	n_1	$t_2\ (\sigma_2)$	n_2	$t_3/t_2\ (\%)$	$t_2/t_1\ (\%)$	$t_4\ (\sigma_4)$
		Ccluster		CclusterR				MPSolve
		10 monic random dense polynomials per degree						
128	128	4.43 (.760)	2598.	1.46 (.235)	463.	7.81	33.1	.031 (.003)
191	191	13.5 (1.82)	3846.	4.40 (.528)	694.	4.20	32.6	.063 (.007)
256	256	23.7 (2.52)	4888.	7.87 (.672)	909.	7.04	33.2	.106 (.013)
391	391	70.9 (9.23)	7494.	22.5 (1.95)	1460.	3.67	31.7	.209 (.037)
512	512	154. (17.9)	9996.	46.1 (6.00)	1840.	7.08	29.9	.392 (.102)
		Bernoulli polynomials						
128	410	3.86	2954	1.25	548	7.48	32.3	0.07
191	689	12.2	4026	4.51	942	8.07	36.8	0.16
256	1056	24.7	5950	10.1	1253	6.57	41.1	0.39
391	1809	75.1	8322	27.4	1907	16.2	36.5	0.97
512	2590	133.	11738	49.9	2645	12.7	37.5	2.32
		Wilkinson polynomials						
128	721	8.43	3786	1.09	14	14.4	12.9	0.17
191	1183	25.4	5916	2.99	18	27.9	11.7	0.51
256	1690	50.7	7500	6.34	18	21.7	12.4	1.17
391	2815	201.	12780	23.1	22	36.2	11.4	4.30
512	3882	379.	14994	51.3	22	35.6	13.5	9.33
		Polynomials with roots on a regular grid						
169	369	7.37	3072	1.99	592	4.03	27.1	0.05
289	741	27.1	5864	10.2	1573	3.18	37.9	0.13
441	1264	81.4	9976	24.4	1713	4.28	29.9	0.56
625	1948	228.	15560	70.2	2508	15.0	30.7	1.16
841	2800	493.	19664	169.	4294	5.75	34.2	3.84
		Mignotte polynomials						
512	256	88.8	9304	28.3	1611	11.0	31.8	0.76
512	512	88.3	9304	29.3	1570	9.20	33.1	0.79
512	1024	101.	9304	32.1	1647	8.62	31.7	0.91
512	2048	106.	9304	33.4	1990	7.50	31.2	1.12
512	4096	102.	9304	50.1	3593	4.88	49.0	1.10

References

1. Becker, R., Sagraloff, M., Sharma, V., Xu, J., Yap, C.: Complexity analysis of root clustering for a complex polynomial. In: Proceedings of the ACM on International Symposium on Symbolic and Algebraic Computation, ISSAC 2016, pp. 71–78. ACM, New York (2016)
2. Becker, R., Sagraloff, M., Sharma, V., Yap, C.: A near-optimal subdivision algorithm for complex root isolation based on Pellet test and Newton iteration. J. Symb. Comput. **86**, 51–96 (2018)
3. Bini, D.A., Robol, L.: Solving secular and polynomial equations: a multiprecision algorithm. J. Comput. Appl. Math. **272**, 276–292 (2014)
4. Fujiwara, M.: Über die obere schranke des absoluten betrages der wurzeln einer algebraischen gleichung. Tohoku Math. J. First Series **10**, 167–171 (1916)
5. Gourdon, X.: Algorithmique du theoreme fondamental de l'algebre. Research Report RR-1852, INRIA (1993). https://hal.inria.fr/inria-00074820
6. Graham, R.L., Yao, F.F.: Finding the convex hull of a simple polygon. J. Algorithms **4**(4), 324–331 (1983)
7. Henrici, P., Gargantini, I.: Uniformly convergent algorithms for the simultaneous approximation of all zeros of a polynomial. In: Constructive Aspects of the Fundamental Theorem of Algebra, pp. 77–113. Wiley-Interscience New York (1969)
8. Imbach, R., Pan, V.Y., Yap, C.: Implementation of a near-optimal complex root clustering algorithm. Math. Softw. - ICMS **2018**, 235–244 (2018)

9. Johansson, F.: Arb: efficient arbitrary-precision midpoint-radius interval arithmetic. IEEE Trans. Comput. **66**, 1281–1292 (2017)
10. Kobel, A., Rouillier, F., Sagraloff, M.: Computing real roots of real polynomials ... and now for real! In: Proceedings of the ACM on International Symposium on Symbolic and Algebraic Computation, ISSAC 2016, pp. 303–310. ACM, New York (2016)
11. Mignotte, M.: On the distance between the roots of a polynomial. Appl. Algebra Eng. Commun. Comput. **6**(6), 327–332 (1995)
12. Pan, V.Y.: Approximating complex polynomial zeros: modified Weyl's quadtree construction and improved Newton's iteration. J. Complex. **16**(1), 213–264 (2000)
13. Pan, V.Y.: Univariate polynomials: nearly optimal algorithms for numerical factorization and root-finding. J. Symb. Comput. **33**(5), 701–733 (2002)
14. Sagraloff, M., Mehlhorn, K.: Computing real roots of real polynomials. J. Symb. Comput. **73**, 46–86 (2016)
15. Schönhage, A.: The fundamental theorem of algebra in terms of computational complexity. Preliminary report, University of Tübingen, Germany (1982)
16. Von Zur Gathen, J., Gerhard, J.: Fast algorithms for Taylor shifts and certain difference equations. In: Proceedings of the 1997 International Symposium on Symbolic and Algebraic Computation, pp. 40–47. ACM (1997)

On First Integrals and Invariant Manifolds in the Generalized Problem of the Motion of a Rigid Body in a Magnetic Field

Valentin Irtegov and Tatiana Titorenko[✉]

Institute for System Dynamics and Control Theory, SB RAS,
134, Lermontov str., Irkutsk 664033, Russia
{irteg,titor}@icc.ru

Abstract. Differential equations describing the motion of a rigid body with a fixed point under the influence of both a magnetic field generated by the Barnett–London effect and potential forces are analyzed. We seek first integrals and invariant manifolds of the equations in the form of polynomials of the second, third, and fourth degrees and conduct the qualitative analysis of the equations in the found particular cases of the existence of additional integrals. Special solutions are found from the necessary extremum conditions of the integrals and their Lyapunov stability is investigated. Computer algebra methods such as the reduction of a polynomial with respect to a list of polynomials, the Gröbner basis method, etc. are used to obtain the integrals and manifolds and to analyze the equations.

1 Introduction

The paper continues our previous work [9] devoted to finding linear invariant manifolds of differential equations in the problem on the rotation of a rigid body with a fixed point in an uniform magnetic field generated by the Barnett–London effect [2,3], taking into account the moment of potential forces. As was noted therein, the influence of the Barnett–London effect on the motion of the body was studied in a number of works in various aspects. Similar problems arise in many applications, e.g., in space dynamics [4], in designing instruments having a contactless suspension system [14]. Our interest is in the qualitative analysis of the equations of motion of the body.

The Euler–Poisson equations of motion of a rigid body with a fixed point in the problem under consideration can be written as [5]:

$$A\dot{\boldsymbol{\omega}} = A\boldsymbol{\omega} \times \boldsymbol{\omega} + B\boldsymbol{\omega} \times \boldsymbol{\gamma} + \boldsymbol{\gamma} \times (C\boldsymbol{\gamma} - \mathbf{s}), \quad \dot{\boldsymbol{\gamma}} = \boldsymbol{\gamma} \times \boldsymbol{\omega}. \tag{1}$$

Here $\boldsymbol{\omega} = (\omega_1, \omega_2, \omega_3)$ is the angular velocity of the body, $\boldsymbol{\gamma} = (\gamma_1, \gamma_2, \gamma_3)$ is the unit vector of the direction of the magnetic field, $\mathbf{s} = (s_1, s_2, s_3)$ is the center of mass of the body, A, B, C are the symmetric matrices of 3rd order:

© Springer Nature Switzerland AG 2021
F. Boulier et al. (Eds.): CASC 2021, LNCS 12865, pp. 157–173, 2021.
https://doi.org/10.1007/978-3-030-85165-1_10

A is the inertia tensor of the body computed at its fixed point, B is the matrix characterizing the magnetic moment of the body, C is the matrix characterizing the action of potential forces on the body.

Equations (1) admit the two first integrals

$$V_1 = A\boldsymbol{\omega} \cdot \boldsymbol{\gamma} = \kappa, \ V_2 = \boldsymbol{\gamma} \cdot \boldsymbol{\gamma} = 1 \tag{2}$$

and, in the general case, are non-integrable. Therefore, the problem of finding invariant manifolds (IMs) and additional first integrals of these equations is of interest for their integrability and analysis. A number of works are devoted to this question, e.g., [5,10,13]. In [5], a linear invariant relation of the Hess type [6] has been found for Eqs. (1). In [10,13], the integrable cases of the equations have been presented when the matrices A, B are diagonal, and potential forces are absent.

In [9], we have proposed a technique to find linear IMs for the equations of type (1). It is a combination of the method of undetermined coefficients with the methods of computer algebra and allows one to obtain both the conditions of the existence of the IMs and the IMs themselves. The aim of this work is to find IMs and first integrals of Eqs. (1) in the form of the polynomials of the 2nd degree and higher and to apply them for the qualitative analysis of these equations. By the same technique as before, we have found the new polynomial IMs and additional first integrals of the 2nd–4th degrees. The latter were used in the qualitative analysis of the equations by the Routh–Lyapunov method [11]. Stationary solutions and IMs were found and their Lyapunov stability was analyzed. The computer algebra system (CAS) "Mathematica" was employed to solve computational problems. The software package [1] developed on its base was used in the analysis of the stability of stationary solutions and IMs.

The paper is organized as follows. In Sect. 2, obtaining the polynomial IMs and integrals of the 2nd–4th degrees for equations (1) by the above-mentioned technique is described. In Sects. 3 and 4, the qualitative analysis of these equations in the particular cases of their integrability is done. In Sect. 5, a conclusion is given.

2   Obtaining Integrals and Invariant Manifolds

For Eqs. (1), we state the problem to find IMs and integrals defined by the polynomials like

$$P = \sum_{\alpha=0}^{n} a_{\alpha} p^{\alpha},$$

where $p^{\alpha} = \omega_1^{\alpha_1} \omega_2^{\alpha_2} \omega_3^{\alpha_3} \gamma_1^{\alpha_4} \gamma_2^{\alpha_5} \gamma_3^{\alpha_6}$, α_i $(1,\ldots,6)$ are the non-negative integers, $\alpha = \sum_{i=1}^{6} \alpha_i$ is the degree of the monomial p^{α}.

In the present work, the cases when $n = 2, 3, 4$ are considered.

2.1 Quadratic Integrals and Invariant Manifolds

Let in Eqs. (1) be $A = diag(A_1, A_2, A_3)$, $B = diag(B_1, B_2, B_3)$, $C = diag(C_1, C_2, C_3)$. IMs and integrals will be sought for these equations in the form:

$$F(\omega_1, \omega_2, \omega_3, \gamma_1, \gamma_2, \gamma_3) = \sum_{i=1}^{3} \left(\sum_{j=i}^{3} (x_{ij}\,\omega_i\omega_j + z_{ij}\,\gamma_i\gamma_j) + \sum_{j=1}^{3} y_{ij}\,\omega_i\gamma_j \right)$$

$$+ f_1\omega_1 + f_2\omega_2 + f_3\omega_3 + f_4\gamma_1 + f_5\gamma_2 + f_6\gamma_3 + f_0 = 0. \tag{3}$$

Here $x_{ij}, y_{ij}, z_{ij}, f_l$ are constant parameters to be determined.

Compute the derivative of F (3) by virtue of Eqs. (1). The derivative $G = G(\omega_i, \gamma_i)$ $(i = 1, 2, 3)$ is a polynomial of the phase variables ω_i, γ_i. Considering G as the polynomial of one phase variable, e.g., ω_1, with the coefficients of the rest of the variables, we can represent it, using the built-in function *PolynomialReduce* of CAS "Mathematica" in the form *PolynomialReduce*$[G, \{F\}, \{\omega_1\}]$, as follows:

$$G = QF + R,$$

where $Q = Q(\omega_2, \omega_3, \gamma_j)$, $R = R(\omega_1, \omega_2, \omega_3, \gamma_j)$ are some polynomials (the degree of R < the degree of F in ω_1). F defines the IMs of Eqs. (1) if $R \equiv 0$, and their integral if $Q = R \equiv 0$.

Equating the coefficients of similar terms in R to zero, we have the system of polynomial equations with respect to $x_{ij}, y_{ij}, y_{ji}, z_{ij}, f_k$ $(i, j = 1, 2, 3; k = 0, \ldots, 6)$:

$$A_2 f_3 s_2 - A_3 f_2 s_3 = 0, \quad (A_1 - A_3)\, f_0 x_{12} = 0, \quad (A_1 - A_3)\,(f_2 x_{11} - f_1 x_{12}) = 0,$$
$$(A_1 - A_3)\, f_3 x_{12} = 0, \quad (A_1 - A_2)\, f_0 x_{13} = 0, \quad (A_1 - A_2)\,(f_3 x_{11} - f_1 x_{13}) = 0,$$
$$(A_1 - A_2)\, f_2 x_{13} = 0, \quad A_3 s_3 x_{12} - A_2 s_2 x_{13} = 0, \quad (A_1 - A_2)\, x_{13} x_{22} = 0,$$
$$A_2 A_3 (A_2 - A_3) f_1 x_{11} + A_1 A_3 (A_1 - A_3) f_2 x_{12} - A_1 A_2 (A_1 - A_2) f_3 x_{13} = 0,$$
$$(A_1 - A_2)\,(x_{12} x_{13} - x_{11} x_{23}) = 0, \quad (A_1 - A_3)\,(x_{12} x_{13} - x_{11} x_{23}) = 0,$$
$$A_2 (B_2 f_3 - A_3 f_6)\, x_{11} + (A_1 - A_2) A_2 f_4 x_{13} - (2 A_3 s_3 x_{22} - A_2 s_2 x_{23})\, x_{11} = 0,$$
$$A_3 (A_2 (A_2 - A_3)\, x_{11} + A_1 (A_1 - A_3)\, x_{22})\, x_{12} - A_1 A_2 (A_1 - A_2)\, x_{13} x_{23} = 0,$$
$$2 A_2 (A_2 - A_3) A_3 x_{11}^2 + A_1 A_3 (A_1 - A_3)(x_{12}^2 - 2 x_{11} x_{22}) \tag{4}$$
$$+ A_1 A_2 (A_1 - A_2)(2 x_{11} x_{33} - x_{13}^2) = 0,$$
$$A_3 (B_3 f_2 - A_2 f_5)\, x_{11} + (A_1 - A_3) A_3 f_4 x_{12} + (A_3 s_3 x_{23} - 2 A_2 s_2 x_{33})\, x_{11} = 0,$$
$$(A_1 - A_3)\, x_{12} x_{33} = 0,$$
$$(A_2 (A_2 - A_3) A_3 x_{11} - A_1 A_2 (A_1 - A_2)\, x_{33})\, x_{13} + A_1 (A_1 - A_3) A_3 x_{12} x_{23} = 0,$$
$$g_l(x_{ij}, y_{ij}, y_{ji}, f_k) = 0 \ (l = 1, \ldots, 29),$$
$$h_m(x_{ij}, y_{ij}, y_{ji}, z_{ij}, f_k) = 0 \ (m = 1, \ldots, 26).$$

Here g_l, h_m are the polynomials of $x_{ij}, y_{ij}, y_{ji}, z_{ij}, f_k$.

So, the problem of seeking the quadratic IMs and integrals of differential Eqs. (1) is reduced to solving the above system of polynomial algebraic equations. It is the overdetermined system of 73 equations with the parameters A_i, B_i, C_i, s_i $(i = 1, 2, 3)$, the number of unknowns is 28.

As can be seen, Eqs. (4) are split up into several subsystems in the variables. The first 18 equations depend only on x_{ij}, f_k. We resolve them with respect to these variables

$$f_1 = f_2 = f_3 = 0, \; f_5 = \frac{2s_2(A_2(A_2 - A_3)\,x_{11} - A_1(A_1 - A_3)\,x_{22})}{A_1 A_2(A_1 - A_2)}, \; f_6 = -\frac{2s_3\,x_{22}}{A_2},$$

$$x_{12} = x_{13} = x_{23} = 0, \; x_{33} = \frac{A_3(A_1(A_1 - A_3)\,x_{22} - A_2(A_2 - A_3)\,x_{11})}{A_1 A_2(A_1 - A_2)} \qquad (5)$$

and substitute the found solution into the rest of the equations. The resulting system consists of 53 equations in the variables $f_0, f_4, x_{11}, x_{22}, y_{ij}, y_{ji}, z_{ij}$. Next, a lexicographical basis with respect to a part of the variables and parameters, e.g., $f_0, f_4, x_{22}, y_{ij}, y_{ji}, z_{ij}, C_1, C_2, C_3, B_1, B_2, s_1, s_2, s_3$ for the polynomials of the system is constructed. As a result, we have a system decomposing into 2 subsystems. These are not represented here for space reasons.

A lexicographical basis with respect to the above variables was computed for the polynomials of each subsystem. One of the bases is written as

$$s_1 = 0, \; s_2 = 0, \; s_3 = 0, \; a_3 B_1 - a_2 B_2 + a_1 B_3 = 0, \; a_3 C_1 - a_2 C_2 + a_1 C_3 = 0,$$
$$(C_2 - C_3)\,x_{11} - A_1(z_{22} - z_{33}) = 0, \; z_{23} = 0, \; z_{13} = 0, \; z_{12} = 0,$$
$$(a_3 B_3 C_1 + a_2(B_2(C_2 - C_3) - B_3 C_2) + a_1 B_3 C_3)\,x_{11} - A_1(a_2 B_2 - a_1 B_3)\,z_{11}$$
$$+ A_1(a_2 B_2 - a_1 B_3)\,z_{33} = 0,$$
$$(a_3 C_1 - a_2 C_2 + a_1 C_3)((C_3 - C_1)\,x_{11} + A_1(z_{11} - z_{33})) = 0, \qquad (6)$$
$$y_{32} = 0, \; y_{31} = 0, \; y_{23} = 0, \; y_{21} = 0, \; y_{13} = 0, \; y_{12} = 0,$$
$$A_3 y_{22} - A_2 y_{33} = 0, \; A_1 y_{33} - A_3 y_{11} = 0,$$
$$A_2 a_3 B_2\,x_{11} - A_1(a_2 B_2 - a_1 B_3)\,x_{22} = 0,$$
$$A_2(a_2 C_2 - a_3 C_1 - a_1 C_3)\,x_{11} - A_1(a_2 C_2 - a_2 C_3)\,x_{22} + A_1 A_2 a_3(z_{11} - z_{33}) = 0,$$
$$(C_1 - C_3)\,x_{22} - A_2(z_{11} - z_{33}) = 0, \; f_4 = 0,$$

where $a_1 = A_1 - A_2, \; a_2 = A_1 - A_3, \; a_3 = A_2 - A_3$.

Equations (6) have the following solution:

$$B_1 = \frac{a_2 B_2 - a_1 B_3}{a_3}, \; C_1 = \frac{a_2 C_2 - a_1 C_3}{a_3}, \; s_1 = s_2 = s_3 = 0,$$

$$x_{22} = \frac{A_2 B_2 a_3\,x_{11}}{A_1(a_2 B_2 - a_1 B_3)}, \; y_{11} = \frac{A_1 y_{33}}{A_3}, \; y_{22} = \frac{A_2 y_{33}}{A_3},$$

$$f_4 = y_{12} = y_{13} = y_{21} = y_{23} = y_{31} = y_{32} = 0, \; z_{11} = \frac{a_2 B_2(C_2 - C_3)\,x_{11}}{A_1(a_2 B_2 - a_1 B_3)} + z_{33},$$

$$z_{22} = \frac{(C_2 - C_3)\,x_{11}}{A_1} + z_{33}, \; z_{12} = z_{13} = z_{23} = 0. \qquad (7)$$

The substitution of (5), (7) into (3) produces the expression

$$\Omega_1 = \left(\omega_1^2 + \frac{a_3\,(A_2 B_2 \omega_2^2 + A_3 B_3 \omega_3^2)}{A_1(a_2 B_2 - a_1 B_3)} + \frac{a_2 B_2(C_2 - C_3)}{A_1(a_2 B_2 - a_1 B_3)}\,\gamma_1^2 + \frac{C_2 - C_3}{A_1}\,\gamma_2^2 \right) x_{11}$$

$$+ \frac{1}{A_3}\,(A_1 \gamma_1 \omega_1 + A_2 \gamma_2 \omega_2 + A_3 \gamma_3 \omega_3)\,y_{33} + (\gamma_1^2 + \gamma_2^2 + \gamma_3^2)\,z_{33} = const \qquad (8)$$

which, as can directly be verified by computation, is the first integral of Eqs. (1) under the following constraints on the parameters of the problem:

$$B_1 = \frac{a_2 B_2 - a_1 B_3}{a_3}, \; C_1 = \frac{a_2 C_2 - a_1 C_3}{a_3}, \; s_1 = s_2 = s_3 = 0.$$

The relation (8) is a linear combination of previously known integrals (the coefficients of y_{33}, z_{33}) and the new integral (the coefficient of x_{11}).

The solution obtained for the 2nd subsystem has the form:

$$B_1 = -\frac{(a_1 + A_1)A_3 B_3}{A_1(a_3 - A_3)}, \; B_2 = -\frac{A_2(a_1 + A_3)B_3}{A_1(a_3 - A_3)}, \; C_2 = C_3 = C_1,$$

$$s_1 = s_2 = s_3 = 0, \; x_{11} = 1, \; x_{22} = 0,$$

$$y_{11} = \frac{2B_3}{A_1}, \; f_4 = y_{12} = y_{13} = y_{21} = y_{22} = y_{23} = y_{31} = y_{32} = 0,$$

$$y_{33} = \frac{2(a_1 + A_1)a_3 A_3 B_3}{a_1 A_1^2(a_3 - A_3)}, \; z_{11} = \frac{a_2 A_2^2(a_1 + A_3)B_3^2}{a_1 A_1^3(a_3 - A_3)^2}, \; z_{22} = \frac{(a_1 + A_1)^2 a_3 A_3 B_3^2}{a_1 A_1^3(a_3 - A_3)^2},$$

$$z_{12} = z_{13} = z_{23} = z_{33} = 0. \tag{9}$$

Having substituted (5) and (9) into (3), we have the expression

$$\Omega_2 = \omega_1^2 - \frac{A_3 a_3}{A_1 a_1}\omega_3^2 + \frac{2B_3}{A_1}\omega_1\gamma_1 + \frac{2(a_1 + A_1)a_3 A_3 B_3}{A_1^2 a_1(a_3 - A_3)}\omega_3\gamma_3$$

$$+ \frac{A_2^2 a_2(a_1 + A_3)B_3^2}{A_1^3 a_1(a_3 - A_3)^2}\gamma_1^2 + \frac{(a_1 + A_1)^2 a_3 A_3 B_3^2}{A_1^3 a_1(a_3 - A_3)^2}\gamma_2^2 = const \tag{10}$$

which is the first integral of Eqs. (1) when the following conditions hold:

$$B_1 = -\frac{(a_1 + A_1)A_3 B_3}{A_1(a_3 - A_3)}, \; B_2 = -\frac{A_2(a_1 + A_3)B_3}{A_1(a_3 - A_3)}, \; C_2 = C_3 = C_1,$$

$$s_1 = s_2 = s_3 = 0. \tag{11}$$

The integrals Ω_1, Ω_2 correspond to the equations of motion for the asymmetric body. The following integrals have been obtained under the different conditions of dynamical symmetry of the body:

1) $K_1 = A_1 B_1 \omega_1^2 + A_3 B_3(\omega_2^2 + \omega_3^2) + B_3(C_1 - C_3)\gamma_1^2 - 2B_3 s_1 \gamma_1$ (12)

    when $A_2 = A_3, \; B_2 = B_3, \; C_2 = C_3, \; s_2 = s_3 = 0$;

2) $K_2 = A_2 A_3(\omega_1^2 + \omega_3^2) - 2A_2 B_2 \omega_2 \gamma_2 - (B_2 B_3 + A_2(C_3 - C_2))\gamma_2^2$

    $- 2A_2 s_2 \gamma_2$;

    when $A_1 = A_3, \; B_1 = B_3, \; C_1 = C_3, \; s_1 = s_3 = 0$;

3) $K_3 = A_2 A_3(\omega_1^2 + \omega_3^2) + 2A_2 B_3(\omega_1 \gamma_1 + \omega_2 \gamma_2) + (B_2 B_3 + A_2(C_3 - C_2))$

    $\times (\gamma_1^2 + \gamma_2^2) - 2A_3 s_3 \gamma_3$

    when $A_1 = A_2, \; B_1 = B_2, \; C_1 = C_2, \; s_1 = s_2 = 0$.

Note that for $A_1 = A_2 = A_3$, $C_i = 0$, $s_i = 0$ $(i = 1, 2, 3)$ we have found the integral previously known [10]:

$$2K = A_1^2(\omega_1^2 + \omega_2^2 + \omega_3^2) - 2A_1(B_1\omega_1\gamma_1 + B_2\omega_2\gamma_2 + B_3\omega_3\gamma_3) + B_1B_3\gamma_2^2$$
$$+ B_2B_3\gamma_1^2 + B_1B_2\gamma_3^2.$$

As to quadratic IMs in the problem under consideration, we have degenerate cases. All the equations of such IMs found by us are complete squares. One of them is given below.

$$\left(\omega_1 - \sqrt{\frac{A_3a_3}{A_1a_1}}\,\omega_3 - \frac{(a_3 - A_3)B_1}{(a_1 + A_1)A_3}\gamma_1 - \sqrt{\frac{a_3}{A_1A_3a_1}}\,B_1\gamma_3\right)^2 = 0. \qquad (13)$$

This solution exists when $C_1 = C_2 = C_3$,

$$B_2 = \frac{A_2(a_1 + A_3)B_1}{(a_1 + A_1)A_3}, \quad B_3 = -\frac{A_1(a_3 - A_3)B_1}{(a_1 + A_1)A_3}, \quad s_2 = 0, \quad s_3 = -\sqrt{\frac{A_1a_3}{a_1A_3}}\,s_1.$$

In fact, Eq. (13) determines a linear IM.

2.2 Integrals and IMs of 3rd and 4th Degrees

To find IMs and integrals defined by the polynomials of 3rd and 4th degrees, homogeneous and non-homogeneous polynomials of the above degrees are used as initial ones. It leads to solving systems of 160–350 polynomial algebraic equations with parameters, the number of unknowns is up to 130.

Four cubic IMs were obtained for Eqs. (1) in the case of the asymmetric body. The equations of two IMs have the form of a complete cube. The equations of the other two IMs are written as follows:

$$\left(A_1\omega_1 + B_3\gamma_1 \pm \frac{\sqrt{A_2 - A_3}\sqrt{A_3}}{\sqrt{A_1}\sqrt{A_1 - A_2}}\left(A_1\omega_3 - \frac{(2A_1 - A_2)B_3\gamma_3}{A_2 - 2A_3}\right)\right)\Omega_2 = 0.$$

Here the first cofactor defines a linear IM of Eqs. (1), and Ω_2 is quadratic integral (10). These exist under constraints (11).

In the case of the dynamically symmetric body, the cubic integral

$$\Omega_3 = \left(\omega_1 + \frac{B_3\gamma_1}{A_1}\right)\left(\omega_2^2 + \omega_3^2 + \frac{2B_1}{A_1}(\omega_2\gamma_2 + \omega_3\gamma_3)\right.$$
$$+ \frac{B_1B_3 - A_1(C_1 - C_3)}{A_1A_3}(\gamma_2^2 + \gamma_3^2)\right) - \frac{s_1}{B_1}(\omega_2^2 + \omega_3^2)$$
$$+ \frac{(B_1B_3 + A_1(C_1 - C_3))s_1}{A_1A_3B_1}(\gamma_2^2 + \gamma_3^2) + \frac{2s_1^2\gamma_1}{A_3B_1} = const,$$

and the integral of 4th degree

$$
\Omega_4 = (\omega_1^2 + \omega_3^2)\left(\omega_1^2 + \omega_3^2 - \frac{4B_2}{A_1}\omega_2\gamma_2 - \frac{B_2B_3(3A_1B_2 + 2D)}{A_1A_2D}\gamma_2^2\right)
$$
$$
-\frac{3B_2^2B_3}{A_2D}(\omega_1\gamma_3 - \omega_3\gamma_1)^2 - \frac{B_2^2}{A_1^2A_2^2D}\Big(A_1B_2(2A_2\omega_2 + B_3\gamma_2)^2
$$
$$
-A_2B_3\left(2A_2B_3\omega_2\gamma_2 + (A_2\omega_2 + B_3\gamma_2)^2\right)\Big)(\gamma_1^2 + \gamma_3^2)
$$
$$
+\frac{2B_2^2B_3}{A_1}\left(\frac{3}{D}\omega_2\gamma_2 - \frac{1}{A_2^2}(\gamma_1^2 + \gamma_2^2 + \gamma_3^2)\right)(\omega_1\gamma_1 + \omega_3\gamma_3) = const, \quad (14)
$$

were found. Here $D = A_1B_2 - A_2B_3$. The conditions of their existence are $A_2 = A_3$, $B_2 = B_3$, $C_2 = C_3$, $s_2 = s_3 = 0$, and $A_3 = A_1$, $B_1 = B_3$, $C_2 = C_3 = C_1$, $s_1 = s_2 = s_3 = 0$, respectively.

Further, the qualitative analysis of Eqs. (1) is done in some of the above presented cases of the existence of additional first integrals.

3 The Equations of Motion with an Additional Quadratic Integral

Let us consider Eqs. (1) when $A_2 = A_3$, $B_2 = B_3$, $C_2 = C_3$, $s_2 = s_3 = 0$. Under these conditions, the equations have the form

$$
A_1\dot{\omega}_1 = B_3(\omega_2\gamma_3 - \omega_3\gamma_2),
$$
$$
A_3\dot{\omega}_2 = (B_3\gamma_1 - (A_1 - A_3)\omega_1)\omega_3 - (B_1\omega_1 + s_1)\gamma_3 - (C_3 - C_1)\gamma_1\gamma_3,
$$
$$
A_3\dot{\omega}_3 = ((A_1 - A_3)\omega_1 - B_3\gamma_1)\omega_2 + (B_1\omega_1 + s_1)\gamma_2 + (C_3 - C_1)\gamma_1\gamma_2,
$$
$$
\dot{\gamma}_1 = \omega_3\gamma_2 - \omega_2\gamma_3, \ \dot{\gamma}_2 = \omega_1\gamma_3 - \omega_3\gamma_1, \ \dot{\gamma}_3 = \omega_2\gamma_1 - \omega_1\gamma_2 \quad (15)
$$

and admit quadratic integral K_1 (12).

Besides K_1, Eqs. (15) have the integrals

$$
\tilde{V}_1 = A_1\omega_1 + A_3(\omega_2 + \omega_3) = c_1, \ V_2 = \sum_{i=1}^{3}\gamma_i^2 = 1 \quad (16)
$$

and the linear integral $V_3 = A_1\omega_1 + B_3\gamma_1 = c_3$ which is directly derived from the equations themselves. Thus, system (15) is completely integrable. We set the problem of seeking stationary solutions and IMs [8] of the system and the analysis of their stability. For this purpose, the Routh–Lyapunov method and some of its generalizations [7] are used. According to this method, stationary solutions and IMs of differential equations under study can be obtained by solving a conditional extremum problem for the first integrals of these equations.

3.1   Seeking Stationary Solutions and Invariant Manifolds

In accordance with the method chosen, we take the nonlinear combination of the first integrals of the problem

$$2\,W = 2\lambda_0 K_1 - 2\lambda_1 \tilde{V}_1 - \lambda_2\,V_2 - \lambda_3 V_3^2 \tag{17}$$

and write down the necessary extremum conditions for W with respect to the variables ω_i, γ_i:

$$
\begin{aligned}
\partial W/\partial\omega_1 &= A_1\left[(\lambda_0 B_1 - \lambda_3 A_1)\,\omega_1 - (\lambda_1 + \lambda_3 B_3)\,\gamma_1\right] = 0,\\
\partial W/\partial\omega_2 &= A_3\,(\lambda_0 B_3\omega_2 - \lambda_1\gamma_2) = 0,\\
\partial W/\partial\omega_3 &= A_3\,(\lambda_0 B_3\omega_3 - \lambda_1\gamma_3) = 0,\\
\partial W/\partial\gamma_1 &= -A_1\,(\lambda_1 + \lambda_3 B_3)\,\omega_1 + \left[(\lambda_0\,(C_1 - C_3) - \lambda_3 B_3)\,B_3 - \lambda_2\right]\gamma_1\\
&\quad -\lambda_0 B_3 s_1 = 0,\\
\partial W/\partial\gamma_2 &= -(\lambda_1 A_3\omega_2 + \lambda_2\gamma_2) = 0, \quad \partial W/\partial\gamma_3 = -(\lambda_1 A_3\omega_3 + \lambda_2\gamma_3) = 0.
\end{aligned}
\tag{18}
$$

First, we seek IMs of maximum dimension, namely, the IMs of codimension 2. In order to solve this problem, a lexicographical basis with respect to $\lambda_0 > \lambda_1 > \lambda_2 > \omega_1 > \gamma_2$ for the polynomials of system (18) is constructed. As a result, the system is transformed to the form:

$$
\begin{aligned}
&\gamma_3\omega_2 - \gamma_2\omega_3 = 0,\\
&(A_3\omega_3 + B_3\gamma_3)\,\gamma_1\omega_3 - (A_1\omega_3 + B_1\gamma_3)\,\gamma_3\omega_1 + ((C_1-C_3)\gamma_1 - s_1)\,\gamma_3^2 = 0,
\end{aligned}
\tag{19}
$$

$$
\begin{aligned}
&\lambda_2[B_1((C_3 - C_1)\gamma_1 + s_1)\,\gamma_3^2 + (A_1 B_3 - A_3 B_1)\,\gamma_1\omega_3^2]\,\gamma_3^2 - \lambda_3 A_3 B_3\omega_3^2\\
&\quad\times[(B_1 B_3\gamma_1 + A_1((C_1 - C_3)\gamma_1 - s_1))\,\gamma_3^2 + A_1(2B_3\gamma_3 + A_3\omega_3)\,\gamma_1\omega_3] = 0,\\
&\lambda_1[B_1\,((C_1 - C_3)\gamma_1 - s_1)\,\gamma_3^2 + (A_3 B_1 - A_1 B_3)\gamma_1\omega_3^2]\,\gamma_3 - \lambda_3 B_3\omega_3\\
&\quad\times[(B_1 B_3\gamma_1 + A_1((C_1 - C_3)\gamma_1 - s_1))\,\gamma_3^2 + A_1(2B_3\gamma_3 + A_3\omega_3)\,\gamma_1\omega_3] = 0,\\
&\lambda_0[B_1((C_3 - C_1)\gamma_1 + s_1)\,\gamma_3^2 + (A_1 B_3 - A_3 B_1)\,\gamma_1\omega_3^2]\\
&\quad+ \lambda_3[(B_1 B_3\gamma_1 + A_1((C_1 - C_3)\gamma_1 - s_1))\,\gamma_3^2 + A_1(2B_3\gamma_3 + A_3\omega_3)\,\gamma_1\omega_3] = 0.
\end{aligned}
\tag{20}
$$

Equations (19) determine an IM of codimension 2 of differential Eqs. (15). It can easily be verified by the definition of IM. Equations (20) allow one to obtain the first integrals of differential equations on this IM. The latter can directly be verified by computation. To do this, it needs to resolve Eqs. (20) with respect to $\lambda_0, \lambda_1, \lambda_2$, and to differentiate the resulting expressions by virtue of the equations of motion on the IM.

Now IMs of minimum dimension are sought. Again we construct a lexicographical basis for the polynomials of system (18), but with respect to $\omega_1 > \gamma_1 > \gamma_2 > \gamma_3 > \lambda_2$. The system takes the form:

$$A_3\lambda_1^2 + B_3\lambda_0\lambda_2 = 0, \tag{21}$$

$$
\begin{aligned}
&\lambda_0 B_3\omega_3 - \lambda_1\gamma_3 = 0, \quad \lambda_0 B_3\omega_2 - \lambda_1\gamma_2 = 0,\\
&[\lambda_0\lambda_1^2 A_1 B_3 + \lambda_3 A_1(\lambda_1^2 A_3 + \lambda_0 B_3^2(\lambda_0(C_1 - C_3) + 2\lambda_1)) - \lambda_0 B_1(A_3\lambda_1^2\\
&\quad+ \lambda_0 B_3^2(\lambda_0(C_1 - C_3) - \lambda_3 B_3))]\,\gamma_1 + \lambda_0^2 B_3^2 s_1(\lambda_0 B_1 - \lambda_3 A_1) = 0,\\
&(\lambda_0\lambda_1^2 A_1 B_3 + \lambda_3 A_1(\lambda_1^2 A_3 + \lambda_0 B_3^2(\lambda_0(C_1\lambda_0 - C_3) + 2\lambda_1)) - \lambda_0 B_1(A_3\lambda_1^2\\
&\quad+ \lambda_0 B_3^2(\lambda_0(C_1 - C_3) - \lambda_3 B_3)))\,\omega_1 + \lambda_0^2 B_3^2 s_1(\lambda_1 + \lambda_3 B_3) = 0.
\end{aligned}
\tag{22}
$$

Equations (22) together with integral V_2 (16) determine a family of one-dimensional IMs of differential Eqs. (15). Here $\lambda_0, \lambda_1, \lambda_3$ are the parameters of the family. Next, find $\lambda_2 = -\lambda_1^2 A_3/(\lambda_0 B_3)$ from Eq. (21) and substitute into (17). We have

$$2\tilde{W} = 2\lambda_0 K_1 - 2\lambda_1 \tilde{V}_1 + \frac{\lambda_1^2 A_3}{\lambda_0 B_3} V_2 - \lambda_3 V_3^2. \tag{23}$$

It is easy to verify by computation that the integral $\tilde{W}$ assumes a stationary value on the elements of the above family of IMs.

In order to find stationary solutions, one needs to add relation V_2 (16) to Eqs. (18) and, for the polynomials of a resulting system, to construct a lexicographical basis with respect to $\omega_1 > \omega_2 > \omega_3 > \gamma_1 > \gamma_2 > \gamma_3 > \lambda_2$. As a result, we have a system of equations decomposing into 3 subsystems. One of them corresponds to Eqs. (22), which the integral V_2 is added to, the other two subsystems are written as:

$$\begin{aligned} &\lambda_2(\lambda_3 A_1 - \lambda_0 B_1) - [\lambda_1^2 A_1 + \lambda_0 B_3(\lambda_3 A_1 - \lambda_0 B_1)(C_1 - C_3 \mp s_1) \\ &+ \lambda_3 B_3(\lambda_0 B_1 B_3 + 2\lambda_1 A_1)] = 0, \end{aligned} \tag{24}$$

$$\begin{aligned} &\gamma_3 = 0, \ \gamma_2 = 0, \ \gamma_1 = \pm 1, \ \omega_3 = 0, \ \omega_2 = 0, \\ &(\lambda_3 A_1 - \lambda_0 B_1)\omega_1 \pm (\lambda_3 B_3 + \lambda_1) = 0. \end{aligned} \tag{25}$$

The Eq. (24) gives

$$\lambda_2 = \frac{\lambda_1^2 A_1 + \lambda_3 B_3(\lambda_0 B_1 B_3 + 2\lambda_1 A_1)}{\lambda_3 A_1 - \lambda_0 B_1} + \lambda_0 B_3(C_1 - C_3 \mp s_1). \tag{26}$$

Equations (25) define the two families of solutions of differential Eqs. (15)

$$\omega_1 = \pm\frac{\lambda_1 + \lambda_3 B_3}{\lambda_0 B_1 - \lambda_3 A_1}, \ \omega_2 = \omega_3 = \gamma_2 = \gamma_3 = 0, \ \gamma_1 = \pm 1, \tag{27}$$

the elements of which deliver a stationary value to the integral W under the corresponding values of λ_2 (26).

From a mechanical point of view, the elements of the families of solutions (27) correspond to permanent rotations of the body about the Ox axis (the system of axes related to the body) with the angular velocity $\omega_1 = \pm(\lambda_1 + \lambda_3 B_3)/(\lambda_0 B_1 - \lambda_3 A_1)$.

It is not difficult to show that the family of IMs (22) belongs to IM (19). For this purpose, we resolve Eqs. (22) with respect to $\omega_1, \gamma_1, \gamma_2, \gamma_3$ and substitute a result into (19). The latter expressions turn into identities. It means that the elements of the family of IMs (22) are submanifolds of IM (19). Similarly, one can show that solutions (27) belong to IM (19) and, under the corresponding values of

$$\lambda_3 = \frac{\lambda_0(\lambda_1^2(B_1 A_3 - A_1 B_3) + \lambda_0^2 B_1 B_3^2(C_1 - C_3 \mp s_1))}{B_1 B_3^3 \lambda_0^2 + A_1(\lambda_1(A_3\lambda_1 + 2\lambda_0 B_3^2) + \lambda_0^2 B_3^2(C_1 - C_3 \mp s_1))},$$

to the elements of the family of IMs (22).

3.2 On the Stability of Stationary Solutions and Invariant Manifolds

In this Section, the algorithms for the analysis of the stability of stationary solutions and IMs on the base of Lyapunov's theorems on the stability of motion are employed. These have been encoded in "Mathematica" and included as some programs in the software package [1]. The programs are used for obtaining the necessary and sufficient conditions of stability. More details of their application can be found in [8].

The Stability of IMs. Let us investigate the stability of the elements of the family of IMs (22). We use the integral $\tilde{W}$ to obtain sufficient conditions.

The deviations are introduced:

$$y_1 = \omega_1 - \omega_{10}, \ y_2 = \gamma_1 - \gamma_{10}, \ y_3 = \lambda_0 B_3 \omega_2 - \lambda_1 \gamma_2, \ y_4 = \lambda_0 B_3 \omega_3 - \lambda_1 \gamma_3,$$

where

$$\omega_{10} = B_3 s_1 (\lambda_1 + \lambda_3 B_3) D^{-1}, \ \gamma_{10} = B_3 s_1 (B_1 - \lambda_3 A_1) D^{-1},$$
$$D = [\lambda_0^2 B_3^2 (C_1 - C_3) + \lambda_1^2 A_3](\lambda_3 A_1 - \lambda_0 B_1) + \lambda_0 B_3 [\lambda_0 \lambda_3 B_1 B_3^2$$
$$+ \lambda_1 A_1 (2\lambda_3 B_3 + \lambda_1)].$$

The 2nd variation of $\tilde{W}$ is written as

$$2\delta^2 \tilde{W} = A_1 (\lambda_0 B_1 - \lambda_3 A_1) y_1^2 + \left(\frac{\lambda_1^2 A_3}{\lambda_0 B_3} + B_3 (\lambda_0 (C_1 - C_3) - \lambda_3 B_3) \right) y_2^2$$
$$- 2A_1 (\lambda_1 + \lambda_3 B_3) y_1 y_2 + \frac{\lambda_1^2 A_3}{\lambda_0 B_3} (y_3^2 + y_4^2).$$

Using the variation of the integral $\delta V_3 = A_1 y_1 + B_3 y_2 = 0$, one can represent the expression $2\delta^2 \tilde{W}$ as follows:

$$2\delta^2 \tilde{W} = \left(\frac{\lambda_0 B_1 B_3^2}{A_1} + \frac{\lambda_1^2 A_3}{\lambda_0 B_3} + (\lambda_0 (C_1 - C_3) + 2\lambda_1) B_3 \right) y_2^2 + \frac{\lambda_1^2 A_3}{\lambda_0 B_3} (y_3^2 + y_4^2).$$

The conditions for the latter quadratic form to be sign definite are sufficient for the stability of the elements of the family of IMs under study. These have the form:

$$\frac{A_3}{\lambda_0 B_3} > 0, \quad \frac{\lambda_0 B_1 B_3^2}{A_1} + \frac{\lambda_1^2 A_3}{\lambda_0 B_3} + (\lambda_0 (C_1 - C_3) + 2\lambda_1) B_3 > 0. \tag{28}$$

Evidently, inequalities (28) are consistent when $A_1 > 0, A_3 > 0, C_1 > C_3 > 0$, $B_1 > 0$, $B_3 > 0$ and $\lambda_0 > 0$, $\lambda_1 > 0$ are fulfilled. The built-in function *Reduce* of CAS "Mathematica" produces the more complete list of the conditions for the consistency of the inequalities. It is rather long, and only some of these conditions are represented here:

$$A_3 > 0, \ C_3 > C_1 > 0, \ B_1 < 0, \ B_3 < 0, \ 0 < A_1 < \frac{B_1 B_3}{C_3 - C_1} \text{ and } \lambda_0 < 0, \ \lambda_1 < 0$$

or

$$A_1 > 0, \ A_3 > 0, \ C_3 > C_1 > 0, \ B_1 < 0, \ B_3 > 0 \text{ and}$$

$$\lambda_1 > 0, \ 0 < \lambda_0 \leq -\frac{2\lambda_1 A_1}{B_1 B_3 + A_1(C_1 - C_3)}.$$

As can be seen, the above conditions of stability are split up into two groups. The first (the constraints on the parameters of the problem) gives the sufficient stability conditions for the elements of the family of IMs (22). The second (the constraints on λ_0, λ_1) isolates those subfamilies of this family, the elements of which are stable.

The Stability of Solutions. Now we investigate the stability of solutions (27). To obtain sufficient conditions the integral W is used under the constraints on λ_2 (26) and $\lambda_3 = (B_1 B_3 \lambda_0 - \lambda_1(A_1 - 2A_3))/(2A_1 B_3 - 2A_3 B_3)$. Under these restrictions, the integral and the solutions take the form, respectively:

$$2\bar{W} = 2\lambda_0 K_1 - 2\lambda_1 V_1 - \frac{B_1 B_3 \lambda_0 + \lambda_1(2A_3\lambda_1 - A_1)}{2A_1 B_3 - 2A_3 B_3} V_3^2$$

$$+ \frac{B_3 \left[2A_3\lambda_1 + B_1 B_3 \lambda_0 + (2A_3\lambda_0 - A_1\lambda_0)(C_1 - C_3 \mp s_1) \right]}{A_1 - 2A_3} V_2,$$

$$\omega_1 = \pm \frac{B_3}{A_1 - 2A_3}, \ \omega_2 = \omega_3 = \gamma_2 = \gamma_3 = 0, \ \gamma_1 = \pm 1. \tag{29}$$

Next, we write down the variations of the integral $\bar{W}$ for the both solutions. The 2nd variation of $\bar{W}$ in the deviations

$$y_1 = \omega_1 \mp \frac{B_3}{A_1 - 2A_3}, \ y_2 = \omega_2, \ y_3 = \omega_3, \ y_4 = \gamma_1 \mp 1, \ y_5 = \gamma_2, \ y_6 = \gamma_3 \tag{30}$$

on the linear manifold

$$\delta K_1 = \pm 2B_3 \left(\frac{A_1 B_1 y_1}{A_1 - 2A_3} + (C_1 - C_3 \mp s_1) y_4 \right) = 0,$$

$$\delta \tilde{V}_1 = \pm A_1 \left(y_1 + \frac{B_3 y_4}{A_1 - 2A_3} \right) = 0, \ \delta V_2 = \pm 2y_4 = 0, \ \delta V_3 = A_1 y_1 + B_3 y_4 = 0$$

is written as $\delta^2 \bar{W} = Q_1 + Q_2$, where

$$2Q_1 = ay_3^2 + by_3 y_6 + cy_6^2, \ 2Q_2 = ay_2^2 + by_2 y_5 + cy_5^2,$$

$$a = \lambda_0 A_3 B_3, \ b = -2\lambda_1 A_3, \ c = B_3 \left(\frac{\lambda_0 B_1 B_3 + 2\lambda_1 A_3}{A_1 - 2A_3} - \lambda_0(C_1 - C_3 - s_1) \right).$$

The conditions for the quadratic forms Q_1 and Q_2 to be sign definite are sufficient for the stability of solutions (29):

$$\lambda_0 A_3 B_3 > 0, \ A_3 \left(\frac{\lambda_0 B_3^2 (\lambda_0 B_1 B_3 + 2\lambda_1 A_3)}{A_1 - 2A_3} - \lambda_1^2 A_2 - \lambda_0^2 B_3^2 (C_1 - C_3 - s_1) \right) > 0.$$

The latter inequalities are consistent under the following constraints on the parameters $A_i, B_i, C_i, s_1, \lambda_0, \lambda_1$:

$A_3 > 0$, $B_1 \neq 0$, $C_1 \neq 0$, $C_3 \neq 0$ and $(A_1 > 2A_3$ or $0 < A_1 < 2A_3)$ and $(B_3 > 0, \lambda_0 > 0$ or $B_3 < 0, \lambda_0 < 0)$ and

$$\lambda_1 \neq 0, \, s_1 > \lambda_1 A_1 \left(\frac{\lambda_1}{\lambda_0^2 B_3^2} - \frac{2}{\lambda_0(A_1 - 2A_3)} \right) - \frac{B_1 B_3}{A_1 - 2A_3} + C_1 - C_3.$$

As in the previous case, we have 2 groups: the sufficient conditions of the stability of solutions (29) and the constraints on the parameters λ_0, λ_1. The latter can be used to select a subfamily of the family of the integrals $\bar{W}$, which will allow one to obtain the best sufficient stability conditions (closest to necessary ones). In order to solve this problem, consider one of the above restrictions on the parameters λ_i:

$$s_1 > \Lambda = \lambda_1 A_1 \left(\frac{\lambda_1}{\lambda_0^2 B_3^2} - \frac{2}{\lambda_0(A_1 - 2A_3)} \right) - \frac{B_1 B_3}{A_1 - 2A_3} + C_1 - C_3.$$

Write down the necessary extremum condition of Λ with respect to λ_1:

$$\frac{\partial \Lambda}{\partial \lambda_1} = \frac{2A_3 \lambda_1}{B_3^2 \lambda_0^2} - \frac{2A_3}{\lambda_0(A_1 - 2A_3)} = 0.$$

It gives $\lambda_1 = B_3^2 \lambda_0 / (A_1 - 2A_3)$. Under this condition, $\delta^2 \check{W}$ takes the form:

$$\delta^2 \check{W} = \tilde{Q}_1 + \tilde{Q}_2,$$

where

$$2\tilde{Q}_1 = \tilde{a} y_3^2 + \tilde{b} y_3 y_6 + \tilde{c} y_6^2, \, 2\tilde{Q}_2 = \tilde{a} y_2^2 + \tilde{b} y_2 y_5 + \tilde{c} y_5^2, \, \tilde{a} = A_3 B_3,$$

$$\tilde{b} = -\frac{2A_3 B_3^2}{A_1 - 2A_3}, \, \tilde{c} = B_3 \left(\frac{B_3(A_1 B_1 + 2A_3(B_3 - B_1))}{(A_1 - 2A_3)^2} - \lambda_0(C_1 - C_3 - s_1) \right).$$

The conditions of sign-definiteness of $\delta^2 \check{W}$ are

$A_3 > 0$, $B_1 \neq 0$, $C_1 \neq 0$, $C_3 \neq 0$ and $B_3 > 0$, $(A_1 > 2A_3$ or $0 < A_1 < 2A_3)$

and $s_1 > C_1 - C_3 - \dfrac{(A_1 B_1 - A_3(2B_1 - B_3))B_3}{(A_1 - 2A_3)^2}.$ (31)

So, solutions (29) are stable when conditions (31) are fulfilled.

The necessary conditions of the stability of solutions (29) are derived on the base of Lyapunov's theorem on stability in the linear approximation [12]. The equations of first approximation, in the case under consideration, in deviations (30) are written as:

$$\dot{y}_1 = 0, \, \dot{y}_2 = \frac{1}{A_3} \left(C_1 - C_3 - s_1 - \frac{B_1 B_3}{A_1 - 2A_3} \right) y_6 - \frac{B_3}{A_1 - 2A_3} y_3,$$

$$\dot{y}_3 = \frac{B_3}{A_1 - 2A_3} y_2 + \frac{1}{A_3} \left(\frac{B_1 B_3}{A_1 - 2A_3} - C_1 + C_3 + s_1 \right) y_5, \, \dot{y}_4 = 0,$$

$$\dot{y}_5 = \frac{B_3}{A_1 - 2A_3} y_6 - y_3, \, \dot{y}_6 = y_2 - \frac{B_3}{A_1 - 2A_3} y_5.$$ (32)

The characteristic equation

$$\frac{\lambda^2}{(A_1 - 2A_3)^4 A_3^2} [(A_1 - 2A_3)^2 A_3 \lambda^2 + B_3(A_1 B_1 + A_3(B_3 - 2B_1))$$

$$- (A_1 - 2A_3)^2 (C_1 - C_3 - s_1)]^2 = 0$$

of system (32) has only zero and purely imaginary roots when the following conditions are satisfied:

$$A_3 > 0, \ B_1 \neq 0, \ B_3 \neq 0, \ C_1 \neq 0, \ C_3 \neq 0, \ (A_1 > 2A_3 \text{ or } 0 < A_1 < 2A_3)$$

$$\text{and } s_1 \geq C_1 - C_3 - \frac{(A_1 B_1 - A_3(2B_1 - B_3))B_3}{(A_1 - 2A_3)^2}.$$

On comparing the latter inequalities with (31) one can conclude that conditions (31) are necessary and sufficient for the stability of solutions (29) with precision up to the boundary of stability.

4   The Equations of Motion with the Additional Integral of the 4th Degree

When $A_3 = A_1$, $B_1 = B_3$, $C_1 = C_2 = C_3$, $s_1 = s_2 = s_3 = 0$, the equations of motion (1) take the form

$$A_1 \dot{\omega}_1 = (A_2 - A_1)\omega_2 \omega_3 + B_2 \omega_2 \gamma_3 - B_3 \omega_3 \gamma_2,$$
$$A_2 \dot{\omega}_2 = B_3(\omega_3 \gamma_1 - \omega_1 \gamma_3),$$
$$A_3 \dot{\omega}_3 = (A_1 - A_3)\omega_1 \omega_2 - B_2 \omega_2 \gamma_1 + B_3 \omega_1 \gamma_2,$$
$$\dot{\gamma}_1 = \omega_3 \gamma_2 - \omega_2 \gamma_3, \ \dot{\gamma}_2 = \omega_1 \gamma_3 - \omega_3 \gamma_1, \ \dot{\gamma}_3 = \omega_2 \gamma_1 - \omega_1 \gamma_2 \qquad (33)$$

and admit the polynomial first integral Ω_4 (14) of 4th degree.

Besides Ω_4, equations (33) have the integrals:

$$\hat{V}_1 = A_2 \omega_2 + A_1(\omega_1 + \omega_3) = c_1, \ V_2 = \sum_{i=1}^{3} \gamma_i^2 = 1,$$

$$V = \omega_1^2 + \frac{A_2 B_2}{A_1 B_3} \omega_2^2 + \omega_3^2 = c_2, \ \bar{V}_3 = A_2 \omega_2 + B_3 \gamma_2 = c_3. \qquad (34)$$

The integral $\bar{V}_3$ has been derived directly from the equations themselves, and V has been found by the technique of Sect. 3.

We set the problem of finding stationary solutions and IMs of differential Eqs. (33) and the analysis of their stability.

4.1   Seeking Stationary Solutions and Invariant Manifolds

First, IMs of maximum dimension will be found by the technique of Sect. 3.1. We choose independent integrals from those of system (33) (such as, e.g., $\hat{V}_1$, V_2, $\bar{V}_3$, Ω_4) and compose the linear combination from them:

$$2\hat{W} = 2\lambda_0 V - 2\lambda_1 \hat{V}_1 - \lambda_2 V_2 - \lambda_3 \Omega_4 \qquad (35)$$

Next, the necessary extremum conditions of $\hat{W}$ with respect to the variables ω_i, γ_i are written:

$$\partial \hat{W}/\partial \omega_i = 0, \ \partial \hat{W}/\partial \gamma_i = 0 \ (i = 1, 2, 3). \tag{36}$$

These are a system of cubic equations with parameters $A_1, A_2, B_2, B_3, \lambda_0$, $\lambda_1, \lambda_2, \lambda_3$. The equations are bulky and these are not presented explicitly here.

We have found the desired IM through the computation of a lexicographical basis for the polynomials of system (36) with respect to $\lambda_0 > \lambda_1 > \omega_2 > \gamma_2$:

$$
\begin{aligned}
&B_2^3 B_3^2 \left(A_2 B_3 - 4A_1 B_2\right) \lambda_3 \gamma_2^4 + [2B_2 B_3 \lambda_3 \left(7A_2 B_3 - 16A_1 B_2\right)(B_2 B_3 \chi_1 \\
&+ 2A_1 A_2 \chi_2) + 16 A_1 (A_1 B_2 - A_2 B_3)(A_1 A_2^2 \lambda_2 - 2B_2^2 B_3 \lambda_3 \chi_3) \\
&+ 24 A_1 B_2^3 B_3^2 \lambda_3 \chi_1] \gamma_2^2 - (4A_1 B_2 - A_2 B_3)\lambda_3 (B_2 B_3 \chi_1 + 2A_1 A_2 \chi_2)^2 = 0, \\
&4A_2 B_2 \lambda_3 (4A_1 B_2 - A_2 B_3)(B_2 B_3 \chi_1 + 2A_1 A_2 \chi_2) \omega_2 \\
&+ B_2^2 B_3^2 (4A_1 B_2 - A_2 B_3) \lambda_3 \gamma_2^3 + [3B_2 B_3 \lambda_3 (12A_1 B_2 - 5A_2 B_3)(B_2 B_3 \chi_1 \\
&+ 2A_1 A_2 \chi_2) - 16 A_1 (A_1 B_2 - A_2 B_3)(A_1 A_2^2 \lambda_2 - 2B_2^2 B_3 \lambda_3 \chi_3) \\
&- 24 A_1 B_2^3 B_3^2 \lambda_3 \chi_1] \gamma_2 = 0, \tag{37}
\end{aligned}
$$

where $\chi_1 = \gamma_1^2 + \gamma_3^2$, $\chi_2 = \omega_1^2 + \omega_3^2$, $\chi_3 = \omega_1 \gamma_1 + \omega_3 \gamma_3$.

It can be verified by the definition of IM that Eqs. (37) determine a family of IMs of codimension 2 of differential Eqs. (33), λ_2, λ_3 are the parameters of the family.

Stationary solutions and IMs of minimum dimension will be obtained from the equations of motion. For this purpose, the right-hand sides of differential Eqs. (33) are equated to zero and then relation $V_2 = 1$ (34) is added to them:

$$
\begin{aligned}
&(A_2 - A_1)\,\omega_2 \omega_3 + B_2 \omega_2 \gamma_3 - B_3 \omega_3 \gamma_2 = 0, \ B_3(\omega_3 \gamma_1 - \omega_1 \gamma_3) = 0, \\
&(A_1 - A_3)\,\omega_1 \omega_2 - B_2 \omega_2 \gamma_1 + B_3 \omega_1 \gamma_2 = 0, \\
&\omega_3 \gamma_2 - \omega_2 \gamma_3 = 0, \ \omega_1 \gamma_3 - \omega_3 \gamma_1 = 0, \ \omega_2 \gamma_1 - \omega_1 \gamma_2 = 0, \\
&\gamma_1^2 + \gamma_2^2 + \gamma_3^2 = 1. \tag{38}
\end{aligned}
$$

For the polynomials of system (38) we construct a lexicographical basis with respect to some part of the phase variables, e.g., $\omega_1 > \omega_2 > \omega_3 > \gamma_1 > \gamma_2$. As a result, the system is transformed to a form which enables us to decompose it into 3 subsystems:

$$1) \ \gamma_2 = 0, \ \gamma_1^2 + \gamma_3^2 - 1 = 0, \ \omega_2 = 0, \ \omega_3 \gamma_1 - \omega_1 \gamma_3 = 0; \tag{39}$$

$$2) \ \gamma_1^2 + \gamma_2^2 + \gamma_3^2 - 1 = 0, \ \omega_1 = 0, \ \omega_2 = 0, \ \omega_3 = 0; \tag{40}$$

$$
\begin{aligned}
3) \ &\gamma_1^2 + \gamma_2^2 + \gamma_3^2 - 1 = 0, \ (B_2 - B_3)\,\gamma_3 - (A_1 - A_2)\,\omega_3 = 0, \\
&(B_3 - B_2)\,\gamma_2 + (A_1 - A_2)\,\omega_2 = 0, \\
&(B_3 - B_2)\,\gamma_1 + (A_1 - A_2)\,\omega_1 = 0. \tag{41}
\end{aligned}
$$

It is not difficult to verify by the definition of IM that Eqs. (39)–(41) define IMs of codimension 4 of differential Eqs. (33).

The differential equations on IM (39) are written as $\dot{\omega}_3 = 0, \dot{\gamma}_3 = 0$. These have the following family of solutions:

$$\omega_3 = \omega_3^0 = const, \; \gamma_3 = \gamma_3^0 = const. \tag{42}$$

Correspondingly, the differential equations on IMs (40), (41) and their solutions have the form: $\dot{\gamma}_1 = 0, \; \dot{\gamma}_3 = 0$ and

$$\gamma_1 = \gamma_1^0 = const, \; \gamma_3 = \gamma_3^0 = const. \tag{43}$$

Equations (39) together with (42) determine the 2 families of solutions for the equations of motion (33):

$$\omega_1 = \pm \frac{\omega_3^0}{\gamma_3^0} \sqrt{1 - \gamma_3^{0^2}}, \; \omega_2 = 0, \; \omega_3 = \omega_3^0, \; \gamma_1 = \pm\sqrt{1 - \gamma_3^{0^2}}, \; \gamma_2 = 0, \; \gamma_3 = \gamma_3^0. \tag{44}$$

Equations (40), (41), and (43) allow us to obtain the other 4 families of solutions:

$$\omega_1 = \omega_2 = \omega_3 = 0, \; \gamma_1 = \gamma_1^0, \; \gamma_2 = \pm\chi, \; \gamma_3 = \gamma_3^0 \tag{45}$$

and

$$\omega_1 = \frac{B_2 - B_3}{A_1 - A_2}\gamma_1^0, \; \omega_2 = \pm\frac{(B_2 - B_3)\chi}{A_1 - A_2}, \; \omega_3 = \frac{B_2 - B_3}{A_1 - A_2}\gamma_3^0, \; \gamma_1 = \gamma_1^0,$$
$$\gamma_2 = \pm\chi, \; \gamma_3 = \gamma_3^0. \tag{46}$$

Here $\chi = \sqrt{1 - \gamma_1^{0^2} - \gamma_3^{0^2}}$.

From a mechanical point of view, the elements of the families of solutions (44) and (46) correspond to permanent rotations of the body, and the elements of the families of solutions (45) correspond to its equilibria.

One can show that the above solutions belong to the family of IMs (37) (or its subfamilies). For this purpose, substitute, e.g., expressions (45) into (37). The latter relations become identities when $\lambda_2 = B_2^2 B_3^2 \lambda_3 / (2A_1^2 A_2^2)$, $\gamma_3^0 = \pm(1 - 2\gamma_1^{0^2})^{1/2}/2$. Thus, the subfamilies of the families of solutions (45) corresponding to $\gamma_3^0 = \pm(1 - 2\gamma_1^{0^2})^{1/2}/2$ belong to a subfamily which is isolated from the family of IMs (37) under the above value of λ_2. We have the same result in the case of solutions (46).

It is not difficult to derive the families of integrals assuming a stationary value on solutions (44)–(46) (the technique is described, e.g., in [8]). A similar problem can be posed for IMs. The following nonlinear combinations of integrals

$$2\Phi_1 = A_1^2 V \hat{V}_1^{-1} + (V_2 - 1)\hat{V}_1 - \bar{V}_3^2, \; \Phi_2 = V + \lambda V_2^2$$

and

$$2\Phi_3 = V - \frac{2(B_2 - B_3)\hat{V}_1}{A_1(A_1 - A_2)} + \frac{(B_2 - B_3)^2 V_2}{(A_1 - A_2)^2} - \frac{(B_2 - B_3)^2 \bar{V}_3^2}{A_1 B_3(A_2(B_1 - 2B_3) + A_1 B_3)}$$

have been found for IM (39), IM (40), and IM (41), respectively. Their necessary extremum conditions are satisfied on the IMs under study.

4.2   On the Stability of Stationary Solutions and Invariant Manifolds

Let us investigate the stability of IM (39), using the integral Φ_1 to obtain sufficient conditions. The analysis of stability is done in some maps of an atlas on this IM. The deviations are introduced:

$$y_1 = \omega_1 \pm \sqrt{1 - \gamma_3^2}\,\frac{\omega_3}{\gamma_3}, \ \ y_2 = \omega_2, \ \ y_3 = \gamma_1 \pm \sqrt{1 - \gamma_3^2}, \ \ y_4 = \gamma_2.$$

The 2nd variation of Φ_1 on the linear manifold

$$\delta V = \mp 2\sqrt{1 - \gamma_3^2}\,\frac{\omega_3}{\gamma_3}\,y_1 = 0, \ \ \delta \hat{V}_1 = \mp A_1 \sqrt{1 - \gamma_3^2}\left(y_1 + \frac{\omega_3}{\gamma_3}\,y_3\right) = 0,$$

$$\delta V_2 = \mp 2\sqrt{1 - \gamma_3^2}\,y_3 = 0, \ \ \delta \bar{V}_3 = A_2 y_2 + B_3 y_4 = 0$$

is written as

$$2\delta^2 \Phi_1 = \left(B_3\left(\frac{B_2 \gamma_3}{A_2 \omega_3} + 2\right) + \frac{A_1 \omega_3}{\gamma_3}\right) y_2^2.$$

The condition of sign-definiteness

$$B_3\left(\frac{B_2 \gamma_3}{A_2 \omega_3} + 2\right) + \frac{A_1 \omega_3}{\gamma_3} > 0$$

of the quadratic form $\delta^2 \Phi_1$ is sufficient for the stability of the IM under study.

Since the integral $\hat{V}_1$ on IM (39) takes the form $\hat{V}_1|_0 = A_1 \omega_3 / \gamma_3 = \tilde{c}_1$, then the latter inequality is true, in particular, under the following constraints on the parameters:

$$(A_1 > 0, \ A_2 > 0, \ B_2 > 0, \ B_3 > 0, \ \tilde{c}_1 > 0) \ \text{or}$$

$$\left(A_1 > 0, \ A_2 > 0, \ B_2 < 0, \ B_2 > 0 \ \text{and} \ ((-B_3 - D < \tilde{c}_1 < 0)\right.$$

$$\text{or} \ D - B_3 < \tilde{c}_1), \ \text{where} \ D = \sqrt{B_3\left(B_3 - \frac{A_1 B_2}{A_2}\right)}.$$

The investigation of the stability of IMs (40), (41) is done similarly. As to the families of solutions (44)–(46) belonging to IMs (39)–(41), their instability in the first approximation was proved.

5   Conclusion

The new additional polynomial integrals and IMs for the differential equations describing the motion of a rigid body with a fixed point under the influence of both a magnetic field generated by the Barnett–London effect and potential forces have been found. These are the integrals of the 2nd–4th degrees for the dynamically symmetric body, the quadratic integrals as well as IMs defined by the polynomials of the 2nd and 3rd degrees in the case of the asymmetric body.

To find them, a combination of the method of undetermined coefficients with computer algebra methods such as the reduction of a polynomial with respect to a list of polynomials, the Gröbner basis method, etc. was applied. The qualitative analysis of the equations in particular cases of the existence of the additional integrals of the 2nd and 4th degrees was done. The stationary solutions corresponding to the permanent rotations and equilibria of the body as well as the IMs of various dimensions have been obtained. With the aid of the software package developed on the base of CAS "Mathematica", the sufficient conditions of the Lyapunov stability have been derived for the found solutions. In some cases, the above conditions were compared with the necessary ones. The presented results show enough the efficiency of the approaches and computational tools which were used.

References

1. Banshchikov, A.V., Burlakova, L.A., Irtegov, V.D., Titorenko, T.N.: Software Package for Finding and Stability Analysis of Stationary Sets. Certificate of State Registration of Software Programs. FGU-FIPS. No. 2011615235 (2011)
2. Barnett, S.J.: Magnetization by rotation. Phys. Rev. **6**(4), 239–270 (1915)
3. Egarmin, I.E.: On the magnetic field of a rotating superconducting body. Astrophysics and Geomagnetic Researches, Moscow. Collected Works, pp. 95–96 (1983)
4. Everitt, C.W.F., et al.: Gravity probe B: final results of a space experiment to test general relativity. Phys. Rev. Lett. **106**, 221101 (2011)
5. Gorr, G.V.: A linear invariant relation in the problem of the motion of a gyrostat in a magnetic field. J. Appl. Math. Mech. **61**(4), 549–552 (1997)
6. Hess, W.: Über die Euler'schen Bewegungsgleichungen und über eine neue partikuläre Lösung des Problems der Bewegung eines starren Körpers um einen festen Punkt. Math. Ann. **37**(2), 153–181 (1890)
7. Irtegov, V.D., Titorenko, T.N.: The invariant manifolds of systems with first integrals. J. Appl. Math. Mech. **73**(4), 379–384 (2009)
8. Irtegov, V., Titorenko, T.: On stationary motions of the generalized Kowalewski Gyrostat and their stability. In: Gerdt, V.P., Koepf, W., Seiler, W.M., Vorozhtsov, E.V. (eds.) CASC 2017. LNCS, vol. 10490, pp. 210–224. Springer, Cham (2017). https://doi.org/10.1007/978-3-319-66320-3_16
9. Irtegov, V., Titorenko, T.: On linear invariant manifolds in the generalized problem of motion of a top in a magnetic field. In: England, M., Koepf, W., Sadykov, T.M., Seiler, W.M., Vorozhtsov, E.V. (eds.) CASC 2019. LNCS, vol. 11661, pp. 246–261. Springer, Cham (2019). https://doi.org/10.1007/978-3-030-26831-2_17
10. Kozlov, V.V.: To the problem of the rotation of a rigid body in a magnetic field. Izv. Akad. Nauk SSSR. MTT **6**, 28–33 (1985)
11. Lyapunov, A.M.: On permanent helical motions of a rigid body in fluid. Collected Works, no. 1, pp. 276–319. USSR Academy Science, Moscow-Leningrad (1954)
12. Lyapunov, A.M.: The General Problem of the Stability of Motion. Taylor & Francis, London (1992)
13. Samsonov, V.A.: On the rotation of a rigid body in a magnetic field. Izv. Akad. Nauk SSSR. MTT **4**, 32–34 (1984)
14. Urman, Y.M.: Influence of the Barnett-London effect on the motion of a superconducting rotor in a nonuniform magnetic field. Tech. Phys. **43**(8), 885–889 (1998). https://doi.org/10.1134/1.1259095

Automatic Differentiation with Higher Infinitesimals, or Computational Smooth Infinitesimal Analysis in Weil Algebra

Hiromi Ishii[(⊠)]

DeepFlow, Inc., 3-16-40, Tsuruse Nishi, Fujimi-shi 354-0026, Japan
h-ishii@math.tsukuba.ac.jp

Abstract. We propose an algorithm to compute the C^∞-ring structure of arbitrary Weil algebra. It allows us to do some analysis with *higher infinitesimals* numerically and symbolically. To that end, we first give a brief description of the (Forward-mode) *automatic differentiation* (AD) in terms of C^∞-rings. The notion of a C^∞-ring was introduced by Lawvere [10] and used as the fundamental building block of *smooth infinitesimal analysis* and *synthetic differential geometry* [11]. We argue that interpreting AD in terms of C^∞-rings gives us a unifying theoretical framework and modular ways to express multivariate partial derivatives. In particular, we can "package" higher-order Forward-mode AD as a Weil algebra, and take tensor products to compose them to achieve multivariate higher-order AD. The algorithms in the present paper can also be used for a pedagogical purpose in learning and studying smooth infinitesimal analysis as well.

Keywords: Automatic differentiation · Smooth infinitesimal analysis · Weil algebras · Smooth algebras and C^∞-rings · Symbolic-numeric algorithms · Symbolic differentiation · Gröbner basis · Zero-dimensional ideals

1 Introduction

Automatic Differentiation (or, *AD* for short) is a method to calculate derivatives of (piecewise) smooth functions accurately and efficiently. AD has a long history of research, and under the recent rise of differentiable programming in machine learning, AD has been attracting more interests than before recently.

Smooth Infinitesimal Analysis (or, *SIA* for short), on the other hand, is an area of mathematics that uses *nilpotent infinitesimals* to develop the theory of real analysis. Its central building blocks are *Weil algebras*, which can be viewed as the real line augmented with nilpotent infinitesimals. Indeed, SIA is a subarea of *Synthetic Differential Geometry* (SDG) initiated by Lawvere [10], which studies

This work was supported by the Research Institute for Mathematical Sciences, an International Joint Usage/Research Center located in Kyoto University.

© Springer Nature Switzerland AG 2021
F. Boulier et al. (Eds.): CASC 2021, LNCS 12865, pp. 174–191, 2021.
https://doi.org/10.1007/978-3-030-85165-1_11

smooth manifolds topos-theoretically, and higher multivariate infinitesimals play crucial roles in building theory of, e.g. vector fields, differential forms and tangent spaces. The key observation of Lawvere is that manifolds can be classified solely by their smooth function ring $C^\infty(M)$, and both such function rings and Weil algebras are special cases of C^∞-rings.

It has been pointed out that AD and SIA have some connection; e.g. even Wikipedia article [14] mentions the connection between first-order Forward-mode AD with the ring $\mathbb{R}[X]/X^2$ of dual numbers. However, a precise theoretical description of this correspondence is not well-communicated, and further generalisation of AD in terms of SIA hasn't been discussed in depth.

The present paper aims at filling this gap, giving a unified description of AD in terms of C^∞-rings and Weil algebras. Furthermore, our main contribution is algorithms to compute the C^∞-ring structure of a general Weil algebra. This enables automatic differentiation done in *arbitrary* Weil algebras other than dual numbers, and, together with tensor products, lets us compute higher-order multivariate partial derivatives in a modular and composable manner, packed as Weil algebra. Such algorithms can also be used to learn and study the theory of SIA and SDG.

This paper is organised as follows. In Sect. 2, we review the basic concepts and facts on C^∞-rings and Weil algebras. This section provides basic theoretical background—but the proofs of proposed algorithms are, however, not directly dependent on the content of this section. So readers can skip this section first and go back afterwards when necessary. Subsequently, we discuss the connection between Forward-mode automatic differentiation and Weil algebras in Sect. 3. There, we see how the notion of Weil algebra and C^∞-ring can be applied to treat higher-order partial ADs in a unified and general setting. Then, in Sect. 4, we give algorithms to compute the C^∞-ring structure of an arbitrary Weil algebra. These algorithms enable us to do *automatic differentiation with higher infinitesimals*, or *computational smooth infinitesimal analysis*. We give some small examples in Sect. 5, using our proof-of-concept implementation [6] in Haskell. Finally, we discuss related and possible future works and conclude in Sect. 6.

2   Preliminaries

In this section, we briefly review classical definitions and facts on Weil algebras and C^∞-rings without proofs, which will be used in Sect. 4. For theoretical detail, we refer readers to Moerdijk–Reyes [11, Chapters I and II] or Joyce [8].

We use the following notational convention:

Definition 1 (Notation). *Throughout the paper, we use the following notation:*

- *$g \circ f$ denotes the composite function from A to C of functions $f : A \to B$ and $g : B \to C$, that is, the function defined by $(g \circ f)(x) = g(f(x))$ for all $x \in A$.*
- *For functions $f_i : Z \to X_i (1 \le i \le n)$, $\langle f_1, \ldots, f_n \rangle$ denotes the product of functions f_i given by the universality of the product objects. That is, $\langle f_1, \ldots, f_n \rangle$ is the function of type $Z \to X_1 \times \cdots \times X_n$ defined by $\langle f_1, \ldots, f_n \rangle(z) = (f_1(z), \ldots, f_n(z)) \in X_1 \times \cdots \times X_n$ for all $z \in Z$*

Definition 2 (Lawvere [10]). *A C^∞-ring A is a product-preserving functor from the category* CartSp *of finite-dimensional Euclidean spaces and smooth maps to the category* Sets *of sets.*

We identify A with $A(\mathbb{R})$ and A^n with $A(\mathbb{R}^n)$. For a map $f : \mathbb{R}^m \to \mathbb{R}$, we call $A(f) : A^m \to A$ the C^∞-lifting of f to A.

Intuitively, a C^∞-ring A is an $\mathbb{R}$-algebra A augmented with m-ary operations $A(f) : A^m \to A$ respecting composition, projection and product for all smooth maps $f : \mathbb{R}^m \to \mathbb{R}$.

One typical example of a C^∞-ring is a formal power series ring:

Theorem 1 (Implicitly in Lawvere [10]; See [11, 1.3 Borel's Theorem]). *The ring $\mathbb{R}[\![X_1, \ldots, X_n]\!]$ of formal power series with finitely many variables has the C^∞-ring structure via Taylor expansion at $\mathbf{0}$. In particular, lifting of a smooth map $f : \mathbb{R}^m \to \mathbb{R}$ is given by:*

$$\mathbb{R}[\![\boldsymbol{X}]\!](f)(g_1, \ldots, g_m) = \sum_{\alpha \in \mathbb{N}^n} \frac{\boldsymbol{X}^\alpha}{\alpha!} D^\alpha(f \circ \langle g_1, \ldots, g_m \rangle)(\mathbf{0}),$$

where $\alpha! = \alpha_1! \ldots \alpha_n!$ is the multi-index factorial and D^α is the partial differential operator to degree α.

The C^∞-rings of central interest in this paper are *Weil algebras*, and have a deep connection with $\mathbb{R}[\![\boldsymbol{X}]\!]$:

Definition 3 (Weil algebra). *A* Weil algebra *W is an associative $\mathbb{R}$-algebra which can be written as $W = \mathbb{R}[X_1, \ldots, X_n]/I$ for some ideal $I \subseteq \mathbb{R}[\boldsymbol{X}]$ such that $\langle X_1, \ldots, X_n \rangle^k \subseteq I$ for some $k \in \mathbb{N}$.*

It follows that a Weil algebra W is finite-dimensional as a $\mathbb{R}$-linear space and hence I is a *zero-dimensional* ideal. A Weil algebra W can be regarded as a real line $\mathbb{R}$ augmented with nilpotent infinitesimals $d_i = [X_i]_I$. In what follows, we identify an element $\boldsymbol{u} \in W$ of a k-dimensional Weil algebra W with a k-dimensional vector $\boldsymbol{u} = (u_1, \ldots, u_k) \in \mathbb{R}^k$ of reals.

Although it is unclear from the definition, Weil algebras have the canonical C^∞-structure. First note that, if I is zero-dimensional, we have $\mathbb{R}[\boldsymbol{X}]/I \simeq \mathbb{R}[\![\boldsymbol{X}]\!]/I$. Hence, in particular, any Weil algebra W can also be regarded as a quotient ring of the formal power series by zero-dimensional ideal. Thus, together with Theorem 1, the following lemma shows that any Weil algebra W has the canonical C^∞-ring structure:

Lemma 1 (Implicitly in Lawvere [10]; See [11, 1.2 Proposition]). *For any C^∞-ring A and a ring-theoretical ideal $I \subseteq A$, the quotient ring A/I again has the canonical C^∞-ring structure induced by the canonical quotient mapping:*

$$(A/I)(f)([x_1]_I, \ldots, [x_m]_I) := [A(f)(x_1, \ldots, x_m)]_I,$$

where $x_i \in A$ and $f : \mathbb{R}^m \xrightarrow{C^\infty} \mathbb{R}$. In particular, the C^∞-structure of Weil algebra W is induced by the canonical quotient mapping to that of $\mathbb{R}[\![\boldsymbol{X}]\!]$.

3 Connection Between Automatic Differentiation and Weil Algebras

In this section, based on the basic facts on C^∞-rings and Weil algebras reviewed in Sect. 2, we describe the connection of automatic differentiation (AD) and Weil algebra.

Forward-mode AD is a technique to compute a value and differential coefficient of given univariate composition of smooth function efficiently. It can be implemented by ad-hoc polymorphism (or equivalently, function overloading). For detailed implementation, we refer readers to Elliott [2] and Kmett's ad package [9].

Briefly speaking, in Forward-mode AD, one stores both the value and differential coefficient simultaneously, say in a form $f(x) + f'(x)d$ for d an indeterminate variable. Then, when evaluating composite functions, one uses the Chain Rule for implementation:

$$\frac{\mathrm{d}}{\mathrm{d}x}(g \circ f)(x) = f'(x)g'(f(x)).$$

The following definitions of functions on dual numbers illustrate the idea:

$$(a_1 + b_1 d) + (a_2 + b_2 d) = (a_1 + a_2) + (b_1 + b_2)d,$$
$$(a_1 + b_1 d) \times (a_2 + b_2 d) = a_1 a_2 + (a_1 b_2 + a_2 b_1)d,$$
$$\cos(a_1 + b_1 d) = \cos(a_1) - b_1 \sin(a_1)d.$$

The last equation for cos expresses the nontrivial part of Forward-mode AD. As mentioned above, we regard $a_1 + b_1 d$ as a pair $(a_1, b_1) = (f(x), f'x)$ of value and differential coefficient of some smooth function f at some point x. So if $a_2 + b_2 d = \cos(a_1 + b_1 d)$, we must have $a_2 = \cos(f(x)) = \cos a_1$ and $b_2 = \frac{\mathrm{d}}{\mathrm{d}x}\cos(f(x)) = -b_1 \sin(a_1)$ by Chain Rule. The first two equations for addition and multiplication suggest us to regard operations on Forward-mode AD as extending the algebraic structure of $\mathbb{R}[d] = \mathbb{R}[X]/X^2$. Indeed, first-order Forward-mode AD can be identified with the arithmetic on *dual numbers*:

Definition 4. *The* dual number ring *is a Weil algebra* $\mathbb{R}[X]/X^2$. *We often write* $d = [X]_I \in \mathbb{R}[d]$ *and* $\mathbb{R}[d] := \mathbb{R}[X]/X^2$.

We use an analogous notation for multivariate versions:

$$\mathbb{R}[d_1, \ldots, d_k] := \mathbb{R}[\boldsymbol{X}]/\langle X_1^2, \ldots, X_k^2 \rangle.$$

Since the dual number ring $\mathbb{R}[d]$ is a Weil algebra, one can apply Theorem 1 and Lemma 1 to compute its C^∞-structure. Letting $f : \mathbb{R} \xrightarrow{C^\infty} \mathbb{R}$ be a univariate smooth function, then we can derive the C^∞-lifting $\mathbb{R}[d](f) : \mathbb{R}[d] \to \mathbb{R}[d]$ as follows:

$$\mathbb{R}[\![X]\!](f)(a+bX)$$

$$= f(a) + \frac{\mathrm{d}}{\mathrm{d}x}(f(a+bx))(0)X + \cdots \quad \text{(by Theorem 1)}$$

$$= f(a) + bf'(a)X + \cdots$$

$$\xrightarrow{X \mapsto d} f(a) + bf'(a)d,$$

$$\therefore \qquad \mathbb{R}[d](f)(a+bd) = f(a) + bf'(a)d. \quad \text{(by Lemma 1)} \qquad (*)$$

One can notice that the derived C^∞-structure in $(*)$ is exactly the same as how to implement individual smooth functions for Forward-mode AD. This describes the connection between Forward-mode AD and dual numbers: Forward-mode AD is just a (partial) implementation of the C^∞-structure of the dual number ring $\mathbb{R}[d]$.

Let us see how this extends to higher-order cases. The most naïve way to compute higher-order derivatives of smooth function is just to successively differentiating it. This intuition can be expressed by duplicating the number of the basis of dual numbers:

Theorem 2. *For any* $f : \mathbb{R} \xrightarrow{C^\infty} \mathbb{R}$ *and* $\boldsymbol{x} \in \mathbb{R}^n$, *we have:*

$$\mathbb{R}[d_1, \ldots, d_k](f)(x + d_1 + \cdots + d_n) = \sum_{0 \le i \le n} f^{(i)}(x)\sigma_n^i(\vec{d}),$$

where, $\sigma_k^i(x_1, \ldots, x_k)$ *denotes the* k-*variate elementary symmetric polynomial of degree* i.

The above can be proven by an easy induction.

However, as one can easily see, terms in $\mathbb{R}[\![\boldsymbol{X}]\!]/\langle X_i^2 \rangle_i$ can grow exponentially and include duplicated coefficients. How could we reduce such duplication and save space consumption? —this is where general Weil algebras beyond (multivariate) dual numbers can play a role. We can get derivatives in more succinct representation with *higher infinitesimal* beyond dual numbers:

Lemma 2. *Let* $I = \langle X^{n+1} \rangle, W = \mathbb{R}[X]/I$ *and* $\varepsilon = [X]_I$ *for* $n \in \mathbb{N}$. *Given* $f : \mathbb{R} \xrightarrow{C^\infty} \mathbb{R}$ *and* $a \in \mathbb{R}$, *we have:*

$$W(f)(a + \varepsilon) = \sum_{k \le n} \frac{f^{(k)}(a)}{k!}\varepsilon^k.$$

In this representation, we have only $(n+1)$-terms, and hence it results in succinct and efficient representation of derivatives.

If we duplicate such higher-order infinitesimals as much as needed, one can likewise compute *multivariate* higher-order derivatives all at once, up to some multidegree β:

Lemma 3. *Let* $I = \left\langle X_i^{\beta_i+1} \mid i \leq m \right\rangle$, $W = \mathbb{R}[X_1, \ldots, X_m]/I$, *and* $\varepsilon_i = [X_i]_I$
for $\beta = (\beta_i)_{i \leq m} \in \mathbb{N}^m$. *For* $f : \mathbb{R}^m \xrightarrow{C^\infty} \mathbb{R}$ *and* $\boldsymbol{a} = (a_i)_{i \leq m} \in \mathbb{R}^m$, *we have:*

$$W(f)(a_1 + \varepsilon_1, \ldots, a_m + \varepsilon_m) = \sum_{\delta_i \leq \beta_i} \frac{D^\delta f}{\delta!}(\boldsymbol{a}) \; \varepsilon_1^{\delta_1} \cdots \varepsilon_m^{\delta_m}.$$

Note that the formal power series ring $\mathbb{R}[\![\boldsymbol{X}]\!]$ can be viewed as the inverse limit of $\mathbb{R}[\boldsymbol{X}]/\langle \boldsymbol{X}^\beta \rangle$'s. In other words, if we take a limit $\beta_i \to \infty$, we can compute any higher derivative up to any finite orders; this is exactly what *Tower-mode* AD aims at, modulo factor $\frac{1}{\beta!}$.

In this way, we can view AD as a technique to compute higher derivatives simultaneously by partially implementing a certain C^∞-ring[1]. Forward-mode AD (of first-order) computes the C^∞-structure of the dual number ring $\mathbb{R}[d]$; Tower-mode AD computes that of the formal power series ring $\mathbb{R}[\![\boldsymbol{X}]\!]$ (modulo reciprocal factorial).

So far, we have used a Weil algebra of form $\mathbb{R}[\![\boldsymbol{X}]\!]/I$. So, do we need to define new ideals by hand whenever one wants to treat multiple variables? The answer is no:

Lemma 4 (See [11, 4.19 Corollary]). *For ideals* $I \subseteq \mathbb{R}[\![\boldsymbol{X}]\!]$ *and* $J \subseteq \mathbb{R}[\![\boldsymbol{Y}]\!]$, *we have:*
$$\mathbb{R}[\![\boldsymbol{X}]\!]/I \otimes_{\mathbb{R}} \mathbb{R}[\![\boldsymbol{Y}]\!]/J \simeq \mathbb{R}[\![\boldsymbol{X}, \boldsymbol{Y}]\!]/(I, J),$$
where $\otimes_{\mathbb{R}}$ *is a tensor product of* C^∞-*rings.*

Thanks to this lemma, we don't have to define I by hand every time, but can take tensor products to compose predefined Weil algebras to compute multivariate and higher-order derivatives. Examples of such calculations will be presented in Sect. 5.

4   Algorithms

In this section, we will present the main results of this paper: concrete algorithms to compute the C^∞-structure of arbitrary Weil algebra and their tensor products. For examples of applications of the algorithm presented here, the reader can skip to the next Sect. 5 to comprehend the actual use case.

4.1   Computing C^∞-Structure of Weil Algebra

Let us start with algorithms to compute the C^∞-structure of a general Weil algebra. Roughly speaking, the algorithm is threefold:

---

[1] Such implementation is inherently a partial approximation: there are $2^{\aleph_0}$-many smooth functions, but there are only countably many computable (floating) functions.

1. A procedure deciding Weil-ness of an ideal and returning data required to compute the C^∞-structure (WEILTEST, Algorithm 1),
2. A procedure to compute the lifting $W(f) : W^m \to W$ to a Weil algebra W from $\mathbb{R}[\![X]\!](f)$ (LIFTWEIL, Algorithm 2), and
3. A procedure to lift smooth map $f : \mathbb{R}^m \to \mathbb{R}$ to the n-variate formal power series ring $\mathbb{R}[\![X]\!]$ (LIFTSERIES, Algorithm 3).

We start with Weil-ness testing. First, we define the basic data needed to compute the C^∞-structure of Weil algebras:

Definition 5 (Weil settings). *The* Weil setting *of a Weil algebra W consists of the following data:*

1. *Monomial basis $\{b_1, \ldots, b_\ell\}$ of W,*
2. *M, the multiplication table of W in terms of the basis,*
3. *$(k_1, \ldots, k_n) \in \mathbb{N}^n$ such that k_i is the maximum satisfying $X_i^{k_i} \notin I$ for each i, and*
4. *NV_W, a table of representations of non-vanishing monomials in W; i.e. for any $\alpha = (\alpha_1, \ldots, \alpha_n) \in \mathbb{N}^n$, if $\alpha_i \leq k_i$ for all i, then $\mathrm{NV}_W(X^\alpha) = (c_1, \ldots, c_k) \in \mathbb{R}^k$ satisfies $[X^\alpha]_I = \sum_i c_i b_i$.*

A basis and multiplication table allow us to calculate the ordinary $\mathbb{R}$-algebra structure of Weil algebra W. The latter two data, $\vec{k}$ and NV_W, are essential in computing the C^∞-structure of W. In theory, (4) is unnecessary if one stores a Gröbner basis of I; but since normal form calculation modulo G can take much time in some case, we don't store G itself and use the precalculated data NV. It might be desirable to calculate NV_W as lazily as possible. Since it involves Gröbner basis computation it is more desirable to delay it as much as possible and do in an on-demand manner.

With this definition, one can decide Weilness and compute their settings:

Algorithm 1 (WeilTest)

Input *An ideal $I \subseteq \mathbb{R}[X_1, \ldots, X_n]$*
Output *Returns the Weil settings of $W = \mathbb{R}[X]/I$ if it is a Weil algebra; otherwise* No.
Procedure WEILTEST

```
1   G ← calcGroebnerBasis(I)
2   If I is not zero-dimensional
3      Return No
4   {b₁,...,b_ℓ} ← Monomial basis of I
5   M ← the Multiplication table of W
6   For i in 1..n
7      pᵢ ← the monic generator of I ∩ ℝ[Xᵢ]
8      If pᵢ is not a monomial
9         Return No
10     kᵢ ← deg(pᵢ) − 1
```

11   $NV_W \leftarrow \{\}$
12   **For** α **in** $\{\alpha \in \mathbb{N}^n | \alpha_i \leq k_i \, \forall i \leq \ell\}$
13      $c_1 b_1 + \cdots + c_\ell b_\ell \leftarrow \overline{\boldsymbol{X}^\alpha}^G$
14      $NV_W(\boldsymbol{X}^\alpha) \leftarrow (c_1, \ldots, c_\ell)$
15   **Return** $(\vec{b}, M, \vec{k}, NV_W)$

Theorem 3. *Algorithm 1 terminates and returns expected values.*

Proof. Algorithms to decide the zero-dimensionality and calculate their multiplication table is well-known (for details, we refer readers to Cox–Little–O'Shea [1, Chapter 2]). So the only non-trivial part is nilpotence detection (Lines 6 to 10). But, again, this is just a variation of radical calculation algorithm for zero-dimensional ideals. Indeed, since each $\mathbb{R}[X_i]$ is a PID, we have $X_i^k \in I \cap R[X_i]$ iff $p_i \mid X_i^k$, hence p_i is a monomial iff X_i is nilpotent in W.

Now that we have the basis and multiplication table at hand, we can calculate the ordinary algebraic operations just by the standard means.

With upper bounds $\vec{k}$ of powers and representations NV_W of non-vanishing monomials, we can now compute the C^∞-structure of an arbitrary Weil algebra, when given a lifting of smooth mapping f to $\mathbb{R}[\boldsymbol{X}]$:

Algorithm 2 (LiftWeil)

Input $I \subseteq \mathbb{R}[\boldsymbol{X}]$, *an ideal where* $W = \mathbb{R}[\boldsymbol{X}]/I$ *is a Weil algebra,* $\mathbb{R}[\boldsymbol{X}](f)$: $\mathbb{R}[\boldsymbol{X}]^m \to \mathbb{R}[\boldsymbol{X}]$, *a lifting of a smooth map* $f : \mathbb{R}^m \to \mathbb{R}$ *to* $\mathbb{R}[\boldsymbol{X}]$, *and* $\vec{u} = (u_1, \ldots, u_m) \in W^m$,.
Output $v = W(f)(\vec{u}) \in W$, *the value of* f *at* $\vec{u}$ *given by* C^∞*-structure.*
Procedure LIFTWEIL

1   $(\vec{b}, \text{M}, \vec{k}, NV_W) \leftarrow \text{WEILTEST}(I)$
2   $g_i \leftarrow (b_1, \ldots, b_k) \cdot u_i \in \mathbb{R}[\boldsymbol{X}]$ for $i \leq \text{m}$
3   $\text{h} = \sum_\alpha c_\alpha \boldsymbol{X}^\alpha \leftarrow \mathbb{R}[\boldsymbol{X}](f)(\vec{g})$
4   $v \leftarrow 0$
5   **For** α **with** $\alpha_i \leq k_i \, \forall i$
6      $v \leftarrow v + c_\alpha NV_W(\boldsymbol{X}^\alpha)$
7   **Return** v

The termination and validity of Algorithm 2 are clear. One might feel it problematic that Algorithm 2 requires *functions* as its input. This can be *any* smooth computable functions on the coefficient type. Practically, we expect a composite function of standard smooth floating-point functions as its argument, for example, it can be $x \mapsto \sin(x)$, $(x, y) \mapsto e^{\sin x} y^2$, and so on. In the modern programming language – like Haskell, Rust, LISP, Ruby, etc. – one don't need to worry about their representation, as we can already freely write *higher-order functions* that take functions or closures as their arguments. Even in the low-level languages such as C/C++, one can use function pointers or whatever to pass an arbitrary function to another function.

Now that we can compute the $\mathbb{R}$-algebraic and C^∞-structure of a Weil algebra solely from its Weil setting, one can hard-code pre-calculated Weil settings for known typical Weil algebras, such as the dual number ring or higher infinitesimal rings of the form $\mathbb{R}[X]/(X^{n+1})$, to reduce computational overheads.

Computing the C^∞-Structure of $\mathbb{R}[\![X]\!]$. So it remains to compute the C^∞-structure of $\mathbb{R}[\![X]\!]$. Thanks to Theorem 1, we know the precise definition of C^∞-lifting to $\mathbb{R}[\![X]\!]$:

$$\mathbb{R}[\![X]\!](f)(g_1, \ldots, g_m) = \sum_{\alpha \in \mathbb{N}^n} \frac{X^\alpha}{\alpha!} D^\alpha (f \circ \langle g_1, \ldots, g_n \rangle)(0).$$

As noted in Sect. 3, as a C^∞-ring, the formal power series ring is isomorphic to multivariate Tower-mode AD. It can be implemented in various ways, such as Lazy Multivariate Tower AD [13], or nested Sparse Tower AD [9, module Numeric.AD.Rank1.Sparse]. For reference, we include a succinct and efficient variant mixing these two techniques in Appendix A.

Both Tower-mode AD and formal power series can be represented as a formal power series. The difference is the interpretation of coefficients in a given series. On one hand, a coefficient of X^α in Tower AD is interpreted as the αth partial differential coefficient $D^\alpha f(a)$, where $a = (g_1(0), \ldots, g_m(0))$. On the other hand, in $\mathbb{R}[\![X]\!]$ it is interpreted as $\frac{D^\alpha f(a)}{\alpha!}$. To avoid the confusion, we adopt the following convention: Tower-mode AD is represented as a function from monomials X^α to coefficient $\mathbb{R}$ in what follows, whilst $\mathbb{R}[\![X]\!]$ as-is. Note that this is purely for notational and descriptional distinctions, and does not indicate any essential difference.

With this distinction, we use the following notation and transformation:

Definition 6. Tower $= \{f | f : \mathbb{N}^n \to \mathbb{R}\}$ *denotes the set of all elements of Tower-mode AD algebra. We denote C^∞-lifting of $f : \mathbb{R}^m \to \mathbb{R}$ to Tower by* Tower$(f) : $ Tower$^m \to$ Tower.

A reciprocal factorial transformation RF $:$ Tower $\to \mathbb{R}[\![X]\!]$ *is defined as follows:*

$$\text{RF}(f) = \sum_{\alpha \in \mathbb{N}^n} \frac{f(\alpha)}{\alpha!} X^\alpha.$$

Then, the inverse reciprocal factorial transformation is given by:

$$\text{RF}^{-1}\left(\sum_{\alpha \in \mathbb{N}^n} c_\alpha X^\alpha\right) = \lambda(X^\alpha).\ \alpha! \cdot c_\alpha.$$

Algorithm 3 (LiftSeries)

Input $f : \mathbb{R}^m \xrightarrow{C^\infty} \mathbb{R}$, *a smooth function which admits Tower AD*, $g_1, \ldots, g_n \in \mathbb{R}[\![X]\!]$, *formal power series.*
Output $\mathbb{R}[\![X]\!](f)(g_1, \ldots, g_m) \in \mathbb{R}[\![X]\!]$, C^∞-*lifting to the formal power series ring.*

Procedure LIFTSERIES

1   $\hat{g}_i \leftarrow \mathrm{RF}^{-1}(g_i)$
2   $\hat{f} \leftarrow \mathrm{Tower}(f)(\hat{g}_1, \ldots, \hat{g}_m)$
3   **Return** $\mathrm{RF}(\hat{f})$

4.2   Tensor Product of Weil Algebras

As indicated by Lemma 4, tensor products enable us to compose multiple Weil algebras into one and use them to compute higher-order multivariate derivatives. Here, we give a simple procedure to compute Weil settings of the tensor product.

Algorithm 4 (WeilTensor)

Input *Weil settings of two Weil algebras* W_1, W_2, *with* $\{b_1^i, \ldots, b_{\ell_i}^i\}$ *a basis,* $(k_1^i, \ldots, k_{n_i}^i)$ *an upper bounds and* M_i *a multiplication table for each* W_i.
Output *Weil settings of* $W_1 \otimes_{\mathbb{R}} W_2$.
Procedure WEILTENSOR

1   $(b_1, \ldots, b_{\ell_1 \ell_2}) \leftarrow \mathrm{CONVOL}(\vec{b}^1, \vec{b}^2)$
2   $\mathsf{M} \leftarrow \{\}$
3   **For** $(\{b_L^1, b_R^1\}, (c_1, \ldots, c_{\ell_1}))$ **in** M_1
4   **For** $(\{b_L^2, b_R^2\}, (d_1, \ldots, d_{\ell_1}))$ **in** M_2
5       $\mathsf{M}(\{b_L^1 b_L^2, \ b_R^1 b_R^2\}) \leftarrow \mathrm{CONVOL}(\vec{c}, \ \vec{d})$
6   $\mathrm{NV}_{W_1 \otimes W_2} \leftarrow \{\}$
7   **For** $(X^\alpha, (c_1, \ldots, c_{\ell_1}))$ **in** NV_{W_1}
8   **For** $(Y^\beta, (d_1, \ldots, d_{\ell_2}))$ **in** NV_{W_2}
9       $\mathrm{NV}_{W_1 \otimes W_2}(X^\alpha Y^\beta) \leftarrow \mathrm{CONVOL}(\vec{c}, \ \vec{d})$
10 **Return** $(b, M, (\vec{k}^1, \vec{k}^2), \mathrm{NV}_{W_1 \otimes W_2})$

Here, CONVOL *is a convolution of two sequences:*

Procedure CONVOL$((c_1, \ldots, c_{\ell_1}), (d_1, \ldots, d_{\ell_2}))$

1   **For** i **in** $1 .. (\ell_1 \times \ell_2)$
2     $\mathsf{j} \leftarrow \lfloor \frac{i}{\ell_2} \rfloor; \ \mathsf{k} \leftarrow i \bmod \ell_2$
3     $a_i \leftarrow c_j d_k$
4   **Return** $(a_1, \ldots, a_{\ell_1 \ell_2})$

The validity proof is routine work.

5   Examples

We have implemented the algorithms introduced in the previous section on top of two libraries: `computational-algebra` package [4,5] and `ad` package [9]. The code is available on GitHub [6].

5.1   Higher-Order Derivatives via Dual Numbers and Higher Infinitesimals

As indicated by Theorem 2 and Lemma 2, to compute higher-order derivatives of univariate functions, we can use tensor products of Dual numbers or higher-order infinitesimals.

Let us first compute higher-order derivatives of $\sin(x)$ up to 3. First, Let us use a tensor product of dual numbers:

```
1 d1, d2, d3 :: Floating a => Weil (D1 |*| D1 |*| D1) a
2 [d1, d2, d3] = map di [0..]
```

Here, `Weil w a` represents the type of Weil algebra with its setting given in `w`, `D1` the dual number ideal $I = (X^2)$, and `|*|` the tensor product operator. Each d_i corresponds to i^{th} infinitesimal.

Next, we calculate higher-order differential coefficients at $x = \frac{\pi}{6}$ up to the third order:

```
>>> (sin (pi/6),  cos (pi/6), -sin (pi/6), -cos (pi/6))
( 0.49999999999999994, 0.8660254037844387, -0.49999999999999994,
  -0.8660254037844387)

>>> sin (pi/6 + d0 + d1 + d2)
-0.8660254037844387 d(0) d(1) d(2) - 0.49999999999999994 d(0) d(1)
  - 0.49999999999999994 d(0) d(2)  - 0.49999999999999994 d(1) d(2)
  + 0.8660254037844387 d(0) + 0.8660254037844387 d(1)
  + 0.8660254037844387 d(2) + 0.49999999999999994
```

It is easy to see that terms of degree i have the coefficients $\sin^{(i)}(\pi/6)$. Since our implementation is polymorphic, if we apply the same function to the type for symbolic computation, say `Symbolic`, we can reconstruct symbolic differentiation and check that the result is indeed correct symbolically:

```
>>> x :: Weil w Symbolic
>>> x = injectCoeff (var "x")

>>> normalise <$> sin (x + d0+d1+d2)
((-1.0) * cos x) d(0) d(1) d(2) + (- (sin x)) d(0) d(1)
  + (- (sin x)) d(0) d(2) + (- (sin x)) d(1) d(2)
  + (cos x) d(0) + (cos x) d(1) + (cos x) d(2) + (sin x)
```

As stated before, the tensor-of-duals approach blows the number of terms exponentially. Let us see how higher infinitesimal works.

```
1 eps :: Floating a => Weil (DOrder 4) a
2 eps = di 0
```

Here, `DOrder n` corresponds to an algebra $\mathbb{R}[X]/(X^n)$. Note that, according to Lemma 2, to calculate an nth derivative we have to use $\mathbb{R}[X]/(X^{n+1})$.

```
>>> (sin (pi/6), cos (pi/6), -sin (pi/6)/2, -cos (pi/6)/6)
( 0.49999999999999994, 0.8660254037844387,
 -0.24999999999999997, -0.14433756729740646)

>>> sin (pi/6 + eps)
-0.14433756729740646 d(0)^3 - 0.24999999999999997 d(0)^2
  + 0.8660254037844387 d(0) + 0.49999999999999994

>>> normalise <$> sin (x + eps)
((-1.0) * cos x / 6.0) d(0)^3 + ((-(sin x)) / 2.0) d(0)^2
  + (cos x) d(0) + (sin x)
```

Note that by Lemma 2, each coefficient is not directly a differential coefficient, but divided by $k!$, that is $f(x + \varepsilon) = \sum_{k \leq 3} \frac{f^{(k)}(x)}{k!} \varepsilon^k$.

Let us see how tensor products of higher Weil algebras can be used to multivariate higher-order partial derivatives. Suppose we want to calculate partial derivatives of $f(x, y) = e^{2x} \sin y$ up to $(2, 1)^{\text{th}}$ order.

```
eps1, eps2 :: Weil (DOrder 3 |*| DOrder 2) a
(eps1, eps2) = (di 0, di 1)

>>> f (2 + eps1) (pi/6 + eps2)
94.5667698566742 d(0)^2 d(1) + 54.59815003314423 d(0)^2
  + 94.5667698566742 d(0) d(1) + 54.59815003314423 d(0)
  + 47.2833849283371 d(1) + 27.299075016572115

>>> normalise <$> f (x + eps1) (y + eps2)
(4.0 * exp (2.0 * x) / 2.0 * cos y) d(0)^2 d(1)
  + (4.0 * exp (2.0 * x) / 2.0 * sin y) d(0)^2
  + (2.0 * exp (2.0 * x) * cos y) d(0) d(1)
  + (2.0 * exp (2.0 * x) * sin y) d(0)
  + (exp (2.0 * x) * cos y) d(1) + (exp (2.0 * x) * sin y)
```

One can see that the coefficient of $d(0)^i d(1)^j$ corresponds exactly to the value $D^{(i,j)} f(x, y)/i!j!$. In this way, we can freely compose multiple Weil algebra to calculate various partial derivatives modularly.

5.2 Computation in General Weil Algebra

All examples so far were about the predefined, specific form of a Weil algebra. Here, we demonstrate that we can determine whether the given ideal defines

Weil algebras with Algorithm 1, and do some actual calculation in arbitrary Weil algebra.

First, we see that WEILTEST rejects invalid ideals:

```
-- R[X,Y]/(X^3 - Y), not zero-dimensional
>>> isWeil (toIdeal [x ^ 3 - y :: Q[x,y]])
Nothing

-- R[X]/(X^2 - 1), which is zero-dimensional but not Weil
>>> isWeil (toIdeal [x ^ 2 - 1 :: Q[x]])
Nothing
```

Next, we try to calculate in arbitrary chosen Weil algebra, $W = \mathbb{R}[x,y]/(x^2 - y^3, y^4)$, whose corresponding meaning in AD is unclear but is a Weil algebra as a matter of fact.

```
i :: Ideal (Rational[x,y])
i = toIdeal [x ^ 2 - y ^ 3, y ^ 4]

>>> isWeil i
Just WeilSettings
  {weilBasis =[[0,0],[0,1], ..., [3,0]]
  , nonZeroVarMaxPowers = [3,3]
  , weilMonomDic =
      [([0,2],[0,0,0,1,0,0,0,0]), ..., ([1,3],[0,0,0,0,0,0,0,1])]
  , table = [((0,0),1),((1,3),d(0)^2), ..., ((3,4),d(0)^3)]
  }
```

Let us see what will happen evaluating $\sin(a + d_0 + d_1)$, where $d_0 = [x]_I$, $d_1 = [y]_I$?

```
>>> withWeil i (sin (pi/4 + di 0 + di 1))
-2.7755575615628914e-17 d(0)^3 - ... + 0.7071067811865476 d(0)
  + 0.7071067811865476 d(1) + 0.7071067811865475

>>> withWeil i (normalise <$> sin (x + di 0 + di 1))
((-1.0) * (-(sin x)) / 6.0 + (-1.0) * cos x / 6.0) d(0)^3
  + ... + (cos x) d(0) + (cos x) d(1) + (sin x)
```

Carefully analysing each output, one can see that the output coincides with what is given by Theorem 1 and Lemma 1.

6   Discussions and Conclusions

We have illustrated the connection between automatic differentiation (AD) and C^∞-rings, especially Weil algebras. Methods of AD can be viewed as techniques to calculate partial coefficients simultaneously by partially implementing the C^∞-lifting operator for certain C^∞-ring. Especially, Forward-mode AD computes the C^∞-structure of the dual number ring $\mathbb{R}[d] = \mathbb{R}[X]/X^2$ and Tower-mode computes that of the formal power series ring $\mathbb{R}[\![X]\!]$.

The dual number ring $\mathbb{R}[d]$ is an archetypical example of Weil algebra, which formalises the real line with nilpotent infinitesimals. We generalised this view to arbitrary Weil algebras beyond dual numbers, enabling us to compute higher-order derivatives efficiently and succinctly. We gave general algorithms to compute the C^∞-structure of Weil algebras. With tensor products, one can easily compose (univariate) higher-order AD corresponding to Weil algebras into multivariate ones.

In this last section, we briefly discuss the possible applications other than AD, related works and future works.

6.1   Possible Applications and Related Works

Beside the reformulation of AD, we can argue that our methods can be used for a pedagogical purpose in teaching *Smooth Infinitesimal Analysis* (SIA) and *Synthetic Differential Geometry* (SDG). In those fields, arguing in the appropriate intuitionistic topos, various infinitesimal spaces corresponding to Weil algebra is used to build a theory, expressed by the following *generalised Kock-Lawvere axiom* [11]:

For any Weil algebra W, the following evaluation map gives an isomorphism:

$$\mathrm{ev} : W \to \mathbb{R}^{\mathrm{Spec}_\mathbb{R} W}$$
$$a \mapsto \lambda f. f(a)$$

This is another way to state the fact that Weil algebras are C^∞-rings, viewed within some topoi. For dual numbers, their meaning is clear: it just couples a value and their (first-order) differential coefficient. However, solely from Kock-Lawvere axiom, it is unclear what the result is in general cases. With the algorithms we have proposed, students can use computers to calculate the map given by the axiom. In SIA and SDG, there are plenty of uses of generalised infinitesimal spaces such as $\mathbb{R}[x_1, \ldots, x_n]/\langle x_i x_j | i, j \leq n\rangle$ or $\mathbb{R}[x]/(x^n)$. Hence, concrete examples for these Weil algebras can help to understand the theory.

In the context of SDG, applying techniques in computer algebra to Weil algebras has attained only little interest. One such example is Nishimura–Osoekawa [12]: they apply zero-dimensional ideal algorithms to compute the generating relation of limits of Weil algebras. However, their purpose is to use computer algebra to ease heavy calculations needed to develop the theory of SDG, and hence they are not interested in computing the C^∞-structure of Weil algebras.

Implementing AD in a functional setting has a long history. See, for example, Elliott [2] for explanation and ad package by Kmett [9] for actual implementation.

In ad package, so-called *Skolem trick*, or *RankN trick* is applied to distinguish multiple directional derivatives. We argue that our method pursues other direction of formulations; we treat higher infinitesimals as first-class citizens, enabling us to treat higher-order AD in a more modular and composable manner.

6.2   Future Works

In SDG, C^∞-ring and higher infinitesimals are used as fundamental building blocks to formulate manifolds, vector fields, differential forms, and so on. Hence, if one can extend our method to treat a general C^∞-ring $C^\infty(M)$ of real-valued smooth functions on M, it can open up a new door to formulate differential geometry on a computer. With such a formulation, we can define differential-geometric objects in more synthetic manner using nilpotent infinitesimals – for example, one can define the tangent space $T_x M$ at $x \in M$ on some manifold M to be the collection of $f : D \to M$ with $f(0) = x$, where D is the set of nilpotents of order two. Another virtue of such system is that we can treat infinitesimal spaces (derived from Weil algebras), manifolds, functions spaces, and vector spaces uniformly – they are all living in the same category. See Moerdijk–Reyes [11] for more theoretical details. One major obstacle in this direction is that, even if $C^\infty(M)$ is finitely *presented* as a C^∞-ring, it is NOT finitely *generated* as an $\mathbb{R}$-algebra, but $2^{\aleph_0}$-generated, by its very nature. Hence, it seems impossible to compute $C^\infty(M)$ in purely symbolic and direct way; we need some workarounds or distinct formulations to overcome such obstacles.

As for connections with AD, there is also plenty of room for further exploration. There are so many "modes" other than Forward- and Tower-modes in AD: for examples, Reverse, Mixed, etc. amongst others. From the point of view of Weil algebras, they are just implementation details. But such details matter much when one takes the efficiency seriously. It might be desirable to extend our formulation to handle such differences in implementation method. For such direction, Elliot [3] proposes the categorical formulation. Exploring how that approach fits with our algebraic framework could be interesting future work, and perhaps also shed a light on the way to realise the aforementioned computational SDG.

Acknowledgments. The author is grateful to Prof. Akira Terui, for encouraging to write this paper and many helpful feedbacks, and to anonymous reviewers for giving constructive comments.

A   Succinct Multivariate Lazy Tower AD

For completeness, we include the referential implementation of the Tower-mode AD in Haskell, which can be used in Algorithm 2. The method presented here is a mixture of Lazy Multivariate Tower [13] and nested Sparse Tower [9]. For details, we refer readers to the related paper by the author in RIMS Kôkyûroku [7].

The idea is simple: we represent each partial derivative as a path in a tree of finite width and infinite heights. A path goes down if the function is differentiated by the 0th variable. It goes right if there will be no further differentiation w.r.t. 0th variable, but differentiations w.r.t. remaining variable can take place. This intuition is depicted by the following illustration of the ternary case:

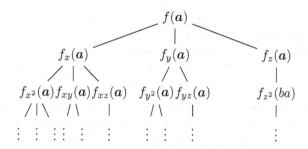

This can be seen as a special kind of infinite trie (or prefix-tree) of alphabets ∂_{x_i}, with available letter eventually decreasing.

This can be implemented by a (co-)inductive type as follows:

```
1 data STower n a where
2    ZS :: !a -> STower 0 a
3    SS :: !a -> STower (n + 1) a -> STower n a
4       -> STower (n + 1) a
```

A tree can have an *infinite height*. Since Haskell is a lazy language, this won't eat up the memory and only necessary information will be gradually allocated. Since making everything lazy can introduce a huge space leak, we force each coefficient `a` when their corresponding data constructors are reduced to weak head normal form, as expressed by field strictness annotation `!a` .

Then a lifting operation for univariate function is given by:

```
1 liftSTower :: forall c n a.
2    (KnownNat n, c a, forall x k. c x => c (STower k x) ) =>
3    (forall x. c x => x -> x) ->
4       -- ^ Function
5    (forall x. c x => x -> x) ->
6       -- ^ its first-order derivative
7    STower n a ->
8    STower n a
9 liftSTower f df (ZS a) = ZS (f a)
10 liftSTower f df x@(SS a da dus)
11    = SS (f a) (da * df x) (liftSTower @c f df dus)
```

Here, we use type-level constraint `c` to represent to a subclass of smooth functions, e.g. `c` = `Floating` for elementary functions. Constraint of form $\forall x k.\ c\ x => c\ (\text{STower } k\ x)$ is an example of so-called *Quantified Constraints*.

This requires ` c ` to be implemented for any succinct Tower AD, provided that their coefficient type, say ` x `, is also an instance of ` c `. This constraint is used recursively when one implements an actual implementation of instance ` c (STower n a) `. For example, **Floating** instance (for elementary floating point operations) can be written as follows:

```
1  instance Floating a => Floating (STower n a) where
2    sin = liftSTower @Floating sin cos
3    cos = liftSTower @Floating cos (negate . sin)
4    exp = liftSTower @Floating exp exp
5    ...
```

In this way, we can implement Tower AD for a class of smooth function closed under differentiation, just by specifying an original and their first derivatives.

More general n-ary case of lifting operator is obtained in just the same way:

```
1  liftNAry :: forall c n a m.
2    ( c a, forall x k. (KnownNat k, c x) => c (STower k x) ) =>
3    -- | f, an m-ary smooth function
4    (forall x. c x => Vec m x -> x) ->
5    -- | partial derivatives of f,
6    -- wrt. i-th variable in the i-th.
7    Vec m (SmoothFun c m) ->
8    Vec m (STower n a) ->
9    STower n a
10 liftNAry f _ Nil = constSS $ f Nil
11 liftNAry f dfs xss =
12   case sing @l of
13     Zero -> ZS (f $ constTerm <$> xss)
14     Succ (k :: SNat k) ->
15       SS (f $ constTerm <$> xss)
16         ( sum
17         $ SV.zipWithSame
18             (\fi gi -> topDiffed gi * runSmooth fi xss)
19             dfs xss
20         )
21         (liftNAry @c f dfs $ diffOther <$> xss)
22
23 diffOther :: STower (n + 1) a -> STower n a
24 diffOther (SS _ _ dus) = dus
```

References

1. Cox, D., Little, J., O'Shea, D.: Using Algebraic Geometry, 2nd edn. Springer, New York (2005). http://www.cs.amherst.edu/~dac/uag.html

2. Elliott, C.: Beautiful differentiation. In: International Conference on Functional Programming (ICFP) (2009). http://conal.net/papers/beautiful-differentiation
3. Elliott, C.: The simple essence of automatic differentiation. In: Proceedings of the ACM on Programming Languages, vol. 2. Association for Computing Machinery, New York, July 2018. https://doi.org/10.1145/3236765
4. Ishii, H.: Computational algebra system in Haskell (2013). https://konn.github.io/computational-algebra
5. Ishii, H.: A purely functional computer algebra system embedded in Haskell. In: Gerdt, V.P., Koepf, W., Seiler, W.M., Vorozhtsov, E.V. (eds.) CASC 2018. LNCS, vol. 11077, pp. 288–303. Springer, Cham (2018). https://doi.org/10.1007/978-3-319-99639-4_20
6. Ishii, H.: smooth: Computational smooth infinitesimal analysis (2020). https://github.com/konn/smooth
7. Ishii, H.: A succinct multivariate lazy multivariate tower AD for Weil algebra computation. In: Fujimura, M. (ed.) Computer Algebra. RIMS Kôkyûroku, vol. 2185, pp. 104–112. Research Institute for Mathematical Sciences, Kyoto University, Kyoto, Japan (2021)
8. Joyce, D.: Algebraic geometry over C^∞-rings (2016)
9. Kmett, E.A.: ad: Automatic differentiation (2010). https://hackage.haskell.org/package/ad
10. Lawvere, F.W.: Categorical dynamics. Topos Theor. Methods Geom. **30**, 1–28 (1979)
11. Moerdijk, I., Reyes, G.E.: Models for Smooth Infinitesimal Analysis. Springer, New York (1991). https://doi.org/10.1007/978-1-4757-4143-8
12. Nishimura, H., Osoekawa, T.: General Jacobi identity revisited again. Int. J. Theor. Phys. **46**(11), 2843–2862 (2007). https://doi.org/10.1007/s10773-007-9397-z
13. Pearlmutter, B., Siskind, J.: Lazy multivariate higher-order forward-mode AD, vol. 42, pp. 155–160 (2007). https://doi.org/10.1145/1190216.1190242
14. Wikipedia: Automatic differentiation (2021). https://en.wikipedia.org/w/index.php?title=Automatic_differentiation&oldid=995938170#Automatic_differentiation_using_dual_numbers

On the Real Stability Radius for Some Classes of Matrices

Elizaveta Kalinina$^{(\boxtimes)}$ and Alexei Uteshev

Faculty of Applied Mathematics, St. Petersburg State University,
7–9 Universitetskaya nab., St. Petersburg 199034, Russia
{e.kalinina,a.uteshev}@spbu.ru
http://www.apmath.spbu.ru

Abstract. We continue investigations on the Frobenius norm real stability radius computation started in the previous publication by the authors (*LNCS*, vol. 12291 (2020)). With the use of the elimination of variables procedure we reduce the problem to the univariate equation solving. The structure of the destabilizing perturbation matrix is also discussed as well as cases of symmetric and orthogonal matrices where the stability radius can be explicitly expressed via the matrix eigenvalues. Several examples are presented.

Keywords: Distance to instability · Stability radius · Real destabilizing perturbation · Frobenius norm

1 Introduction

Matrix $A \in \mathbb{R}^{n \times n}$ is called **stable** (**Routh – Hurwitz stable**) if all its eigenvalues are situated in the open left half plane of the complex plane. For a stable matrix A, some perturbation $E \in \mathbb{R}^{n \times n}$ may lead to that eigenvalues of $A + E$ cross the imaginary axis, i.e., to loss of stability. Given some norm $|| \cdot ||$ in $\mathbb{R}^{n \times n}$, the smallest perturbation E that makes $A + E$ unstable is called the **destabilizing real perturbation**. It is connected with the notion of the **distance to instability (stability radius) under real perturbations** that is formally defined as

$$\beta_{\mathbb{R}}(A) = \min\{||E|| \,|\, \eta(A + E) \geq 0, E \in \mathbb{R}^{n \times n}\}. \tag{1}$$

Here $\eta(\cdot)$ denotes the **spectral abscissa** of the matrix, i.e., the maximal real part of its eigenvalues.

The present paper is devoted to the choice of Frobenius norm in (1), and thereby it is an extension of the investigation by the authors started in [10,11]. It should be mentioned that while the 2-norm variant of the problem and the application of pseudospectrum to its solution have been explored intensively [2,3,7,12] including numerical computations of spectral norm of a matrix [13], there are just a few studies [1,6,9] on the Frobenius norm counterpart. The treatment of the latter is considered as far more complex than the former due

© Springer Nature Switzerland AG 2021
F. Boulier et al. (Eds.): CASC 2021, LNCS 12865, pp. 192–208, 2021.
https://doi.org/10.1007/978-3-030-85165-1_12

to the fundamental difference between the spectral and Frobenius norms. We refer to the paper [11] for the discussion of the practical applications of the stated problem and for the related references. The major difficulty in utilization of numerical procedures for estimation of (1) is that none of them is able to guarantee the convergence to the global minimum of the distance function. As an alternative to this approach, we attack the problem with the combination of symbolical and numerical methods.

It is known that the set of stable matrices in $\mathbb{R}^{n \times n}$ is bounded by two manifolds, namely the one consisting of singular matrices and the other containing the matrices with a pair of eigenvalues of the opposite signs. Both boundaries are algebraic manifolds. The distance from the matrix A to the manifold of singular matrices is estimated via the least singular value of A. More difficult is the treatment of the second alternative that is in the focus of the present paper. In Sect. 3, the so-called **distance equation** [11,14] is constructed, i.e., the univariate equation whose zero set contains all the critical values of the squared distance function. We also detail the structures of the nearest matrix B_* and the corresponding matrix of the smallest perturbation E_* such that $B_* = A + E_*$. The result is presented on the feasibility of simultaneous quasi-triangular Schur decomposition for the matrices B_* and E_*.

It is utilized in Sect. 4 and in Sect. 5 for the classes of stable matrices where the distance to instability $\beta_{\mathbb{R}}(A)$ can be explicitly expressed via the eigenvalues of A. These happen to be symmetric and orthogonal matrices.

Remark. All the numerical computations were performed in CAS Maple 15.0 (**LinearAlgebra** package and functions **discrim**, and **resultant**). We present the results of the approximate computations with the 10^{-6} accuracy.

2   Algebraic Preliminaries

Let $M = [m_{jk}]_{j,k=1}^{n} \in \mathbb{R}^{n \times n}$ be an arbitrary matrix and

$$f(z) = \det(zI - M) = z^n + a_1 z^{n-1} + \ldots + a_n \in \mathbb{R}^n \qquad (2)$$

be its characteristic polynomial. Find the real and imaginary part of $f(x + iy)$ ($\{x, y\} \subset \mathbb{R}$):

$$f(z) = f(x + iy) = \Phi(x, y^2) + iy\Psi(x, y^2),$$

where

$$\Phi(x, Y) = f(x) - \frac{1}{2!}f''(x)Y + \frac{1}{4!}f^{(4)}(x)Y^2 - \ldots,$$

$$\Psi(x, Y) = f'(x) - \frac{1}{3!}f^{(3)}(x)Y + \frac{1}{5!}f^{(5)}(x)Y^2 - \ldots.$$

Compute the resultant of polynomials $\Phi(0, Y)$ and $\Psi(0, Y)$ in terms of the coefficients of (2):

$$K(f) := \mathcal{R}_Y (\Phi(0, Y), \Psi(0, Y))$$

$$= \mathcal{R}_Y (a_n - a_{n-2}Y + a_{n-4}Y^2 + \ldots, a_{n-1} - a_{n-3}Y + a_{n-5}Y^2 + \ldots). \quad (3)$$

Polynomial $f(z)$ possesses a root with the zero real part iff either $a_n = 0$ or $K(f) = 0$. This results in the following statement [11].

Theorem 1. *Equations*

$$\det M = 0 \quad (4)$$

and

$$K(f) := \mathcal{R}_Y (\Phi(0, Y), \Psi(0, Y)) = 0 \quad (5)$$

*define implicit manifolds in $\mathbb{R}^{n^2}$ that compose the boundary for the **domain of stability**, i.e., the domain in the matrix space $\mathbb{R}^{n \times n}$*

$$\mathbb{P} = \{\text{vec}\,(M) \in \mathbb{R}^{n^2} | M \text{ is stable}\}. \quad (6)$$

Here vec($\cdot$) stands for the vectorization of the matrix:

$$\text{vec}\,(M) = [m_{11}, m_{21}, \ldots, m_{n1}, m_{12}, \ldots, m_{n2}, \ldots, m_{1n}, \ldots, m_{nn}]^\top.$$

Therefore, the distance to instability from a stable matrix A is computed as the smallest of the distances to the two algebraic manifolds in $\mathbb{R}^{n^2}$. The Euclidean distance to the set of singular matrices equals the minimal singular value $\sigma_{\min}(A)$ of the matrix A. If $\beta_{\mathbb{R}}(A) = \sigma_{\min}(A)$, then the destabilizing perturbation is given by the rank-one matrix

$$E_* = -A V_* V_*^\top, \quad (7)$$

where V_* stands for the normalized right singular-vector of A corresponding to $\sigma_{\min}(A)$.

More complicated is the problem of distance evaluation from A to the manifold (5) corresponding to the matrices with a pair of eigenvalues of opposite signs (i.e., either $\pm\lambda$ or $\pm i\beta$ for $\{\lambda, \beta\} \subset \mathbb{R} \setminus \{0\}$). First of all, the function (3) treated w.r.t. the entries of the matrix M, is not convex. Indeed, for $n = 3$, the characteristic polynomial of the Hessian of this function is as follows

$$z^9 - 4a_1 z^8 - \left(3 \sum_{j,k=1}^{3} m_{jk}^2 + 7 a_1^2 \right) z^7 + \cdots + 4 \left(\sum_{j,k=1}^{3} m_{jk}^2 + a_1^2 + a_2 \right) [K(f)]^2 z$$

$$-8 [K(f)]^3.$$

It cannot possess all its (real) zeros of the same sign, and thus, the Hessian is not a sign definite matrix. Therefore, one may expect that any gradient-based numerical procedure applied for searching the minimum of the distance function related to the stated problem will meet the traditional trouble of recognizing the local minima.

The general problem of finding the Euclidean distance in a multidimensional space from a point to an implicitly defined algebraic manifold can be solved via the construction of the so-called **distance equation** [11,14], i.e., the univariate equation whose zero set contains all the critical values of the squared distance function. In the next section, we develop an approach for the construction of this equation for the case of the manifold (5).

3   Distance to the Manifold (5)

The starting point in this construction is the following result [15].

Theorem 2. *Distance from a stable matrix $A \in \mathbb{R}^{n \times n}$ to the manifold (5) equals*

$$\sqrt{z_{\min}} \qquad (8)$$

where

$$z_{\min} = \min_{\{X,Y\} \in \mathbb{R}^n} \{||AX||^2 + ||AY||^2 - (X^\top AY)^2 - (Y^\top AX)^2\} \qquad (9)$$

subject to the constraints

$$||X|| = 1, ||Y|| = 1, \ X^\top Y = 0, \qquad (10)$$
$$(X^\top AY)(Y^\top AX) \leq 0.$$

All vector norms here are 2-norms.

If $\beta_{\mathbb{R}}(A)$ equals the value (8) that is attained at the columns X_* and Y_*, then the destabilizing perturbation is computed by the formula

$$E_* = (aX_* - AY_*)Y_*^\top + (bY_* - AX_*)X_*^\top \ \text{ where } a := X_*^\top AY_*, b := Y_*^\top AX_*. \ (11)$$

It is known [5] that the matrix (11) has rank 2.

Theorem 3 [11]. *If $a \neq -b$, then the matrix (11) has a unique nonzero eigenvalue*

$$\lambda_* = -X_*^\top AX_* = -Y_*^\top AY_* \qquad (12)$$

of the multiplicity 2.

In what follows, we will consider the most general case $a \neq -b$.

Constructive computation of (8) is a nontrivial task. Utilization of numerical optimization procedures results in convergence to several local minima (including those satisfying inappropriate condition $a + b = 0$). In [11], the approach was proposed reducing the problem to that of finding an unconstrained minimum of an appropriate rational function; unfortunately, the approach is applicable only for the particular case of the third order matrices.

To treat the general case, we convert the constrained optimization problem (9)–(10) to a new one with lesser number of variables and constraints. Denote the objective function in (9) by $F(X, Y)$, and consider the Lagrange function

$$L(X, Y, \tau_1, \tau_2, \mu) := F(X, Y) - \tau_1(X^\top X - 1) - \tau_2(Y^\top Y - 1) - \mu(X^\top Y)$$

with the Lagrange multipliers τ_1, τ_2 and μ. Its derivatives with respect to X and Y yield the system

$$2A^\top AX - 2(X^\top AY)AY - 2(Y^\top AX)A^\top Y - 2\tau_1 X - \mu Y = 0, \qquad (13)$$
$$2A^\top AY - 2(Y^\top AX)AX - 2(X^\top AY)A^\top X - 2\tau_2 Y - \mu X = 0. \qquad (14)$$

Together with conditions (10), this algebraic system contains $2n + 3$ variables in a nonlinear manner. We will make some manipulations aiming at reducing twice the number of these variables.

Equation (13) together with two of conditions (10) are those providing the Lagrange equations for the constrained optimization problem

$$\min_{X \in \mathbb{R}^n} F(X, Y) \ s.t. \ X^\top X = 1, \ X^\top Y = 0.$$

Since $F(X, Y)$ is a quadratic function w.r.t. X:

$$F(X, Y) = X^\top \mathfrak{A}(Y)X + \mathfrak{b}(Y),$$

where

$$\mathfrak{A}(Y) := A^\top A - AYY^\top A^\top - A^\top YY^\top A, \ \mathfrak{b}(Y) := Y^\top A^\top AY,$$

one can apply the traditional method of finding its critical values [4]. First, resolve (13) w.r.t. X

$$X = \frac{\mu}{2}(\mathfrak{A} - \tau_1 I)^{-1}Y. \tag{15}$$

Substitute this into $X^\top X = 1$:

$$\frac{\mu^2}{4} Y^\top (\mathfrak{A} - \tau_1 I)^{-2} Y - 1 = 0 \tag{16}$$

and into $X^\top Y = 0$:

$$\frac{\mu}{2} Y^\top (\mathfrak{A} - \tau_1 I)^{-1} Y = 0. \tag{17}$$

Next, introduce a new variable z responsible for the critical values of F:

$$z - F(X, Y) = 0$$

and substitute here (15). Skipping some intermediate computations, one arrives at

$$\Phi(Y, \tau_1, \mu, z) := z - \frac{\mu^2}{4} Y^\top (\mathfrak{A} - \tau_1 I)^{-1} Y - \tau_1 - \mathfrak{b}(Y) = 0. \tag{18}$$

Next step consists of the elimination of the parameters τ_1 and μ from (16)–(18). It can be readily verified that $\partial \Phi / \partial \mu$ coincides, up to a sign, with the left-hand side of (17). One may expect that $\partial \Phi / \partial \tau_1$ coincides with the left-hand side of (16). This is not the fact:

$$\partial \Phi / \partial \tau_1 + \{\text{left-hand side of (16)}\} \equiv -2. \tag{19}$$

Introduce the functions

$$\widetilde{\Phi}(Y, \tau_1, \mu, z) := \begin{vmatrix} \mathfrak{A} - \tau_1 I & \mu/2Y \\ \mu/2Y^\top & z - \tau_1 - \mathfrak{b}(Y) \end{vmatrix}_{(n+1) \times (n+1)}, \quad \mathfrak{F}(\tau_1) := \det(\mathfrak{A} - \tau_1 I). \tag{20}$$

Due to Schur complement formula, one has

$$\Phi \equiv \widetilde{\Phi}/\mathfrak{F}(\tau_1). \tag{21}$$

Replace Φ by $\widetilde{\Phi}$. From (18) deduce

$$\widetilde{\Phi} = 0. \tag{22}$$

From (17) one gets that

$$\partial \widetilde{\Phi}/\partial \mu = 0. \tag{23}$$

Under condition (22), the following relation is valid

$$\frac{\partial \Phi}{\partial \tau_1} \equiv \frac{\widetilde{\Phi}'_{\tau_1}\mathfrak{F} - \mathfrak{F}'_{\tau_1}\widetilde{\Phi}}{\mathfrak{F}^2} = \frac{\widetilde{\Phi}'_{\tau_1}}{\mathfrak{F}}.$$

In view of (19), replace (16) by

$$\widetilde{\Phi}'_{\tau_1} + 2\mathfrak{F} = 0. \tag{24}$$

Finally, eliminate τ_1 and μ from (22), (23) and (24) (elimination of μ is simplified by the fact that the polynomial $\widetilde{\Phi}$ is a quadratic one w.r.t. this parameter):

$$Y^\top A \cdot A^\top Y + \tau_1 - z = 0.$$

The resulting equation

$$G(z, Y) = 0 \tag{25}$$

is an algebraic one w.r.t. its variables.

Conjecture 1. *One has*

$$\deg_z G(z, Y) = n - 1, \quad \deg_Y G(z, Y) = 2n,$$

and the coefficient of z^{n-1} equals $Y^\top Y$.

Equation (25) represents z as an implicit function of Y. We need to find the minimum of this function subject to the constraint $Y^\top Y = 1$. This can be done via direct elimination of either of variables $y_1, y_2, \ldots, y_n$, say y_1, from the equations (25) and $Y^\top Y = 1$ and further computation of the (absolute) minimum of the implicitly defined function of the variables $y_2, \ldots, y_n$. The elimination procedure for these variables consists of the successive resultant computations and results, on expelling some extraneous factors, in the distance equation $\mathcal{F}(z) = 0$.

Conjecture 2. *Generically, one has*

$$\deg \mathcal{F}(z) = \binom{n}{2}^2,$$

while the number of real zeros of $\mathcal{F}(z)$ is $\geq \binom{n}{2}$.

Real zeros of $\mathcal{F}(z) = 0$ are the critical values of the squared distance function. In all the examples we have computed, the true distance is provided by the square root of the least positive zero of this equation[1].

Example 1. For the upper triangular matrix

$$A = \begin{bmatrix} -5 & 3 & -4 \\ 0 & -7 & 8 \\ 0 & 0 & -11 \end{bmatrix},$$

the distance equation to the manifold (5) is as follows:

$$\mathcal{F}(z) := 2761712704 \, z^9 - 8117525391152 \, z^8 + 9928661199130545 \, z^7$$

$$-6661449509594611833 \, z^6 + 2725873911089976326856 \, z^5$$

$$-71008439770247880837 3248 \, z^4 + 11790439291722852243095 1424 \, z^3$$

$$-1194140591782836282449690 6240 \, z^2 + 653700309832952667775747 751936 \, z$$

$$-13855088524292326555552906739712 = 0$$

with real zeros

$$z_{\min} \approx 49.502398, \quad z_2 \approx 178.803874, \quad z_3 \approx 207.566503.$$

Distance to (5) equals $\sqrt{z_{\min}} \approx 7.035794$, and it is provided by the perturbation matrix

$$E_* \approx \begin{bmatrix} 4.346976 & 0.523508 & -0.557899 \\ 0.705685 & 3.592395 & 1.164459 \\ -1.972167 & 3.053693 & 1.430776 \end{bmatrix}.$$

Spectrum of the matrix $B_* = A + E_*$ is $\approx \{-13.629850, \pm 1.273346 \, \mathbf{i}\}$.

The perturbation matrix corresponding to the zero z_2 of the distance equation is

$$E_2 \approx \begin{bmatrix} 3.435003 & -5.117729 & -0.980014 \\ -3.957240 & 6.004731 & -0.650159 \\ -0.242289 & -0.207877 & 9.360120 \end{bmatrix}.$$

Spectrum of the matrix $B_2 = A + E_2$ is $\approx \{-4.200144, \pm 1.517560\}$.

□

Example 2. For the matrix

$$A = \begin{bmatrix} -1 & -4 & -1 & 0 \\ 2 & -3 & 2 & 0 \\ 4 & 1 & -5 & -0.02 \\ 0 & 0 & 0.1 & -1 \end{bmatrix},$$

---

[1] For the general problem of distance to arbitrary algebraic manifold, this is not always the case.

the distance to the manifold (5) equals $\sqrt{z_{\min}}$ where $z_{\min} \approx 10.404067$. Vectors providing this value, as the solution to the constrained optimization problem (9)–(10), are as follows[2]:

$$X_* \approx \begin{bmatrix} -0.262202 \\ -0.089560 \\ -0.242204 \\ 0.929820 \end{bmatrix}, \quad Y_* \approx \begin{bmatrix} 0.719155 \\ 0.148735 \\ 0.571599 \\ 0.366015 \end{bmatrix}.$$

The perturbation matrix is determined via (11):

$$E_* \approx \begin{bmatrix} 1.550382 & 0.346249 & 1.256766 & 0.018654 \\ -1.735702 & -0.386136 & -1.405552 & -0.066067 \\ -0.125734 & -0.027972 & -0.101818 & -0.004775 \\ -0.061674 & -0.048946 & -0.083641 & 1.057733 \end{bmatrix}.$$

The only nonzero eigenvalue (12) of this matrix is $\lambda_* \approx 1.060080$. The spectrum of the corresponding nearest to A matrix $B_* = A + E_*$ is

$$\mu_1 \approx -5.937509, \mu_2 \approx -1.942329, \mu_{3,4} = \pm 0.066088\,\mathrm{i}.$$

Just for the sake of curiosity, let us find the real Schur decomposition [8] for the matrices B_* and E_*. The orthogonal matrix

$$P \approx \begin{bmatrix} 0.326926 & -0.579063 & -0.541040 & 0.514858 \\ -0.403027 & 0.627108 & -0.529829 & 0.404454 \\ -0.029186 & 0.045432 & 0.652787 & 0.755614 \\ 0.854304 & 0.518994 & -0.020604 & 0.019594 \end{bmatrix}$$

furnishes the lower quasi-triangular Schur decomposition for B_*:

$$P^\top B_* P \approx \begin{bmatrix} 0 & 0.159482 & 0 & 0 \\ -0.027386 & 0 & 0 & 0 \\ -0.974903 & 1.383580 & \mu_1 & 0 \\ 2.170730 & -3.675229 & -2.733014 & \mu_2 \end{bmatrix}.$$

Eigenvalues of the upper left-corner block of this matrix

$$\begin{bmatrix} 0 & 0.159482 \\ -0.027386 & 0 \end{bmatrix}$$

equal $\mu_{3,4}$.

Surprisingly, it turns out that the matrix P provides also the upper quasi-triangular Schur decomposition for E_*:

$$P^\top E_* P \approx \begin{bmatrix} \lambda_* & 0 & -0.172898 & 1.393130 \\ 0 & \lambda_* & 0.251668 & -2.474365 \\ 0 & 0 & 0 & 0 \\ 0 & 0 & 0 & 0 \end{bmatrix}.$$

$\square$

---

[2] Due to symmetry of the problem w.r.t. the entries of X and Y, the optimal solution is evaluated up to a sign.

The discovered property is confirmed by the following result.

Theorem 4. *Let $A \in \mathbb{R}^{n \times n}$ be a stable matrix, B_* and E_* be the nearest to A matrix in the manifold (5) and the destabilizing perturbation correspondingly: $B_* = A + E_*$. There exists an orthogonal matrix $P \in \mathbb{R}^{n \times n}$ such that the matrix $P^\top E_* P$ contains only two nonzero rows while the matrix $P^\top B_* P$ is of the lower quasi-triangular form.*

Proof. Let the orthogonal matrix P furnish the lower quasi-triangular Schur decomposition for B_*:

$$P^\top B_* P = \left[\begin{array}{ccccc} \widetilde{b}_{11} & \widetilde{b}_{12} & 0 & \dots & 0 \\ \widetilde{b}_{21} & \widetilde{b}_{22} & 0 & \dots & 0 \\ \hline & & \widetilde{\mathbf{B}} & & \end{array} \right],$$

where $\widetilde{\mathbf{B}} \in \mathbb{R}^{(n-2) \times n}$ is the lower quasi-triangular matrix while the matrix

$$\begin{bmatrix} \widetilde{b}_{11} & \widetilde{b}_{12} \\ \widetilde{b}_{21} & \widetilde{b}_{22} \end{bmatrix} \tag{26}$$

has its eigenvalues of the opposite signs, i.e., $\widetilde{b}_{11} + \widetilde{b}_{22} = 0$.

It turns out that the matrix P provides also the upper quasi-triangular Schur decomposition for E_*:

$$P^\top E_* P = \left[\begin{array}{ccccc} \lambda_* & 0 & e_{13} & \dots & e_{1n} \\ 0 & \lambda_* & e_{23} & \dots & e_{2n} \\ \hline & & \mathbb{O}_{(n-2) \times n} & & \end{array} \right], \tag{27}$$

where λ_* is defined by (12). Indeed, represent $P^\top E_* P$ as a stack matrix:

$$P^\top E_* P = \begin{bmatrix} \mathbf{E}_1 \\ \mathbf{E}_2 \end{bmatrix} \quad \text{where} \quad \mathbf{E}_1 \in \mathbb{R}^{2 \times n}, \; \mathbf{E}_2 \in \mathbb{R}^{(n-2) \times n}.$$

Then

$$P^\top A P + \begin{bmatrix} \mathbf{E}_1 \\ \mathbb{O} \end{bmatrix} = \mathfrak{B} \quad \text{where} \quad \mathfrak{B} := \left[\begin{array}{ccccc} \widetilde{b}_{11} & \widetilde{b}_{12} & 0 & \dots & 0 \\ \widetilde{b}_{21} & \widetilde{b}_{22} & 0 & \dots & 0 \\ \hline & & \widetilde{\mathbf{B}} - \mathbf{E}_2 & & \end{array} \right] \tag{28}$$

and, consequently,

$$A + P \begin{bmatrix} \mathbf{E}_1 \\ \mathbb{O} \end{bmatrix} P^\top = P \mathfrak{B} P^\top.$$

Matrix $\mathfrak{B}$ still lies in the manifold (5); so does the matrix $P \mathfrak{B} P^\top$. If $\mathbf{E}_2 \neq \mathbb{O}$, then the latter is closer to A than B_* since

$$\left\| P \begin{bmatrix} \mathbf{E}_1 \\ \mathbb{O} \end{bmatrix} P^\top \right\| = \|\mathbf{E}_1\| < \sqrt{\|\mathbf{E}_1\|^2 + \|\mathbf{E}_2\|^2} = \|E_*\|.$$

This contradicts the assumption. Therefore, the matrix $P^\top E_* P$ contains only two nonzero rows, namely those composing the matrix $\mathbf{E}_1$.

Furthermore, the matrix E_* has a single real eigenvalue λ_* of the multiplicity 2 (Theorem 3). Consider the second order submatrix located in the upper-left corner of $P^\top E_* P$:

$$\begin{bmatrix} e_{11} & e_{12} \\ e_{21} & e_{22} \end{bmatrix}. \tag{29}$$

This submatrix has the double eigenvalue λ_*, and its norm is the minimal possible. Hence, it should have the following form

$$\begin{bmatrix} \lambda_* & 0 \\ 0 & \lambda_* \end{bmatrix}.$$

Indeed, let us find the minimum of the norm of (29) under the constraints

$$(e_{11} - e_{22})^2 + 4e_{12}e_{21} = 0, \quad e_{11} + e_{22} = 2\lambda_*$$

by the Lagrange multiplier method. We have the Lagrangian function

$$F(e_{11}, e_{22}, e_{12}, e_{21}, \mu, \nu) = \sum_{j,k=1}^{2} e_{jk}^2 + \mu((e_{11} - e_{22})^2 + 4e_{12}e_{21}) + \nu(e_{11} + e_{22} - 2\lambda_*),$$

where μ and ν are the Lagrange multipliers. We obtain the system of equations:

$$e_{11} + \mu(e_{11} - e_{22}) + \nu = 0,$$
$$e_{22} - \mu(e_{11} - e_{22}) + \nu = 0,$$
$$e_{12} + 2\mu e_{21} = 0,$$
$$e_{21} + 2\mu e_{12} = 0,$$
$$(e_{11} - e_{22})^2 + 4\,e_{12}e_{21} = 0,$$
$$e_{11} + e_{22} - 2\lambda_* = 0$$

whence it follows that

$$e_{12}(1 - 4\mu^2) = 0,$$
$$e_{21}(1 - 4\mu^2) = 0,$$
$$e_{22} = 2\lambda_* - e_{11},$$
$$\nu = -\lambda_*,$$
$$(e_{11} - \lambda_*)(1 + 2\mu) = 0,$$
$$(e_{11} - \lambda_*)^2 + e_{12}e_{21} = 0.$$

- If $\mu \neq \pm 1/2$, then $a_{12} = e_{21} = 0$ and $e_{11} = e_{22} = \lambda_*$.
- If $\mu = 1/2$, then $e_{12} = -e_{21}$, after that by the fifth equation, $e_{11} = \lambda_*$, by the third equation $e_{22} = \lambda_*$, and by the last equation, $e_{12} = -e_{21} = 0$.
- If $\mu = -1/2$, then $e_{12} = e_{21}$ and by the last equation, $e_{11} = \lambda_*$ and $e_{12} = 0$. $\qquad\square$

We next investigate some classes of matrices where the distance to instability can be directly expressed via the eigenvalues.

4   Symmetric Matrix

Theorem 5. *Let* $\lambda_1, \lambda_2, \ldots, \lambda_n$ *be the eigenvalues of a stable symmetric matrix* A *arranged in descending order:*

$$\lambda_n \le \lambda_{n-1} \le \ldots \le \lambda_2 \le \lambda_1 < 0.$$

The distance from A *to the manifold (5) equals*

$$|\lambda_1 + \lambda_2|/\sqrt{2}.$$

Proof. For a symmetric matrix A, the nearest in the manifold (5) matrix B_* possesses two real eigenvalues of the opposite signs. Indeed, in this case, the block (26) becomes symmetric: $\widetilde{b}_{12} = \widetilde{b}_{21}$, and its eigenvalues equal $\pm\alpha$ where $\alpha := \sqrt{\widetilde{b}_{11}^2 + \widetilde{b}_{12}^2}$.

Since orthogonal transformations preserve the lengths of vectors and angles between them, we can consider our problem for diagonal matrix $A_d = \mathrm{diag}\{\lambda_1, \lambda_2, \ldots, \lambda_n\}$. It is evident that the matrix $E_{d*} = \mathrm{diag}\{\lambda_*, \lambda_*, 0, \ldots, 0\}$ where $\lambda_* = -(\lambda_1 + \lambda_2)/2$ is such that the matrix $B_{d*} = A_d + E_{d*}$ belongs to the manifold (5). The distance from A_d to B_{d*} equals $|\lambda_1 + \lambda_2|/\sqrt{2}$. We need to prove that this matrix E_{d*} gives us the destabilizing perturbation, i.e., its Frobenius norm is the smallest.

Assume the converse, i.e., there exist matrices $\widetilde{E}_{d*}, \widetilde{B}_{d*}$ and $\widetilde{P}$ satisfying Theorem 4 such that the norm of the matrix $\widetilde{E}_{d*}$ that coincides with the norm of the matrix

$$\widetilde{P}^\top \widetilde{E}_{d*}\widetilde{P} = \left[\begin{array}{cc|cc} \widetilde{b}_{11} & \widetilde{b}_{12} & 0 & \ldots 0 \\ \widetilde{b}_{12} & \widetilde{b}_{22} & 0 & \ldots 0 \\ \hline & & \widetilde{\mathbf{B}} & \end{array}\right] - \widetilde{P}^\top A_d \widetilde{P} = \left[\begin{array}{cc|ccc} \widetilde{\lambda}_* & 0 & \widetilde{e}_{13} & \cdots & \widetilde{e}_{1n} \\ 0 & \widetilde{\lambda}_* & \widetilde{e}_{23} & \cdots & \widetilde{e}_{2n} \\ \hline & & \mathbb{O}_{(n-2)\times n} & & \end{array}\right]$$

is smaller than $\|E_{d*}\|$. Consider the matrix $\widetilde{A} = \widetilde{P}^\top A_d \widetilde{P} = [\widetilde{a}_{ij}]_{i,j=1}^n$. Since $\widetilde{b}_{11} = -\widetilde{b}_{22}$, one gets $\widetilde{\lambda}_* = -(\widetilde{a}_{11} + \widetilde{a}_{22})/2$. Let us estimate this value:

$$\begin{aligned} -2\widetilde{\lambda}_* &= \lambda_1(p_{11}^2 + p_{12}^2) + \lambda_2(p_{21}^2 + p_{22}^2) + \ldots + \lambda_n(p_{n1}^2 + p_{n2}^2) \\ &= \lambda_1(p_{11}^2 + p_{21}^2 + \ldots + p_{n1}^2) - \lambda_1(p_{21}^2 + p_{31}^2 + \ldots + p_{n1}^2) \\ &\quad + \lambda_2(p_{12}^2 + p_{22}^2 + \ldots + p_{n2}^2) - \lambda_2(p_{12}^2 + p_{32}^2 + \ldots + p_{n2}^2) \\ &\quad + \lambda_1 p_{12}^2 + \lambda_2 p_{21}^2 + \lambda_3(p_{31}^2 + p_{32}^2) + \ldots + \lambda_n(p_{n1}^2 + p_{n2}^2) \\ &= \lambda_1 + \lambda_2 + (\lambda_2 - \lambda_1)p_{21}^2 + (\lambda_3 - \lambda_1)p_{31}^2 + \ldots + (\lambda_n - \lambda_1)p_{n1}^2 \\ &\quad + (\lambda_1 - \lambda_2)p_{12}^2 + (\lambda_3 - \lambda_2)p_{32}^2 + \ldots + (\lambda_n - \lambda_2)p_{n2}^2 \\ &\le \lambda_1 + \lambda_2 + (\lambda_2 - \lambda_1)p_{21}^2 + (\lambda_2 - \lambda_1)p_{31}^2 + \ldots + (\lambda_2 - \lambda_1)p_{n1}^2 \\ &\quad + (\lambda_1 - \lambda_2)p_{12}^2 + (\lambda_3 - \lambda_2)p_{32}^2 + \ldots + (\lambda_n - \lambda_2)p_{n2}^2 \\ &= \lambda_1 + \lambda_2 + \left[(\lambda_2 - \lambda_1) - (\lambda_2 - \lambda_1)p_{11}^2 - (\lambda_2 - \lambda_1)p_{12}^2\right] \\ &\quad + (\lambda_3 - \lambda_2)p_{32}^2 + \ldots + (\lambda_n - \lambda_2)p_{n2}^2 \le \lambda_1 + \lambda_2. \end{aligned}$$

Both values are non-positive, therefore

$$\tilde{\lambda}_*^2 \geq \left(\frac{\lambda_1 + \lambda_2}{2}\right)^2.$$

Finally, we obtain

$$||\tilde{E}_{d*}|| \geq \tilde{\lambda}_* \sqrt{2} \geq \lambda_* \sqrt{2} = ||E_{d*}||,$$

and it is clear that $E_{d*} = \text{diag}\{\lambda_*, \lambda_*, 0, \ldots, 0\}$ provides the destabilizing perturbation for A_d.

$\square$

Corollary 1. *Destabilizing perturbation providing the distance in Theorem 5 is given as the rank 2 matrix*

$$E_* = -\frac{1}{2}(\lambda_1 + \lambda_2)\left(P_{[1]}P_{[1]}^\top + P_{[2]}P_{[2]}^\top\right) \tag{30}$$

where $P_{[1]}$ and $P_{[2]}$ are the normalized eigenvectors of A corresponding to the eigenvalues λ_1 and λ_2 correspondingly.

Example 3. For the matrix

$$A = \frac{1}{9}\begin{bmatrix} -121 & -14 & 34 \\ -14 & -94 & 20 \\ 34 & 20 & -118 \end{bmatrix}$$

with eigenvalues $\lambda_1 = -9, \lambda_2 = -10, \lambda_3 = -18$, the orthogonal matrix

$$P = \frac{1}{3}\begin{bmatrix} 1 & 2 & 2 \\ 2 & -2 & 1 \\ 2 & 1 & -2 \end{bmatrix}$$

reduces it to the diagonal form $P^\top A P = \text{diag}\{\lambda_1, \lambda_2, \lambda_3\}$. Distance from A to the manifold (5) equals

$$\frac{1}{\sqrt{2}}|9 + 10| \approx 13.435028.$$

The corresponding destabilizing matrix is determined by (30)

$$E_* = \frac{1}{18}\begin{bmatrix} 95 & -38 & 76 \\ -38 & 152 & 38 \\ 76 & 38 & 95 \end{bmatrix}.$$

It is of interest to watch how the general form of the distance equation transforms for this example:

$$\mathcal{F}(z) = (z - 729/2)(z - 361/2)(z - 392)(z - 545)^2(z - 1513/2)^2(z - 1145/2)^2 = 0.$$

$\square$

Conjecture 3. *Let $\{\lambda_j\}_{j=1}^n$ be the spectrum of a symmetric matrix A. Denote*

$$\left\{ \Lambda_{jk} := \frac{1}{2}(\lambda_j + \lambda_k)^2 \,\Big|\, 1 \le j < k \le n \right\}.$$

Distance equation for A can be represented as

$$\prod_{1 \le j < k \le n} (z - \Lambda_{jk}) \cdot \prod (z - (\Lambda_{jk} + \Lambda_{\ell s}))^2 = 0.$$

The second product is extended to all the possible pairs of indices (j,k) and (ℓ, s) such that $j < k, \ell < s$ and $j \ne \ell, k \ne s$.

Corollary 2. *In notation of Theorem 5 and Corollary 1, the distance to instability for a stable symmetric matrix A equals $|\lambda_1|$ with the destabilizing perturbation $E_* = -\lambda_1 P_{[1]} P_{[1]}^\top$.*

Though this corollary makes the result of Theorem 5 redundant for solving the problem of distance to instability evaluation for *symmetric* matrices, it, nevertheless, might be useful for establishing the upper bound for this distance for *arbitrary* matrices.

Theorem 6. *Let $A \in \mathbb{R}^{n \times n}$ be a stable matrix. Denote by $d(\cdot)$ the distance to the manifold (5). One has:*

$$d(A) \le \sqrt{\left\| \frac{1}{2}(A - A^\top) \right\|^2 + d^2 \left(\frac{1}{2}(A + A^\top) \right)}.$$

Proof follows from the fact that the skew-symmetric matrix $A - A^\top$ is normal to the symmetric matrix $A + A^\top$ with respect to the inner product in $\mathbb{R}^{n \times n}$ introduced by $\langle A_1, A_2 \rangle := \text{trace}(A_1^\top A_2)$.

For instance, this theorem yields the estimation $d(A) < 5.654250$ for the matrix of Example 2.

5   Orthogonal Matrix

Now we consider how to find the distance to instability for a stable orthogonal matrix $A \in \mathbb{R}^{n \times n}$. We assume that this matrix has at least one pair of non-real eigenvalues.

Theorem 7. *Let $\cos \alpha_j \pm \mathrm{i} \sin \alpha_j$ $j \in \{1, \ldots, k\}$ be the non-real eigenvalues of an orthogonal matrix A arranged in descending order of their real parts:*

$$\cos \alpha_k \le \cos \alpha_{k-1} \le \ldots \le \cos \alpha_1 < 0.$$

(All the other eigenvalues of A, if any, equal (-1)). The distance from A to the manifold (5) equals $\sqrt{2}|\cos \alpha_1|$.

Proof. First, there exists an orthogonal transformation bringing the matrix A to the block diagonal form

$$A_J = \begin{bmatrix} \mathbf{A}_1 \cdots & & & & \\ & \ddots & & \mathbb{O} & \\ & & \mathbf{A}_k & & \\ & & & -1 & \\ & \mathbb{O} & & & \ddots \\ & & & & & -1 \end{bmatrix} \quad \text{where } \mathbf{A}_\ell := \begin{bmatrix} \cos\alpha_\ell & -\sin\alpha_\ell \\ \sin\alpha_\ell & \cos\alpha_\ell \end{bmatrix}, \; \ell \in \{1, \ldots, k\}.$$

It is evident that the matrix

$$E_{J*} = \operatorname{diag}\{-\cos\alpha_1, -\cos\alpha_1, 0, \ldots, 0\} \tag{31}$$

is such that the matrix $B_{J*} = A_J + E_{J*}$ belongs to the manifold (5). The distance from A_J to B_{J*} equals $\sqrt{2}|\cos\alpha_1|$. We need to prove that this matrix E_{J*} provides the destabilizing perturbation, i.e., its Frobenius norm is the smallest.

Assume the converse, i.e., there exist matrices $\widetilde{E}_{J*}, \widetilde{B}_{J*}$ and $\widetilde{P}$ satisfying Theorem 4 such that the norm of the matrix $\widetilde{E}_{J*}$ that coincides with the norm of the matrix

$$\widetilde{P}^\top \widetilde{E}_{J*} \widetilde{P} = \begin{bmatrix} \widetilde{b}_{11} & \widetilde{b}_{12} & 0 & \ldots & 0 \\ \widetilde{b}_{21} & \widetilde{b}_{22} & 0 & \ldots & 0 \\ \hline & & \widetilde{\widetilde{\mathbf{B}}} & & \end{bmatrix} - \widetilde{P}^\top A_J \widetilde{P} = \begin{bmatrix} \widetilde{\lambda}_* & 0 & \widetilde{e}_{13} & \cdots & \widetilde{e}_{1n} \\ 0 & \widetilde{\lambda}_* & \widetilde{e}_{23} & \cdots & \widetilde{e}_{2n} \\ \hline & & \mathbb{O}_{(n-2)\times n} & & \end{bmatrix}$$

is smaller than $\|E_{J*}\|$. Consider the matrix $\widetilde{A} = \widetilde{P}^\top A_J \widetilde{P} = [\widetilde{a}_{ij}]_{i,j=1}^n$. Since $\widetilde{b}_{11} = -\widetilde{b}_{22}$, one gets $\widetilde{\lambda}_* = -(\widetilde{a}_{11} + \widetilde{a}_{22})/2$. Let us estimate this value:

$$-2\widetilde{\lambda}_* = (p_{11}^2 + p_{21}^2)\cos\alpha_1 + (p_{31}^2 + p_{41}^2)\cos\alpha_2 + \ldots + (p_{n-1,1}^2 + p_{n1}^2)\cos\alpha_k$$

$$+ (p_{12}^2 + p_{22}^2)\cos\alpha_1 + (p_{32}^2 + p_{42}^2)\cos\alpha_2 + \ldots + (p_{n-1,2}^2 + p_{n2}^2)\cos\alpha_k$$

$$- p_{k+1,1}^2 - \ldots - p_{n1}^2 - p_{k+1,2}^2 - \ldots - p_{n2}^2.$$

Add (and subtract) the terms $p_{31}^2 + p_{41}^2 + \ldots + p_{n-1,1}^2 + p_{n1}^2$ and $p_{32}^2 + p_{42}^2 + \ldots + p_{n-1,2}^2 + p_{n2}^2$ to the coefficients of $\cos\alpha_1$ to obtain the sums of squares of the first and the second columns of the matrix $\widetilde{P}$:

$$-2\widetilde{\lambda}_* = 2\cos\alpha_1 + (\cos\alpha_2 - \cos\alpha_1)(p_{31}^2 + p_{41}^2 + p_{32}^2 + p_{42}^2) + \ldots$$

$$+ (\cos\alpha_k - \cos\alpha_1)(p_{k-1,1}^2 + p_{k1}^2 + p_{k-1,2}^2 + p_{k2}^2)$$

$$- \cos\alpha_1(p_{k+1,1}^2 + p_{k+1,2}^2 + \ldots + p_{n1}^2 + p_{n2}^2) - p_{k+1,1}^2 - p_{k+1,2}^2 - \ldots - p_{n1}^2 - p_{n2}^2$$

$$= 2\cos\alpha_1 + (\cos\alpha_2 - \cos\alpha_1)(p_{31}^2 + p_{41}^2 + p_{32}^2 + p_{42}^2) + \ldots$$

$$+ (\cos\alpha_k - \cos\alpha_1)(p_{k-1,1}^2 + p_{k1}^2 + p_{k-1,2}^2 + p_{k2}^2)$$

$$+ (-1 - \cos\alpha_1)(p_{k+1,1}^2 + p_{k+1,2}^2 + \ldots + p_{n1}^2 + p_{n2}^2).$$

Since

$$\cos\alpha_k - \cos\alpha_1 \leq \cos\alpha_{k-1} - \cos\alpha_1 \leq \ldots \leq \cos\alpha_2 - \cos\alpha_1 \leq 0, -1 - \cos\alpha_1 < 0,$$

the following inequality holds

$$-2\widetilde{\lambda}_* \leq 2\cos\alpha_1.$$

Finally, we obtain

$$||\widetilde{E}_{J*}|| \geq \widetilde{\lambda}_* \sqrt{2} \geq \lambda_* \sqrt{2} = ||E_{J*}||,$$

and it is clear that the matrix (31) provides the destabilizing perturbation for A_J.

□

Corollary 3. *Destabilizing perturbation providing the distance in Theorem 7 is given as*

$$E_* = -\cos\alpha_1 \left[\Re(P_{[1]}) \Re(P_{[1]})^\top + \Im(P_{[1]}) \Im(P_{[1]})^\top \right] \tag{32}$$

where $\Re(P_{[1]})$ and $\Im(P_{[1]})$ are the normalized real and imaginary parts of the eigenvector of A corresponding to the eigenvalue $\cos\alpha_1 + \mathrm{i}\sin\alpha_1$.

Matrix (32) is, evidently, symmetric. In view of Theorem 1, the following result is valid:

Corollary 4. *If $\eta(\cdot)$ denotes the spectral abscissa of the matrix, then the stability radius of the orthogonal matrix A can be evaluated by the formula*

$$\beta_{\mathbb{R}}(A) = \begin{cases} \sqrt{2}\eta(-A) & \text{if } -1 \notin \{\lambda_1, \ldots, \lambda_n\}, \\ \min\{1, \sqrt{2}\eta(-A)\} & \text{otherwise.} \end{cases}$$

Example 4. For the matrix

$$A = \frac{1}{3} \begin{bmatrix} -2 & -2 & 1 \\ 1 & -2 & -2 \\ -2 & 1 & -2 \end{bmatrix}$$

with the eigenvalues $\lambda_1 = -1, \lambda_{2,3} = -\frac{1}{2} \pm \mathrm{i}\frac{\sqrt{3}}{2}$, the orthogonal matrix

$$P = \frac{1}{\sqrt{6}} \begin{bmatrix} \sqrt{2} & 2 & 0 \\ \sqrt{2} & -1 & -\sqrt{3} \\ \sqrt{2} & -1 & \sqrt{3} \end{bmatrix}$$

reduces it to the form

$$P^\top A P = \frac{1}{2} \begin{bmatrix} -2 & 0 & 0 \\ 0 & -1 & \sqrt{3} \\ 0 & -\sqrt{3} & -1 \end{bmatrix}.$$

The distance from A to instability equals $1/\sqrt{2} \approx 0.707106$. The corresponding destabilizing matrix is determined by (32)

$$E_* = \frac{1}{6} \begin{bmatrix} 2 & -1 & -1 \\ -1 & 2 & -1 \\ -1 & -1 & 2 \end{bmatrix}.$$

Distance equation for the matrix A transforms into

$$\mathcal{F}(z) := (z - 1/2)(z - 15/8)^2(z^2 - 3z + 9)(z - 5)^4 = 0.$$

$\square$

The results of the present section can evidently be extended to the case of matrices orthogonally equivalent to the block-diagonal matrices with real blocks of the types

$$[\lambda] \quad \text{and} \quad r \begin{bmatrix} \cos\alpha & -\sin\alpha \\ \sin\alpha & \cos\alpha \end{bmatrix} ; \quad r > 0, \cos\alpha < 0, \lambda < 0.$$

6 Conclusion

We treat the problem of the Frobenius norm real stability radius evaluation in the framework of symbolic computations, i.e., we look for the reduction of the problem to univariate algebraic equation solving. Though the obtained results clear up some issues of the problem, the latter, in its general statement, remains still open.

As it is mentioned in Introduction, the main problem of exploiting the numerical procedures for finding the distance to instability estimations is that of reliability of the results. The results of the present paper can supply these procedures with testing samples of matrix families with trustworthy estimations of the distance to instability value.

Acknowledgments. The authors are grateful to the anonymous referees for valuable suggestions that helped to improve the quality of the paper.

References

1. Bobylev, N.A., Bulatov, A.V., Diamond, Ph.: Estimates of the real structured radius of stability of linear dynamic systems. Autom. Remote Control **62**, 505–512 (2001)
2. Embree, M., Trefethen, L.N.: Generalizing eigenvalue theorems to pseudospectra theorems. SIAM J. Sci. Comput. **23**(2), 583–590 (2002)
3. Freitag, M.A., Spence, A.: A Newton-based method for the calculation of the distance to instability. Linear Algebra Appl. **435**, 3189–3205 (2011)
4. Gantmakher, F.R.: The Theory of Matrices, vol. I, II. Chelsea, New York (1959)
5. Guglielmi, N., Lubich, C.: Low-rank dynamics for computing extremal points of real pseudospectra. SIAM J. Matrix Anal. Appl. **34**, 40–66 (2013)

6. Guglielmi, N., Manetta, M.: Approximating real stability radii. IMA J. Numer. Anal. **35**(3), 1401–1425 (2014)
7. Hinrichsen, D., Pritchard, A.J.: Mathematical Systems Theory I: Modelling, State Space Analysis, Stability and Robustness. Springer, Heidelberg (2005)
8. Horn, R.A., Johnson, Ch.: Matrix Analysis, 2nd edn. Cambridge University Press, New York (2013)
9. Katewa, V., Pasqualetti, F.: On the real stability radius of sparse systems. Automatica **113**, 108685 (2020)
10. Kalinina, E.A., Smol'kin, Yu.A., Uteshev, A.Yu.: Stability and distance to instability for polynomial matrix families. Complex perturbations. Linear Multilin. Algebra. https://doi.org/10.1080/03081087.2020.1759500
11. Kalinina, E.A., Smol'kin, Y.A., Uteshev, A.Y.: Routh – Hurwitz stability of a polynomial matrix family. Real perturbations. In: Boulier, F., England, M., Sadykov, T.M., Vorozhtsov, E.V. (eds.) CASC 2020. LNCS, vol. 12291, pp. 316–334. Springer, Cham (2020). https://doi.org/10.1007/978-3-030-60026-6_18
12. Qiu, L., Bernhardsson, B., Rantzer, A., Davison, E.J., Young, P.M., Doyle, J.C.: A formula for computation of the real stability radius. Automatica **31**(6), 879–890 (1995)
13. Rump, S.M.: Verified bounds for singular values, in particular for the spectral norm of a matrix and its inverse. BIT Numer. Math. **51**(2), 367–384 (2011)
14. Uteshev, A.Yu., Goncharova, M.V.: Metric problems for algebraic manifolds: analytical approach. In: Constructive Nonsmooth Analysis and Related Topics – CNSA 2017 Proceedings 7974027 (2017)
15. Van Loan, C.F.: How near is a stable matrix to an unstable matrix? In: Datta, B.N., et al. (eds.) Linear Algebra and Its Role in Systems Theory 1984, Contemporary Mathematics, vol. 47, pp. 465–478. American Mathematical Society, Providence, Rhode Island (1985). https://doi.org/10.1090/conm/047

Decoupling Multivariate Fractions

François Lemaire$^{(\boxtimes)}$ and Adrien Poteaux

Univ. Lille, CNRS, Inria, Centrale Lille, UMR 9189 CRIStAL, F-59000 Lille, France
{francois.lemaire,adrien.poteaux}@univ-lille.fr

Abstract. We present a new algorithm for computing compact forms of multivariate fractions. Given a fraction presented as a quotient of two polynomials, our algorithm builds a tree where internal nodes are operators, and leaves are fractions depending on pairwise disjoint sets of variables. The motivation of this work is to obtain compact forms of fractions, which are more readable and meaningful for the user or the modeler, and better suited for interval arithmetic.

Keywords: Multivariate fractions · Decoupling · Compact form

1 Introduction

This article presents a new algorithm decouple for computing compact forms of multivariate fractions. Informally, given a multivariate fraction given as a quotient P/Q, Algorithm decouple computes a (usually) more compact representative of P/Q in the form of a tree where internal nodes are operators $+$, $\times$ and $\div$, and where leaves are fractions depending on pairwise disjoint sets of variables. As a consequence, the fraction P/Q is usually written as a sum, product or quotient of expressions which may also contain fractions. As an example, our algorithm rewrites the fraction

$$\frac{a_0 b_1 a_3 + a_0 b_1 b_2 + a_0 a_2 + a_1 a_3 + a_1 b_2}{b_1 a_3 + b_1 b_2 + a_2}$$

as

$$a_0 + \frac{a_1}{-\dfrac{a_2}{-a_3 - b_2} + b_1},$$

and rewrites the fraction

$$-\frac{x\left(d\,x^2 + dxk_1 + dxk_2 + dk_1 k_2 + V_1 x + V_2 x + V_1 k_2 + V_2 k_1\right)}{(k_1 + x)(k_2 + x)}$$

as

$$-dx - \frac{V_1 x}{k_1 + x} - \frac{V_2 x}{k_2 + x}.$$

Our algorithm also works with polynomials, and in that case the expressions returned are free of quotients. For example, our algorithm rewrites $ab + ax + bx + cd + cx + dx + 2x^2$ as $(x + b)(x + a) + (x + c)(x + d)$.

© Springer Nature Switzerland AG 2021
F. Boulier et al. (Eds.): CASC 2021, LNCS 12865, pp. 209–231, 2021.
https://doi.org/10.1007/978-3-030-85165-1_13

This work was mainly motivated by the following reasons. A compact expression is usually easier to read and understand for a user/modeler. Moreover, if the variables appear in the least places (ideally only once), the interval arithmetic should yield sharper results.

Computer algebra software are usually focused on polynomials rather than fractions. Extracting the numerator of a fraction can produce some expression swell, especially if the fraction is given as a sum of different fractions with different denominators. When fractions are reobtained after applying a polynomial-based method, our algorithm can help to recover different fractions with different denominators again.

In order to decompose a fraction into several terms, our method uses a decoupling technique on the variables. Roughly speaking, as the term decoupling suggests, our method tries to split a fraction into different terms involving disjoint sets of variables. As a consequence, our method does nothing on a univariate fraction, even if the fraction can be written in a compact way using nested fractions.

Simplification of multivariate fractions has already been considered. The Leĭnartas decomposition is presented in [7] (see [8, Theorem 2.1] for an English presentation). It decomposes a fraction into a sum of fractions, using computations on the varieties associated to the irreducible factors of the fraction denominator. Also, [9] presents a partial decomposition for multivariate fractions, based on successive univariate partial decompositions. In both cases, multivariate fractions are rewritten in a more compact way, as a sum of several fractions (thus nested fractions are never produced).

Our method does not work the same way, and produces a different output. Our method can produce nested fractions such as $a_0 + \cfrac{a_1}{-\cfrac{a_2}{-a_3 - b_2} + b_1}$ mentioned earlier in the introduction. However, our method does no simplification on fractions which cannot be decoupled. For example, our algorithm performs no simplification on the fraction $F = \frac{x^2 y + x y^2 + x y + x + y}{x y (x y + 1)}$ taken from [8, Example 2.5], whereas [7,8] computes $F = \frac{1}{x y + 1} + \frac{x+y}{x y}$, and [9] computes $F = \frac{1}{x} + \frac{1}{x y + 1} + \frac{1}{y}$.

It is also worth mentioning [10] which provides "Ten commandments" around expression simplifications, especially Sects. 3 and 4 which discuss some techniques for partially factoring the numerators and denominators of a fraction. Also, a method for computing Horner's schemes for multivariate polynomials is given in [3]. Finally, [11] presents a choice of nice functionalities a computer algebra software should provide for helping the user with expression manipulations.

We implemented our algorithm decouple in Maple 2020. All examples presented in the paper run under ten seconds (on a i7-8650U CPU 1.90 GHz running Linux), and the memory footprint in under 180 Mbytes.

Organization of the Paper. Section 2 defines the decouplings of fractions and the splittable fractions. Theorem 1 which characterizes the splittable fractions is presented, and the existence and uniqueness of the so-called finest partition (of variables) is proven. Section 3 presents our algorithm decouple, with elements of proofs. Section 4 presents some examples. Finally, Sect. 5 presents some complexity results and implementation remarks.

Notations. In this article, $\mathbb{K}$ denotes any field of characteristic zero[1]. Take a fraction F in $\mathbb{K}(X)$, where X contains n variables. For brevity, the partial derivatives $\frac{\partial F}{\partial x}$, $\frac{\partial^2 F}{\partial x \partial y}$ and $\frac{\partial^{j+k} F}{\partial x^j \partial y^k}$ are also written F_x, $F_{x,y}$ and F_{x^j,y^k}. We denote by $\text{Supp}(F)$ the set $\{x \in X | F_x \neq 0\}$; it is simply the variables on which F really depends. We denote by $\text{Def}(F)$ the domain of definition of F, which is the set of values of $\mathbb{K}^n$ which does not cancel the denominator of F.

For any subset $Y \subseteq X$ of size m, and any $Y^0 \in \mathbb{K}^m$, $F(Y = Y^0)$ designates the partial evaluation of F for the variables Y at Y^0. This partial evaluation is only defined if the denominator of F does not identically vanish at $Y = Y^0$. Partitions of a set X will usually be denoted $(X_i)_{1 \leq i \leq p}$ and $(Y_i)_{1 \leq i \leq q}$, or simply (X_i) and (Y_i).

2   Decoupled and Splittable Fractions

2.1   Definitions

Definition 1 (Expression Tree). *An* Expression Tree *in $a_1, \ldots, a_p$ over a field $\mathbb{K}$ is a finite tree satisfying:*

- *each internal node is a binary operator: either $+$, $\times$, or $\div$,*
- *each leaf is either a variable a_i, or an element of $\mathbb{K}$,*
- *if the tree contains two or more nodes, then any subtree encodes a nonzero fraction in the variables $a_1, \ldots, a_p$.*

Proposition 1 (Expression Tree and associated fraction). *The third item of Definition 1 ensures that no division by zero can occur. As a consequence, any Expression Tree encodes a fraction in the a_i variables. Moreover, any fraction can be encoded by an Expression Tree (note the Expression Tree is not unique). If A is an Expression Tree in $a_1, \ldots, a_p$, we simply denote its associated fraction by $A(a_1, \ldots, a_p)$. Please note that zero can still be encoded by the tree with only one root node equal to zero. Finally, the tree*

$$\overset{+}{\underset{-6 \quad 6}{\diagup \diagdown}}$$

is not an Expression Tree since it violates the third item of Definition 1.

Definition 2 (Decoupled Expression Tree (DET)). *A* Decoupled Expression Tree *in the variables $a_1, \ldots, a_p$ is an Expression Tree where each a_i appears exactly once.*

---

[1] Fields of characteristic nonzero have not been considered by the authors, as they raise some difficulties. Indeed, most results and algorithms presented here rely on evaluation and differentiation, which are difficult to handle in nonzero characteristic.

is a **DET** encoding $11a_2 + 5/a_1$.

Proposition 2 (Interval arithmetic). *Assume $\mathbb{K}$ is $\mathbb{Q}$ or $\mathbb{R}$. Consider a fraction $F(a_1, \ldots, a_p)$ which can be represented as a **DET** A. If each a_i lies in some interval I_i, and if evaluating the tree A using interval arithmetic never inverses intervals containing zero, then the evaluation computes $F(I_1, \ldots, I_p)$.*

Proof. We prove it by induction on the number of nodes. The base case with one node is immediate. If the number of nodes is higher than 2, the induction hypothesis can be applied on both left and right subtrees, yielding two intervals I and J. The evaluation of the complete tree consists in evaluating either $I + J$, $I \times J$, or $I \div J$. In all these cases, interval arithmetic gives an exact interval image (i.e. not overestimated), since both subtrees involve distinct variables (A is a **DET**), and because (by assumption) no interval containing zero is inverted.

Remark 1. When inverting an interval containing zero occurs during the evaluation of a **DET**, difficulties arise, as the following example shows. Take $F = \frac{x}{1+x}$, whose image on the interval $I = [0, 1]$ is $F(I) = [0, 1/2]$. The fraction F can be written as the **DET** $\frac{1}{1+\frac{1}{x}}$ whose evaluation is delicate because $\frac{1}{x}$ is not defined at $x = 0$. However, if F is written as the **DET** $1 - \frac{1}{1+x}$, Proposition 2 applies.

In order to generalize Proposition 2 for tackling intervals containing zero, multi-intervals and handling intervals containing infinity may be required.

Definition 3 (Decoupling of a fraction). *Let F a fraction of $\mathbb{K}(X)$. We call decoupling of F a triple $(A, (F_i)_{1 \le i \le p}, (X_i)_{1 \le i \le p})$ where:*

 - *A is a **DET** in the variables $a_1, \ldots, a_p$ over $\mathbb{K}$,*
 - *$(X_i)_{1 \le i \le p}$ is a partition of $\mathrm{Supp}(F)$,*
 - *each F_i is a fraction of $\mathbb{K}(X_i)$ with $\mathrm{Supp}(F_i) = X_i$,*
 - *$F = A(F_1, \ldots, F_p)$ where $A(F_1, \ldots, F_p)$ designates the fraction associated to A evaluated on the F_i.*

In that case, we say that the partition (X_i) decouples the fraction F.

Remark 2. Any constant fraction F admits the decoupling $(F, \emptyset, \emptyset)$. Any non constant fraction $F \in \mathbb{K}(X)$ admits the (trivial) decoupling $(a_1, (F), (\mathrm{Supp}(F)))$.

Definition 4 (Splittable fraction). *A fraction F of $\mathbb{K}(X)$ is said* splittable *if there exists a partition $(X_i)_{1 \le i \le p}$ of $\mathrm{Supp}(F)$ with $p \ge 2$, such that (X_i) decouples F. Otherwise, the fraction is said* nonsplittable.

Remark 3. Constant and univariate fractions are nonsplittable.

2.2   Characterization of Splittable Fractions

Theorem 1 below gives a characterization of splittable fractions. It is central for the decouple algorithm (Algorithm 1). Indeed the decouple algorithm checks the four different cases and either calls itself recursively if one case succeeds or concludes that the fraction is nonsplittable.

Lemma 1. *Take a splittable fraction F of $\mathbb{K}(X)$. Then for any nonzero constant c, the fractions $c + F$, $c \times F$, c/F, and F/c are splittable.*

Proof. For each fraction $c + F$, $c \times F$, c/F, and F/c, it suffices to adjust the tree A of a decoupling $(A, (F_i)_{1 \leq i \leq p}, (X_i)_{1 \leq i \leq p})$ of F.

Theorem 1 (Splittable characterization). *A fraction F of $\mathbb{K}(X)$ is splittable if and only if the fraction F can be written in one of the following forms:*

$$\textbf{C1} \quad G + H \qquad\qquad \textbf{C2} \quad c + GH$$

$$\textbf{C3} \quad c + \frac{1}{G + H} \qquad \textbf{C4} \quad c + \frac{d}{1 + GH} \quad ,$$

where

- *c and d are in $\mathbb{K}$, and $d \neq 0$,*
- *(Y, Z) is a partition of $\mathrm{Supp}(F)$,*
- *$G \in \mathbb{K}(Y)$ and $H \in \mathbb{K}(Z)$, with $\mathrm{Supp}(G) = Y$ and $\mathrm{Supp}(H) = Z$.*

Proof. The right to left implication is immediate.

Let us prove the left to right implication. Assume F is splittable, and consider a decoupling $(A, (F_i)_{1 \leq i \leq p}, (X_i)_{1 \leq i \leq p})$ of F with $p \geq 2$. Since the fraction is splittable, it is necessarily non constant, and the root of the tree A is necessarily an operator. As a consequence, the tree A has the shape

$$
\begin{array}{c}
o \\
{}^{\diagup} \quad {}^{\diagdown} \\
L \quad R
\end{array} .
$$

Substituting the F_i's in the L and R trees, one gets two fractions F_L and F_R. There are two cases:

Case 1. Both fractions F_L and F_R are nonconstant. They have by construction some disjoint supports. If the operator o is $+$, then F can be written as $F_L + F_R$ as in the case **C1**. If the operator is $\times$ (resp. $\div$), then F can be written as in the case **C2**, with $c = 0$, $G = F_L$, and $H = F_R$ (resp. $1/F_R$).

Case 2. Among the fractions F_R and F_R, one is constant, and the other one is nonconstant. The nonconstant fraction is splittable by Lemma 1. We consider the following scenario by induction: either the splittable fraction satisfies Case 1, concluding the induction, either we are once again in the Case 2. This process can only happen a finite number of times (since the tree A is finite). We can thus assume that the splittable fraction can be written in one of the four cases.

Assume first that F_R is constant and that the operator is $+$. If F_L has the form **C1** $G + H$, then $F = G + (H + F_R)$. If F_L has form **C2**, **C3** or **C4**, then F has the same form as F_L (by replacing c by $c + F_R$). By a similar argument, F has the same form as F_L is the operator is $\times$ or $\div$.

Assume now that F_L is constant. It is easy to show that F has the same form as F_R is the operator is $+$ or $\times$. If the operator is $\div$, some more computations are needed. If F_R has form **C1**, then F_L/F_R has form **C3** (with $c = 0$). If F_R has form **C2** with $F_R = c + GH$, then F_L/F_R has form **C2** if $c = 0$, and form **C4** otherwise. If F_R has form **C3** with $F_R = c + \frac{1}{G+H}$, then F_L/F_R has form **C1** if $c = 0$, and form **C3** otherwise. If F_R has form **C4** with $F_R = c + \frac{d}{1+GH}$, then F_L/F_R has form **C2** if either $c = 0$ or $c + d = 0$, and form **C4** otherwise. $\square$

Remark 4. Anticipating Propositions 8 and 9, the constant c of Theorem 1 is unique for the cases **C2** and **C3**. Anticipating Proposition 10, the values of c and d in the case **C4** of Theorem 1 are not unique, because a fraction $c + \dfrac{d}{1+GH}$ can also be written as $(c + d) + \dfrac{-d}{1 + \frac{1}{G}\frac{1}{H}}$, which is also of the form **C4**.

2.3   Basic Lemmas Around Fractions

This section gives some lemmas around the evaluation of fractions for some variables. Those lemmas would be quite obvious to prove for polynomials, but fractions deserve special treatment because of the possible cancellations of the denominators at some evaluation points.

Lemma 2. *Consider a fraction F of $\mathbb{K}(X)$. If the fraction F cancels at any point $X^0 \in \mathrm{Def}(F)$, then the fraction F is the zero fraction.*

Proof. Write F as P/Q where P and Q are polynomials of $\mathbb{K}[X]$. Denote $X = \{x_1, \ldots, x_n\}$. Using a Kronecker substitution (see [4, exercise 8.4, page 247] and references therein), there exists a substitution ϕ of the form $x_1 \mapsto u^{a_1}, \ldots, x_n \mapsto u^{a_n}$, where u is a new variable and the a_i are positive integers, such that ϕ is injective on the sets of monomials occurring in P and Q.

The polynomial $\phi(Q)$ is nonzero and univariate, so there exists an integer u_0 such that $\phi(Q)(u) \neq 0$ for any integer $u \geq u_0$. As a consequence, the set of points $S = \{(u^{a_1}, \ldots, u^{a_n}) | u \in \mathbb{N}, u \geq u_0\}$ is included in $\mathrm{Def}(F)$.

Since F cancels on $\mathrm{Def}(F)$ by assumption, P cancels on the set S, implying that $\phi(P)(u)$ cancels for any integer $u \geq u_0$. Since $\phi(P)$ is univariate, $\phi(P)$ is the zero polynomial. Since the transformation ϕ is injective on the monomials, P is also the zero polynomial, hence $F = 0$. $\square$

Lemma 3. *Consider a nonzero fraction F of $\mathbb{K}(X)$ and a variable $x \in X$. There exists a finite subset S of $\mathbb{K}$ such that for any $x^0 \in \mathbb{K}\backslash S$, the partial evaluation $F(x = x^0)$ is well-defined and nonzero, and $\mathrm{Supp}(F(x = x^0)) = \mathrm{Supp}(F)\backslash\{x\}$.*

Proof. The lemma is immediate if x does not belong to the support of F. Now assume $x \in \mathrm{Supp}(F)$. Consider the fraction $H = F \prod_{y \in \mathrm{Supp}(F)} F_y$, which by construction is nonzero since F is nonzero. The fraction can be seen as a univariate fraction H of $\bar{\mathbb{K}}(x)$, where $\bar{\mathbb{K}} = \mathbb{K}(X \setminus \{x\})$. Consider the set $\bar{S} \subseteq \bar{\mathbb{K}}$ of elements $\bar{x}_0 \in \bar{\mathbb{K}}$ either canceling the numerator or the denominator of H. This set $\bar{S}$ is finite. Take $S = \bar{S} \cap \mathbb{K}$, which is also finite. Then for any element $x^0 \in \mathbb{K} \setminus S$, the fraction $H(x = x^0)$ is well-defined and nonzero. This ends the proof since $H(x = x^0) \neq 0$ implies $F(x = x^0) \neq 0$, and $F_y(x = x^0) \neq 0$ for any $y \in \mathrm{Supp}(X)$. □

The following lemma is a generalization of Lemma 3 for evaluating two different fractions simultaneously.

Lemma 4. *Consider two nonzero fractions F and G of $\mathbb{K}(X)$. For any variable $x \in X$, there exists a finite subset S of $\mathbb{K}$ such that for any $x^0 \in \mathbb{K} \setminus S$, the partial evaluations $F(x = x^0)$ and $G(x = x^0)$ are well-defined and nonzero, $\mathrm{Supp}(F(x = x^0)) = \mathrm{Supp}(F) \setminus \{x\}$, and $\mathrm{Supp}(G(x = x^0)) = \mathrm{Supp}(G) \setminus \{x\}$.*

Proof. The proof is similar to that of Lemma 3, simply replace the fraction H by $F(\prod_{y \in \mathrm{Supp}(F)} F_y) G(\prod_{y \in \mathrm{Supp}(G)} G_y)$. □

Lemma 5. *Consider a nonconstant univariate fraction F of $\mathbb{K}(x)$. For any finite set of values $S \subseteq \mathbb{K}$, there exists a value $x^0 \in \mathbb{K}$ such that $F(x^0)$ is well-defined and $F(x^0) \notin S$.*

Proof. Let us assume that the image of the fraction F is included in S. We prove that this leads to a contradiction. Since F is univariate, there exists an integer u_0 such that the denominator Q does not cancel on the set $D = \{u \in \mathbb{N} | u \geq u_0\}$. Since F is defined on D, and D is infinite, and S is finite, there exists a value v of S such that $F(u) = v$ for an infinite number of integers $u \geq u_0$. This implies that the numerator of $F - v$ cancels on an infinite number of integers, hence $F - v$ is the zero fraction. Contradiction since F is nonconstant. □

2.4 Finest Decoupling Partition

We prove in this section that for any fraction F, there exists a unique most refined partition decoupling F. The following definition is classical.

Definition 5 (Finer partition). *A partition $(X_1, \ldots, X_p)$ of some set X is finer than a partition $(Y_1, \ldots, Y_q)$ of X if each X_i is included in some Y_j. The finer-than relation is a partial order.*

Definition 6 (Partition deprived of one element). *Consider a partition $(X_i)_{1 \leq i \leq p}$ of some set X, and a variable $x \in X$. Up to a renaming of the X_i, assume that $x \in X_p$.*

Build a partition (Y_i) of $X \setminus \{x\}$ in the following way: if X_p is equal to $\{x\}$, then take the partition $(Y_i)_{1 \leq i \leq p-1}$ where $Y_i = X_i$ for $1 \leq i \leq p-1$. Otherwise take the partition $(Y_i)_{1 \leq i \leq p}$ where $Y_i = X_i$ for $1 \leq i \leq p-1$, and $Y_p = X_p \setminus \{x\}$.

The partition (Y_i) is called the partition (X_i) deprived of x.

The following proposition shows how to specialize a variable in a decoupling.

Proposition 3 (Specialization of a decoupling). *Let us consider a decoupling* $(A, (F_i)_{1 \leq i \leq p}, (X_i)_{1 \leq i \leq p})$ *of some fraction* F *of* $\mathbb{K}(X)$ *and a variable* $x \in \operatorname{Supp}(F)$. *Denote* (Y_i) *the partition* (X_i) *deprived of* x.

Then there exists an $x^0 \in \mathbb{K}$ *such that the partition* (Y_i) *decouples* $F(x = x^0)$.

Proof. Up to a renaming of the X_i, assume that $x \in X_p$. Assume that the set X_p equals $\{x\}$. Assigning a value a^0 to the variable a_p in the **DET** A may not yield a **DET** because of the third condition of Definition 1. However, there only exists a finite set S of "unlucky" values a^0 which break the third condition of Definition 1. By Lemma 5 on the univariate fraction $F_p(x)$ and S, there exists an x^0 such that $(A(a_p = F_p(x^0)), (F_i)_{1 \leq i \leq p-1}, (X_i)_{1 \leq i \leq p-1})$ is a decoupling of $F(x = x^0)$.

Now assume that the $\{x\}$ is strictly included in X_p. By Lemma 3, there exists a value x^0 such that $F_p(x = x^0)$ is well-defined, and $\operatorname{Supp}(F_p(x = x^0)) = X_p \backslash \{x\}$. Thus, replacing F_p by $F_p(x = x^0)$ and X_p by $X_p \backslash \{x\}$ in the decoupling $(A, (F_i)_{1 \leq i \leq p}, (X_i)_{1 \leq i \leq p})$ of F yield a decoupling for $F(x = x^0)$. $\qquad\square$

The following proposition is a generalization of Proposition 3 for specializing two different decouplings of the same fraction F.

Proposition 4 (Simultaneous specialization of two decouplings). *Consider two decouplings* $(A, (G_i)_{1 \leq i \leq p}, (X_i)_{1 \leq i \leq p})$ *and* $(B, (H_i)_{1 \leq i \leq q}, (U_i)_{1 \leq i \leq q})$ *of the same fraction* F *of* $\mathbb{K}(X)$, *and a variable* $x \in \operatorname{Supp}(F)$. *Denote* (Y_i) *the partition* (X_i) *deprived of* x, *and* (V_i) *the partition* (U_i) *deprived of* x.

Then there exists a value $x^0 \in \mathbb{K}$ *such that both partitions* (Y_i) *and* (V_i) *decouples* $F(x = x^0)$.

Proof. The proof is similar to that of Proposition 3. The only difficulty is the choice of an x^0 which is suitable for both decouplings. Up to a renaming of the X_i and U_i, assume that $x \in X_p$ and $x \in U_q$. If both X_p and U_q are equal to $\{x\}$, then there is a finite number of values for x^0 to avoid, hence Lemma 5 concludes. Assume X_p is the singleton $\{x\}$ and U_q strictly contains x. By Lemmas 3 and 5, there is also a finite number of values for x^0 to avoid, which ends the proof. By symmetry, we need not consider the case where X_p strictly contains x and U_q is the singleton $\{x\}$. Finally, if x is strictly included in X_p and in U_q, Lemma 4 concludes. $\qquad\square$

Lemma 6. *Consider a fraction* $F \in \mathbb{K}(X)$, *and a* **DET** C *in one variable* a_1. *Denote* $C(F)$ *the fraction obtained by evaluating* C *on* $a_1 = F$. *If the fraction* $C(F)$ *is splittable, then* F *is also splittable.*

Proof. Consider a **DET** C in one variable a_1. It can be shown by induction that the fraction $C(a_1)$ associated to C is an homography, i.e. $C(a_1) = \dfrac{u^0 + v^0 a_1}{u^1 + v^1 a_1}$ where the u^0, v^0, u^1 and v^1 are in $\mathbb{K}$, and satisfy $u^0 v^1 - u^1 v^0 \neq 0$. Indeed, the variable a_1 is an homography, and adding a constant to an homography, multiplying an homography by a nonzero constant, or taking the inverse of an homography yield an homography. Since an homography is invertible, and its inverse is also an homography, $C(a_1)$ is invertible and its inverse $D(a_1)$ is an homography, which can easily be encoded by a **DET** in one variable.

Since $C(F)$ is splittable, adding D to the top of the tree of the decoupling of F yields a decoupling of $D(C(F))$ which is equal to F, hence F is splittable. □

Proposition 5 (Finest partition). *Consider a fraction $F \in \mathbb{K}(X)$. There exists a unique finest partition (X_i) of $\mathrm{Supp}(F)$ decoupling F. A decoupling $(A, (F_i), (X_i))$ of F is said finest if (X_i) is the finest partition decoupling F.*

Proof. The set S of partitions decoupling F is not empty by Remark 2, and is also finite. Since the finer-than relation is a partial order (Definition 5), the existence of finest partitions is guaranteed. We now prove that all finest partitions are in fact equal, which is the difficult part of the proof.

The proposition is immediate for constant fractions. Consider a non constant fraction $F \in \mathbb{K}(X)$, and two different finest partitions $(X_i)_{1 \le i \le p}$ and $(Y_i)_{1 \le i \le q}$ decoupling F, along with some corresponding decouplings $(A, (G_i), (X_i))$ and $(B, (H_i), (Y_i))$.

Since the two partitions (X_i) and (Y_i) are different, there exists a X_k intersecting at least two different sets of the (Y_i) partition. Without loss of generality, let us assume that the set X_1 intersects the sets $Y_1, Y_2, \ldots, Y_r$ with $r \ge 2$, and does not intersect the remaining sets $Y_{r+1}, \ldots, Y_q$. See Fig. 1 for an illustration. We prove below that the set X_1 can be further refined into $X_1 \cap Y_1, \ldots, X_1 \cap Y_r$, leading to a contradiction since (X_i) is finest.

Let us apply successively Proposition 4 on all variables of $X_2 \cup X_3 \cup \cdots \cup X_p$, thus obtaining some values $X_2^0, \ldots, X_p^0$. We obtain two different decouplings for $\bar{F} = F(X_2 = X_2^0, X_3 = X_3^0, \ldots, X_p = X_p^0)$. The first one (obtained from $(A, (G_i), (X_i))$ is $(C, (G_1), (X_1))$ where C is the (univariate) tree $A(a_2 = G_2(X_2^0), \ldots, a_p = G_p(X_p^0))$. The second one (obtained from $(B, (H_i), (Y_i)))$ is $(D, (R_i)_{1 \le i \le r}, (U_i)_{1 \le i \le r})$ where (U_i) is the partition $(X_1 \cap Y_1, \ldots, X_1 \cap Y_r)$ of X_1. As a consequence, the fraction $\bar{F}$ is splittable. Since $\bar{F} = C(G_1)$ is splittable, the fraction G_1 is also splittable by Lemma 6. This contradicts the fact that (X_i) is finest, since G_1 could be split in the decoupling $(A, (G_i), (X_i))$ of F. □

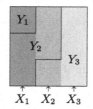

Fig. 1. Two partitions (X_i) and (Y_i) of X. The sets X_1, X_2 and X_3 are the rectangles in dark gray, gray and light gray. The set X_1 intersects the sets Y_1 and Y_2, but not Y_3.

2.5   Decomposition into a Sum and Product

In this section, we give necessary and sufficient conditions for decomposing a fraction $F \in \mathbb{K}(X)$ with $\mathrm{Supp}(F) = X$, into a sum $G + H$ or a product GH, where $G \in \mathbb{K}(Y)$, $H \in \mathbb{K}(Z)$, and (Y, Z) is a partition of X.

Over the reals or the complexes, the conditions are immediate to show using converging Taylor expansions for example. However, we show them in a more general context for any field $\mathbb{K}$ of characteristic zero, such as for example $\mathbb{Q}(a, b, c)$. We avoid here the use of converging Taylor expansions, which would require us to equip $\mathbb{K}$ with a norm. By the way, the authors of [2] required a normed vector space, which was in fact not required by using techniques presented here.

Proposition 6 (Decomposition into sum). *Let $F \in \mathbb{K}(X)$ with $\mathrm{Supp}(F) = X$, and (Y, Z) a partition of X. Then there exist two fractions $G \in \mathbb{K}(Y)$ and $H \in \mathbb{K}(Z)$ such that $F = G + H$ if and only if $F_{y,z} = 0$ for any $(y, z) \in (Y, Z)$.*

Proof. The left to right implication is immediate. To prove the right to left implication, we assume for simplicity that X only contains two elements y and z. Consider a point $X^0 = (y^0, z^0) \in \mathrm{Def}(F)$. Without loss of generality, using a shift on variables y and z, let us assume that $X^0 = (0, 0)$.

Take $G = F(z = 0)$ and $H = F(y = 0) - F(0, 0)$, and take $U = F - (G + H)$. Then $U_{y,z} = F_{y,z}$ is also the zero fraction. Moreover, U cancels on the varieties $y = 0$ and $z = 0$, whenever U is well-defined. We now show that the fraction U is the zero fraction, which proves that $F = G + H$ as required.

Write U as P/Q with P and Q polynomials. Since $P = QU$ and using a classical Taylor expansion on P, one gets

$$P = \sum_{j \geq 0, k \geq 0} \frac{1}{j!k!} (QU)_{y^j, z^k}(0, 0) y^j z^k, \tag{1}$$

where only a finite terms are non zero since P is a polynomial (hence no convergence arguments are needed here).

Since $U_{y,z}$ is the zero fraction, then all terms with $j \geq 1$ and $k \geq 1$ in Eq. (1) are zero. We finish the proof by showing (using the symmetry on y and z) that any term $(QU)_{y^j}(0, 0)$ is zero, which proves that P is the zero polynomial.

By Lemma 2, the fraction $U(z = 0)$ is the zero fraction, hence $(QU)(z = 0)$ is the zero polynomial. Using the fact that evaluating at $z = 0$ and differentiating w.r.t. y commute, $(QU)_{y^j}(0, 0) = ((QU)(z = 0))_{y^j}(y = 0) = 0$.   □

Remark 5. Proposition 6 can be interpreted using a graph. Indeed, with notations of Proposition 6, and writing $X = \{x_1, \ldots, x_n\}$, consider the undirected graph with nodes x_i and with edges the (x_i, x_j) such that $G_{x_i, x_j} \neq 0$. Then the fraction F can be written as a sum if and only if the graph admits at least two connected components.

The next proposition is the equivalent of Proposition 6 for decomposition a fraction as a product instead of a sum. From an analytical point of view, decomposing a fraction F as a product GH corresponds to decomposing $\ln F$ as the sum of $\ln G$ and $\ln H$. The differentiation conditions of Proposition 6 applied on $\ln F$, yield $(\ln F)_{y,z} = \left(\frac{F_y}{F}\right)_z = 0$. This condition, which does not involve a logarithm, is used in the following Proposition.

Proposition 7 (Decomposition into product). *Consider $F \in \mathbb{K}(X)$ with* $\mathrm{Supp}(F) = X$, *and* (Y,Z) *a partition of X. Then there exist two fractions $G \in$* $\mathbb{K}(Y)$ *and* $H \in \mathbb{K}(Z)$ *such that $F = GH$ if and only if $\left(\frac{F_y}{F}\right)_z = 0$ for any* $(y,z) \in (Y,Z)$.

Proof. The left to right implication is immediate. To prove the right to left implication, we assume for simplicity that X only contains two elements y and z. The fraction F is not constant since its support X is not empty. By contraposition of Lemma 2, there exists a point $X^0 \in \mathrm{Def}(F)$ such that $F(X^0) \neq 0$. Without loss of generality, using a shift on variables y and z, let us assume that $X^0 = (0,0)$.

Take $G = F(z = 0)$ and $H = F(y = 0)/F(0,0)$ and consider $U = F/(GH) - 1$. We prove below that the fraction U is equal to 0, thus showing that $F = GH$.

Write U as $\frac{P}{Q}$ with P and Q polynomials. Since U is zero on $z = 0$, then by Lemma 2, the fraction $U(z = 0)$ is the zero fraction. Using the commutativity argument at the end of Proposition 6 proof, $U_{y^j}(0,0) = 0$ for any nonnegative integer j. By symmetry on y and z, $U_{z^k}(0,0) = 0$ for any nonnegative integer k.

The condition $\left(\frac{F_y}{F}\right)_z = 0$ can be rewritten as $F_{y,z} = \frac{F_y F_z}{F}$. This implies that $U_{yz} = \frac{U_y U_z}{U+1}$. By an inductive argument on $k + l$, and using the fact that $U_{y^j}(0,0) = 0$ and $U_{z^k}(0,0) = 0$ for any nonnegative integers j and k, one proves that $U_{y^j,z^k}(0,0) = 0$ for any nonnegative integers j and k. Using Eq. (1), the polynomial P is zero, hence $U = 0$ which ends the proof.   □

3   Algorithm **decouple**

Algorithm decouple takes as input a fraction F and a list X, such that $F \in \mathbb{K}(X)$, and returns a finest decoupling of F. Unless F is a constant, or a univariate fraction, the four cases of Theorem 1 are sequentially checked by calling the four so-called functions checkC1 , ..., checkC4. If one of them succeeds (returning some G and H plus other results), Algorithm 1 calls itself on G and H and builds the final result. Otherwise, if no case succeeds, the fraction is proved to be nonsplittable (by Theorem 1) and F is returned.

The main difficulty in the process is to prove that the four checkC1 , ..., checkC4 functions are correct, which is done in the four following subsections.

Algorithm 1: decouple(F, X)

Input: A fraction $F \in \mathbb{K}(X)$ and a list $X = [x_1, \ldots, x_n]$
Output: A finest decoupling $(A, [F_1, \ldots, F_p], [X_1, \ldots, X_p])$ of F

1   **if** F is constant **then return** $(F, [\,], [\,])$;
2   **else if** F does not depend on x_1 **then return** decouple$(F, [x_2, \ldots, x_n])$;
3   **else if** F only depends on x_1 **then return** $(a_1, [F], [\{x_1\}])$;
4   **else if** checkC1(F, X) returns G, Y, H, Z **then**
5 | $(A_G, \bar{G}, \bar{Y}) := $ decouple(G, Y) ;
6 | $(A_H, \bar{H}, \bar{Z}) := $ decouple(H, Z) ;
7 | let r be the length of $\bar{G}$
8 | shift the variables of A_H by r i.e. replace each a_i by a_{i+r} in A_H

9 | **return** ($A_G \overset{+}{\frown} A_H$, $\bar{G} + \bar{H}, \bar{Y} + \bar{Z}$)
10 | /* where $\bar{G} + \bar{H}$ and $\bar{Y} + \bar{Z}$ are list concatenations   */
11 **else if** checkC2(F, X) returns c, G, Y, H, Z **then**
12 | proceed as in Lines 5 to 8 ;

13 | **return** ($c \overset{+}{\frown} A_G \overset{\times}{\frown} A_H$, $\bar{G} + \bar{H}, \bar{Y} + \bar{Z}$)
14 **else if** checkC3(F, X) returns c, G, Y, H, Z **then**
15 | proceed as in Lines 5 to 8 ;

16 | **return** ($c \overset{+}{\underset{1}{\frown}} \overset{\div}{\frown} A_G \overset{+}{\frown} A_H$, $\bar{G} + \bar{H}, \bar{Y} + \bar{Z}$)
17 **else if** checkC4(F, X) returns c, d, G, Y, H, Z **then**
18 | proceed as in Lines 5 to 8 ;

19 | **return** ($c \overset{+}{\underset{d}{\frown}} \overset{\div}{\underset{1}{\frown}} \overset{+}{\frown} A_G \overset{\times}{\frown} A_H$, $\bar{G} + \bar{H}, \bar{Y} + \bar{Z}$)
20 **else return** $(a_1, [F], [\text{Supp}(F)])$;

3.1   Algorithm checkC1 $(F = G + H)$

Following Proposition 6 and Remark 5, Algorithm checkC1 computes (using Algorithm 3) the connected component Y containing the node x_1 of the undirected graph with vertices the x_i, and with edges the (x_i, x_j) such that $F_{x_i, x_j} \neq 0$. If this component Y is strictly included in the support of F, then one can split F as a sum of two fractions $G + H$ as in the case **C1**, using some (random) evaluation to compute the (non-unique) G and H fractions.

Algorithm 2: checkC1(F, X)

Input: A fraction $F \in \mathbb{K}(X)$ s.t. $x_1 \in \mathrm{Supp}(F)$ and a list $X = [x_1, \ldots, x_n]$

Output: Succeeds by returning G, Y, H, Z if F can be written as $G + H$ (as in the case **C1**), and fails otherwise

1 $Y := \mathsf{connectedVariablesSum}(F, X)$;

2 $Z := \mathrm{Supp}(F) \backslash Y$;

3 **if** Z is empty **then** FAIL ;

4 **else**

5      $G := F(Z = Z^0)$ where Z^0 is a random point such that $F(Z = Z^0)$ is well-defined ;

6      $H := F - G$;

7   succeed by returning G, Y, H, Z ;

Algorithm 3: connectedVariablesSum(F, X)

Input: A fraction $F \in \mathbb{K}(X)$ and a list $X = [x_1, \ldots, x_n]$

Output: Return the connected component containing x_1 of the undirected graph with nodes x_i, and with edges the (x_i, x_j) such that $F_{x_i, x_j} \neq 0$.

1 $visited := \{\}$;

2 $todo := \{x_1\}$;

3 **while** $todo$ is not empty **do**

4   pick and extract some variable v from $todo$;

5      $visited := visited \cup \{v\}$;

6      $V := \mathrm{Supp}(F_v)$;

7      $todo := todo \cup (V \backslash visited)$;

8 **return** visited

3.2 Algorithm checkC2 $(F = c + GH)$

Algorithm checkC2 proceeds similarly to Algorithm checkC1 but it first needs to compute a constant candidate c such that $F - c$ can be written as a product as in the case **C2**.

Proposition 8. *Take a fraction $F \in \mathbb{K}(X)$ of the form **C2** (i.e. $F = c + GH$) where $\mathrm{Supp}(G) = Y$, $\mathrm{Supp}(H) = Z$ and (Y, Z) is a partition of $\mathrm{Supp}(F)$. Then $c = F - \frac{F_y F_z}{F_{y,z}}$ for any $(y, z) \in (Y, Z)$.*

Moreover, if for some $(u, v) \in X^2$, the expression $F - \frac{F_u F_v}{F_{u,v}}$ is well-defined and constant, then it is equal to the c defined above.

Proof. The first part of the proposition is a simple computation (note that the formula for c is well-defined because $F_{y,z} = G_y H_z$, which is nonzero).

For the second part of the proposition, there is nothing to prove if $(u, v) \in (Y, Z)$, or $(u, v) \in (Z, Y)$. Assume (by symmetry) that both u and v lies in Y, and that $F - \frac{F_u F_v}{F_{u,v}}$ is well-defined and constant.

Simple computations show that $F - \frac{F_u F_v}{F_{u,v}} = c + (G - \frac{G_u G_v}{G_{u,v}})H$. Since this expression is constant, the term $G - \frac{G_u G_v}{G_{u,v}}$ is necessarily zero (otherwise, the expression would not be constant since the supports of G and H are distinct), which ends the proof. □

Remark 6. The case $G - \frac{G_u G_v}{G_{u,v}} = 0$ in the previous proof occurs for example if the fraction G can itself be written as a product of two fractions M and N of disjoint supports, with $u \in \mathrm{Supp}(M)$ and $v \in \mathrm{Supp}(N)$.

Proposition 8 ensures that Algorithm 5 can stop as soon as it finds a constant candidate c. Indeed, if F has form **C2**, then the constant candidate c is correct by Proposition 8. If F has not form **C2**, and if a constant candidate c is computed (which can happen by Remark 7), then the call to checkProd$(F - c)$ at Line 2 of Algorithm 4 will detect that F has not form **C2**.

Remark 7. Fix $X = \{x, y, z\}$. The following fraction $F = 3 + (x + z)/(y + z)$ yields $F - \frac{F_x F_y}{F_{x,y}} = 3$. However, it can be shown (using Algorithm decouple) that the fraction F cannot be written as **C2**. This does not contradict Proposition 8, since Algorithm 2 will detect that $F - 3$ cannot be decomposed as a non trivial product. Finally, note that F is splittable (of the form **C2**) if we take for example $X = \{x, y\}$ and $\mathbb{K} = \mathbb{Q}(z)$.

Algorithm 4: checkC2(F, X)

Input: A fraction $F \in \mathbb{K}(X)$ and a list $X = [x_1, \ldots, x_n]$
Output: Succeed by returning G, Y, H, Z if F can be written as $c + GH$ (as in the case **C2**), and fails otherwise
1 **if** findConstantCase2(F, X) returns a constant c **then**
2   **if** checkProd$(F - c, X)$ returns G, Y, H, Z **then**
3   **return** c, G, Y, H, Z
4   **else** FAIL ;
5 **else** FAIL ;

Algorithm 5: findConstantCase2(F, X)

Input: A fraction $F \in \mathbb{K}(X)$ and a list $X = [x_1, \ldots, x_n]$
Output: Either return some constant candidate c for case **C2**, or fails.
1 **for** i from 2 to n **do**
2   **if** $F_{x_1, x_i} \neq 0$ **then**
3        $c := F - \dfrac{F_{x_1} F_{x_i}}{F_{x_1, x_i}}$;
4   **if** $c \in \mathbb{K}$ **then return** c ;
5 FAIL

Algorithm 6: checkProd(F, X)

Input: A fraction $F \in \mathbb{K}(X)$ with $x_1 \in \mathrm{Supp}(F)$, and a list $X = [x_1, \ldots, x_n]$
Output: Succeed by returning G, Y, H, Z if F can be written as GH (i.e. as in the case **C2** with $c = 0$), and fails otherwise

1 $Y := \mathsf{connectedVariablesProd}(F, X)$;
2 $Z := \mathrm{Supp}(F) \backslash Y$;
3 **if** Z is empty **then** FAIL ;
4 **else**
5      $G := F(Z = Z^0)$ where Z^0 is a random point such that $F(Z = Z^0)$ is well-defined and nonzero ;
6      $H := F/G$;
7   succeed by returning G, Y, H, Z

Algorithm 7: connectedVariablesProd(F, X)

Input: A fraction $F \in \mathbb{K}(X)$ and a list $X = [x_1, \ldots, x_n]$
Output: Return the connected component containing x_1 of the undirected graph with nodes x_i, and with edges the (x_i, x_j) s.t. $\left(\frac{F_{x_i}}{F} \right)_{x_j} \neq 0$.

1 Same algorithm as Algorithm 3 except F_v is replaced by $\dfrac{F_v}{F}$ in Line 6

3.3 Algorithm checkC3 $(F = c + 1/(G + H))$

Algorithm checkC3 proceeds similarly to Algorithm checkC2 but with a different formula for computing c, G, and H. Once a candidate c is found, Algorithm checkC3 tries to decompose $1/(F - c)$ into a sum $G + H$ using Algorithm checkC1.

Proposition 9. *Take a fraction $F \in \mathbb{K}(X)$ of the form **C3** (i.e. $c + 1/(G + H)$) where $\mathrm{Supp}(G) = Y$, $\mathrm{Supp}(H) = Z$ and (Y, Z) is a partition of $\mathrm{Supp}(F)$. Then $c = F - 2\frac{F_y F_z}{F_{y,z}}$ for any $(y, z) \in (Y, Z)$.*

Moreover, if for some $(u, v) \in X^2$, the expression $F - 2\frac{F_u F_v}{F_{u,v}}$ is well-defined and constant, then it is equal to c defined above.

Proof. The first part of the proof is once again a simple computation. For the second part, there is nothing to prove if $(u, v) \in (Y, Z)$ or $(u, v) \in (Z, Y)$. Assume (by symmetry) that both u and v lies in Y, and that the expression $F - 2\frac{F_u F_v}{F_{u,v}}$ is well-defined and constant.

Computations yields $F - 2\frac{F_u F_v}{F_{u,v}} = c + \dfrac{G_{u,v}}{G_{u,v}(G + H) - 2G_u G_v}$. This expression is equal to c when $G_{u,v} = 0$. If $G_{u,v} \neq 0$, the numerator of the expression is free of Z, but the support of denominator contains Z, hence a contradiction since the expression is constant. $\qquad\square$

Algorithm 8: checkC3(F, X)

Input: A fraction $F \in \mathbb{K}(X)$ and a list $X = [x_1, \ldots, x_n]$
Output: Succeed by returning c, G, Y, H, Z if F can be written as
$c + 1/(G + H)$ (as in the case **C3**), and fails otherwise

1 **if** findConstantCase3(F, X) returns a constant c **then**
2 | $\quad$ $U := 1/(F - c)$;
3 | $\quad$ **if** checkC1(U, X) returns G, Y, H, Z **then return** c, G, Y, H, Z ;
4 | $\quad$ **else** FAIL ;
5 **else** FAIL ;

Algorithm 9: findConstantCase3(F, X)

Input: A fraction $F \in \mathbb{K}(X)$ and a list $X = [x_1, \ldots, x_n]$
Output: Either return some constant candidate c for case **C3**, or fails.

1 Same algorithm as Algorithm 5 except Line 3 is replaced by $c := F - 2\dfrac{F_{x_1} F_{x_i}}{F_{x_1, x_i}}$

3.4   Algorithm checkC4 $(F = c + d/(1 + GH))$

Algorithm checkC4 proceeds similarly to Algorithms checkC2 and checkC3. Once candidates c and d are found, Algorithm checkC4 tries to decompose $d/(F - c) - 1$ into a product GH using Algorithm checkProd.

However the computations for finding the candidates c and d are more difficult, because c and d are solutions of quadratic equations. As a consequence, some fractions of $\mathbb{K}(X)$ are nonsplittable in $\mathbb{K}(X)$, but are splittable in $\bar{\mathbb{K}}(X)$ where $\bar{\mathbb{K}}$ is some extension of $\mathbb{K}$. Here is a quite easy example demonstrating this fact.

Example 1. The fraction $F = \frac{xy+a}{x+y} \in \mathbb{K}(x, y)$, where $a \in \mathbb{K}$, can be written as

$$F = -b + \cfrac{2b}{1 - \left(1 - \frac{2}{\frac{x}{b}+1}\right)\left(1 - \frac{2}{\frac{y}{b}+1}\right)}$$

if b satisfies $b^2 = a$. As a consequence, the fraction F is splittable in $\mathbb{K}(x, y)$ if a is a square in $\mathbb{K}$, and nonsplittable in $\mathbb{K}(x, y)$ otherwise.

Propositions 10 and 11 below explain the process used by Algorithm 11 for finding the candidates c and d.

Proposition 10. *Take a fraction $F \in \mathbb{K}(X)$ of the form **C4** (i.e. $c + d/(1 + GH)$) where $\mathrm{Supp}(G) = Y$, $\mathrm{Supp}(H) = Z$, c and d constants, with $d \neq 0$.*
Then, for any $(y, z) \in (Y, Z)$, we have

$$\frac{1}{F - c} + \frac{1}{J - c} = \frac{2}{d}, \tag{2}$$

where $J = F - 2\frac{F_y F_z}{F_{y,z}}$. Moreover, the couple (c, d) is unique up to the (involutive) transformation $(c, d) \mapsto (c + d, -d)$.

Proof. Take $(y, z) \in (Y, Z)$. Note that J is well-defined since $F_{yz} = \frac{2dG_y H_z}{(1+GH)^3}$, which is nonzero. Computations show that $J = c + \frac{d}{1-GH}$, and Eq. (2) follows. Eq. (2) can be rewritten as

$$- (c + d/2)S + c(c + d) + P = 0, \tag{3}$$

where $S = F + J$ and $P = FJ$. One proves that S is nonconstant. Indeed if S were constant, then $2c + d(\frac{1}{1+GH} + \frac{1}{1-GH})$ would be constant, $\frac{1}{1+GH} + \frac{1}{1-GH}$ would be constant, hence $G^2 H^2$ would be constant, a contradiction since G and H are nonconstant with disjoint supports.

Since S is non constant, there exist X^0 and X^1 such that where $S(X^0) \neq S(X^1)$. Substituting those values in (3) yield a invertible linear system, hence unique values for $\bar{a} = -(c + d/2)$ and $\bar{b} = c(c + d)$.

Finally, d is solution of $d^2 = 4(\bar{a}^2 - \bar{b})$, and $c = -\bar{a} - d/2$. Hence the couple (c, d) is unique, up to the (involutive) transformation $(c, d) \mapsto (c + d, -d)$. $\square$

Proposition 11. *Take the same hypotheses as in Proposition 10. Take $(u, v) \in X^2$ and assume $F_{u,v} \neq 0$. Consider $J = F - 2\frac{F_u F_v}{F_{u,v}}$, and $S = F + J$ and $P = FJ$. Assume S is not constant. Consider the (unique) solution $(\bar{a}, \bar{b})$ of $aS + b + P = 0$, with $\bar{a}$ and $\bar{b}$ constants, if such a solution exists. Then, if $4(\bar{a}^2 - \bar{b})$ is nonzero and admits a squareroot $\bar{d}$ in $\mathbb{K}$, then $(\bar{c}, \bar{d})$, where $\bar{c} = -\bar{a} - \bar{d}/2$, is either (c, d) or $(c + d, -d)$.*

Proof. If $(u, v) \in (Y, Z)$ or $(u, v) \in (Z, Y)$, Proposition 10 concludes. Assume (by symmetry) that both u and v lies in Y. Computations show that $J = c + d\frac{G_{u,v}}{G_{u,v} + (GG_{u,v} - 2G_u G_v)H}$. If $G_{u,v} = 0$, then $J = c$. It implies that $S = F + c$, $P = cF$. As a consequence, S is not constant, and $(\bar{a}, \bar{b}) = (-c, c^2)$ is the unique solution of $aS + b + P = 0$. In that case, $4(\bar{a}^2 - \bar{b}) = 0$, which ends the proof. Now assume that $G_{u,v} \neq 0$. The fraction J can then be rewritten as $J = c + d\dfrac{1}{1 + \bar{G}H}$ where $\bar{G} = G - 2\frac{G_u G_v}{G_{u,v}}$.

Let us first consider the case $\bar{G} = -G$ (which happens for example if G can be written as a product, see Remark 6). This implies $J = c + d\frac{1}{1-GH}$, and the proof ends by following the proof of Proposition 10.

Now consider that $\bar{G} \neq -G$. By taking the numerator of the equation $aS + b + P = 0$, tedious computations[2] yield:

$$G\bar{G}(2ac + c^2 + b) H^2 + (2ac + c^2 + b + (a + c)d)(\bar{G} + G) H +$$

$$(2ac + c^2 + b + 2(a + c)d + d^2) = 0. \tag{4}$$

Since the supports of G and H are disjoint, and H is nonconstant, the previous equation can only hold if the three coefficients in H are the zero fractions. This implies that the three constants $u_2 = 2ac + c^2 + b$, $u_1 = 2ac + c^2 + b + (a + c)d$ and $u_0 = 2ac + c^2 + b + 2(a + c)d + d^2$ are zero. Expanding $u_2 - 2u_1 + u_0 = 0$ yields $d^2 = 0$, a contradiction, which ends the proof. $\square$

---

[2] Use your favorite computer algebra system!.

Algorithm 10: checkC4(F, X)

Input: A fraction $F \in \mathbb{K}(X)$ and a list $X = [x_1, \ldots, x_n]$
Output: Succeed by returning c, d, G, Y, H, Z if F can be written as
$c + d/(1 + GH)$ (as in the case **C4**), and fails otherwise

1 **if** findConstantsCase4(F, X) returns a couple (c, d) **then**
2    $U := d/(F - c) - 1$;
3   **if** checkProd(U, X) returns G, Y, H, Z **then**
4   **return** c, d, G, Y, H, Z
5   **else** FAIL ;
6 **else** FAIL ;

Algorithm 11: findConstantsCase4(F, X)

Input: A fraction $F \in \mathbb{K}(X)$ and a list $X = [x_1, \ldots, x_n]$
Output: Either return some couple candidate $(c, d) \in \mathbb{K}^2$ for case **C4**, or fails.

1 **for** i from 2 to n **do**
2   **if** $F_{x_1, x_i} \neq 0$ **then**
3      $J := F - 2\frac{F_{x_1} F_{x_i}}{F_{x_1, x_i}}$;
4      $S := F + J$;
5      $P := F \times J$;
6   **if** S is not constant **then**
7   find two random points X^0 and X^1 non canceling the denominators
       of F and J, such that $S(X^0) \neq S(X^1)$;
8   find the solution $(\bar{a}, \bar{b})$ of the linear system $aS(X^0) + b + P(X^0) = 0$,
       $aS(X^1) + b + P(X^1) = 0$;
9   **if** (the fraction $\bar{a}S + \bar{b} + P$ is the zero fraction, and if $4(\bar{a}^2 - \bar{b})$ is
       nonzero and admits a squareroot $\bar{d} \in \mathbb{K}$, **then**
10          $\bar{c} := -\bar{a} - \bar{d}/2$;
11   succeed by returning $(\bar{c}, \bar{d})$

12 FAIL

---

4 Examples

Example 2. The polynomial $p = ab + ax + bx + cd + cx + dx + 2x^2$ can be decoupled in $\mathbb{K}(a, b, c, d)$ with $\mathbb{K} = \mathbb{Q}(x)$ into $(x + b)(x + a) + (x + c)(x + d)$.

Note that p is not splittable in $\mathbb{Q}(a, b, c, d, x)$.

Example 3. We present here a worked out example to illustrate how the decouple algorithm works. To make the walkthrough readable, we do not fully detail all values returned by the algorithms. Consider the fraction $F = x^2 + x + 4 + \frac{y+1}{z + \frac{2}{1+tu}}$ taken in $\mathbb{Q}(x, y, z, t, u)$, whose expanded form is

$$\frac{tux^2z + tuxz + tuy + 4tuz + x^2z + tu + 2x^2 + xz + 2x + y + 4z + 9}{tuz + z + 2}.$$

When calling decouple($F, [x, y, z, t, u]$), the call to checkC1 succeeds. Indeed, the graph considered during the call to connectedVariablesSum is

$$
\boxed{\begin{array}{c} y \ - \ u \\ x \quad \diagdown\!\!\!\!\diagup \\ t \ - \ z \end{array}}\ ,
$$

which admits two connected components. The connected component containing the vertex x is simply $\{x\}$, so F can be written as the sum $Q + R$, with $Q = F(y = -2, z = 0, t = 1, u = 1) = x^2 + x + 3 \in \mathbb{K}(x)$ and $R = F - Q = \frac{tuy+tuz+tu+y+z+3}{tuz+z+2} \in \mathbb{K}(y, z, t, u)$. Please note that the previous evaluation is chosen randomly in checkC1, we just picked a possible one for the example.

Then the function decouple performs recursive calls on Q and R. The call to decouple($Q, [x]$) simply returns Q itself. When calling decouple($R, [y, z, t, u]$), the call to checkC2 succeeds. Indeed, the constant $c = R - \frac{R_y R_z}{R_{y,z}} = 1$ is computed by findConstantCase2. Then checkProd($S, [y, z, t, u]$) where $S = R - 1$ is able to split S as a product TU, where $T = S(z = 0, t = 1, u = 1) = y + 1 \in \mathbb{K}(y)$ and $U = S/T = \frac{tu+1}{tuz+z+2} \in \mathbb{K}(z, t, u)$. Indeed, the graph considered in connectedVariablesProd($S, [y, z, t, u]$) is

$$
\boxed{\begin{array}{c} u \\ y \quad \diagup\ \diagdown \\ t \ - \ z \end{array}}\ ,
$$

which admits two connected components.

Then the function decouple performs recursive calls on T and U. The call to decouple($T, [y]$) simply returns T. When calling decouple($U, [z, t, u]$), the call to checkC3 succeeds. Indeed, the constant $c = U - \frac{U_z U_t}{U_{z,t}} = 0$ is computed by findConstantCase3. Then checkC1($1/U, [z, t, u]$) is able to split $1/U$ as a sum $V + W$ where $V = 1/U(t = 1, u = 0) = z + 2 \in \mathbb{K}(z)$ and $W = 1/U - V = -\frac{2tu}{1+tu}$.

Then the function decouple performs recursive calls on V and W. The call to decouple($V, [z]$) simply returns V. Finally, when calling decouple($W, [t, u]$), checkC4 succeeds. Algorithm findConstantsCase4 computes $c = 0$ and $d = -2$ and checkProd($-d/(W - c) - 1, [t, u]$) decomposes $-d/(W - c) - 1 = \frac{1}{tu}$ as a product $\frac{1}{t}$ times $\frac{1}{u}$.

Putting everything together, decouple($F, [x, y, z, t, u]$) returns a tree encoding the fraction

$$
(x^2 + x + 3) + (1 + \frac{y + 1}{z + 2 - \frac{2}{1 + \frac{1}{tu}}}).
$$

Please note that the output would be different (and slightly more compact) if Algorithm findConstantsCase4 were returning $c = -2$ and $d = 2$, instead of $c = 0$ and $d = -2$ (see Proposition 10).

Example 4. The main point of this example is to show how Eq. (5) below can be rewritten into Eq. (6). We however quickly explain how to derive Eq. (5) using [1, 6].

Consider the following reactions, which simulate a gene G regulated by the protein P it produces: $G + P \overset{a}{\underset{b}{\rightleftharpoons}} H$, $G \overset{e}{\rightarrow} G + M$, $M \overset{f}{\rightarrow} M + P$, $M \xrightarrow{V_m, k_m} \emptyset$, $P \xrightarrow{V_p, k_p} \emptyset$. The three first reactions follow the classical mass action law, and the two last are Michaelis-Menten degradations. Assuming the binding/unbinding of the protein is fast, the following dynamical system can be obtained:

$$H'(t) = -G'(t) = \frac{a((fM(t) - V_p)P(t) + fk_pM(t))G(t)}{(aG(t) + aP(t) + b)(k_p + P(t))}, \tag{5}$$

$$M'(t) = \frac{(eG(t) - V_m)M(t) + ek_mG(t)}{k_m + M(t)},$$

$$P'(t) = \frac{((fM(t) - V_p)P(t) + fk_pM(t))(aP(t) + b)}{(aG(t) + aP(t) + b)(k_p + P(t))}.$$

The right hand sides are quite compact, and one clearly sees some denominators like $k_p + P(t)$ and $k_m + M(t)$ coming for the Michaelis-Menten degradations, and $aG(t) + aP(t) + b$ coming from the fast binding/unbinding hypothesis.

Using Algorithm decouple on the right hand sides of Eq. (5) seen as fractions of $\mathbb{K}(V_m, k_m, V_p, k_p, a, b, e, f, G, H, M)$ with $\mathbb{K} = \mathbb{Q}(P)$, one gets

$$H'(t) = -G'(t) = \frac{fM(t) - \dfrac{V_pP(t)}{k_p + P(t)}}{1 + \dfrac{\frac{b}{a} + P(t)}{G(t)}}, \tag{6}$$

$$M'(t) = -\frac{V_m}{\dfrac{k_m}{M(t)} + 1} + eG(t), \tag{7}$$

$$P'(t) = \frac{fM(t) - \dfrac{V_pP(t)}{k_pP(t)}}{1 + \dfrac{G(t)}{P(t)\left(1 + \frac{b}{aP(t)}\right)}}.$$

Eq. (6) might be of interest for a modeler. For example, the expression of $M'(t)$ in (6) clearly shows that $M'(t)$ is the contribution of two reactions (the degradation of M and the production of M by the gene), whereas it is quite hidden in (5). Expression of $M'(t)$ in (6) clearly indicates a contribution $fM(t) - \frac{V_pP(t)}{k_p+P(t)}$ (the production of P minus the degradation of P) divided by the special correction term $-\left(1 + \frac{\frac{b}{a}+P(t)}{G(t)}\right)$ that comes from the fast binding/unbinding hypothesis.

Please remark that Eq. (6) are not obtained anymore if one considers P as a variable instead of putting it in the base field. The reason is that P appears in too many places, which prevents a "nice" decoupling.

Also, note the term $\frac{V_m}{\frac{k_m}{M(t)}+1}$ in the expression of $M'(t)$ in (6). This term is probably a bit odd for a modeler, who would rather prefer the more classical form $\frac{V_m M(t)}{k_m+M(t)}$.

As a last comment, using the `intpakX` package [5], here are the intervals obtained by using either Eq. (5) or (6), on the intervals $G = [0.4, 0.7]$, $M = [10.0, 15.0]$, $P = [50.0, 100.0]$, $V_m = [130.0, 250.0]$, $k_m = [100.0, 200.0]$, $V_p = [80.0, 160.0]$, $k_p = [100.0, 200.0]$, $a = [10.0, 20.0]$, $b = [5.0, 10.0]$, $e = [3.1, 4.5]$, $f = [7.8, 11.6]$:

Value for	$H'(t)$	$G'(t)$	$M'(t)$	$P'(t)$
Eq. (5)	$[-0.07, 8.10]$	$[-8.10, 0.07]$	$[-32.79, -2.97]$	$[-10.53, 1163.61]$
Eq. (6)	$[-0.39, 2.21]$	$[-2.21, 0.39]$	$[-31.37, -3.04]$	$[-28.55, 160.04]$

Except for the interval for $P'(t)$, the differences between the intervals using Eq. (5) or (6) is here rather minor.

Example 5. The following example is a bit artificial but illustrates how compact fractions can become big when being developed. Consider the fraction

$$F = \frac{a_0 + \frac{a_1}{b_1 + \frac{a_2}{b_2 + a_3}}}{c_0 + \frac{c_1}{d_1 + \frac{c_2}{d_2 + c_3}}} + \frac{e_0 + \frac{e_1}{f_1 + \frac{e_2}{f_2 + e_3}}}{g_0 + \frac{g_1}{h_1 + \frac{g_2}{h_2 + g_3}}}$$

which is in a completely decoupled form since each variable only appears once.

Developing F as a reduced fraction P/Q yields a polynomial P of degree 10 with 450 monomials, and a polynomial Q of degree 10 with 225 monomials. Our algorithm `decouple` recovers from P/Q the fraction F with some minor sign differences

$$\frac{-a_0 - \frac{a_1}{-\frac{a_2}{-a_3 - b_2} + b_1}}{-c_0 - \frac{c_1}{-\frac{c_2}{-d_2 - c_3} + d_1}} + \frac{-e_0 - \frac{e_1}{f_1 + \frac{e_2}{f_2 + e_3}}}{-g_0 + \frac{g_1}{-\frac{g_2}{-g_3 - h_2} - h_1}}.$$

Finally, if each variables is replaced by the interval $[1.0, 5.0]$, the reduced fraction P/Q yields the interval $[0.140 \times 10^{-5}, 0.284 \times 10^7]$, whereas the decoupled form yields $[0.237, 16.8]$.

5   Implementation and Complexity

5.1   Complexity

Algorithm `decouple` performs $O(n^2)$ operations over $\mathbb{K}(X)^3$, where n is the number of variables of X. Indeed, Algorithm `decouple` performs at most two recursive calls on a partition of X, plus at most $O(n)$ arithmetic operations: each "check" algorithm performs a linear number of operations over $\mathbb{K}(X)$ (including their subalgorithms), and there is no other operation in $\mathbb{K}(X)$ in Algorithm `decouple`.

---

[3] We count here only arithmetic operations and differentiations. Note that complexity is not the main point of this paper, so that we do not go into much details here.

Note that we are not considering the complexity over $\mathbb{K}$, which is much higher. Indeed, differentiations, additions, are intensively used and may produce very large fractions. Also, reduced forms of fractions are computed intensively, causing a lot of gcd computations. Some techniques are mentioned in the next section, in order to limit this problem. Finally, if we consider operations over $\mathbb{K}$, our algorithm is Las Vegas, as there are some random evaluations in Algorithms 2 and 11.

5.2   Implementation

Algorithm decouple has been coded in the Maple 2020 computer algebra system. All examples presented in the paper run under ten seconds (on a i7-8650U CPU 1.90 GHz running Linux), and the memory footprint in under 180 Mbytes.

Our implementation has also been intensively stress-tested in the following way. It is easy to compute splittable fractions by building a tree representing a decoupling. Expanding this tree yields a (usually large) fraction which is given to Algorithm decouple, which then recovers the initial decoupling.

Some heuristics have been used in our code to limit potential costly computations. For example, when testing that a fraction is zero, some evaluations are first performed, and the fraction is only developed if all evaluations return zero.

One difficulty in Algorithm 11 is to decide whether the equation $d^2 = 4(\bar{a}^2 - \bar{b})$ admits solution for d in the field $\mathbb{K}$. For the moment, we simply chose to use an expression with a radical for d, thus assuming d exists.

Acknowledgments. This work has been supported by the interdisciplinary bilateral project ANR-17-CE40-0036 and DFG-391322026 SYMBIONT. We also want to thank the reviewers for their useful comments and suggestions which helped improve this article.

References

1. Boulier, F., Lefranc, M., Lemaire, F., Morant, P.E.: Model reduction of chemical reaction systems using elimination. Math. Comput. Sci. **5**, 289–301 (2011). http://hal.archives-ouvertes.fr/hal-00184558, Presented at the international conference MACIS 2007, submitted to Mathematics in Computer Science, Special Issue on Polynomial System Solving in July 2008
2. Boulier, F., Lemaire, F.: Finding first integrals using normal forms modulo differential regular chains. In: Gerdt, V.P., Koepf, W., Seiler, W.M., Vorozhtsov, E.V. (eds.) CASC 2015. LNCS, vol. 9301, pp. 101–118. Springer, Cham (2015). https://doi.org/10.1007/978-3-319-24021-3_8
3. Ceberio, M., Kreinovich, V.: Greedy algorithms for optimizing multivariate Horner schemes. SIGSAM Bull. **38**(1), 8–15 (2004). https://doi.org/10.1145/980175.980179
4. von zur Gathen, J., Gerhard, J.: Modern Computer Algebra, 3rd edn. Cambridge University Press, Cambridge (2013). https://doi.org/10.1017/CBO9781139856065
5. Geulig, I., Krämer, W., Grimmer, M.: The intpakX V1.2 package (2005). http://www2.math.uni-wuppertal.de/wrswt/software/intpakX/

6. Lemaire, F., Ürgüplü, A.: MABSys: modeling and analysis of biological systems. In: Horimoto, K., Nakatsui, M., Popov, N. (eds.) ANB 2010. LNCS, vol. 6479, pp. 57–75. Springer, Heidelberg (2012). https://doi.org/10.1007/978-3-642-28067-2_4
7. Leĭnartas, E.K.: Factorization of rational functions of several variables into partial fractions. Soviet Math. (Iz. VUZ) **22**(10), 35–38 (1978)
8. Raichev, A.: Leĭnartas's partial fraction decomposition (2012). arXiv:1206.4740
9. Stoutemyer, D.R.: Multivariate partial fraction expansion. ACM Commun. Comput. Algebra **42**(4), 206–210 (2009). https://doi.org/10.1145/1504341.1504346
10. Stoutemyer, D.R.: Ten commandments for good default expression simplification. J. Symb. Comput. **46**(7), 859–887 (2011). https://doi.org/10.1016/j.jsc.2010.08.017, special Issue in Honour of Keith Geddes on his 60th Birthday
11. Stoutemyer, D.R.: A computer algebra user interface manifesto (2013). arXiv:1305.3215v1

Towards Extending Fulton's Algorithm for Computing Intersection Multiplicities Beyond the Bivariate Case

Marc Moreno Maza and Ryan Sandford$^{(\boxtimes)}$

Department of Computer Science, The University of Western Ontario,
London, Canada
moreno@csd.uwo.ca, rsandfo@uwo.ca

Abstract. We provide a procedure which partially extends Fulton's intersection multiplicty algorithm to the general case, using a generalization of his seven properties. This procedure leads to a novel, standard basis free approach for computing intersection multiplicities beyond the case of two planar curves, which can cover cases the current standard basis free techniques cannot.

1 Introduction

The study of singularities in algebraic sets is one of the driving application areas of computer algebra and has motivated the development of numerous algorithms and software, see the books [2,4] for an overview. One important question in that area is the computation of intersection multiplicities. The first algorithmic solution was proposed by Mora, for which a modern presentation is given in [4]. Mora's approach relies on the computation of standard bases. An alternative approach has been investigated in the 2012 and 2015 CASC papers [1,6], following an observation made by Fulton in [3, Section 3-3] where he exhibits an algorithm for computing the intersection multiplicity of two plane curves.

Fulton's algorithm is based on 7 properties (see Sect. 2.4 of the present paper) which uniquely define the intersection multiplicity of two plane curves at the origin, and yield a procedure for computing it, see Algorithm 1. If the input is a pair (f_0, g_0) of bivariate polynomials over some algebraically closed field $\mathbb{K}$, then Fulton's 7 properties acts as a set of *rewrite rules* replacing (f_0, g_0), by a sequence of pairs $(f_1, g_1), (f_2, g_2), \ldots$ of bivariate polynomials over $\mathbb{K}$, which preserves the intersection multiplicity at the origin. This process may split the computation and terminates in each branch once reaching a pair for which the intersection multiplicity at the origin can be determined. This is an elegant process, which, experimentally, outperforms Mora's algorithm, as reported in [9].

Extending Fulton's algorithm to a general setting was discussed but not solved in [1,6]. Given n polynomials $f_1, \ldots, f_n \in \mathbb{K}[x_1, \ldots, x_n]$ generating a zero-dimensional ideal, and a point $p \in \mathbf{V}(f_1, \ldots, f_n)$, the authors of [1,6] propose an algorithmic criterion for reducing the intersection multiplicity of p

© Springer Nature Switzerland AG 2021
F. Boulier et al. (Eds.): CASC 2021, LNCS 12865, pp. 232–251, 2021.
https://doi.org/10.1007/978-3-030-85165-1_14

in $\mathbf{V}(f_1, \ldots, f_n)$, to computing another intersection multiplicity with $n-1$ polynomials in $n-1$ variables. For this criterion to be applicable, a transversality condition must hold. Unfortunately, this assumption is not generically true.

The present paper makes three contributions towards the goal of extending Fulton's algorithm to the general, multivariate case.

1. In Sect. 3, we propose and prove an adaptation of Fulton's algorithm to handle polynomials in three variables. For $f, g, h \in \mathbb{K}[x, y, z]$ which form a regular sequence in the local ring at $p \in \mathbb{A}^3$, the proposed algorithm either returns the intersection multiplicity of p in $\mathbf{V}(f, g, h)$, or returns "Fail". We show that this algorithm can cover cases which were out of reach of the algorithmic criterion [1,6].
2. In Sect. 4, we extend the algorithm proposed in Sect. 3 to the general setting of n-polynomials in n variables, where $n \geq 2$.
3. In Sect. 5, we prove that if n polynomials $f_1, \ldots, f_n \in \mathbb{K}[x_1, \ldots, x_n]$ form both a triangular set and a regular sequence in the local ring at $p \in \mathbb{A}^n$, then the intersection multiplicity of p in $\mathbf{V}(f_1, \ldots, f_n)$ can be obtained immediately by evaluating $f_1, \ldots, f_n$.

The result of Sect. 5 has two important consequences. First, it provides an optimization for Fulton's algorithm as well as for the algorithms of Sects. 3 and 4: indeed, when these algorithms are applied to a triangular regular sequence, they immediately return the intersection multiplicity at p of such input system. Second, this result suggests a new direction towards the goal of extending Fulton's algorithm: develop an algorithm which would decide whether an arbitrary regular sequence $f_1, \ldots, f_n$ (in the local ring at p) can be transformed into a triangular regular sequence.

Lastly, the present paper considers only the theoretical aspects of extending Fulton's algorithm. The current implementation, and other interesting topics such as optimizations, relative performance, and complexity analysis, will be discussed in a future paper.

2   Preliminaries

2.1   Notation

Let $\mathbb{K}$ be an algebraically closed field. Let $\mathbb{A}^n$ denote $\mathbb{A}^n(\mathbb{K})$, the affine space of dimension n over $\mathbb{K}$. Assume variables $x_1, \ldots, x_n$ are ordered $x_1 \succ \ldots \succ x_n$. We define the degree of the zero polynomial to be $-\infty$ with respect to any variable.

If I is an ideal of $\mathbb{K}[x_1, \ldots, x_n]$, we denote by $\mathbf{V}(I)$ the algebraic set (aka variety) consisting of the common zeros to all polynomials in I. An algebraic set $\mathbf{V}$ is irreducible, whenever $\mathbf{V} = \mathbf{V}_1 \cup \mathbf{V}_2$ for some algebraic sets $\mathbf{V}_1, \mathbf{V}_2$, implies $\mathbf{V} = \mathbf{V}_1$ or $\mathbf{V} = \mathbf{V}_2$. The ideal of an algebraic set $\mathbf{V}$, denoted by $\mathbf{I}(\mathbf{V})$, is the set of all polynomials which vanish on all points in $\mathbf{V}$. For $f_1, \ldots, f_n \in \mathbb{K}[x_1, \ldots, x_n]$, we say $\mathbf{V}(f_1), \ldots, \mathbf{V}(f_n)$ have a common component which passes through $p \in \mathbb{A}^n$ if when we write $\mathbf{V}(f_1, \ldots, f_n)$ as a union of its irreducible components, say $\mathbf{V}_1 \cup \ldots \cup \mathbf{V}_m$, there is a $\mathbf{V}_i$ which contains p. Similarly, we say $f_1, \ldots, f_n$ have a common component through p when $\mathbf{V}(f_1), \ldots, \mathbf{V}(f_n)$ have a common component which passes through p. We say an algebraic set is zero-dimensional if it contains only finitely many points in $\mathbb{A}^n$.

2.2   Local Rings and Intersection Multiplicity

Definition 1. *Let $\mathbf{V}$ be an irreducible algebraic set with $p \in \mathbf{V}$. We define the local ring of $\mathbf{V}$ at p as*

$$\mathcal{O}_{\mathbf{V},p} := \left\{ \frac{f}{g} \mid f, g \in \mathbb{K}[x_1, \ldots, x_n]/\mathbf{I}(\mathbf{V}) \text{ where } g(p) \neq 0 \right\}.$$

Often, we will refer to the local ring of $\mathbb{A}^n$ at p, in which case we will simply say the local ring at p and write

$$\mathcal{O}_{\mathbb{A}^n,p} := \left\{ \frac{f}{g} \mid f, g \in \mathbb{K}[x_1, \ldots, x_n] \text{ where } g(p) \neq 0 \right\}.$$

Local rings have a unique maximal ideal. In the case of $\mathcal{O}_{\mathbb{A}^n,p}$ all elements which vanish on p are in the maximal ideal and all of those that do not are units. Hence, given an element $f \in \mathbb{K}[x_1, \ldots, x_n]$ we can test whether f is invertible in $\mathcal{O}_{\mathbb{A}^n,p}$ by testing $f(p) \neq 0$.

Definition 2. *Let $f_1, \ldots f_n \in \mathbb{K}[x_1, \ldots, x_n]$. We define the intersection multiplicity of $f_1, \ldots, f_n$ at $p \in \mathbb{A}^n$ as the dimension of the local ring at p modulo the ideal generated by $f_1, \ldots, f_n$ in the local ring at p, as a vector space over $\mathbb{K}$. That is,*

$$\operatorname{Im}(p; f_1, \ldots, f_n) := \dim_{\mathbb{K}}(\mathcal{O}_{\mathbb{A}^n,p}/\langle f_1, \ldots, f_n \rangle).$$

The following observation allows us to write the intersection multiplicity of a system of polynomials as the intersection multiplicity of a smaller system of polynomials, in fewer variables, when applicable. It follows from an isomorphism between the respective residues of local rings in the definition of intersection multiplicity.

Remark 1. Let $f_1, \ldots f_n \in \mathbb{K}[x_1, \ldots, x_n]$ and $p = (p_1, \ldots, p_n) \in \mathbb{A}^n$. If there are some f_i such that $f_i = x_i - p_i$, say $f_m, \ldots, f_n$ where $1 < m \leq n$, then

$$\operatorname{Im}(p; f_1, \ldots, f_n) = \operatorname{Im}((p_1, \ldots, p_{m-1}); F_1, \ldots, F_{m-1}),$$

where F_j is the image of f_j modulo $\langle x_m - p_m, \ldots, x_n - p_n \rangle$.

2.3   Regular Sequences

Regular sequences are one of the primary tools leveraged in our approach to compute intersection multiplicities. Given a regular sequence, Corollary 1, along side Propositions 3 and 4, describe a set of permissible modifications which maintain regularity.

Later we will encounter a property of intersection multiplicities which requires the input polynomials form a regular sequence. Hence, our approach will be to start with a regular sequence, perform a set of operations on the input system which are permissible as to maintain being a regular sequence, and compute the intersection multiplicity.

Proposition 1 can be found in [5, Section 3-1] and Proposition 2 in [7, Section 6–15]. We believe Propositions 3, 4, and 5 can also be found in the literature but include proofs for completeness, as we refer to these propositions frequently in later sections.

Definition 3. *Let R be a commutative ring and M an R module. Let $r_1, \ldots, r_d$ be a sequence of elements in R. Then $r_1, \ldots, r_d$ is an M-regular sequence if r_i is not a zero divisor on $M/\langle r_1, \ldots, r_{i-1}\rangle M$ for all $i = 1, \ldots, d$ and $M \neq \langle r_1, \ldots, r_d\rangle M$.*

When $R, M = \mathcal{O}_{\mathbb{A}^n, p}$, we will often refer to a M-regular sequence as a regular sequence in $\mathcal{O}_{\mathbb{A}^n, p}$ or simply as a regular sequence.

Proposition 1. *Let $r_1, \ldots, r_d$ form a regular sequence in a Noetherian local ring R, and suppose all r_i are in the maximal ideal, then any permutation of $r_1, \ldots, r_d$ is a regular sequence in R.*

Corollary 1. *Let $f_1, \ldots, f_n \in \mathbb{K}[x_1, \ldots, x_n]$ where $f_1, \ldots, f_n$ vanish on some $p \in \mathbb{A}^n$ and form a regular sequence in $\mathcal{O}_{\mathbb{A}^n, p}$. Then any permutation of $f_1, \ldots, f_n$ is a regular sequence in $\mathcal{O}_{\mathbb{A}^n, p}$.*

Proof: Since $f_1, \ldots, f_n$ vanish at p they are in the maximal ideal of $\mathcal{O}_{\mathbb{A}^n, p}$. The conclusion follows from Proposition 1. □

With Corollary 1, we can now give a more intuitive explanation of regular sequences in the local ring at p. Regular sequences in the local ring at p can be thought of as systems which behave nicely at p. That is, if $f_1, \ldots, f_n \in \mathbb{K}[x_1, \ldots, x_n]$ is a regular sequence in the local ring at p, no f_i is zero, a zero-divisor, or a unit modulo any subset of the remaining polynomials. Moreover, we can say there is no pair f_i, f_j where $i \neq j$, modulo any subset of the remaining polynomials, which has a common component through p.

Proposition 2. *If $f_1, \ldots, f_n \in \mathbb{K}[x_1, \ldots, x_n]$ is a regular sequence in $\mathcal{O}_{\mathbb{A}^n, p}$ then the irreducible component of $\mathbf{V}(f_1, \ldots, f_n)$ which passes through p is zero-dimensional.*

We may assume $\mathbf{V}(f_1, \ldots, f_n)$ is equal to its component which contains p since the other components do not affect the intersection multiplicity.

Proposition 3. *Let* $f_1, \ldots, f_n \in \mathbb{K}[x_1, \ldots, x_n]$ *where* $f_1, \ldots, f_n$ *vanish on some* $p \in \mathbb{A}^n$. *Fix some* $g \in \{f_1, \ldots, f_n\}$ *and choose some subset* $I \subseteq \{i \in \mathbb{N} \mid 1 \le i \le n, f_i \ne g\}$. *For each* $i = 1, \ldots, n$, *define*

$$F_i^I = \begin{cases} f_i & \text{if } i \notin I \\ s_i f_i - r_i g & \text{if } i \in I \end{cases},$$

where s_i, r_i *are in* $\mathbb{K}[x_1 \ldots, x_n]$ *and each* s_i *is invertible in* $\mathcal{O}_{\mathbb{A}^n, p}$.

Then $f_1, \ldots, f_n$ *forms a regular sequence in* $\mathcal{O}_{\mathbb{A}^n, p}$ *if and only if* $F_1^I, \ldots, F_n^I$ *forms a regular sequence in* $\mathcal{O}_{\mathbb{A}^n, p}$.

Proof: By Corollary 1, $f_1, \ldots, f_n$ is a regular sequence under permutation, thus we may reorder so that all polynomials with indices in I are at the end of the sequence. That is, we may assume $I = \{i \in \mathbb{N} \mid N < i \le n\}$ for some $N \in \mathbb{N}$. Moreover, we may reorder so that $g = f_N$.

It suffices to show F_k^I is regular modulo $\langle F_1^I, \ldots, F_{k-1}^I \rangle$ for each k such that $N < k \le n$. First observe,

$$\begin{aligned} \langle F_1^I, \ldots, F_k^I \rangle &= \langle f_1, \ldots, f_N, s_{N+1} f_{N+1} - r_{N+1} f_N, \ldots, s_k f_k - r_k f_N \rangle \\ &= \langle f_1, \ldots, f_N, s_{N+1} f_{N+1}, \ldots, s_k f_k \rangle \\ &= \langle f_1, \ldots, f_k \rangle. \end{aligned}$$

Hence, we will show F_k^I is regular modulo $\langle f_1, \ldots, f_{k-1} \rangle$. Suppose it was not, thus there are $q, a_1, \ldots, a_{k-1}$ in $\mathcal{O}_{\mathbb{A}^n, p}$ where $q \notin \langle f_1, \ldots, f_{k-1} \rangle$ such that,

$$\begin{aligned} q F_k^I &= a_1 f_1 + \ldots + a_{k-1} f_{k-1} \\ q s_k f_k - q r_k f_N &= a_1 f_1 + \ldots + a_{k-1} f_{k-1} \\ q f_k &= s_k^{-1} (a_1 f_1 + \ldots + (q r_k + a_N) f_N + \ldots + a_{k-1} f_{k-1}). \end{aligned}$$

Since $q \notin \langle f_1, \ldots, f_{k-1} \rangle$, this contradicts the regularity of f_k modulo $\langle f_1, \ldots, f_{k-1} \rangle$. The converse follows by the same argument. $\square$

Proposition 4. *Let* $f_1, \ldots, f_n \in \mathbb{K}[x_1, \ldots, x_n]$ *where* $f_1, \ldots, f_n$ *vanish on some* $p \in \mathbb{A}^n$. *Suppose for some* i *we have* $f_i = q_1 q_2$ *for some* $q_1, q_2 \in \mathbb{K}[x_1, \ldots, x_n]$ *which are not units in* $\mathcal{O}_{\mathbb{A}^n, p}$. *Then* $f_1, \ldots, f_n$ *is a regular sequence in* $\mathcal{O}_{\mathbb{A}^n, p}$ *if and only if both* $f_1, \ldots, q_1, \ldots, f_n$ *and* $f_1, \ldots, q_2, \ldots, f_n$ *are regular sequences in* $\mathcal{O}_{\mathbb{A}^n, p}$.

Proof: Suppose $f_1, \ldots, f_n$ is a regular sequence in $\mathcal{O}_{\mathbb{A}^n, p}$. By Corollary 1 we may assume $i = n$. We may assume neither $q_1, q_2 \in \langle f_1, \ldots, f_{n-1} \rangle$ since otherwise, the result clearly holds.

Suppose f_n is not regular, then $q q_1 q_2 = q f_n = Q_1 f_1 + \ldots + Q_{n-1} f_{n-1}$ for some $q, Q_1, \ldots, Q_{n-1} \in \mathcal{O}_{\mathbb{A}^n, p}$ where $q \notin \langle f_1, \ldots, f_{n-1} \rangle$. If $q q_1 \notin \langle f_1, \ldots, f_{n-1} \rangle$ then q_2 is a zero divisor since $q_2 \notin \langle f_1, \ldots, f_{n-1} \rangle$. If $q q_1 \in \langle f_1, \ldots, f_{n-1} \rangle$ then since $q_1 \notin \langle f_1, \ldots, f_{n-1} \rangle$, q_1 is a zero divisor.

Suppose one of q_1, q_2 was a zero divisor, say q_1 and write $q q_1 = Q_1 f_1 + \ldots + Q_{n-1} f_{n-1}$ for some $q, Q_1, \ldots, Q_{n-1} \in \mathcal{O}_{\mathbb{A}^n, p}$ where $q \notin \langle f_1, \ldots, f_{n-1} \rangle$. Observe we have $q_2 Q_1 f_1 + \ldots + q_2 Q_{n-1} f_{n-1} = q q_1 q_2 = q f$. Since $q_2 \notin \langle f_1, \ldots, f_{n-1} \rangle$, f is a zero divisor. $\square$

Proposition 5. *Let $f_1, \ldots, f_n$ be polynomials in $\mathbb{K}[x_1, \ldots, x_n]$ which vanish on p. Suppose $f_1, \ldots, f_n$ form a regular sequence in $\mathbb{K}[x_1, \ldots, x_n]$, then $f_1, \ldots, f_n$ form a regular sequence in $\mathcal{O}_{\mathbb{A}^n, p}$.*

Proof: The case where $n = 1$ is straight forward, assume $n > 1$. Suppose $f_1, \ldots, f_n$ is not a regular sequence in $\mathcal{O}_{\mathbb{A}^n, p}$. Then there is some $i > 1$ such that f_i is not regular modulo $\langle f_1, \ldots, f_{i-1} \rangle$. Write,

$$\frac{Q_1}{q_1} f_1 + \ldots + \frac{Q_{i-1}}{q_{i-1}} f_{i-1} = \frac{Q}{q} f_i,$$

for some $Q_1, \ldots, Q_{i-1}, q_1, \ldots, q_{i-1}, Q, q \in \mathbb{K}[x_1, \ldots, x_n]$ where $q_1, \ldots, q_{i-1}$ do not vanish on p and $Q \notin \langle f_1, \ldots, f_{i-1} \rangle$. Observe we have,

$$(\widehat{q_1} \cdot \ldots \cdot q_{i-1}q)Q_1 f_1 + \ldots + (q_1 \cdot \ldots \cdot \widehat{q_{i-1}}q)Q_{i-1}f_{i-1} = (q_1 \cdot \ldots \cdot q_{i-1})Q f_i,$$

where $q_1 \cdot \ldots \cdot \widehat{q_j} \cdot \ldots \cdot q_{i-1}$ is the product of $q_1 \cdot \ldots \cdot q_{i-1}$ with q_j omitted. Since $Q \notin \langle f_1, \ldots, f_{i-1} \rangle$ and since none of $q_1, \ldots, q_{i-1}$ vanish on p and all of $f_1, \ldots, f_{i-1}$ vanish on p, we must have $(q_1 \cdot \ldots \cdot q_{i-1})Q \notin \langle f_1, \ldots, f_{i-1} \rangle$, hence f_i is not regular modulo $\langle f_1, \ldots, f_{i-1} \rangle$ in the polynomial ring. $\quad \square$

Unlike Corollary 1, and Propositions 3 and 4, Proposition 5 does not give a permissible modification we can make to a regular sequence. Instead, Proposition 5 states that to test for a regular sequence in the local ring, it is sufficient to test for a regular sequence in the polynomial ring.

As mentioned earlier, our approach initially requires the input system to be a regular sequence. Proposition 5 tells us this is a reasonable requirement which can be tested using techniques for polynomial ideals.

2.4   Bivariate Intersection Multiplicity

It is shown in [3, Section 3-3] that the following seven properties characterize intersection multiplicity of bivariate curves. Moreover, these seven properties lead to a constructive procedure which computes the intersection multiplicity of bivariate curves, which is given in Algorithm 1.

Proposition 6 (Fulton's Properties). *Let $p = (p_1, p_2) \in \mathbb{A}^2$ and $f, g \in \mathbb{K}[x, y]$.*

- *(2-1) $\text{Im}(p; f, g)$ is a non-negative integer when $\mathbf{V}(f)$ and $\mathbf{V}(g)$ have no common component at p, otherwise $\text{Im}(p; f, g) = \infty$.*
- *(2-2) $\text{Im}(p; f, g) = 0$ if and only if $p \notin \mathbf{V}(f) \cap \mathbf{V}(g)$.*
- *(2-3) $\text{Im}(p; f, g)$ is invariant under affine changes of coordinates on $\mathbb{A}^2$.*
- *(2-4) $\text{Im}(p; f, g) = \text{Im}(p; g, f)$.*

– (2-5) $\mathrm{Im}(p; f, g) \geq m_f m_g$ where m_f and m_g are the respective tailing degrees of f and g expressed in $\mathbb{K}[x - p_1, y - p_2]$. Moreover, $\mathrm{Im}(p; f, g) = m_f m_g$ when $\mathbf{V}(f)$ and $\mathbf{V}(g)$ intersect transversally, i.e. have no tangent lines in common.
– (2-6) $\mathrm{Im}(p; f, gh) = \mathrm{Im}(p; f, g) + \mathrm{Im}(p; f, h)$ for any $h \in \mathbb{K}[x, y]$.
– (2-7) $\mathrm{Im}(p; f, g) = \mathrm{Im}(p; f, g + hf)$ for any $h \in \mathbb{K}[x, y]$.

Algorithm 1: Fulton's algorithm

---

1 **Function** $\mathrm{im}(p; f, g)$
    Input: Let: $x \succ y$
      1. $p \in \mathbb{A}^2$ the origin.
      2. $f, g \in \mathbb{K}[x, y]$ such that $\gcd(f, g)(p) \neq 0$.

    Output: $\mathrm{Im}(p; f, g)$

2   **if** $f(p) \neq 0$ **or** $g(p) \neq 0$ **then**   /* Red */
3   **return** 0
4     $r \leftarrow \deg_x (f(x, 0))$
5     $s \leftarrow \deg_x (g(x, 0))$
6   **if** $r > s$ **then**   /* Green */
7   **return** $\mathrm{im}(p; g, f)$
8   **if** $r < 0$ **then**   /* Yellow, $y \mid f$ */
9   write $g(x, 0) = x^m (a_m + a_{m+1}x + \dots)$
10   **return** $m + \mathrm{im}(p; \mathrm{quo}(f, y; y), g)$
11   **else**   /* Blue */
12         $g' = \mathrm{lc}(f(x, 0)) \cdot g - (x)^{s-r} \mathrm{lc}(g(x, 0)) \cdot f$
13   **return** $\mathrm{im}(p; f, g')$

The following proposition was proved by Fulton in [3, Section 3-3]. It is included here for the readers convenience, as we will use similar arguments in later sections.

Proposition 7. Algorithm 1 is correct and terminates.

Proof: By (2-3) we may assume p is the origin. Let f, g be polynomials in $\mathbb{K}[x, y]$ with no common component through the origin. By (2-1), $\mathrm{Im}(p; f, g)$ is finite. We induct on $\mathrm{Im}(p; f, g)$ to prove termination. Suppose $\mathrm{Im}(p; f, g) = 0$, then by (2-2), at least one of f or g does not vanish at the origin and Algorithm 1 correctly returns zero.

Now suppose $\mathrm{Im}(p; f, g) = n > 0$ for some $n \in \mathbb{N}$. Let r, s be the respective degrees of f, g evaluated at $(x, 0)$. By (2-4) we may reorder f, g to ensure $r \leq s$. Notice $r, s \neq 0$ since f, g vanish at the origin.

If $r < 0$, then f is a univariate polynomial in y which vanishes at the origin, hence f is divisible by y. By (2-6) we have,

$$\mathrm{Im}(p; f, g) = \mathrm{Im}(p; y, g) + \mathrm{Im}(p; \mathrm{quo}(f, y; y), g) \,.$$

By definition of intersection multiplicity $\mathrm{Im}(p;\, y, g) = \mathrm{Im}(p;\, y, g(x, 0))$. Since $g(x, 0)$ vanishes at the origin and since g has no common component with f at the origin, $g(x, 0)$ is a non-zero univariate polynomial divisible by x. Write $g(x, 0) = x^m(a_m + a_{m+1}x + \ldots)$ for some $a_m, a_{m+1}, \ldots \in \mathbb{K}$ where m is the largest positive integer such that $a_m \neq 0$. Applying (2-6), (2-5), and (2-2) yields

$$\mathrm{Im}(p;\, f, g) = m + \mathrm{Im}(p;\, \mathrm{quo}(f, y; y), g).$$

Thus, Algorithm 1 returns correctly when $r < 0$. Moreover, we can compute $\mathrm{Im}(p;\, \mathrm{quo}(f, y; y), g) < n$ by induction.

Now suppose $0 < r < s$. By (2-7), replacing g with g' preserves the intersection multiplicity. Notice such a substitution strictly decreases the degree in x of $g(x, 0)$. After finitely many iterations, we will obtain curves F, G such that $\mathrm{Im}(p;\, f, g) = \mathrm{Im}(p;\, F, G)$ and the degree in x of $F(x, 0) < 0$. □

2.5   A Generalization of Fulton's Properties

The following theorem gives a generalization of Fulton's Properties for n polynomials in n variables. This generalization of Fulton's Properties was first discovered by the authors of [6] and proved in [9].

Theorem 1. Let $f_1, \ldots, f_n$ be polynomials in $\mathbb{K}[x_1, \ldots, x_n]$ such that $\mathbf{V}(f_1, \ldots f_n)$ is zero-dimensional. Let $p = (p_1, \ldots, p_n) \in \mathbb{A}^n$. The $\mathrm{Im}(p;\, f_1, \ldots, f_n)$ satisfies (n-1) to (n-7) where:

- (n-1) $\mathrm{Im}(p;\, f_1, \ldots, f_n)$ is a non-negative integer.
- (n-2) $\mathrm{Im}(p;\, f_1, \ldots, f_n) = 0$ if and only if $p \notin \mathbf{V}(f_1, \ldots, f_n)$.
- (n-3) $\mathrm{Im}(p;\, f_1, \ldots, f_n)$ is invariant under affine changes of coordinates on $\mathbb{A}^n$.
- (n-4) $\mathrm{Im}(p;\, f_1, \ldots, f_n) = \mathrm{Im}(p;\, \sigma(f_1, \ldots, f_n))$ where σ is any permutation.
- (n-5) $\mathrm{Im}(p;\, (x_1 - p_1)^{m_1}, \ldots, (x_n - p_n)^{m_n}) = m_1 \cdots m_n$ for any $m_1, \ldots, m_n \in \mathbb{N}$.
- (n-6) $\mathrm{Im}(p;\, f_1, \ldots, f_{n-1}, gh) = \mathrm{Im}(p;\, f_1, \ldots, f_{n-1}, g) + \mathrm{Im}(p;\, f_1, \ldots, f_{n-1}, h)$ for any $g, h \in \mathbb{K}[x_1, \ldots, x_n]$ such that $f_1, \ldots, f_{n-1}, gh$ is a regular sequence in $\mathcal{O}_{\mathbb{A}^n, p}$.
- (n-7) $\mathrm{Im}(p;\, f_1, \ldots, f_n) = \mathrm{Im}(p;\, f_1, \ldots, f_{n-1}, f_n + g)$ for any $g \in \langle f_1, \ldots, f_{n-1} \rangle$.

3   Trivariate Fulton's Algorithm

In this section we show how the n-variate generalization of Fulton's properties can be used to create a procedure to compute intersection multiplicity in the trivariate case. Later we will see this approach generalizes to the n-variate case, although, it is helpful to first understand the algorithms behaviour in the trivariate case.

This procedure is not complete since the syzygy computations, analogous to those used in Algorithm 1, do not necessarily preserve intersection multiplicity under (n-7). When this is the case, the procedure returns Fail to signal an error.

When the procedure succeeds, we obtain a powerful tool for computing intersection multiplicities in the trivariate case. This allows us to compute intersection multiplicities that previously could not be computed by other, standard basis free approaches, namely that of [1] and [9].

Throughout this section we assume $p \in \mathbb{A}^3$ is the origin.

Definition 4. *Let f be in $\mathbb{K}[x, y, z]$ where $x \succ y \succ z$. We define the modular degree of f with respect to a variable $v \in V$ as $\deg_v (f \mod \langle V_{<v} \rangle)$, where $V = \{x, y, z\}$ is the set of variables and $V_{<v}$ is the set of all variables less than v in the given ordering. If $V_{<v} = \emptyset$, we define the modular degree of f with respect to v to be the degree of f with respect to v. Write $\mathrm{moddeg}(f, v)$ to denote the modular degree of f with respect to v.*

Remark 2. The definition of modular degree can be generalized to a point $p = (p_1, p_2, p_3) \in \mathbb{A}^3$ by replacing $V_{<v}$ with $V_{<v,p} = \{x - p_1, y - p_2, z - p_3\}$ in Definition 4.

The modular degree is used to generalize the computation of r, s in Algorithm 1. If we fix some variable v, the modular degree with respect to v is the degree of a polynomial modulo all variables smaller than v in a given ordering.

Below we formally define cases in terms of the colour they are highlighted with in Algorithm 2. Although not necessary, using a name to distinguish between cases rather then a set of conditions makes the proof far more readable, especially when the set of cases is small, as is the case for trivariate intersection multiplicity.

In the n-variate case, we will see that some of these cases are not distinct and in fact, instances of the same case. We will describe this in more detail later. For now, we make this distinction to illustrate the similarities to Algorithm 1 and to help the reader build intuition for this procedure in a more general setting.

Definition 5 (Colour Cases). *Consider $f, g, h \in \mathbb{K}[x, y, z]$.*

1. *We say we are in the red case if one of f, g, h does not vanish on p.*
2. *We say we are in the blue case if:*
   (a) We are not in the red case.
   (b) The modular degrees of f, g, h in x are in ascending order.
   (c) At least one of f or g has modular degree in x greater than zero.
3. *We say we are in the orange case if:*
   (a) We are not in the red case.
   (b) The modular degrees of f, g, h in x are in ascending order.
   (c) Both f and g have modular degrees in x less than zero.
4. *We say we are in the yellow case if:*
   (a) We are in the orange case.
   (b) The modular degrees of f, g, h in x and the modular degrees of f, g in y are in ascending order.

(c) The modular degree of f in y is less than zero.

5. *We say we are in the pink case if:*
   (a) *We are in the orange case.*
   (b) *The modular degrees of f, g, h in x and the modular degrees of f, g in y are in ascending order.*
   (c) *The modular degree of f in y is greater than zero.*

Remark 3. Note that when we are not in the red case for f, g, h the modular degrees of f, g, h can never be zero as f, g, h vanish at p.

Algorithm 2 generalizes Fulton's approach in the trivariate case. The key to generalizing Fulton's approach to 3 polynomials in 3 variables is generalizing the splitting computation. When the yellow case holds, we can split the intersection multiplicity computation into the sum of smaller intersection multiplicity computations. Thus, the rest of the algorithm is designed to reduce to the yellow case, or return Fail, in finitely many iterations.

At this time there is no clear way to characterize when Algorithm 2 fails since it is difficult to determine before runtime which cases will be reached after rewriting and splitting. Namely, it is difficult to characterize all inputs which will eventually reach a branch which satisfies the conditions of the pink case. Given an input that does satisfy the conditions of pink case, it is easy to check whether Algorithm 2 fails in that iteration, as we will see in the proof of Theorem 2.

Theorem 2. *Algorithm 2 correctly computes the intersection multiplicity of a regular sequence $f, g, h \in \mathbb{K}[x, y, z]$ or returns Fail.*

Proof: Let $f, g, h \in \mathbb{K}[x, y, z]$ be a regular sequence in $\mathcal{O}_{\mathbb{A}^3, p}$. By $(n\text{-}3)$ we may assume p is the origin. By Proposition 2, $\mathbf{V}(f, g, h)$ is zero-dimensional, hence by $(n\text{-}1)$, $\mathrm{Im}(p; f, g, h) \in \mathbb{N}$.

To prove termination we induct on $\mathrm{Im}(p; f, g, h)$ and show that when Algorithm 2 does not fail, we can either compute $\mathrm{Im}(p; f, g, h)$ directly or strictly decrease $\mathrm{Im}(p; f, g, h)$ through splitting.

Suppose $\mathrm{Im}(p; f, g, h) = 0$, then by $(n\text{-}2)$, one of f, g, h does not vanish on p, hence, Algorithm 2 correctly returns zero. Assume that $\mathrm{Im}(p; f, g, h) = N$ for some positive $N \in \mathbb{N}$.

By $(n\text{-}4)$ and Corollary 1, we may reorder f, g, h so that their modular degrees with respect to x are in ascending order.

Suppose f, g, h satisfy the conditions of the blue case, that is, at most one polynomial has modular degree in x less than zero. Depending on how many polynomials have modular degree in x less than zero, we perform slightly different syzygy computations, since there is no need to reduce a modular degree in x of a polynomial that already has modular degree in x less than zero. Notice the syzygy computations in the blue case preserve intersection multiplicity by $(n\text{-}7)$ and regular sequences by Proposition 3. Since the modular degrees in x of the resulting polynomials is strictly decreasing, we will reach the orange case in finitely many iterations.

By $(n\text{-}4)$ and Corollary 1, we may reorder f, g so that their modular degrees with respect to y are in ascending order.

Suppose f, g, h satisfy the conditions of the pink case. Define,

$$L_f = \mathrm{lc}(f(x, y, 0); y),$$

$$L_g = \mathrm{lc}(g(x, y, 0); y).$$

If L_f is not a unit in $\mathcal{O}_{\mathbb{A}^n, p}$ and does not divide L_g, Algorithm 2 returns Fail since $(n\text{-}7)$ cannot be applied to the syzygy computations.

Suppose either $L_f(p) \neq 0$ or $L_f \mid L_g$. Then the respective syzygy computations preserve intersection multiplicity by $(n\text{-}7)$ and regular sequences by Proposition 3. Moreover, if g' is the polynomial resulting from either of the respective syzygy computations, then $\mathrm{moddeg}(g', y) < \mathrm{moddeg}(g, y)$ and $\mathrm{moddeg}(g', x) < 0$. The latter statement follows from both f and g having modular degree in x less than zero as a result of being in the orange case. Since the modular degree of g' with respect to y strictly decreases, we will reach the yellow case or return Fail in finitely many iterations.

Suppose f, g, h satisfy the conditions of the yellow case. Since $\mathrm{moddeg}(f, x) < 0$, $\mathrm{moddeg}(f, y) < 0$, f is non-zero, and f vanishes at the origin, we have $z \mid f$.

By Proposition 4, the sequence z, g, h is regular, hence $g(x, y, 0)$ is non-zero and vanishes at the origin. Since $\mathrm{moddeg}(g, x) < 0$ holds, we have $y \mid g(x, y, 0)$.

Write $f = zq_f$, $g(x, y, 0) = yq_g$, and $m_h = max(m \in \mathbb{Z}^+ \mid h(x, 0, 0) \equiv 0$ mod $\langle x^m \rangle)$. By $(n\text{-}6)$ and Proposition 4, it is correct to compute:

$$\begin{aligned}
\mathrm{Im}(p; f, g, h) &= \mathrm{Im}(p; q_f, g, h) + \mathrm{Im}(p; z, q_g, h) + \mathrm{Im}(p; z, y, h) \\
&= \mathrm{Im}(p; q_f, g, h) + \mathrm{Im}(p; z, q_g, h) + m_h \\
&= \mathrm{Im}(p; q_f, g, h) + \mathrm{Im}(p; q_g, h(x, y, 0)) + m_h.
\end{aligned}$$

Since m_h is a positive integer, we have:

$$\mathrm{Im}(p; q_f, g, h), \mathrm{Im}(p; q_g, h(x, y, 0)) < \mathrm{Im}(p; f, g, h) = N.$$

Thus, when Algorithm 2, called on the input q_f, g, h, does not fail, termination follows from induction. $\square$

To illustrate the utility of this approach we will work through an example where the available standard basis free techniques used to compute intersection multiplicity fail. A full description of these techniques can be found in [1] and [9], although we give a brief overview below.

Suppose for $f_1, \ldots, f_n \in \mathbb{K}[x_1, \ldots, x_n]$, we have $\mathbf{V}(f_1, \ldots, f_n)$ is a zero-dimensional, that is, $\mathrm{Im}(p; f_1, \ldots, f_n) \in \mathbb{N}$, and at least one of $f_1, \ldots, f_n$, say f_n is non-singular at p. Theorem 1 of [1], states that when the above conditions hold, and under an additional transversality constraint between $\mathbf{V}(f_1, \ldots, f_{n-1})$ and $\mathbf{V}(f_n)$, an n-variate intersection multiplicity can be reduced to an $n-1$-variate intersection multiplicity computation.

In [9], the above reduction is combined with an additional reduction procedure referred to as cylindrification. The idea behind this second reduction procedure is to use pseudo-division by a polynomial, say f_n, to reduce the degree of $f_1, \ldots, f_{n-1}$ with respect to some variable, say x_n. The cylindrification procedure assumes that f_n has a term containing x_n with a non-zero coefficient invertible in $\mathcal{O}_{\mathbb{A}^n, p}$.

The following example contains 3 polynomials which are singular at p, hence the above reduction cannot be applied. Moreover, one can check that applying cylindrification does not reduce the input in a way that the first reduction criterion holds. Hence, the current standard basis free techniques fail. Additionally, this can be verified using the *Maple* implementation of the techniques in [9].

Example 1. Compute $\text{Im}\left(p; zy^2, y^5 - z^2, x^5 - y^2\right)$ using Algorithm 2.

Notice, $zy^2, y^5 - z^2, x^5 - y^2$ form a regular sequence. We compute the modular degrees with respect to x: $r_x < 0, s_x < 0, t_x = 5$, hence, we begin in the orange case. Since additionally, $r_y < 0$, we are in the yellow case and the computation reduces to:

$$\text{Im}\left(p; zy^2, y^5 - z^2, x^5 - y^2\right) = \text{Im}\left(p; y^2, y^5 - z^2, x^5 - y^2\right) + \text{Im}\left(p; y^4, x^5 - y^2\right) + 5.$$

Start with $\text{Im}\left(p; y^4, x^5 - y^2\right)$, applying Fulton's bivariate algorithm we get,

$$\begin{aligned}
\text{Im}\left(p; y^4, x^5 - y^2\right) &= \text{Im}\left(p; y^3, x^5 - y^2\right) + 5 \\
&= \text{Im}\left(p; y^2, x^5 - y^2\right) + 10 \\
&= \text{Im}\left(p; y, x^5 - y^2\right) + 15 \\
&= 20.
\end{aligned}$$

Next we compute $\text{Im}\left(p; y^2, y^5 - z^2, x^5 - y^2\right)$. Here we have modular degrees in x: $r_x < 0, s_x < 0, t_x = 5$, thus we are in the orange case. Computing the modular degrees in y we get: $r_y = 2, s_y = 5$, hence we enter the pink case. The leading coefficient in y of $y^5 - z^2$ evaluated at $z = 0$ is a unit, hence the pink case computation is valid. Thus, let $g' = (y^5 - z^2) - y^3(y^2) = -z^2$ and compute $\text{Im}\left(p; y^2, -z^2, x^5 - y^2\right)$.

Computing the modular degrees with respect to y we get: $r_y = 2, s_z < 0$, hence we reorder y^2 and $-z^2$. Again, we enter the yellow case and the computation reduces to

$$\text{Im}\left(p; -z^2, y^2, x^5 - y^2\right) = \text{Im}\left(p; -z, y^2, x^5 - y^2\right) + \text{Im}\left(p; y, x^5 - y^2\right) + 5.$$

Clearly $\text{Im}\left(p; y, x^5 - y^2\right) = 5$ by Fulton's bivariate algorithm. The computation $\text{Im}\left(p; -z, y^2, x^5 - y^2\right)$ immediately satisfies the yellow case, hence we may split,

$$\begin{aligned}
\text{Im}\left(p; -z, y^2, x^5 - y^2\right) &= \text{Im}\left(p; -1, y^2, x^5 - y^2\right) + \text{Im}\left(p; y, x^5 - y^2\right) + 5 \\
&= 0 + 5 + 5 \\
&= 10.
\end{aligned}$$

Combining the intermediate computations, we get,

$$\text{Im}\left(p; zy^2, y^5 - z^2, x^5 - y^2\right) = 45.$$

Algorithm 2: Trivariate Fulton's Algorithm

---

1 **Function** $\mathrm{im}_3(p; f, g, h)$

    Input: Let: $x \succ y \succ z$

      1. $p \in \mathbb{A}^3$ the origin.

      2. $f, g, h \in \mathbb{K}[x, y, z]$ such that f, g, h form a regular sequence in $\mathcal{O}_{\mathbb{A}^3, p}$ or one of f, g, h is a unit in $\mathcal{O}_{\mathbb{A}^3, p}$.

    Output: $\mathrm{Im}(p; f, g, h)$ or Fail

2   **if** $f(p) \neq 0$ **or** $g(p) \neq 0$ **or** $h(p) \neq 0$ **then**   /* Red */

3   **return** 0

4     $r_y \leftarrow \mathrm{moddeg}(f, y)$, $r_x \leftarrow \mathrm{moddeg}(f, x)$

5     $s_y \leftarrow \mathrm{moddeg}(g, y)$, $s_x \leftarrow \mathrm{moddeg}(g, x)$

6     $t_y \leftarrow \mathrm{moddeg}(h, y)$, $t_x \leftarrow \mathrm{moddeg}(h, x)$

7   Reorder f, g, h so that $r_x \leq s_x \leq t_x$ /* Green */

8   **if** $r_x < 0$ **and** $s_x < 0$ **then**   /* Orange */

9   Reorder f, g so that $r_y \leq s_y$ /* Green */

10   **if** $r_y < 0$ **then**   /* Yellow */

11             $m_h \leftarrow max(m \in \mathbb{N} \mid h \mod \langle y, z \rangle = x^m(a_0 + a_1 x + \ldots))$

12             $q_f \leftarrow \mathrm{quo}(f, z; z)$

13             $q_g \leftarrow \mathrm{quo}(g(x, y, 0), y; y)$

14   **return** $\mathrm{im}_3(p; q_f, g, h) + \mathrm{im}(p; q_g, h(x, y, 0)) + m_h$

15   **else**   /* Pink */

16             $L_f \leftarrow \mathrm{lc}(f(x, y, 0); y)$

17             $L_g \leftarrow \mathrm{lc}(g(x, y, 0); y)$

18   **if** $L_f(p) \neq 0$ **then**

19                 $g' \leftarrow L_f g - y^{s_y - r_y} L_g f$

20   **return** $\mathrm{im}_3(p; f, g', h)$

21   **else if** $L_f \mid L_g$ **then**

22                 $g' \leftarrow g - y^{s_y - r_y} \frac{L_g}{L_f} f$

23   **return** $\mathrm{im}_3(p; f, g', h)$

24   **else**

25   **return** Fail

26   **else**   /* Blue */

27   **if** $r_x < 0$ **then**

28             $h' \leftarrow \mathrm{lc}(g(x, 0, 0); x)h - x^{t_x - s_x}\mathrm{lc}(h(x, 0, 0); x)g$

29   **return** $\mathrm{im}_3(p; f, g, h')$

30   **else**

31             $g' \leftarrow \mathrm{lc}(f(x, 0, 0); x)g - x^{s_x - r_x}\mathrm{lc}(g(x, 0, 0); x)f$

32             $h' \leftarrow \mathrm{lc}(f(x, 0, 0); x)h - x^{t_x - r_x}\mathrm{lc}(h(x, 0, 0); x)f$

33   **return** $\mathrm{im}_3(p; f, g', h')$

4   Generalized Fulton's Algorithm

In this section, we give a generalization of Algorithm 1 using properties $(n\text{-}1)$ to $(n\text{-}7)$. Unfortunately, the natural generalization using these properties does not characterize intersection multiplicities as in the bivariate case. There are two main reasons for this.

First, property $(n\text{-}6)$ requires the input polynomials form a regular sequence in order to split. In the bivariate case, splitting with $(2\text{-}6)$ was always possible. Thus, for our generalization, we must assume our input is a regular sequence whenever the intersection multiplicity is not zero.

Second, syzygy computations do not necessarily preserve intersection multiplicity in the n-variate case. In particular, if a leading coefficient used in the syzygy computation is not invertible in the local ring, $(n\text{-}7)$ may not be applicable. In the bivariate case, all leading coefficients considered in such a computation were units in the local ring. When such a case arises, other techniques must be used to complete the computation, and hence our generalization will signal an error.

Throughout this section we assume $p \in \mathbb{A}^n$ is the origin and $n > 1$.

Definition 6. *Let f be in $\mathbb{K}[x_1, \ldots, x_n]$ where $x_1 \succ \ldots \succ x_n$. We define the modular degree of f with respect to a variable $v \in V$ as $\deg_v (f \mod \langle V_{<v} \rangle)$, where $V = \{x_1, \ldots, x_n\}$ is the set of variables and $V_{<v}$ is the set of all variables less than v in the given ordering. If $V_{<v} = \emptyset$, we define the modular degree of f with respect to v to be the degree of f with respect to v. Write $\operatorname{moddeg}(f, v)$ to denote the modular degree of f with respect to v.*

Remark 4. The definition of modular degree can be generalized to a point $p = (p_1, \ldots, p_n) \in \mathbb{A}^n$ by replacing $V_{<v}$ with $V_{<v,p} = \{x_1 - p_1, \ldots, x_n - p_n\}$ in Definition 6.

Remark 5. When $f_1, \ldots, f_n \in \mathbb{K}[x_1, \ldots, x_n]$ form a regular sequence in $\mathcal{O}_{\mathbb{A}^n, p}$, the modular degrees of $f_1, \ldots, f_n$ can never be zero since $f_1, \ldots, f_n$ vanish at p.

Unlike in the trivariate case, it is no longer practical to partition the algorithm into coloured cases. Moreover, we will see that this does not accurately reflect the structure of the procedure. The main reason for this is that several of the cases we encountered in the past are instances of the same, more general case.

Roughly speaking, Algorithm 3 can be divided into 2 key parts. The first is the main loop which modifies the input using syzygy computations and reordering polynomials. The second is the splitting part, which occurs as a result of the main loop successfully terminating.

The purpose of the main loop, in the j-th iteration, is to create $n - j$ polynomials with modular degrees less than zero in x_j and in any variable larger than x_j. When we examine Algorithm 2 in this context, we see the orange and yellow case were simply conditions necessary to move forward an iteration in the main loop. Moreover, the syzygy computations in the blue and pink case were separate instances of the same process, which is used to reduce modular degrees for different iterations of the main loop. We highlight line 7 of Algorithm 3 with the colour orange to illustrate the similarities between moving forward an iteration in the loop and satisfying the orange case in Algorithm 2.

Recall in Algorithm 2 there were several possible syzygy computations that could be performed in the blue case, the deciding factor being, how many of the input polynomials had modular degree in x less than zero. Extending this to the context of the n-variate algorithm, in each iteration of the main loop, we check how many polynomials already satisfy the condition required to move forward an iteration. As in the blue case, this determines how many syzygy computations to perform and which polynomials will be used in said computations. To illustrate these similarities, we highlight line 11 of Algorithm 3 with the colour blue.

When the main loop terminates, assuming the procedure did not fail, our input system will have a of triangular shape with respect to modular degrees. That is, consider R, the $n \times n$ matrix of modular degrees, where $R_{i,j}$ is the modular degree of f_i with respect to x_j. Upon successful termination of the main loop, any entry of R which lies above the anti-diagonal will be negative infinity. Lemma 1, describes the implications of this triangular shape in terms of splitting intersection multiplicity computations. To illustrate the similarities between this splitting procedure, and the procedure used in the yellow case of Algorithm 2, we highlight line 22 of Algorithm 3 with the colour yellow.

As in the trivariate case, we cannot clearly characterize all cases for which Algorithm 3 fails before runtime, due to the difficulty in determining how an input will be rewritten and split. Nonetheless, it is still easy to determine whether an input will cause Algorithm 3 to fail in a given iteration of the main loop, as described in the proof of Theorem 3.

Lemma 1. *Let $f_1, \ldots, f_n$ be polynomials in $\mathbb{K}[x_1, \ldots, x_n]$ which form a regular sequence in $\mathcal{O}_{\mathbb{A}^n, p}$ where p is the origin. Let $V = \{x_1, \ldots, x_n\}$ and let $V_{>v} = \{x_i \in V \mid x_i > v\}$. Define the map $J : \{1, \ldots, n-1\} \to \{2, \ldots, n\}$ such that $J(i) = n - i + 1$.*

Suppose for all $i = 1, \ldots, n-1$ we have $\mathrm{moddeg}(f_i, v) < 0$ for all $v \in V_{>x_{J(i)}}$. Then, we have $x_{J(i)} \mid f_i(x_1, \ldots, x_{J(i)}, 0, \ldots, 0)$. Moreover, if we define $q_i = quo(f_i(x_1, \ldots, x_{J(i)}, 0, \ldots, 0), x_{J(i)}; x_{J(i)})$ then,

$$\mathrm{Im}(p; f_1, \ldots, f_n) = \mathrm{Im}(p; q_1, f_2, \ldots, f_n) + \mathrm{Im}(p; x_n, q_2, \ldots, f_n)$$
$$+ \ldots + \mathrm{Im}\big(p; x_n, \ldots, x_{J(i)+1}, q_i, f_{i+1}, \ldots, f_n\big) + \cdots$$
$$+ \mathrm{Im}(p; x_n, x_{n-1}, \ldots, q_{n-1}, f_n) + m_n,$$

where $m_n = max(m \in \mathbb{Z}^+ \mid f_n(x_1, 0, \ldots, 0) \equiv 0 \mod \langle x_1^m \rangle)$.

Proof: First we will show that we can write $f_i(x_1, \ldots, x_{J(i)}, 0, \ldots, 0) = x_{J(i)} q_i$ for all $i = 1, \ldots, n-1$.

Suppose $x_n, \ldots, x_{J(i)+1}, f_i, \ldots, f_n$ is a regular sequence for some $1 \leq i < n$. The hypothesis $\mathrm{moddeg}(f_i, x_1), \ldots, \mathrm{moddeg}(f_i, x_{J(i)-1}) < 0$ and the fact that f_i is regular modulo $\langle x_{J(i)+1}, \ldots, x_n \rangle$ and vanishes at the origin implies $x_{J(i)}$ divides $f_i(x_1, \ldots, x_{J(i)}, 0, \ldots, 0)$.

Algorithm 3: Generalized Fulton's Algorithm

---

1 **Function** $\text{im}_n(p; f_1, \ldots, f_n)$

   Input: Let: $x_1 \succ \ldots \succ x_n$, $n \geq 2$

   1. $p \in \mathbb{A}^n$ the origin.
   2. $f_1, \ldots, f_n \in \mathbb{K}[x_1, \ldots, x_n]$ such that $f_1, \ldots, f_n$ form a regular sequence in $\mathcal{O}_{\mathbb{A}^n, p}$ or one such f_i is a unit in $\mathcal{O}_{\mathbb{A}^n, p}$.

   Output: $\text{Im}(p; f_1, \ldots, f_n)$ or Fail

2 **if** $f_i(p) \neq 0$ for any $i=1,\ldots,n$ **then**   /* Red */
3 | **return** 0

4 **for** $i = 1, \ldots, n$ **do**
5 | **for** $j = 1, \ldots, n - 1$ **do**
6 | | $r_j^{(i)} \leftarrow \text{moddeg}(f_i, x_j)$

7 **for** $j = 1, \ldots, n - 1$ **do**   /* Orange */
8 | Reorder $f_1, \ldots, f_{n-j+1}$ so that $r_j^{(1)} \leq \ldots \leq r_j^{(n-j+1)}$ /* Green */
9 | $m \leftarrow min(i \mid r_j^{(i)} > 0)$ or $m \leftarrow \infty$ if no such i exists
10 | **if** $m \leq (n - j)$ **then**
11 | | **for** $i = m + 1, \ldots, n - j + 1$ **do**   /* Blue */
12 | | | $d \leftarrow r_j^{(i)} - r_j^{(m)}$
13 | | | $L_m \leftarrow \text{lc}(f_m(x_1, \ldots, x_j, 0, \ldots, 0); x_j)$
14 | | | $L_i \leftarrow \text{lc}(f_i(x_1, \ldots, x_j, 0, \ldots, 0); x_j)$
15 | | | **if** $L_m(p) \neq 0$ **then**
16 | | | | $f_i' \leftarrow L_m f_i - x_j^d L_i f_m$
17 | | | **else if** $L_m \mid L_i$ **then**
18 | | | | $f_i' \leftarrow f_i - x_j^d \frac{L_i}{L_m} f_m$
19 | | | **else**
20 | | | | **return** Fail
21 | | **return** $\text{im}_n(p; f_1, \ldots, f_m, f_{m+1}', \ldots, f_{n-j+1}', \ldots, f_n)$

22   /* Yellow */
23 $m_n \leftarrow max(m \in \mathbb{Z}^+ \mid f_n(x_1, 0, \ldots, 0) \equiv 0 \mod \langle x_1^m \rangle)$
24 **for** $i = 1, \ldots, n - 1$ **do**
25 | $q_i \leftarrow \text{quo}(f_i(x_1, \ldots, x_{n-i+1}, 0, \ldots, 0), x_{n-i+1}; x_{n-i+1})$

26 **return**
27 $\text{im}_n(p; q_1, f_2, \ldots, f_n)$
28 $+ \text{im}_{n-1}(p; q_2(x_1, \ldots, x_{n-1}, 0), \ldots, f_n(x_1, \ldots, x_{n-1}, 0))$
29 $+$

30 $\vdots$
31 $+\text{im}_2(p; q_{n-1}(x_1, x_2, 0, \ldots, 0), f_n(x_1, x_2, 0, \ldots, 0))$
32 $+m_n$

To show $x_n, \ldots, x_{J(i)+1}, f_i, \ldots, f_n$ is a regular sequence for all $1 \leq i < n$, it suffices to show $x_n, f_2, \ldots, f_n$ is a regular sequence, since repeated applications of Proposition 4, and the above implication will yield the desired result.

Observe $moddeg(f_1, x_1), \ldots, moddeg(f_1, x_{n-1}) < 0$ and f_1 is a non-zero polynomial which vanishes at the origin, and hence, must be divisible by x_n. By applying Proposition 4 we get $x_n, f_2, \ldots, f_n$ is a regular sequence.

Since $f_1, \ldots, f_n$ is a regular sequence we may apply $(n\text{-}6)$ to get

$$\text{Im}(p; f_1, \ldots, f_n) = \text{Im}(p; x_n, f_2, \ldots, f_n) + \text{Im}(p; q_1, f_2, \ldots, f_n).$$

By definition of intersection multiplicity,

$$\text{Im}(p; x_n, f_2, \ldots, f_n) = \text{Im}(p; x_n, f_2(x_1, \ldots, x_{n-1}, 0), \ldots, f_n(x_1, \ldots, x_{n-1}, 0)).$$

Continuing in this way we get,

$$\text{Im}(p; f_1, \ldots, f_n) = \text{Im}(p; q_1, f_2, \ldots, f_n) + \text{Im}(p; x_n, q_2, \ldots, f_n) + \cdots$$
$$+ \text{Im}(p; x_n, x_{n-1}, \ldots, q_{n-1}, f_n) + \text{Im}(p; x_n, \ldots, x_2, f_n).$$

By definition of intersection multiplicity,

$$\text{Im}(p; x_n, \ldots, x_2, f_n) = max(m \in \mathbb{Z}^+ \mid f_n(x_1, 0, \ldots, 0) \equiv 0 \mod \langle x_1^m \rangle),$$

which completes the proof. □

Corollary 2. *When the conditions of Lemma 1 hold,*

$$\text{Im}(p; f_1, \ldots, f_n) = \text{Im}(p; q_1, f_2, \ldots, f_n)$$
$$+ \text{Im}(p; q_2(x_1, \ldots, x_{n-1}, 0), \ldots, f_n(x_1, \ldots, x_{n-1}, 0)) +$$
$$\vdots$$
$$+ \text{Im}(p; q_{n-1}(x_1, x_2, 0, \ldots, 0), f_n(x_1, x_2, 0, \ldots, 0))$$
$$+ m_n.$$

Proof: Follows from Lemma 1 and the definition of intersection multiplicity. □

Theorem 3. *Algorithm 3 correctly computes the intersection multiplicity of a regular sequence $f_1, \ldots, f_n \in \mathbb{K}[x_1, \ldots, x_n]$ or returns Fail.*

Proof: Let $f_1, \ldots, f_n \in \mathbb{K}[x_1, \ldots, x_n]$ be a regular sequence in $\mathcal{O}_{\mathbb{A}^n, p}$. By $(n\text{-}3)$ we may assume p is the origin. By Proposition 2, $\mathbf{V}(f_1, \ldots, f_n)$ is zero-dimensional, hence by $(n\text{-}1)$ we may assume $\text{Im}(p; f_1, \ldots, f_n) \in \mathbb{N}$.

To prove termination we induct on $\text{Im}(p; f_1, \ldots, f_n)$, and show that when Algorithm 3 does not return Fail, we can either compute $\text{Im}(p; f_1, \ldots, f_n)$ directly or strictly decrease $\text{Im}(p; f_1, \ldots, f_n)$ through splitting.

Suppose $\text{Im}(p; f_1, \ldots, f_n) = 0$, then by $(n\text{-}2)$, one of $f_1, \ldots, f_n$ does not vanish at p, hence Algorithm 3 correctly returns zero. Thus, we may assume $\text{Im}(p; f_1, \ldots, f_n) = N$ for some positive $N \in \mathbb{N}$.

First, we claim that either Algorithm 3 returns Fail or the input polynomials can be modified while preserving intersection multiplicity such that they satisfy the conditions of Lemma 1. Moreover, we claim such modifications can be performed in finitely many iterations. To modify the input such that they satisfy the conditions of Lemma 1, we proceed iteratively.

Fix some x_j where $1 \le j \le n - 1$, and suppose $f_1, \ldots, f_{n-j+k}$ all have modular degree in x_{j-k} less than zero for any $1 \le k < j$ whenever $j > 1$. Notice $f_1, \ldots, f_{n-j+1}$ are the polynomials which have modular degree less than zero in all variables greater then x_j. By $(n\text{-}4)$ and Corollary 1 we may rearrange $f_1, \ldots, f_{n-j+1}$ so that their modular degrees with respect to x_j are ascending.

To satisfy the conditions of Lemma 1, in the j-th iteration we must have $n - j$ polynomials in $\{f_1, \ldots, f_{n-j+1}\}$ with modular degree in x_j less than zero. Since the modular degrees are in ascending order we may compute,

$$m = \begin{cases} min(i \mid \operatorname{moddeg}(f_i, x_j) > 0) & \text{if such an } i \text{ exists,} \\ \infty & \text{otherwise.} \end{cases}$$

If $m > n - j$ then $f_1, \ldots, f_{n-j}$ satisfy the conditions of Lemma 1 for the variable x_j and hence we are done.

Suppose $m \le n - j$. We will use f_m in a syzygy computation with f_i for all $i = m + 1, \ldots, n - j + 1$ to reduce the modular degree of each f_i with respect to x_j. Define,

$$L_m = \operatorname{lc}(f_m(x_1, \ldots, x_j, 0, \ldots, 0); x_j),$$

$$L_i = \operatorname{lc}(f_i(x_1, \ldots, x_j, 0, \ldots, 0); x_j),$$

and

$$d = \operatorname{moddeg}(f_i, x_j) - \operatorname{moddeg}(f_m, x_j).$$

If $L_m(p) = 0$ and there is an i such that $L_i \nmid L_m$, then $(n\text{-}7)$ will not preserve intersection multiplicity under the syzygy computation since L_m is not a unit in the local ring. When this case occurs, we return Fail.

Suppose either $L_m(p) \ne 0$ or for all i we have $L_m \mid L_i$. In which case, $(n\text{-}7)$ allows us to replace f_i with $f_i' = L_m f_i - x^d L_i f_m$ or $f_i' = f_i - x^d \frac{L_i}{L_m} f_m$ respectively. Moreover, Proposition 3 tells us such a substitution preserves regular sequences.

Notice if $j > 1$, then $\operatorname{moddeg}(f_i', x_{j-k}) < 0$ for all $1 \le k < j$, since, by assumption, both f_i and f_m have modular degree in x_{j-k} less than zero. Thus, making such a substitution preserves the assumptions of our hypothesis. Lastly, since $\operatorname{moddeg}(f_i', x_j) < \operatorname{moddeg}(f_i, x_j)$, we will have $n - j$ polynomials with modular degree in x_j less than zero or return Fail, in finitely many iterations.

Thus we may now assume $f_1, \ldots, f_n$ satisfy the conditions of Lemma 1, hence the algorithm correctly splits computations by Lemma 1 and Corollary 2.

To show termination, we may suppose none of the split computations fail, since in such a case, termination is immediate. Since m_n, as defined in Lemma 1, is a positive integer, each term has intersection multiplicity strictly less than $\operatorname{Im}(p; f_1, \ldots, f_n) = N$ and hence termination follows by induction. $\square$

5   Triangular Regular Sequences

In this section we consider input systems with a triangular shape. We observe that under a mild constraint, such a system is a regular sequence. Moreover, the triangular shape combined with being a regular sequence allows us to compute the intersection multiplicity of such a system using $(n\text{-}6)$.

At this time there are no known triangular decomposition techniques that preserve intersection multiplicity for a polynomial ideal in the local ring; although, if such a technique were to be discovered, the following observation could lead to a complete algorithm for computing intersection multiplicity.

Definition 7. *The main variable of a polynomial $f \in \mathbb{K}[x_1, \ldots, x_n]$ where $x_1 \succ \ldots \succ x_n$ is the largest variable x_i such that $\mathrm{lc}(f; x_i)$ is non-zero.*

Theorem 4 (McCoy's Theorem). *Let f be a non-zero polynomial in $R[x]$ where R is a commutative ring. Then f is a regular element of $R[x]$ if and only if ever non-zero $s \in R$ is such that $sf \neq 0$.*

McCoy's Theorem is a well-known result proven in [8].

Corollary 3. *Consider a sequence $t_1, \ldots, t_n$ such that for $i = 1, \ldots, n$, each t_i is a non-zero polynomial in $\mathbb{K}[x_i, \ldots, x_n]$ with main variable x_i.*

If at least one non-zero coefficient of t_{i-1} is invertible modulo $\langle t_i, \ldots, t_n \rangle$ for all $1 < i \leq n$, then $t_1, \ldots, t_n$ is a regular sequence in $\mathbb{K}[x_1, \ldots, x_n]$. If $t_1, \ldots, t_n$ also vanish on $p \in \mathbb{A}^n$ then $t_1, \ldots, t_n$ is a regular sequence in $\mathcal{O}_{\mathbb{A}^n, p}$.

Proof: The first statement follows from Theorem 4, the second statement follows from the first statement and Proposition 5.   □

Proposition 8. *Consider a sequence $t_1, \ldots, t_n$ such that for $i = 1, \ldots, n$, each t_i is a non-zero polynomial in $\mathbb{K}[x_i, \ldots, x_n]$ with main variable x_i.*

Suppose each $t_1, \ldots, t_n$ vanish at the origin, which we denote by p, and suppose at least one non-zero coefficient of t_{i-1} is invertible modulo $\langle t_i, \ldots, t_n \rangle$ for $1 < i \leq n$.

Then we may write $t_i(x_i, 0, \ldots, 0)$ as $x_i^{m_i} f_i$ where m_i is the least positive integer such that $f_i \in \mathbb{K}[x_i]$ does not vanish at the origin. Moreover,

$$\mathrm{Im}(p; t_1, \ldots, t_n) = m_1 \cdot \ldots \cdot m_n.$$

Proof: The result is trivial for $n = 1$, so we may assume $n > 1$. Since $t_i(x_i, 0, \ldots, 0)$ is a non-zero univariate polynomial in $\mathbb{K}[x_i]$ which vanishes at the origin, we may write $t_i(x_i, 0, \ldots, 0) = x_i^{m_i} f_i$ for a positive integer m_i and f_i a unit in the local ring at p.

By Corollary 3, $t_1, \ldots, t_n$ is a regular sequence in $\mathcal{O}_{\mathbb{A}^n, p}$. Hence, we may apply $(n\text{-}6)$ and Proposition 4 repeatedly and finally $(n\text{-}5)$ to get,

$$
\begin{aligned}
\mathrm{Im}(p;\, t_1, \ldots, t_n) &= \mathrm{Im}(p;\, t_1, \ldots, t_{n-1}, x_n^{m_n} f_n) \\
&= \mathrm{Im}(p;\, t_1, \ldots, t_{n-1}, x_n^{m_n}) + \mathrm{Im}(p;\, t_1, \ldots, f_n) \\
&= m_n \mathrm{Im}(p;\, t_1, \ldots, t_{n-1}(x_{n-1}, 0), x_n) + 0 \\
&= m_n \mathrm{Im}\left(p;\, t_1, \ldots, x_{n-1}^{m_{n-1}} f_{n-1}, x_n\right) \\
&= m_n m_{n-1} \mathrm{Im}(p;\, t_1, \ldots, x_{n-1}, x_n) + 0 \\
&\;\;\vdots \\
&= m_1 \cdot \ldots \cdot m_n \mathrm{Im}(p;\, x_1, \ldots, x_n) \\
&= m_1 \cdot \ldots \cdot m_n.
\end{aligned}
$$

$\square$

References

1. Alvandi, P., Maza, M.M., Schost, É., Vrbik, P.: A standard basis free algorithm for computing the tangent cones of a space curve. In: Gerdt, V.P., Koepf, W., Seiler, W.M., Vorozhtsov, E.V. (eds.) CASC 2015. LNCS, vol. 9301, pp. 45–60. Springer, Cham (2015). https://doi.org/10.1007/978-3-319-24021-3_4
2. Cox, D., Little, J., O'Shea, D.: Using Algebraic Geometry. Graduate Text in Mathematics, vol. 185. Springer, New York (1998). https://doi.org/10.1007/978-1-4757-6911-1
3. Fulton, W.: Algebraic Curves - An Introduction to Algebraic Geometry (reprint from 1969). Addison-Wesley, Advanced book classics (1989)
4. Greuel, G.M., Pfister, G.: A Singular Introduction to Commutative Algebra. Springer, Heidelberg (2012). https://doi.org/10.1007/978-3-540-73542-7
5. Kaplansky, I.: Commutative Rings, 3rd edn. The University of Chicago Press, Chicago (1974). Ill.-London, revised edn
6. Marcus, S., Maza, M.M., Vrbik, P.: On Fulton's algorithm for computing intersection multiplicities. In: Gerdt, V.P., Koepf, W., Mayr, E.W., Vorozhtsov, E.V. (eds.) CASC 2012. LNCS, vol. 7442, pp. 198–211. Springer, Heidelberg (2012). https://doi.org/10.1007/978-3-642-32973-9_17
7. Matsumura, H.: Commutative Algebra, Mathematics Lecture Note Series, vol. 56, 2nd edn. Benjamin/Cummings Publishing Co. Inc., Reading (1980)
8. McCoy, N.H.: Remarks on divisors of zero. Amer. Math. Mon. **49**, 286–295 (1942). https://doi.org/10.2307/2303094
9. Vrbik, P.: Computing intersection multiplicity via triangular decomposition. Ph.D. thesis, The University of Western Ontario (2014)

On the Pseudo-Periodicity of the Integer Hull of Parametric Convex Polygons

Marc Moreno Maza and Linxiao Wang[(✉)]

University of Western Ontario, London, ON, Canada
{mmorenom,lwang739}@uwo.ca

Abstract. Consider a rational convex polygon given by a system of linear inequalities $A\vec{x} \leq \vec{b}$, where A is a matrix over $\mathbb{Z}$, with m rows and 2 columns, and $\vec{b}$ is an integer vector. The coordinates $b_1, \ldots, b_m$ of $\vec{b}$ are treated as parameters while the coefficients of A have fixed values. We observe that for every $1 \leq i \leq m$, there exists a positive integer T_i so that, when each $b_1, \ldots, b_m$ is large enough, the vertex sets V and V' of the respective integer hulls of $P := P(b_1, \ldots, b_{i-1}, b_i, b_{i+1}, \ldots, b_m)$ and $P' := P(b_1, \ldots, b_{i-1}, b_i + T_i, b_{i+1}, \ldots, b_m)$, respectively, are in a "simple" one-to-one correspondence. We state and prove explicit formulas for the pseudo-period T_i and that correspondence between V and V'. This result and the ingredients of its proof lead us to propose a new algorithm for computing the integer hull of a rational convex polygon.

Keywords: Parametric convex polygon · Integer hull · Pseudo-periodic functions

1 Introduction

The integer points of rational polyhedral sets are of great interest in various areas of scientific computing. Two such areas are *combinatorial optimization* (in particular integer linear programming) and *compiler optimization* (in particular, the analysis, transformation and scheduling of for-loop nests in computer programs), where a variety of algorithms solve questions related to the points with integer coordinates belonging to a given polyhedron. Another area is at the crossroads of computer algebra and polyhedral geometry, with topics like toric ideals and Hilbert bases, see for instance [16] by Thomas.

One can ask different questions about the integer points of a polyhedral set, ranging from "whether or not a given rational polyhedron has integer points" to "describing all such points". Answers to that latter question can take various forms, depending on the targeted application. For plotting purposes, one may want to enumerate all the integer points of a 2D or 3D polytope. Meanwhile, in the context of combinatorial optimization or compiler optimization, more concise descriptions are sufficient and more effective.

For a rational convex polyhedron $P \subseteq \mathbb{Q}^d$, defined either by the set of its facets or that of its vertices, one such description is the *integer hull* P_I of P, that

© Springer Nature Switzerland AG 2021
F. Boulier et al. (Eds.): CASC 2021, LNCS 12865, pp. 252–271, 2021.
https://doi.org/10.1007/978-3-030-85165-1_15

is, the convex hull of $P \cap \mathbb{Z}^d$. The set P_I is itself polyhedral and can be described either by its facets, or its vertices. One important family of algorithms for computing the vertex set of P_I relies on the so-called *cutting plane method*, originally introduced by Gomory in [7] to solve integer linear programs. Chvátal [3] and Schrijver [13] developed a procedure to compute P_I based on that latter method. Schrijver gave a full proof and a complexity study of this method in [12]. Another approach for computing P_I uses the *branch and bound method*, introduced by Land and Doig in the early 1960s in [8]. This method recursively divides P into sub-polyhedra, then the vertices of the integer hull of each part of the partition are computed.

In addition to finding the description of the whole integer hull P_I another problem that is well studied is that of counting the integer points in a rational polyhedron. A well-known theory on that latter subject was proposed by Pick [11]. In particular, the celebrated Pick's theorem provides a formula for the area of a simple polygon P with integer vertex coordinates, in terms of the number of integer points within P and on its boundary. In the 1990s, Barvinok [1] created an algorithm for counting the integer points inside a polyhedron, which runs in polynomial time, for a fixed dimension of the ambient space. Later studies such as [21] gave a simpler approach for lattice point counting, which divides a polygon into *right-angle triangles* and calculates the number of lattice points within each such triangle. In 2004, the software package LattE presented in [9] for lattice point enumeration, offers the first implementation of Barvinok's algorithm.

In practice, polyhedral sets are often *parametric*. Consider for instance the for-loop nest, written in a programming language (say C) of a dense matrix multiplication algorithm. At compile time, the upper bound of the value range of each loop counter is a symbol. To be more precise, the iterations of that for-loop nest are the integer points of a polyhedral set P given by a system of linear inequalities $A\vec{x} \leq \vec{b}$ where A is a matrix with integer coefficients, $\vec{b}$ is a vector of symbols (actually the parameters of the polyhedral set) and $\vec{x}$ is the vector of the loop counters. At execution time, different values of $\vec{b}$ yield different shapes and numbers of vertices for P_I. So what can be done at compile time? This is the question motivating this paper. But before we present our results, let us continue our literature review, returning to the problem of counting the number of integer points in (parametric) polytopes. Verdoolaege, Seghir, Beyls, Loechner and Bruynooghe present in [17] a novel method for that latter problem, based on Barvinok's decomposition for counting the number of integer points in a non-parametric polytope. In [15], Seghir, Loechner and Meister deal with the more general problem of counting the number of images by an affine integer transformation of the lattice points contained in a parametric polytope.

Since the present paper is concerned with the integer hull of a parametric polyhedron, it is natural to ask for the number of vertices in an integer hull of a polyhedron. Note that this problem only considers the vertices not all the lattice points. The earliest study by Cook, Hartmann, Kannan and McDiarmid, in [4], shows that the number of vertices of P_I is related to the *size* (as defined in [12]) of the coefficients of the inequalities that describe P. More recent studies such as [18] and [2] use different approaches to reach similar or slightly improved estimates.

We turn our attention to the main result of our paper. We consider a rational convex polygon (that is, a rational polyhedral set of dimension 2) given by a system of linear inequalities $A\vec{x} \leq \vec{b}$, where A is a matrix over $\mathbb{Z}$, with m rows and $d = 2$ columns, and $\vec{b}$ is an integer vector. The coordinates $b_1, \ldots, b_m$ of $\vec{b}$ are treated as parameters, while the coefficients of A have fixed values. We observe that for every $1 \leq i \leq m$, there exists a positive integer T_i so that, when each $b_1, \ldots, b_m$ is large enough, the vertex sets V and V' of the respectively integer hulls of

$$P := P(b_1, \ldots, b_{i-1}, b_i, b_{i+1}, \ldots, b_m)$$

and

$$P' := P(b_1, \ldots, b_{i-1}, b_i + T_i, b_{i+1}, \ldots, b_m),$$

respectively, are in "simple" one-to-one correspondence. Here, simple, means that one can construct a partition $V_1, \ldots, V_c$ of V and a partition $V'_1, \ldots, V'_c$ of V', together with vectors $\vec{u}_1, \ldots, \vec{u}_c$ of $\mathbb{Z}^2$ so that every vertex of V'_i is the image of a vertex of V_i by the translation of $\vec{u}_i$, for all $1 \leq i \leq c$. Section 5 offers various examples, including animated images, which illustrate our result. Watching those animations requires to use a modern document viewer like Okular. The animations are also available at https://github.com/lxwangruc/parametric_integer_hull.

While the arguments yielding to our main result are elementary, the proof is relatively long and technical. The first and main step is a study of the *pseudo-periodicity* of a parametric angular section, see Sect. 3. Since a convex polygon is an intersection of finitely many angular sectors, angular sectors are the building blocks of our main result, see Sect. 4, where the partitions of $V_1, \ldots, V_c$ of V, $V'_1, \ldots, V'_c$ of V', and the vectors $\vec{u}_1, \ldots, \vec{u}_c$ are explicitly given. This result and the ingredients of its proof lead us to propose a new algorithm for computing the integer hull of a rational convex polygon, see Sect. 6.

We note that in [10] Meister presents a new method for computing the integer hull of a parameterized rational polyhedron. The author introduces a concept of periodic polyhedron (with facets given by equalities depending on periodic numbers). Hence, the word "periodic" means that the polyhedron can be defined in a periodic manner which is different from our perspective.

Last but not least, we recall the work of Eugème Ehrhart from his articles [6] and [5]. For each integer $n \geq 1$, Ehrhart defined the *dilation* of the polyhedron P by n as the polyhedron $nP = \{nq \in \mathbb{Q}^d \mid q \in P\}$. Ehrhart studied the number of lattice points in nP, that is:

$$i(P, n) = \#(nP \cap \mathbb{Z}^d) = \#\{q \in P \mid nq \in Z^d\}.$$

He proved that there exists an integer $N > 0$ and polynomials $f_0, f_1, \ldots, f_{N-1}$ such that $i(P, n) = f_i(n)$ if $n \equiv i \mod N$. The quantity $i(P, n)$ is called the *Ehrhart quasi-polynomial* of P, in the dilation variable n. Ehrhart's study on quasi-polynomials is focused on counting the lattice points and can be seen as a higher-dimensional generalization of Pick's theorem. Meanwhile our research on the pseudo-periodicity of a parametric convex polygon studies the number and coordinates of the vertices of the integer hull.

2   Preliminaries

In this review of polyhedral geometry, we follow the concepts and notations of Schrijver's book [12], As usual, we denote by $\mathbb{Z}$, $\mathbb{Q}$ and $\mathbb{R}$ the ring of integers, the field of rational numbers and the field of real numbers. Unless specified otherwise, all matrices and vectors have their coefficients in $\mathbb{Z}$. A subset $P \subseteq \mathbb{Q}^d$ is called a *convex polyhedron* (or simply a *polyhedron*) if $P = \{\vec{x} \in \mathbb{Q}^d \mid A\vec{x} \leq \vec{b}\}$ holds, for a matrix $A \in \mathbb{Q}^{m \times d}$ and a vector $\vec{b} \in \mathbb{Q}^m$, where m and d are positive integers; we call the linear system $\{A\vec{x} \leq \vec{b}\}$ an *H-representation* of P. Hence, a polyhedron is the intersection of finitely many affine half-spaces. Here an affine half-space is a set of the form $\{\vec{x} \in \mathbb{Q}^d \mid \vec{w}^t\vec{x} \leq \delta\}$ for some nonzero vector $\vec{w} \in \mathbb{Z}^d$ and an integer number δ. When $d = 2$, as in the rest of this paper, the term *convex polygon* is used for convex polyhedron.

A non-empty subset $F \subseteq P$ is a *face* of P if $F = \{\vec{x} \in P \mid A'\vec{x} = \vec{b}'\}$ for some subsystem $A'\vec{x} \leq \vec{b}'$ of $A\vec{x} \leq b$. A face distinct from P and with maximum dimension is a *facet* of P. The *lineality space* of P is $\{\vec{x} \in \mathbb{Q}^d \mid A\vec{x} = \vec{0}\}$ and P is said *pointed* if its lineality space has dimension zero. Note that, in this paper, we only consider pointed polyhedra. For a pointed polyhedron P, the inclusion-minimal faces are the *vertices* of P.

We are interested in computing P_I the *integer hull* of P, that is, the smallest convex polyhedron containing the integer points of P. In other words, P_I is the intersection of all convex polyhedra containing $P \cap \mathbb{Z}^d$. If P is pointed, then $P = P_I$ if and only if every vertex of P is integral [14]. Therefore, the convex hull of all the vertices of P_I is P_I itself.

In this paper, we also talk about parametric polyhedra. In particular, we use the notation $P(\vec{b}) = \{\vec{x} \mid A\vec{x} \leq \vec{b}\}$ where $\vec{b}$ is unknown and $P(b_i) = \{\vec{x} \mid A\vec{x} \leq \vec{b}\}$ where b_i is an unknown coordinate of the vector $\vec{b}$.

3   The Integer Hull of an Angular Sector

Lemma 1 is an elementary result which gives a necessary and sufficient condition for a line in the affine plane to have integer points. With Lemma 2, we show that every angular sector S without integer points on its facets can be replaced by a angular sector S' with integer points on both of its facets and so that S and S' have the same integer hull. With Lemma 3, we perform another reduction step: we show how the computation of the integer hull of an angular sector with integer points on its facets can be reduced to that of the integer hull of a triangle with at least two integer vertices.

Theorem 1 is our main result specialized to the case of a parametric angular sector. In other words, Theorem 1 describes the pseudo-periodical phenomenon observed when varying one of the "right-hand side" parameters over a sufficiently large range of consecutive integer values. In fact, Theorem 1 precisely gives a formula for the period as well as a formula for transforming the integer hull of the parametric angular sector over a period.

Definition 1. *An* angular sector *in an affine plane is defined by the intersection of two half-planes whose boundaries intersect in a single point, called the* vertex *of that angular sector.*

Lemma 1. *In the affine plane, with Cartesian coordinates (x, y), consider a line with equation $ax + cy = b$ where a, b and c are all integers so that there is no common divisor among them, that is, $\gcd(a, b, c) = 1$. Then, three cases arise:*

- *Case 1. If $a \neq 0$ and $c \neq 0$ then there are integer points along the line if and only if a and c are coprime. Moreover, if $\gcd(a, c) = 1$ holds, then a point (x, y) on the line is integral if and only if we have:*

$$x \equiv \frac{b}{a} \quad \text{mod } c.$$

- *Case 2. If $a = 0$, then c must equal to 1 for the line to have integer points. Moreover, if $c = 1$, then a point (x, y) on the line is integral if and only if x is an integer.*
- *Case 3. If $c = 0$, then a must equal to 1 for the line to have integer points. Moreover, if $a = 1$ holds, then a point (x, y) on the line is integral if and only if y is an integer.*

PROOF ▷ For Case 1, the y coordinate of a point (x, y) on the line must satisfy:

$$y = \frac{b - ax}{c}$$

For each integer x, the above y is an integer if and only if we have:

$$b - ax \equiv 0 \quad \text{mod } c.$$

Therefore, every point (x, y) on the line is an integer point if and only if x is an integer satisfying

$$b \equiv ax \quad \text{mod } c.$$

If $\gcd(a, c) = 1$ holds, then a is invertible modulo c and every integer x congruent to $\frac{b}{a}$ mod c is a solution. If a and c are not coprime and if the above equation has a solution in x then $\gcd(a, b, c) = 1$ cannot hold, which is a contradiction. Therefore, the line admits integer points if and only if $\gcd(a, c) = 1$ holds. Moreover, when this holds, those points (x, y) satisfy:

$$x \equiv \frac{b}{a} \quad \text{mod } c,$$

For Case 2, with $a = 0$, the condition becomes $\gcd(b, c) = 1$ and the line now writes $cy = b$. Therefore, $\frac{b}{c}$ must be integer in order to have integer points on the line, which means c must equal to 1. Case 3 is similar to Case 2. ◁

Lemma 2. *In the affine plane, with Cartesian coordinates (x, y), let S be a angular sector defined by*

$$\begin{cases} a_1 x + c_1 y \leq b_1 \\ a_2 x + c_2 y \leq b_2 \end{cases}.$$

Then, one can find another angular sector S', given by

$$\begin{cases} a_1 x + c_1 y \leq b_1' \\ a_2 x + c_2 y \leq b_2 \end{cases}.$$

such that $\frac{a_1}{g}$ and $\frac{c_1}{g}$ are coprime where $g = \gcd(a_1, c_1, b_1') \geq 1$ and so that the integer hull of S' is the same as that of S.

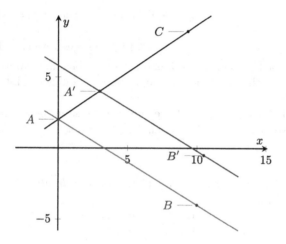

Fig. 1. The integer hull of sector BAC is the same as that of sector $B'AC'$

PROOF ▷ Let A be the vertex of S. Let B (resp. C) be a point on the facet of S with equation $a_1 x + c_1 y = b_1$ (resp. $a_2 x + c_2 y = b_2$). The general idea is to construct S' by sliding A to the vertex A' of S' along the line (AC), with the facets of S' being given by $(A'C)$ and $(A'B')$ so that

1. $(A'B')$ and (AB) are parallel lines with no integer points between them, meanwhile
2. $(A'B')$ has integer points.

Details follow, including corner cases. Three cases arise:

- Case 1. If a_1 and c_1 are non-zero integers and coprime, then, by Lemma 1, one can choose $S' = S$, thus $A' = A$ and $b_1' = b_1$.
- Case 2. If a_1 and c_1 are non-zero but a_1 is not coprime to c_1, then we have $g := \gcd(a_1, c_1) > 1$. Let C have coordinate (x_C, y_C). Two cases arise.

- Case 2.1. If $y_C > -\frac{a_1}{c_1} x_C + \frac{b_1}{c_1}$ (as in Fig. 1), then we can choose $b'_1 = \lceil \frac{b_1}{g} \rceil g$. Since $b'_1 > b_1$ and C is above (AB), the line $(A'B')$ is closer to C than (AB). We want to prove that there's no integer point between $(A'B')$ and (AB). Assume, by contradiction, there is an integer point X between $(A'B')$ and (AB). Then, a line $a_1 x + c_1 y = b''_1$ must pass through X such that $b_1 < b''_1 < b'_1$ and $b''_1 \mod g \equiv 0$ both hold. Since we chose $b'_1 = \lfloor \frac{b_1}{g} \rfloor g$, the integer b''_1 cannot exist. Therefore, there is no integer point between $(A'B')$ and (AB). Since all the integer points in S are also in S', the integer hull of S' must be the same as that of S.
  - Case 2.2. If $y_C < -\frac{a_1}{c_1} x_C + \frac{b_1}{c_1}$ holds, then we can choose $b'_1 = \lfloor \frac{b_1}{g} \rfloor g$. And the proof is similar to that of the previous case.
- Case 3. Now we consider the case where either a_1 or c_1 is zero. Three cases arise:
  - Case 3.1. Assume $a_1 = 0$, if $\frac{b_1}{c_1}$ is an integer, then we can choose $b'_1 = b_1$, that is $S' = S$.
  - Case 3.2. If $a_1 = 0$ and $\frac{b_1}{c_1}$ is not an integer, then we can choose b_1 to be $\lfloor \frac{b_1}{c_1} \rfloor \times c_1$ or $\lceil \frac{b_1}{c_1} \rceil \times c_1$ depending on the relationship between C and (AB). Similarly to the discussion above, there is no integer point between (AB) and $(A'B')$.
  - Case 3.3. Finally, If $c_1 = 0$, we can use the same proof as when $a_1 = 0$, except we need to see if $\frac{b_1}{a_1}$ is an integer or not.

◁

Lemma 3. *In the affine plane, with Cartesian coordinates (x, y), let S be an angular sector defined by*

$$\begin{cases} a_1 x + c_1 y \leq b_1 \\ a_2 x + c_2 y \leq b_2 \end{cases},$$

where $\gcd(a_i, b_i, c_i) = 1$ for $i \in \{1, 2\}$ and a_i, b_i, c_i are all integers (see Fig. 2). We assume that both facets of S admit integer points. Let S_I be the integer hull of S and let A be the vertex of S. Let B and C be integer points on each facet of S, with $A \neq B$ and $A \neq C$, chosen so that there is no integer point between A and B (on the facet given by A and B) and no integer point between A and C (on the facet given by A and C). Then, one of the following properties hold:

1. *A is an integer point and $S = S_I$,*
2. *A is not an integer point and the vertex set V of S_I is equal to the vertex set V' of the integer hull $\triangle_I$ of the triangle $\triangle ABC$.*

PROOF ▷ We write $S = \triangle ABC \cup T$, where T is the convex hull of $\{B, C\} \cup (S \backslash \triangle ABC)$. Therefore, we have:

$$S_I = \triangle_I \cup T_I, \tag{1}$$

where T_I is the integer hull of T. The convex polygon T has 2 vertices (namely B and C, which are integer points) and 3 facets (the segment $[B, C]$ and two unbounded facets). From Lemma 1, the two unbounded facets of T have infinitely many integer points. It follows that $T_I = T$ holds. Therefore, with Eq. (1) we deduce:

$$S_I = \triangle_I \cup T. \tag{2}$$

We consider two cases for the vertex A.

1. Assume that A is an integer point. Then, all points A, B, C are integer points, and since $\triangle ABC$ is pointed, we deduce $\triangle_I = \triangle ABC$. Thus, with Eq. (2) we deduce $S = S_I$, as desired.
2. If A is not an integer point, if suffices to observe from Eq. (2) that all vertices of T are vertices of $\triangle_I$ which yield the conclusion.

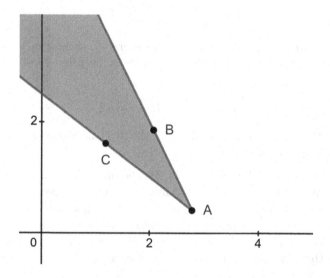

Fig. 2. Finding the integer hull of an angular sector

◁

Theorem 1. *Let us consider a parametric angular sector* $S(b_i)$ *defined by*

$$\begin{cases} a_1\, x + c_1\, y \le b_1 \\ a_2\, x + c_2\, y \le b_2 \end{cases},$$

where $\gcd(a_i, b_i, c_i) = 1$ *for* $i \in \{1, 2\}$ *and* a_i, b_i, c_i *are all integers,* $b_i \in \{b_1, b_2\}$. *Let* $S_I(b_i)$ *be the integer hull of* $S(b_i)$. *Then, there exists an integer* T *and a vector* $\vec{u}$ *such that* $S_I(b_i + T)$ *is the translation of* $S_I(b_i)$ *by* $\vec{u}$.
The integer T *is given by* $\frac{1}{g_2}\, |a_2\, c_1 - a_1\, c_2|$ *or* $\frac{1}{g_1}\, |a_2\, c_1 - a_1\, c_2|$ *and*

$$\vec{u} = \left(\frac{c_2\, T}{a_2\, c_1 - a_1\, c_2}, \frac{a_2\, T}{a_2\, c_1 - a_1\, c_2} \right)$$

or

$$\vec{u} = \left(\frac{c_1\, T}{a_1\, c_2 - a_2\, c_1}, \frac{a_1\, T}{a_1\, c_2 - a_2\, c_1} \right)$$

for $b_i = b_1$ or $b_i = b_2$ respectively, where $g_i = \gcd(a_i, c_i)$. Note that $a_2\, c_1 - a_1\, c_2 \neq 0$ holds.

PROOF ▷ Let A be the vertex of $S(b)$. Let $B(x_B, y_B)$ be a point such that

$$\begin{cases} a_1\, x_B + c_1\, y_B = b_1 \\ a_2\, x_B + c_2\, y_B \leq b_2 \end{cases}$$

and $C(x_C, y_C)$ be a point such that

$$\begin{cases} a_1\, x_C + c_1\, y_C \leq b_1 \\ a_2\, x_C + c_2\, y_C = b_2 \end{cases}$$

with $A \neq B$ and $A \neq C$. Without loss of generality, assume $b_i = b_2$ and $T = \frac{1}{g_1}|a_2\, c_1 - a_1\, c_2|$. Consider the angular sector S' is given by

$$\begin{cases} a_1\, x + c_1\, y \leq b_1 \\ a_2\, x + c_2\, y \leq b_2' = b_2 + T \end{cases}, \tag{3}$$

where A' is the vertex of S' and B' is on the facet of S' contained in the line AB). We distinguish three cases.

- Case 1. Assume that for each $i \in \{1, 2\}$, the integers a_i and c_i are non-zero coprime. With this assumption, the integer T becomes $|a_2\, c_1 - a_1\, c_2|$. Let D and E be two integer points where $\overrightarrow{AD} = t\,\overrightarrow{AC}$ and $\overrightarrow{AE} = k\,\overrightarrow{AB}$ where t and k are positive real numbers. Such points exist since a_i and c_i are coprime integers for $i \in \{1, 2\}$. We choose D and E so that there is no other integer point on the segments $[A, D]$ and $[A, E]$. The points D' and E' are defined in a similar way on the angular sector S' (see Fig. 3).

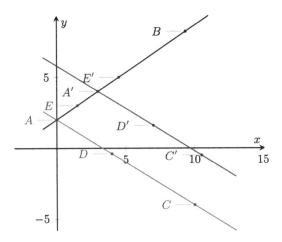

Fig. 3. We want to prove that $\overrightarrow{AE} = \overrightarrow{A'E'}$ and $\overrightarrow{AD} = \overrightarrow{A'D'}$

We shall prove that the integer hull of $\triangle ADE$ is a translation of the integer hull of $\triangle A'D'E'$. This fact will follow from the following two vector equalities:

$$\overrightarrow{AE} = \overrightarrow{A'E'} \text{ and } \overrightarrow{AD} = \overrightarrow{A'D'}, \tag{4}$$

which we shall prove now. Let (x_A, y_A) be the coordinates of A. Since A is the vertex of S, we have:

$$x_A = \frac{b_2 c_1 - b_1 c_2}{a_2 c_1 - a_1 c_2} = x_1 + x_0,$$

where $x_1 = \lfloor x_A \rfloor$ and $x_0 = x_A - x_1$. The coordinate of A', $(x_{A'}, y_{A'})$, would become

$$x_{A'} = \frac{b_2' c_1 - b_1 c_2}{a_2 c_1 - a_1 c_2} = \frac{b_2 c_1 - b_1 c_2}{a_2 c_1 - a_1 c_2} + \frac{T c_1}{T} = x_A + c_1 = x_1 + c_1 + x_0.$$

Proof of $\overrightarrow{AE} = \overrightarrow{A'E'}$. By definition of the point E, its x-coordinate has the form

$$x_E = x_A - x_0 + \Delta x_1 = x_1 + \Delta x_1, \tag{5}$$

where Δx_1 is a integer number. Since a_1 and c_1 are non-zero and coprime, from Lemma 1, we have:

$$x_E \equiv \frac{b_1}{a_1} \qquad \mod c_1$$

$$\Delta x_1 + x_1 \equiv \frac{b_1}{a_1} \qquad \mod c_1$$

$$\Delta x_1 \equiv \frac{b_1}{a_1} - x_1 \mod c_1$$

Similarly, the x-coordinate $x_{E'}$ of E' satisfies $x_{E'} = x_{A'} - x_0 + \Delta x_1' = x_1 + c_1 + \Delta x_1'$, where $\Delta x_1'$ is a integer number. From Lemma 1 we have:

$$x_{E'} \equiv \frac{b_1}{a_1} \qquad \mod c_1$$

$$\Delta x_1' + x_1 + c_1 \equiv \frac{b_1}{a_1} \qquad \mod c_1$$

$$\Delta x_1' \equiv \frac{b_1}{a_1} - x_1 - c_1 \qquad \mod c_1$$

$$\Delta x_1' \equiv \frac{b_1}{a_1} - x_1 \equiv \Delta x_1 \mod c_1$$

Since we choose E (resp. E') as close as possible to A (resp. A') we can assume that $\Delta x_1' - \Delta x_1$ is less than c_1. Thus we have

$$\Delta x_1' = \Delta x_1. \tag{6}$$

Therefore, we have

$$x_E - x_A = \Delta x_1 - x_0 = x_{E'} - x_{A'}. \tag{7}$$

Since A, A', E, E' are all on the line $a_1 x + c_1 y = b_1$, we easily deduce:

$$y_E - y_A = \frac{-a_1 (\Delta x_1 - x_0)}{c_1} = y_{E'} - y_{A'}. \tag{8}$$

With Eqs. 7 and 8 we have proved:

$$\overrightarrow{AE} = \overrightarrow{A'E'}. \tag{9}$$

Proof of $\overrightarrow{AD} = \overrightarrow{A'D'}$. Let $x_D = x_A - x_0 + \Delta x_2 = x_1 + \Delta x_2$, where Δx_2 is a integer number. From Lemma 1 we know that

$$x_D \equiv \frac{b_2}{a_2} \qquad \mathrm{mod}\ c_2$$

$$\Delta x_2 + x_1 \equiv \frac{b_2}{a_2} \qquad \mathrm{mod}\ c_2$$

$$\Delta x_2 \equiv \frac{b_2}{a_2} - x_1 \ \mathrm{mod}\ c_2$$

Similarly, let $x_{D'} = x_{A'} - x_0 + \Delta x_2' = x_1 + c_1 + \Delta x_2'$, where $\Delta x_2'$ is a integer number. From Lemma 1 we know that

$$x_{D'} \equiv \frac{b_2'}{a_2} \qquad\qquad \mathrm{mod}\ c_2$$

$$\Delta x_2' + x_1 + c_1 \equiv \frac{b_2'}{a_2} \qquad\qquad \mathrm{mod}\ c_2$$

$$\Delta x_2' \equiv \frac{b_2'}{a_2} - x_1 - c_1 \qquad\qquad \mathrm{mod}\ c_2$$

$$\Delta x_2' \equiv \frac{b_2 + (a_2 c_1 - a_1 c_2)}{a_2} - x_1 - c_1 \ \ \mathrm{mod}\ c_2$$

$$\Delta x_2' \equiv \frac{b_2}{a_2} + \frac{(a_2 c_1 - a_1 c_2)}{a_2} - x_1 - c_1 \ \ \mathrm{mod}\ c_2$$

$$\Delta x_2' \equiv \frac{b_2}{a_2} + c_1 - \frac{n a_1 c_2}{a_2} - x_1 - c_1 \qquad \mathrm{mod}\ c_2$$

$$\Delta x_2' \equiv \frac{b_2}{a_2} - \frac{a_1 c_2}{a_2} - x_1 \qquad\qquad \mathrm{mod}\ c_2$$

$$\Delta x_2' \equiv \frac{b_2}{a_2} - x_1 \equiv \Delta x_2 \qquad\qquad \mathrm{mod}\ c_2$$

Therefore, we have

$$x_D - x_A = \Delta x_2 - x_0 = x_{D'} - x_{A'}. \tag{10}$$

Since A, D are all on the line $a_2 x + c_2 y = b_2$, we have

$$y_D - y_A = \frac{-a_2 \left(\Delta x_2 - x_0 \right)}{c_2}. \tag{11}$$

And A', D' are all on the line $a_2 x + c_2 y = b_2 + (a_2 c_1 - a_1 c_2)$, we have

$$y'_D - y'_A = \frac{-a_2 \left(\Delta x_2 - x_0 \right)}{c_2} = y_D - y_A. \tag{12}$$

From Eq. 10 and 12 we know that

$$\overrightarrow{AD} = \overrightarrow{A'D'}.$$

So far we have proved that $\overrightarrow{AE} = \overrightarrow{A'E'}$ and $\overrightarrow{AD} = \overrightarrow{A'D'}$ both hold, which imply:

$$\overrightarrow{AA'} = \overrightarrow{DD'} = \overrightarrow{EE'}. \tag{13}$$

With the assumption that D, E, D', E' are all integer points, we deduce that for any integer point F in $\triangle ADE$, there is an integer point F' in $\triangle A'D'E'$ such that

$$\overrightarrow{FF'} = \overrightarrow{AA'}. \tag{14}$$

Therefore, the integer hulls of $\triangle ADE$ is a translation of that of $\triangle A'D'E'$. Finally, with Lemma 3, we conclude hat (in this Case 1) there exists a vector

$$\vec{u} = \overrightarrow{AA'} = \left(\frac{c_1 T}{a_1 c_2 - a_2 c_1}, \frac{a_1 T}{a_1 c_2 - a_2 c_1} \right)$$

and an integer $T = |a_2 c_1 - a_1 c_2|$ such that $S_I(b_2 + T)$ is a translation of $S_I(b_2)$ by $\vec{u}$.

- Case 2. Consider the case where a_2 and c_2 are coprime integers while a_1 and c_1 are not coprime. From Lemma 2 we know that we can find another line $a_1 x + c_1 y = b'_1$ such that $\frac{a_1}{g}$ and $\frac{c_1}{g}$ are coprime, where $g = g_1 = \gcd(a_1, c_1, b'_1) \geq 1$. Then, we can claim that if we re-define (AB) as $\frac{a_1}{g_1} x + \frac{c_1}{g_1} y = \frac{b'_1}{g_1}$, we will not lose any integer point in the new sector comparing to our original sector. Therefore, we have reduced this second case to the previous one.
- Case 3. Consider the case where a_1 and c_1 are coprime integers while a_2 and c_2 are not coprime. Similar to Case 2, we can find another line

$$a_2 x + c_2 y = b'_2 \tag{15}$$

such that $\frac{a_2}{g}$ and $\frac{c_2}{g}$ are coprime where $g = g_2 = \gcd(a_2, c_2, b'_2) \geq 1$, also the new line is not further to C than line (AC). Then we can say that if we re-define (AC) as $\frac{a_2}{g_2} x + \frac{c_2}{g_2} y = \frac{b'_2}{g_2}$, we will not lose any integer point in the new sector comparing to our original sector. Using Case 1 we can prove that $T = \left| \frac{a_2 c_1}{g_2} - \frac{a_1 c_2}{g_2} \right| = \frac{1}{g_2} |a_2 c_1 - a_1 c_2|$ w.r.t $\frac{b'_2}{g_2}$. Therefore, returning to the original b_2 (which is b'_2 as in Eq. (15) plus some integer constant), we have $T = g_2 \left| \frac{a_2 c_1}{g_2} - \frac{a_1 c_2}{g_2} \right| = |a_2 c_1 - a_1 c_2|$.

◁

4   The Integer Hull of a Convex Polygon

4.1   Case of a Triangle

We start by a fundamental case, that of a triangle P, say defined by

$$\begin{cases} a_1\,x + c_1\,y \le b_1 \\ a_2\,x + c_2\,y \le b_2 \\ a_3\,x + c_3\,y \le b_3 \end{cases}$$

with $\gcd(a_i, b_i, c_i) = 1$ for $i \in \{1, 2, 3\}$. We further assume $\gcd(a_i, c_i) = 1$ for $i \in \{1, 2, 3\}$, case to which one can reduce using Lemma 2. Note that P is the intersection of three angular sectors S_1, S_2, S_3 that are defined by

$$\begin{cases} a_1\,x + c_1\,y \le b_1 \\ a_2\,x + c_2\,y \le b_2 \end{cases},$$

$$\begin{cases} a_2\,x + c_2\,y \le b_2 \\ a_3\,x + c_3\,y \le b_3 \end{cases},$$

$$\begin{cases} a_1\,x + c_1\,y \le b_1 \\ a_3\,x + c_3\,y \le b_3 \end{cases},$$

respectively. Hence, we have $P = \bigcap_{i=1}^{3} S_i$.

Lemma 4. *Let P_I and S_{iI} be the integer hulls of P and S_i, respectively. Then, we have $P_I = \bigcap_{i=1}^{3} S_{iI}$.*

PROOF ▷ Any integer point $A \in P_I$ must be in P, that is $A \in S_i$ for $i \in \{1, 2, 3\}$. Since A is an integer point, the fact $A \in S_i$ holds implies that $A \in S_{iI}$ holds as well. Therefore, the point A must be in the intersection of S_{iI} for $i \in \{1, 2, 3\}$. Similarly, any integer point $B \in \bigcap_{i=1}^{3} S_{iI}$ must satisfy $B \in S_i$ for $i \in \{1, 2, 3\}$. Thus we have $B \in \bigcap_{i=1}^{3} S_i = P$. Since B is an integer point in P, we deduce $B \in P_I$. ◁

Lemma 5. *For a line defined by $ax + cy = b$, with a, b, c non-zero integers, and $\gcd(a, c) = 1$, and for two points $A(x_A, y_A)$ and $B(x_B, y_B)$ on that line, there are at least two integer points on the segment $[A, B]$ if and only if we have: $|x_A - x_B| \ge |c|$.*

PROOF ▷ By Lemma 1, and under the hypotheses of this lemma, a point on the line $ax + cy = b$ is an integer point if and only its x-coordinate satisfies

$$x \equiv \frac{b}{a} \mod c.$$

Therefore, the distance between the x-values of any two consecutive integer points should be c. The conclusion follows. ◁

Lemma 6. *Let V, V_1, V_2, V_3 be the vertex sets of $P_I, S_{1I}, S_{2I}, S_{3I}$, respectively. Then, we have $V = V_1 \cup V_2 \cup V_3$ and the pairwise intersections of the V_i's are all empty, if the following three inequalities all hold:*

$$\begin{cases} \left| \frac{b_2 c_1 - b_1 c_2}{a_2 c_1 - a_1 c_2} - \frac{b_1 c_3 - b_3 c_1}{a_1 c_3 - a_3 c_1} \right| \geq |c_1| \\ \left| \frac{b_2 c_1 - b_1 c_2}{a_2 c_1 - a_1 c_2} - \frac{b_2 c_3 - b_3 c_2}{a_2 c_3 - a_3 c_2} \right| \geq |c_2| \\ \left| \frac{b_3 c_1 - b_1 c_3}{a_3 c_1 - a_1 c_3} - \frac{b_2 c_3 - b_3 c_2}{a_2 c_3 - a_3 c_2} \right| \geq |c_3| \end{cases} \tag{16}$$

PROOF ▷ From Lemma 5, there are at least two integer point on each facet of the triangle, whenever the three inequalities of (16) all hold. To find the vertex sets V_i, $i \in \{1, 2, 3\}$, we need to find the closest integer points to each of the three vertices of P, see Lemma 3. Since there are at least two integer points on each facet, then the triangles we find for S_i according to Lemma 3 do not overlap with each other. Therefore, $V = V_1 \cup V_2 \cup V_3$ and the pairwise intersections of the V_i's are all empty. ◁

Theorem 2. *Let $P(b_i)$ be a parametric triangle where $b_i \in \{b_1, b_2, b_3\}$, and $P_I(b_i)$ is the integer hull of $P(b_i)$. We say that $|b_i|$ is large enough whenever the following three inequalities all hold:*

$$\begin{cases} \left| \frac{b_2 c_1 - b_1 c_2}{a_2 c_1 - a_1 c_2} - \frac{b_1 c_3 - b_3 c_1}{a_1 c_3 - a_3 c_1} \right| \geq |c_1| \\ \left| \frac{b_2 c_1 - b_1 c_2}{a_2 c_1 - a_1 c_2} - \frac{b_2 c_3 - b_3 c_2}{a_2 c_3 - a_3 c_2} \right| \geq |c_2| \\ \left| \frac{b_3 c_1 - b_1 c_3}{a_3 c_1 - a_1 c_3} - \frac{b_2 c_3 - b_3 c_2}{a_2 c_3 - a_3 c_2} \right| \geq |c_3| \end{cases}$$

There exists an integer T and 3 vectors $\vec{u}, \vec{v}$ and $\vec{w}$, such that for $|b|$ large enough, the integer hull $P_I(b + T)$ can be obtained from $P_I(b)$ as follows.

As defined above, denoting S_1, S_2, S_3 the angular sectors of $P(b)$ and by S_{1I}, S_{2I}, S_{3I} their respective integer hulls, the integer hull of $P(T + b)$ is the intersection of $f_u(S_{1I}), f_v(S_{2I}), f_w(S_{3I})$ where f_u, f_v, f_w are the translations of vectors $\vec{u}, \vec{v}$ and $\vec{w}$ respectively. Specifically, when $b = b_1$ we have

$$T = \text{lcm} \left(\frac{1}{g_2} |a_2 c_1 - a_1 c_2|, \frac{1}{g_3} |a_3 c_1 - a_1 c_3| \right).$$

Similar results apply to other b_i as well.

PROOF ▷ Without loss of generality, assume $b_i = b_1$. For S_1, defined by $a_1 x + c_1 y \geq b_1, a_2 x + c_2 y \geq b_2$, we know from Theorem 1 that there exists an integer

$$T_1 = \frac{1}{g_2} |a_2 c_1 - a_1 c_2|$$

and a vector

$$\vec{h_1} = \left(\frac{c_2 T_1}{a_2 c_1 - a_1 c_2}, \frac{a_2 T_1}{a_2 c_1 - a_1 c_2} \right)$$

such that $S_{1I}(b_1 + T_1)$ is the translation of $S_{1I}(b_1)$ by $\vec{h_1}$.

Similarly, for S_3, defined by $a_1 x + c_1 y \geq b_1, a_3 x + c_3 y \geq b_3$, there exists an integer

$$T_3 = \frac{1}{g_3} |a_3 c_1 - a_1 c_3|$$

and a vector

$$\vec{h_3} = \left(\frac{c_3 T_3}{a_3 c_1 - a_1 c_3}, \frac{a_3 T_3}{a_3 c_1 - a_1 c_3} \right)$$

such that $S_{3I}(b_1 + T_3)$ is the translation of $S_{3I}(b_1)$ by $\vec{h_3}$.

As for S_2, it is not affected by the change in b_1, which means for any integer k, $S_{2I}(b_1 + k)$ is the same as $S_{2I}(b_1)$, in other words, $S_{2I}(b_1 + k)$ is the translation of $S_{2I}(b_1)$ by the zero vector.

Combining the three sectors, we have proved that for $T = \text{lcm}(T_1, T_3)$, and the three vectors $\vec{u} = \frac{T}{T_1} \vec{h_1}, \vec{v} = \frac{T}{T_2} \vec{h_3}, \vec{w} = (0,0)$, the sets $f_u(S_{1I}(b_1))$, $f_v(S_{2I}(b_1))$, $f_w(S_{3I}(b_1))$ are the same as the sets $S_{1I}(b_1 + T)$, $S_{2I}(b_1 + T)$, $S_{3I}(b_1 + T)$ respectively. Also as we have proved in Lemma 4 that $P_I = \bigcap_{i=1}^{3} S_{iI}$. Therefore, $P_I(T + b_1)$ is the intersection of $f_u(S_{1I}(b_1)), f_v(S_{2I}(b_1)), f_w(S_{3I}(b_1))$ where f_u, f_v, f_w are the translations of vectors $\vec{u}, \vec{v}, \vec{w}$ respectively.

The proofs for $b_i = b_2$ or $b_i = b_3$ are similar. ◁

4.2 Convex Polygon of Arbitrary Shape

With Theorem 2 proved, we can extend it to a convex polygon of any shape.

Theorem 3. *Let $P(b)$ be a parametric polygon given by*

$$a_i x + c_i y \leq b_i,$$

where $i \in \{1, \ldots, n\}$ and the parameter $b \in \{b_1, \ldots, b_n\}$ and $P_I(b)$ be the integer hull of $P(b)$. Specifically, $a_i x + c_i y \geq b_i$ and $a_{i+1} x + c_{i+1} y \geq b_{i+1}$ define an angular sector S_i of P, for all $1 \leq i \leq n$, with the convention $i + 1 = 1$ if $i = n$. Then, there exist an integer T and n vectors $\vec{v_1}, \ldots, \vec{v_n}$, such that, for $|b|$ large enough, $P_I(b + T)$ can be obtained from $P_I(b)$ as follows. Denoting by S_{iI} the integer hull of the angular sector S_i, for all $1 \leq i \leq n$, the integer hull $P_I(b + T)$ of $P(T + b)$ is the intersection of $f_{v_i}(S_{iI})$, where f_{v_i} are the translations of vectors $\vec{v_i}$. Specifically, for $1 \leq m \leq n$, when $b = b_m$ we have

$$T = \text{lcm} \left(\frac{1}{g_{m-1}} |a_{m-1} c_m - a_m c_{m-1}|, \frac{1}{g_{m+1}} |a_{m+1} c_m - a_m c_{m+1}| \right),$$

here we have $m - 1 = n$ when $m = 1$, and $m + 1 = 1$ when $m = n$.

The condition $|b_m|$ large enough means that all of the following inequalities hold:

$$\begin{cases} \left| \frac{b_{m+1} c_m - b_m c_{m+1}}{a_{m+1} c_m - a_m c_{m+1}} - \frac{b_m c_{m-1} - b_{m-1} c_m}{a_m c_{m-1} - a_{m-1} c_m} \right| \geq |c_m| \\ \left| \frac{b_{m+1} c_m - b_m c_{m+1}}{a_{m+1} c_m - a_m c_{m+1}} - \frac{b_{m+1} c_{m+2} - b_{m+2} c_{m+1}}{a_{m+1} c_{m+2} - a_{m+2} c_{m+1}} \right| \geq |c_{m+1}| \\ \left| \frac{b_m c_{m-1} - b_{m-1} c_m}{a_m c_{m-1} - a_{m-1} c_m} - \frac{b_{m-2} c_{m-1} - b_{m-1} c_{m-2}}{a_{m-2} c_{m-1} - a_{m-1} c_{m-2}} \right| \geq |c_{m-1}| \end{cases} \quad (17)$$

PROOF ▷ Without lose of generality, let's assume $b = b_1$. For S_1, defined by $a_1 x + c_1 y \geq b_1, a_2 x + c_2 y \geq b_2$, we know from Theorem 1 that we choose the integer

$$T_1 = \frac{1}{g_2} |a_2 c_1 - a_1 c_2|$$

and the vector

$$\vec{h_1} = \left(\frac{c_2 T_1}{a_2 c_1 - a_1 c_2}, \frac{a_2 T_1}{a_2 c_1 - a_1 c_2} \right)$$

such that $S_{1I}(b_1 + T_1)$ is the translation of $S_{1I}(b_1)$ by $\vec{h_1}$. Similarly, for S_n, defined by $a_1 x + c_1 y \geq b_1, a_n x + c_n y \geq b_n$, we choose the integer

$$T_n = \frac{1}{g_n} |a_n c_1 - a_1 c_n|$$

and the vector

$$\vec{h_n} = \left(\frac{c_n T_n}{a_n c_1 - a_1 c_n}, \frac{a_n T_n}{a_n c_1 - a_1 c_n} \right)$$

such that $S_{nI}(b_1 + T_n)$ is the translation of $S_{nI}(b_1)$ by $\vec{h_n}$.

As for each $j \in \{2, \ldots, n-1\}$, the angular sector S_j is not effected by the change in b_1, which means for any integer k, the sets $S_{jI}(b_1 + k)$ and $S_{jI}(b_1)$ are the same, in other words, $S_{jI}(b_1 + k)$ is the translation of $S_{jI}(b_1)$ by the zero vector.

Combining all n sectors, we have proved that for $T = \text{lcm}(T_1, T_n)$, and the n vectors $\vec{v_1} = \frac{T}{T_1} \vec{h_1}, \vec{v_n} = \frac{T}{T_n} \vec{h_n}, \vec{v_j} = (0,0)$ for $j \in \{2, \ldots, n-1\}$, the set $f_{v_i}(S_{iI}(b_1))$, for $i \in \{1, \ldots, n\}$, is the same as the set $S_{iI}(b_1 + T)$.

Also as we have proved in Lemma 4, we have $P_I = \bigcap_{i=1}^{n} S_{iI}$. Therefore, $P_I(T + b_1)$ is the intersection of $f_{v_i}(S_{iI}(b_1))$ where f_{v_i} is the translation of vector $\vec{v_1}$. ◁

5 Examples

In this section, we give some examples to show the periodic phenomenon that we proved in the previous sections.

Consider a simple parametric polytope. Figure 4 shows a triangle $P(b)$ defined by

$$\begin{cases} x - 4y \leq -4 \\ -2x + y \leq 0 \\ x + y \leq b \end{cases}.$$

First, we look at the angular sector $S(b)$ given by $x - 4y \leq -4$ and $x + y \leq b$ (see Fig. 4a[1]). According to Theorem 1, the integer hull of $S(b - 5n)$ is a transformation of that of $S(b - 5(n-1))$ by $(\vec{4,1})$ for any $n \geq 1$.

---

[1] Also available at https://github.com/lxwangruc/parametric_integer_hull.

We can extend this observation to the triangle $P(b)$. Using Theorem 2 when $|b| \geq 11$, the integer hull of $P(b - 15n)$ is a translation of $P(b - 15(n - 1))$ by $(\vec{0,0}), (\vec{12,3}), (\vec{5,10})$ for $n \geq 1$.

Figure 4b shows the integer hulls of $P(b)$ where $-26 \leq b \leq -11$, the points in the figure are the vertices of the integer hull. We can see that the integer hull of $P(-26)$ is a translation of that of $P(-11)$.

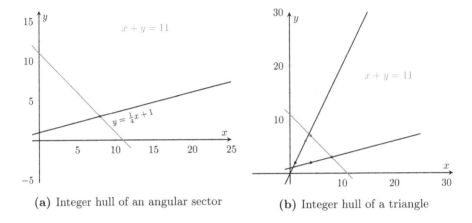

(a) Integer hull of an angular sector   (b) Integer hull of a triangle

Fig. 4. The periodic phenomenon in a simple example. The dots are the vertices of the integer hull.

Consider a more complicated example. In order to have a clear view, we only look at one angular sector $S(b)$ given by

$$\begin{cases} -103\,x + 43\,y \leq 172 \\ 59\,x + 83\,y \ \ \leq b \end{cases}.$$

By Theorem 1, we have $T = 11086$ and the integer hull of $S(b + nT)$ is a transformation of that of $S(b)$. We pick $b = 90 \times 83$ and $n = 83$ so that the integer hull of $S(83 \times (90 + 11086 + i))$ is a transformation of that of $S(83 \times (90 + i))$. Figure 5 shows the first 15 iterations of the vertices of the integer hull of each sector.

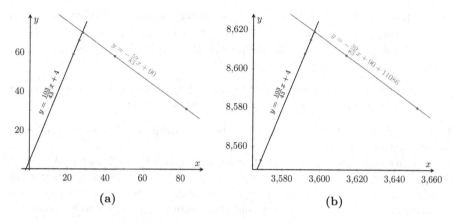

Fig. 5. A more complicated example. The red dots are the vertices of the integer hull of the sector. (Color figure online)

6   A New Integer Hull Algorithm

The most natural application of our conclusions from the previous sections is to use the periodic phenomenon to study the integer hull of a parametric polyhedron. Before discussing that application, we propose an algorithm, based on the results of Sect. 3, for computing the integer hull of a rational convex polygon P.

We assume that P has at least one integer point and writes $P = \{\vec{x} \mid A\vec{x} \leq \vec{b}\}$, for a matrix $A \in \mathbb{Z}^{m \times 2}$ and a vector $\vec{b} \in \mathbb{Z}^m$, where m is a positive integer. It is easy to determine:

1. the equations of the facets $F_1, \ldots, F_f$ of P, each of them having a form $a_i\, x + c_i\, y \geq b_i$. Note that if a facet has no integer point, we use Lemma 2 to replace it with a new facet that has integer points, without modifying the integer hull of P.
2. the coordinates of the vertices $V_1, \ldots, V_f$ of P, so that $[V_i, V_{i+1}] = F_i$, with the conventions $V_{f+1} = V_1$ and $F_0 = F_f$.

To compute the integer hull P_I of P, we compute its vertices. We transform V so that it becomes the vertex set of P_I. We visit each vertex V_i of V and do the following:

1. if the coordinates of V_i are integers, we keep V_i in V,
2. otherwise:
   (a) we compute the vertex set U of the integer hull of the angular sector defined by F_{i-1} and F_i with V_i as its vertex. In the current implementation of the algorithm, we first find the integer points A, B on F_i and F_{i-1} that are closest to V_i. If no such A or B exists, we pick $A = V_{i-1}$ and $B = V_{i+1}$. Then we use the *triangle rasterisation algorithm* [20] on $\triangle V_i A B$ to find the integer points that are likely to be the vertices of the integer hull of

the angular sector. That is, we find all the integer points that are closest to the edges $[V_i A]$ and $[V_i B]$. Then, we compute the *convex hull* [19] of all the possible integer points plus A, B to find the vertex set U.

(b) we replace V_i with U.

If the given P is a parametric convex polygon, where b_i is unknown, we propose the following steps to compute the vertices of P_I:

1. determine the smallest $|b_i|$ so that the constrains in Theorem 3 hold (See inequalities 17).
2. compute the period T and the transformation vectors in Theorem 3
3. compute the integer hull of every non-parametric polyhedron in this period.
4. when the values of the parameters are available, using the corresponding solution from the previous step and the vectors from step 2 to compute the integer hull of the P with the given parameters.

Note that we can finish the first three steps "off-line", once the parameters are given the only computation that needs to be done is the translations which could be done in linear time. This method is both time and space efficient if the period T is short.

References

1. Barvinok, A.I.: A polynomial time algorithm for counting integral points in polyhedra when the dimension is fixed. Math. Oper. Res. **19**(4), 769–779 (1994). https://doi.org/10.1287/moor.19.4.769
2. Berndt, S., Jansen, K., Klein, K.: New bounds for the vertices of the integer hull. In: Le, H.V., King, V. (eds.) 4th Symposium on Simplicity in Algorithms, SOSA 2021, Virtual Conference, January 11–12, 2021, pp. 25–36. SIAM (2021). https://doi.org/10.1137/1.9781611976496.3
3. Chvátal, V.: Edmonds polytopes and a hierarchy of combinatorial problems. Discret. Math. **4**(4), 305–337 (1973). https://doi.org/10.1016/0012-365X(73)90167-2
4. Cook, W.J., Hartmann, M., Kannan, R., McDiarmid, C.: On integer points in polyhedra. Combinatorica **12**(1), 27–37 (1992). https://doi.org/10.1007/BF01191202
5. Ehrhart, E.: Polynômes arithmétiques et méthode des polyédres en combinatoire. International Series of Numerical Mathematics, Birkhäuser Verlag, Basel 35 (1977)
6. Erhart, E.: Sur un problème de géométrie diophantienne linéaire. i. J. für die reine und angewandte Mathematik **226**, 1–29 (1967)
7. Gomory, R.E.: Outline of an algorithm for integer solutions to linear programs and an algorithm for the mixed integer problem. In: Jünger, M., et al. (eds.) 50 Years of Integer Programming 1958–2008, pp. 77–103. Springer, Heidelberg (2010). https://doi.org/10.1007/978-3-540-68279-0_4
8. Land, A., Doig, A.: An automatic method of solving discrete programming problems. Econometrica: J. Econom. Soc. **28**, 497–520 (1960)
9. Loera, J.A.D., Hemmecke, R., Tauzer, J., Yoshida, R.: Effective lattice point counting in rational convex polytopes. J. Symb. Comput. **38**(4), 1273–1302 (2004). https://doi.org/10.1016/j.jsc.2003.04.003
10. Meister, B.: Stating and manipulating periodicity in the polytope model: applications to program analysis and optimization. Ph.D. thesis, Strasbourg 1 (2004)

11. Pick, G.: Geometrisches zur zahlenlehre. Sitzenber. Lotos (Prague) **19**, 311–319 (1899)
12. Rajan, A.: Theory of linear and integer programming, by Alexander Schrijver, Wiley, New York, 1986, 471 pp. price $71.95. Networks **20**(6), 801 (1990). https://doi.org/10.1002/net.3230200608
13. Schrijver, A.: On cutting planes. Combinatorics **79**, 291–296 (1980)
14. Schrijver, A.: Theory of Linear and Integer Programming. Wiley-Interscience Series in Discrete Mathematics and Optimization. Wiley, Hoboken (1999)
15. Seghir, R., Loechner, V., Meister, B.: Integer affine transformations of parametric $\mathbb{Z}$-polytopes and applications to loop nest optimization. ACM Trans. Archit. Code Optim. **9**(2), 8:1–8:27 (2012). https://doi.org/10.1145/2207222.2207224
16. Thomas, R.R.: Integer programming: algebraic methods. In: Floudas, C.A., Pardalos, P.M. (eds.) Encyclopedia of Optimization, 2nd edn., pp. 1624–1634. Springer, Heidelberg (2009). https://doi.org/10.1007/978-0-387-74759-0_285
17. Verdoolaege, S., Seghir, R., Beyls, K., Loechner, V., Bruynooghe, M.: Counting integer points in parametric polytopes using Barvinok's rational functions. Algorithmica **48**(1), 37–66 (2007). https://doi.org/10.1007/s00453-006-1231-0
18. Veselov, S., Chirkov, A.Y.: Some estimates for the number of vertices of integer polyhedra. J. Appl. Ind. Math. **2**(4), 591–604 (2008)
19. Wikipedia contributors: Convex hull – Wikipedia, the free encyclopedia (2021). https://en.wikipedia.org/w/index.php?title=Convex_hull&oldid=1024617697. Accessed 1 July 2021
20. Wikipedia contributors: Rasterisation – Wikipedia, the free encyclopedia (2021). https://en.wikipedia.org/w/index.php?title=Rasterisation&oldid=1027759975. Accessed 1 July 2021
21. Yanagisawa, H.: A simple algorithm for lattice point counting in rational polygons (2005)

Relaxed NewtonSLRA
for Approximate GCD

Kosaku Nagasaka[✉]

Kobe University, 3 -11 Tsurukabuto, Kobe, Nada-ku 657-8501, Japan
nagasaka@main.h.kobe-u.ac.jp

Abstract. We propose a better algorithm for approximate GCD in terms of robustness and distance, based on the NewtonSLRA algorithm that is a solver for the structured low rank approximation (SLRA) problem. Our algorithm mainly enlarges the tangent space in the Newton-SLRA algorithm and adapts it to a certain weighted Frobenius norm. By this improvement, we prevent a convergence to a local optimum that is possibly far from the global optimum. We also propose some modification using a sparsity on the NewtonSLRA algorithm for the subresultant matrix in terms of computing time.

Keywords: Approximate GCD · Structured low rank approximation · NewtonSLRA algorithm · Weighted Frobenius norm

1 Introduction

Approximate GCD is one of classical and important problems in symbolic-numeric algorithms that finds a non-trivial greatest common divisor (GCD) of polynomials in a certain specified neighborhood of the given polynomials. For example, approximate GCD is used for a nearby non-trivial Smith form of a matrix polynomial [14], applications in signal processing [20], rational function approximation [1, 21] and so on. This problem was introduced implicitly by Dunaway [10] to extract the squarefree part of the given (numerical) polynomial, and there were several fundamental studies [8, 11, 12, 18, 23–26] on the early stage of approximate GCD (e.g. quasi GCD by Schönhage and QRGCD by Corless et al.).

At present, there are mainly two approaches: simple optimization and structured matrix. UVGCD [33], Fastgcd [2] and GPGCD [6, 29] are some typical algorithms that solve a certain optimization problem to compute their approximate GCD and/or cofactors directly (e.g. the Gauss–Newton algorithm with QR decomposition). The structured total least norm (STLN) based algorithms [16, 17, 34] and the structured low rank approximation (SLRA) based algorithms [27, 30] are some typical ones based on structured matrices that basically compute a perturbed matrix of the column full rank matrix (e.g. the subresultant matrix). Moreover, we note that there are also algorithms [4, 7, 21, 28, 31, 32] using

This work was supported by JSPS KAKENHI Grant Number 19K11827.

© Springer Nature Switzerland AG 2021

F. Boulier et al. (Eds.): CASC 2021, LNCS 12865, pp. 272–292, 2021.
https://doi.org/10.1007/978-3-030-85165-1_16

other bases (e.g. the Bernstein basis) instead of the monomial basis. For further information, see [3,13,30] for fundamental references of approximate GCD.

In this paper, we propose a better algorithm in terms of robustness and distance, based on the NewtonSLRA algorithm by Schost and Spaenlehauer [27] which is a solver for the SLRA problem. Our algorithm mainly enlarges the tangent space (i.e., orthogonality is relaxed) in the NewtonSLRA algorithm and adapts it to a certain column weighted Frobenius norm. By these improvements, we try to prevent a convergence to a local optimum that is possibly far from the global optimum. We also propose some modification using a sparsity on the NewtonSLRA algorithm for the subresultant matrix in terms of computing time (note that the NewtonSLRA algorithm is not specific to approximate GCD).

After the following preliminary subsections including some terminology and problem description, we start with the brief review of known NewtonSLRA algorithm in Sect. 2. Our theoretical contribution is given in Sect. 3, and our result of some performance test is given in Sect. 4.

1.1 Definitions and Notations

We assume that polynomials over the reals, $f(x) = \sum_{i=0}^{m} f_i x^i \in \mathbb{R}[x]$ and $g(x) = \sum_{i=0}^{n} g_i x^i \in \mathbb{R}[x]$ are given with the assumption $m \geq n$ (this is not required in nature but for simplicity's sake). We denote the set of matrices of size $p \times q$ by $\mathbb{R}^{p \times q}$ which is endowed with the inner product $\langle M_1, M_2 \rangle = \text{trace}(M_1 M_2^T)$ where M^T is the transpose of matrix M, and the set of matrices of rank $r \in \mathbb{N}$ by $\mathcal{D}_r \subset \mathbb{R}^{p \times q}$. For an affine subspace $\mathcal{S} \subset \mathbb{R}^{p \times q}$, we denote its underlying vector space by $\mathcal{S}^0$, its tangent space at M by $T_M \mathcal{S}$, and the orthogonal projection of M on $\mathcal{S}$ by $\Pi_{\mathcal{S}}(M)$. For vectors and matrices, $\|\cdot\|_2$ and $\|\cdot\|_F$ denote the Euclidean norm (2-norm) and the Frobenius norm (deduced from the inner product above), respectively. By this Frobenius norm, we denote the open and closed balls centered at $M \in \mathbb{R}^{p \times q}$ and of radius ρ by $\mathcal{B}_\rho(M), \overline{\mathcal{B}_\rho(M)} \subset \mathbb{R}^{p \times q}$, respectively. M^{-1} and $M^\dagger$ are the inverse and Moore–Penrose pseudo-inverse of matrix M, respectively. We define the angle between linear subspaces (cf. [9, Chap. 9]) and the transversally condition as follows (note that we focus on approximate GCD hence the notations and assumptions are a little bit different from Schost and Spaenlehauer [27]).

Definition 1 (Angle Between Subspaces). *Let $\mathcal{S}_1, \mathcal{S}_2 \subset \mathbb{R}^{p \times q}$ be two linear subspaces. We define their angle $\alpha(\mathcal{S}_1, \mathcal{S}_2) = 0$ if $\mathcal{S}_1 \subset \mathcal{S}_2$ or $\mathcal{S}_2 \subset \mathcal{S}_1$. Otherwise, let $\alpha(\mathcal{S}_1, \mathcal{S}_2) \in [0, \pi/2] \subset \mathbb{R}$ be defined by*

$$\alpha(\mathcal{S}_1, \mathcal{S}_2) = \arccos\left(\max\left\{\langle x, y \rangle : \begin{array}{l} x \in \mathbb{S} \cap \mathcal{S}_1 \cap (\mathcal{S}_1 \cap \mathcal{S}_2)^\perp, \\ y \in \mathbb{S} \cap \mathcal{S}_2 \cap (\mathcal{S}_1 \cap \mathcal{S}_2)^\perp \end{array}\right\}\right)$$

where $\mathbb{S}$ denotes the unit sphere and $\mathcal{S}^\perp$ denotes the orthogonal complement of a linear subspace $\mathcal{S}$ of $\mathbb{R}^{p \times q}$.   ◁

Definition 2 (Transversally Condition). *Let $\mathcal{S}$ be an affine subspace of $\mathbb{R}^{p \times q}$. We say that $\mathcal{S}$ and $\mathcal{D}_r$ intersect transversally at $\zeta \in \mathcal{S} \cap \mathcal{D}_r$ if $\text{codim}(\mathcal{S}^0 \cap T_\zeta \mathcal{D}_r^0) = \text{codim}(\mathcal{S}^0) + \text{codim}(T_\zeta \mathcal{D}_r^0)$ where codim denotes the codimension in $\mathbb{R}^{p \times q}$.*   ◁

The coefficient vector (in the descending term order) of $p(x) \in \mathbb{R}[x]$ of degree k is denoted by $\overrightarrow{p} \in \mathbb{R}^{k+1}$. We denote the polynomial norm of $p(x)$ by $\|p\|_2$ that is defined as $\|p\|_2 = \|\overrightarrow{p}\|_2$. For a pair $(f, g) \in \mathbb{R}[x] \times \mathbb{R}[x]$, we define its norm as $\|(f, g)\|_2 = \sqrt{\|f\|_2^2 + \|g\|_2^2}$.

The subresultant matrix of order r of $f(x)$ and $g(x)$ is denoted by $\mathrm{Syl}_r(f, g) \in \mathbb{R}^{(m+n-r) \times (m+n-2r)}$ and is defined as follows ($n - r$ columns for $\overrightarrow{f}$ and $m - r$ columns for $\overrightarrow{g}$).

$$\mathrm{Syl}_r(f, g) = \begin{pmatrix} C_{n-r-1}(f) & C_{m-r-1}(g) \end{pmatrix} \tag{1.1}$$

where $C_k(p)$ denotes the convolution matrix of kth order of $p(x) \in \mathbb{R}[x]$ such that $C_k(p)\overrightarrow{q} = \overrightarrow{h}$ and $h(x) = p(x)q(x)$ for any polynomial $q(x)$ of degree k. We have the following well-known lemma which is very important for many approximate GCD algorithms.

Lemma 1. *For the largest integer r such that $\mathrm{Syl}_r(f, g)$ is not column full rank, let $\overrightarrow{v}$ be a non-zero vector in the null space of $\mathrm{Syl}_r(f, g)$ and $g_1(x), f_1(x) \in \mathbb{R}[x]$ be polynomials whose coefficient vectors are the first $n - r$ elements and the last $m - r$ elements of $\overrightarrow{v}$, respectively. Then, $f(x)/f_1(x)$ and $-g(x)/g_1(x)$ are the polynomial GCD of $f(x)$ and $g(x)$, and their degree is $r + 1$.* ◁

1.2   Problem Description and SLRA

In the literature, there are so many definitions for approximate GCD. In this paper, we focus on the following approximate GCD, and note that this and similar definitions are widely used in the former studies [13,16,17,20–22,27,29, 30,34], and often used in a combination with degree search strategies (cf. [30, Section 1][22]).

Definition 3 (approximate GCD). *For the degree $k \in \mathbb{N}$, we compute the polynomial $d(x) \in \mathbb{R}[x]$ called "approximate GCD" of degree k, which minimizes $\|(\Delta_f, \Delta_g)\|_2$ (called **perturbation**) and satisfies*

$$f(x) + \Delta_f(x) = f_1(x)d(x), \quad g(x) + \Delta_g(x) = g_1(x)d(x), \quad \deg(d) = k$$

for some polynomials $\Delta_f(x), \Delta_g(x), f_1(x), g_1(x) \in \mathbb{R}[x]$ such that

$$\deg(\Delta_f) \leq \deg(f), \quad \deg(\Delta_g) \leq \deg(g). \qquad ◁$$

Remark 1.1. As also noted in [3,16], the coefficients of approximate GCD are not uniquely determined. Moreover, one may be interested in approximate GCD of degree k for polynomials whose exact GCD is of higher degree than k. In this case, any possible combination of factors gives its approximate GCD. However, for such polynomials, the given degree k is not appropriate. The degree search strategy in use must continue searching a more appropriate degree. ◁

Algorithm 1. Approximate GCD by SLRA

Input: $f(x), g(x) \in \mathbb{R}[x]$ and $k \in \mathbb{N}$
Output: $d(x) \in \mathbb{R}[x]$, approximate GCD of degree k
1: construct a SLRA problem in Definition 4 with
$$M = \mathrm{Syl}_{k-1}(f, g), \mathcal{S} = \mathcal{S}_{k-1}(f, g) \text{ and } r = m + n - 2k + 1;$$
2: solve the SLRA problem and let M^* be the resulting matrix;
3: construct $f(x) + \Delta_f(x)$ and $g(x) + \Delta_g(x)$ back from M^*;
4: compute $d(x)$ from $\mathrm{Syl}_{k-1}(f + \Delta_f, g + \Delta_g)$;
5: **return** $d(x)$;

By Lemma 1, the approximate GCD problem can be considered as the following constrained optimization.

$$\min_{\Delta_f, \Delta_g} \| (\Delta_f, \Delta_g) \|_2$$
$$\text{subject to } \mathrm{rank}(\mathrm{Syl}_{k-1}(f + \Delta_f, g + \Delta_g)) < m + n - 2k + 2.$$

This means that we want to compute a nearby low rank matrix of $\mathrm{Syl}_{k-1}(f + \Delta_f, g + \Delta_g)$ that is structured (as in the definition of subresultant matrix). Therefore, the approximate GCD problem is reduced to the structured low rank approximation (SLRA) problem. We note that computing the global optimum for this problem is not easy since it is non-convex due to the rank constraint (see also [19] for further references in low rank approximation). Hence most of algorithms (including ours) will compute a local optimum or some enough small perturbation. In this paper, following Schost and Spaenlehauer [27], we define the SLRA problem as follows.

Definition 4 (Structured Low Rank Approximation, SLRA). *Let $\mathcal{S} \subset \mathbb{R}^{p \times q}$ be an affine subspace of $\mathbb{R}^{p \times q}$ (i.e., this defines the structure of matrices). For the given $M \in \mathcal{S}$ and $r \in \mathbb{N}$, find a matrix $M^* \in \mathcal{S} \cap \mathcal{D}_r$ such that $\| M - M^* \|_F$ is "small".* ◁

For the SLRA problem, one of the first iterative methods (the convergence ratio is linear) is proposed by Cadzow [5] and is based on alternating projections. The first quadratic convergent method is the NewtonSLRA algorithm by Schost and Spaenlehauer [27]. Actually the approximate GCD is one of applications of the algorithm in their paper. Following them, we use the NewtonSLRA algorithm for computing approximate GCD.

Let $\mathcal{S}_{k-1}(f, g)$ be the set of subresultant matrices of order $k-1$ of $f(x) + \Delta_f(x)$ and $g(x) + \Delta_g(x)$ whose degrees are less than or equal to m and n, respectively. This set plays the set of structured matrices and is $\mathcal{S}$ in Definition 4. As a consequence of the discussion above we have Algorithm 1. We note that there are several ways to extract $d(x)$ from the subresultant matrix $\mathrm{Syl}_{k-1}(f + \Delta_f, g + \Delta_g)$ on the line 4. For example, at first we extract cofactors $f_1(x)$ and $g_1(x)$ by computing the null space of $\mathrm{Syl}_{k-1}(f + \Delta_f, g + \Delta_g)$ by Lemma 1 and approximate GCD $d(x)$ can be computed by the least squares with the convolution matrices of $f_1(x)$ and $g_1(x)$, unknown vector $\overrightarrow{d}$ and the r.h.s. constant vector $(\overrightarrow{f}^T, \overrightarrow{g}^T)^T$.

1.3 Our Contributions

We give some resolutions (improvements) to the following issues of the Newton-SLRA algorithm [27], to make the algorithm better.

1) Time complexity due to the inner product.
One iteration of the NewtonSLRA algorithm mainly computes the singular value decomposition and solves a certain underdetermined linear system (least squares) as in the next section. But additionally, $O((m+n)k)$ times matrix-vector products and inner products are required. Our resolution reduces such matrix-vector products to element-wise vector products that will be given in Sect. 3.1.

2) Uncontrollable convergence point in some sense.
Schost and Spaenlehauer gave the theorem that the iterations by the Newton-SLRA algorithm converges to a good local approximation [27, Theorem 2]. However, even though it behaves to the first order as the optimum, approximate GCDs computed by the NewtonSLRA algorithm sometimes have $O(1)$ perturbations even if the expected value is 1.0e-2 or so, as in Sect. 4. Our resolution enlarges the tangent space and tries to prevent a local limit point from being far from the global optimum, that will be given in Sect. 3.2.

3) Mismatch between the Euclidean and Frobenius norms.
The target functions of approximate GCD and SLRA are $\| (\Delta_f, \Delta_g) \|_2$ and $\| M - M^* \|_F$, respectively, and they are not the same. The difference is made by the difference between numbers of columns corresponding to $f(x)$ and $g(x)$ (i.e., $n - k + 1$ and $m - k + 1$, respectively, as in (1.1)). Our resolution makes the difference smaller that will be given in Sect. 3.3.

2 NewtonSLRA Algorithm

In this section, we briefly review the NewtonSLRA algorithm as Algorithm 2. We note that there are the NewtonSLRA/1 and NewtonSLRA/2 algorithms proposed by Schost and Spaenlehauer [27]. However, we treat only the NewtonSLRA/1 algorithm since they are essentially the same, the only difference is performance depending on the problem, and the NewtonSLRA/1 algorithm is better for approximate GCD (see their paper [27, Section 5.1] for detail).

The outline of the NewtonSLRA/1 algorithm is as follows. It basically follows the alternating projection method (or called the lift and projection method) by Cadzow [5] that is formed by the following two steps: 1) lifting M_i up to the desired rank matrix in $\mathcal{D}_r$ by the well known Eckart-Young theorem (cf. [15, Theorem 2.4.8]), 2) projecting it back to the structured matrix in $\mathcal{S}$ by the orthogonal projection on $\mathcal{S}$. The NewtonSLRA/1 algorithm also has the following similar two steps: 1) the lifting step is exactly the same as the alternating projection method (this corresponds to $\tilde{M}$ on the line 2 of Algorithm 2), 2) projecting it back to the structured matrix in $\mathcal{S} \cap T_{\tilde{M}} \mathcal{D}_r$ by the orthogonal projection on $\mathcal{S} \cap T_{\tilde{M}} \mathcal{D}_r$ (this corresponds to the lines 3-7 of Algorithm 2). This difference in the projection methods makes the NewtonSLRA algorithm being with the following local quadratic convergence property.

Algorithm 2. One iteration of NewtonSLRA/1 [27]

Input: $M \in \mathcal{S} \subset \mathbb{R}^{p \times q}$, $r \in \mathbb{N}$ and $\{B_1, \ldots, B_d\}$: an orthonormal basis of $\mathcal{S}^0$
Output: $\Pi_{\mathcal{S} \cap T_{\tilde{M}} \mathcal{D}_r}(M)$ where $\tilde{M} = \Pi_{\mathcal{D}_r}(M)$

1: $U \Sigma V^T :=$ the singular value decomposition of M
         and let $U = (\overrightarrow{u_1}, \ldots, \overrightarrow{u_p})$ and $V = (\overrightarrow{v_1}, \ldots, \overrightarrow{v_q})$;
2: $\tilde{M} := U_r \Sigma_r V_r^T$ where U_r, V_r are the first r columns of U, V,
         respectively, and Σ_r is the top-left $r \times r$ sub-matrix of Σ;
3: **for** $i \in \{1, \ldots, p-r\}$, $j \in \{1, \ldots, q-r\}$ **do**
4:     $N_{(i-1)(q-r)+j} := \overrightarrow{u_{r+i}} \, \overrightarrow{v_{r+j}}^T$;
5:     $A := (a_{k,\ell}) \in \mathbb{R}^{(p-r)(q-r) \times d}$, $a_{k,\ell} = \langle N_k, B_\ell \rangle$;
6:     $\overrightarrow{b} := (b_k) \in \mathbb{R}^{(p-r)(q-r)}$, $b_k = \langle N_k, \tilde{M} - M \rangle$;
7: **return** $M + \sum_{\ell=1}^{d} (A^\dagger \overrightarrow{b})_\ell B_\ell$;

Theorem 1 (Convergence Property [27, Theorem 1]). *Let ζ be in $\mathcal{S} \cap \mathcal{D}_r$ such that $\Pi_{\mathcal{D}_r}$ is C^2 around ζ and $\mathcal{S}$ and $\mathcal{D}_r$ intersect transversally at ζ. There exist $\nu, \gamma, \gamma' > 0$ such that, for all M_0 in $\mathcal{S} \cap \mathcal{B}_\nu(\zeta)$, the sequence (M_i) given by $M_{i+1} = \varphi(M_i)$ is well defined and converges toward a matrix $M_\infty \in W$, and*

- *$\| M_{i+1} - M_\infty \|_F \leq \gamma \| M_i - M_\infty \|_F^2$ for all $i \geq 0$,*
- *$\| \Pi_W(M_0) - M_\infty \|_F \leq \gamma' \| \Pi_W(M_0) - M_0 \|_F^2$*

where φ is Algorithm 2 as a mapping, U is an open neighborhood of $\mathcal{D}_r$ at ζ and $W = \mathcal{S} \cap \mathcal{D}_r \cap U$. ◁

As for the time complexity and actual implementation, we do not have to compute $N_{(i-1)(q-r)+j}$, A and $\overrightarrow{b}$ as is on the lines 4, 5 and 6 in Algorithm 2. Instead we compute them as follows (cf. Schost and Spaenlehauer [27, Section 3]).

$$\langle \overrightarrow{u} \, \overrightarrow{v}^T, M \rangle = \overrightarrow{u}^T M \overrightarrow{v} \quad \text{for } M \in \mathbb{R}^{p \times q}.$$

This part can be done in $O(pdq(p-r)(q-r))$ over reals. Computing $\tilde{M}$ is done in $O(pqr)$ and computing the Moore–Penrose pseudo-inverse is done in $O(d(p-r)^2(q-r)^2)$. Therefore, one iteration of the NewtonSLRA/1 requires the singular value decomposition and $O(pqd(p-r)(q-r) + pqr)$ arithmetic operations.

Remark 2.1 (Time Complexity Specific to Approximate GCD). For computing an approximate GCD of degree k, of $f(x)$ and $g(x)$, all the parameters in the NewtonSLRA/1 algorithm become $p = m + n - k + 1$, $q = m + n - 2k + 2$, $r = m + n - 2k + 1$, $d = m + n + 2$, $\mathcal{S} = \mathcal{S}_{k-1}(f, g)$ and $M = \mathrm{Syl}_{k-1}(f, g)$. This means that one iteration of the NewtonSLRA/1 requires the singular value decomposition and $O((m+n-k)(m+n-2k)(m+n)k)$ arithmetic operations. ◁

We note that $O(m^3 k)$ (since $m \geq n$) is a little bit larger than other one of STLN based algorithms [16] computes the QR decomposition for the least squares, of matrices of sizes $(m+n+3) \times (m+n+k+3)$ and $(2m+2n-k+2) \times (2m+2n-2k+1)$, respectively, hence they are $O(m^3)$. However, as in the next section, $O(m^3 k)$ can be reduced to the same order.

3 Improvements

In this section, we show our improvements of the NewtonSLRA/1 algorithm, as introduced in Sect. 1.3.

3.1 Subresultant Specific Better Complexity

As in Remark 2.1, we consider to compute an approximate GCD of degree k, of $f(x)$ and $g(x)$, by the NewtonSLRA/1 algorithm. In this case, the given orthonormal basis of $\mathcal{S}_{k-1}(f,g)$ will be made from

$$\{\bar{B}_1,\ldots,\bar{B}_d\} = \left\{\overline{\mathrm{Syl}_{k-1}(f,g)}^{f_m}, \ldots, \overline{\mathrm{Syl}_{k-1}(f,g)}^{f_0}, \right.$$
$$\left. \overline{\mathrm{Syl}_{k-1}(f,g)}^{g_n}, \ldots, \overline{\mathrm{Syl}_{k-1}(f,g)}^{g_0}\right\} \tag{3.1}$$

where $\overline{\mathrm{Syl}_{k-1}(f,g)}^{h}$ denotes $\mathrm{Syl}_{k-1}(f,g)$ of symbolic $f(x)$ and $g(x)$ with the substitution $f_m = \cdots = f_0 = g_n = \cdots = g_0 = 0$ but $h = 1$, such that

$$\mathrm{Syl}_{k-1}(f,g) = f_m\bar{B}_1 + \cdots + f_0\bar{B}_{m+1} + g_n\bar{B}_{m+2} + \cdots + g_0\bar{B}_d.$$

Therefore, its orthonormalized basis is given by

$$\{B_1,\ldots,B_d\} = \{\eta_1^{-1}\bar{B}_1, \ldots, \eta_{m+1}^{-1}\bar{B}_{m+1}, \eta_{m+2}^{-1}\bar{B}_{m+2}, \ldots, \eta_d^{-1}\bar{B}_d\}$$

where $\eta_i = \sqrt{n-k+1}$ $(i \leq m+1)$ and $\eta_i = \sqrt{m-k+1}$ $(m+2 \leq i)$.

Remark 3.1. We note that removing some of B_is fixes a priori corresponding coefficients. For example, this can be used to keep polynomials monic.   ◁

In the NewtonSLRA algorithm, we compute the matrix A with the elements $a_{(i-1)(q-r)+j,\ell} = \vec{u}_i^T B_\ell \vec{v}_j$, and the complexity of each element is $O(pq)$ for $\vec{u}_i^T B_\ell$ and $O(q)$ for $(\vec{u}_i^T B_\ell)\vec{v}_j$. However, since we have $B_i = \eta_i^{-1}\bar{B}_i$ and $\bar{B}$ is a sparse matrix (i.e. only $n-k+1$ or $m-k+1$ non-zero elements), $\vec{u}_i^T B_\ell$ can be computed in $O(m)$ as

$$\begin{cases} \vec{u}_i^T B_\ell = (u_{i,\ell}\eta_\ell^{-1} \cdots u_{i,\ell+n-k}\eta_\ell^{-1} \overbrace{0 \cdots 0}^{m-k+1}) & (\ell \leq m+1) \\ \vec{u}_i^T B_\ell = (\underbrace{0 \cdots 0}_{n-k+1} u_{i,\ell-m-1}\eta_\ell^{-1} \cdots u_{i,\ell-k-1}\eta_\ell^{-1}) & (m+2 \leq \ell) \end{cases},$$

where $\vec{u}_i^T = (u_{i1} \cdots u_{ip})$.

As a consequence, computing A and $\vec{b}$ is done in $O(m^2k)$, computing $\tilde{M}$ and updating M are done in $O((m+n)(m+n-k)(m+n-2k))$, and computing the Moore–Penrose pseudo-inverse is done in $O((m+n)k^2)$. Therefore, we have the following lemma and this means that this is faster than the original NewtonSLRA/1 algorithm though our modification is only applicable for approximate GCD.

Lemma 2. *One iteration of the NewtonSLRA/1 algorithm for computing approximate GCD requires the singular value decomposition and $O(m^3)$ arithmetic operations.*   ◁

3.2 Relaxed NewtonSLRA Algorithm

The quadratic convergence property of the NewtonSLRA algorithm is depending on the angle between the tangent space and the affine subspace, that is reflected to the constants in Theorem 1. Hence it may happen that the angle is small and the algorithm converges to a point that is relatively far from the global optimum, as in Sect. 4. Therefore, in the followings, we propose the relaxed NewtonSLRA algorithm that enlarges the tangent space to prevent from the generated sequence being far from the initial point on the early stage of iterations. In other words, this modification is intended to decrease the number of constraints of the least squares on the last line of the NewtonSLRA/1 algorithm.

Assumption 3.1 (Size of Matrix and Deficiency). In this section, we assume $p > q$ and $r = q-1$ that mean the case specific to the subresultant matrix for computing non-linear approximate GCD (especially for shorter proofs).   ◁

Let $U\Sigma V^T$ be the singular value decomposition of M, and let U and V be $(\vec{u_1} \cdots \vec{u_p})$ and $(\vec{v_1} \cdots \vec{v_q})$, respectively. In the NewtonSLRA/1 algorithm, the tangent space of $\mathcal{D}_r^0$ at M and its normal space $N_M\mathcal{D}_r^0$ are given as follows.

$$T_M\mathcal{D}_r^0 = \mathrm{Im}(M) \otimes \mathbb{R}^q + \mathbb{R}^p \otimes \mathrm{Ker}(M)^\perp, \quad N_M\mathcal{D}_r^0 = \mathrm{Ker}(M^T) \otimes \mathrm{Ker}(M).$$

Moreover, we have that $\{\vec{u_1}, \ldots, \vec{u_r}\}$, $\{\vec{v_1}, \ldots, \vec{v_r}\}$, $\{\vec{u_{r+1}}, \ldots, \vec{u_p}\}$ and $\{\vec{v_{r+1}}, \ldots, \vec{v_q}\}$ $(= \{\vec{v_q}\}$ since $r = q - 1$ by the assumption) are bases of $\mathrm{Im}(M)$, $\mathrm{Ker}(M)^\perp$, $\mathrm{Ker}(M^T)$ and $\mathrm{Ker}(M)$, respectively.

In our algorithm, instead of these tangent and normal spaces, we define the following relaxed tangent space $\mathcal{T}_{O,M}\mathcal{D}_r^0$ and relaxed normal space $\mathcal{N}_{O,M}\mathcal{D}_r^0$ at M from O such that $M - O$ is orthogonal to $T_M\mathcal{D}_r^0$ and $M \neq O$.

$$\mathcal{T}_{O,M}\mathcal{D}_r^0 = (\mathcal{N}_{O,M}\mathcal{D}_r^0)^\perp, \quad \mathcal{N}_{O,M}\mathcal{D}_r^0 = \mathrm{span}(M - O).$$

For $O \notin \mathcal{D}_r$ and $M = \Pi_{\mathcal{D}_r}(O)$, by Assumption 3.1, we have

$$\mathcal{T}_{O,M}\mathcal{D}_r^0 = \mathrm{span}(\vec{u_1}, \ldots, \vec{u_r}, \vec{u_{r+2}}, \ldots, \vec{u_p}) \otimes \mathbb{R}^q + \mathbb{R}^p \otimes \mathrm{Ker}(M)^\perp,$$
$$\mathcal{N}_{O,M}\mathcal{D}_r^0 = \mathrm{span}(\vec{u_{r+1}}) \otimes \mathrm{Ker}(M).$$

As a consequence of these modifications above, we propose the relaxed NewtonSLRA algorithm as Algorithm 3 and it has the following convergence property (note that the mapping φ is different from Theorem 1).

Theorem 2 (Convergence Property). *Let ζ be in $\mathcal{S} \cap \mathcal{D}_r$ such that $\Pi_{\mathcal{D}_r}$ is C^2 around ζ and $\mathcal{S}$ and $\mathcal{D}_r$ intersect transversally at ζ. There exist $\nu, \gamma, \gamma' > 0$ such that, for all M_0 in $\mathcal{S} \cap \mathcal{B}_\nu(\zeta)$, the sequence (M_i) given by $M_{i+1} = \varphi(M_i)$ is well defined and converges toward a matrix $M_\infty \in W$ and*

- *$\|M_{i+1} - M_\infty\|_F \leq \gamma \|M_i - M_\infty\|_F^2$ for all $i \geq 0$,*
- *$\|\Pi_W(M_0) - M_\infty\|_F \leq \gamma' \|\Pi_W(M_0) - M_0\|_F^2$*

*where φ **is Algorithm 3 as a mapping**, U is an open neighborhood of $\mathcal{D}_r$ at ζ and $W = \mathcal{S} \cap \mathcal{D}_r \cap U$.*   ◁

Algorithm 3. One iteration of relaxed NewtonSLRA

Input: $M \in \mathcal{S} \subset \mathbb{R}^{p \times q}$, $r \in \mathbb{N}$ (s.t. $p > q$ and $r = q - 1$)
and $\{B_1, \ldots, B_d\}$: an orthonormal basis of $\mathcal{S}^0$

Output: $\Pi_{\mathcal{S} \cap T_{M,\tilde{M}} \mathcal{D}_r}(M)$ where $\tilde{M} = \Pi_{\mathcal{D}_r}(M)$

1: $U \Sigma V^T :=$ the singular value decomposition of M
and let $U = (\vec{u_1}, \ldots, \vec{u_p})$ and $V = (\vec{v_1}, \ldots, \vec{v_q})$;

2: $\tilde{M} := U_r \Sigma_r V_r^T$ as in Algorithm 2;

3: $A := (a_{1,\ell}) \in \mathbb{R}^{1 \times d}$, $a_{1,\ell} = \langle \vec{u_{r+1}} \vec{v_q}^T, B_\ell \rangle$;

4: $\vec{b} := (b_1) \in \mathbb{R}^1$, $b_1 = \langle \vec{u_{r+1}} \vec{v_q}^T, \tilde{M} - M \rangle$;

5: **return** $M + \sum_{\ell=1}^d (A^\dagger \vec{b})_\ell B_\ell$;

The proof of Theorem 2 is exactly the same as that for Theorem 1, which is based on the following Proposition 4 and Proposition 5. However, the proofs of these propositions are a little bit different from [27] but the difference is not large since $T_{M,\Pi_{\mathcal{D}_r}(M)} \mathcal{D}_r^0 \supset T_{\Pi_{\mathcal{D}_r}(M)} \mathcal{D}_r^0$ and the property of the tangent space used in the proofs is basically that $M - \Pi_{\mathcal{D}_r}(M)$ is orthogonal to $T_{\Pi_{\mathcal{D}_r}(M)} \mathcal{D}_r^0$. Therefore, in the following, we show only lemmas and propositions that are affected by our relaxation.

Lemma 3 (cf. [27, Lemma 4.5]).
There exists an open neighborhood U of ζ such that

$$\inf_{y \in \mathcal{D}_r \cap U, \, x \in \lfloor \mathcal{S} \cap U \rfloor_y} \alpha(T_{x,y} \mathcal{D}_r^0, \mathcal{S}^0) > 0$$

where $\lfloor \mathcal{S} \cap U \rfloor_y = \{x \in \mathcal{S} \cap U \mid y - x \in (T_y \mathcal{D}_r^0)^\perp, \, x \neq y\}$.   ◁

Proof. Suppose that the lemma is not valid hence there exist $y \in \mathcal{D}_r \cap U$, $x \in \lfloor \mathcal{S} \cap U \rfloor_y$ such that $\alpha(T_{x,y} \mathcal{D}_r^0, \mathcal{S}^0) = 0$. This means $T_{x,y} \mathcal{D}_r^0 \subset \mathcal{S}^0$ or $\mathcal{S}^0 \subset T_{x,y} \mathcal{D}_r^0$. By [27, Lemma 4.5], we have $\inf_{y \in \mathcal{D}_r \cap U} \alpha(T_y \mathcal{D}_r^0, \mathcal{S}^0) > 0$, and $T_{x,y} \mathcal{D}_r^0 \subset \mathcal{S}^0$ is not satisfied since $T_y \mathcal{D}_r^0 \subset T_{x,y} \mathcal{D}_r^0$. As for $\mathcal{S}^0 \subset T_{x,y} \mathcal{D}_r^0$, let $x' \in \lfloor \mathcal{S} \cap U \rfloor_y$ and $c \in \mathbb{R}$ be such that $y - x' = c(y - x)$ and $c \neq 1$, we have $x' - x \in \mathcal{S}^0$ hence $y - x \in S^0$. This means $S^0 \not\subset T_{x,y} \mathcal{D}_r^0$ since $y - x \notin T_{x,y} \mathcal{D}_r^0$ by the definition. Therefore, we have $\alpha(T_{x,y} \mathcal{D}_r^0, \mathcal{S}^0) \neq 0$.   □

Let $\lambda, \rho > 0$ be such that $U = \mathcal{B}_\rho(\zeta)$ satisfies Lemma 3 and lemmas by Schost and Spaenlehauer [27, Lemma 2.3,4.5,4.6 and 4.7], and K, K' and δ be defined as follows.

$$\alpha_0 = \inf_{y \in \mathcal{D}_r \cap \overline{\mathcal{B}_\rho(\zeta)}, \, x \in \lfloor \mathcal{S} \cap \overline{\mathcal{B}_\rho(\zeta)} \rfloor_y} \alpha(T_{x,y} \mathcal{D}_r^0, \mathcal{S}^0),$$

$$C_{\mathcal{D}_r} = \sup_{v \in \overline{\mathcal{B}_\rho(\zeta)}} \|D^2 \Pi_{\mathcal{D}_r}(v)\|_F, \quad K = C_{\mathcal{D}_r}/\sin(\alpha_0) + \sqrt{2}\lambda,$$

$$C_W = \sup_{z \in \mathcal{B}_\rho(\zeta)} \|D\Pi_W(z)\|_F, \quad K' = C_W K,$$

$$\delta > 0 \text{ such that } C_{\mathcal{D}_r}^2 \delta^2 \leq 1/2 \text{ and } 2\delta + K\delta^2 \leq \rho.$$

In the rest of this subsection, for simplicity's sake, we use the following notations: for $x \in \mathcal{B}_\delta(\zeta)$, let $y = \Pi_{\mathcal{D}_r}(x)$, $w = \Pi_W(x)$, $z = \Pi_{T_{x,y} \mathcal{D}_r}(w)$, w' be the orthogonal projection of x on the affine space parallel to $\mathcal{S} \cap T_y \mathcal{D}_r$ containing w, and $z' = \Pi_{T_{x,y} \mathcal{D}_r}(w')$.

Proposition 1 (cf. [27, Proposition 4.8]).
For $x \in \mathcal{B}_\delta(\zeta)$, we have $\|z - w\|_F < C_{\mathcal{D}_r} \|x - w\|_F^2$.   ◁

Proof. As in the proof of [27, Proposition 4.8], we have y, $w \in \mathcal{B}_\rho(\zeta)$ and $\| y - w \|_F \leq 2\delta$. Since y and w are fixed points of $\Pi_{\mathcal{D}_r}$, all the points of the line segment between y and w are in $\mathcal{B}_\rho(\zeta)$, and $\mathcal{T}_{x,y}\mathcal{D}_r^0 \supset \mathcal{T}_y\mathcal{D}_r^0$, by a Taylor approximation of $\Pi_{\mathcal{D}_r}$ between y and w, we have

$$w - y = \Pi_{\mathcal{D}_r}(w) - \Pi_{\mathcal{D}_r}(y) = \Pi_{\mathcal{T}_{x,y}\mathcal{D}_r^0}(w - y) + r$$

with $\|r\|_F \leq C_{\mathcal{D}_r} \|w - y\|_F^2 / 2$. Since $y + \Pi_{\mathcal{T}_{x,y}\mathcal{D}_r^0}(w - y) = \Pi_{\mathcal{T}_{x,y}\mathcal{D}_r}(w) = z$, we have $\| z - w \|_F \leq C_{\mathcal{D}_r} \|y - w\|_F^2 / 2 \leq 2C_{\mathcal{D}_r}\delta^2$ hence $C_{\mathcal{D}_r} \|z - w\|_F \leq 1$. $x - y$ and $w - z$ are orthogonal to $\mathcal{T}_{x,y}\mathcal{D}_r^0$ and $y - z$ hence we have

$$\|y - w\|_F^2 = \|y - z\|_F^2 + \|z - w\|_F^2 \leq \|x - w\|_F^2 + \|z - w\|_F^2 .$$

Therefore, we have

$$\|z - w\|_F \leq \frac{C_{\mathcal{D}_r}}{2} \|y - w\|_F^2 \leq \frac{C_{\mathcal{D}_r}}{2}(\|x - w\|_F^2 + \|z - w\|_F^2)$$
$$\leq \frac{C_{\mathcal{D}_r}}{2} \|x - w\|_F^2 + \frac{1}{2} \|z - w\|_F .$$

This means $\|z - w\|_F < C_{\mathcal{D}_r} \|x - w\|_F^2$.   □

Lemma 4. *For $x \in \mathcal{B}_\delta(\zeta)$, $w' - x$ is orthogonal to $(\mathcal{S} \cap \mathcal{T}_{x,y}\mathcal{D}_r)^0$.*   ◁

Proof. At first, by Lemma 2.3 [27] with our assumptions, $\mathcal{S} \cap \mathcal{T}_y\mathcal{D}_r$ is not empty hence $\mathcal{S} \cap \mathcal{T}_{x,y}\mathcal{D}_r$ is not empty since $\mathcal{T}_y\mathcal{D}_r \subset \mathcal{T}_{x,y}\mathcal{D}_r$. This means $(\mathcal{S} \cap \mathcal{T}_{x,y}\mathcal{D}_r)^0 = \mathcal{S}^0 \cap \mathcal{T}_{x,y}\mathcal{D}_r^0$. By the construction, $w' - x$ is parallel to $y - x$ and $\mathcal{T}_{x,y}\mathcal{D}_r^0 = \text{span}(y - x)^\perp$ hence $w' - x$ is orthogonal to $(\mathcal{S} \cap \mathcal{T}_{x,y}\mathcal{D}_r)^0$.   □

Proposition 2 (cf. [27, Proposition 4.8]).
For $x \in \mathcal{B}_\delta(\zeta)$, we have $\|\varphi(x) - w\|_F \leq \frac{C_{\mathcal{D}_r}}{\sin(\alpha_0)} \|x - w\|_F^2 + \|w' - w\|_F$.   ◁

Proof. Let θ be the angle between $w' - \varphi(x)$ and $z' - \varphi(x)$ that are in $\mathcal{S}^0$ and $\mathcal{T}_{x,y}\mathcal{D}_r^0$, respectively. As in the proof [27, Proposition 4.8], $z' - \varphi(x)$ is in the orthogonal complement of $(\mathcal{S} \cap \mathcal{T}_{x,y}\mathcal{D}_r)^0$ since $z' - \varphi(x) = (z' - w') + (w' - x) + (x - \varphi(x))$ which are orthogonal to $(\mathcal{S} \cap \mathcal{T}_{x,y}\mathcal{D}_r)^0$ by Lemma 4. As in the proof of Lemma 4, we have $(\mathcal{S} \cap \mathcal{T}_{x,y}\mathcal{D}_r)^0 = \mathcal{S}^0 \cap \mathcal{T}_{x,y}\mathcal{D}_r^0$. Therefore, we have $z' - \varphi(x) \in \mathcal{T}_{x,y}\mathcal{D}_r^0 \cap (\mathcal{S}^0 \cap \mathcal{T}_{x,y}\mathcal{D}_r^0)^\perp$ and $w' - \varphi(x) \in \mathcal{S}^0$ hence by Lemma 4.4 [27] we have

$$\cos(\theta) = \left\langle \frac{z' - \varphi(x)}{\|z' - \varphi(x)\|_F}, \frac{w' - \varphi(x)}{\|w' - \varphi(x)\|_F} \right\rangle \leq \cos(\alpha(\mathcal{T}_{x,y}\mathcal{D}_r^0, \mathcal{S}^0)) \leq \cos(\alpha_0).$$

Since $w' - z'$ is orthogonal to $\mathcal{T}_{x,y}\mathcal{D}_r^0$ and $\varphi(x) - z' \in \mathcal{T}_{x,y}\mathcal{D}_r^0$ hence $\|w' - z'\|_F = \sin(\theta) \|w' - \varphi(x)\|_F$, we have

$$\|\varphi(x) - w'\|_F \leq \|z' - w'\|_F / \sin(\alpha_0).$$

We have $\|z-w\|_F = \|z'-w'\|_F$ by the construction hence we have $\|\varphi(x)-w'\|_F \leq C_{\mathcal{D}_r} \|x-w\|_F^2 / \sin(\alpha_0)$ by Proposition 1. Therefore, we have

$$\|\varphi(x) - w\|_F \leq \frac{C_{\mathcal{D}_r}}{\sin(\alpha_0)} \|x-w\|_F^2 + \|w'-w\|_F$$

by the inequality $\|\varphi(x) - w\|_F \leq \|\varphi(x) - w'\|_F + \|w'-w\|_F$.   □

Proposition 3 (cf. [27, Proposition 4.8]).
For $x \in \mathcal{B}_\delta(\zeta)$, we have $\|w-w'\|_F \leq \sqrt{2}\lambda \|x-w\|_F^2$.   ◁

Proof. Let θ' be the angle between $w'-w$ and $x-w$. Since $x-w'$ is orthogonal to $w'-w$, we have $\|w-w'\|_F = \cos(\theta') \|x-w\|_F$. By Lemma 4.4 [27] we have

$$\cos(\theta') \leq \cos(\alpha(\mathcal{S}^0 \cap T_y\mathcal{D}_r^0, (\mathcal{S}^0 \cap T_y\mathcal{D}_r^0)^\perp))$$

since $w'-w$ is in $(\mathcal{S} \cap T_y\mathcal{D}_r)^0 = \mathcal{S}^0 \cap T_y\mathcal{D}_r^0$, and $x-w$ is orthogonal to $T_wW^0 = (\mathcal{S} \cap T_w\mathcal{D}_r)^0$ by the transversality assumption. By Lemma 4.7 [27], there exists a constant λ such that

$$\|w-w'\|_F \leq \lambda \|y-w\|_F \|x-w\|_F .$$

As in the proof of Proposition 1, we have $\|z-w\|_F \leq C_{\mathcal{D}_r}\delta \|y-w\|_F$ and $\|y-w\|_F^2 \leq \|x-w\|_F^2 + \|z-w\|_F^2$. Therefore, we have $\|y-w\|_F \leq \sqrt{2} \|x-w\|_F$ hence $\|w-w'\|_F \leq \sqrt{2}\lambda \|x-w\|_F^2$.   □

Proposition 4 (cf. [27, Proposition 4.8]).
For $x \in \mathcal{B}_\delta(\zeta)$, $\varphi(x)$ is in $\mathcal{B}_\rho(\zeta)$ and we have

$$\|\varphi(x) - \Pi_W(x)\|_F \leq K \|x - \Pi_W(x)\|_F^2,$$
$$\|\Pi_W(\varphi(x)) - \Pi_W(x)\|_F \leq K' \|x - \Pi_W(x)\|_F^2 .$$

◁

Proof. By Propositions 2 and 3, and $w = \Pi_W(x)$, we have

$$\|\varphi(x) - w\|_F \leq \frac{C_{\mathcal{D}_r}}{\sin(\alpha_0)} \|x-w\|_F^2 + \sqrt{2}\lambda \|x-w\|_F^2 = K \|x - \Pi_W(x)\|_F^2 .$$

As in the proof of [27, Proposition 4.8], we have $\|\zeta-w\|_F < 2\delta$ and $\|x-w\|_F < \delta$. We have $\|\zeta - \varphi(x)\|_F < \rho$ since $2\delta + K\delta^2 \leq \rho$ and

$$\|\zeta - \varphi(x)\|_F \leq \|\zeta-w\|_F + \|\varphi-w\|_F < 2\delta + K \|x-w\|_F^2 < 2\delta + K\delta^2.$$

As in the proof of [27, Proposition 4.8], a first-order Taylor expansion of Π_W along the line segment between $\varphi(x)$ and w gives

$$\begin{aligned}
\|\Pi_W(\varphi(x)) - \Pi_W(x)\|_F &= \|\Pi_W(\varphi(x)) - \Pi_W(w)\|_F \\
&\leq C_W \|\varphi(x) - w\|_F \leq C_W \times K \|x-w\|_F^2 \leq K' \|x-w\|_F^2 .
\end{aligned}$$

□

With the above proposition, by following exactly the same way (induction) of Proposition 4.9 [27], we have the following proposition where $\kappa = K + K'$ and $\nu > 0$ such that $\kappa\nu < 1/2$ and $4\nu < \delta$.

Proposition 5 (cf. [27, Proposition 4.9]). *Let x_0 be in $\mathcal{B}_\nu(\zeta)$. One can define sequences $(x_i)_{i\geq0}$ and $(w_i)_{i\geq0}$ of elements of $\mathbb{R}^{p\times q}$ such that $\| x_0 - w_0 \|_F \leq \nu$ and, for $i \geq 0$, $x_i \in \mathcal{B}_\delta(\zeta)$, $w_i = \Pi_W(x_i)$, $x_i = \varphi(x_{i-1})$ $(i \geq 1)$, $\| x_i - w_i \|_F \leq \kappa \| x_{i-1} - w_{i-1} \|_F^2$ $(i \geq 1)$, and $\| w_i - w_{i-1} \|_F \leq \kappa \| x_{i-1} - w_{i-1} \|_F^2$ $(i \geq 1)$.* ◁

3.3 Column Weighted Frobenius Norm

In the both of original and relaxed NewtonSLRA algorithms, let the solution of least squares on the last line be $\overrightarrow{h}$ hence $\overrightarrow{h} = A^\dagger \overrightarrow{b}$. Consider that this iteration is for computing approximate GCD of $f(x)$ and $g(x)$, we have the perturbed polynomials $f(x) + \Delta_f(x)$ and $g(x) + \Delta_g(x)$ as follows.

$$\begin{pmatrix} \overrightarrow{f + \Delta_f} \\ \overrightarrow{g + \Delta_g} \end{pmatrix} = \begin{pmatrix} \overrightarrow{f} \\ \overrightarrow{g} \end{pmatrix} + \mathrm{diag}(\eta_1^{-1}, \ldots, \eta_d^{-1})\, \overrightarrow{h}.$$

Since $\{B_1, \ldots, B_d\}$ is an orthonormal basis of $\mathcal{S}^0$, each iteration minimizes the Frobenius norm of the correction matrix $\sum_{\ell=1}^{d}(A^\dagger \overrightarrow{b})_\ell B_\ell$ and its value is $\| \overrightarrow{h} \|_2$. Actually each iteration computes the nearest intersection point between two subspaces in the Frobenius norm. However, as for approximate GCD, we have $\| (\Delta_f, \Delta_g) \|_2 = \| \mathrm{diag}(\eta_1^{-1}, \ldots, \eta_d^{-1}) \overrightarrow{h} \|_2$ hence this is not minimized (i.e., not the nearest point) in the polynomial 2-norm if $m \neq n$ (i.e., $\eta_1 \neq \eta_d$).

To make this difference smaller, we introduce the following column weighted inner product $\langle M_1, M_2 \rangle_W$ and norm $\| M \|_W$.

$$\langle M_1, M_2 \rangle_W = \langle M_1 W, M_2 W \rangle = \mathrm{tr}(W^T M_1^T M_2 W),$$
$$\| M \|_W = \sqrt{\langle M, M \rangle_W} = \sqrt{\langle MW, MW \rangle} = \| MW \|_F$$

where W is a diagonal invertible matrix and in this paper we use

$$W = \mathrm{diag}(\overbrace{\eta_1^{-1}, \ldots, \eta_1^{-1}}^{n-k+1}, \overbrace{\eta_{m+2}^{-1}, \ldots, \eta_{m+2}^{-1}}^{m-k+1}).$$

Lemma 5. *Let us consider $\mathcal{S}_{k-1}(f,g)$ as an affine subspace of inner product space endowed with $\langle M_1, M_2 \rangle_W$. Then, $\{\bar{B}_1, \ldots, \bar{B}_d\}$ in (3.1) is an orthonormal basis of $\mathcal{S}_{k-1}(f,g)$.* ◁

Proof. By the construction of $\{\bar{B}_1, \ldots, \bar{B}_d\}$, clearly it spans $\mathcal{S}_{k-1}(f,g)$ hence we only show that it is already orthogonalized and normalized. For any pair $\bar{B}_i$ and $\bar{B}_j$, there exist $h_i, h_j \in \{f_m, \ldots, f_0, g_n, \ldots, g_0\}$ such that

$$\langle \bar{B}_i, \bar{B}_j \rangle_W = \langle \overline{\mathrm{Syl}_{k-1}(f,g)}^{h_i} W, \overline{\mathrm{Syl}_{k-1}(f,g)}^{h_j} W \rangle.$$

We have

$$\langle \bar{B}_i, \bar{B}_j \rangle_W = \langle \overline{\mathrm{Syl}_{k-1}(\eta_1^{-1}f, \eta_{m+2}^{-1} g)}^{h_i}, \overline{\mathrm{Syl}_{k-1}(\eta_1^{-1}f, \eta_{m+2}^{-1} g)}^{h_j} \rangle.$$

If $i \neq j$, all the non-zero elements of these two matrices are placed at different indices hence we have $\langle \bar{B}_i, \bar{B}_j \rangle_W = 0$. Otherwise $(i = j)$, we have

$$\langle \bar{B}_i, \bar{B}_i \rangle_W = \begin{cases} \overbrace{\eta_1^{-2} + \cdots + \eta_1^{-2}}^{n+k-1} = 1 & (i \leq m+1) \\ \overbrace{\eta_{m+2}^{-2} + \cdots + \eta_{m+2}^{-2}}^{m+k-1} = 1 & (i \geq m+2) \end{cases}.$$

$\square$

To make the NewtonSLRA/1 and relaxed NewtonSLRA algorithms being compatible with the column weighted inner product and its Frobenius norm, we give the column weighted Frobenius norm version of the Eckart–Young theorem as follows.

Theorem 3. *For $M \in \mathbb{R}^{p \times q}$ and $r \in \mathbb{N}$, let $U\Sigma V^T$ be the singular value decomposition of MW, and let U_r, V_r be the first r columns of U, V, respectively, and Σ_r be the top-left $r \times r$ sub-matrix of Σ. We have*

$$U_r \Sigma_r V_r^T W^{-1} = \mathrm{argmin}_{M_r \in \mathcal{D}_r} \| M - M_r \|_W . \qquad \lhd$$

Proof. Since W is a diagonal matrix and is invertible, the proof just follows from that for the Frobenius norm version of the Eckart–Young theorem as follows.

$$\begin{aligned} \| M - M_r \|_W^2 &= \| MW - M_r W \|_F^2 = \sum_{i=1}^{\min(p,q)} \sigma_i(MW - M_r W)^2 \\ &\geq \sum_{i=r+1}^{\min(p,q)} \sigma_i(MW)^2 = \| MW - U_r \Sigma_r V_r^T \|_F^2 \\ &= \| M - U_r \Sigma_r V_r^T W^{-1} \|_W^2 \end{aligned}$$

where we denote the ith largest singular value of A by $\sigma_i(A)$. $\square$

Moreover, since the orthogonality of M in terms of the column weighted Frobenius norm is just the orthogonality of MW in terms of the Frobenius norm, and we have $\mathrm{Im}(MW) = \mathrm{Im}(M)$ and $\mathrm{Ker}((MW)^T) = \mathrm{Ker}(W^T M^T) = \mathrm{Ker}(M^T)$, we have the following.

$$T_M \mathcal{D}_r^0 = \mathrm{Im}(M) \otimes \mathbb{R}^q + \mathbb{R}^p \otimes \mathrm{Ker}_W(MW)^\perp, \quad N_M \mathcal{D}_r^0 = \mathrm{Ker}(M^T) \otimes \mathrm{Ker}_W(MW)$$

where $\mathrm{Ker}_W(A) = \{ W^{-1} \vec{x} \mid \vec{x} \in \mathrm{Ker}(A) \}$. The relaxed tangent and relaxed normal spaces for $O \notin \mathcal{D}_r$ and $M = \Pi_{\mathcal{D}_r}(O)$ are as follows, where $U = (\vec{u_1} \cdots \vec{u_p})$, $V = (\vec{v_1} \cdots \vec{v_q})$ and $U\Sigma V^T$ is the singular value decomposition of MW.

$$\begin{aligned} T_{O,M} \mathcal{D}_r^0 &= \mathrm{span}(\vec{u_1}, \ldots, \vec{u_r}, \vec{u_{r+2}}, \ldots, \vec{u_p}) \otimes \mathbb{R}^q + \mathbb{R}^p \otimes \mathrm{Ker}_W(M)^\perp, \\ N_{O,M} \mathcal{D}_r^0 &= \mathrm{span}(\vec{u_{r+1}}) \otimes \mathrm{span}(W^{-1}\vec{v_q}). \end{aligned}$$

As a consequence, we have the weighted NewtonSLRA algorithm as Algorithm 4. The correctness of this iteration is given by the following lemma.

Algorithm 4. One iteration of weighted NewtonSLRA

Input: $M \in \mathcal{S} \subset \mathbb{R}^{p \times q}$, $r \in \mathbb{N}$, $W \in \mathbb{R}^{q \times q}$ and $\{\bar{B}_1, \ldots, \bar{B}_d\}$: an orthonormal basis of $\mathcal{S}^0$
Output: $\Pi_{\mathcal{S} \cap T_{\tilde{M}} \mathcal{D}_r}(M)$ where $\tilde{M} = \Pi_{\mathcal{D}_r}(M)$ in terms of $\|\cdot\|_W$
1: $U \Sigma V^T :=$ the singular value decomposition of MW

$\qquad\qquad\qquad$ and let $U = (\vec{u_1}, \ldots, \vec{u_p})$ and $V = (\vec{v_1}, \ldots, \vec{v_q})$;
2: $\tilde{M} := U_r \Sigma_r V_r^T W^{-1}$ as in Algorithm 2 except for W^{-1};
3: **for** $i \in \{1, \ldots, p - r\}$, $j \in \{1, \ldots, q - r\}$ **do**
4: $\qquad N_{(i-1)(q-r)+j} := \vec{u_{r+i}} \, \vec{v_{r+j}}^T W^{-1}$;
5: $A := (a_{k,\ell}) \in \mathbb{R}^{(p-r)(q-r) \times d}$, $a_{k,\ell} = \langle N_k, \bar{B}_\ell \rangle_W$;
6: $\vec{b} := (b_k) \in \mathbb{R}^{(p-r)(q-r)}$, $b_k = \langle N_k, \tilde{M} - M \rangle_W$;
7: **return** $M + \sum_{\ell=1}^{d} (A^\dagger \vec{b})_\ell \bar{B}_\ell$;

Lemma 6. *Algorithm 4 works correctly under our assumptions.* ◁

Proof. Let $\varphi(M)$ denote $M + \sum_{\ell=1}^{d}(A^\dagger \vec{b})_\ell \bar{B}_\ell$ on the line 7. At first we prove $\varphi(M) \in \mathcal{S} \cap T_{\tilde{M}} \mathcal{D}_r$. By the assumption we have $M \in \mathcal{S}$ and $\{\bar{B}_1, \ldots, \bar{B}_d\}$ is an orthonormal basis of $\mathcal{S}^0$, we have $\varphi(M) \in \mathcal{S}$. As for $\varphi(M) \in T_{\tilde{M}} \mathcal{D}_r$, we show $\varphi(M) - \tilde{M} \in T_{\tilde{M}} \mathcal{D}_r^0$ and in fact we have

$$
\begin{aligned}
\langle N_k, \varphi(M) - \tilde{M} \rangle_W &= \langle N_k, M + \sum_{\ell=1}^{d}(A^\dagger \vec{b})_\ell \bar{B}_\ell - \tilde{M} \rangle_W \\
&= \langle N_k, M - \tilde{M} \rangle_W + \langle N_k, \sum_{\ell=1}^{d}(A^\dagger \vec{b})_\ell \bar{B}_\ell \rangle_W = 0.
\end{aligned}
$$

Next, we prove that $\|\varphi(M) - M\|_W$ is minimized. Since $\varphi(M) \in \mathcal{S} \cap T_{\tilde{M}} \mathcal{D}_r$, we can let $\varphi(M) = M + \sum_{\ell=1}^{d} x_\ell \bar{B}_\ell$ for some unknowns $\vec{x} = (x_\ell)$. By Lemma 5, we have

$$
\|\varphi(M) - M\|_W = \|\sum_{\ell=1}^{d} x_\ell \bar{B}_\ell\|_W = \|\vec{x}\|_2 \, .
$$

$A^\dagger \vec{b}$ on the line 7 is the minimum solution of the least squares (underdetermined linear system) hence $\varphi(M) = \Pi_{\mathcal{S} \cap T_{\tilde{M}} \mathcal{D}_r}(M)$. $\qquad\qquad\square$

As for the weighted/relaxed NewtonSLRA algorithm (Algorithm 5) we have the same lemma whose proof is the same way above.

Lemma 7. *Algorithm 5 works correctly under our assumptions.* ◁

Moreover, both of the relaxed and weighted/relaxed NewtonSLRA algorithms have the same convergent property as in Theorem 1 and Theorem 2 though we omit the theorem/proof since they are the same with the exception of the weighted part.

Remark 3.2. Our algorithms with the weighted Frobenius norm do not guarantee that the resulting perturbation is smaller than the original algorithm since this modification is just for each iteration and it does not guarantee any better resulting perturbation in total. ◁

Algorithm 5. One iteration of weighted/relaxed NewtonSLRA

Input: $M \in \mathcal{S} \subset \mathbb{R}^{p \times q}$, $r \in \mathbb{N}$ (s.t. $p > q$ and $r = q - 1$), $W \in \mathbb{R}^{q \times q}$
and $\{B_1, \ldots, B_d\}$: an orthonormal basis of $\mathcal{S}^0$
Output: $\Pi_{\mathcal{S} \cap \mathcal{T}_{M, \tilde{M}} \mathcal{D}_r}(M)$ where $\tilde{M} = \Pi_{\mathcal{D}_r}(M)$ in terms of $\|\cdot\|_W$

1: $U \Sigma V^T :=$ the singular value decomposition of MW
and let $U = (\vec{u_1}, \ldots, \vec{u_p})$ and $V = (\vec{v_1}, \ldots, \vec{v_q})$;
2: $\tilde{M} := U_r \Sigma_r V_r^T W^{-1}$ as in Algorithm 2 except for W^{-1};
3: $A := (a_{1,\ell}) \in \mathbb{R}^{1 \times d}$, $a_{1,\ell} = \langle \vec{u_{r+1}} \vec{v_q}^T W^{-1}, B_\ell \rangle_W$;
4: $\vec{b} := (b_1) \in \mathbb{R}^1$, $b_1 = \langle \vec{u_{r+1}} \vec{v_q}^T W^{-1}, \tilde{M} - M \rangle_W$;
5: **return** $M + \sum_{\ell=1}^d (A^\dagger \vec{b})_\ell B_\ell$;

Algorithm 6. Approximate GCD by improved NewtonSLRA

Input: $f(x), g(x) \in \mathbb{R}[x]$ and $k \in \mathbb{N}$
(options: $\varepsilon_c, \varepsilon_r \in \mathbb{R}_{\geq 0}$, $max_i \in \mathbb{N}$ and $weighted \in \{T, F\}$)
Output: $d(x) \in \mathbb{R}[x]$, approximate GCD of degree k

1: $M_0 := \mathrm{Syl}_{k-1}(f, g)$ and $r := m + n - 2k + 1$;
2: **for** $i \in \{1, 2, \ldots, max_i\}$ **do**
3:    compute M_i from M_{i-1}
- by Algorithm 3 if $weighted = F$; (switch to Alg. 2 if $\sigma_{r+1}(M_{i-1}) \leq \varepsilon_r$)
- by Algorithm 5 if $weighted = T$; (switch to Alg. 4 if $\sigma_{r+1}(M_{i-1}W) \leq \varepsilon_r$)
4:    **if** $\|A^\dagger \vec{b}\|_2$ (computed on the last line) $\leq \varepsilon_c$ **then**
5:       **break** the **for** loop;
6: construct $f(x) + \Delta_f(x)$ and $g(x) + \Delta_g(x)$ back from the result;
7: compute $d(x)$ from $\mathrm{Syl}_{k-1}(f + \Delta_f, g + \Delta_g)$;
8: **return** $d(x)$;

---

4   Numerical Experiments

We have implemented all the algorithms in this paper (including the Newton-SLRA/1 algorithm) in the collection of C programs for computing approximate GCDs introduced by the author[1] [22]. Algorithm 6 is the top level function we implemented. Basically we have compared with the UVGCD algorithm [33] and the STLN based algorithm [16] since they are the two best algorithms according to the wide range of numerical experiments by the author [22].

All the experiments in this section have been done by single-threaded programs compiled with GNU C Compiler 5.4.0 (optimized with -O2 -march= native), ATLAS 3.11.39 (as BLAS) and reference LAPACK 3.9.0 (through LAPACKE) on Ubuntu 16.04 LTS (x86_64, kernel 4.4.0) with Intel Xeon E5-2687W v4 and 256GB of memory. Moreover, for each pair $(f(x), g(x))$, we computed approximate GCDs of $(f(x), g(x))$ and $(g(x), f(x))$, and averaged them since their matrix factorization computed without column pivoting are usually different (a little bit in general though) due to numerical errors.

---

[1] All the C programs and data will be available via email upon request or at the webpage: https://wwwmain.h.kobe-u.ac.jp/~nagasaka/research/snap/.

Table 1. Result of better complexity (noise=1.0e-8)

half(small)	ite	time (sec.)	perturb	#f
uvgcd	2.0	7.9860e-3	5.7729e-9	0
stlngcd	2.0	2.5113e-2	5.7729e-9	0
newtonslra/1	2.0	1.4256e-1	5.7729e-9	0
improved(F, ∞)	2.0	1.5260e-2	5.7729e-9	0

We note some implementation remarks. In the tables, "uvgcd" denotes the UVGCD algorithm [33], however, we use the singular value decomposition (LAPACK's dgesdd) for computing singular vectors instead of the method (QR decomposition and solving triangular linear system iteratively from a random vector) in [33] since sometimes this randomness makes the computed singular vectors not appropriate for the iteration. Moreover, the Gauss–Newton method continues the iteration until the norm of correction vector is less than or equal to the given threshold (i.e., ε_c in Algorithm 6) since otherwise the resulting perturbation could be much larger. "stlngcd" denotes the STLN based algorithm [16], "newtonslra/1" denotes Algorithm 6 with the NewtonSLRA/1 algorithm as is, and "improved($weighted, \varepsilon_r$)" denotes Algorithm 6 as is (note that improved($weighted = F, \varepsilon_r = \infty$) means just with our modification in Sect. 3.1). Additionally, as a reference, we denote the algorithm by "improved($weighted, \varepsilon_r$) +uvgcd" that calls uvgcd with the output of improved($weighted, \varepsilon_r$) as initial value. After getting the resulting structured matrix, all the methods for computing the final approximate GCD are the same (i.e., cofactors from singular value decomposition and approximate GCD by the least squares). Moreover, we use LAPACK's dgesdd for singular value decomposition, and LAPACK's dgelsy for QR decomposition.

4.1 Subresultant Specific Better Complexity

As for the performance of the improvement in Sect. 3.1, we have generated the following set of polynomial pairs (call it **half(small)**) that is the same set of polynomials used for the experiments in [22]: For $\ell = 10$, we have generated 100 pairs of polynomials of degree 10ℓ, of unit 2-norm. Each pair has the GCD of degree 5ℓ and each factor has integer coefficients randomly chosen from $[-99, 99]$ before normalization. We added the same degree polynomials whose 2-norm is 10^{-8}, and made them re-normalized again.

Table 1 shows the result computed with $\varepsilon_c = 1.0e-8$ and $max_i = 8192$, where "ite." and "#f" denote the averages of number of iterations and number of polynomial pairs whose perturbation is not smaller than 10^{-7}, respectively. According to this result, our improvement works well (10 times faster).

Table 2. Result of relaxed NewtonSLRA (noise=1.0e-2)

half(large)	ite	time (sec.)	perturb	#f
uvgcd	507.3*	8.3763e-1	7.4101e-3	0.0
stlngcd	393.8*	3.1277e-0	1.2918e-2	3.5
newtonslra/1	5.56	3.6152e-1	2.3861e-2	8.0
improved(F, ∞)	5.56	3.5819e-2	2.3862e-2	8.0
improved(F, 1.0e-3)	10.15	5.4137e-2	2.0162e-2	7.0
improved(F, 1.0e-4)	66.44	2.8067e-1	1.5068e-2	4.0
improved(F, 1.0e-5)	638.8*	2.5754e-0	1.1769e-2	2.0
improved(F, 1.0e-6)	1567.5*	6.3315e-0	1.1648e-2	2.0
improved(F, 1.0e-4)+uvgcd	–	8.4933e-1	6.8757e-3	0.0

Table 3. Result of weighted NewtonSLRA (noise=1.0e-2)

asym(large)	ite	time (sec.)	perturb	#f
newtonslra/1	4.68	4.3339e-1	1.8564e-2	3.0
improved(F, ∞)	4.68	6.9391e-2	1.8564e-2	3.0
improved(T, ∞)	31.44	3.9531e-1	1.3588e-2	3.0
improved(T, 1.0e-6)	88.10	1.0521e-0	1.2384e-2	3.0

4.2   Relaxed NewtonSLRA Algorithm

To see the performance of the relaxed NewtonSLRA algorithm, we have generated a set of polynomial pairs (call it **half(large)**) similar to **half(small)** but we added the same degree polynomials whose 2-norm is 10^{-2} instead of 10^{-8}.

Table 2 shows the result computed with $\varepsilon_c = 1.0e-8$ and $max_i = 8192$, where "*" denotes that some of pairs reached the maximum iterations and the threshold of "#f" is 10^{-1}. According to this result, our relaxed NewtonSLRA algorithm works well since the average of perturbations and number of failures are smaller as ε_r is smaller. However, the resulting perturbations are a little bit larger than the UVGCD algorithm though our algorithm is in balance with the computing time and the perturbation.

4.3   Column Weighted Frobenius Norm

To see the performance of the column weighted NewtonSLRA algorithm, we have generated a set of polynomial pairs (call it **asym(large)**) similar to **half(large)** but each pair has the GCD of degree ℓ instead of 5ℓ and degrees of each pair of polynomials are 2ℓ and 18ℓ.

Table 3 shows the result computed with $\varepsilon_c = 1.0e-8$ and $max_i = 8192$ where the threshold of "#f" is 10^{-1}. According to this result, our column weighted NewtonSLRA algorithm works well though the convergence speed is slower than the NewtonSLRA/1 algorithm.

Table 4. Result of ill-conditioned polynomials

with $k = 1000$	ite	time (sec.)	perturb	#f
uvgcd	656.8*	2.2697e+2	3.1529e-2	2.0
uvgcd$_{16}$	11.4*	4.2856e-0	1.2865e+2	5.0
stlngcd	833.4*	2.5641e+3	1.6322e-2	0.5
stlngcd$_{16}$	10.7*	3.2587e+1	1.5336e-2	0.0
newtonslra/1	7.85	9.1670e+1	1.9806e-2	0.5
improved(F, ∞)	7.85	4.5850e-0	1.9440e-2	0.5
improved(F, 1.0e-2)	7.85	4.6663e-0	1.9440e-2	0.5
improved(F, 1.0e-3)	8.50	3.8587e-0	1.8723e-2	0.0
improved(F, 1.0e-4)	62.35	4.4467e-0	2.2711e-2	0.0
improved(F, 1.0e-3)+uvgcd	–	1.6443e+2	2.4252e-2	2.0
with $k = 1002$	ite	time (sec.)	perturb	#f
uvgcd	2.25	1.1481e-0	3.1580e-3	0.0
stlngcd	2.25	7.5260e-0	3.1580e-3	0.0
improved(F, 1.0e-3)	3.00	1.4714e-0	3.1580e-3	0.0

4.4 Ill-Conditioned Polynomials

The following 20 pairs of polynomials that were used in [30].

$$f(x) = \left\lceil d(x) \sum_{i=0}^{3} x^i \right\rceil + \epsilon_f(x), \; g(x) = \left\lceil d(x) \sum_{i=0}^{3} (-x)^i \right\rceil + \epsilon_g(x)$$

where $d(x)$ is a polynomial of degree 1000, whose coefficients are random integers in $[-5, 5]$, $\lceil \cdot \rfloor$ denotes the normalization in terms of 2-norm, and $\epsilon_f(x)$ and $\epsilon_g(x)$ are noise polynomials whose coefficient vectors are Gaussian zero-mean i.i.d. random vectors with standard deviation 1.0e-4. We note that this set of polynomial pairs are similar to polynomials $(g(x) = \left\lceil d(x) \sum_{i=0}^{4} (-x)^i \right\rceil + \epsilon_g(x))$ in [3, Example 8.3.1], however, they are quite different. Though the expected maximum degree of approximate GCD of $f(x)$ and $g(x)$ above is 1002, in this experiment, we also computed approximate GCDs of degree 1000 as in [30].

Table 4 shows the result computed with $\varepsilon_c = 1.0e-8$ and $max_i = 8192$ (but $max_i = 16$ for uvgcd$_{16}$ and stlngcd$_{16}$), where the threshold of "#f" is 10^{-1}. According to this result, our algorithm works well though giving the best choice of the threshold ε_r is not easy.

4.5 Polynomials with Multiple Roots

To see the performance for polynomials with multiple roots (clusters of roots after adding noise polynomials), we have generated a set of polynomial pairs (call it **mult(large)**) similar to **half(large)** but each pair has the GCD of

Table 5. Result of polynomials with multiple roots

mult(large)	ite	time (sec.)	perturb	#f
uvgcd	4598.2*	7.4609e-0	7.3866e-4	0.0
uvgcd$_{16}$	16.0*	3.0840e-2	1.5746e-0	12.0
stlngcd	4524.6*	3.8227e+1	1.1269e-2	2.5
stlngcd$_{16}$	16.0*	1.4192e-1	2.7403e-2	7.5
newtonslra/1	23.26	1.4035e-0	8.6582e-3	2.0
improved(F, ∞)	23.13	1.2745e-1	4.8640e-3	1.0
improved(F, 1.0e-3)	23.14	1.3183e-1	4.3044e-3	1.0
improved(F, 1.0e-4)	29.76	1.5741e-1	4.5151e-3	1.0
improved(F, 1.0e-5)	522.2*	2.0680e-0	2.1616e-3	0.0
improved(F, 1.0e-3)+uvgcd	–	7.3543e-0	7.8047e-4	0.0

degree 5ℓ that is the ℓth power of a polynomial of degree 5 (i.e., 5 distinct roots whose multiplicities are $\ell = 10$).

Table 5 shows the result computed with $\varepsilon_c = 1.0e\text{-}8$ and $max_i = 8192$ (but $max_i = 16$ for uvgcd$_{16}$ and stlngcd$_{16}$) where the threshold of "#f" is 10^{-1}. According to this result, our relaxed NewtonSLRA algorithm works well and is in balance with the computing time and the perturbation.

References

1. Alcázar, J.G., Quintero, E.: Affine equivalences of trigonometric curves. Acta Appl. Math. **170**, 691–708 (2020)
2. Bini, D.A., Boito, P.: Structured matrix-based methods for polynomial ϵ-GCD: analysis and comparisons. In: ISSAC 2007, pp. 9–16. ACM, New York (2007)
3. Boito, P.: Structured Matrix Based Methods for Approximate Polynomial GCD, vol. 15. Edizioni della Normale, Pisa (2011)
4. Bourne, M., Winkler, J.R., Su, Y.: A non-linear structure-preserving matrix method for the computation of the coefficients of an approximate greatest common divisor of two Bernstein polynomials. J. Comput. Appl. Math. **320**, 221–241 (2017)
5. Cadzow, J.A.: Signal enhancement-a composite property mapping algorithm. IEEE Trans. Acoust. Speech Signal Process. **36**(1), 49–62 (1988)
6. Chi, B., Terui, A.: The GPGCD algorithm with the Bézout matrix. In: Boulier, F., England, M., Sadykov, T.M., Vorozhtsov, E.V. (eds.) Computer Algebra in Scientific Computing, pp. 170–187. Springer International Publishing, Cham (2020)
7. Corless, R.M., Rafiee Sevyeri, L.: Approximate GCD in a Bernstein basis. In: Gerhard, J., Kotsireas, I. (eds.) Maple in Mathematics Education and Research, pp. 77–91. Springer International Publishing, Cham (2020)
8. Corless, R.M., Watt, S.M., Zhi, L.: QR factoring to compute the GCD of univariate approximate polynomials. IEEE Trans. Signal Process. **52**(12), 3394–3402 (2004)

9. Deutsch, F.: Best Approximation in Inner Product Spaces. CMS Books in Mathematics/Ouvrages de Mathématiques de la SMC, vol. 7. Springer-Verlag, New York (2001)

10. Dunaway, D.K.: Calculation of zeros of a real polynomial through factorization using Euclid's algorithm. SIAM J. Numer. Anal. **11**, 1087–1104 (1974)

11. Emiris, I.Z., Galligo, A., Lombardi, H.: Numerical univariate polynomial GCD. In: The mathematics of numerical analysis (Park City, UT, 1995), Lectures in Applied Mathematics-American Mathematical Society, vol. 32, pp. 323–343, Providence, RI (1996)

12. Emiris, I.Z., Galligo, A., Lombardi, H.: Certified approximate univariate GCDs. J. Pure Appl. Algebra **117**(118), 229–251 (1997). algorithms for algebra (Eindhoven, 1996)

13. Fazzi, A., Guglielmi, N., Markovsky, I.: An ODE-based method for computing the approximate greatest common divisor of polynomials. Numer. Algorithms **81**(2), 719–740 (2019)

14. Giesbrecht, M., Haraldson, J., Labahn, G.: Computing nearby non-trivial Smith forms. J. Symbolic Comput. **102**, 304–327 (2021)

15. Golub, G.H., Van Loan, C.F.: Matrix computations. Johns Hopkins Studies in the Mathematical Sciences, Johns Hopkins University Press, Baltimore, MD, Fourth Edition (2013)

16. Kaltofen, E., Yang, Z., Zhi, L.: Approximate greatest common divisors of several polynomials with linearly constrained coefficients and singular polynomials. In: ISSAC 2006, pp. 169–176. ACM, New York (2006)

17. Kaltofen, E., Yang, Z., Zhi, L.: Structured low rank approximation of a Sylvester matrix. In: Symbolic-numeric computation, pp. 69–83. Trends Math., Birkhäuser, Basel (2007)

18. Karmarkar, N., Lakshman, Y.N.: Approximate polynomial greatest common divisors and nearest singular polynomials. In: ISSAC 1996, pp. 35–39. ACM, New York (1996)

19. Markovsky, I.: Low-rank approximation: Algorithms, Implementation, Applications. Communications and Control Engineering Series, 2nd edn. Springer, Cham (2019)

20. Markovsky, I., Fazzi, A., Guglielmi, N.: Applications of polynomial common factor computation in signal processing. In: Deville, Y., Gannot, S., Mason, R., Plumbley, M.D., Ward, D. (eds.) Latent Variable Analysis and Signal Separation, pp. 99–106. Springer International Publishing, Cham (2018)

21. Nagasaka, K.: Approximate GCD by Bernstein basis, and its applications. In: ISSAC 2020, pp. 372–379. ACM, New York (2020)

22. Nagasaka, K.: Toward the best algorithm for approximate GCD of univariate polynomials. J. Symbolic Comput. **105**, 4–27 (2021)

23. Noda, M.T., Sasaki, T.: Approximate GCD and its application to ill-conditioned algebraic equations. In: Proceedings of the International Symposium on Computational Mathematics (Matsuyama, 1990). vol. 38(1–3), pp. 335–351 (1991)

24. Pan, V.Y.: Computation of approximate polynomial GCDs and an extension. Inform. and Comput. **167**(2), 71–85 (2001)

25. Sasaki, T., Noda, M.T.: Approximate square-free decomposition and root-finding of ill-conditioned algebraic equations. J. Inform. Process. **12**(2), 159–168 (1989)

26. Schönhage, A.: Quasi-GCD computations. J. Complexity **1**(1), 118–137 (1985)

27. Schost, E., Spaenlehauer, P.J.: A quadratically convergent algorithm for structured low-rank approximation. Found. Comput. Math. **16**(2), 457–492 (2016)

28. Sevyeri, L., Corless, R.M.: Approximate GCD in Lagrange bases. In: 2020 22nd International Symposium on Symbolic and Numeric Algorithms for Scientific Computing (SYNASC), pp. 40–47. IEEE Computer Society, Los Alamitos, CA, USA (Sep 2020)
29. Terui, A.: GPGCD: an iterative method for calculating approximate GCD of univariate polynomials. Theoret. Comput. Sci. **479**, 127–149 (2013)
30. Usevich, K., Markovsky, I.: Variable projection methods for approximate (greatest) common divisor computations. Theoret. Comput. Sci. **681**, 176–198 (2017)
31. Winkler, J.R., Goldman, R.N.: The Sylvester resultant matrix for Bernstein polynomials. In: Curve and surface design (Saint-Malo, 2002), pp. 407–416. Mod. Methods Math., Nashboro Press, Brentwood, TN (2003)
32. Winkler, J.R., Yang, N.: Resultant matrices and the computation of the degree of an approximate greatest common divisor of two inexact Bernstein basis polynomials. Comput. Aided Geom. Design **30**(4), 410–429 (2013)
33. Zeng, Z.: The numerical greatest common divisor of univariate polynomials. In: Randomization, relaxation, and complexity in polynomial equation solving, Contemp. Math. Amer. Math. Soc., vol. 556, pp. 187–217, Providence, RI (2011)
34. Zhi, L., Yang, Z.: Computing approximate GCD of univariate polynomials by structure total least norm. MM Res. Preprints **24**, 375–387 (2004)

Simplification of Nested Real Radicals Revisited

Nikolay N. Osipov$^{(\boxtimes)}$ and Alexey A. Kytmanov

Siberian Federal University, Svobodny 79, Krasnoyarsk 660041, Russia

Abstract. The problem of simplification of nested radicals over arbitrary number fields was studied by many authors. The case of real radicals over real number fields is somewhat easier to study (at least, from theoretical point of view). In particular, an efficient (i.e., a polynomial-time) algorithm of simplification of at most doubly nested radicals is known. However, this algorithm does not guarantee complete simplification for the case of radicals with nesting depth more than two. In the paper, we give a detailed presentation of the theory that provides an algorithm which simplifies triply nested reals radicals over $\mathbb{Q}$. Some examples of triply nested real radicals that cannot be simplified are also given.

Keywords: Nested radicals · Simplification · Computer algebra systems

1 Introduction

The problem of simplification plays a significant role in symbolic computations. For symbolic expressions of special kinds, this problem can be solved more or less reasonably, so that we can use efficient algorithms for simplification implemented in *computer algebra systems* (CAS) of a general kind. In our paper, we discuss a simplification problem for the so-called *nested radical expressions* (i.e., expressions containing the signs of square root, cubic root, etc.). This is the simplest class of elementary algebraic expressions for which the simplification problem seems to be quite complicated. Usually, simplifying means decreasing of the *depth* of a given nested radical expression. The main difficulties arise due to the existence of unexpected non-trivial relations between nested radicals.

The trivial identity of the type

$$\sqrt{2} + \sqrt{8} = \sqrt{18} \tag{1}$$

with "usual" (i.e., non-nested) radicals is clear. Besicovitch [2] proved that the non-trivial identities with non-nested radicals over the field of rational numbers $\mathbb{Q}$ do not exist (i.e., after reducing proportional terms in such an equality, we must obtain $0 = 0$). However, there exist more interesting identities which seem unexpected. For instance,

$$\sqrt{5 + 2\sqrt{6}} = \sqrt{2} + \sqrt{3}, \quad \sqrt{4 + 3\sqrt{2}} = \sqrt[4]{2} + \sqrt[4]{8}. \tag{2}$$

© Springer Nature Switzerland AG 2021
F. Boulier et al. (Eds.): CASC 2021, LNCS 12865, pp. 293–313, 2021.
https://doi.org/10.1007/978-3-030-85165-1_17

We can easily verify these equalities by squaring or using the following elementary formula

$$\sqrt{A \pm \sqrt{B}} = \sqrt{\frac{A + \sqrt{A^2 - B}}{2}} \pm \sqrt{\frac{A - \sqrt{A^2 - B}}{2}} \qquad (3)$$

that can also be used (basically) for denesting the square nested radicals of arbitrary depth. Some more exotic identities with nested radicals were proposed by Ramanujan:

$$\sqrt[3]{\sqrt[3]{2} - 1} = \sqrt[3]{\frac{1}{9}} - \sqrt[3]{\frac{2}{9}} + \sqrt[3]{\frac{4}{9}}, \qquad \sqrt{\sqrt[3]{5} - \sqrt[3]{4}} = \frac{\sqrt[3]{2} + \sqrt[3]{20} - \sqrt[3]{25}}{3}.$$

Here, it is not so clear how the left hand side could be reduced to the right-hand side. Slightly simpler equalities of the type

$$\sqrt[3]{10 + \sqrt{108}} + \sqrt[3]{10 - \sqrt{108}} = 2$$

are provided by Cardano's formula for solving a cubic equation.

The first algorithm for determining whether a given nested radical can be denested was introduced by S. Landau [8]. This algorithm works with nested radicals over an arbitrary algebraic number field (a subfield L of the field of complex numbers $\mathbb{C}$ such that the extension $L/\mathbb{Q}$ is finite) and involves complex roots of unity. The bottleneck of Landau's algorithm seems to be in necessity of computing the *Galois group* for polynomials which is, probably, even a more difficult problem.

The case of real radicals over real number fields is somewhat easier to study (a root function is single-valued over real numbers). A polynomial-time algorithm of simplification of at most doubly nested radicals has been known for a long period of time [4]. However, this algorithm does not guarantee complete simplification for the case of radicals with nesting depth more than two. An algorithm which either simplifies (i.e., reduces nesting depth) triply nested radicals over the field $\mathbb{Q}$ or proves that such simplification is impossible was firstly proposed in [11].

The simplest case of nested square real radicals was treated by Borodin et al. [6]. The corresponding algorithm for simplifying works correctly with the equalities of the type (2). It was implemented in some CAS (for instance, Maple [12]).

In this paper, we propose a much more detailed description of the algorithm from [11] which simplifies triply nested radicals over $\mathbb{Q}$. Also, we generalize the method for finding all the roots of a given polynomial from $\mathbb{Q}[x]$ in the so-called *complete radical extension* $R(\mathbb{Q})$ (see Theorem 4). We provide new explicit examples of triply nested radicals over $\mathbb{Q}$ that cannot be simplified (see Example 7). In addition, we propose some impossible equalities with double nested radicals over $\mathbb{Q}$ (see Proposition 3).

The paper is organized as follows.

In Sect. 2, we give some preliminary results about the set of solutions over $\mathbb{C}$ for a special class of polynomial systems (see Proposition 1 and its corollaries). For solving these systems, we propose using the Gröbner bases technique together with the well-known Theorem of Finiteness (see [1, Theorem 6.54]).

Sect. 3 contains main definitions and results about non-nested real radicals over an arbitrary real field (in particular, Theorem 1 which was firstly proved by Mordell [10]).

In Sect. 4, we explain how a double nested real radical over an arbitrary real field can be denested if possible.

In Sect. 5 and 6, we propose and discuss some new results about simplifying triply nested real radicals.

2   Special Polynomial Systems with Zero-Dimensional Variety of Solutions

Let L, $F \subset \mathbb{C}$ be two number fields with $L \subset F$. Suppose that the extension F/L is finite and $N = [F : L]$ is its degree (in particular, this extension is an algebraic extension). Denote by $\{\omega_1, \ldots, \omega_N\}$ a fixed L-basis of the field F (such a basis can be arbitrary). For a fixed polynomial

$$f \in L[x], \quad \deg f = q > 1,$$

we introduce the polynomials $p_j \in L[x_1, \ldots, x_N]$ $(j = 1, \ldots, N)$ using the representation

$$
\begin{aligned}
&f(x_1\omega_1 + \ldots + x_N\omega_N) \\
&= p_1(x_1, \ldots, x_N)\omega_1 + \ldots + p_N(x_1, \ldots, x_N)\omega_N.
\end{aligned}
\tag{4}
$$

Denote by ψ_j $(j = 1, \ldots, N)$ all the isomorphisms of F into $\mathbb{C}$ over L (which are the identity map on L). For each $j = 1, \ldots, N$, we also have

$$
\begin{aligned}
&f(x_1\psi_j(\omega_1) + \ldots + x_N\psi_j(\omega_N)) \\
&= p_1(x_1, \ldots, x_N)\psi_j(\omega_1) + \ldots + p_N(x_1, \ldots, x_N)\psi_j(\omega_N),
\end{aligned}
\tag{5}
$$

which are immediate consequences of (4). For any fixed N-tuple $(a_1, \ldots, a_N) \in \mathbb{C}^N$, we consider the following system of polynomial equations

$$
\begin{cases}
p_1(x_1, \ldots, x_N) = a_1, \\
\ldots \\
p_N(x_1, \ldots, x_N) = a_N.
\end{cases}
\tag{6}
$$

Proposition 1. *For any* $(a_1, \ldots, a_N) \in \mathbb{C}^N$, *the system* (6) *has only a finite set of solutions* $(x_1, \ldots, x_N)$ *in* $\mathbb{C}^N$.

Proof. Let us introduce the number $\theta = a_1\omega_1 + \ldots + a_N\omega_N$ and its (formal) conjugates

$$\theta^{(j)} = a_1\psi_j(\omega_1) + \ldots + a_N\psi_j(\omega_N) \quad (j = 1, \ldots, N).$$

Let $(x_1, \ldots, x_N) \in \mathbb{C}^N$ be an arbitrary solution of the system (6). From (5), it follows that $(x_1, \ldots, x_N)$ satisfies a linear system of the form

$$
\begin{cases}
x_1 \psi_1(\omega_1) + \ldots + x_N \psi_1(\omega_N) = c_1, \\
\ldots \\
x_1 \psi_N(\omega_1) + \ldots + x_N \psi_N(\omega_N) = c_N,
\end{cases}
\tag{7}
$$

where the number $c_j \in \mathbb{C}$ $(j = 1, \ldots, N)$ is a root of the polynomial

$$
f_j = f - \theta^{(j)} \quad (j = 1, \ldots, N).
$$

Thus, we obtain finitely many (q^N at most) linear systems of the form (7). It remains to observe that the determinant

$$
\Delta = \det \begin{bmatrix} \psi_1(\omega_1) & \ldots & \psi_1(\omega_N) \\ \ldots\ldots\ldots\ldots\ldots\ldots \\ \psi_N(\omega_1) & \ldots & \psi_N(\omega_N) \end{bmatrix}
$$

of the linear system (7) does not vanish for any L-basis $\{\omega_1, \ldots, \omega_N\}$ of the field F. Indeed, Δ^2 is equal to the discriminant of given L-basis that is non-zero because of separability of the extension F/L (this is well known; see, e.g., [5, Sect. "Algebraic Supplement"]). Therefore, each linear system (7) has a unique solution $(x_1, \ldots, x_N)$. This completes the proof. $\qquad\square$

Remark 1. Clearly, system (6) has at most q solutions $(x_1, \ldots, x_N)$ in L^N. If $(a_1, \ldots, a_N) \in L^N$ then $\theta = a_1 \omega_1 + \ldots + a_N \omega_N \in F$ and finding of all the solutions $(x_1, \ldots, x_N)$ of (6) in L^N is equivalent to finding the roots of the polynomial $f - \theta$ in the field F.

We now give some consequences of Proposition 1 for the important case of monomial

$$
f = x^q.
\tag{8}
$$

Corollary 1. *Let $(a_1, \ldots, a_N) \neq (0, \ldots, 0)$. Then, for each $j = 1, \ldots, N$, the system*

$$
\begin{cases}
x_0 p_1(x_1, \ldots, x_N) = a_1, \\
\ldots \\
x_0 p_N(x_1, \ldots, x_N) = a_N, \\
x_j = 1
\end{cases}
\tag{9}
$$

has only a finite set of solutions $(x_0, x_1, \ldots, x_N)$ in $\mathbb{C}^{N+1}$.

Proof. In our case, all the polynomials $p_j(x_1, \ldots, x_N)$ defined by (4) are homogeneous polynomials of degree q. Put $x_0 = t^q$ where t is a new variable. Then system (9) reduces to the system

$$
\begin{cases}
p_1(tx_1, \ldots, tx_N) = a_1, \\
\ldots \\
p_N(tx_1, \ldots, tx_N) = a_N, \\
x_j = 1.
\end{cases}
$$

Since $(a_1, \ldots, a_N) \neq (0, \ldots, 0)$, we conclude that $t \neq 0$. From Proposition 1, it follows that

$$(y_1, \ldots, y_N) = (tx_1, \ldots, tx_N) \in A$$

where $A \subset \mathbb{C}^N$ is a finite set. Consequently, the product tx_j can take at most a finite set of different values. At the same time, $x_j = 1$ in (9). Thus, all the possible values of t form a finite set. Now, the statement of Corollary 1 is clear.

$\square$

Corollary 2. *For each $j = 1, \ldots, N$, the system*

$$\begin{cases} p_2(x_1, \ldots, x_N) = 0, \\ \ldots \\ p_N(x_1, \ldots, x_N) = 0, \\ x_j = 1 \end{cases} \tag{10}$$

has only a finite set of solutions $(x_1, \ldots, x_N)$ in $\mathbb{C}^N$.

Proof. Consider the system

$$\begin{cases} p_1(x_1, \ldots, x_N) = 1, \\ p_2(x_1, \ldots, x_N) = 0, \\ \ldots \\ p_N(x_1, \ldots, x_N) = 0 \end{cases}$$

which possesses a finite set $B \subset \mathbb{C}^N$ of solutions. Then any solution $(x_1, \ldots, x_N)$ of the subsystem

$$\begin{cases} p_2(x_1, \ldots, x_N) = 0, \\ \ldots \\ p_N(x_1, \ldots, x_N) = 0 \end{cases}$$

can be represented as $(ty_1, \ldots, ty_N)$ with some $(y_1, \ldots, y_N) \in B$. Because $x_j = 1$ in (10), we have $ty_j = 1$. Therefore, the variable t can take values only in a finite set. Corollary 2 is proved.

$\square$

Remark 2. Corollary 2 can also be derived from Corollary 1.

Suppose that, for the field L, we have an algorithm for finding all the roots in L of any given polynomial in $L[x]$ (for instance, $L = \mathbb{Q}$ or some finite extension of $\mathbb{Q}$ are suitable). Then, for the systems (6), (9) and (10) in the case $(a_1, \ldots, a_N) \in L^N$, we can find all their solutions over L. This can be deduced from Proposition 1, Corollary 1 and the following theorem (see, for instance, [1, Theorem 6.54] or [7, Sect. 3.1.3]).

Theorem of Finiteness. *Let $G(S)$ be a Gröbner basis for a system S of polynomial equations in N variables $x_1, \ldots, x_N$ with respect to the pure lexicographic order. Then the system S has a finite set of solutions in $\mathbb{C}^N$ if and only if each variable x_j occurs as an isolated variable in some leading monomial of $G(S)$.*

For an integer $q > 1$, denote by F^q the set of qth powers of all numbers from the field F, i.e.,

$$F^q = \{\alpha^q : \alpha \in F\}.$$

As usual, L^* denotes the multiplicative group of the field L.

Definition 1. *A non-zero number $\theta \in F$ is called an almost q-power in F over L if there exists a number $a \in L^*$ such that $\theta/a \in F^q$.*

Due to the assumptions about the field L (see above), it follows that there exist the following algorithms.

Algorithm I. An algorithm that determines whether a non-zero number $\theta \in F$ belongs to the set F^q.

Algorithm II. An algorithm that determines whether a non-zero number $\theta \in F$ is an almost q-power in F over L.

Indeed, let $\theta = a_1\omega_1 + \ldots + a_N\omega_N$ be a fixed non-zero number from the field F. To implement Algorithm I, we need to solve the system (6) for the case (8) (recall that f and $p_1, \ldots, p_N$ are connected by (4)) which is possible. Similarly, for implementation of Algorithm II, we need to (and, indeed, are able to) solve system (9) for all $j = 1, \ldots, N$.

In order to illustrate these algorithms, let us consider an example.

Example 1. Let $L = \mathbb{Q}$ and $F = \mathbb{Q}(\sqrt[3]{2})$. Then for L-basis of F we can take

$$\omega_1 = 1, \quad \omega_2 = \sqrt[3]{2}, \quad \omega_3 = \sqrt[3]{4}$$

(here the values of all radicals are assumed to be real). In particular, $N = 3$. For the polynomial $f(x) = x^2$, we obtain

$$p_1(x_1, x_2, x_3) = x_1^2 + 4x_2x_3,$$
$$p_2(x_1, x_2, x_3) = 2x_1x_2 + 2x_3^2,$$
$$p_3(x_1, x_2, x_3) = 2x_1x_3 + x_2^2.$$

For $(a_1, a_2, a_3) = (1, 1, 0)$, consider the system (6) and the systems (9) where $j \in \{1, 2, 3\}$. Using the technique of Gröbner bases and any suitable CAS (for instance, Maple [12] which contains the corresponding module Groebner), it is easy to verify that all these systems have no solutions over $\mathbb{Q}$. Consequently, we can conclude that

$$\theta = 1 + \sqrt[3]{2} \notin (\mathbb{Q}(\sqrt[3]{2}))^2$$

and, moreover, the number θ is not an almost square in $\mathbb{Q}(\sqrt[3]{2})$ over $\mathbb{Q}$.

Obviously, the simplest case is $N = 2$ and $q = 2$. Constructing the algorithms I and II in this case, we can use the following elementary assertion which is valid for an arbitrary field L of characteristic $\neq 2$.

Proposition 2. *Let $F = L(\omega)$ where $\omega \notin L$, but $\omega^2 \in L$. For the number*

$$\theta = a_1 + a_2\omega \in F$$

with some $a_1, a_2 \in L$ and $a_2 \neq 0$, the following statements hold.
(i) $\theta \in F^2$ if and only if $a_1^2 - a_2^2\omega^2 \in L^2$ and exactly one of the numbers

$$\frac{a_1 \pm \sqrt{a_1^2 - a_2^2\omega^2}}{2}$$

belongs to L^2.
(ii) θ is an almost square in F over L if and only if $a_1^2 - a_2^2\omega^2 \in L^2$.

Proof. (i) Suppose that $\theta = (x + y\omega)^2$ for some $x, y \in L$. Then

$$x^2 + y^2\omega^2 = a_1, \quad 2xy = a_2.$$

Eliminating y, we get the equation

$$4x^4 - 4a_1x^2 + a_2^2\omega^2 = 0$$

which can be rewritten as $(2x^2 - a_1)^2 = a_1^2 - a_2^2\omega^2$. Thus, the number $a_1^2 - a_2^2\omega^2$ must be a square in L (i.e., belongs to L^2). If $a_1^2 - a_2^2\omega^2 = d^2$ with some $d \in L$ then

$$x^2 = \frac{a_1 \pm d}{2}.$$

This means that one of the numbers $(a_1 \pm d)/2$ must be a square in L. Since

$$\frac{a_1 - d}{2} \cdot \frac{a_1 + d}{2} = \frac{a_2^2\omega^2}{4}$$

and $\omega \notin L$, exactly one of the numbers $(a_1 \pm d)/2$ can be a square in L.
Suppose that $a_1^2 - a_2^2\omega^2 = d^2$ for some $d \in L$ and, moreover,

$$\frac{a_1 \pm d}{2} = z^2$$

where $z \in L$ and the sign is fixed. Clearly, z must be non-zero. Setting

$$x = z, \quad y = \frac{a_2}{2z},$$

we obtain the representation $\theta = (x + y\omega)^2$ as desired.
(ii) Suppose that $\theta = a(x + y\omega)^2$ with some $x, y \in L$ and $0 \neq a \in L$. Then

$$x^2 + y^2\omega^2 = b_1, \quad 2xy = b_2$$

where $b_1 = a_1/a$ and $b_2 = a_2/a$. As above, we conclude that

$$b_1^2 - b_2^2\omega^2 = \frac{a_1^2 - a_2^2\omega^2}{a^2} = w^2$$

for some $w \in L$. Thus, $a_1^2 - a_2^2\omega^2 = (aw)^2$. Hence the number $a_1^2 - a_2^2\omega^2$ must be a square in L.

If $a_1^2 - a_2^2\omega^2 = d^2$ for some $d \in L$ then we can take

$$x = 1, \quad y = \frac{a_2}{a_1 + d}, \quad a = \frac{a_1 + d}{2}.$$

It can easily be verified that the representation $\theta = a(x + y\omega)^2$ is valid. $\square$

3   Real Radicals over a Real Field

Let $P \subset \mathbb{R}$ be a real number field. For the field P, we will suppose that there exist the following algorithms:

Algorithm (a). An algorithm that determines the sign of number $a \in P$.

Algorithm (b). An algorithm that determines whether a non-zero number $a \in P$ belongs to the set P^q where q is an arbitrary prime number.

For example, the field $P = \mathbb{Q}$ satisfies these conditions as well as $P = \mathbb{Q}(\sqrt{2})$ and many other fields of real algebraic numbers.

Definition 2. *A number $\alpha \in \mathbb{R}$ is called a real radical of degree $n > 1$ over P if $\alpha^n \in P$ and $\alpha^n \notin P^q$ for any prime $q \mid n$.*

From now on by "radical" we will mean "real radical". It is easy to see that a non-zero number $\alpha \in \mathbb{R}$ is a radical of degree n over P if and only if $\alpha^i \notin P$ ($1 \leqslant i < n$), but $\alpha^n \in P$. Moreover, if α is a radical of degree n over P then the corresponding polynomial

$$f_\alpha = x^n - \alpha^n \in P[x]$$

is irreducible over P (and, consequently, f_α is the minimal polynomial for algebraic number α). In particular, the system $\{1, \alpha, \ldots, \alpha^{n-1}\}$ is a P-basis of the field $P(\alpha) \subset \mathbb{R}$.

Remark 3. For any field L, there is a criterion of irreducibility for an arbitrary binomial

$$x^n - a \in L[x]$$

(see, for instance, [9, Ch. VI, Sect. 9]). The irreducibility of f_α over P can be derived using this criterion but can also be established by elementary arguments.

For a given field P, consider an arbitrary number $\alpha = \sqrt[m]{b}$ where $0 < b \in P$ and $m > 1$. Using Algorithms (a) and (b), we can determine whether α is a radical over P or $\alpha \in P$ (the fact that $\alpha^m \in P$ yields impossibility of the other variants). Moreover, in the first case, we can obtain the canonical representation $\alpha = \sqrt[n]{a}$ with some $0 < a \in P$ (i.e., in this representation, n is the degree of α). In the second case, we can find $0 < a \in P$ such that $\alpha = a$.

For $(n_1, \ldots, n_s) \in \mathbb{N}^s$, denote

$$I_{(n_1,\ldots,n_s)} = \{(i_1, \ldots, i_s) \in \mathbb{Z}^s : 0 \leqslant i_k < n_k \text{ for each } k = 1, \ldots, s\}.$$

Definition 3. *The radicals $\alpha_1, \ldots, \alpha_s$ over P of degrees $n_1, \ldots, n_s$ respectively are called multiplicatively independent if the condition*

$$\prod_{k=1}^{s} \alpha_k^{i_k} \in P^*,$$

where $(i_1, \ldots, i_s) \in I_{(n_1, \ldots, n_s)}$ holds only for $(i_1, \ldots, i_s) = (0, \ldots, 0)$.

For an arbitrary collection of radicals $\rho_1, \ldots, \rho_t$ over P, there exists a system of multiplicatively independent radicals $\alpha_1, \ldots, \alpha_s$ over P such that both systems of radicals generate the same subgroup in the multiplicative factor-group $\mathbb{R}^*/P^*$:

$$\langle \alpha_1 P^*, \ldots, \alpha_s P^* \rangle = \langle \rho_1 P^*, \ldots, \rho_t P^* \rangle.$$

This result follows from the well-known structure theorem about finite abelian groups which states that any finite abelian group can be represented as a product of finite cyclic groups. In particular, we have

$$P(\rho_1, \ldots, \rho_t) = P(\alpha_1, \ldots, \alpha_s). \tag{11}$$

Furthermore, if ρ_l-s are represented in the form $\rho_l = \sqrt[m_l]{b_l}$ where $0 < b_l \in P$ then the construction of suitable α_k-s in the form $\alpha_k = \sqrt[n_k]{a_k}$ where $0 < a_k \in P$ and n_k is the degree of α_k can be performed via the algorithms (a) and (b).

Theorem 1. *If $\alpha_1, \ldots, \alpha_s$ are multiplicatively independent radicals over P of degrees $n_1, \ldots, n_s$ respectively then*

$$[P(\alpha_1, \ldots, \alpha_s) : P] = \prod_{k=1}^{s} n_k \tag{12}$$

and the numbers

$$\alpha_{(i_1, \ldots, i_s)} = \prod_{k=1}^{s} \alpha_k^{i_k} \quad \text{with} \quad (i_1, \ldots, i_s) \in I_{(n_1, \ldots, n_s)} \tag{13}$$

form a P-basis of the field $P(\alpha_1, \ldots, \alpha_s)$.

Proof. See, e.g., [10]. □

Note that all the numbers $\alpha_{(i_1, \ldots, i_s)}$ with $(i_1, \ldots, i_s) \neq (0, \ldots, 0)$ are radicals over P (namely, the degree of $\alpha_{(i_1, \ldots, i_s)}$ is equal to the least common multiple of the integers $n_k / \gcd(i_k, n_k)$, $k = 1, \ldots, s$).

Corollary 3. *Let $\rho_1, \ldots, \rho_t$ be arbitrary radicals over P. If*

$$\frac{\rho_l}{\rho_{l'}} \notin P^* \quad \text{for all} \quad l \neq l' \tag{14}$$

then the numbers $1, \rho_1, \ldots, \rho_t$ are linearly independent over P.

Proof. Indeed, there is a suitable system of multiplicatively independent radicals $\alpha_1, \ldots, \alpha_s$ over P such that (11) holds and each ρ_l can be represented in the form $a\alpha_{(i_1,\ldots,i_s)}$ where $a \in P^*$ and the numbers $\alpha_{(i_1,\ldots,i_s)}$ are defined by (13). Due to (14), the correspondence $l \mapsto (i_1, \ldots, i_s)$ must be injective. Hence the numbers $1, \rho_1, \ldots, \rho_t$ are linearly independent over P because they represent some part of the P-basis formed by the numbers (13).   □

Corollary 4. *If α is a radical over P and $\alpha \in P(\alpha_1, \ldots, \alpha_s)$ then*

$$\alpha = a\alpha_{(i_1,\ldots,i_s)}$$

for some $(i_1, \ldots, i_s) \in I_{(n_1,\ldots,n_s)}$ and $a \in P^*$.

Proof. The proof follows from Corollary 3 if for $\rho_1, \ldots, \rho_t$ we consider the collection of numbers $\alpha_{(i_1,\ldots,i_s)}$ with $(i_1, \ldots, i_s) \neq (0, \ldots, 0)$ additioned by the radical α.   □

Remark 4. For the cases of $P = \mathbb{Q}$ or $P = \mathbb{Q}(\omega)$ with a real algebraic number ω, there is an algorithm [3] which provides checking condition (14) in polynomial time depending on all the parameters that determine the numbers ω and ρ_l-s.

4   Simplification of Doubly Nested Real Radicals

In this section, we will make some additional assumptions about the given field $P \subset \mathbb{R}$ and its extensions. Namely, suppose that there exists

(c) an algorithm that finds all the roots in the field P of a given polynomial from $P[x]$.

Fix an arbitrary system of multiplicatively independent radicals $\alpha_1, \ldots, \alpha_s$ over P of degrees $n_1, \ldots, n_s$ respectively. Consider the field

$$\widetilde{P} = P(\alpha_1, \ldots, \alpha_s).$$

Suppose that there exists

(d) an algorithm that determines the sign of the number $\theta \in \widetilde{P}$.

For convenience of notation, denote by N the degree of the extension $\widetilde{P}/P$ (i.e., N is equal to (12)) and let $\omega_1, \ldots, \omega_N$ be the P-basis of the field $\widetilde{P}$ formed by the numbers (13). Based on the results from Sect. 2, for any given number

$$\theta = a_1\omega_1 + \ldots + a_N\omega_N \in \widetilde{P}$$

and any prime q, we can determine whether θ belongs to the set $\widetilde{P}^q$ (in fact, we need to apply the algorithm I for the fields $L = P$ and $F = \widetilde{P}$). Thus, under the assumptions on the fields P and $\widetilde{P}$, there exists an algorithm that, for a number $\beta = \sqrt[m]{\theta}$ with $0 < \theta \in \widetilde{P}$ and $m > 1$, determines whether β is a radical over $\widetilde{P}$. Moreover, in the case when β is a radical over $\widetilde{P}$, we can represent β in the form $\beta = \sqrt[r]{\eta}$ where $0 < \eta \in \widetilde{P}$ and r is the degree of β.

Definition 4. *Let P be a given real field. The field obtained by adjoining all the real radicals over P is called a complete radical extension of P and denoted by $R(P)$.*

Remark 5. It is easy to see that $P \subset P_1$ implies $R(P) \subset R(P_1)$.

If a number β is a radical over $\widetilde{P}$ then, clearly, $\beta \notin \widetilde{P}$. Yet, it is possible that $\beta \in R(P) \supset \widetilde{P}$. Theorem 2 below provides a method to determine it. We need the following auxiliary result.

Lemma 1. *Let ρ_1, ..., ρ_t be arbitrary radicals over P for which the condition (14) holds. Then any number*

$$\sigma = c_0 + c_1\rho_1 + \ldots + c_t\rho_t$$

where all $c_l \in P$ and are non-zero for $l = 1, \ldots, t$ is a primitive element of the extension $P(\rho_1, \ldots, \rho_t)/P$, i.e.,

$$P(\rho_1, \ldots, \rho_t) = P(\sigma).$$

Proof. See Theorem 3 in [11]. □

Theorem 2. *Suppose that $0 < \eta \in \widetilde{P}$ and $\beta = \sqrt[r]{\eta}$ is a radical over $\widetilde{P}$ of degree r. If $\beta \in R(P)$ then there exists some $j \in \{1, \ldots, N\}$ such that the number η/ω_j is an almost r-power in $\widetilde{P}$ over P.*

Proof. Let $\beta \in R(P)$. Then there are some radicals ρ_1, ..., ρ_t over P such that

$$\beta = c_0 + c_1\rho_1 + \ldots + c_t\rho_t \tag{15}$$

where all $c_l \in P$ and are non-zero for $l = 1, \ldots, t$. Moreover, we can assume that the radicals ρ_1, ..., ρ_t satisfy the condition (14). Show that there exist a radical ρ over P and a non-zero number $\zeta \in \widetilde{P}$ such that

$$\rho = \zeta\beta. \tag{16}$$

Indeed, Lemma 1 yields that $P(\rho_1, \ldots, \rho_t) = P(\beta)$. Hence, $\rho_l = f_l(\beta)$ for some polynomials $f_l \in P[x]$ $(l = 1, \ldots, t)$. Since $\beta^r = \eta \in \widetilde{P}$, we obtain

$$\rho_l \in \widetilde{P}(\beta) \quad (l = 1, \ldots, t).$$

Each ρ_l is either an element of $\widetilde{P}$ or a radical over $\widetilde{P}$ (because ρ_l is a radical over P and $P \subset \widetilde{P}$). Applying Corollary 4 to the fields $\widetilde{P}$ and $\widetilde{P}(\beta)$, we arrive at

$$\rho_l = \zeta_l\beta^{k_l}, \quad 0 \neq \zeta_l \in \widetilde{P}, \quad 0 \leqslant k_l < r \quad (l = 1, \ldots, t).$$

Now, (15) can be rewritten as

$$\beta = c_0 + c_1\zeta_1\beta^{k_1} + \ldots + c_t\zeta_t\beta^{k_t}.$$

Since β is a radical over $\widetilde{P}$ of degree r, there is $l \in \{1, \ldots, t\}$ for which $k_l = 1$. Setting $\rho = \rho_l$ and $\zeta = \zeta_l$, we obtain (16) as desired.

From (16), we deduce

$$\rho^r = \zeta^r \beta^r = \zeta^r \eta \in \widetilde{P}.$$

Moreover, the number ρ^r is either an element of P or a radical over P (we recall that ρ is a radical over P). By Corollary 4 applied to the field $\widetilde{P}$, we obtain $\rho^r = a\omega_j$ for some $a \in P^*$ and $j \in \{1, \ldots, N\}$. Thus, we have

$$\frac{\eta}{\omega_j} = \frac{a}{\zeta^r} = a \left(\frac{1}{\zeta}\right)^r.$$

It means that the number η/ω_j is an almost r-power in $\widetilde{P}$ over P. This completes the proof. $\qquad \Box$

Remark 6. Theorem 2 was firstly proved in [4] using various techniques. Also, there was proposed an algorithm that provides verification of the condition $\beta \in R(P)$ in polynomial time for the case $P = \mathbb{Q}$ or $P = \mathbb{Q}(\omega)$ where ω is an algebraic number. The proof of Theorem 2 proposed above is new.

Corollary 5. *Let $0 < \theta \in \widetilde{P}$. If q is a prime then $\theta \in (R(P))^q$ if and only if, for some $j \in \{1, \ldots, N\}$, the number θ/ω_j is an almost q-power in $\widetilde{P}$ over P.*

Proof. Let $\beta = \sqrt[q]{\theta}$. Since q is a prime, then $\beta \in \widetilde{P}$ or β is a radical over $\widetilde{P}$ of degree q. Now, the part"only if"follows immediately from Theorem 2. The part"if"is obvious. $\qquad \Box$

Thus, for a given number of the form $\beta = \sqrt[m]{\theta}$ where $0 < \theta \in \widetilde{P}$ and $m > 1$, we can determine whether β is a radical over $R(P)$ or $\beta \in R(P)$. Moreover, if β is a radical over $R(P)$ then we can represent β as

$$\beta = \sqrt[m]{a\omega_j} \sqrt[r]{\eta},$$

where $0 < \eta \in \widetilde{P}$ and r is the degree of β (also $a \in P^*$ and $j \in \{1, \ldots, N\}$).

To illustrate this, let us consider two examples.

Example 2. Let $P = \mathbb{Q}$ and $\widetilde{P} = \mathbb{Q}(\sqrt[3]{2})$. Consider the number

$$\theta = 1 + \sqrt[3]{2} \in \mathbb{Q}(\sqrt[3]{2}).$$

In Example 1, we showed that θ is not an almost square in $\mathbb{Q}(\sqrt[3]{2})$ over $\mathbb{Q}$. In particular, $\beta = \sqrt{\theta}$ is a square radical over $\mathbb{Q}(\sqrt[3]{2})$. One can show that this is also valid for the numbers

$$\frac{\theta}{\sqrt[3]{2}} = 1 + \frac{1}{2}\sqrt[3]{4}, \quad \frac{\theta}{\sqrt[3]{4}} = \frac{1}{2}\sqrt[3]{2} + \frac{1}{2}\sqrt[3]{4}.$$

From Theorem 2, it follows that the number $\beta = \sqrt{1 + \sqrt[3]{2}}$ does not belong to $R(\mathbb{Q})$ and, consequently, is a square radical over $R(\mathbb{Q})$.

Example 3. Let $P = \mathbb{Q}$ and $\widetilde{P} = \mathbb{Q}(\sqrt{2})$. Consider the number

$$\theta = 12 + 9\sqrt{2} \in \mathbb{Q}(\sqrt{2}).$$

Using Proposition 2, one can show that $\theta \notin (\mathbb{Q}(\sqrt{2}))^2$, but the number

$$\frac{\theta}{\sqrt{2}} = 9 + 6\sqrt{2}$$

is an almost square in $\mathbb{Q}(\sqrt{2})$ over $\mathbb{Q}$. Namely, we have

$$9 + 6\sqrt{2} = 3 \cdot (1 + \sqrt{2})^2.$$

Thus, being a square radical over $\mathbb{Q}(\sqrt{2})$, the number $\beta = \sqrt{\theta} = \sqrt{12 + 9\sqrt{2}}$ is not a square radical over $R(\mathbb{Q})$. In fact, we obtain

$$\beta = \sqrt{3\sqrt{2} \cdot (1 + \sqrt{2})^2} = \sqrt[4]{18} \cdot (1 + \sqrt{2}) = \sqrt[4]{18} + \sqrt[4]{72} \in R(\mathbb{Q}).$$

The following example is more complicated and seems unexpected but, theoretically, we are dealing with the same phenomenon as in the trivial identities of the type (1).

Example 4. Consider the equality

$$\sqrt{3 + \sqrt{2}} + \sqrt{3 - \sqrt{2}} = \sqrt{6 + 2\sqrt{7}}. \tag{17}$$

Here all the numbers

$$\beta_1 = \sqrt{3 + \sqrt{2}}, \quad \beta_2 = \sqrt{3 - \sqrt{2}}, \quad \beta_3 = \sqrt{6 + 2\sqrt{7}}$$

are square radicals over $R(\mathbb{Q})$. This can be shown similarly to Example 2 (the proof is technically easier because we can apply Proposition 2). Since β_l-s are linearly dependent, among them there is at least one pair which are proportional over $R(\mathbb{Q})$ (see Corollary 3 with respect to $P = R(\mathbb{Q})$). In fact, we have

$$\frac{\beta_2}{\beta_1} = \frac{3}{7}\sqrt{7} - \frac{1}{7}\sqrt{14}, \quad \frac{\beta_3}{\beta_1} = 1 + \frac{3}{7}\sqrt{7} - \frac{1}{7}\sqrt{14}, \tag{18}$$

i.e., all the radicals β_l are pairwise proportional over $R(\mathbb{Q})$. Relations (18) can be found using Theorem 2 together with Proposition 2 (due to the fact that all involving radicals are of degree two). Simplifying β_2/β_1, we can also use the elementary identity (3) (and this would be simpler).

We proceed with some further observations on the identity (17). In the left-hand side of (17), there are numbers of the form

$$\sqrt{a + b\sqrt{2}} \quad (a, b \in \mathbb{Q}), \tag{19}$$

the sum of which is a number of the form

$$\sqrt{c + d\sqrt{7}} \quad (c, d \in \mathbb{Q}). \tag{20}$$

To be short, we will call the numbers (19) and (20) *white* and *black*, respectively. The identity (17) means that a black number can be represented as a sum of several white numbers. There are various identities of this kind, for instance,

$$\sqrt{5 + 3\sqrt{2}} + \sqrt{27 + 9\sqrt{2}} + \sqrt{26 - 14\sqrt{2}} = \sqrt{54 + 18\sqrt{7}}.$$

We call a white number (19) *interesting* if both coefficients a and b are positive. One can observe that in the previous identity (as well as in (17)), not all the white numbers are interesting. Below (see Proposition 3), we prove that it is not a simple coincidence. For convenience purposes, we reformulate Theorem 2 for square nested radicals.

Let $P \subset \mathbb{R}$ be a number field and $\omega \in \mathbb{R}$ be a square radical over P. Consider the numbers

$$\rho = \sqrt{a + b\omega} \tag{21}$$

with $a, b \in P$ and $a + b\omega > 0$. The following assertion answers how complicated the simplifying expressions for a double radical (21) could be, if exists.

Lemma 2. *Suppose $\rho = \sqrt{a + b\omega} \in R(P)$. Then there exist x, y, and $z > 0$ in P, such that either (i) $a + b\omega = z(x + y\omega)^2$, or (ii) $a + b\omega = z\omega(x + y\omega)^2$.*

Proof. This is a particular case of Theorem 2 where $\widetilde{P} = P(\omega)$. □

Proposition 3. *No black number (20) can be equal to a sum of interesting white numbers (19).*

Proof. Let

$$\sum_k r_k = r,$$

where $r_k = \sqrt{a_k + b_k\sqrt{2}}$ are interesting white numbers, $r = \sqrt{c + d\sqrt{7}}$ is a black number. Then

$$\sum_k r_k^2 + \sum_{k \neq l} \rho_{k,l} = r^2, \tag{22}$$

where $\rho_{k,l} = 2r_k r_l = \sqrt{A_{k,l} + B_{k,l}\sqrt{2}}$ with $A_{k,l} > 0$ and $B_{k,l} > 0$. Note that $\rho_{k,l} \in R(\mathbb{Q})$ for any $k \neq l$. Indeed, if some $\rho_{k,l} \notin R(\mathbb{Q})$ then the number in the left-hand side of (22) could not belong to $R(\mathbb{Q})$. The latter is due to the fact that after combining like terms in the left-hand side of (22), the radicals over $R(\mathbb{Q})$ would still remain. Lemma 2 yields

$$A_{k,l} + B_{k,l}\sqrt{2} = z_{k,l}(x_{k,l} + y_{k,l}\sqrt{2})^2\omega,$$

where either $\omega = 1$, or $\omega = \sqrt{2}$, and $x_{k,l}$, $y_{k,l}$, $z_{k,l}$ are rationals with $z_{k,l} > 0$. Since $2z_{k,l}x_{k,l}y_{k,l} = B_{k,l}$ when $\omega = 1$, and $4z_{k,l}x_{k,l}y_{k,l} = A_{k,l}$ when $\omega = \sqrt{2}$, $x_{k,l}y_{k,l} > 0$, we can assume that $x_{k,l} > 0$ and $y_{k,l} > 0$ so that

$$\rho_{k,l} = (x_{k,l} + y_{k,l}\sqrt{2})\sqrt{z_{k,l}}\sqrt{\omega}.$$

But (22) is contradictory in this case. Indeed, after combining like terms in the left-hand side there will remain $\sqrt{2}$ with positive rational coefficient (since it must contain the terms $r_k^2 = a_k + b_k\sqrt{2}$ with $b_k > 0$), and the right-hand side does not contain $\sqrt{2}$. This completes the proof. $\qquad\square$

In the last part of this section, we briefly discuss the question about simplification of sums containing nested radicals. The following theorem reduces the problem of denesting a sum of several nested radicals to the (formally, simpler) problem of simplification of each radical in this sum.

Theorem 3. *Suppose* $\rho_1, \ldots, \rho_t$ *are radicals over* $\widetilde{P}$ *satisfying*

$$\frac{\rho_l}{\rho_{l'}} \notin \widetilde{P}^* \quad \text{for all} \quad l \neq l'.$$

If all $\zeta_l \in \widetilde{P}$ *are non-zero then*

$$\sigma = \zeta_1\rho_1 + \ldots + \zeta_t\rho_t \in R(P)$$

if and only if $\rho_l \in R(P)$ *for each* l.

Proof. Let $\sigma \in R(P)$. From Lemma 1 applied to the field $\widetilde{P}$, it follows that

$$\widetilde{P}(\rho_1, \ldots, \rho_t) = \widetilde{P}(\sigma).$$

Therefore, $\rho_l = g_l(\sigma)$ for a polynomial $g_l \in \widetilde{P}[x]$ $(l = 1, \ldots, t)$. Thus, $\rho_l \in R(P)$ for each l. The converse assertion is obvious. This completes the proof. $\qquad\square$

5   Examples of Triply Nested Real Radicals over $\mathbb{Q}$ that Cannot Be Simplified

Radicals with nesting depth more than two can also be denested according to the scheme described in the previous section.

For instance, the radical

$$\sqrt{2 + \sqrt{6} + \sqrt{4 + 4\sqrt{6}}}$$

triply nested over $\mathbb{Q}$ can be denested. For this purpose, we treat it as a doubly nested radical over the field $P = \mathbb{Q}(\sqrt{6})$ which yields

$$\sqrt{2 + \sqrt{6} + \sqrt{4 + 4\sqrt{6}}} = 1 + \sqrt{1 + \sqrt{6}}.$$

The following example shows that such a trick does not work in general.

Example 5. The radical

$$\gamma = \sqrt{1 + 2\sqrt{6} + \sqrt{20 + 2\sqrt{6}}}$$

(which is similar to the previous one) cannot be denested as a doubly nested radical over $P = \mathbb{Q}(\sqrt{6})$. Indeed, the number $\omega = \sqrt{20 + 2\sqrt{6}}$ is a square radical over P since the equality

$$20 + 2\sqrt{6} = (u + v\sqrt{6})^2$$

is impossible for any rationals u and v because the necessary condition from Proposition 2 (which requires that $20^2 - 6 \cdot 2^2$ must be a square of a rational number) does not hold. Now, putting $a = 1 + 2\sqrt{6}$ and $b = 1$, we can apply Lemma 2 together with Proposition 2. Finally, we need to check that both numbers

$$a^2 - b^2\omega^2 = 5 + 2\sqrt{6}, \qquad \frac{a^2 - b^2\omega^2}{-\omega^2} = -\frac{38 + 15\sqrt{6}}{188}$$

are not squares in P which is actually true. Thus, $\gamma \notin R(P)$, i.e., γ cannot be simplified as a doubly nested radical over P. On the other hand, we observe that $\gamma^2 \in R(P)$. This means that γ is a square radical over $R(P)$.

At the same time, we have

$$\gamma = \sqrt{\frac{1 + \sqrt{2} + \sqrt{3} + 2\sqrt{6}}{2}} + \sqrt{\frac{1 - \sqrt{2} - \sqrt{3} + 2\sqrt{6}}{2}} = \rho_1 + \rho_2.$$

This equality can be established if we start with a wider field P'. Indeed, in the field $P' = \mathbb{Q}(\sqrt{2}, \sqrt{3}) \supset P$ we have the equality

$$5 + 2\sqrt{6} = (\sqrt{2} + \sqrt{3})^2$$

that provides the desired simplification.

Remark 7. In fact, ρ_1 and ρ_2 are square radicals over $R(P)$ as well as γ. Since (by Corollary 3) we have no nontrivial identities with non-nested radicals, the equality $\gamma = \rho_1 + \rho_2$ implies that ρ_1, ρ_2, and γ are pairwise proportional over $R(P)$ (cf. (17)). This is actually true because $\rho_1\rho_2 = \omega \in R(P)$.

Certainly, taking $P = R(\mathbb{Q})$, we can guarantee complete simplification (and, particularly, the impossibility of denesting over $\mathbb{Q}$). In the following examples, we give some triply nested radicals over $\mathbb{Q}$ that cannot be simplified.

Example 6. Let $P = R(\mathbb{Q})$. Show that the number

$$\gamma = \sqrt{1 + \sqrt{1 + \sqrt[3]{2}}}$$

is a square radical over $R(P) = R(R(\mathbb{Q}))$. In Example 2, we have shown that

$$\beta = \sqrt{1 + \sqrt[3]{2}}$$

is a square radical over $R(\mathbb{Q})$. Denote $\theta = 1 + \beta$. We need to show that

$$\theta \notin (R(R(\mathbb{Q})))^2. \tag{23}$$

For this purpose, we have to show that both numbers θ and

$$\frac{\theta}{\beta} = 1 + \frac{\beta}{1 + \sqrt[3]{2}}$$

are not almost squares in $R(\mathbb{Q})(\beta)$ over $R(\mathbb{Q})$. Using Proposition 2, it suffices to show that

$$1 - \beta^2 = -\sqrt[3]{2} \notin (R(\mathbb{Q}))^2, \quad 1 - \frac{1}{\beta^2} = \frac{2}{3} + \frac{1}{3}\sqrt[3]{2} - \frac{1}{3}\sqrt[3]{4} \notin (R(\mathbb{Q}))^2.$$

The first is obvious (all the numbers are real), the second can be obtained as in Example 2. Thus, $\gamma = \sqrt{\theta} = \sqrt{1 + \beta}$ is a radical over $R(R(\mathbb{Q}))$. Consequently, its nesting depth is three. So, it is the minimum depth possible for the nested radical γ (in the case of real radicals over $\mathbb{Q}$).

The following example is similar to the previous one. At the same time, it requires a lot more computations to arrive at the expected result.

Example 7. Show that the number

$$\gamma = \sqrt{1 + \sqrt[3]{1 + \sqrt{2}}} \tag{24}$$

is a square radical over $R(R(\mathbb{Q}))$. We start by noticing that

$$\beta = \sqrt[3]{1 + \sqrt{2}}$$

is a cubic radical over $R(\mathbb{Q})$ which can be verified by checking $1 + \sqrt{2} \notin (R(\mathbb{Q}))^3$. For $\theta = 1 + \beta$, we need to show (23) again, but this time we must prove that the numbers θ and

$$\frac{\theta}{\beta} = 1 + \frac{\beta^2}{1 + \sqrt{2}}, \quad \frac{\theta}{\beta^2} = \frac{\beta}{1 + \sqrt{2}} + \frac{\beta^2}{1 + \sqrt{2}}$$

are not almost squares in $R(\mathbb{Q})(\beta)$ over $R(\mathbb{Q})$. However, we cannot use Proposition 2 as in Example 6 because β is not a square radical.

Below, we prove that θ is not an almost square in $R(\mathbb{Q})(\beta)$ over $R(\mathbb{Q})$ (we can proceed similarly for θ/β and θ/β^2 and get the same result).

    I. Suppose that

$$1 + \beta = x_0(x_1 + x_2\beta + x_3\beta^2)^2$$

where all $x_j \in R(\mathbb{Q})$ (see Definition 1). We need to apply Corollary 1 for the field $L = R(\mathbb{Q})$. In our case, the system (9) is the following:

$$\begin{cases} x_0(x_1^2 + (2 + 2\sqrt{2})x_2x_3) = 1, \\ x_0(2x_1x_2 + (1 + \sqrt{2})x_3^2) = 1, \\ x_0(2x_1x_3 + x_2^2) = 0, \\ x_j = 1, \end{cases} \tag{25}$$

where $j \in \{1, 2, 3\}$. For instance, take $j = 2$. One can compute a Gröbner basis of (25) that contains a univariate polynomial of the form

$$h = 4x^4 - 8x^3 + (4 - 4\sqrt{2})x + 1 - \sqrt{2} \tag{26}$$

with respect to $x = x_3$. Using a modified version of the corresponding algorithm from [11] (see Theorem 4 below), we aim at proving that the polynomial $h \in \mathbb{Q}(\sqrt{2})[x]$ has no roots in $R(\mathbb{Q})$.

II. Assume $\sigma \in R(\mathbb{Q})$ is a root of h. Then there exist multiplicatively independent radicals $\alpha_1, \ldots, \alpha_s$ over $P_1 = \mathbb{Q}(\sqrt{2})$ of degrees $n_1, \ldots, n_s$ respectively such that

$$P_1(\sigma) = P_1(\alpha_1, \ldots, \alpha_s).$$

In particular, we have

$$\prod_{k=1}^{s} n_k = [P_1(\sigma) : P_1] = 4$$

because h is irreducible over P_1. Therefore, there are only two cases: (i) $s = 2$, $n_1 = n_2 = 2$, and (ii) $s = 1$, $n_1 = 4$.

Let α be one of the unknown radicals α_k $(k = 1, \ldots, s)$. Then

$$\alpha = y_1 + y_2\sigma + y_3\sigma^2 + y_4\sigma^3,$$

where all $y_j \in P_1$ and there is $j \in \{2, 3, 4\}$ such that $y_j \neq 0$ (without of loss of generality, we can assume $y_j = 1$).

Let us consider the case (i). In this case, we obtain $\alpha^2 \in P_1$, so that we can use Corollary 2. Let $j = 2$ (and, consequently, $y_2 = 1$). Then the corresponding system (10) can be rewritten as

$$\begin{cases} -(1 - \sqrt{2})y_3^2 - \frac{9}{2}(1 - \sqrt{2})y_4^2 - \frac{9}{2}(1 - \sqrt{2})y_3y_4 + 2y_1 - 2(1 - \sqrt{2})y_4 = 0, \\ -\frac{9}{4}(1 - \sqrt{2})y_4^2 + 2y_1y_3 - 2(1 - \sqrt{2})y_3y_4 + 1 = 0, \\ 2y_3^2 + (7 + \sqrt{2})y_4^2 + 2y_1y_4 + 8y_3y_4 + 2y_3 + 4y_4 = 0. \end{cases}$$

A Gröbner basis (which can be computed, for instance, using Maple Groebner package) of this system contains a univariate polynomial

$$g = 711y_4^7 - (3500 + 1372\sqrt{2})y_4^6 + \ldots \in P_1[y_4] \tag{27}$$

of degree 7 having no roots in P_1. The same result can be obtained for the cases $j = 3$ and $j = 4$. Thus, the case (i) is impossible.

In the case (ii), we can proceed in the same way. In this case, the complexity of computing Gröbner basis for corresponding systems of the form (10) increases significantly. In particular, an analog of polynomial (27) is of degree 49 and its coefficients are of the form $a + b\sqrt{2}$ with integers $a, b \approx 10^{60}$. Omitting computations, we conclude that the case (ii) is also impossible. Therefore, polynomial (26) has no roots in the field $R(\mathbb{Q})$ (in fact, we have proved that it has no roots in the field $R(\mathbb{Q}(\sqrt{2}))$ that includes $R(\mathbb{Q})$, see Remark 5). Hence, for $j = 2$, system (25) has no solutions (x_0, x_1, x_2, x_3) over $R(\mathbb{Q})$. The remaining cases of $j \in \{1, 3\}$ can be considered in a similar way. Finally, we conclude that the number (24) is a square radical over $R(R(\mathbb{Q}))$.

The final part of Example 7 suggests a generalization of the corresponding result from [11]. Let $P_1 \subset \mathbb{R}$ be a real field for which there is an algorithm for factoring any polynomial in $P_1[x]$ (in particular, we can find all the roots in P_1 of a given polynomial in $P_1[x]$). For instance, for P_1 one may take $\mathbb{Q}(\omega)$ where ω is a real algebraic number.

Theorem 4. *There is an algorithm that finds all the roots of a given polynomial $h \in P_1[x]$ in $R(P_1)$.*

Proof. Without loss of generality, assume that h is irreducible over P_1. Let $\sigma \in R(P_1)$ be a root of h. By Lemma 1 with $P = P_1$, there exist multiplicatively independent radicals $\alpha_1, \ldots, \alpha_s$ (with degrees $n_1, \ldots, n_s$, respectively) over P_1 such that

$$P_1(\sigma) = P_1(\alpha_1, \ldots, \alpha_s), \quad [P_1(\sigma) : P_1] = \prod_{k=1}^{s} n_k = N,$$

where $N = \deg h$ is a fixed positive integer. In particular, there exists at most a finite set of such s-tuples $(n_1, \ldots, n_s)$. Fix one of them and fix $k \in \{1, \ldots, s\}$. Then, for the unknown radical α_k of degree n_k, we have

$$\alpha_k = y_1 + y_2\sigma + \ldots + y_N\sigma^{N-1},$$

where all $y_j \in P_1$ and there exists $j_0 > 1$ such that $y_{j_0} \neq 0$ (in fact, such y_{j_0} can be assumed to be equal to 1). Using Corollary 2 and Gröbner bases technique, we can solve the system

$$\begin{cases} p_2^{(k)}(y_1, \ldots, y_N) = 0, \\ \ldots \\ p_N^{(k)}(y_1, \ldots, y_N) = 0, \\ y_{j_0} = 1 \end{cases} \tag{28}$$

over the field P_1 for all $j_0 \in \{2, \ldots, N\}$ (in (28), the polynomials $p_1^{(k)}, \ldots, p_N^{(k)}$ are defined by (4) with $\omega_j = \sigma^{j-1}$ and $f = x^{n_k}$). Let $(y_1, \ldots, y_N) \in P_1^N$ be an arbitrary solution of system (28). Then

$$b_k = \alpha_k^{n_k} = p_1^{(k)}(y_1, \ldots, y_N) \in P_1.$$

Thus, we find all possible values of the radical α_k of the fixed degree n_k.

Finally, whenever h has a root in $R(P_1)$, then it must belong to one of the fields

$$\widetilde{P_1} = P_1(\sqrt[n_1]{b_1}, \ldots, \sqrt[n_s]{b_s}), \qquad (29)$$

where all the possible $(n_1, \ldots, n_s) \in \mathbb{N}^s$ and the corresponding $(b_1, \ldots, b_s) \in P_1^s$ can be computed. Thus, for finding all the roots h in $R(P_1)$, it suffices to find all the roots h in each field $\widetilde{P_1}$ of the form (29). This can be done by means of Proposition 1 (furthermore, for the frequently used case $P_1 = \mathbb{Q}(\omega)$, there exist easier methods implemented in some CASs). $\qquad \Box$

6 Concluding Remarks

Theorem 4 provides some improvements of the algorithm for solving polynomial equations over $R(\mathbb{Q})$ proposed in [11]. Indeed, in the previous version of the algorithm, we had to operate on the auxiliary polynomial

$$H = h\bar{h} = 16x^8 - 64x^7 + \ldots \in \mathbb{Q}[x]$$

instead of the given polynomial (26). Here

$$\bar{h} = 4x^4 - 8x^3 + (4 + 4\sqrt{2})x + 1 + \sqrt{2}$$

is a polynomial having conjugate (with respect to $\mathbb{Q}(\sqrt{2})/\mathbb{Q}$) coefficients. It is clear that the further computations would be very difficult to implement (due to impossibility of computing a Gröbner basis of the corresponding polynomial system in a reasonable time).

The complexity of the algorithm that provides denesting of a given triply nested radical strongly depends on complexity of the algorithm that solves polynomial systems of a special class (see Proposition 1 and its Corollaries 1 and 2). At the moment, we can only use the Gröbner basis technique which is, obviously, not the best option.

We finish with the following example which is, apparently, impossible to handle via the methods presented here. Consider the equation

$$x^4 - x - 1 = 0. \qquad (30)$$

Both real roots of (30) are nested radicals of depth four over $\mathbb{Q}$. Namely, they can be written in the form

$$x = \frac{\left(\left(\frac{1}{2} + \left(\frac{283}{108}\right)^{1/2}\right)^{1/3} + \left(\frac{1}{2} - \left(\frac{283}{108}\right)^{1/2}\right)^{1/3}\right)^{1/2}}{2}$$

$$\pm \frac{\left(-\left(\frac{1}{2} + \left(\frac{283}{108}\right)^{1/2}\right)^{1/3} - \left(\frac{1}{2} - \left(\frac{283}{108}\right)^{1/2}\right)^{1/3} + 2\left(\left(\frac{1}{2} + \left(\frac{283}{108}\right)^{1/2}\right)^{1/3} + \left(\frac{1}{2} - \left(\frac{283}{108}\right)^{1/2}\right)^{1/3}\right)^{-1/2}\right)^{1/2}}{2}$$

that is provided by Ferrari's method. It is very likely that this expression cannot be denested (using only the real radicals), but how can we prove it?

Acknowledgments. This work is supported by the Krasnoyarsk Mathematical Center and financed by the Ministry of Science and Higher Education of the Russian Federation in the framework of the establishment and development of regional Centers for Mathematics Research and Education (Agreement No. 075-02-2020-1534/1).

References

1. Becker, T., Weispfenning, V.: A Computational Approach to Commutative Algebra. Graduate Texts in Mathematics, vol. 141. Springer-Verlag, New York (1993). https://doi.org/10.1007/978-1-4612-0913-3
2. Besicovitch, A.S.: On the linear independence of fractional powers of integers. J. London Math. Soc. **15**, 3–6 (1940)
3. Blömer, J.: Computing sums of radicals in polynomial time. In: Proceedings of the 32nd Annual Symposium on Foundations of Computer Science, pp. 670–677 (1991)
4. Blömer, J.: How to denest Ramanujan's nested radicals. In: Proceedings of the 33nd Annual Symposium on Foundations of Computer Science, pp. 447–456 (1992)
5. Borevich, Z.I., Shafarevich, I.R.: Number Theory. Academic Press, London (1966)
6. Borodin, A., et al.: Decreasing the nesting depth of expressions involving square roots. J. Symb. Comput. **1**, 169–188 (1985)
7. Davenport, J., Siret, Y., Tournier, E.: Calcul formel: Systèmes et algorithmes de manipulations algébriques. Masson, Paris (1987)
8. Landau, S.: Simplification of nested radicals. SIAM J. Comput. **21**, 85–109 (1992)
9. Lang, S.: Algebra. Springer, New York (2002). https://doi.org/10.1007/978-1-4613-0041-0
10. Mordell, L.J.: On the linear independence of algebraic numbers. Pacific J. Math. **3**, 625–630 (1953)
11. Osipov, N.N.: On the simplification of nested real radicals. Program. Comput. Softw. **23**(3), 142–146 (1997)
12. Maplesoft. https://www.maplesoft.com

Parametric Toricity of Steady State Varieties of Reaction Networks

Hamid Rahkooy[2] and Thomas Sturm[1,2,3(⊠)]

[1] CNRS, Inria, and the University of Lorraine, Nancy, France
thomas.sturm@loria.fr
[2] MPI Informatics, Saarland Informatics Campus, Saarbrücken, Germany
hamid.rahkooy@mpi-inf.mpg.de
[3] Saarland University, Saarland Informatics Campus, Saarbrücken, Germany

Abstract. We study real steady state varieties of the dynamics of chemical reaction networks. The dynamics are derived using mass action kinetics with parametric reaction rates. The models studied are not inherently parametric in nature. Rather, our interest in parameters is motivated by parameter uncertainty, as reaction rates are typically either measured with limited precision or estimated. We aim at detecting toricity and shifted toricity, using a framework that has been recently introduced and studied for the non-parametric case over both the real and the complex numbers. While toricity requires that the variety specifies a subgroup of the direct power of the multiplicative group of the underlying field, shifted toricity requires only a coset. In the non-parametric case these requirements establish real decision problems. In the presence of parameters we must go further and derive necessary and sufficient conditions in the parameters for toricity or shifted toricity to hold. Technically, we use real quantifier elimination methods. Our computations on biological networks here once more confirm shifted toricity as a relevant concept, while toricity holds only for degenerate parameter choices.

Keywords: Chemical reaction networks · Logic computation · Mass action kinetics · Parameter uncertainty · Real computation · Scientific computation · Symbolic computation · Toric varieties

1 Introduction

We study the kinetics of reaction networks in the sense of *Chemical Reaction Network Theory* [22]. This covers also biological networks that are not reaction networks in a strict sense, e.g., epidemic models and signaling networks. The kinetics of reaction networks is given by ordinary differential equations (ODE) $\dot{\mathbf{x}} = \mathbf{f}$ with polynomial vector field $\mathbf{f} \in \mathbb{Z}[\mathbf{k}, \mathbf{x}]$, where $\mathbf{k}$ are positive scalar reaction rates and $\mathbf{x}$ are concentrations of species over time. Such ODE are

Electronic supplementary material The online version of this chapter (https://doi.org/10.1007/978-3-030-85165-1_18) contains supplementary material, which is available to authorized users.

© Springer Nature Switzerland AG 2021
F. Boulier et al. (Eds.): CASC 2021, LNCS 12865, pp. 314–333, 2021.
https://doi.org/10.1007/978-3-030-85165-1_18

typically derived using mass action kinetics [22, Sect. 2.1.2]. For fixed choices $\mathbf{k}^* \in \mathbb{R}^s_{>0}$, the real variety $V_{\mathbf{k}^*}(\mathbf{f}) = \{\, \mathbf{x}^* \in \mathbb{R}^n \mid \mathbf{f}(\mathbf{k}^*, \mathbf{x}^*) = 0 \,\}$ describes the set of steady states of the system.

One famous example is the Michaelis–Menten network [39], which describes an enzymatic reaction as follows:

$$S + E \underset{k^{\mathrm{off}}}{\overset{k^{\mathrm{on}}}{\rightleftharpoons}} ES \xrightarrow{k^{\mathrm{cat}}} P + E. \tag{1}$$

Here one has reaction rates $\mathbf{k} = (k^{\mathrm{on}}, k^{\mathrm{off}}, k^{\mathrm{cat}})$ and species concentrations $\mathbf{x} = (x_1, \ldots, x_4)$ for the substrate S, the enzyme E, the enzyme-substrate complex ES, and the product P, respectively. The vector field of the ODE is given by $\mathbf{f} = (f_1, \ldots, f_4)$ as follows, where $f_2 = -f_3$:

$$\begin{aligned}
f_1 &= -k^{\mathrm{on}} x_1 x_2 + k^{\mathrm{off}} x_3 \\
f_2 &= -k^{\mathrm{on}} x_1 x_2 + (k^{\mathrm{off}} + k^{\mathrm{cat}}) x_3 \\
f_3 &= k^{\mathrm{on}} x_1 x_2 - (k^{\mathrm{off}} + k^{\mathrm{cat}}) x_3 \\
f_4 &= k^{\mathrm{cat}} x_3.
\end{aligned} \tag{2}$$

For an intuition about mass action kinetics consider the reaction $S + E \xrightarrow{k^{\mathrm{on}}} ES$ in (1). The summand $-k^{\mathrm{on}} x_1 x_2$ in the differential equation $\dot{x}_1 = f_1 = -k^{\mathrm{on}} x_1 x_2 + k^{\mathrm{off}} x_3$ describes a decrease of the concentration x_1 of S that is proportional to the product $x_1 x_2$ of concentrations of S and E with a positive proportionality factor k^{on}. The product $x_1 x_2$ of concentrations models the probability that one molecule of S and one molecule of E encounter each other in a perfectly stirred reactor.

For steady state of the Michaelis–Menten kinetics, f_4 in (2) imposes $x_3 = 0$. Biologically speaking, steady state requires that the concentration of the enzyme-substrate complex become zero. Next, $f_1, \ldots, f_3$ impose that either $x_1 = 0$ and x_2 can be freely chosen, or vice versa. That is, the concentration of either substrate or enzyme must become zero. The concentration x_4 of the product can always be freely chosen. It turns out that $V_{\mathbf{k}}(\mathbf{f}) \neq \emptyset$, and $V_{\mathbf{k}}(\mathbf{f})$ does not depend on $\mathbf{k}$ at all.

Let us look at 1-site phosphorylation [43, 53], which gives a slightly more complex network as follows:

$$S_0 + E \underset{k^{\mathrm{off}}}{\overset{k^{\mathrm{on}}}{\rightleftharpoons}} ES_0 \xrightarrow{k^{\mathrm{cat}}} S_1 + E \qquad S_1 + F \underset{\ell^{\mathrm{off}}}{\overset{\ell^{\mathrm{on}}}{\rightleftharpoons}} FS_1 \xrightarrow{\ell^{\mathrm{cat}}} S_0 + F. \tag{3}$$

Here we have $\mathbf{k} = (k^{\mathrm{on}}, \ldots, \ell^{\mathrm{cat}})$, $\mathbf{x} = (x_1, \ldots, x_6)$ for concentrations of species S_0, S_1, ES_0, FS_1, E, F, respectively. The vector field of the ODE is given by $\mathbf{f} = (f_1, \ldots, f_6)$ with

$$\begin{aligned}
f_1 &= -k^{\mathrm{on}} x_1 x_5 + k^{\mathrm{off}} x_3 + \ell^{\mathrm{cat}} x_4 \\
f_3 &= k^{\mathrm{on}} x_1 x_5 - (k^{\mathrm{cat}} + k^{\mathrm{off}}) x_3 \\
f_4 &= \ell^{\mathrm{on}} x_2 x_6 - (\ell^{\mathrm{cat}} + \ell^{\mathrm{off}}) x_4.
\end{aligned} \tag{4}$$

Similarly to f_2 in (2), f_2, f_5, f_6 here are linear combinations of $\mathbf{f}' = (f_1, f_3, f_4)$ and thus $V_{\mathbf{k}}(\mathbf{f}) = V_{\mathbf{k}}(\mathbf{f}')$. In contrast to the Michaelis–Menten kinetics we now find steady states where all species concentrations are non-zero. One such steady state is

$$\mathbf{x}^* = \left(1, 1, 1, \frac{k^{\text{cat}}}{\ell^{\text{cat}}}, \frac{k^{\text{cat}} + k^{\text{off}}}{k^{\text{on}}}, \frac{k^{\text{cat}} \ell^{\text{cat}} + k^{\text{cat}} \ell^{\text{off}}}{\ell^{\text{cat}} \ell^{\text{on}}}\right)^T. \tag{5}$$

Notice that this particular steady state exists uniformly in $\mathbf{k}$ and that denominators cannot vanish, due to our requirement that $\mathbf{k} > 0$.

For the non-parametric case, i.e., for fixed $\mathbf{k}^* \in \mathbb{R}^s_{>0}$, comprehensive computational experiments on reaction networks in [28] have identified *shifted toricity* as a structural property that occurs frequently but not generally. Assuming that $V_{\mathbf{k}^*}(\mathbf{f})$ is irreducible, the set $V_{\mathbf{k}^*}(\mathbf{f})^* = V_{\mathbf{k}^*}(\mathbf{f}) \cap \mathbb{R}^{*n}$ is *shifted toric* if it forms a multiplicative coset of $\mathbb{R}^{*n}$ [29]. Here $\mathbb{R}^*$ is the multiplicative group of the field of real numbers, and $\mathbb{R}^{*n}$ is its direct power. For the sake of this clear and simple algebraic setting we do not take into consideration the positivity of $\mathbf{x}$ here. Instead, shifted tori can be algorithmically intersected with the positive first orthant later on.

The notion of shifted toricity historically originates from the consideration of additive groups. In our setting, the "shift" is geometrically not a translation but a scaling of the torus. For the natural sciences, structural properties like shifted toricity provide *qualitative* insights into nature, as opposed to quantitative information like numeric values of coordinates of some fixed points. For symbolic computation, our hope is that structural properties can be exploited for the development of more efficient algorithms.

Our program for this article is the generalization of the concept of shifted toricity to the parametric case, along with the development of suitable computational methods, accompanied by computational experiments. For instance, for our 1-site phosphorylation we will automatically derive in Sect. 4.4 that

(i) $V_{\mathbf{k}}(\mathbf{f})^*$ forms a coset for all admissible choices of $\mathbf{k}$, and
(ii) $V_{\mathbf{k}}(\mathbf{f})^*$ forms a group if and only if $k^{\text{on}} - k^{\text{off}} = \ell^{\text{on}} - \ell^{\text{off}} = k^{\text{cat}} = \ell^{\text{cat}}$.

Chemical reaction network theory [22] generally studies specific structural properties of networks like (1) and (3), such as our shifted toricity. There is a consensus in chemical reaction network theory that meaningful structural properties of networks would not refer to specific values of the rate constants $\mathbf{k}$, as Feinberg explicitly states in his excellent textbook: *The network itself will be our object of study, not the network endowed with a particular set of rate constants* [22, p.19]. In reality, exact rate constants are hardly ever known. They are either measured in experiments with a certain finite precision, or they are estimated, often only in terms of orders of magnitude. Furthermore, even if we had perfect positive real values for the rate constants $\mathbf{k}$, recall that according to mass action kinetics their co-factors are products of certain species concentrations $\mathbf{x}$, which only approximate probabilities as they would hold under hypothetical ideal conditions. Hence, we are looking primarily for results like (i) above. Result (ii) might seem appealing from a mathematical viewpoint, but it has hardly any relevance in nature. Bluntly speaking, a metabolism whose functioning depends on any of the equations in (ii) could not be evolutionarily successful.

What is the motivation for looking at admissible parameter values at all? Why not just derive yes/no decisions under suitable existential or universal quantification of the parameters? First, just as the equations in (ii) hardly ever hold in reality, the same arguments support the hypothesis that derived inequalities, in the sense of logically negated equations, in $\mathbf{k}$ would hardly ever fail and may thus be acceptable. Second, we are working in real algebra here. Even if there are no order inequalities in the input, they will in general be introduced by the computation. For instance, when asking whether there exists $x_1 \in \mathbb{R}$ such that $x_1^2 = k_1 - 10^6 k_2$, an equivalent condition is given by $k_1 \geq 10^6 k_2$. Such a condition that one reaction rate be larger than another by several orders of magnitude is meaningful and might provide useful insights into a model. It should be clear at this point that our parametric considerations are not aimed at uniform treatment of families of similar problems. Rather, we are concerned with a formally clean treatment of parameter uncertainty.

Let us summarize the main characteristics of our approach taken here:

1. Our domain of computation are the real numbers in contrast to the complex numbers. This is the natural choice for reaction networks. It allows us to consequently use the information $\mathbf{k} > 0$ throughout the computation. There is a perspective to discover further polynomial ordering inequalities in $\mathbf{k}$ with the derivation of equivalent conditions for shifted toricity, even though the input is purely equational.
2. We take a logic approach, using polynomial constraints, arbitrary Boolean combinations of these constraints, and first-order quantification. In this way, the logical connection between the occurring constraints is shifted from meta-mathematical reasoning to object mathematics. This ensures that human intuition is not mixed up with automatically derived results. The long-term goal is to develop robust fully automatic methods and to make corresponding implementations in software accessible to natural scientists. Technically, we employ real quantifier elimination methods, normal form computations, and various simplification techniques.
3. Our approach aims at the geometric shape of the real variety in contrast to the syntactic shape of generators of the polynomial ideal. On the one hand, there is a strong relation between toricity of the variety and binomiality of the ideal [18], and Gröbner bases are mature symbolic computation tool in this regard. The relation between toricity and binomiality has even been generalized to shifted toricity [28,29]. On the other hand, real quantifier elimination methods are an equally mature tool, and they allow to operate directly on the real steady state variety, which is the object of interest from the point of view of natural sciences. Particularly with parameters, order inequalities enter the stage. They should not be ignored, and their derivation from the ideal would not be straightforward.

Our definitions of toricity and shifted toricity are inspired by Grigoriev and Milman's work on *binomial varieties* [29]. In joint work with Grigoriev and others, we have systematically applied them to both complex and real steady state varieties of reaction networks [28]. We have furthermore studied the connection between complex and real shifted toricity [45]. Toric dynamical systems have been studied by Feinberg [20] and by Horn and Jackson [32]. Craciun et al. [12] showed that toric dynamical systems correspond to *complex balancing* [22]. There are further definitions in the literature, where the use of the term "toric" is well motivated. Gatermann et al. considered *deformed toricity* for steady state ideals [23]. The exact relation between the principle of complex balancing and various definitions of toricity has obtained considerable attention in the last years [24,40,43]. Complex balancing itself generalizes *detailed balancing*, which has widely been used in the context of chemical reaction networks [21,22,32]. Gorban et al. [25,26] related reversibility of chemical reactions in detailed balance to binomiality of the corresponding varieties. Historically, the principle of detailed balancing has attracted considerable attention in the sciences. It was used by Boltzmann in 1872 in order to prove his H-theorem [2], by Einstein in 1916 for his quantum theory of emission and absorption of radiation [17], and by Wegscheider [55] and Onsager [41] in the context of *chemical kinetics*, which led to Onsager's Nobel prize in Chemistry in 1968. Pérez–Millán et al. [43] consider steady state ideals with binomial generators. They present a sufficient linear algebra condition on the *stoichiometry matrix* of a reaction network in order to test whether the steady state ideal has binomial generators. Conradi and Kahle proposed a corresponding heuristic algorithm. They furthermore showed that the sufficient condition is even equivalent when the ideal is homogenous [11,33,34]. Based on the above-mentioned linear algebra condition, MESSI systems have been introduced in [42]. Another linear algebra approach to binomiality has been studied in [44]. Recently, binomiality of steady state ideals was used to infer network structure of chemical reaction networks out of measurement data [54].

Bradford et al. [5,6] and England et al. [19] have worked on multistationarity of reaction networks with parametric rate constants. Pérez–Millán et al., in their above-mentioned work [43], have also discussed the parametric case, remarkably, already in 2012. We have taken various of our examples in the present article from [43], which allows the reader to directly compare our results obtained here over the real numbers with the existing ones over the complex numbers.

In Sect. 2, we make precise our notions of toricity and shifted toricity. We choose a strictly formal approach leading to characterizing first-order logic formulas over the reals. This prepares the application of real quantifier elimination methods. In Sect. 3, we summarize basic concepts from real quantifier elimination theory and related simplification techniques to the extent necessary to understand our computational approach. In Sect. 4, we present systematic computations on biological networks taken from the literature and from established biological databases for such models [8]. In Sect. 5, we summarize our findings and draw conclusions.

2   Tori Are Groups, and Shifted Tori Are Cosets

We start with some notational conventions. For a vector $\mathbf{v} = (v_1, \ldots, v_n)$ equations $\mathbf{v} = 0$ have to be read as $v_1 = 0 \wedge \ldots \wedge v_n = 0$, which is equivalent to $\mathbf{v} = (0, \ldots, 0)$. Inequalities $\mathbf{v} \neq 0$ have to be read as $v_1 \neq 0 \wedge \ldots \wedge v_n \neq 0$, which is *not* equivalent to $\mathbf{v} \neq (0, \ldots, 0)$. Similarly, inequalities $\mathbf{v} > 0$ serve as shorthand notations for $v_1 > 0 \wedge \ldots \wedge v_n > 0$. Other ordering relations will not occur with vectors. All arithmetic on vectors is component-wise. Logic formulas as above are mathematical objects that can contain equations. For better readability we use "$\doteq$" to express equality between formulas.

Consider polynomials $\mathbf{f} \in \mathbb{Z}[\mathbf{k}, \mathbf{x}]^m$ with parameters $\mathbf{k} = (k_1, \ldots, k_s)$ and variables $\mathbf{x} = (x_1, \ldots, x_n)$. For fixed choices $\mathbf{k}^* \in \mathbb{R}^s_{>0}$ of $\mathbf{k}$, the corresponding real variety of $\mathbf{f}$ is given by

$$V_{\mathbf{k}^*}(\mathbf{f}) = \{ \mathbf{x}^* \in \mathbb{R}^n \mid \mathbf{f}(\mathbf{k}^*, \mathbf{x}^*) = 0 \}. \tag{6}$$

We consider the multiplicative group $\mathbb{R}^* = \mathbb{R} \backslash \{0\}$, note that the direct product $\mathbb{R}^{*n}$ establishes again a group, and define

$$V_{\mathbf{k}^*}(\mathbf{f})^* = V_{\mathbf{k}^*}(\mathbf{f}) \cap \mathbb{R}^{*n} \subseteq \mathbb{R}^{*n}. \tag{7}$$

This set $V_{\mathbf{k}^*}(\mathbf{f})^*$ is a *torus* if it forms an irreducible subgroup of $\mathbb{R}^{*n}$. For this purpose, we allow ourselves to call $V_{\mathbf{k}^*}(\mathbf{f})^*$ irreducible if $V_{\mathbf{k}^*}(\mathbf{f})$ is irreducible, equivalently, if $\langle \mathbf{f}(\mathbf{k}^*, \mathbf{x}) \rangle$ is a prime ideal over $\mathbb{R}$. More generally, $V_{\mathbf{k}^*}(\mathbf{f})^*$ is a *shifted torus* if it forms an irreducible coset of $\mathbb{R}^{*n}$ [28,29].

In this article, we focus on the discovery of coset and group structures. This is only a very mild limitation, as a closer look at the geometric relevance of the irreducibility requirement shows: If we discover a coset but irreducibility does not hold, then we are, from a strictly geometrical point of view, faced with finitely many shifted tori instead of a single one. If we disprove the coset property and irreducibility does not hold, then some but not all of the irreducible components might be shifted tori, and they could be discovered via decomposition of the variety. The same holds for groups vs. tori.

It should be noted that the primality of $\langle \mathbf{f}(\mathbf{k}^*, \mathbf{x}) \rangle$ over $\mathbb{R}$ in contrast to $\mathbb{Q}$ is a computationally delicate problem already in the non-parametric case. Starting with integer coefficients, prime decomposition would require the construction of suitable real extension fields during computation. Our parametric setting would require in addition the introduction of suitable finite case distinctions on the vanishing of coefficient polynomials in $\mathbf{k}$.

The definition typically used for a set $C \subseteq \mathbb{R}^{*n}$ to form a coset of $\mathbb{R}^{*n}$ goes as follows: There exists $\mathbf{g} \in \mathbb{R}^{*n}$ such that $\mathbf{g}^{-1}C$ forms a subgroup of $\mathbb{R}^{*n}$. We are going to use a slightly different but equivalent characterization: $\mathbf{g}^{-1}C$ forms a subgroup of $\mathbb{R}^{*n}$ for all $\mathbf{g} \in C$. A proof for the equivalence can be found in [28, Proposition 21]. We now present four first-order logic formulas $\varphi_1, \ldots, \varphi_4$. They state, uniformly in $\mathbf{k}$, certain properties that can be combined to express that $V_{\mathbf{k}}(\mathbf{f})^*$ forms a coset or a group:

1. *Non-emptiness*
   There exists $\mathbf{x} \in \mathbb{R}^{*n}$ such that $\mathbf{x} \in V_{\mathbf{k}}(\mathbf{f})$:

$$\varphi_1 \doteq \exists \mathbf{x}(\mathbf{x} \neq 0 \wedge \mathbf{f} = 0). \tag{8}$$

2. *Shifted completeness under inverses*
   For all $\mathbf{g}$, $\mathbf{x} \in \mathbb{R}^{*n}$, if $\mathbf{g}$, $\mathbf{gx} \in V_{\mathbf{k}}(\mathbf{f})$, then $\mathbf{gx}^{-1} \in V_{\mathbf{k}}(\mathbf{f})$:

$$\varphi_2 \doteq \forall \mathbf{g} \forall \mathbf{x}(\mathbf{g} \neq 0 \wedge \mathbf{x} \neq 0 \wedge \mathbf{f}[\mathbf{x} \leftarrow \mathbf{g}] = 0 \wedge \mathbf{f}[\mathbf{x} \leftarrow \mathbf{g} \cdot \mathbf{x}] = 0$$
$$\longrightarrow \mathbf{f}[\mathbf{x} \leftarrow \mathbf{g} \cdot \mathbf{x}^{-1}] = 0). \tag{9}$$

   Here $[\mathbf{x} \leftarrow \mathbf{t}]$ denotes substitution of terms $\mathbf{t}$ for variables $\mathbf{x}$. In the equation $\mathbf{f}[\mathbf{x} \leftarrow \mathbf{g} \cdot \mathbf{x}^{-1}] = 0$ we tacitly drop the principal denominator of the left hand side to obtain a polynomial. This is admissible due to the premise that $\mathbf{x} \neq 0$.

3. *Shifted completeness under multiplication*
   For all $\mathbf{g}$, $\mathbf{x}$, $\mathbf{y} \in \mathbb{R}^{*n}$, if $\mathbf{g}$, $\mathbf{gx}$, $\mathbf{gy} \in V_{\mathbf{k}}(\mathbf{f})$, then $\mathbf{gxy} \in V_{\mathbf{k}}(\mathbf{f})$:

$$\varphi_3 \doteq \forall \mathbf{g} \forall \mathbf{x} \forall \mathbf{y}(\mathbf{g} \neq 0 \wedge \mathbf{x} \neq 0 \wedge \mathbf{y} \neq 0 \wedge \mathbf{f}[\mathbf{x} \leftarrow \mathbf{g}] = 0 \wedge$$
$$\mathbf{f}[\mathbf{x} \leftarrow \mathbf{g} \cdot \mathbf{x}] = 0 \wedge \mathbf{f}[\mathbf{x} \leftarrow \mathbf{g} \cdot \mathbf{y}] = 0 \longrightarrow \mathbf{f}[\mathbf{x} \leftarrow \mathbf{g} \cdot \mathbf{x} \cdot \mathbf{y}] = 0). \tag{10}$$

4. *Neutral element*
   $(1, \ldots, 1) \in V_{\mathbf{k}}(\mathbf{f})$:

$$\varphi_4 \doteq \mathbf{f}[\mathbf{x} \leftarrow (1, \ldots, 1)] = 0. \tag{11}$$

In these terms we can define formulas σ and τ, which state the $V_{\mathbf{k}}(\mathbf{f})^*$ is a coset or group, respectively:

$$\sigma \doteq \varphi_1 \wedge \varphi_2 \wedge \varphi_3, \quad \tau \doteq \varphi_2 \wedge \varphi_3 \wedge \varphi_4. \tag{12}$$

For the non-parametric case, these formulas have been derived and discussed in [28, Sect. 3.2]. In the absence of parameters they were logic sentences, which are either true or false over the real numbers. Real decision produces were used to automatically derive either "true" or "false." In our parametric setting here, they contain $\mathbf{k}$ as free variables and thus establish exact formal conditions in $\mathbf{k}$, which become either "true" or "false" after making choices of real values for $\mathbf{k}$.

3   Real Quantifier Elimination and Simplification

In the presence of parameters, the natural generalization of a decision procedure is an effective *quantifier elimination* procedure for the real numbers [15, 48, 49]. In fact, most real decision procedures are actually quantifier elimination procedures themselves, which apply quantifier elimination to their parameter-free input and subsequently evaluate the variable-free quantifier elimination result to either "true" or "false." Plenty of approaches have been proposed for real quantifier elimination, e.g. [1, 10, 27, 35, 38, 50, 56, 57], but only few of them have led to publicly available implementations with a long-term support strategy [7, 9, 13, 47, 51].

Given a first-order formula φ built from polynomial constraints with integer coefficients, quantifier elimination computes a formula φ' that is equivalent to φ over the reals, formally $\mathbb{R} \models \varphi \longleftrightarrow \varphi'$, but does not contain any quantifiers. We allow ourselves to call φ' *the result* of the quantifier elimination, although it is not uniquely determined by φ.

The following example, which is discussed in more detail in [48, Sect. 2.1], gives a first idea: On input of

$$\varphi \doteq \forall x_1 \exists x_2 (x_1^2 + x_1 x_2 + k_2 > 0 \wedge x_1 + k_1 x_2^2 + k_2 \leq 0), \tag{13}$$

quantifier elimination computes the result $\varphi' \doteq k_1 < 0 \wedge k_2 > 0$, which provides a necessary and sufficient condition in $\mathbf{k}$ for φ to hold. Another application of quantifier elimination has been used already in the introduction of this article: Consider $\mathbf{f} = (f_1, f_3, f_4)$ with f_1, f_3, f_4 as in (4). Then compute $\varphi_2, \ldots, \varphi_4$ as in (9)–(11) and τ as in (12). On input of τ, quantifier elimination delivers the result $\tau' \doteq k^{\mathrm{on}} - k^{\mathrm{off}} = \ell^{\mathrm{on}} - \ell^{\mathrm{off}} = k^{\mathrm{cat}} = \ell^{\mathrm{cat}}$. This is a necessary and sufficient condition in $\mathbf{k}$ for $V_{\mathbf{k}}(\mathbf{f})^*$ to form a group, which has already been presented in (ii) on p. 322.

For an existential formula like φ_1 in (8), quantifier elimination computes a result φ_1' that provides necessary and sufficient conditions in $\mathbf{k}$ for the existence of choices for $\mathbf{x}$ that satisfy the constraints in φ_1. By definition, quantifier elimination does not derive any information on possible choices of $\mathbf{x}$. In other words, quantifier elimination talks about solvability, not about solutions. However, quantifier elimination via virtual substitution [35,38,49,56], which we use here primarily, can optionally provide sample solutions for $\mathbf{x}$. This is known as *extended quantifier elimination* [36]. We have used extended quantifier elimination to compute the uniform steady state $\mathbf{x}^*$ in (5) in the introduction, besides the actual quantifier elimination result "true."

Successful practical application of quantifier elimination by virtual substitution goes hand in hand with strong and efficient automatic simplification of intermediate and finite results. We use essentially a collection of techniques specified in [14, Sect. 5.2] as the "standard simplifier." In particular, we exploit the concept of an *external theory* introduced in [14] with $\mathbf{k} > 0$ as our theory. This means that all simplifications are performed modulo the assumption $\mathbf{k} > 0$ without explicitly adding this information to the input formula φ. As a consequence, the quantifier elimination result φ' is equivalent only modulo $\mathbf{k} > 0$, formally $\mathbb{R} \models \mathbf{k} > 0 \longrightarrow (\varphi \longleftrightarrow \varphi').$[1]

Note that, in contrast to $\mathbf{k} > 0$ for the rate constants, we never require $\mathbf{x} > 0$ for the species concentrations although chemical reaction network theory assumes both to be positive. The reason is that the concepts of toricity used here have been defined in terms of varieties and multiplicative groups without any reference to order. It might be interesting to review these concepts with respect

---

[1] Alternatively, one could temporarily introduce constants $\mathbf{k}$ and state equivalence in an extended theory of real closed fields: $\mathrm{Th}(\mathbb{R}) \cup \{\mathbf{k} > 0\} \models \varphi \longleftrightarrow \varphi'$. This point of view is common in algebraic model theory and has been taken in [14].

to the particular situation encountered here. However, this is beyond the scope of this article and should be settled in a non-parametric context first.

We convert our final results to disjunctive normal form [14, Sect. 7] and apply simplification methods based on Gröbner bases [14, Sect. 4.3]. A disjunctive normal form is a finite case distinction over systems of constraints. It has been our experience that users prefer such a presentation of the computed information in comparison to arbitrary boolean combinations, even at the price of larger output. In general, this normal form computation can get quite expensive in time and space, because quantifier elimination by virtual substitution on universal formulas like $\varphi_2, \ldots, \varphi_4$ in (9)–(11) tends to produce conjunctions of disjunctions rather than vice versa. Luckily, our results are rather small.

Having said this, we have devised *quantifier elimination-based simplification* as another heuristic simplification step for our results ψ here. It checks via quantifier elimination for every single constraint γ in ψ whether

$$\mathbb{R} \models \forall \mathbf{k}(\mathbf{k} > 0 \longrightarrow \gamma) \longleftrightarrow \text{true} \quad \text{or} \quad \mathbb{R} \models \exists \mathbf{k}(\mathbf{k} > 0 \wedge \gamma) \longleftrightarrow \text{false}. \quad (14)$$

When such constraints γ are found, they are replaced in ψ with the respective truth value, and then the standard simplifier in applied to ψ once more. Quantifier elimination-based simplification preserves disjunctive normal forms.

As an example consider $\mathbf{k} = (k_{12}, k_{13}, k_{21}, k_{23}, k_{31}, k_{32})^T$ and $\psi \doteq \gamma_1 \vee \gamma_2$, where

$$\gamma_1 \doteq k_{31} - k_{32} = 0$$
$$\gamma_2 \doteq 16k_{12}k_{21} + 8k_{12}k_{23} + 8k_{13}k_{21} + 4k_{13}k_{23} + k_{31}^2 - 2k_{31}k_{32} + k_{32}^2 \leq 0. \quad (15)$$

If one recognizes that $k_{31}^2 - 2k_{31}k_{32} + k_{32}^2 = (k_{31} - k_{32})^2$ and furthermore takes into consideration that $\mathbf{k} > 0$, it becomes clear that γ_2 is not satisfiable. The argument can be seen as a generalization of sum-of-squares decomposition, which is not supported within our simplification framework [14]. Quantifier elimination-based simplification recognizes that the condition on the right hand side of (14) holds for γ_2. It replaces γ_2 with "false" in ψ, which yields $\gamma_1 \vee$ false. Finally, the standard simplifier is applied, and γ_1 is returned.

4   Computational Experiments

All our computations have been conducted on an AMD EPYC 7702 64-Core Processor. On the software side, we have used SVN revision 5797 of the computer algebra system Reduce with its computer logic package Redlog [13,30,31]. Reduce is open source and freely available on SourceForge.[2] On these grounds, we have implemented systematic Reduce scripts, which essentially give algorithms and could be turned into functions as a next step. In few places, global Redlog options have been adjusted manually in order to optimize the efficiency of quantifier elimination for a particular example. The scripts and the log files of the computations are available as supplementary material with this article.

---

[2] https://sourceforge.net/projects/reduce-algebra/.

4.1   An Artificial Triangle Network

We start with an artificial network introduced by Pérez–Millán et al. [43, p.1033, Ex. 2.3]:

$$2\,A \underset{k_{21}}{\overset{k_{12}}{\rightleftharpoons}} 2\,B \underset{k_{32}}{\overset{k_{23}}{\rightleftharpoons}} A + B \underset{k_{13}}{\overset{k_{31}}{\rightleftharpoons}} 2\,A. \tag{16}$$

There are reaction rates $\mathbf{k} = (k_{12}, k_{13}, k_{21}, k_{23}, k_{31}, k_{32})^T$ and species concentrations $\mathbf{x} = (x_1, x_2)^T$ for abstract species A and B, respectively. Its kinetics is described by an ODE $\dot{\mathbf{x}} = \mathbf{f}$ with a polynomial vector field $\mathbf{f} = (f_1, f_2)^T$ as follows:

$$f_1 = f_2 = (-2k_{12} - k_{13})x_1^2 + (2k_{21} + k_{23})x_2^2 + (k_{31} - k_{32})x_1 x_2. \tag{17}$$

We form φ_1 according to (8), and extended quantifier elimination yields $\varphi_1' \doteq$ true along with a uniform witness

$$\mathbf{x}^* = \left(1, -\frac{\sqrt{16k_{12}k_{21}+8k_{12}k_{23}+8k_{13}k_{21}+4k_{13}k_{23}+k_{31}^2-2k_{31}k_{32}+k_{32}^2}-k_{31}+k_{32}}{4k_{21}+2k_{23}}\right)^T. \tag{18}$$

Notice that $\mathbf{k} > 0$ ensures that the denominator cannot vanish.

Next, we consider φ_2 and obtain $\varphi_2' \doteq k_{31} - k_{32} = 0$ with the help of quantifier elimination-based simplification. In fact, this is the example for quantifier elimination-based simplification discussed in the previous section. From φ_3 we also obtain $\varphi_3' \doteq k_{31} - k_{32} = 0$.

Hence, $V_{\mathbf{k}}(\mathbf{f})^*$ forms a coset of $\mathbb{R}^{*2}$ if and only if $\mathbb{R} \models \sigma'$, where

$$\sigma' = k_{31} - k_{32} = 0. \tag{19}$$

The same condition has been derived with a different method in [43]. For $V_{\mathbf{k}}(\mathbf{f})^*$ to form even a subgroup of $\mathbb{R}^{*2}$ we must add to σ' the condition $\varphi_4 \doteq \mathbf{f}[\mathbf{x} \leftarrow (1,1)] = 0$. This yields

$$\tau' \doteq k_{31} - k_{32} = 0 \wedge 2k_{12} + k_{13} - 2k_{21} - k_{23} = 0. \tag{20}$$

The overall CPU time for the computations in this section was $0.867\,\mathrm{s}$. Details on input problem sizes can be found in Table 1.

Table 1. Problem sizes and computation times for Sect. 4.1–Sect. 4.3

Section	network	$|\mathbf{k}|$	$|\mathbf{x}|$	$|\mathbf{f}|$	# quantifiers			time
					φ_1	φ_2	φ_3	
4.1	Triangle	6	2	2	2	4	6	$0.845\,\mathrm{s}$
4.2	EnvZ-OmpR	14	9	9	9	18	27	$2.172\,\mathrm{s}$
4.3	TGF-β	8	6	6	6	12	18	$26.477\,\mathrm{s}$

4.2   Escherichia Coli Osmoregulation System

Our next example is a model of the escherichia coli osmoregulation system (EnvZ-OmpR). It has been introduced by Shinar and Feinberg [46, (S60) in the supporting online material] and also discussed in [43, p.1043, Example 3.15]:

$$
\begin{array}{ll}
XD \underset{k_{21}}{\overset{k_{12}}{\rightleftharpoons}} X \underset{k_{32}}{\overset{k_{23}}{\rightleftharpoons}} XT \xrightarrow{k_{34}} X_P & XT + Y_P \underset{k_{98}}{\overset{k_{89}}{\rightleftharpoons}} XTY_P \xrightarrow{k_{9,10}} XT + Y \\[2mm]
X_P + Y \underset{k_{65}}{\overset{k_{56}}{\rightleftharpoons}} X_PY \xrightarrow{k_{67}} X + Y_P & XD + Y_P \underset{k_{12,11}}{\overset{k_{11,12}}{\rightleftharpoons}} XDY_P \xrightarrow{k_{12,13}} XD + Y.
\end{array}
\tag{21}
$$

There are 14 reaction rates $\mathbf{k}$ and species concentrations $\mathbf{x} = (x_1, \ldots, x_9)^T$ for $XD, X, XT, X_P, Y, X_{PY}, Y_P, XTY_P, XDY_P$, respectively. Its kinetics is described by an ODE $\dot{\mathbf{x}} = \mathbf{f}$ with a polynomial vector field $\mathbf{f} = (f_1, \ldots, f_9)^T$ as follows:

$$
\begin{aligned}
f_1 &= -k_{12}x_1 + k_{21}x_2 - k_{11,12}x_1x_7 + (k_{12,11} + k_{12,13})x_9 \\
f_2 &= k_{12}x_1 + (-k_{21} - k_{23})x_2 + k_{32}x_3 + k_{67}x_6 \\
f_3 &= k_{23}x_2 + (-k_{32} - k_{34})x_3 - k_{89}x_3x_7 + (k_{98} + k_{9,10})x_8 \\
f_4 &= k_{34}x_3 - k_{56}x_4x_5 + k_{65}x_6 \\
f_5 &= -k_{56}x_4x_5 + k_{65}x_6 + k_{9,10}x_8 + k_{12,13}x_9 \\
f_6 &= k_{56}x_4x_5 + (-k_{65} - k_{67})x_6 \\
f_7 &= k_{67}x_6 - k_{89}x_3x_7 + k_{98}x_8 - k_{11,12}x_1x_7 + k_{12,11}x_9 \\
f_8 &= k_{89}x_3x_7 + (-k_{98} - k_{9,10})x_8 \\
f_9 &= k_{11,12}x_1x_7 + (-k_{12,11} - k_{12,13})x_9.
\end{aligned}
\tag{22}
$$

We compute $\varphi_1' \doteq \varphi_2' \doteq \varphi_3' \doteq \sigma \doteq$ true, which means that $V_{\mathbf{k}}(\mathbf{f})^*$ forms a coset for all admissible choices of reaction rates $\mathbf{k}$. Again, extended quantifier elimination delivers, in addition to φ_1', a uniform parametric witness $\mathbf{x}^*$ for the non-emptiness of $V_{\mathbf{k}}(\mathbf{f})^*$. We obtain the following equivalent condition in $\mathbf{k}$ for $V_{\mathbf{k}}(\mathbf{f})^*$ to form even a group:

$$
\begin{aligned}
\varphi_4' \doteq \tau \doteq\ & k_{89} - k_{9,10} - k_{98} = 0 \wedge k_{12,13} - k_{67} + k_{89} - k_{98} = 0 \\
& \wedge k_{12,13} - k_{56} + k_{65} + k_{89} - k_{98} = 0 \wedge k_{12,13} - k_{34} + k_{89} - k_{98} = 0 \\
& \wedge k_{12,13} - k_{23} + k_{32} + k_{89} - k_{98} = 0 \wedge k_{12} - k_{21} = 0 \\
& \wedge k_{11,12} - k_{12,11} - k_{12,13} = 0.
\end{aligned}
\tag{23}
$$

The overall CPU time for the computations in this section was 0.651 s. Details on input problem sizes can be found in Table 1.

4.3   TGF-β Pathway

The TGF-β signaling pathway plays a central role in tissue homeostasis and morphogenesis, as well as in numerous diseases such as fibrosis and cancer [52].

It is featured as model no. 101 in the BioModels repository [8].[3] We consider here a variant, which ignores a discrete event changing ligand concentration at time $t = 2500$. A non-parametric instance of this variant has been studied in [28] with respect to toricity and in [37] with respect to multiple time scale reduction.

$$\text{RII} + \text{RI} \xrightarrow{\text{ka}\cdot\text{ligand}} \text{IRIRII} \qquad\qquad \text{RI endo} \xrightarrow{\text{kr}} \text{RI}$$
$$\text{IRIRII} \xrightarrow{\text{kcd}} \emptyset \qquad\qquad \text{IRIRII\_endo} \xrightarrow{\text{kr}} \text{RI} + \text{RII}$$
$$\text{IRIRII} \xrightarrow{\text{klid}} \emptyset \qquad\qquad \emptyset \xrightarrow{\text{pRII}} \text{RII}$$
$$\text{IRIRII} \xrightarrow{\text{ki}} \text{IRIRII\_endo} \qquad\qquad \text{RII} \xrightarrow{\text{kcd}} \emptyset$$
$$\emptyset \xrightarrow{\text{pRI}} \text{RI} \qquad\qquad \text{RII} \xrightarrow{\text{ki}} \text{RII\_endo}$$
$$\text{RI} \xrightarrow{\text{kcd}} \emptyset \qquad\qquad \text{RII\_endo} \xrightarrow{\text{kr}} \text{RII}.$$
$$\text{RI} \xrightarrow{\text{ki}} \text{RI\_endo}$$

$$\tag{24}$$

There are 8 parameters $\mathbf{k}$ and species concentrations $\mathbf{x} = (x_1, \ldots, x_6)^T$ corresponding to RI, RII, IRIRII, IRIRII_endo, RI_endo, RII_endo, respectively. The dynamics of the network is described by an ODE $\dot{\mathbf{x}} = \mathbf{f}$ with a polynomial vector field $\mathbf{f} = (f_1, \ldots, f_6)^T$ as follows:

$$f_1 = -\text{ka} \cdot \text{ligand} \cdot x_1 x_2 - \text{kcd} \cdot x_1 - \text{ki} \cdot x_1 + \text{kr} \cdot x_4 + \text{kr} \cdot x_5 + \text{pri}$$
$$f_2 = -\text{ka} \cdot \text{ligand} \cdot x_1 x_2 - \text{kcd} \cdot x_2 - \text{ki} x_2 + \text{kr} \cdot x_4 + \text{kr} \cdot x_6 + \text{prii}$$
$$f_3 = \text{ka} \cdot \text{ligand} \cdot x_1 x_2 - \text{kcd} \cdot x_3 - \text{ki} \cdot x_3 - \text{klid} \cdot x_3$$
$$f_4 = \text{ki} \cdot x_3 - \text{kr} \cdot x_4$$
$$f_5 = \text{ki} \cdot x_1 - \text{kr} \cdot x_5$$
$$f_6 = \text{ki} \cdot x_2 - \text{kr} \cdot x_6.$$

$$\tag{25}$$

For fixed choices $\mathbf{k}^*$ of parameters as specified in the BioModels repository we had shown in [28] that $V_{\mathbf{k}^*}(\mathbf{f})^*$ is not a coset. Our parametric approach here allows to investigate to what extent this negative result depends on the specific choices $\mathbf{k}^*$. We compute $\varphi_1' \doteq$ true along with a witness for $V_{\mathbf{k}}(\mathbf{f})^* \neq \emptyset$ for all admissible choices of $\mathbf{k}$. Next, we obtain $\varphi_2' \doteq \varphi_3' \doteq$ false, i.e., shifted completeness under inverses and multiplication fails for all admissible choices of $\mathbf{k}$. It follows that $\sigma \doteq \tau \doteq$ false, i.e., $V_{\mathbf{k}}(\mathbf{f})^*$ is generally not a coset and not a group.

The synthesis and degradation reactions[4] in (24) cause absolute summands in f_1 and f_2 in the dynamics (25). Although there is a connection between cosets and the existence of binomial generators of the ideal, those summands are not an immediate reason to exclude cosets. Consider, e.g., the abstract example

---

[3] https://www.ebi.ac.uk/biomodels/BIOMD0000000101.

[4] i.e., the ones with "$\emptyset$" on their left hand side or right hand side, respectively.

$\mathbf{g} = (-x_1 - x_2 + k_1, x_2 + x_3 + k_2)$, where $V_{\mathbf{k}}(\mathbf{g})^*$ is a coset for all admissible choices of k_1, k_2. On the other hand, we have mentioned in the introduction that toricity is related to complex balance. TGF-β cannot not have complex balance, because there is a nonzero flux through the system: receptors are produced, they cycle, and are degraded. One cannot transfer information without dissipation. This observation generally applies to signaling models.

The overall CPU time for the computations in this section was 26.477 s. Details on input problem sizes can be found in Table 1.

4.4 N-Site Phosphorylation-Dephosphorylation Cycle

The n-site phosphorylation network in the form discussed here has been taken from Wang and Sontag [53]. Pérez–Millán et al. have discussed n-site phosphorylation for generic n [43, Sect. 4.1]; the cases $n = 1$ and $n = 2$ are discussed explicitly as Ex. 2.1 and Ex. 3.13, respectively. We have used the case $n = 1$ in the introduction.

For a fixed positive integer n, the n-site phosphorylation reaction network is given by

$$S_0 + E \underset{k_0^{\text{off}}}{\overset{k_0^{\text{on}}}{\rightleftharpoons}} ES_0 \overset{k_0^{\text{cat}}}{\longrightarrow} S_1 + E \qquad S_1 + F \underset{\ell_0^{\text{off}}}{\overset{\ell_0^{\text{on}}}{\rightleftharpoons}} FS_1 \overset{\ell_0^{\text{cat}}}{\longrightarrow} S_0 + F$$

$$\vdots \qquad\qquad\qquad\qquad \vdots$$

$$S_{n-1} + E \underset{k_{n-1}^{\text{off}}}{\overset{k_{n-1}^{\text{on}}}{\rightleftharpoons}} ES_{n-1} \overset{k_{n-1}^{\text{cat}}}{\longrightarrow} S_n + E \qquad S_n + F \underset{\ell_{n-1}^{\text{off}}}{\overset{\ell_{n-1}^{\text{on}}}{\rightleftharpoons}} FS_n \overset{\ell_{n-1}^{\text{cat}}}{\longrightarrow} S_{n-1} + F.$$

$$\tag{26}$$

Its dynamics is described by the following ODE with $6n$ parameters $\mathbf{k}_n = (k_0^{\text{on}}, \ldots, \ell_{n-1}^{\text{cat}})$ and $3n + 3$ variables

$$\mathbf{x}_n = (s_0, \ldots, s_n, c_0, \ldots, c_{n-1}, d_1, \ldots, d_n, e, f) \tag{27}$$

for concentrations of species S_0, ..., S_n, ES_0, ..., ES_{n-1}, FS_1, ..., FS_n, E, F, respectively:

$$\dot{s}_0 = -k_0^{\text{on}} s_0 e + k_0^{\text{off}} c_0 + \ell_0^{\text{cat}} d_1$$
$$\dot{s}_i = -k_i^{\text{on}} s_i e + k_i^{\text{off}} c_i + k_{i-1}^{\text{cat}} c_{i-1} - \ell_{i-1}^{\text{on}} s_i f + \ell_{i-1}^{\text{off}} d_i + \ell_i^{\text{cat}} d_{i+1}$$
$$\dot{c}_j = k_j^{\text{on}} s_j e - (k_j^{\text{off}} + k_j^{\text{cat}}) c_j$$
$$\dot{d}_k = \ell_{k-1}^{\text{on}} s_k f - (\ell_{k-1}^{\text{off}} + \ell_{k-1}^{\text{cat}}) d_k,$$
$$i = 1, \ldots, n-1, \quad j = 0, \ldots, n-1, \quad k = 1, \ldots, n. \tag{28}$$

Let $\mathbf{f}_n = (f_1, \ldots, f_{3n-1})$ denote the vector field of (28). We may ignore here the equations for $\dot{s}_n$, $\dot{e}$, and $\dot{f}$, whose right hand sides are linear combinations of $\mathbf{f}_n$.

For $n \in \{1, \ldots, 5\}$ we obtain the following computational results:

(i) $V_{\mathbf{k}}(\mathbf{f})^* \neq \emptyset$ for all admissible choices of $\mathbf{k}$; we also obtain a uniform witness in terms of $\mathbf{k}$;

(ii) $V_{\mathbf{k}}(\mathbf{f})^*$ forms a coset for all admissible choices of $\mathbf{k}$;
(iii) $V_{\mathbf{k}}(\mathbf{f})^*$ forms a group if and only if

$$\bigwedge_{i=0}^{n-1} k_i^{\mathrm{on}} - k_i^{\mathrm{off}} = \ell_i^{\mathrm{on}} - \ell_i^{\mathrm{off}} = k_i^{\mathrm{cat}} = \ell_i^{\mathrm{cat}}. \tag{29}$$

Wang and Sontag, in their article [53], were interested in quantitative information on the numbers of steady states of the dynamics (28). Our results here provide qualitative information on the structure of the set of steady states. We could automatically deduce that there is always at least one steady state, for which we find a uniform witness in $\mathbf{k}$. In fact, extended quantifier elimination could even enumerate steady states, because one can exclude in the input formula the ones already found, and rerun. More important, we know that the set $S \subseteq \mathbb{R}^{*n}$ of all steady states forms a coset. That is, for all choices of $\mathbf{k}$ and all $\mathbf{g} \in S$, the set $G = \mathbf{g}^{-1}S$ is complete under component-wise multiplication and inverses. The set S itself has this completeness property only for choices of parameters satisfying the equations (29) exactly, which one cannot expect from a practical point of view.

As one possible application of our results, assume that experiments have delivered three steady states $\mathbf{x}_1, \ldots, \mathbf{x}_3$. Then, e.g., the following are steady states, too:

$$\mathbf{x}_1(\mathbf{x}_1^{-1}\mathbf{x}_2 \cdot \mathbf{x}_1^{-1}\mathbf{x}_3) = \mathbf{x}_1^{-1}\mathbf{x}_2\mathbf{x}_3, \quad \mathbf{x}_1(\mathbf{x}_1^{-1}\mathbf{x}_2)^{-1} = \mathbf{x}_1^2\mathbf{x}_2. \tag{30}$$

Here we use multiplication with $\mathbf{x}_1^{-1}$ for switching from S to G, exploit there completeness under multiplication and inverses, respectively, and finally use multiplication with $\mathbf{x}_1$ for switching back to S.

The computation times are collected in Table 2. The formula φ_3 for $n = 5$ is the formally largest quantifier elimination problem considered in this article. We have eliminated here 54 real quantifiers in an 84-dimensional space, which took 1 h 6 min. For $n \geq 6$, the computations did not finish within 6 h.

Table 2. Problem sizes and computation times for n-site phosphorylation in Sect. 4.4

n	$|\mathbf{k}|$	$|\mathbf{x}|$	$|\mathbf{f}|$	# quantifiers			time
				φ_1	φ_2	φ_3	
1	6	6	2	6	12	18	0.500 s
2	12	9	5	9	18	27	1.131 s
3	18	12	8	12	24	36	5.911 s
4	24	15	11	15	30	45	33.790 s
5	30	18	14	18	36	54	3963.204 s
≥ 6	$6n$	$3(n+1)$	$3n-1$	$3(n+1)$	$6(n+1)$	$9(n+1)$	> 6 h

4.5   Excitatory Post-Synaptic Potential Acetylcholine Event

The excitatory post-synaptic potential acetylcholine event model (EPSP-ACh) has been introduced by Edelstein et al. [16]. It also appears as model no. 1 in the BioModels repository [8]:[5]

$$\text{Basal} \underset{k_0^r}{\overset{k_0^f}{\rightleftharpoons}} \text{BasalACh} \underset{k_1^r}{\overset{k_1^f}{\rightleftharpoons}} \text{BasalACh}_2$$

$$\text{Active} \underset{k_3^r}{\overset{k_3^f}{\rightleftharpoons}} \text{ActiveACh} \underset{k_4^r}{\overset{k_4^f}{\rightleftharpoons}} \text{ActiveACh}_2$$

$$\text{Intermediate} \underset{k_7^r}{\overset{k_7^f}{\rightleftharpoons}} \text{IntermediateACh} \underset{k_8^r}{\overset{k_8^f}{\rightleftharpoons}} \text{IntermediateACh}_2$$

$$\text{Desensitized} \underset{k_{12}^r}{\overset{k_{12}^f}{\rightleftharpoons}} \text{DesensitizedACh} \underset{k_{13}^r}{\overset{k_{13}^f}{\rightleftharpoons}} \text{DesensitizedACh}_2$$

$$\text{Basal} \underset{k_5^r}{\overset{k_5^f}{\rightleftharpoons}} \text{Active} \underset{k_9^r}{\overset{k_9^f}{\rightleftharpoons}} \text{Intermediate} \underset{k_{14}^r}{\overset{k_{14}^f}{\rightleftharpoons}} \text{Desensitized}$$

$$\text{BasalACh} \underset{k_6^r}{\overset{k_6^f}{\rightleftharpoons}} \text{ActiveACh} \underset{k_{10}^r}{\overset{k_{10}^f}{\rightleftharpoons}} \text{IntermediateACh} \underset{k_{15}^r}{\overset{k_{15}^f}{\rightleftharpoons}} \text{DesensitizedACh}$$

$$\text{BasalACh}_2 \underset{k_2^r}{\overset{k_2^f}{\rightleftharpoons}} \text{ActiveACh}_2 \underset{k_{11}^r}{\overset{k_{11}^f}{\rightleftharpoons}} \text{IntermediateACh}_2 \underset{k_{16}^r}{\overset{k_{16}^f}{\rightleftharpoons}} \text{DesensitizedACh}_2.$$

$$(31)$$

There are 34 reaction rates $\mathbf{k}$ and species concentrations $\mathbf{x} = (x_1, \ldots, x_{12})^T$ for BasalACh2, IntermediateACh, ActiveACh, Active, BasalACh, Basal, DesensitizedACh2, Desensitized, IntermediateACh2, DesensitizedACh, Intermediate, ActiveACh2, respectively. The kinetics is described by an ODE $\dot{\mathbf{x}} = \mathbf{f}$ with a polynomial vector field $\mathbf{f} = (f_1, \ldots, f_{12})^T$ as follows:

$$f_1 = k_1^f x_5 - k_1^r x_1 - k_2^f x_1 + k_2^r x_{12}$$

$$f_2 = k_7^f x_{11} - k_7^r x_2 - k_8^f x_2 + k_8^r x_9 + k_{10}^f x_3 - k_{10}^r x_2 - k_{15}^f x_2 + k_{15}^r x_{10}$$

$$f_3 = k_4^r x_{12} + k_6^f x_5 - k_6^r x_3 - k_{10}^f x_3 + k_{10}^r x_2 + k_3^f x_4 - k_3^r x_3 - k_4^f x_3$$

$$f_4 = k_5^f x_6 - k_5^r x_4 - k_9^f x_4 + k_9^r x_{11} - k_3^f x_4 + k_3^r x_3$$

$$f_5 = k_0^f x_6 - k_6^f x_5 + k_6^r x_3 - k_0^r x_5 - k_1^f x_5 + k_1^r x_1$$

$$f_6 = -k_0^f x_6 - k_5^f x_6 + k_5^r x_4 + k_0^r x_5$$

$$f_7 = k_{13}^f x_{10} - k_{13}^r x_7 + k_{16}^f x_9 - k_{16}^r x_7$$

$$f_8 = -k_{12}^f x_8 + k_{12}^r x_{10} + k_{14}^f x_{11} - k_{14}^r x_8$$

$$f_9 = k_8^f x_2 - k_8^r x_9 + k_{11}^f x_{12} - k_{11}^r x_9 - k_{16}^f x_9 + k_{16}^r x_7$$

$$f_{10} = k_{12}^f x_8 - k_{12}^r x_{10} - k_{13}^f x_{10} + k_{13}^r x_7 + k_{15}^f x_2 - k_{15}^r x_{10}$$

---

[5] https://www.ebi.ac.uk/biomodels/BIOMD0000000001.

$$f_{11} = -k_7^f x_{11} + k_7^r x_2 + k_9^f x_4 - k_9^r x_{11} - k_{14}^f x_{11} + k_{14}^r x_8$$
$$f_{12} = -k_4^r x_{12} - k_{11}^f x_{12} + k_{11}^r x_9 + k_2^f x_1 - k_2^r x_{12} + k_4^f x_3. \tag{32}$$

In the presentation of the model in the BioModels repository, occurrences of reaction rates $\mathbf{k}$ are generally multiplied with the volume of a compartment compl. This amounts in (32) to a corresponding factor for all $\mathbf{f}$, which would not affect our computations here and can be equivalently dropped. It is noteworthy that our framework would allow to handle occurrences of various different compartment volumes as extra parameters in $\mathbf{k}$.

Our computations for this model did not finish within 24 h, even when fixing all forward reaction rates k_i^f to their values specified in the BioModels repository. This is a bit surprising, because with regard to $|\mathbf{k}|$, $|\mathbf{x}|$, and $|\mathbf{f}|$, the problem is smaller than 5-site phosphorylation, which we successfully computed in the previous section. Furthermore, $\mathbf{f} = 0$ is a system of parametric *linear* equations. It seems that there is an immense combinatorial explosion in the size of parametric coefficient polynomials caused by iterated solving for certain variables and plugging in.

5   Conclusions

Geometric definitions of shifted toricity and toricity of a real steady state variety V require that $V \cap \mathbb{R}^{*n}$ forms a multiplicative coset or group, respectively. We have proposed a formal framework, based on first-order logic and real quantifier elimination, to test this in the presence of parameters. Computational experiments succeeded on dynamics of reaction networks with up to 54 species and 30 parameters.

With all our computations on real-world networks here, we have found that the coset property is independent of the choice of parameters. This result is desirable from the viewpoint of chemical reaction theory, which postulates that relevant properties of networks do not depend on reaction rates. Given the coset property, the stronger group property holds only for degenerate choices of parameters in the sense that they satisfy algebraic equations. In the context of our framework, this is not too surprising. The equivalent conditions in the parameters for the group property are obtained by plugging in 1 for all species concentrations in the defining equations of V. Our conclusion is that the coset property without algebraic conditions on the parameters is the relevant concept.

We have used above a strict notion of *algebraic*, which excludes order inequalities. Recall that we had advertised in the introduction that our approach is capable of producing semi-algebraic conditions on the parameters, which can include inequalities. Such inequalities come into existence during quantifier elimination as sign conditions on discriminants of non-linear polynomials. With the Triangle network in Sect. 4.1 they almost made their way into the output but were removed in the last moment by quantifier elimination-based simplification. One of them has been presented in (15). Beyond that, our computations did not produce any order constraints on the parameters. It is an interesting question, maybe also for the natural sciences, whether there is a systematic reason for their absence. A positive answer would also support alternative purely algebraic approaches to toricity, e.g., based on binomial ideals.

Acknowledgments. This work has been supported by the interdisciplinary bilateral project ANR-17-CE40-0036/DFG-391322026 SYMBIONT [3,4]. We are grateful to our project partner Ovidiu Radulescu for helping us understand part of the biological background.

References

1. Basu, S., Pollack, R., Roy, M.F.: On the combinatorial and algebraic complexity of quantifier elimination. J. ACM **43**(6), 1002–1045 (1996). https://doi.org/10.1145/235809.235813
2. Boltzmann, L.: Lectures on Gas Theory. University of California Press, Berkeley and Los Angeles (1964)
3. Boulier, F., et al.: The SYMBIONT project: symbolic methods for biological networks. ACM Commun. Comput. Algebra **52**(3), 67–70 (2018). https://doi.org/10.1145/3313880.3313885
4. Boulier, F., et al.: The SYMBIONT project: symbolic methods for biological networks. F1000Research **7**(1341) (2018). https://doi.org/10.7490/f1000research.1115995.1
5. Bradford, R., et al.: A case study on the parametric occurrence of multiple steady states. In: Proceedings of the ISSAC 2017, pp. 45–52. ACM (2017). https://doi.org/10.1145/3087604.3087622
6. Bradford, R., et al.: Identifying the parametric occurrence of multiple steady states for some biological networks. J. Symb. Comput. **98**, 84–119 (2020). https://doi.org/10.1016/j.jsc.2019.07.008
7. Brown, C.W.: QEPCAD B: a program for computing with semi-algebraic sets using CADs. ACM SIGSAM Bull. **37**(4), 97–108 (2003). https://doi.org/10.1145/968708.968710
8. Chelliah, V., et al.: BioModels: ten-year anniversary. Nucl. Acids Res. **43**(D1), D542–D548 (2015). https://doi.org/10.1093/nar/gku1181
9. Chen, C., Moreno Maza, M.: Quantifier elimination by cylindrical algebraic decomposition based on regular chains. J. Symb. Comput. **75**, 74–93 (2016). https://doi.org/10.1016/j.jsc.2015.11.008
10. Collins, G.E., Hong, H.: Partial cylindrical algebraic decomposition for quantifier elimination. J. Symb. Comput. **12**(3), 299–328 (1991). https://doi.org/10.1016/S0747-7171(08)80152-6
11. Conradi, C., Kahle, T.: Detecting binomiality. Adv. Appl. Math. **71**, 52–67 (2015). https://doi.org/10.1016/j.aam.2015.08.004
12. Craciun, G., Dickenstein, A., Shiu, A., Sturmfels, B.: Toric dynamical systems. J. Symb. Comput. **44**(11), 1551–1565 (2009). https://doi.org/10.1016/j.jsc.2008.08.006
13. Dolzmann, A., Sturm, T.: REDLOG: computer algebra meets computer logic. ACM SIGSAM Bull. **31**(2), 2–9 (1997). https://doi.org/10.1145/261320.261324
14. Dolzmann, A., Sturm, T.: Simplification of quantifier-free formulae over ordered fields. J. Symb. Comput. **24**(2), 209–231 (1997). https://doi.org/10.1006/jsco.1997.0123

15. Dolzmann, A., Sturm, T., Weispfenning, V.: Real quantifier elimination in practice. In: Matzat, B.H., Greuel, G.M., Hiss, G. (eds.) Algorithmic Algebra and Number Theory, pp. 221–247. Springer, Heidelberg (1998). https://doi.org/10.1007/978-3-642-59932-3_11

16. Edelstein, S.J., Schaad, O., Henry, E., Bertrand, D., Changeux, J.P.: A kinetic mechanism for nicotinic acetylcholine receptors based on multiple allosteric transitions. Biol. Cybern. **75**(5), 361–379 (1996). https://doi.org/10.1007/s004220050302

17. Einstein, A.: Strahlungs-emission und -absorption nach der Quantentheorie. Verh. Dtsch. Phys. Ges. **18**, 318–323 (1916)

18. Eisenbud, D., Sturmfels, B.: Binomial ideals. Duke Math. J. **84**(1), 1–45 (1996). https://doi.org/10.1215/S0012-7094-96-08401-X

19. England, M., Errami, H., Grigoriev, D., Radulescu, O., Sturm, T., Weber, A.: Symbolic versus numerical computation and visualization of parameter regions for multistationarity of biological networks. In: Gerdt, V.P., Koepf, W., Seiler, W.M., Vorozhtsov, E.V. (eds.) CASC 2017. LNCS, vol. 10490, pp. 93–108. Springer, Cham (2017). https://doi.org/10.1007/978-3-319-66320-3_8

20. Feinberg, M.: Complex balancing in general kinetic systems. Arch. Rational Mech. Anal. **49**(3), 187–194 (1972). https://doi.org/10.1007/BF00255665

21. Feinberg, M.: Stability of complex isothermal reactors–I. The deficiency zero and deficiency one theorems. Chem. Eng. Sci. **42**(10), 2229–2268 (1987). https://doi.org/10.1016/0009-2509(87)80099-4

22. Feinberg, M.: Foundations of Chemical Reaction Network Theory. AMS, vol. 202. Springer, Cham (2019). https://doi.org/10.1007/978-3-030-03858-8

23. Gatermann, K.: Counting stable solutions of sparse polynomial systems in chemistry. In: Symbolic Computation: Solving Equations in Algebra, Geometry, and Engineering, Contemporary Mathematics, vol. 286, pp. 53–69. AMS, Providence (2001). https://doi.org/10.1090/conm/286/04754

24. Gatermann, K., Wolfrum, M.: Bernstein's second theorem and Viro's method for sparse polynomial systems in chemistry. Adv. Appl. Math. **34**(2), 252–294 (2005). https://doi.org/10.1016/j.aam.2004.04.003

25. Gorban, A.N., Mirkes, E.M., Yablonski, G.S.: Thermodynamics in the limit of irreversible reactions. Physica A **392**(6), 1318–1335 (2013). https://doi.org/10.1016/j.physa.2012.10.009

26. Gorban, A.N., Yablonski, G.S.: Extended detailed balance for systems with irreversible reactions. Chem. Eng. Sci. **66**(21), 5388–5399 (2011). https://doi.org/10.1016/j.ces.2011.07.054

27. Grigoriev, D.: Complexity of deciding Tarski algebra. J. Symb. Comput. **5**(1–2), 65–108 (1988). https://doi.org/10.1016/S0747-7171(88)80006-3

28. Grigoriev, D., Iosif, A., Rahkooy, H., Sturm, T., Weber, A.: Efficiently and effectively recognizing toricity of steady state varieties. Math. Comput. Sci. **15**(2), 199–232 (2021). https://doi.org/10.1007/s11786-020-00479-9

29. Grigoriev, D., Milman, P.D.: Nash resolution for binomial varieties as Euclidean division. A priori termination bound, polynomial complexity in essential dimension 2. Adv. Math. **231**(6), 3389–3428 (2012). https://doi.org/10.1016/j.aim.2012.08.009

30. Hearn, A.C.: Reduce: a user-oriented interactive system for algebraic simplification. In: Proceedings of the Symposium on Interactive Systems for Experimental Applied Mathematics. ACM (1967). https://doi.org/10.1145/2402536.2402544

31. Hearn, A.C.: Reduce: the first forty years. In: Algorithmic Algebra and Logic: Proceedings of the A3L 2005, pp. 19–24. BOD, Norderstedt (2005)

32. Horn, F., Jackson, R.: General mass action kinetics. Arch. Rational Mech. Anal. **47**(2), 81–116 (1972). https://doi.org/10.1007/BF00251225
33. Kahle, T.: Decompositions of binomial ideals. Ann. Inst. Stat. Math. **62**(4), 727–745 (2010). https://doi.org/10.1007/s10463-010-0290-9
34. Kahle, T.: Decompositions of binomial ideals. J. Softw. Algebra Geom. **4**(1), 1–5 (2012). https://doi.org/10.2140/jsag.2012.4.1
35. Košta, M.: New concepts for real quantifier elimination by virtual substitution. Doctoral dissertation, Saarland University, Germany (2016). https://doi.org/10.22028/D291-26679
36. Košta, M., Sturm, T., Dolzmann, A.: Better answers to real questions. J. Symb. Comput. **74**, 255–275 (2016). https://doi.org/10.1016/j.jsc.2015.07.002
37. Kruff, N., Lüders, C., Radulescu, O., Sturm, T., Walcher, S.: Algorithmic reduction of biological networks with multiple time scales. Math. Comput. Sci. **15**(3), 499–534 (2021). https://doi.org/10.1007/s11786-021-00515-2
38. Loos, R., Weispfenning, V.: Applying linear quantifier elimination. Comput. J. **36**(5), 450–462 (1993). https://doi.org/10.1093/comjnl/36.5.450
39. Michaelis, L., Menten, M.L.: Die Kinetik der Invertinwirkung. Biochemische Zeitschrift **49**, 333–369 (1913)
40. Müller, S., Feliu, E., Regensburger, G., Conradi, C., Shiu, A., Dickenstein, A.: Sign conditions for injectivity of generalized polynomial maps with applications to chemical reaction networks and real algebraic geometry. Found. Comput. Math. **16**(1), 69–97 (2016). https://doi.org/10.1007/s10208-014-9239-3
41. Onsager, L.: Reciprocal relations in irreversible processes. I. Phys. Rev. **37**(4), 405 (1931). https://doi.org/10.1103/PhysRev.37.405
42. Pérez Millán, M., Dickenstein, A.: The structure of MESSI biological systems. SIAM J. Appl. Dyn. Syst. **17**(2), 1650–1682 (2018). https://doi.org/10.1137/17M1113722
43. Pérez Millán, M., Dickenstein, A., Shiu, A., Conradi, C.: Chemical reaction systems with toric steady states. Bull. Math. Biol. **74**(5), 1027–1065 (2012). https://doi.org/10.1007/s11538-011-9685-x
44. Rahkooy, H., Radulescu, O., Sturm, T.: A linear algebra approach for detecting binomiality of steady state ideals of reversible chemical reaction networks. In: Boulier, F., England, M., Sadykov, T.M., Vorozhtsov, E.V. (eds.) CASC 2020. LNCS, vol. 12291, pp. 492–509. Springer, Cham (2020). https://doi.org/10.1007/978-3-030-60026-6_29
45. Rahkooy, H., Sturm, T.: First-order tests for Toricity. In: Boulier, F., England, M., Sadykov, T.M., Vorozhtsov, E.V. (eds.) CASC 2020. LNCS, vol. 12291, pp. 510–527. Springer, Cham (2020). https://doi.org/10.1007/978-3-030-60026-6_30
46. Shinar, G., Feinberg, M.: Structural sources of robustness in biochemical reaction networks. Science **327**(5971), 1389–1391 (2010). https://doi.org/10.1126/science.1183372
47. Strzebonski, A.W.: Cylindrical algebraic decomposition using validated numerics. J. Symb. Comput. **41**(9), 1021–1038 (2006). https://doi.org/10.1016/j.jsc.2006.06.004
48. Sturm, T.: A survey of some methods for real quantifier elimination, decision, and satisfiability and their applications. Math. Comput. Sci. **11**(3–4), 483–502 (2017). https://doi.org/10.1007/s11786-017-0319-z
49. Sturm, T.: Thirty years of virtual substitution: foundations, techniques, applications. In: Proceedings of the ISSAC 2018, pp. 11–16. ACM (2018). https://doi.org/10.1145/3208976.3209030

50. Tarski, A.: A decision method for elementary algebra and geometry. Prepared for publication by J.C.C. McKinsey. RAND Report R109, 1 August 1948, Revised May 1951, Second Edition, RAND, Santa Monica, CA (1957)
51. Tonks, Z.: A poly-algorithmic quantifier elimination package in maple. In: Gerhard, J., Kotsireas, I. (eds.) MC 2019. CCIS, vol. 1125, pp. 171–186. Springer, Cham (2020). https://doi.org/10.1007/978-3-030-41258-6_13
52. Vilar, J.M.G., Jansen, R., Sander, C.: Signal processing in the TGF-β superfamily ligand-receptor network. PLoS Comput. Biol. **2**(1), e3 (2006). https://doi.org/10.1371/journal.pcbi.0020003
53. Wang, L., Sontag, E.D.: On the number of steady states in a multiple futile cycle. J. Math. Biol. **57**(1), 29–52 (2008). https://doi.org/10.1007/s00285-007-0145-z
54. Wang, S., Lin, J.R., Sontag, E.D., Sorger, P.K.: Inferring reaction network structure from single-cell, multiplex data, using toric systems theory. PLoS Comput. Biol. **15**(12), e1007311 (2019). https://doi.org/10.1371/journal.pcbi.1007311
55. Wegscheider, R.: Über simultane Gleichgewichte und die Beziehungen zwischen Thermodynamik und Reactionskinetik homogener Systeme. Monatsh. Chem. Verw. Tl. **22**(8), 849–906 (1901). https://doi.org/10.1007/BF01517498
56. Weispfenning, V.: Quantifier elimination for real algebra–the quadratic case and beyond. Appl. Algebra Eng. Commun. Comput. **8**(2), 85–101 (1997). https://doi.org/10.1007/s002000050055
57. Weispfenning, V.: A new approach to quantifier elimination for real algebra. In: Caviness, B.F., Johnson, J.R. (eds.) Quantifier Elimination and Cylindrical Algebraic Decomposition. Texts and Monographs in Symbolic Computation (A Series of the Research Institute for Symbolic Computation, Johannes-Kepler-University, Linz, Austria), pp. 376–392. Springer, Vienna (1998). https://doi.org/10.1007/978-3-7091-9459-1_20

Testing Binomiality of Chemical Reaction Networks Using Comprehensive Gröbner Systems

Hamid Rahkooy[2]($\boxtimes$) (iD) and Thomas Sturm[1,2,3] (iD)

[1] CNRS, Inria, and the University of Lorraine, Nancy, France
`thomas.sturm@loria.fr`
[2] MPI Informatics, Saarland Informatics Campus, Saarbrücken, Germany
`hamid.rahkooy@mpi-inf.mpg.de`
[3] Saarland University, Saarland Informatics Campus, Saarbrücken, Germany

Abstract. We consider the problem of binomiality of the steady state ideals of biochemical reaction networks. We are interested in finding polynomial conditions on the parameters such that the steady state ideal of a chemical reaction network is binomial under every specialisation of the parameters if the conditions on the parameters hold. We approach the binomiality problem using Comprehensive Gröbner systems. Considering rate constants as parameters, we compute comprehensive Gröbner systems for various reactions. In particular, we make automatic computations on n-site phosphorylations and biomodels from the Biomodels repository using the grobcov library of the computer algebra system Singular.

Keywords: Binomial ideals · Toric varieties · Chemical reaction networks · Mass action kinetics · Scientific computation · Symbolic computation · Gröbner bases · Comprehensive Gröbner bases

1 Introduction

A *chemical reaction* is a transformation between two sets of chemical objects called chemical *complexes*. The objects that form a chemical complex are chemical *species*. In fact, complexes are formal sums of chemical species representing the left and the right hand sides of chemical reactions. A *chemical reaction network* is a set of chemical reactions. For example,

$$E + S \underset{k_{-1}}{\overset{k_1}{\rightleftharpoons}} ES \overset{k_2}{\longrightarrow} E + P \tag{1}$$

is a chemical reaction network with one reversible reaction and one non-reversible reaction. This reaction network is a well-known network, called the *Michaelis–Menton* reaction network.

A *kinetics* of a chemical reaction network is an assignment of a rate function to each reaction in the network. The rate function depends on the concentrations

© Springer Nature Switzerland AG 2021
F. Boulier et al. (Eds.): CASC 2021, LNCS 12865, pp. 334–352, 2021.
https://doi.org/10.1007/978-3-030-85165-1_19

of the species. A kinetics for a chemical reaction network is called *mass-action* if for each reaction in the network, the rate function is a monomial in terms of the concentrations of the species, such that the exponents are given by the numbers of molecules of the species consumed in the reaction, multiplied by a constant called *rate constant*. In the Michaelis–Menton reaction, k_1, k_{-1}, k_2 are the rate constants. In this article, we assume mass-action kinetics.

A system of autonomous ordinary differential equations can be used to describe the change in the concentration of each species over time in a reaction. For example, in the Michaelis–Menton reaction, let the variables s, p, c, e represent the concentrations of the species S, P, ES, E respectively. The ordinary differential equations (ODEs) describing change of the concentrations of the species for this reaction network are the following:

$$\dot{s} = f_s = -k_1 se + k_{-1} c, \tag{2}$$

$$\dot{p} = f_p = k_2 c, \tag{3}$$

$$\dot{c} = f_c = k_1 se - (k_{-1} + k_2)c, \tag{4}$$

$$\dot{e} = -f_c. \tag{5}$$

Solutions of the polynomials f_s, f_p, f_c and $-f_c$ give us the concentrations of the species in which the system is in equilibrium. In fact, the solutions of f_s, f_p, f_c and $-f_c$ are called the steady states of the chemical reaction network. Accordingly, the ideal generated by f_s, f_p, f_c and $-f_c$, i.e., $I = \langle f_s, f_p, f_c, -f_c \rangle \subseteq \mathbb{K}[k_1, k_{-1}, k_2][s, p, c, e]$, where $\mathbb{K}$ is a field, is called the *steady state ideal* of the Michaelis–Menton network. For a thorough introduction on chemical reaction network theory, refer to Feinberg's Book [22] and his lecture notes [21]. We follow the notation of Feinberg's book in this article.

A *binomial ideal* is an ideal that is generated by a set of binomials. In this article, we consider the problem of binomiality of steady state ideals when the rate constants are specialised over a field extension of $\mathbb{K}$, that is, when the rate constants have been assigned values from an extension of $\mathbb{K}$, typically the closure of $\mathbb{K}$. More precisely, we are interested in conditions over the rate constants (typically given by polynomial equations on rate constants), such that for every values of the rate constants in the extension field, the steady state ideal is binomial under those conditions. In this article, we often use parameters instead of rate constants, an indication that they can be specialised. Therefore, we consider the *parametric binomiality problem*.

Let us consider the steady state ideal of the Michaelis–Menton reaction:

$$I = I = \langle f_s, f_p, f_c \rangle \subseteq \mathbb{K}[k_1, k_{-1}, k_2][s, p, c, e], \tag{6}$$

given by Eqs. (2)–(4). One can observe that $f_c = -f_s + f_p$. Hence, $I = \langle f_s, f_p \rangle$. Having fixed the term ordering induced by $c > s > e$, one may consider further reducing f_s by f_p, i.e., $f_s - f_p = (k_{-1} - k_1)c - k_1 se$. As the rate constants in a chemical reaction take values, $k_{-1} - k_1$ may vanish. In this case, if the leading term of $f_s - f_p$ vanishes, then it will be a monomial, and therefore, the reduced Gröbner basis of I will be the monomial ideal generated by $\{k_2 c, -k_1 se\}$, given that $k_2 \neq 0$ and $k_{-1} \neq 0$. This example shows that the Gröbner basis of the steady state ideal (and the steady states of the reaction) can change depending on the values of the rate constants. Therefore, we must consider distinct cases for the parameters when analysing a reaction network. Thinking purely in terms of computer algebra, this example illustrates the idea behind *Comprehensive Gröbner bases*. In this article, we investigate the conditions on the parameters of a steady state ideal (or equivalently on the rate constants of a reaction) such that the steady state ideal is binomial when those conditions on the parameters hold.

In the literature, a slightly different notions of binomiality has been considered. Eisenbud and Sturmfels in [16] call an ideal binomial if it is generated by polynomials with at most two terms. Some authors, e.g., Pérez-Milán et al. [40], have studied the binomiality of steady state ideals according to the definition in [16]. However, in this article, our definition does not include those ideals that include monomials. This difference in the definition, obviously, affects the steady state variety of binomial chemical reaction networks in practice.

Binomial ideals and toric varieties have rich history in chemical reaction networks theory. Binomiality corresponds to detailed balance, which is a very important concept in thermodynamics. Detailed balance means that at thermodynamic equilibrium, the forward and backward rates should be equal for all reactions. Detailed balance has been historically used by Einstein [15], Wegscheider [48] and by Onsager [38]. Some of the subsystems of molecular devices can satisfy binomiality conditions. Another interesting point to study binomiality is because the analysis of properties such as multi-stationarity and stability are easier to establish for binomial systems. Toricity, also known as complex, or cyclic, or semi-detailed balance is also known since Boltzmann that has used it as a sufficient condition for deriving his famous H-theorem [2]. Toricity implies binomiality, but the converse is not true. A toric variety is indeed irreducible, however a binomial steady state ideal may have an irreducible variety, which would not be toric. However, every variety of a binomial ideal includes a toric variety as its irreducible component. A toric system must obey constraints on the rates constants, such as the well known Weigscheider—Kolmogorov condition, which implies the equality of the products of forward and backward rates constants in cycles of reversible reactions.

Mathematicians have considered binomiality and toricity and investigated their properties thoroughly. Among the existing literature are the work by Fulton [23], Sturmfels [45] and Eisenbud et al. [16]. Binomiality implies *detailed balancing* of reversible chemical reactions, which has been studied by Gorban et al. [24,25] and Grigoriev and Weber [28]. Toric dynamical systems have been studied by Feinberg [20] and Horn and Jackson [30]. Over the real numbers Craciun et al. have studied the toricity problem in [9]. In the latter work, it hs been shown that *complex balanced systems* are the same as toric dynamical systems, although *toric steady states* are different from that. Binomiality implies much simpler criteria for multistationarity [14,44].

Pérez-Milán, et al. presented sufficient linear algebra conditions with inequalities for binomiality of the steady state ideals [40]. The idea in the latter has been developed in [39], where MESSI reactions have been introduced. Conradi and Kahle have proved in [8] that for homogenous ideals the latter sufficient condition is necessary as well, and introduced an algorithm for that case. Their algorithm has been implemented in Maple and Macaulay II in [31,32]. A geometric view towards toricity of chemical reaction networks has been given by Grigoriev et al. in [27], where shifted toricity has been introduced, algorithms presented for testing shifted toricity and complexity bounds and experimental results are discussed. In [27], the two main tools from computer algebra, quantifier elimination [12,26,49] and Gröbner bases [5,6,18,19] are used in order to test shifted toricity of chemical reaction networks. Also recently, the authors introduced a first order logic test for toricity [43]. An efficient linear algebra method for testing unconditional binomiality has been presented in [42] and a graph-theoretical equivalent of the method is given in [41].

Testing binomiality of an ideal is a difficult problem, both from a theoretical and a practical point of view. A typical method to test binomiality is via computing a Gröbner basis. It has been shown that computing a Göbner basis is EXPSPACE-complete [36], which shows the difficulty of the binomiality problem from the computational point of view. The approach proposed for testing binomiality of steady state ideals in [8,40] relies on linear algebra. In this approach the computations are done without considering the values of the parameters. Also large matrices are constructed in this approach.

Existing work on binomiality of chemical reaction networks typically ignores specialisation of the parameters, often treating them as variables and carrying on the computations. For instance, fixing an ordering in which the parameters are smaller than the variables, e.g., lexicographic ordering, one may consider computing a Gröbner basis of the steady state ideal and then eliminating the variables. Then the elimination ideal will be in the ring of parameters and may result in conditions on the parameters such that the original ideal is binomial. However, this approach does not consider the fact that in the process of computations, some terms can be vanished, if parameters are specialised.

In contrast, our approach is to use comprehensive Gröbner bases, which considers specialisations of the parameters. A comprehensive Gröbner basis of an ideal is a finite set of polynomials on the parameters and the variables, such that it is a Gröbner basis under every value assignment in the parameters. Therefore, a steady state ideal is binomial if its comprehensive Gröbner basis is binomial. This observation reduces testing binomiality of a steady state ideal under specialisation into testing binomiality of a comprehensive Gröbner basis. Computing a comprehensive Gröbner basis results in a partitioning of the ambient space into certain varieties and computations of certain set of polynomials associated to each of those varieties, such that if the parameters are specialised from the variety, the associated polynomial set is a Gröbner basis. Such a partition with its associated polynomial sets is called a Gröbner system. Computing comprehensive Gröbner bases is at least as difficult as computing Gröbner bases. Hence, testing binomiality via comprehensive Gröbner bases is a hard problem.

The concept of comprehensive Gröbner bases has been introduced by Weispfenning in his seminal work [50]. He later introduced canonical comprehensive Gröbner bases in [51]. A source of introduction to comprehensive Gröbner basis is Becker and Weispfenning's book [1]. Weispfenning also worked on the relation between comprehensive Gröbner bases and regular rings [52]. Later, several authors worked on the topic and introduced more efficient algorithms and polished the theory of comprehensive Gröbner bases. Suzuki-Sati's approach to Gröbner bases is presented in [46]. Montes has worked extensively on comprehensive Gröbner bases, introduced several algorithms and developed the theory [11,37]. In particular, Montes' book, the Gröbner Cover [35] is a great source for computations, among other interesting aspects, that can be used as a guide to the Singular library grobcov.lib [13] for computing comprehensive Gröbner bases. Among the most efficient algorithms for computing comprehensive Gröbner bases are the algorithms given by Kapur et al. [33,34]. Dehghani and Hashemi studied Gröbner walk and FGLM for comprehensive Gröbner bases [10,29] and implemented several algorithms for computing comprehensive Gröbner bases and related topics in Maple [29].[1]

To the best of our knowledge, to this date, comprehensive Gröbner bases have not been used in chemical reaction networks theory. Previous studies on binomiality of steady state ideals have considered Gröbner bases, linear algebra on stoichiometric matrices, etc., however, never have considered the change in the polynomials during computations when the values are assigned to the parameters. For instance, it is known that detailed balancing holds under some polynomial conditions on the parameters.

However, the fact that specialisation of the rate constants may affect the computations has not beed considered. The authors' previous work on toricity [27,43] considers the toricity problem when the parameters have already been assigned real positive values. Other articles of the authors have considered unconditional binomiality, that is, when the rate constants are considered variables [41,42]. The present article is the original work that consideres specialisation of the parameters and uses comprehensive Gröbner bases to study the binomiality under specialisations.

The plan of the article is as follows. Section 1 gives an introduction to the necessary concepts of chemical reaction network theory, reviews the literature and presents the idea of the present article. Section 2 explains the preliminaries required on comprehensive Gröbner systems, explains the main concepts and sketches the idea behind computing comprehensive Gröbner bases. Section 3 includes the main computations, where we show our computations on n-phosphorylations and biochemical reactions and present the benchmarks. We furthermore compare our computations using comprehensive Gröbner bases with some earlier work on the binomiality problem that does not take into account the specialisation of the rate constants. In Sect. 4 we summarise our results and draw some conclusions.

---

[1] https://amirhashemi.iut.ac.ir/sites/amirhashemi.iut.ac.ir/files//file_basepage/
pggw_0.txt.

2 Preliminaries on Comprehensive Gröbner Systems

We review the required definitions, theorems and an algorithm on comprehensive Gröbner systems, mainly from the original work of Weispfenning [50] and Kapur, et al.'s work [34].

Let $\mathbb{K}$ be a field, $R = \mathbb{K}[U] = \mathbb{K}[u_1, \ldots, u_m]$ be the ring of polynomials over $\mathbb{K}$ in the indeterminates $u_1, \ldots, u_m$ and let $S = \mathbb{K}[U][X] = \mathbb{K}[u_1, \ldots, u_m][x_1, \ldots, x_n]$ be the ring of polynomials over $\mathbb{K}[U]$ with the indeterminates $x_1, \ldots, x_n$. Assume that $X \cap U = \emptyset$. We call $u_1, \ldots, u_m$ the parameters of the ring S and $x_1, \ldots, x_n$ the variables of S. In fact, the coefficients of every polynomial in S are themselves polynomials in parameters. For every $\alpha = (\alpha_1, \ldots, \alpha_n) \in \mathbb{N}^n$, by X^α we denote $x_1^{\alpha_1} \ldots x_n^{\alpha_n}$ and by U^α we denote $u_1^{\alpha_1} \ldots u_n^{\alpha_n}$. In this paper, $\mathbb{K}$ is either $\mathbb{R}$ or $\mathbb{C}$. By the variety of an ideal I (or a set of polynomials F), we mean the set of solutions of the ideal I (or the set of polynomials F) and we denote it by $V(I)$ (or $V(F)$).

Let $<_1$ and $<_2$ be term orders on $\mathbb{K}[U]$ and $\mathbb{K}[X]$, respectively. We define a block order $<$ produced by the latter on $\mathbb{K}[U][X]$. Firstly, define $u_i < x_j$ for all $1 \le i \le m, 1 \le j \le n$. Secondly, define $X^{\alpha_1} U^{\beta_1} < X^{\alpha_2} U^{\beta_2}$ if either $X^{\alpha_1} < X^{\alpha_2}$ or $(X^{\alpha_1} = X^{\alpha_2} \wedge U^{\alpha_1} < U^{\alpha_2})$. A polynomial of the form $c_\alpha p(U) X^\alpha$, where $\alpha \in \mathbb{N}^n$, $c_\alpha \in \mathbb{K}$ and $p(U) \in R$, is called a term in $\mathbb{K}[U][X]$. A monomial is a term of the form X^α. Leading monomial, leading term and leading coefficient of the polynomials in $\mathbb{K}[U][X]$ are defined with respect to the block ordering $<$.

A specialisation of S is a ring-homomorphism from the ring of parameters $R = \mathbb{K}[U]$ into some field $\mathbb{L}$, i.e., $\sigma : R \to \mathbb{L}$. Obviously $\mathbb{K}$ is embedded in $\mathbb{L}$. We consider $\mathbb{L}$ to be an algebraically closed field in this paper. Every specialisation is uniquely determined by its restriction to $\mathbb{K}$ and its images on the parameters $u_1, \ldots, u_m$ and vice versa. A specialisation $\sigma : R \to \mathbb{L}$ has a canonical extension to a ring-homomorphism $\bar{\sigma} : S \to \mathbb{L}[x_1, \ldots, x_n]$, i.e., for every $f = \sum_{i \in I} a_i(U) X^{\alpha_i}, \bar{\sigma}(f) = \sum_{i \in I} \sigma(a_i(U)) X^{\alpha_i}$, where $a_i(U) \in R$ and X^{α_i} is a monomial in $\mathbb{K}[X]$. Following Weispfenning's notation, we denote $\bar{\sigma}$ by σ as well. Specialisation of a set of polynomials F by σ, denoted by $\sigma(F)$, is defined to be the set of specialisations of the polynomials in F. Accordingly, a specialisation of an ideal I by σ is defined, and is denoted by $\sigma(I)$. Following Kapur, et al. [34], in this paper we only consider specialisations induced by the elements $a \in \mathbb{L}^m$, that is, $\sigma_a : f \to f(a)$, where $f \in R$.

Below we mention the definition of comprehensive Gröbner system and comprehensive Gröbner basis, which are due to Weispfenning. We follow Kapur et al.'s notation in [34].

Definition 1 (Comprehensive Gröbner System). *Let I be an ideal in S generated by a finite set $F \subseteq S$ and $\mathbb{L}$ be a an algebraically closed field containing $\mathbb{K}$. Assume that $V_1, W_1, \ldots, V_r, W_r$ are varieties in $\mathbb{L}^n$, and $G_1, \ldots, G_r$ are finite sets of polynomials in S. A set of tripples $\mathcal{G} = \{(V_1, W_1, G_1), \ldots, (V_r, W_r, G_r)\}$ is called a comprehensive Gröbner system of I on $V = \bigcup_{i=1}^r V_i \backslash W_i$, if for every $a \in V$ and every specialisation σ_a of S, $\sigma_a(G_i)$ is a Gröbner basis of $\sigma_a(I)$ in $\mathbb{L}[X]$ when a is in $V(V_i) \backslash V(W_i)$, for $i = 1, \ldots, r$. If $V = \mathbb{L}^m$, we simply call $\mathcal{G}$ a comprehensive*

Gröbner system of I. Each (V_i, W_i, G_i) is called a branch of $\mathcal{G}$. A comprehensive Gröbner system $\mathcal{G}$ of I is called faithful, if every element of G_i is in I.

Definition 2 (Comprehensive Gröbner Basis). *Let I be an ideal in S and $\mathbb{L}$ be an algebraically closed field containing $\mathbb{K}$. Assume that V is a subset of $\mathbb{L}^m$. A finite subset G of I is called a comprehensive Gröbner basis of I on V, if for all specialisations $\sigma_a : R \to \mathbb{L}$ of S, where $a \in V$, the set $\sigma_a(G)$ is a Gröbner basis of the ideal generated by $\sigma_a(I)$ in $\mathbb{L}[X]$. If $V = \mathbb{L}^m$, we simply call G a comprehensive Gröbner basis of I. A comprehensive Gröbner basis G of I is called faithful, if every element of G is in I.*

Having defined comprehensive Gröbner bases, Weispfenning proved the existence of a comprehensive Gröbner basis for every ideal in S [50]. In the latter reference, he gave a non-constructive proof first, and an algorithm later.

Following the first algorithm proposed by Weispfenning, algorithms for computing a comprehensive Gröbner basis essentially construct a faithful comprehensive Gröbner system $\mathcal{G} = \{(V_1, W_1, G_1), \ldots, (V_r, W_r, G_r)\}$. Then the union $G = \cup_{i=1}^{r} G_i$ will be a comprehensive Gröbner basis. Roughly speaking, the varieties V_i and W_i are typically obtained by considering the monomials that are vanished by specialisations, and simultaneously, using a Gröbner basis computation algorithm, a Gröbner basis under the conditions imposed by the specialisations is computed. Below we present a modified version of Kapur, et al.'s algorithm by Dehghani and Hashemi from [29]. "Other cases" in line 16 of the algorithm refers to those cases that the Gröbner basis is 1. Dehghani and Hashemi group all those cases together with the aim of speeding the computations up. In line 13, MDBasis computes a minimal Dickson basis for a given set of polynomials in S. For more details, refer to [29].

3   Testing Binomiality of Chemical Reaction Networks Using Comprehensive Gröbner Systems

In this section we present computations on biochemical networks, using comprehensive Gröbner bases, in order to test binomiality of the corresponding steady state ideals.

In [9, 16, 39], the authors call an ideal binomial if there exists a basis for the ideal whose polynomials have at most two terms. In particular, as it is discussed in the latter references, one can see that an ideal is binomial if and only if its reduced Gröbner bases with respect to every term order is binomial. Our definition of binomiality is as in [41, 42], which is slightly different from [9, 16, 39]. We call an ideal binomial if there exists a basis for the ideal whose polynomials have exactly two terms. That is, we do not consider monomials in the basis. Similar to the definition of binomiality in [9, 16, 39], one can easily observe that, for the case of our definition, an ideal is binomial if and only if its reduced Gröbner bases with respect to every term order is binomial. In terms of parametric polynomial rings, i.e., $\mathbb{K}[U][X]$, we discuss the binomiality using

---

Algorithm 1. PGBMAIN

Input: 1. $N, W \subseteq \mathbb{K}[U]$ finite;   2. $F \subseteq \mathbb{K}[U][X]$ finite

Output: PGB a Gröbner system of F on $V(N) \setminus V(W)$

1: $PGB := \emptyset$
2: **if** $V(N) \setminus V(W) = \emptyset$ **then**
3:     **return** $\emptyset$
4: **end if**
5: $G := \text{ReducedGroebnerBasis}(F \cup N, <)$
6: **if** $1 \in G$ **then**
7:     **return** $\{(N, W, \{1\})\}$
8: **end if**
9: $G_r := G \cap \mathbb{K}[U]$
10: **if** $V(G_r) \setminus V(W) = \emptyset$ **then**
11:     **return** PGB
12: **else**
13:     $G_m := \text{MDBasis}(G \setminus G_r)$
        $h = lcm(h_1, \ldots, h_k)$ with $h_i = LC_{<_1}(g_i)$ for each $g_i \in G_m$
14:     **if** $V(G_r) \setminus V(W \times \{h\}) \neq \emptyset$ **then**
15:         $PGB := PGB \cup \{G_r, W \times \{h\}, G_m\}$
16:     **end if**
17:     **return** $PGB \cup \bigcup_{h_i \in \{h_1, \ldots, h_k\}} \text{PGBMAIN}(G_r \cup \{h_i\}, W \times \{h_1 h_2 \ldots h_{i-1}\}, G \setminus G_r) \cup \{(\text{Other Cases}, \{1\})\}$
18: **end if**

---

a comprehensive Gröbner system. That is in particular the case for the steady state ideals of chemical reaction networks.

As computing a comprehensive Gröbner basis is done via computing the branches of a comprehensive Gröbner system, we basically compute the latter and check the binomiality of the Gröbner basis at each branch. Then a comprehensive Gröbner basis of a steady state ideal will be binomial if and only if the Gröbner basis at each branch of a comprehensive system is binomial. One can consider the generic comprehensive Gröbner bases, introduced in [50], however as it is mentioned in the latter reference, computing a generic comprehensive Gröbner basis is not feasible in practice.

In this paper, for our computations on the steady state ideals of the chemical reaction networks, we consider $\mathbb{L} = \bar{\mathbb{K}}$, the algebraic closure of $\mathbb{K}$. In practice, for the computation purpose, the coefficient field is considered to be $\mathbb{Q}$, extended by the parameters, i.e., $\mathbb{Q}(k_1, \ldots, k_m)$; hence the comprehensive Gröbner system computations are carried out over $\mathbb{Q}(k_1, \ldots, k_m)[x_1, \ldots, x_n]$.

Our computations are carried out via version 4.2.0 of the computer algebra system Singular [13][2], the grobcov package (whose latest version is available at A. Montes' website)[3]. For instructions on the grobcov package we refer the reader to the book [35] and examples by A. Montes. We have done fully automated

---

[2] http://www.singular.uni-kl.de.
[3] https://mat.upc.edu/en/people/antonio.montes.

computations on sets of examples, in particular on biochemical models from the BioModels' repository [7][4]. Our computations have been done on a 2.48 MHz AMD EPYC 7702 64-Core Processor in a Debian GNU/Linux 10 machine with 211 GB memory.

3.1 n-Site Phosphorylation

Multisite phosphorylation–dephosphorylation cycles or n-site phosphorylations (for $n \in \mathbb{N}$) are studied by Wang and Sontag in [47] in terms of multi-stationarity. Pérez-Milán et al. in [40] have shown that for every $n \in \mathbb{N}$, n-site phosphorylation has a binomial steady state. As mentioned earlier, in the latter reference, the authors did not take into account the specialisations of the constant rates. In this subsection, we first do some reductions on a basis of the steady state ideal of n-phosphorylations and prove its binomiality. This essentially gives us the unconditional binomiality of n-phosphorylation, defined and investigated in [41,42]. Our algebraic maniplations below are simple and avoid the criterion presented by Pérez-Milán et al. in [40].

Using Wang and Sontag's notation in [47] for the variables and parameters, for a fixed positive integer n, the n-site phosphorylation reaction network is the following:

$$S_0 + E \underset{k_{\mathrm{off}_0}}{\overset{k_{\mathrm{on}_0}}{\rightleftharpoons}} ES_0 \xrightarrow{k_{\mathrm{cat}_0}} S_1 + E$$

$$\vdots$$

$$S_{n-1} + E \underset{k_{\mathrm{off}_{n-1}}}{\overset{k_{\mathrm{on}_{n-1}}}{\rightleftharpoons}} ES_{n-1} \xrightarrow{k_{\mathrm{cat}_{n-1}}} S_n + E$$

$$S_1 + F \underset{l_{\mathrm{off}_0}}{\overset{l_{\mathrm{on}_0}}{\rightleftharpoons}} FS_1 \xrightarrow{l_{\mathrm{cat}_0}} S_0 + F$$

$$\vdots$$

$$S_n + F \underset{l_{\mathrm{off}_{n-1}}}{\overset{l_{\mathrm{on}_{n-1}}}{\rightleftharpoons}} FS_n \xrightarrow{l_{\mathrm{cat}_{n-1}}} S_{n-1} + F$$

The parameters of the reaction network are $k_{\mathrm{on}_0}, \ldots, k_{\mathrm{on}_{n-1}}, k_{\mathrm{off}_0}, \ldots, k_{\mathrm{off}_{n-1}},$ $k_{\mathrm{cat}_0}, \ldots, k_{\mathrm{cat}_{n-1}}, l_{\mathrm{on}_0}, \ldots, l_{\mathrm{on}_{n-1}}, l_{\mathrm{off}_0}, \ldots, l_{\mathrm{off}_{n-1}}, l_{\mathrm{cat}_0}, \ldots, l_{\mathrm{cat}_{n-1}}$. Let the variables $s_0, \ldots, s_n, c_0, \ldots, c_{n-1}, d_1, \ldots, d_n, e, f$ represent the concentrations of the species $S_0, \ldots, S_n, ES_0, \ldots, ES_{n-1}, FS_1, \ldots, FS_n, E, F$ respectively. The ODEs describing change of the concentrations of the species for this reaction network are the following:

$$\dot{s}_0 = P_0 = - k_{\mathrm{on}_0} s_0 e + k_{\mathrm{off}_0} c_0 + l_{\mathrm{cat}_0} d_1,$$
$$\dot{s}_i = P_i = - k_{\mathrm{on}_i} s_i e + k_{\mathrm{off}_i} c_i + k_{\mathrm{cat}_{i-1}} c_{i-1} - l_{\mathrm{on}_{i-1}} s_i f + l_{\mathrm{off}_{i-1}} d_i + l_{\mathrm{cat}_i} d_{i+1},$$
$$i = 1, \ldots, n-1,$$

---

[4] https://www.ebi.ac.uk/biomodels.

$$\dot{c}_j = Q_j = k_{\mathrm{on}_j} s_j e - (k_{\mathrm{off}_j} + k_{\mathrm{cat}_j}) c_j, \quad j = 0, \ldots, n-1,$$

$$\dot{d}_k = R_k = l_{\mathrm{on}_{k-1}} s_k f - (l_{\mathrm{off}_{k-1}} + l_{\mathrm{cat}_{k-1}}) d_k, \quad k = 1, \ldots, n.$$

The ODEs for s_n, e and f are linear combinations of the above ODEs, hence they are redundant and we skip them in this article.

In order to show unconditional binomiality of the steady state ideal of n-phosphorylation, we perform reductions on the generators of the steady state ideal so that a binomial basis is obtained. First of all, note that polynomials Q_j and R_k are already binomial. Reducing P_0 with respect to Q_0, we obtain

$$\begin{aligned}
P_0' &= P_0 + Q_0 \\
&= -k_{\mathrm{on}_0} s_0 e + k_{\mathrm{off}_0} c_0 + l_{\mathrm{cat}_0} d_1 \\
&\quad + k_{\mathrm{on}_0} s_0 e - (k_{\mathrm{off}_0} + k_{\mathrm{cat}_0}) c_0 \\
&= l_{\mathrm{cat}_0} d_1 + k_{\mathrm{cat}_0} c_0,
\end{aligned}$$

which is a binomial.

Now we reduce P_i with respect to P_0', Q_j and R_k as follows. First we reduce P_i with respect to R_I:

$$\begin{aligned}
P_i + R_i &= \\
&\quad -k_{\mathrm{on}_i} s_i e + k_{\mathrm{off}_i} c_i + k_{\mathrm{cat}_{i-1}} c_{i-1} - l_{\mathrm{on}_{i-1}} s_i f + l_{\mathrm{off}_{i-1}} d_i + l_{\mathrm{cat}_i} d_{i+1} \\
&\quad + l_{\mathrm{on}_{i-1}} s_i f - (l_{\mathrm{off}_{i-1}} + l_{\mathrm{cat}_{i-1}}) d_i \\
&= -k_{\mathrm{on}_i} s_i e + k_{\mathrm{off}_i} c_i + k_{\mathrm{cat}_{i-1}} c_{i-1} + l_{\mathrm{cat}_i} d_{i+1} - l_{\mathrm{cat}_{i-1}} d_i.
\end{aligned}$$

Then we reduce the result with respect to Q_i:

$$\begin{aligned}
P_i + R_i + Q_i &= \\
&\quad -k_{\mathrm{on}_i} s_i e + k_{\mathrm{off}_i} c_i + k_{\mathrm{cat}_{i-1}} c_{i-1} + l_{\mathrm{cat}_i} d_{i+1} - l_{\mathrm{cat}_{i-1}} d_i \\
&\quad + k_{\mathrm{on}_i} s_i e - (k_{\mathrm{off}_i} + k_{\mathrm{cat}_i}) c_i \\
&= k_{\mathrm{cat}_{i-1}} c_{i-1} + l_{\mathrm{cat}_i} d_{i+1} - l_{\mathrm{cat}_{i-1}} d_i + k_{\mathrm{cat}_i} c_i.
\end{aligned}$$

For $i = 1$, the above can be reduced with respect to P_0':

$$\begin{aligned}
P_1' = P_1 + R_1 + Q_1 - P_0' &= k_{\mathrm{cat}_0} c_0 + l_{\mathrm{cat}_1} d_1 - l_{\mathrm{cat}_0} d_1 + k_{\mathrm{cat}_1} c_1 \\
&\quad - (l_{\mathrm{cat}_0} d_1 + k_{\mathrm{cat}_0} c_0) \\
&= l_{\mathrm{cat}_1} d_1 + k_{\mathrm{cat}_1} c_1,
\end{aligned}$$

which is a binomial.

Similarly, for $i = 2, \ldots, n$, P_i can be reduced to a binomial with respect to R_i, Q_I and P_{i-1}'. Therefore, a binomial basis can be obtained this way for the steady state ideal.

As the algebraic manipulations above do not take into account the specialisations of the parameters, we computed comprehensive Gröbner system of the steady state ideals for the cases $n = 1, 2$ to test the binomiality under specialisations. 1-site phosphorylation and 2-site phosphorylations have been studied in [40] using the criteria presented in that article as well.

Example 1 (1-site phosphorylation, [40] Example 2.1).

$$S_0 + E \underset{k_{\mathrm{off}_0}}{\overset{k_{\mathrm{on}_0}}{\rightleftharpoons}} ES_0 \overset{k_{\mathrm{cat}_0}}{\longrightarrow} S_1 + E$$

$$S_1 + F \underset{l_{\mathrm{off}_0}}{\overset{l_{\mathrm{on}_0}}{\rightleftharpoons}} FS_1 \overset{l_{\mathrm{cat}_0}}{\longrightarrow} S_0 + F.$$

Let the variables representing the change of the concentrations of the species S_0, S_1, ES_0, FS_1, E, F be s_0, s_1, c_0, d_1, e, f respectively, and let the parameters be $k_{\mathrm{on}_0}, k_{\mathrm{off}_0}, k_{\mathrm{cat}_0}, l_{\mathrm{on}_0}, l_{\mathrm{off}_0}, l_{\mathrm{cat}_0}$.

The steady state ideal for 1-site phosphorylation reaction is generated by

$$\dot{s}_0 = -k_{\mathrm{on}_0} s_0 e + k_{\mathrm{off}_0} c_0 + l_{\mathrm{cat}_0} d_1,$$
$$\dot{s}_1 = -k_{\mathrm{on}_1} s_1 e + k_{\mathrm{off}_1} c_1 + k_{\mathrm{cat}_0} c_0 - l_{\mathrm{on}_0} s_1 f + l_{\mathrm{off}_0} d_1,$$
$$\dot{c}_0 = k_{\mathrm{on}_0} s_0 e - (k_{\mathrm{off}_0} + k_{\mathrm{cat}_0}) c_0,$$
$$\dot{d}_1 = l_{\mathrm{on}_0} s_1 f - (l_{\mathrm{off}_0} + l_{\mathrm{cat}_0}) d_1.$$

We skip the ODEs for e and f as they are linear combination of the other ODEs. Renaming the variables as

$$s_0 = x_1, s_1 = x_2, c_0 = x_3, d_1 = x_4, e = x_5, f = x_6,$$

we computed the comprehensive Gröbner system for the steady state ideal using Singular. It contains 25 branches, out of which 6 are binomial. We recall that in this article, a binomial ideal is an ideal that is generated by a set of binomials (not including monomials). For the last branch, V_{25} and W_{25} are the zero sets of the following sets of polynomials in $\mathbb{Q}[k_{\mathrm{on}_0}, k_{\mathrm{off}_0}, k_{\mathrm{cat}_0}, l_{\mathrm{on}_0}, l_{\mathrm{off}_0}, l_{\mathrm{cat}_0}][x_1, \ldots, x_6]$ respectively:

$$\{l_{\mathrm{cat}_0}, k_{\mathrm{on}_0}\},$$
$$\{k_{\mathrm{off}_0} k_{\mathrm{cat}_0} l_{\mathrm{on}_0} + k_{\mathrm{cat}_0}^2 l_{\mathrm{on}_0}\}.$$

The corresponding Gröbner basis is

$$\{f_1 = k_{\mathrm{cat}_0} x_3,$$
$$f_2 = l_{\mathrm{on}_0} x_2 x_6 - l_{\mathrm{off}_0} x_4\},$$

which obviously is not binomial.

An example of a branch with binomial Gröbner basis is branch 24, for which V_{24} and W_{24} are the zero sets of the following sets, respectively:

$$\{k_{\mathrm{off}_0} + k_{\mathrm{cat}_0}, k_{\mathrm{on}_0}\},$$
$$\{l_{\mathrm{on}_0} k_{\mathrm{cat}_0}\}.$$

The corresponding Gröbner basis is

$$\{f_1 = k_{\mathrm{cat}_0} x_3 + l_{\mathrm{cat}_0} x_4,$$
$$f_2 = l_{\mathrm{on}_0} x_2 x_6 + (-l_{\mathrm{off}_0} - l_{\mathrm{cat}_0}) x_4\}.$$

Example 2 (2-site phosphorylation, [40] Example 3.13). The steady state ideal for the 2-site phosphorylation reaction is generated by

$$\dot{s}_0 = P_0 = - k_{\mathrm{on}_0} s_0 e + k_{\mathrm{off}_0} c_0 + l_{\mathrm{cat}_0} d_1,$$
$$\dot{s}_1 = P_1 = - k_{\mathrm{on}_1} s_1 e + k_{\mathrm{off}_1} c_1 + k_{\mathrm{cat}_0} c_0 - l_{\mathrm{on}_0} s_1 f + l_{\mathrm{off}_0} d_1 + l_{\mathrm{cat}_1} d_2,$$
$$\dot{c}_0 = Q_0 = k_{\mathrm{on}_0} s_0 e - (k_{\mathrm{off}_0} + k_{\mathrm{cat}_0}) c_0,$$
$$\dot{c}_0 = Q_1 = k_{\mathrm{on}_1} s_1 e - (k_{\mathrm{off}_1} + k_{\mathrm{cat}_1}) c_1,$$
$$\dot{d}_1 = R_1 = l_{\mathrm{on}_0} s_1 f - (l_{\mathrm{off}_0} + l_{\mathrm{cat}_0}) d_1,$$
$$\dot{d}_2 = R_2 = l_{\mathrm{on}_1} s_2 f - (l_{\mathrm{off}_1} + l_{\mathrm{cat}_1}) d_2,$$

where the variables are

$$s_0, s_1, s_2, c_0, c_1, d_1, d_2, e, f$$

and the parameters are

$$k_{\mathrm{on}_0}, k_{\mathrm{on}_1}, k_{\mathrm{off}_0}, k_{\mathrm{off}_1}, k_{\mathrm{cat}_0}, k_{\mathrm{cat}_1}, l_{\mathrm{on}_0}, l_{\mathrm{on}_1}, l_{\mathrm{off}_0}, l_{\mathrm{off}_1}, l_{\mathrm{cat}_0}, l_{\mathrm{cat}_1}.$$

We have computed a comprehensive Gröbner system for this system using Singular. It has 1187 branches, out of which 36 are binomial. The last branch of the comprehensive Gröbner system is as follows. V_{1187} is the zero set of $l_{\mathrm{off}_1} + l_{\mathrm{cat}_1}$ and W_{1187} is the zero set of the following polynomial:

$$\begin{aligned}
& k_{\mathrm{on}_0} k_{\mathrm{on}_1} k_{\mathrm{off}_0} k_{\mathrm{off}_1} k_{\mathrm{cat}_0} k_{\mathrm{cat}_1} l_{\mathrm{on}_0} l_{\mathrm{on}_1} l_{\mathrm{off}_0} l_{\mathrm{cat}_0} l_{\mathrm{cat}_1} \\
& + k_{\mathrm{on}_0} k_{\mathrm{on}_1} k_{\mathrm{off}_0} k_{\mathrm{off}_1} k_{\mathrm{cat}_0} k_{\mathrm{cat}_1} l_{\mathrm{on}_0} l_{\mathrm{on}_1} l_{\mathrm{cat}_0}^2 l_{\mathrm{cat}_1} \\
& + k_{\mathrm{on}_0} k_{\mathrm{on}_1} k_{\mathrm{off}_0} k_{\mathrm{cat}_0} k_{\mathrm{cat}_1}^2 l_{\mathrm{on}_0} l_{\mathrm{on}_1} l_{\mathrm{off}_0} l_{\mathrm{cat}_0} l_{\mathrm{cat}_1} \\
& + k_{\mathrm{on}_0} k_{\mathrm{on}_1} k_{\mathrm{off}_0} k_{\mathrm{cat}_0} k_{\mathrm{cat}_1}^2 l_{\mathrm{on}_0} l_{\mathrm{on}_1} l_{\mathrm{cat}_0}^2 l_{\mathrm{cat}_1} \\
& + k_{\mathrm{on}_0} k_{\mathrm{on}_1} k_{\mathrm{off}_1} k_{\mathrm{cat}_0}^2 k_{\mathrm{cat}_1} l_{\mathrm{on}_0} l_{\mathrm{on}_1} l_{\mathrm{off}_0} l_{\mathrm{cat}_0} l_{\mathrm{cat}_1} \\
& + k_{\mathrm{on}_0} k_{\mathrm{on}_1} k_{\mathrm{off}_1} k_{\mathrm{cat}_0}^2 k_{\mathrm{cat}_1} l_{\mathrm{on}_0} l_{\mathrm{on}_1} l_{\mathrm{cat}_0}^2 l_{\mathrm{cat}_1} \\
& + k_{\mathrm{on}_0} k_{\mathrm{on}_1} k_{\mathrm{cat}_0}^2 k_{\mathrm{cat}_1}^2 l_{\mathrm{on}_0} l_{\mathrm{on}_1} l_{\mathrm{off}_0} l_{\mathrm{cat}_0} l_{\mathrm{cat}_1} \\
& + k_{\mathrm{on}_0} k_{\mathrm{on}_1} k_{\mathrm{cat}_0}^2 k_{\mathrm{cat}_1}^2 l_{\mathrm{on}_0} l_{\mathrm{on}_1} l_{\mathrm{cat}_0}^2 l_{\mathrm{cat}_1}.
\end{aligned}$$

Renaming the variables as

$$s_0 = x_1, s_1 = x_2, s_2 = x_3, c_0 = x_4, c_1 = x_5, d_1 = x_6, d_2 = x_7, e = x_8, f = x_9,$$

the Gröbner basis for every specialisation of the parameters in $V_{1187} \backslash W_{1187}$ is the following:

$$f_1 = k_{\mathrm{cat}_1} x_5 - l_{\mathrm{cat}_1} x_7,$$
$$f_2 = k_{\mathrm{cat}_0} x_4 - l_{\mathrm{cat}_0} x_6,$$
$$f_3 = l_{\mathrm{on}_1} x_3 x_9,$$
$$f_4 = l_{\mathrm{on}_0} x_2 x_9 + (-l_{\mathrm{off}_0} - l_{\mathrm{cat}_0}) x_6,$$

$$f_5 = (k_{on_1}l_{off_0} + k_{on_1}l_{cat_0})x_6x_8 + (-k_{off_1}l_{on_0})x_5x_9 + (-l_{on_0}l_{cat_1})x_7x_9,$$

$$f_6 = (k_{on_1})x_2x_8 + (-k_{off_1})x_5 + (-l_{cat_1})x_7,$$

$$f_7 = (k_{on_0})x_1x_8 + (-k_{off_0})x_4 + (-l_{cat_0})x_6,$$

$$f_8 = (l_{on_1}l_{off_0} + l_{on_1}l_{cat_0})x_3x_6,$$

$$f_9 = (k_{on_1}k_{off_0}k_{cat_1}l_{cat_0} + k_{on_1}k_{cat_0}k_{cat_1}l_{cat_0})x_2x_6$$
$$+ (-k_{on_0}k_{off_1}k_{cat_0}l_{cat_1} - k_{on_0}k_{cat_0}k_{cat_1}l_{cat_1})x_1x_7,$$

$$f_{10} = (k_{on_0}k_{off_1}l_{on_0}l_{cat_1} + k_{on_0}k_{cat_1}l_{on_0}l_{cat_1})x_1x_7x_9$$
$$+ (-k_{on_1}k_{off_0}k_{cat_1}l_{off_0} - k_{on_1}k_{off_0}k_{cat_1}l_{cat_0})x_4x_6$$
$$+ (-k_{on_1}k_{cat_1}l_{off_0}l_{cat_0} - k_{on_1}k_{cat_1}l_{cat_0}^2)x_6^2,$$

$$f_{11} = (k_{on_0}k_{off_1}k_{cat_0}l_{on_1}l_{off_0}l_{cat_1} + k_{on_0}k_{off_1}k_{cat_0}l_{on_1}l_{cat_0}l_{cat_1}$$
$$+ k_{on_0}k_{cat_0}k_{cat_1}l_{on_1}l_{off_0}l_{cat_1} + k_{on_0}k_{cat_0}k_{cat_1}l_{on_1}l_{cat_0}l_{cat_1})x_1x_3x_7.$$

One can observe that the above branch of the comprehensive Gröbner system is not binomial.

We carried on the computations for comprehensive Gröbner system of the steady state ideal of n-phosphorylation for $n = 2, 3, 4, 5$ in Singular with the time limit of six hours. The results of the computations are summarised in Table 1. In this table, DNF refers to did not finish.

Table 1. Comprehensive Gröbner system of n-Phosphorylations

	#branches	#binomial branches	% of binomial branches	Time(s)
2−phosph.	1187	36	3.03	24
3−phosph.	57857	216	0.37	2231
4−phosph.	−	−	−	DNF
5−phosph.	−	−	−	DNF

As the number of variables and parameters grow drastically when n increases, comprehensive Gröbner system computations did not finish in a reasonable time period for $n \geq 4$.

We also computed a comprehensige Groöbner system of 2-phosphorylation in Maple, using Dehghani and Hashemi's PWWG package[5], which uses a modification of Kapur et al.'s algorithm so that the branches with Gröbner basis $\{1\}$ are ignored [29]. According to the authors' experiments in [29], this modification results in speed-up of the computations. However, even for 2-phosphorylation the computations did not finish in six hours in Maple.

As we see from the computations in this subsection, there are several branches of teh n-phosphorylations that are not binomial. This means that for certain

---

[5] https://amirhashemi.iut.ac.ir/sites/amirhashemi.iut.ac.ir/files//file_basepage/pggw_0.txt.

values of the rate constants, n-phosphorylation is not binomial, while the computations without taking into account the specialisations of the rate constants leads to the binomiality.

3.2 BioModels

Our main benchmark for computing comprehensive Gröbner system of steady state ideals, are the biochemical models from the BioModels repository [7], which is typically used for such computations. As a first example, we present biomodel 629 and the corresponding computations in the following example.

Example 3 (BIOMD0000000629, [7]). The corresponding ODEs for biomodel 629 are the following:

$$\dot{x}_1 = -k_2 x_1 x_3 + k_3 x_2,$$
$$\dot{x}_2 = k_2 x_1 x_3 - k_3 x_2 - k_4 x_2 x_4 + k_5 x_5,$$
$$\dot{x}_3 = -k_2 x_1 x_3 + k_3 x_2,$$
$$\dot{x}_4 = -k_4 x_2 x_4 + k_5 x_5,$$
$$\dot{x}_5 = k_4 x_2 x_4 - k_5 x_5,$$

where $k_1, \ldots, k_5$ are the parameters and $x_1, \ldots, x_5$ are the variables. Comprehensive Göbner system computation over the ring $\mathbb{Q}[k_1, \ldots, k_5][x_1, \ldots, x_5]$ in Singular results in 10 branches with the following conditions and Gröbner bases (Table 2).

Table 2. Comprehensive Gröbner system of BIOMD0000000629

Branch	V	W	GB
1	0	$k_2 k_4$	$k_4 x_2 x_4 - k_5 x_5, k_2 x_1 x_3 - k_3 x_2$
2	k_4	$k_2 k_5$	$k_5 x_5, k_2 x_1 x_3 - k_3 x_2$
3	k_5, k_2	k_2	$k_2 x_1 x_3 - k3 x_2$
4	k_5, k_4, k_2	k_3	$k_3 x_2$
5	k_5, k_4, k_3, k_2	1	0
6	k_4, k_2	$k_3 k_5$	$k_5 x_5, k_3 x_2$
7	k_4, k_3, k_2	k_5	$k_5 x_5$
8	k_2	k_5, k_4, k_3	$k_3 k_5 x_5, k_3 x_2$
9	k_3, k_2	k_4	$k_4 x_2 x_4 - k_5 x_5$
10	k_5, k_2	$k_3 k_4$	$k_3 x_2$

There are three branches with binomial Gröbner basis for biomodel 629. All the branches have either monomial or binomial Gröbner basis.

In Table 3, we present the results of our computations for some biomodels from the Biomodels repository [7]. As computing comprehensive Gröbner system of systems with large number of variables is very expensive, we have considered those biomodels that have relatively small number of species (correspondingly, relatively small number of variables), so that the computations took less than ten minutes for those biomodels. In Table 3, one can find the number of branches of the corresponding comprehensive Gröbner systems, the number of branches that are binomial, and their percentage. Except for biomodels 271 and 519 that have no binomial branch, all other biomodels have at least one binomial branch. For two biomodels (283 and 486), at least half of their branches are binomial.

The largest biomodel we have considered is model 26. We note that this model is a MAPK reaction network. It has been studied in [17], where the authors associated a graph to the CRN and used a trick based on vertex cover in order to reduce the number of the polynomials in the steady state ideal into 2 polynomials.

Table 3. Branches of comprehensive Gröbner systems of biomodels

Model	#branches	#binomial branches	% of binomial branches
26	46870	164	0.35
40	35	6	17.00
92	10	4	40.00
101	81	11	13.40
104	4	1	25.00
156	25	5	20.00
159	36	6	16.66
178	24	2	8.33
194	19	5	26.31
233	18	5	27.78
267	12	2	16.67
271	92	0	0.00
272	44	7	15.91
282	18	4	22.22
283	2	1	50.00
289	351	43	12.25
321	26	5	19.23
363	15	2	13.33
459	40	9	22.50
486	3	2	66.67
519	128	0	0.00
546	15	1	6.67
629	10	4	40.00

4 Conclusion

We address the problem of binomiality of the steady state ideal of a chemical reaction network. The binomiality problem has been widely considered in the literature of mathematics and chemical reaction network theory and is still an active research area. Finding binomiality and toricity is a hard problem from both a theoretical and a practical point of view. The computational methods typically rely on Gröbner bases.

The authors have recently investigated binomiality and toricity in several papers. We have given efficient algorithms for testing toricity in [27]. We also have considered the binomiality from a first-order logic point of view and gave efficient computational results and studied biomodels systematically via quantifier elimination [27,43]. Other than those, we have considered the concept of unconditional binomiality, which considers rate constants as variables, and gave polynomial time linear algebra and graph theoretical approaches for detecting binomiality [41,42].

The existing work on binomiality of steady state ideals do not take into account the effect of assigning values to the rate constats during the computations. In the present work, we consider the problem of binomiality when the parameters can be specialised. Our approach to this parametric binomiality problem is naturally based on comprehensive Gröbner bases. We make systematic computations on n-phosphorylations and biomodels and detect the branches of the Gröbner systems that are binomial. Our computations via comprehensive Gröbner systems show that in several cases, the comprehensive Gröbner bases for steady state ideals are not binomial, while using other methods, e.g., considering rate constants as variables or doing computations without considering the effect of specialisation, one may consider those steady state ideal as binomial ideals.

As in this paper the concept of comprehensive Gröbner bases is used for the first time on chemical reaction network theory, we propose using this approach for studying further properties of chemical reaction networks.

Acknowledgments. This work has been supported by the interdisciplinary bilateral project ANR-17-CE40-0036/DFG-391322026 SYMBIONT [3,4]. We would like to thank A. Hashemi and M. Dehghani for the discussions on comprehensive Gröbner bases and providing us with their Maple package.

References

1. Becker, T., Weispfenning, V., Kredel, H.: Gröbner Bases - A Computational Approach to Commutative Algebra. Graduate Texts in Mathematics, vol. 141. Springer, Heidelberg (1993). https://doi.org/10.1007/978-1-4612-0913-3
2. Boltzmann, L.: Lectures on Gas Theory. University of California Press, Berkeley and Los Angeles (1964)
3. Boulier, F., et al.: The SYMBIONT project: symbolic methods for biological networks. ACM Commun. Comput. Algebra **52**(3), 67–70 (2018). https://doi.org/10.1145/3313880.3313885

4. Boulier, F., et al.: The SYMBIONT project: symbolic methods for biological networks. F1000Research **7**(1341) (2018). https://doi.org/10.7490/f1000research. 1115995.1

5. Buchberger, B.: Ein Algorithmus zum Auffinden der Basiselemente des Restklassenringes nach einem nulldimensionalen Polynomideal. Doctoral dissertation, Mathematical Institute, University of Innsbruck, Austria (1965)

6. Buchberger, B.: Ein Algorithmisches Kriterium für die Lösbarkeit eines algebraischen Gleichungssystems. Aequationes Mathematicae **3**, 374–383 (1970)

7. Chelliah, V., et al.: BioModels: ten-year anniversary. Nucl. Acids Res. **43**, D542–D548 (2015). https://doi.org/10.1093/nar/gku1181

8. Conradi, C., Kahle, T.: Detecting binomiality. Adv. Appl. Math. **71**, 52–67 (2015). https://doi.org/10.1016/j.aam.2015.08.004

9. Craciun, G., Dickenstein, A., Shiu, A., Sturmfels, B.: Toric dynamical systems. J. Symb. Comput. **44**(11), 1551–1565 (2009). https://doi.org/10.1016/j.jsc.2008.08. 006

10. Darmian, M.D., Hashemi, A.: Parametric FGLM algorithm. J. Symb. Comput. **82**, 38–56 (2017). https://doi.org/10.1016/j.jsc.2016.12.006

11. Darmian, M.D., Hashemi, A., Montes, A.: Erratum to "a new algorithm for discussing Gröbner bases with parameters". [J. Symbolic Comput. 33(1–2) (2002) 183–208]. J. Symb. Comput. **46**(10), 1187–1188 (2011). https://doi.org/10.1016/j. jsc.2011.05.002

12. Davenport, J.H., Heintz, J.: Real quantifier elimination is doubly exponential. J. Symb. Comput. **5**(1–2), 29–35 (1988). https://doi.org/10.1016/S0747-7171(88)80004-X

13. Decker, W., Greuel, G.M., Pfister, G., Schönemann, H.: Singular 4-2-0 – a computer algebra system for polynomial computations (2020). http://www.singular.uni-kl. de

14. Dickenstein, A., Pérez Millán, M., Anne, S., Tang, X.: Multistatonarity in structured reaction networks. Bull. Math. Biol. **81**, 1527–1581 (2019). https://doi.org/ 10.1007/s11538-019-00572-6

15. Einstein, A.: Strahlungs-emission und -absorption nach der Quantentheorie. Verh. Dtsch. Phys. Ges. **18**, 318–323 (1916)

16. Eisenbud, D., Sturmfels, B.: Binomial ideals. Duke Math. J. **84**(1), 1–45 (1996). https://doi.org/10.1215/S0012-7094-96-08401-X

17. England, M., Errami, H., Grigoriev, D., Radulescu, O., Sturm, T., Weber, A.: Symbolic versus numerical computation and visualization of parameter regions for multistationarity of biological networks. In: Gerdt, V.P., Koepf, W., Seiler, W.M., Vorozhtsov, E.V. (eds.) CASC 2017. LNCS, vol. 10490, pp. 93–108. Springer, Cham (2017). https://doi.org/10.1007/978-3-319-66320-3_8

18. Faugère, J.C.: A new efficient algorithm for computing Gröbner bases (F4). J. Pure Appl. Algebra **139**(1–3), 61–88 (1999). https://doi.org/10.1145/780506.780516

19. Faugère, J.C.: A new efficient algorithm for computing Gröbner bases without reduction to zero (F5). In: Mora, T. (ed.) ISSAC 2002, pp. 75–83. ACM (2002). https://doi.org/10.1145/780506.780516

20. Feinberg, M.: Complex balancing in general kinetic systems. Arch. Ration. Mech. Anal. **49**(3), 187–194 (1972). https://doi.org/10.1007/BF00255665

21. Feinberg, M.: Lectures on chemical reaction networks (1979)

22. Feinberg, M.: Foundations of Chemical Reaction Network Theory. AMS, vol. 202. Springer, Cham (2019). https://doi.org/10.1007/978-3-030-03858-8

23. Fulton, W.: Introduction to Toric Varieties, Annals of Mathematics Studies, vol. 131. Princeton University Press (1993)

24. Gorban, A.N., Kolokoltsov, V.N.: Generalized mass action law and thermodynamics of nonlinear Markov processes. Math. Model. Nat. Phenom. **10**(5), 16–46 (2015). https://doi.org/10.1051/mmnp/201510503

25. Gorban, A.N., Yablonsky, G.S.: Three waves of chemical dynamics. Math. Model. Nat. Phenom. **10**(5), 1–5 (2015). https://doi.org/10.1051/mmnp/201510501

26. Grigorev, D.: Complexity of deciding Tarski algebra. J. Symb. Comput. **5**(1–2), 65–108 (1988). https://doi.org/10.1016/S0747-7171(88)80006-3

27. Grigoriev, D., Iosif, A., Rahkooy, H., Sturm, T., Weber, A.: Efficiently and effectively recognizing toricity of steady state varieties. Math. Comput. Sci. **15**, 199–232 (2020). https://doi.org/10.1007/s11786-020-00479-9

28. Grigoriev, D., Weber, A.: Complexity of solving systems with few independent monomials and applications to mass-action kinetics. In: Gerdt, V.P., Koepf, W., Mayr, E.W., Vorozhtsov, E.V. (eds.) CASC 2012. LNCS, vol. 7442, pp. 143–154. Springer, Heidelberg (2012). https://doi.org/10.1007/978-3-642-32973-9_12

29. Hashemi, A., Darmian, M.D., Barkhordar, M.: Gröbner systems conversion. Math. Comput. Sci. **11**(1), 61–77 (2017). https://doi.org/10.1007/s11786-017-0295-3

30. Horn, F., Jackson, R.: General mass action kinetics. Arch. Ration. Mech. Anal. **47**(2), 81–116 (1972). https://doi.org/10.1007/BF00251225

31. Iosif, A., Rahkooy, H.: Analysis of the Conradi-Kahle algorithm for detecting binomiality on biological models. arXiv preprint arXiv:1912.06896 (2019)

32. Iosif, A., Rahkooy, H.: MapleBinomials, a Maple package for testing binomiality of ideals (2019). https://doi.org/10.5281/zenodo.3564428

33. Kapur, D.: Comprehensive Gröbner basis theory for a parametric polynomial ideal and the associated completion algorithm. J. Syst. Sci. Complex. **30**(1), 196–233 (2017). https://doi.org/10.1007/s11424-017-6337-8

34. Kapur, D., Sun, Y., Wang, D.: An efficient method for computing comprehensive Gröbner bases. J. Symb. Comput. **52**, 124–142 (2013). https://doi.org/10.1016/j.jsc.2012.05.015

35. Montes, A.: The Gröbner Cover. ACM, vol. 27. Springer, Cham (2018). https://doi.org/10.1007/978-3-030-03904-2

36. Mayr, E.W., Meyer, A.R.: The complexity of the word problems for commutative semigroups and polynomial ideals. Adv. Math. **46**(3), 305–329 (1982). https://doi.org/10.1016/0001-8708(82)90048-2

37. Montes, A.: A new algorithm for discussing Gröbner bases with parameters. J. Symb. Comput. **33**(2), 183–208 (2002). https://doi.org/10.1006/jsco.2001.0504

38. Onsager, L.: Reciprocal relations in irreversible processes. I. Phys. Rev. **37**(4), 405 (1931). https://doi.org/10.1103/PhysRev.37.405

39. Pérez Millán, M., Dickenstein, A.: The structure of MESSI biological systems. SIAM J. Appl. Dyn. Syst. **17**(2), 1650–1682 (2018). https://doi.org/10.1137/17M1113722

40. Pérez Millán, M., Dickenstein, A., Shiu, A., Conradi, C.: Chemical reaction systems with toric steady states. Bull. Math. Biol. **74**(5), 1027–1065 (2012). https://doi.org/10.1007/s11538-011-9685-x

41. Rahkooy, H., Montero, C.V.: A graph theoretical approach for testing binomiality of reversible chemical reaction networks. In: 22nd International Symposium on Symbolic and Numeric Algorithms for Scientific Computing, SYNASC 2020, Timisoara, Romania, September 1–4, 2020, pp. 101–108. IEEE (2020). https://doi.org/10.1109/SYNASC51798.2020.00027

42. Rahkooy, H., Radulescu, O., Sturm, T.: A linear algebra approach for detecting binomiality of steady state ideals of reversible chemical reaction networks. In: Boulier, F., England, M., Sadykov, T.M., Vorozhtsov, E.V. (eds.) CASC 2020. LNCS, vol. 12291, pp. 492–509. Springer, Cham (2020). https://doi.org/10.1007/978-3-030-60026-6_29

43. Rahkooy, H., Sturm, T.: First-order tests for toricity. In: Boulier, F., England, M., Sadykov, T.M., Vorozhtsov, E.V. (eds.) CASC 2020. LNCS, vol. 12291, pp. 510–527. Springer, Cham (2020). https://doi.org/10.1007/978-3-030-60026-6_30

44. Sadeghimanesh, A., Feliu, E.: The multistationarity structure of networks with intermediates and a binomial core network. Bull. Math. Biol. **81**, 2428–2462 (2019). https://doi.org/10.1007/s11538-019-00612-1

45. Sturmfels, B.: Gröbner Bases and Convex Polytopes, University Lecture Series, vol. 8. AMS, Providence, RI (1996). https://doi.org/10.1112/S0024609396272376

46. Suzuki, A., Sato, Y.: An alternative approach to comprehensive Gröbner bases. J. Symb. Comput. **36**(3–4), 649–667 (2003). https://doi.org/10.1016/S0747-7171(03)00098-1

47. Wang, L., Sontag, E.D.: On the number of steady states in a multiple futile cycle. J. Math. Biol. **57**(1), 29–52 (2008). https://doi.org/10.1007/s00285-007-0145-z

48. Wegscheider, R.: Über simultane Gleichgewichte und die Beziehungen zwischen Thermodynamik und Reactionskinetik homogener Systeme. Monatsh. Chem. Verw. Tl. **22**(8), 849–906 (1901). https://doi.org/10.1007/BF01517498

49. Weispfenning, V.: The complexity of linear problems in fields. J. Symb. Comput. **5**(1–2), 3–27 (1988). https://doi.org/10.1016/S0747-7171(88)80003-8

50. Weispfenning, V.: Comprehensive Gröbner bases. J. Symb. Comput. **14**(1), 1–30 (1992). https://doi.org/10.1016/0747-7171(92)90023-W

51. Weispfenning, V.: Canonical comprehensive Gröbner bases. J. Symb. Comput. **36**(3–4), 669–683 (2003). https://doi.org/10.1016/S0747-7171(03)00099-3

52. Weispfenning, V.: Comprehensive Gröbner bases and regular rings. J. Symb. Comput. **41**(3–4), 285–296 (2006). https://doi.org/10.1016/j.jsc.2003.05.003

Primitive Recursive Ordered Fields and Some Applications

Victor Selivanov[1](✉) and Svetlana Selivanova[2]

[1] A. P. Ershov Institute of Informatics Systems, and S. L. Sobolev Institute
of Mathematics, Novosibirsk, Russia
vseliv@iis.nsk.su
[2] KAIST, School of Computing, Daejeon, Republic of Korea

Abstract. We establish primitive recursive versions of some known facts about computable ordered fields of reals and computable reals and apply them to several problems of algebra and analysis. In particular, we find a primitive recursive analogue of Ershov-Madison's theorem about the computable real closure, relate primitive recursive fields of reals to the field of primitive recursive reals, give sufficient conditions for primitive recursive root-finding and for computing solution operators of symmetric hyperbolic systems of partial differential equations.

Keywords: Ordered field · Real closure · Primitive recursion · Polynomial · Splitting · Root-finding · Solution operators of PDEs

1 Introduction

In [23], computable ordered fields of reals were related to the field of computable reals and used to prove computability of some problems in algebra and analysis (notably, spectral problems for symmetric matrices and computing solutions of symmetric hyperbolic systems of partial differential equations (PDEs) uniformly on matrix coefficients) in the rigorous sense of computable analysis [27]. The proposed sufficient conditions for computability are very broad but do not yield any complexity upper bounds because they use algorithms based on unbounded search through countable sets. We note that the situation here is rather subtle, e.g. the spectral decomposition of a symmetric 2×2-matrix is not computable [28] but it becomes computable (even for $n \times n$-matrices uniformly on n) if matrix coefficients range over any fixed computable ordered field of reals.

V. Selivanov—The work is supported by Mathematical Center in Akademgorodok under agreement No. 075-15-2019-1613 with the Ministry of Science and Higher Education of the Russian Federation.

S. Selivanova—The work is partially supported by RFBR-JSPS Grant 20-51-50001, by the National Research Foundation of Korea (grant 2017R1E1A1A03071032), by the International Research & Development Program of the Korean Ministry of Science and ICT (grant 2016K1A3A7A03950702), and by the NRF Brain Pool program (grant 2019H1D3A2A02102240).

© Springer Nature Switzerland AG 2021
F. Boulier et al. (Eds.): CASC 2021, LNCS 12865, pp. 353–369, 2021.
https://doi.org/10.1007/978-3-030-85165-1_20

In [24], the PTIME-presentability of the ordered field $\mathbb{R}_{alg}$ of algebraic reals and PTIME-computability of some problems on algebraic numbers established in [1] were applied to find non-trivial upper complexity bounds for the aforementioned problems in algebra and analysis. A weak point here is that this approach applies only to problems with coefficients in $\mathbb{R}_{alg}$ because $\mathbb{R}_{alg}$ is currently the only known PTIME-presentable real closed ordered field.

Another weak point is that complexity classes like PTIME or PSPACE are often not closed under important constructions. E.g. the spectral decomposition of an algebraic symmetric $n \times n$-matrix is PTIME-computable for any fixed n, but not uniformly on n. The same holds for the problem of root-finding for polynomials in $\mathbb{R}_{alg}[x]$ [1]. For differential equations, PTIME is in many cases preserved for analytic/polynomial initial data: [3,12] for ordinary differential equations (ODEs), [15] for PDEs. However, for more general functional classes the situation is different: solving ODEs with a Lipshitz continuous PTIME computable right-hand part is PSPACE-complete [11]. Computing the solutions of the Dirichlet problem for the Poisson equation [13] and periodic boundary value problem for the heat equation [14], is #P_1-complete; according to [14,15], for a large class of linear evolutionary PDEs, the difference scheme method is in general in PSPACE, for some particular cases in #P, when applied to fixed real PTIME computable initial data.

Thus, it seems reasonable to investigate properties of the aforementioned problems for natural complexity classes in between PTIME and COMPUTABLE, to obtain better closure properties and efficient solutions of wider classes of problems. An obvious candidate here is the class PR of primitively recursive functions having a prominent role in computability theory and proof theory.

Recently, there was a renewed interest in primitively recursive (PR) structures (see e.g. [2] and references therein) which are recognized as a principal model for an emerging new paradigm of computability—the so called online computability (see e.g. [4]). PR-solvability of a problem yields a solution algorithm which does not use an exhaustive search through a structure (usually written as unbounded WHILE...DO, REPEAT...UNTIL, or μ operator); thus, it becomes possible to count working time of the algorithm. Although the upper complexity bounds for a PR-algorithm may be awfully large, this is a principal improvement compared with the general computability. As stressed in [2], PR-presentability of a structure may often be improved even to PTIME-presentability.

Thus, PR-presentability of structures (and PR-computability in general) seems important for the following reasons: it is in some respect close to feasible computability, is technically easier than, say PTIME-computability, and has much better closure properties. In this paper we investigate PR-versions of some results in [23,24]. The PR versions have their own flavour and complement the results in [23,24].

In particular, we find a PR-version (for Ahchimedean case) of the Ershov-Madison theorem on the computable real closure [7,17], relate PR ordered fields of reals to the field of PR reals, propose (apparently, new) notions of PR-computability in analysis and apply them to obtain new results on computability of PDE-solutions. Our notion of PR Archimedean field of reals uses the idea of PR Skolem functions which was earlier used by R. L. Goodstein in [10] in his development of a version of constructive analysis.[1] Our approach to PR computability in analysis sketched below is also related to the approach by W. Gomaa (see [9], comments after Remark 1) to PR computability on the reals.[2]

More specifically, we identify a class of PRAS-fields (PR Archimedean fields of reals with PR-splitting) such that the above-mentioned problems over any such field are PR-computable. These results complement and contrast the results in [23,24], as well as some results in [1]. E.g., the class of PRAS-fields is shown to be richer than the class of PTIME-presentable fields but the union of this class is a proper subset of the set of PR reals (in contrast with the corresponding fact in [23]). In the applications section, we show how this applies to spectral problems and (PR) solving of symmetric hyperbolic systems of PDEs. For the latter example the solution is computed numerically (via difference schemes) while the algebraic part is performed symbolically; this part also requires introducing definitions of PR real functions and operators.

In programming terms, we identify an important class of number fields and related algorithmic problems of algebra and analysis which may be programmed without using the above-mentioned unbounded cycle operators.

After some preliminaries in the next section, we prove in Sect. 3 the PR Ershov-Madison theorem and some of its corollaries; in particular, we give a sufficient condition for the existence of PR root-finding algorithms in the PR real and algebraic closure of a PRAS-field. In Sect. 4 we examine the PR-versions of results in [23] on the relations of computable ordered fields of reals to the field of computable reals. In Sect. 5 we describe the above-mentioned applications to linear algebra and analysis.

2   PR Ordered Fields

We start with recalling some basic notions related to computable structures (see e.g. [6,19,25] for additional details).

A *numbering* is any function with domain $\mathbb{N}$. A *numbering of a set* B is a surjection β from $\mathbb{N}$ onto B; sometimes we write β_n or βn instead of the "canonical" $\beta(n)$. For numberings β and γ, β is *reducible* to γ (in symbols $\beta \leq \gamma$) iff $\beta = \gamma \circ f$ for some computable function f on $\mathbb{N}$, and β is *equivalent* to γ (in symbols $\beta \equiv \gamma$) iff $\beta \leq \gamma$ and $\gamma \leq \beta$. Let $\nu : \mathbb{N} \to B$ be a numbering. A relation $P \subseteq B^n$ on B is ν-*computable* if the relation $P(\nu(k_1), \ldots, \nu(k_n))$ on $\mathbb{N}$ is computable. A function $f : B^n \to B$ is ν-*computable* if $f(\nu(k_1), \ldots, \nu(k_n)) = \nu g(k_1, \ldots, k_n)$ for some computable function $g : \mathbb{N}^n \to \mathbb{N}$. More generally, given another numbering $\mu : \mathbb{N} \to C$, a function $f : B^n \to C$ is (ν, μ)-*computable* if $f(\nu(k_1), \ldots, \nu(k_n)) = \mu g(k_1, \ldots, k_n)$ for some computable function $g : \mathbb{N}^n \to \mathbb{N}$.

---

[1] We are grateful to Vasco Brattka for the hint to Goodstein's monography.

[2] We are grateful to an anonymous reviewer for the hint to the survey by W. Gomaa.

Definition 1. *A structure* $\mathbb{B} = (B; \sigma)$ *of a finite signature* σ *is called constructivizable iff there is a numbering* β *of* B *such that all signature predicates and functions, and the equality predicate, are* β-*computable. Such* β *is called a constructivization of* $\mathbb{B}$, *and the pair* $(\mathbb{B}, \beta)$ *is called a constructive structure.*

PR-versions of the notions above are obtained by changing "computable" to "PR". They were introduced in [19]. In particular, for numberings β and γ, β is *PR-reducible* to γ (in symbols $\beta \leq_{PR} \gamma$) iff $\beta = \gamma \circ f$ for some PR function f on $\mathbb{N}$, and β is *PR-equivalent* to γ (in symbols $\beta \equiv_{PR} \gamma$) iff $\beta \leq_{PR} \gamma$ and $\gamma \leq_{PR} \beta$. For $\nu : \mathbb{N} \to B$, a relation $P \subseteq B^n$ on B is ν-PR if the relation $P(\nu(k_1), \ldots, \nu(k_n))$ on $\mathbb{N}$ is PR. A function $f : B^n \to B$ is ν-PR if $f(\nu(k_1), \ldots, \nu(k_n)) = \nu g(k_1, \ldots, k_n)$ for some PR function $g : \mathbb{N}^n \to \mathbb{N}$. A structure $\mathbb{B} = (B; \sigma)$ is *PR-constructivizable* iff there is a numbering β of B such that all signature predicates and functions, and the equality predicate, are β-PR. Such β is called a *PR-constructivization* of $\mathbb{B}$, and the pair $(\mathbb{B}, \beta)$ is called a *PR structure*. Definition and basic properties of PR functions may be found e.g. in [20].

A structure $\mathbb{B}$ is *fully PR-presentable (FPR-presentable, or punctual)* if it is isomorphic to a PR structure with universe $\mathbb{N}$. Let us characterise this class of structures (discussed in [2] as important for capturing the online structures) in our terms. We call a numbering ν *PR-infinite* if there is a PR function f such that $\nu(f(i)) \neq \nu(f(j))$ whenever $i \neq j$.

Proposition 2. *A structure* $\mathbb{B}$ *is FPR-presentable iff it has a PR-constructivization* β *which is PR-infinite.*

Proof. We consider the less obvious direction. Let β be a PR-constructivization which is PR-infinite via f. Let $h(n) = max\{f(0), \ldots, f(n)\}$ and let $g(0) = 0$ and $g(n+1) = \mu x.\forall i \leq n(\beta(x) \neq \beta(g(i)))$. Since B is infinite, g is total and injective. Then h is PR and $g(n+1) = \mu x \leq h(n).\forall i \leq n(\beta(x) \neq \beta(g(i)))$, hence g is also PR. The numbering $\gamma = \beta \circ g$ is PR-reducible to β and injective. Conversely, $\beta \leq_{PR} \gamma$ via the PR function $u(n) = \mu x \leq n.\beta(n) = \beta(x)$. Thus, γ is a bijective numbering of B PR-equivalent to β, so it is a bijective PR-constructivization of $\mathbb{B}$. Copying interpretations of signature symbols from $\mathbb{B}$ to $\mathbb{N}$ via γ^{-1} we obtain a PR-copy of $\mathbb{B}$ with universe $\mathbb{N}$. □

Note that any PR-constructivization β of an associative commutative ring with 1 of characteristic 0 is PR infinite. Since in the sequel we consider only rings and fields of characteristic 0, most PR-constructivizable structures below are FPR-presentable.

Importantly, all usual encodings and decodings of constructive objects (like pairs, triples, finite strings, terms, formulas and so on) used in computability theory and its applications may be done using PR functions [20]. For instance, there is a PR bijection $\langle n_1, n_2 \rangle$ between $\mathbb{N} \times \mathbb{N}$ and $\mathbb{N}$. With some abuse we use similar notation $\langle n_1, n_2, n_3 \rangle$ to encode triples and finite strings of natural numbers. We fix bijective PR-constructivizations $\zeta, \varkappa$ of the ring $\mathbb{Z}$ of integers and of the ordered field $\mathbb{Q}$ of rationals, resp.

We freely use basic notions and facts about (ordered) rings and fields (see e.g. [26]). We consider fields and ordered fields in signatures $\{+, \cdot, -, ^{-1}, 0, 1\}$ and $\{+, \cdot, -, ^{-1} \leq, 0, 1\}$ resp.; for (ordered) rings the symbol $^{-1}$ is of course removed. Theory of computable rings and fields is very rich (see e.g. [6,25]) but the PR analogue of this theory does not seem to be considered seriously so far. Many PR analogues of results in [6,25,26] are straightforward, in the proofs below we just mention this, sometimes with references. We mention some examples of such results. With any numbering β of a ring $\mathbb{B}$ we associate the numbering β^* of the ring $\mathbb{B}[x]$ of polynomials over $\mathbb{B}$ with variable x as follows: $\beta^*(\langle i_0, \ldots, i_n \rangle) = \beta(i_0)x^0 + \cdots + \beta(i_n)x^n$ where $\langle i_0, \ldots, i_n \rangle$ is a PR coding of the finite non-empty strings of natural numbers. Iterating this construction, we obtain for each n the numbering $\beta^{[n]}$ of $\mathbb{B}[x_0, \ldots, x_n]$ (identifying $\mathbb{B}[x_0, \ldots, x_{n+1}]$ with $\mathbb{B}[x_0, \ldots, x_n][x_{n+1}]$): $\beta^{[0]} = \beta^*$, $\beta^{[n+1]} = (\beta^{[n]})^*$. Clearly, if β is a PR-constructivization then so is every $\beta^{[0]}$, and the evaluation function $ev_n : \mathbb{B}[x_0, \ldots, x_n] \times \mathbb{B}^n \to \mathbb{B}$ is PR w.r.t. the corresponding numberings. If $(\mathbb{B}, \beta)$ is a PR field then $(\mathbb{B}^*, \beta^*)$ is a PR integral domain and the usual functions and relations of polynomial arithmetic (like the functions $\deg(p)$ returning the degree of $p \in \mathbb{B}[x]$, the functions p/q, $rest(p, q)$, $\gcd(p, q)$, $res(p, q)$, p' returning resp. the quotient, remainder, greatest common divisor, resultant and derivative, and the relations "p divides q", "p_1, p_2 are relatively prime", "p is square-free", are β^*-PR.

3 PR Real Closure

By a classical theorem of Artin and Schreier, for any ordered field $\mathbb{A}$ there exists an algebraic ordered extension $\widehat{\mathbb{A}} \supseteq \mathbb{A}$ which is real closed. Yu. L. Ershov [7] and independently E. W. Madison [17] proved a computable version of the Artin-Schreier theorem: if $\mathbb{A}$ is constructivizable then so is also $\widehat{\mathbb{A}}$. We search for a PR analogue of the Ershov-Madison theorem. Though we have not found a complete analogue, we describe one for Archimedean ordered fields. Every such field embeds in $\mathbb{R}$, so we always assume that $\mathbb{A} \subseteq \mathbb{R}$. In fact, we can also assume that $\widehat{\mathbb{A}} \subseteq \mathbb{R}$ since $\widehat{\mathbb{A}}$ is isomorphic to the ordered field of real roots of non-zero polynomials from $\mathbb{A}[x]$. So, from now on we always assume that $\mathbb{A}$ and $\widehat{\mathbb{A}}$ are ordered subfields of $\mathbb{R}$, i.e. $\alpha, \widehat{\alpha} : \mathbb{N} \to \mathbb{R}$, and $\widehat{\mathbb{A}}$ is the set of real roots of non-zero polynomials over $\mathbb{A}$.

Note that if $\alpha : \mathbb{N} \to \mathbb{R}$ is a constructivization of $\mathbb{A}$ then $(\mathbb{A}, \alpha)$ is computably Archimedean, i.e. $\alpha(n) \leq f(n)$ for some computable function f. The PR-version of the last fact, probably, does not hold in general. Our proof below works only for *PR-Archimedean fields* which we define as the PR ordered subfields $(\mathbb{A}, \alpha)$ of $\mathbb{R}$ such that $\alpha(n) \leq f(n)$, for some PR function f.

Given α, we define $\widehat{\alpha}$ by essentially the same construction as in [17]. Let $P(i, k)$ mean that either α_i^* is the zero polynomial (i.e., all coefficients of α_i^* are zero) or α_i^* has at most k real roots. Then $\widehat{\alpha}(\langle i, k \rangle)$ is defined as follows: if $P(i, k)$ then $\widehat{\alpha}(\langle i, k \rangle) = 0$, otherwise $\widehat{\alpha}(\langle i, k \rangle)$ is the $(k+1)$-st (w.r.t. $<$) real root b of α_i^* (i.e., $\alpha_i^*(b) = 0$ and there are precisely k real roots of α_i^* strictly below b). We are ready to prove the PR Ershov-Madison theorem.

Theorem 3. *If* $(\mathbb{A}, \alpha)$ *is a PR-Archimedean subfield of* $\mathbb{R}$ *then so is also* $(\widehat{\mathbb{A}}, \widehat{\alpha})$.

Theorem follows from facts 1—7 below. Most of them just show that some standard algebraic functions are PR. The proofs are close to the corresponding proofs in [1, 16] which show that $\mathbb{R}_{\text{alg}}$ is PTIME-presentable.

1. There is a PR function f such that all real roots of any non-zero polynomial $\alpha_i^* \in \mathbb{A}[x]$ are in the interval $(-f(i), f(i))$. In particular, $\widehat{\alpha}(\langle i, k \rangle) < f(i)$ for all i, k (so $(\widehat{\mathbb{A}}, \widehat{\alpha})$ is PR-Archimedean provided that it is a PR ordered field).

Proof. By the notation in Sect. 2, $\alpha_i^* = \alpha(i_0)x^0 + \ldots + \alpha(i_n)x^n$. Since α_i^* is non-zero, we have $\alpha(i_m) \neq 0$ where m is the degree of α_i^*. As is well known, all real roots of α_i^* are in $(-M_i; M_i)$ where $M_i = 1 + a|\alpha(i_m)^{-1}| \in A$ and $a = max\{|\alpha(i_j)| : j < m\}$. Since $(\mathbb{A}, \alpha)$ is PR-Archimedean, there is a PR-function f with $M_i \leq f(i)$. The second assertion follows from the definition of $\widehat{\alpha}(\langle i, k \rangle)$. □

2. Given a polynomial $p \in \mathbb{A}[x]$ of degree > 1, one can primitive recursively find the Sturm sequence of polynomials $\text{sseq}(p) = (p_0, p_1, \ldots, p_m)$ in $\mathbb{A}[x]$ with the following property: the number of real roots of p in any interval $(a, b]$ equals $v(a) - v(b)$ where $v(c)$, for $c \in \mathbb{R}$, is the sign alternation number in the sequence $(p_0(c), p_1(c), \ldots, p_m(c))$.

Proof. By the definition of sseq, $p_0 = p$, $p_1 = p'$ is the derivative of p, and for $j > 1$, p_j is the negative remainder after dividing p_{j-1} by p_{j-2} (thus, $\text{sseq}(p)$ is a small variation of the sequence from the Euclidean algorithm for p, p'). By the remarks in Sect. 2, $\text{sseq}(p)$ can be found primitive recursively. □

3. Given a non-zero polynomial $p \in \mathbb{A}[x]$ and $a, b \in \mathbb{Q}$, one can primitive recursively find the number of real roots of p in the interval $(a, b]$, as well as the number of all real roots of p.

Proof. Follows from facts 1 and 2. □

4. Given a non-zero polynomial $p \in \mathbb{A}[x]$ with at least two distinct (complex) roots, one can primitive recursively find a positive rational number $\delta_p < \Delta_p$ where Δ_p is the smallest distance between distinct roots of p.

Proof. Without loss of generality we can think that p has no multiple roots (otherwise, we can take $p/\gcd(p, p')$ instead of p). By Mahler's theorem (see corollary of Theorem 2 in [18]),

$$\Delta_p > \sqrt{3}m^{-\frac{m+2}{2}}|D(p)|^{\frac{1}{2}}L(p)^{-(m-1)}$$
$$> m^{-(m+2)}|D(p)|^{\frac{1}{2}}L(p)^{-(m-1)}$$

where $D(p)$ is the discriminant of p, and $L(p) = |\alpha(i_0)| + \ldots + |\alpha(i_m)|$. Since $D(p) \in A$ and p has no multiple roots, $D(p) \neq 0$. Since $(\mathbb{A}, \alpha)$ is PR-Archimedean, we can find a positive rational δ_p below $m^{-(m+2)}|D(p)|^{\frac{1}{2}}L(p)^{-(m-1)}$. □

5. Given a non-zero polynomial $p \in \mathbb{A}[x]$ and a positive rational ε, one can primitive recursively find a sequence $I_1 < \cdots < I_l$ (where $l \geq 0$ is the number of real roots of p) of pairwise disjoint rational intervals of length $\leq \varepsilon$ which separate the real roots of p, i.e. every I_j contains precisely one real root of p.

Proof. Follows from the previous facts using the bisection method. □

6. Operations $+, \cdot, -, ^{-1}$ on $\widehat{A}$ are $\widehat{\alpha}$-PR.

Proof. All operations are considered similarly, so we give details only for $+$; we describe a PR function $f : \mathbb{N} \times \mathbb{N} \to \mathbb{N}$ with $\widehat{\alpha}(m) + \widehat{\alpha}(m') = \widehat{\alpha}(f(m, m'))$. Let $m = \langle i, k \rangle$ and $m' = \langle i', k' \rangle$. By the definition of $P(i, k)$, this relation is PR. If $P(i, k)$ then we set $f(m, m') = m'$. If $\neg P(i, k)$ and $P(i', k')$ then we set $f(m, m') = m$. Finally, let both $P(i, k)$ and $P(i', k')$ be false, i.e. $\widehat{\alpha}(m) = c$ is the $(k+1)$-st real root of $p = \alpha_i^*$ and $\widehat{\alpha}(m') = d$ is the $(k'+1)$-st real root of $q = \alpha_{i'}^*$. It suffices to primitive recursively find $s, t \in \mathbb{N}$ such that $\neg P(s, t)$ and $c+d$ is the $(t+1)$-st real root of $r = \alpha_s^* \in \mathbb{A}[x]$ (then we can set $f(m, m') = \langle s, t \rangle$).

By (the proof of) Theorem 6 in [16], one can primitive recursively find a (resultant) polynomial r which has $c + d$ as a root, so we can find s with $r = \alpha_s^*$. For any rational intervals $(a, b) \ni c$ and $(a', b') \ni d$, the interval $I = (a + a', b + b')$ contains $c + d$, and its length may be made arbitrarily small. Using fact 5, we can primitive recursively find a sequence $I_1 < \cdots < I_l$ of rational intervals which separate all real roots of r such that I intersects precisely one interval $I_t, t \leq l$, of this sequence. Then $c + d \in I_t$, hence it remains to set $f(m, m') = \langle s, t \rangle$. □

7. The relation $\leq$ on $\widehat{A}$ is $\widehat{\alpha}$-PR.

Proof. By fact 6, it suffices to show that the relation $0 \leq \widehat{\alpha}(m)$ is PR. Let again $m = \langle i, k \rangle$. By the definition of $\widehat{\alpha}(m)$ we have: $0 \leq \widehat{\alpha}(m)$ iff either $P(i, k)$ or $(\neg P(i, k)$ and the $(k + 1)$-st real root of α_i^* is non-negative).

Consider the case when $P(i, k)$ is false. By fact 5, we can primitive recursively find a sequence $I_1 < \cdots < I_l$ (where $l > k$ is the number of real roots of α_i^*) of pairwise disjoint rational intervals of length $\leq \varepsilon$ such that every I_j contains precisely one real root of α_i^*. Then $\widehat{\alpha}(m) \in I_{k+1}$. Assume first that $\alpha_i^*(0) = 0$ (i.e., $\alpha(i_0) = 0$). Then $0 \in I_j$ for a unique $j \leq l$, hence $0 \leq \widehat{\alpha}(m)$ iff $j \leq k + 1$.

In the case $\alpha_i^*(0) \neq 0$, we consider the polynomial $q = x\alpha_i^* \in A[x]$ which satisfies $q(0) = 0$. Computing the sequence $I_1 < \cdots < I_l$ for polynomial q in place of α_i^* and applying the argument of the previous paragraph we see that $0 \leq \widehat{\alpha}(m)$ iff $j < k + 1$. Altogether, these arguments and the primitive recursiveness of relation $P(i, k)$ complete the proof. □

By a classical theorem of Steinitz, for any field $\mathbb{A}$ there exists its algebraic closure $\overline{\mathbb{A}} \supseteq \mathbb{A}$. M. Rabin [22] proved a computable version of the Steinitz theorem: if $\mathbb{A}$ is constructivizable then so is also $\overline{\mathbb{A}}$. Though we do not yet know a complete PR-analogue of Rabin's theorem, we can deduce a partial one from Theorem 3. Recall (see e.g. Chapters 10, 11 of [26]) that a real closed field $\mathbb{B}$ is never algebraically closed but its algebraic closure $\overline{\mathbb{B}}$ is constructed very easily, by adjoining a root of $x^2 + 1$. Thus, $\overline{\mathbb{B}}$ is isomorphic to $\mathbb{B} \times \mathbb{B}$ where the arithmetic on pairs is similar to that of the field $\mathbb{C}$ of complex numbers. If $(\mathbb{A}, \alpha)$ is a constructive ordered subfield of $\mathbb{R}$, let $\bar{\alpha}$ be the induced numbering of $\overline{\mathbb{A}}$ (considered as a subfield of $\mathbb{C}$), i.e. $\bar{\alpha}\langle n_1, n_2 \rangle = (\widehat{\alpha}(n_1), \widehat{\alpha}(n_2))$. The following is an immediate corollary of Theorem 3.

Corollary 4. *If $(\mathbb{A}, \alpha)$ is a PR-Archimedean ordered subfield of $\mathbb{R}$ then $(\overline{\mathbb{A}}, \overline{\alpha})$ is a PR subfield of $\mathbb{C}$.*

We say that a computable field $(\mathbb{B}, \beta)$ *has computable root-finding* (cf. [8]) if, given a polynomial $p \in \mathbb{B}[x]$ of degree > 1, one can compute a (possibly, empty) list of all roots of p in $\mathbb{B}$, and also the length of the list (i.e., the number pf roots). Theorem 4.43 in [8] implies that if $\mathbb{B}$ is of characteristic 0 then $(\mathbb{B}, \beta)$ has computable root-finding iff it has computable splitting (i.e., given $p \in \mathbb{B}[x]$, one can compute a decomposition of p to polynomials irreducible in $\mathbb{B}[x]$). As usual, the notion of PR root-finding is obtained by changing "computable" to "PR" in the definition above. The proof of Theorem 4.43 in [8] works for the PR-version, so we have the following.

Proposition 5. *Let $(\mathbb{B}, \beta)$ be a PR field of characteristic 0. Then $(\mathbb{B}, \beta)$ has PR root-finding iff it has PR splitting.*

Every computable algebraically closed field has computable root-finding, but the proof makes use of the unbounded search. The next theorem shows that the PR-version of this holds at least for some fields considered above. To shorten formulations, we denote by $\mathrm{pra}(\mathbb{R})$ (resp. $\mathrm{pras}(\mathbb{R})$) the set of all $\alpha : \mathbb{N} \to \mathbb{R}$ such that $(\mathbb{A}, \alpha)$, $A = rng(\alpha)$, is a PR-Archimedean ordered subfield of $\mathbb{R}$ (resp., a PR-Archimedean ordered subfield with PR splitting). We always denote by $\mathbb{A}, \widehat{\mathbb{A}}, \overline{\mathbb{A}}$ the (ordered) fields associated with $\alpha, \widehat{\alpha}, \overline{\alpha}$, resp.

Theorem 6. *If $\alpha \in \mathrm{pras}(\mathbb{R})$ then both $(\widehat{\mathbb{A}}, \widehat{\alpha})$ and $(\overline{\mathbb{A}}, \overline{\alpha})$ have PR root-finding.*

Under the assumption $\alpha \in \mathrm{pras}(\mathbb{R})$ we first establish some auxiliary facts.

1. Given a polynomial $p \in \mathbb{A}[x_0, \ldots, x_k]$ and irreducible $p_0, \ldots, p_k \in \mathbb{A}[x]$ of positive degrees, one can primitive recursively find $q \in \mathbb{A}[x]$ of positive degree such that, for all complex roots b_i of p_i, $i \leq k$, $p(b_0, \ldots, b_k)$ is a root of q.

Proof Sketch. Let $r^+, r^{\cdot}$ be binary operators on $\mathbb{A}[x]$ such that all sums (resp. products) of complex roots of p, q are among the roots of $r^+(p, q)$ (resp. $r^{\cdot}(p, q)$). By the proof of Theorem 6 in [16], operators $r^+, r^{\cdot}$ are given by explicit formulas (based on resultants) which show they are α^*-PR. We associate with any term $t = t(x_0, \ldots, x_k)$ of signature $\{+, \cdot, c_0, c_1, \ldots\}$ the polynomial $q_t \in \mathbb{A}[x]$ as follows: $q_{c_n} = x - \alpha(n)$, $q_{x_i} = p_i$, $q_{t_1+t_2} = r^+(q_{t_1}, q_{t_2})$, $q_{t_1 \cdot t_2} = r^{\cdot}(q_{t_1}, q_{t_2})$. By induction on t one easily checks that, for all complex roots b_i of p_i, $i \leq k$, $t^{\mathbb{A}}(b_0, \ldots, b_k)$ is a root of q_t. Then, given $p \in \mathbb{A}[x_0, \ldots, x_k]$ one can primitive recursively find a σ-term $t = t(x_0, \ldots, x_k)$ such that $p(b_0, \ldots, b_k) = t^{\mathbb{A}}(b_0, \ldots, b_k)$ for all $b_0, \ldots, b_k \in A$. Thus, we can take $q = q_t$. □

2. Given a non-zero polynomial $r \in \mathbb{A}[x]$, one can primitive recursively find $q_1, q_2 \in \mathbb{A}[x]$ such that, for any complex root $b = (b_1, b_2)$ of r, the real part b_1 is a root of q_1 and the imaginary part b_2 is a root of q_2.

Proof. Let $q_1 = q$ be the polynomial obtained from the algorithm of fact 1 for $p(x_0, x_1) = \frac{1}{2}(x_0 + x_1)$ and $p_0 = p_1 = r$. For any complex root $b = (b_1, b_2)$ of r we then have: $p(b, \bar{b}) = b_1$, b is a root of p_0, and $\bar{b}$ is a root of p_1 where $\bar{b} = (b_1, -b_2) = b_1 - ib_2$ is the complex conjugate of b and i is the imaginary unit. Thus, q_1 has the desired property.

Let now $q = a_0 + a_1 x + a_2 x^2 + \cdots$ be the polynomial obtained from the algorithm of fact 1 for $p(x_0, x_1) = \frac{1}{2}(x_0 - x_1)$ and $p_0 = p_1 = r$. For any complex root $b = (b_1, b_2)$ of r we then have: $p(b, \bar{b}) = ib_2$, b is a root of p_0, and $\bar{b}$ is a root of p_1. Thus, $q(ib_2) = 0$, hence also $q(-ib_2) = 0$. Summing up the last two equalities we see that $q_2(b_2) = 0$ where $q_2 = a_0 + a_2 x^2 + \cdots$. Thus, q_2 has the desired property. □

3. Given polynomials $p = b_0 x^0 + \cdots + b_n x^n \in \overline{\mathbb{A}}[x]$ and $q_0, \ldots, q_n \in \mathbb{A}[x]$ such that $q_i(b_i) = 0$ for each $i \leq n$, one can primitive recursively find $r \in \mathbb{A}[x]$ such that all complex roots of p are among the roots of r.

Proof. The proof is essentially the same as in the Algorithm 3 of [16], hence we give only a sketch. Since $(\mathbb{A}, \alpha)$ has PR splitting, we may without loss of generality think that $q_0, \ldots, q_n$ are irreducible. By the PR-version of the primitive element theorem ([26], Sect. 46), we may primitive recursively find $b \in \overline{\mathbb{A}}$ and irreducible $t, p_0, \ldots, p_n \in \mathbb{A}[y]$ such that $\mathbb{A}(b) = \mathbb{A}(b_0, \ldots, b_n)$ $t(b) = 0$, and $p_i(b) = b_i$ for all $i \leq n$. Let $s = \gcd(t, p_n)$. Without loss of generality, $\deg(s) = 0$ (otherwise, replace t by t/s). Then the resultant $r = \operatorname{res}(t, q)$, where $q = p_0 x^0 + \cdots + p_n x^n \in \mathbb{A}[y][x]$, has the desired properties. □

Proof of Theorem 6. Given $p \in \overline{\mathbb{A}}[x]$, we have to primitive recursively find all complex roots of p. By fact 3 we can find $r \in \mathbb{A}[x]$ such that all complex roots of p are among the roots of r. By fact 2, we can find $q_1, q_2 \in \mathbb{A}[x]$ such that, for any complex root $b = (b_1, b_2)$ of r, the real part b_1 is a root of q_1 and the imaginary part b_2 is a root of q_2. By the definition of $\overline{\alpha}$, we can find the lists $b_{1,0} < \cdots < b_{1,m}$ and $b_{2,0} < \cdots < b_{2,n}$ of all real roots of q_1 and q_2, respectively. Then all complex roots of p are among $(b_{1,i}, b_{2,j})$ where $i \leq m, j \leq n$. Substituting these numbers one by one in p, we primitive recursively find all complex roots of p.

It remains to show that $(\widehat{\mathbb{A}}, \widehat{\alpha})$ has PR root-finding. Let $p \in \widehat{\mathbb{A}}[x]$; we have to find a list of all real roots of p. Since $\widehat{\alpha} \leq_{PR} \overline{\alpha}$, we have $\widehat{\alpha}^* \leq_{PR} \overline{\alpha}^*$. By the previous paragraph, we can compute the list of all complex roots of p. Choosing the real numbers from this list, we obtain a list of all real roots of p. □

4 PR-Archimedean Fields vs. PR Reals

Here we search for a PR-analogue of the following fact from [23]: for any finite set $F \subseteq \mathbb{R}_c$ there is a computable real closed ordered subfield $(\mathbb{B}, \beta)$ of $\mathbb{R}_c$ such that

$F \subseteq B$ (see also a more general Theorem 4.1 in [21] obtained independently). This implies that $\mathbb{R}_c = \bigcup\{A \mid \alpha \in , (\mathbb{R})\} = \bigcup\{A \mid \alpha \in \mathrm{cs}(\mathbb{R})\}$ where $\mathbb{R}_c$ is the set of computable reals, and $, (\mathbb{R}), \mathrm{cs}(\mathbb{R})$ are the computable analogues of $\mathrm{pra}(\mathbb{R}), \mathrm{pras}(\mathbb{R})$. The PR-analogue of $\mathbb{R}_c$ is the ordered field $\mathbb{R}_p$ of PR reals (see e.g. Section 4 of [5] and references therein, we sometimes use slightly different notation; also recall that equality in $\mathbb{R}_c$ is not computable [27]). Recall that a real number a is PR if $a = \lim_n q_n$ for a PR sequence $\{q_n\}$ of rational numbers which is fast Cauchy, i.e. $|q_n - q_{n+1}| < 2^{-n}$ for all n. There is a natural numbering π of $\mathbb{R}_p$ which is a computable sequence of computable reals such that $+, \cdot, -$ are π-PR.

For any $\alpha \in \mathrm{pra}(\mathbb{R})$, let $\mathbb{R}_p(\alpha)$ be the set of PR reals b such that the sign of polynomials in $\mathbb{A}[x]$ at b is checked primitive recursively. Formally, for any real b, let $\mathrm{sign}(b)$ be $0, 1, 2$ depending on whether b is zero, positive, or negative. Then $\mathbb{R}_p(\alpha)$ is the set of all $b \in \mathbb{R}_p$ such that the function $i \mapsto \mathrm{sign}(\alpha_i^*(b))$ is PR. More generally, for any $n \geq 0$, let $\mathbb{R}_p^{[n]}(\alpha)$ be the set of strings $\bar{b} = (b_0, \ldots, b_n)$ of PR reals such that the function $i \mapsto \mathrm{sign}(\alpha_i^{[n]}(b_0, \ldots, b_n))$ is PR where $\alpha^{[n]}$ is the numbering of $\mathbb{A}[x_0, \ldots, x_n]$ from Sect. 2. Note that $\mathbb{R}_p(\alpha) = \mathbb{R}_p^{[0]}(\alpha)$.

Proposition 7. *1. If $\alpha, \beta \in \mathrm{pra}(\mathbb{R})$ and $\alpha \leq_{PR} \beta$ then $\mathbb{R}_p(\beta)^{[n]} \subseteq \mathbb{R}_p(\alpha)^{[n]}$.*
2. For all $\alpha \in \mathrm{pra}(\mathbb{R})$ and n we have: $\mathbb{R}_p(\alpha)^{[n]} \subseteq \mathbb{R}_p(\varkappa)^{[n]}$.
3. For any $\alpha \in \mathrm{pra}(\mathbb{R})$ we have $\alpha \leq_{PR} \pi$, hence $rng(\alpha) \subseteq \mathbb{R}_p(\alpha)$.

Proof. 1. Let $\bar{b} \in \mathbb{R}_p(\beta)$, so $i \mapsto \mathrm{sign}(\beta_i^*(\bar{b}))$ is PR. Since $\alpha \leq_{PR} \beta$, we have $\alpha^{[n]} \leq_{PR} \beta^{[n]}$, so $\alpha_i^{[n]} = \beta_{f(i)}^{[n]}$ for some PR function f. Then $\mathrm{sign}(\alpha_i^{[n]}(\bar{b})) = \mathrm{sign}(\beta_{f(i)}^{[n]}(\bar{b}))$, hence $i \mapsto \mathrm{sign}(\alpha_i^{[n]}(\bar{b}))$ is PR.

2. The assertion follows from item 1 because, clearly, $\varkappa \leq_{PR} \alpha$.

3. Since $(\mathbb{A}, \alpha)$ is PR-Archimedean, $-f(n) < \alpha(n) < f(n)$ for some PR function f. Using bisection method, we construct a uniformly PR sequence $\{g_n\}$ of PR functions $g_n : \mathbb{N} \to \mathbb{Q}$ such that $\{g_n(i)\}_i$ is a fast Cauchy sequence converging to $\alpha(n)$. By the definition of π, $\alpha \leq_{PR} \pi$ and $rng(\alpha) \subseteq \mathbb{R}_p(\alpha)$.   □

By items 2 and 3 above, $\alpha \in \mathrm{pra}(\mathbb{R})$ implies $rng(\alpha) \subseteq \mathbb{R}_p(\varkappa)$, hence all PR ordered fields of reals are contained in $\mathbb{R}_p(\varkappa)$. The next proposition shows which elements of $\mathbb{R}_p(\varkappa)$ can be included into some PR ordered field of reals.

Proposition 8. *Let $\alpha \in \mathrm{pras}(\mathbb{R})$ and $\bar{b} \in \mathbb{R}_p^n$. Then $\bar{b} \in \mathbb{R}_p^{[n]}(\alpha)$ iff there exists $\beta \in \mathrm{pras}(\mathbb{R})$ such that $\alpha \leq_{PR} \beta$ and $b_0, \ldots, b_n \in B$.*

Proof. If $\beta \in \mathrm{pras}(\mathbb{R})$, $\alpha \leq_{PR} \beta$, and $b_0, \ldots, b_n \in B = rng(\beta)$, then $i \mapsto \mathrm{sign}(\alpha_i^{[n]}(\bar{b}))$ is PR, hence $\bar{b} \in \mathbb{R}_p^{[n]}(\alpha)$. Conversely, let $\bar{b} \in \mathbb{R}_p^{[n]}(\alpha)$. First we consider the case when $b_0, \ldots, b_n$ are algebraically independent over $\mathbb{A}$, hence $\mathrm{sign}(\alpha_i^{[n]}(\bar{b})) \in \{1, 2\}$ for every i with $\alpha_i^{[n]} \neq 0$. Then $\mathbb{A}(b_0, \ldots, b_n)$ with the induced numbering γ is a PR field because it is isomorphic to the field $\mathbb{A}(x_0, \ldots, x_n)$ of rational functions. The elements of $\mathbb{A}(b_0, \ldots, b_n)$ have the form $p(\bar{b})/q(\bar{b})$ for some $p, q \in \mathbb{A}[x_0, \ldots, x_n]$, $q \neq 0$. Since $p(\bar{b})/q(\bar{b}) > 0$ iff both

$p(\bar{b}), q(\bar{b})$ are positive or both $p(\bar{b}), q(\bar{b})$ are negative, γ is a PR constructivization of $\mathbb{A}(b_0, \ldots, b_n)$. Then $\gamma \in \mathrm{pras}(\mathbb{R})$, hence we can take $\beta = \gamma$.

Now let $\bar{b} \in \mathbb{R}_p^n$ be arbitrary. Without loss of generality (after suitable renum-
bering of $b_0, \ldots, b_n$ if necessary), let $j \leq n$ be the unique number such that
$b_0, \ldots, b_{j-1}$ are algebraically independent over $\mathbb{A}$ while $b_j, \ldots, b_n$ are algebraic
over $\mathbb{A}(b_0, \ldots, b_{j-1})$. Let γ be defined as in the previous paragraph for $j > 0$
(with n replaced by $j - 1$) and $\gamma = \alpha$ for $j = 0$. By the previous paragraph, we
can take $\beta = \hat{\gamma}$.   □

How rich are the collections $\mathrm{pra}(\mathbb{R})$ and $\mathrm{pras}(\mathbb{R})$? By the PR-version of a
well-known fact, $\varkappa \in \mathrm{pras}(\mathbb{R})$. The class $\mathrm{pras}(\mathbb{R})$ is closed under $\alpha \mapsto \hat{\alpha}$, hence
$\hat{\varkappa} \in \mathrm{pras}(\mathbb{R})$, in particular $\mathbb{R}_{\mathrm{alg}} \subseteq \mathbb{R}_{\mathrm{p}}(\varkappa)$. Proposition 8 provides conditions
under which finite sets of reals may be included into some PR ordered subfield
of $\mathbb{R}$. We show that many transcendental reals satisfy these conditions.

Theorem 9. *1. For any $\alpha \in \mathrm{pras}(\mathbb{R})$ and any non-empty rational interval I
    there exists $b \in I \cap \mathbb{R}_{\mathrm{p}}(\alpha)$ which is transcendental over $\mathbb{A}$.*
*2. For any $\alpha \in \mathrm{pras}(\mathbb{R})$ there exists a uniformly PR infinite sequence $b_0, b_1, \ldots$
    of reals which are algebraically independent over $\mathbb{A}$ and satisfy $\bar{b} \in \mathbb{R}_{\mathrm{p}}^{[n]}(\alpha)$ for
    every n.*

Proof. 1. We define by induction PR sequences $\{q_j\}$ of rational numbers and
$\{I_j\}$ of rational open intervals such that $q_0 \in I_0 = I$ and, for every j, $I_j \supseteq [I_{j+1}]$
where $[I_{j+1}]$ is the closure of I_{j+1}, and $q_{j+1} \in I_{j+1} \subseteq (q_j - 2^{-j}, q_j + 2^{-j})$.
Then we set $b = \lim_j q_j$ which automatically guarantees that $\{q_j\}$ is fast Cauchy
and hence $b \in \mathbb{R}_{\mathrm{p}}$. The remaining properties of b are obtained by taking some
additional care.

Let $I_0 = I$ and q_0 be any rational number in I_0. Assume by induction that
we already have defined q_j, I_j for $j \leq n$ which satisfy the properties above
for $j < n$. Then we define q_{n+1}, I_{n+1} as follows. If the polynomial α_n^* is zero
or has no real roots, choose q_{n+1}, I_{n+1} arbitrarily such that $I_n \supseteq [I_{n+1}]$ and
$q_{n+1} \in I_{n+1} \subseteq (q_n - 2^{-n}, q_n + 2^{-n})$. Otherwise, use fact 5 in the proof of
Theorem 3 to primitive recursively find a non-empty rational open interval J
such that $[J] \subseteq I_n$ and $[J]$ contains no real root of α_n^*; then α_n^* is either positive
on $[J]$ or negative on $[J]$, and this alternative is checked primitive recursively.
Now choose q_{n+1}, I_{n+1} as above but with the additional property $I_{n+1} \subseteq J$.
Then the sequences $\{q_j\}, \{I_j\}$ are PR and satisfy the properties specified in the
previous paragraph.

Note that $b \in I_n$ for all n, and if α_n^* is non-zero then it is either positive or
negative on $I_{n+1} \ni b$, hence $\alpha_n^*(b) \neq 0$; therefore, b is transcendental over $\mathbb{A}$. If α_n^*
is zero then $\mathrm{sign}(\alpha_n^*(b)) = 0$, otherwise $\mathrm{sign}(\alpha_n^*(b)) = 1, 2$ depending on whether
α_n^* is positive on $[J]$ or is negative on $[J]$. Therefore, the function $n \mapsto \mathrm{sign}(\alpha_n^*(b))$
is PR and hence $b \in \mathbb{R}_{\mathrm{p}}(\alpha)$.

2. Note that the construction $\alpha \mapsto b$ in item 1 is PR in the sense that,
given an index for $\alpha \in \mathrm{pras}(\mathbb{R})$ (i.e., a code of tuple of indices for PR functions
representing the equality and the signature symbols, and also of the splitting
function), one can primitive recursively find a π-index for b and a PR-index of
the function $n \mapsto \mathrm{sign}(\alpha_n^*(b))$.

Let $b_0 = b$. Since the construction in Proposition 8 is PR, we can primitive recursively find an index of $\beta \in \mathrm{pras}(\mathbb{R})$ with $rng(\beta) = \mathbb{A}(b)$. Since the construction in Theorem 3 is PR, we can primitive recursively find an index of $\widehat{\beta} \in \mathrm{pras}(\mathbb{R})$ with $rng(\widehat{\beta}) = \widehat{\mathbb{A}(b)}$.

Taking $\widehat{\beta}$ in place of α, we primitive recursively find an index of some b_1 transcendental over $\widehat{\mathbb{A}(b_0)}$. It is easy to check that b_0, b_1 are algebraically independent over $\mathbb{A}$ and $(b_0, b_1) \in \mathbb{R}_{\mathrm{p}}^{[2]}(\widehat{\beta})$. Iterating this process indefinitely, we obtain a desired sequence $b_0, b_1, \dots$. □

The previous proposition implies that the algebraic closures of $\mathbb{Q}(x_0, \dots, x_n)$ and of $\mathbb{Q}(x_0, x_1, \dots)$ are PR-constructivizable. It also shows that the collection $\mathrm{pras}(\mathbb{R})$ is rather rich. In particular, for $n = 0$ it together with Proposition 8 implies the following.

Corollary 10. *We have $\mathbb{R}_{\mathrm{p}}(\varkappa) = \bigcup\{A \mid \alpha \in \mathrm{pra}(\mathbb{R})\} = \bigcup\{A \mid \alpha \in \mathrm{pras}(\mathbb{R})\}$.*

This corollary is a partial PR-analogue of some facts mentioned in the beginning of this section. The full analogue does not hold because $\mathbb{R}_{\mathrm{p}}(\varkappa)$ is contained in the set $\mathbb{R}_4$ of reals with PR continuous fraction representation, and the inclusion $\mathbb{R}_4 \subseteq \mathbb{R}_{\mathrm{p}}$ is strict [5]. We guess that the inclusion $\mathbb{R}_{\mathrm{p}}(\varkappa) \subseteq \mathbb{R}_4$ is also strict. Thus, in contrast with the general computability, it is harder to determine which PR reals may be included into PR ordered fields of reals.

An important problem is to determine, given concrete PR reals $\bar{b} \in \mathbb{R}_{\mathrm{p}}^n$, whether the function $i \mapsto \mathrm{sign}(\alpha_i^{[n]}(\bar{b}))$ is PR. In general the problem looks very difficult and related to the theory of transcendental numbers. For some concrete numbers it might be shown that they are in $\mathbb{R}_{\mathrm{p}}(\varkappa)$. For instance, this is the case for the Euler number e and for the circle number π. Indeed, in the appendix to [10] it is proved that both e and π are PR-transcendental. From the definition of PR-transcendental number in [10] it follows that every such number is in $\mathbb{R}_{\mathrm{p}}(\varkappa)$. By Proposition 8, both $\mathbb{Q}(e)$ and $\mathbb{Q}(\pi)$ are PRAS-fields. By Theorem 3, so are also $\widehat{\mathbb{Q}(e)}$ and $\widehat{\mathbb{Q}(\pi)}$.

5   Applications to Spectral Problems and PDEs

Here we propose definitions of PR functions on the reals and some functional spaces which are used to investigate PR-versions of results in [23,24] on computabilty and complexity of solution operators for some PDEs. Since this is related to linear algebra, we start with PR-versions of some results in this field.

As is well known, the eigenvalues of symmetric real matrices are real. *Spectral decomposition* of such a matrix $A \in M_n(\mathbb{R})$ is a pair $((\lambda_1, \dots, \lambda_n), (\mathbf{v}_1, \dots, \mathbf{v}_n))$ where $\lambda_1 \leq \cdots \leq \lambda_n$ is the non-decreasing sequence of eigenvalues of A and $\mathbf{v}_1, \dots, \mathbf{v}_n$ is a corresponding orthonormal basis of eigenvectors, i.e. $A\mathbf{v}_i = \lambda_i \mathbf{v}_i$ for $i = 1, \dots, n$. A *matrix pencil* is a pair (A, B) of real non-degenerate symmetric matrices such that A is positive definite. *Spectral decomposition* of such a pencil is a tuple

$$((\lambda_1, \dots, \lambda_n), (\mathbf{v}_1, \dots, \mathbf{v}_n), (\mu_1, \dots, \mu_n), (\mathbf{w}_1, \dots, \mathbf{w}_n))$$

such that $((\lambda_1,\ldots,\lambda_n),(\mathbf{v}_1,\ldots,\mathbf{v}_n))$ and $((\mu_1,\ldots,\mu_n),(\mathbf{w}_1,\ldots,\mathbf{w}_n))$ are spectral decompositions of the symmetric matrices A and D^*L^*BLD respectively, where L is the matrix formed by vectors $\mathbf{v}_1,\ldots,\mathbf{v}_n$ written as columns, L^* is the transposition of L, and $D = \mathrm{diag}\{\frac{1}{\sqrt{\lambda_1}},\frac{1}{\sqrt{\lambda_2}},\ldots,\frac{1}{\sqrt{\lambda_n}}\}$. The next proposition follows easily from Theorem 6 and corresponding results in [23,24]. In all formulations of this section α is a fixed element of $\mathrm{pras}(\mathbb{R})$ and $\widehat{\mathbb{A}}$ is the real closure of $\mathbb{A}$.

Proposition 11. *Given n, a symmetric matrix $A \in M_n(\widehat{\mathbb{A}})$, and a matrix pencil (A,B) with $A,B \in M_n(\widehat{\mathbb{A}})$, one can primitive recursively find spectral decompositions of A and (A,B) uniformly in n.*

A central notion of computable analysis [27] is that of a computable function over the reals going back to A. Turing; we sketch a PR-version.

First we recall a nice characterization of unary PR functions due to R. Robinson (see e.g. Section 3.5 in [20]). Consider the structure $(\mathcal{N}; +, \circ, J, \mathbf{s}, \mathbf{q})$ where $\mathcal{N} = \mathbb{N}^{\mathbb{N}}$ is the set of unary functions on $\mathbb{N}$, $+$ and $\circ$ are binary operations on $\mathcal{N}$ defined by $(p+q)(n) = p(n) + q(n)$ and $(p \circ q)(n) = p(q(n))$, J is a unary operation on $\mathcal{N}$ defined by $J(p)(n) = p^n(0)$ where $p^0 = id_{\mathbb{N}}$ and $p^{n+1} = p \circ p^n$, $\mathbf{s}$ and $\mathbf{q}$ are distinguished elements defined by $\mathbf{s}(n) = n+1$ and $\mathbf{q}(n) = n - [\sqrt{n}]^2$ where, for $x \in \mathbb{R}$, $[x]$ is the unique integer m with $m \le x < m+1$. For any $n \ge 0$, any term $t = t(v_1,\ldots,v_n)$ of signature τ with variables among a fixed list $v_1,\ldots,v_n$ of pairwise distinct variables determines the n-ary operator $\mathbf{t}$ on $\mathcal{N}$ by setting $\mathbf{t}(g_1,\ldots,g_n)$ to be the value of t for $v_i = g_i$.

The Gödel numbering $\{t_e^{(n)}\}$ of all such terms $t(v_1,\ldots,v_n)$ induces the numbering $\{\mathbf{t}_e^{(n)}\}$ of n-ary PR operators on $\mathcal{N}$. Similar to the ideas of [27], we can use a suitable surjection $\gamma : \mathcal{N} \to \mathbb{R}$ to transfer primitive recursiveness on $\mathcal{N}$ to that on $\mathbb{R}$ (and, may be, to more complicated spaces). Namely, we define $\gamma(q) = \lim_n \varkappa(\tilde{q}(n))$ and call this γ the *Cauchy representation* of $\mathbb{R}$. Now, a function $f : \mathbb{R}^{n+1} \to \mathbb{R}$ is called PR if $f(\gamma(p_0),\ldots,\gamma(p_n)) = \gamma(g(p_0,\ldots,p_n))$ for some PR function $g : \mathcal{N}^{n+1} \to \mathcal{N}$. This definition is adapted to partial functions f in the obvious way. Clearly, the PR functions on the reals are computable, and in fact they form a very restricted subclass of the computable functions. Nevertheless, many practically important functions are PR, in particular the functions $+,\cdot,-$ on $\mathbb{R}$ and $\mathbb{C}$ are PR.

Using the notions above, we can define PR metric spaces and PR-computability of functions between such spaces using standard Cauchy representations (the only difference with the classical definition in [27] is that now the distance between points in the specified dense set is uniformly PR). Below we use functional spaces which are subsets of the set $C(\mathbb{R}^m,\mathbb{R}^n) \simeq C(\mathbb{R}^m,\mathbb{R})^n$ of integrable continuous functions $\varphi : \mathbb{R}^m \to \mathbb{R}^n$ equipped with the L_2-norm. In particular, we deal with the space $C(Q,\mathbb{R}^n) \simeq C(Q,\mathbb{R})^n$ (resp. $C^k(Q,\mathbb{R}^n)$) of continuous (resp. k-time continuously differentiable) functions $\varphi : Q \to \mathbb{R}^n$ equipped with the L_2-norm. We also use the sup-norm and the sL_2-norm on $C(Q \times [0,T],\mathbb{R}^n)$ where $T > 0$. Whenever we want to emphasize the norm we use notation like $C_{L_2}(Q,\mathbb{R}^n)$, $C_s(Q,\mathbb{R}^n)$ or $C_{sL_2}(Q \times [0,T],\mathbb{R}^n)$. Discrete versions of these norms are used on grid functions. All the corresponding computable metric spaces are PR. Multilinear interpolations of rational grid functions will play the role of approximations to the solutions of Cauchy problem. We refer to [23, 24] for additional information on the Godunov difference scheme mentioned below.

We apply the introduced notions to investigate when the solution operators for symmetric hyperbolic systems of PDEs are PR. For simplicity we discuss here only the Cauchy initial value problem (the boundary value problems are considered similarly) stated as follows:

$$
\begin{cases}
A\frac{\partial \mathbf{u}}{\partial t} + \sum_{i=1}^{m} B_i \frac{\partial \mathbf{u}}{\partial x_i} = f(t, x_1, \ldots, x_m), \ t \geq 0, \\
\mathbf{u}|_{t=0} = \varphi(x_1, \ldots, x_m),
\end{cases}
\tag{1}
$$

where $A = A^* > 0$ and $B_i = B_i^*$ are non-degenerate symmetric $n \times n$-matrices, $t \geq 0$, $x = (x_1, \ldots, x_m) \in Q = [0, 1]^m$, $\varphi : Q \to \mathbb{R}^n$, $f : [0, +\infty) \times Q \to \mathbb{R}^n$ and $\mathbf{u} : [0, +\infty) \times Q \rightharpoonup \mathbb{R}^n$ is a partial function acting on the domain H of existence and uniqueness of the Cauchy problem (1). The set H is known to be (see e.g. [24] for references and additional information) the intersection of semi-spaces

$$
t \geq 0, \ x_i - \mu_{\max}^{(i)} t \geq 0, \ x_i - 1 - \mu_{\min}^{(i)} t \leq 0
$$
$$
(i = 1, \ldots, m)
$$

where $\mu_{\min}^{(i)}, \mu_{\max}^{(i)}$ are the minimum and maximum of the eigenvalues of $A^{-1}B_i$.

The next immediate corollary of Proposition 11 shows that we can primitive recursively compute H. Our algorithms for solving the Cauchy problem are for technical reasons presented only for the case when H satisfies the condition $\mu_{\min}^{(i)} < 0 < \mu_{\max}^{(i)}$ for all $i = 1, \ldots, m$ (which implies that H is compact); this condition often holds for natural physical systems.

Proposition 12. *Given $m, n \geq 1$ and $A, B_1 \ldots, B_m \in M_n(\widehat{\mathbb{A}})$ as in (1), one can primitive recursively (uniformly in m, n) compute $\mu_{\max}^{(1)}, \ldots, \mu_{\max}^{(m)}, \mu_{\min}^{(1)}, \ldots, \mu_{\min}^{(m)}$ and check the condition $\mu_{\min}^{(i)} < 0 < \mu_{\max}^{(i)}$ for all $i = 1, \ldots, m$. Thus, the algorithm finds the domain H satisfying the condition above, or reports on the absence of such a domain.*

We also need another immediate corollary of Proposition 11. First we compute the spectral decomposition $((\lambda_1, \ldots, \lambda_n), (\mathbf{v}_1, \ldots, \mathbf{v}_n))$ of $A \in M_n(\widehat{\mathbb{A}})$. Let $\lambda_{max}, \lambda_{min}$ be respectively the maximum and minimum of $\lambda_1, \ldots, \lambda_n$. Let L be the orthonormal matrix formed by vectors $\mathbf{v}_1, \ldots, \mathbf{v}_n$ written in columns, so $L^* A L = \Lambda = \mathrm{diag}\{\lambda_1, \lambda_2, \ldots, \lambda_n\}$, and let $D = \Lambda^{-\frac{1}{2}}$. For each $i = 1, \ldots, m$, let $((\mu_1^{(i)}, \ldots, \mu_n^{(i)}), (\mathbf{w}_1^i, \ldots, \mathbf{w}_n^i))$ be the spectral decomposition of the symmetric matrix $D^* L^* B_i L D$. Let $\mu_{max}^{(i)}, \mu_{min}^{(i)}$ be respectively the maximum and minimum of $\mu_1^{(i)}, \ldots, \mu_n^{(i)}$. Let $M_i = \mathrm{diag}\{\mu_1^{(i)}, \ldots, \mu_n^{(i)})\}$ and K_i be the orthonormal matrix formed by vectors $\mathbf{w}_1^i, \ldots, \mathbf{w}_n^i$ written in columns, so $K_i^* D^* L^* B_i L D K_i = M_i$. Let $T_i = LDK_i$ for each $i = 1, \ldots, m$.

Proposition 13. *Given $m, n \geq 1$ and $A, B_1 \ldots, B_m \in M_n(\widehat{\mathbb{A}})$ as in (1), one can primitive recursively (uniformly in m, n) compute $A^{-1}, T_i, T_i^{-1}, \lambda_{max}, \lambda_{min}, \mu_{max}^{(i)}, \mu_{min}^{(i)}, \mu_k^{(i)}$ ($i = 1, \ldots, m, k = 1, \ldots, n$) specified above.*

Now we can formulate our results about PR-computability of the solution operator for (1). The proof of the next result is a simplified version of the proof of Theorem 5.1 in [23] (formulated for $f = 0$). We start with computations in Propositions 12 and 13 and then compute with the Godunov scheme as in [23]; all computations are precise computations within $\widehat{\mathbb{A}}$, and all estimates in [23] apply.

Theorem 14. *Let $M, p \geq 2$ be integers. Then the operator $(A, B_1, \ldots, B_m, \varphi) \mapsto \mathbf{u}$ for (1) is a PR-computable function from the space $S_+ \times S^m \times C_s^{p+1}(Q, \mathbb{R}^n)$ to $C_{sL_2}^p(H, \mathbb{R}^n)$ where S and S^+ are respectively the sets of all symmetric and symmetric positively definite matrices from $M_n(\widehat{\mathbb{A}})$, $\|\frac{\partial \varphi}{\partial x_i}\|_s \leq M$, and $\|\frac{\partial^2 \varphi}{\partial x_i \partial x_j}\|_s \leq M$ for $i, j = 1, 2, \ldots, m$.*

Proof Sketch. We first make precise computations as in Propositions 12 and 13 and then compute with the Godunov scheme as in [24]; all computations are precise within the field $\widehat{\mathbb{A}}$ and all the estimates in the proof of Theorem 5.2 apply. □

For fixed $A, B_1 \ldots, B_m \in M_n(\widehat{\mathbb{A}})$, Theorem 14 of course implies PR-computability of the solution operator $\varphi \mapsto \mathbf{u}$ for (1). The next result (which is a PR-version of Theorem 5.1 in [23]) shows that the assumption $A, B_1 \ldots, B_m \in M_n(\widehat{\mathbb{A}})$ may be weakened to $A, B_1 \ldots, B_m \in \mathbb{R}_p$.

Theorem 15. *Let $M, p \geq 2$ be integers and $A, B_1, \ldots, B_m \in M_n(\mathbb{R}_p)$ be fixed matrices satisfying the conditions in (1). Then the solution operator $\varphi \mapsto \mathbf{u}$ for (1) is a PR-computable function (uniformly in m, n) from $C_s^{p+1}(Q, \mathbb{R}^n)$ to $C_{sL_2}^p(H, \mathbb{R}^n)$, $\|\frac{\partial \varphi}{\partial x_i}\|_s \leq M$, and $\|\frac{\partial^2 \varphi}{\partial x_i \partial x_j}\|_s \leq M$ for $i, j = 1, 2, \ldots, m$.*

Proof Sketch. All data from Propositions 12 and 13 will have fixed coefficients in $\mathbb{R}_p$ because this field is real closed (Peter Hertling, private communication with permission to mention it here). With these data at hand, all computations in the Godunov scheme are made within $\mathbb{R}_p$ using only the operations $+, \cdot, -$. It is not hard to see that these computations are PR. □

We conclude with the following PR-version of results in [24]. The formulation is broader than in [24] because now the algorithm is uniform on m, n, a and works not only with algebraic numbers. The proof is almost the same as in [24], using Propositions 12 and 13 as stronger versions of the corresponding facts in [24]. This time all computations are precise and performed within $\widehat{\mathbb{A}}$.

Theorem 16. *Given integers $m, n, a \geq 1$, matrices $A, B_1 \ldots, B_m \in M_n(\widehat{\mathbb{A}})$, and rational functions $\varphi_1 \ldots, \varphi_n \in \widehat{\mathbb{A}}(x_1 \ldots, x_m)$, $f_1 \ldots, f_n \in \widehat{\mathbb{A}}(t, x_1 \ldots, x_m)$ as in (1), one can primitive recursively compute a rational $T > 0$ with $H \subseteq [0, T] \times Q$, a spatial rational grid step h dividing 1, a time grid step τ dividing T and an h, τ-grid function $v : G_N^\tau \to \widehat{\mathbb{A}}$ such that $\|\mathbf{u} - \widetilde{v \mid_H}\|_{sL_2} < a^{-1}$.*

6   Conclusion

We hope that the present paper demonstrates that PR computations is a natural next step in the investigation of the interaction between symbolic and numeric computations because it provides a natural borderline between problems in algebra and analysis computable in principle and more feasible problems. Although PR functions were thoroughly investigated in computability theory and proof theory, their study in computable structure theory and computable analysis seems still in the very beginning. A natural next step to filling the huge gap between PTIME and PR (in the context of this paper) would be development of a similar theory for the Grzegorczyk classes.

Practical realization of algorithms considered in this paper requires of course establishing of much better upper complexity bounds. In particular, it would be interesting to establish PTIME-presentability of real closures of the fields $\mathbb{Q}(e)$ and $\mathbb{Q}(\pi)$ (or prove that these real closures are not PTIME-presentable).

Acknowledgments. The authors thank Pavel Alaev, Sergey Goncharov, Valentina Harizanov, Peter Hertling, Iskander Kalimullin, Julia Knight, Russell Miller and Andrey Morozov for useful discussions. The first author is grateful to Arcadia University and Xizhong Zheng for the hospitality, support, and useful discussions.

References

1. Alaev, P., Selivanov, V.: Polynomial-time presentations of algebraic number fields. In: Manea, F., Miller, R.G., Nowotka, D. (eds.) CiE 2018. LNCS, vol. 10936, pp. 20–29. Springer, Cham (2018). https://doi.org/10.1007/978-3-319-94418-0_2
2. Bazhenov, N., Downey, R., Kalimullin, I., Melnikov, A.: Foundations of online structure theory. Bull. Symb. Logic **25**(2), 141–181 (2019)
3. Bournez, O., Graça, D.S., Pouly, A.: Solving analytic differential equations in polynomial time over unbounded domains. In: Murlak, F., Sankowski, P. (eds.) MFCS 2011. LNCS, vol. 6907, pp. 170–181. Springer, Heidelberg (2011). https://doi.org/10.1007/978-3-642-22993-0_18
4. Borodin, A., El-Yaniv, R.: Online Computation and Competitive Analysis. Cambridge University Press, Cambridge (1998)
5. Chen, Q., Su, K., Zheng, X.: Primitive recursive real numbers. Math. Logic Q. **53**(4/5), 365–380 (2007)
6. Ershov, Yu.L., Goncharov, S.S.: Constructive models. Novosibirsk, Scientific Book (1999). (in Russian, there is an English Translation)
7. Ershov, Yu.L.: Numbered fields. In: Proceedings of 3rd International Congress for Logic, Methodology and Philosophy of Science, 1967, Amsterdam, pp. 31–35 (1968)
8. Fröhlich, A., Shepherdson, J.C.: Effective procedures in field theories. Philos. Trans. Lond. R. Soc. **248**(950), 407–432 (1956)
9. Gomaa, W.: Algebraic characterizations of computable analysis real functions. Int. J. Unconv. Comput. **7**(4), 245–272 (2011)
10. Goodstein, R.L.: Recursive Analysis. Amsterdam, North Holland (1961)
11. Kawamura, A.: Lipschitz continuous ordinary differential equations are polynomial-space complete. Comput. Complex. **19**(2), 305–332 (2010)

12. Kawamura, A., Steinberg, F., Thies, H.: Parameterized complexity for uniform operators on multidimensional analytic functions and ODE solving. In: Proceedings of 25th International Workshop on Logic, Language, Information, and Computation (WOLLIC), pp. 223–236 (2018)

13. Kawamura, A., Steinberg, F., Ziegler, M.: On the computational complexity of the Dirichlet problem for Poisson's equation. Math. Struct. Comput. Sci. **27**(8), 1437–1465 (2017)

14. Koswara, I., Pogudin, G., Selivanova, S., Ziegler, M.: Bit-complexity of solving systems of linear evolutionary partial differential equations. In: Santhanam, R., Musatov, D. (eds.) CSR 2021. LNCS, vol. 12730, pp. 223–241. Springer, Cham (2021). https://doi.org/10.1007/978-3-030-79416-3_13

15. Koswara, I., Selivanova, S., Ziegler, M.: Computational complexity of real powering and improved solving linear differential equations. In: van Bevern, R., Kucherov, G. (eds.) CSR 2019. LNCS, vol. 11532, pp. 215–227. Springer, Cham (2019). https://doi.org/10.1007/978-3-030-19955-5_19

16. Loos, R.: Computing in algebraic extensions. In: Buchberger, B., Collins, G.E., Loos, R. (eds.) Computer Algebra. Computing Supplementum, vol. 4. Springer, Vienna (1982). https://doi.org/10.1007/978-3-7091-3406-1_12

17. Madison, E.W.: A note on computable real fields. J. Symb. Logic **35**(2), 239–241 (1970)

18. Mahler, K.: An inequality for the discriminant of a polynomial. Michigan Math. J. **11**, 257–262 (1964)

19. Mal'cev, A.I.: The Metamathematics of Algebraic Systems, North Holand, Amsterdam, pp. 148–214 (1971)

20. Mal'cev, A.I.: Algorithms and Recursive Functions. Fizmatgiz, Moscow (1964). (Russian, English translation: Wolters-Noordhoff, 1970)

21. Miller, R., Ocasio, G.V.: Degree spectra of real closed fields. Arch. Math. Logic **58**, 387–411 (2019)

22. Rabin, M.O.: Computable algebra, general theory and theory of computable fields. Trans. Am. Math. Soc. **95**(2), 341–360 (1960)

23. Selivanova, S., Selivanov, V.: Computing solution operators of boundary-value problems for some linear hyperbolic systems of PDEs. Log. Methods Comput. Sci. **13**(4:13), 1–31 (2017)

24. Selivanova, S.V., Selivanov, V.L.: Bit complexity of computing solutions for symmetric hyperbolic systems of PDEs with guaranteed precision. Computability **10**(2), 123–140 (2021). https://doi.org/10.3233/COM-180215

25. Stoltenberg-Hansen, V., Tucker, J.V.: Computable rings and fields. In: Griffor, E. (ed.) Handbook of Computability Theory, pp. 363–447. Elsevier (1999)

26. van der Waerden, B.L.: Algebra. Springer, Berlin (1967). https://doi.org/10.1007/978-3-662-22183-9

27. Weihrauch, K.: Computable Analysis. TTCSAES. Springer, Heidelberg (2000). https://doi.org/10.1007/978-3-642-56999-9

28. Ziegler, M., Brattka, V.: A computable spectral theorem. In: Blanck, J., Brattka, V., Hertling, P. (eds.) CCA 2000. LNCS, vol. 2064, pp. 378–388. Springer, Heidelberg (2001). https://doi.org/10.1007/3-540-45335-0_23

Exact Real Computation of Solution Operators for Linear Analytic Systems of Partial Differential Equations

Svetlana Selivanova[1], Florian Steinberg[2], Holger Thies[3(✉)], and Martin Ziegler[1]

[1] School of Computing, KAIST, Daejeon, Republic of Korea
[2] Inria, Saclay, France
[3] Kyoto University, Kyoto, Japan
thies.holger.5c@kyoto-u.ac.jp

Abstract. We devise and analyze the bit-cost of solvers for linear evolutionary systems of Partial Differential Equations (PDEs) with given analytic initial conditions. Our algorithms are rigorous in that they produce approximations to the solution up to guaranteed absolute error $1/2^n$ for *any* desired number n of output bits. Previous work has shown that smooth (i.e. infinitely differentiable but non-analytic) initial data does not yield polynomial-time computable solutions unless it holds P=NP (or stronger complexity hypotheses). We first resume earlier complexity investigations of the Cauchy-Kovalevskaya Theorem about linear PDEs with analytic matrix coefficients: from qualitative polynomial-time solutions for any fixed polynomial-time computable analytic initial conditions, to quantitative parameterized bit-cost analyses for any given analytic initial data, as well as turn devised algorithms into computational practice. We secondly devise a parameterized polynomial-time solver for the Heat and the Schrödinger equation with given analytic initial data: PDEs not covered by Cauchy-Kovalevskaya. Reliable implementations and empirical performance evaluation (including testing on the Elasticity and Acoustic systems examples) in the Exact Real Computation (ERC) paradigm confirm the theoretical predictions and practical applicability of our algorithms. These involve new continuous abstract data types operating on power and Fourier series without rounding error.

Keywords: Computable analysis · Exact real computation · Partial differential equations · Power series · Fourier series · Parametrized complexity · Polynomial-time algorithms

1 Introduction and Summary of Contributions

We turn the rigorous theoretical approach to computing with continuous data (see [2,22]) into numerical practice for computing solutions of Partial Differential Equations (PDEs) with guaranteed *arbitrary* output precision. We adapt classical analytic series techniques for solving initial-value problems (IVP) for Cauchy-Kovalevskaya type systems by means of the *Exact Real Computation* (ERC) approach [19].

© Springer Nature Switzerland AG 2021
F. Boulier et al. (Eds.): CASC 2021, LNCS 12865, pp. 370–390, 2021.
https://doi.org/10.1007/978-3-030-85165-1_21

This approach allows to conveniently implement imperative algorithms involving real numbers, converging sequences, and smooth functions: equivalent, but without appealing, to Turing machines as in the underlying Computable Analysis approach. ERC differs from traditional Reliable Numerics in considering real numbers as exact entities (as opposed to intervals [20]) while guaranteeing output approximations up to error $1/2^n$ (as opposed to intermediate precision propagation), where $n \in \mathbb{N}$ is a given error parameter, representing the (arbitrary given) number of bits of the output. See [1,3,4,14] for rigorous complexity analysis and implementation in ERC packagers of ordinary differential equations (ODEs).

In this paper we develop a turnkey solver in agreement with complexity predictions [16]. We consider Cauchy-Kovalevskaya type systems of linear partial differential equations (PDEs) with variable coefficients and given initial values:

$$\partial_t \boldsymbol{u}(\boldsymbol{x}, t) = f_1(\boldsymbol{x})\partial_1 \boldsymbol{u} + \cdots + f_d(\boldsymbol{x})\partial_d \boldsymbol{u} \qquad \boldsymbol{u}(\boldsymbol{x}, 0) \equiv \boldsymbol{v}(\boldsymbol{x}) \ . \tag{1}$$

In particular, such equations of mathematical physics, as the Acoustics, Elasticity and Maxwell systems are examples of (1). Also, many higher-order equations can be reduced to first-order systems (1) by introducing additional unknown functions [5, P.228], e.g. the Wave Equation $u_{tt} = \Delta u$ is equivalent to the Acoustics system.

In [15,16] we have proved that the finite difference approach, adapted to the ERC paradigm, is in the complexity class PSPACE, w.r.t. n, with fixed polynomial time computable initial functions and matrix coefficients. It can be improved at best to #P (believed to be strictly between P and PSPACE) in the constant periodic case even for analytic polynomial time computable initial functions, since so are the exponential-size matrix powering and inner product. See Remark 7 below why difference schemes are not suitable for uniform computation of operators.

The power series approach on the other hand does yield [16] a polynomial time algorithm w.r.t. n for fixed polynomial time computable analytic functions:

Fact 1 (Polynomial-Time Cauchy – Kovalevskaya, [16]). *Let* $f_1, \ldots, f_d :$ $[-1; 1]^d \to \mathbb{C}^{d' \times d'}$ *and* $v : [-1; 1]^d \to \mathbb{C}^{d'}$ *denote matrix/vector functions, analytic on some open neighborhood of* $[-1; 1]^d$ *and consider the system of linear partial differential equations* (1).

If $f_1, \ldots f_d$ *and* $v_1, \ldots, v_d$ *are computable in polynomial time, then the unique analytic local solution* $\boldsymbol{u} : [-\varepsilon; +\varepsilon]^{d+1} \ni (\boldsymbol{x}, t) \mapsto \boldsymbol{u}(\boldsymbol{x}, t) \in \mathbb{C}^{d'}$ *to Eq.* (1) *(here* $[-\varepsilon, \varepsilon]$ *is within the domain of existence and uniqueness determined by the Cauchy-Kovalevskaya theorem) is again computable in polynomial time.*

In this work we improve this nonuniform result to a uniform algorithm, where the right-hand side functions $f_1, \ldots, f_d$ and the initial value v are not fixed but given as input to the algorithm, together with certain parameters that quantitatively capture their convergence behaviour:

Definition 2. *Fix* $d \in \mathbb{N}$.

a) *Consider a multi-index $\alpha \in \mathbb{N}^d$ and $x \in \mathbb{R}^d$. Abbreviate $x^\alpha := x_1^{\alpha_1} \cdots x_d^{\alpha_d}$ and $\partial^\alpha := \partial_1^{\alpha_1} \cdots \partial_d^{\alpha_d}$ and $\alpha! = \alpha_1! \cdots \alpha_d!$ and $|\alpha| = \alpha_1 + \cdots + \alpha_d$.*

b) *Consider a complex multi-sequence $(a_\alpha) : \mathbb{N}^d \to \mathbb{C}$. A pair (M, L) with $M, L \in \mathbb{N}$ is called a* coefficient bound *for (a_α) if it satisfies*

$$|a_\alpha| \leq M \cdot L^{|\alpha|} \quad \text{for all} \quad \alpha \in \mathbb{N}^d. \tag{2}$$

c) *Consider a complex function f analytic in some neighborhood of $[-1; 1]^d$. A pair (M, L) with $M, L \in \mathbb{N}$ is called a* coefficient bound *for f if it is a coefficient bound for the multi-sequence $\partial^\alpha f(x)/\alpha!$ for every $x \in [-1; 1]^d$. Same for a complex function f analytic on the* hyper-torus

$$\Omega = \left([0; 1) \bmod 1\right)^d.$$

The latter means that, for some L and for every $x \in \Omega$,

$$\left(-1/L, +1/L\right)^d \ni y \mapsto f(x + y \bmod 1) = \sum_\alpha f_\alpha y^\alpha$$

is a converging power series, with complex Taylor coefficient sequence (f_α) depending on x. Here $1/L$ is a radius of convergence of f.

See Sect. 3 for explanation and intuition behind these notions. Using the notions, we can turn Fact 1 into a uniform algorithm where the inputs are (encodings of) the right-hand side and initial condition functions and provide worst-case complexity bounds polynomial in the output precision and the parameters of the functions:

Theorem 3. *Fix $d \in \mathbb{N}$ and consider the solution operator that maps any analytic right-hand sides $f_1, \ldots, f_d : [-1; 1]^d \to \mathbb{C}^{d' \times d'}$ and initial condition $v : [-1; 1]^d \to \mathbb{C}^{d'}$ and "small" enough $t \in \mathbb{C}$ to the solution $u = u(t, \cdot)$ of (1).*

This operator is computable in time polynomial in $n + L + \log M$ where n is the output precision, $L, M \in \mathbb{N}$ are as in Definition 2 and $v, f_1, \ldots, f_d$ are given via their (componentwise) Taylor expansions around $\mathbf{0}$ as well as (M, L) as coefficient bounds to $v, f_1, \ldots, f_d$ componentwise.

The Heat and Schrödinger's equations, on the other hand, are not covered by the Cauchy-Kovalevskaya Theorem. Nevertheless, we provide a polynomial time algorithm for the case where the initial value function is analytic.

Theorem 4. *The proofs of these statements can be found in Sect. 4.1 and Sect. 4.2, respectively.*

Fix $d \in \mathbb{N}$ and consider the following linear partial differential equations on the d-dimensional hypercube with periodic boundary conditions

$$\Omega = \left([0; 1) \bmod 1\right)^d,$$

that is, analytic initial data $v : [0; 1]^d \to \mathbb{C}$ satisfying

$$\partial^\alpha v(x_1, \ldots, x_{j-1}, 0, x_{j+1}, \ldots, x_d) = \partial^\alpha v(x_1, \ldots, x_{j-1}, 1, x_{j+1}, \ldots, x_d) \tag{3}$$

for all $\alpha \in \mathbb{N}^d$, *all* $j = 1, 2 \ldots, d$ *and all* $x \in \Omega$; *similarly for the solution* $u(t, \cdot) : [0; 1]^d \to \mathbb{C}$ *for all* $t > 0$. *Recall that* $\Delta = \partial_1^2 + \partial_2^2 + \cdots + \partial_d^2$ *denotes the Laplace operator.*

a) Consider the Heat equation

$$u_t = \Delta u, \quad u(0, \cdot) = v. \tag{4}$$

b) Consider the Schrödinger equation of a free particle

$$u_t = i\Delta u, \quad u(0, \cdot) = v. \tag{5}$$

For any $t > 0$ *and for any initial data* v *given by coefficient bounds* (M, L) *and* v *'s power series expansion at each* $x = (2\ell+1)/(2L) \in \Omega$, $\ell \in \{0, 1, \ldots, L-1\}^d$, *the unique analytic solution* $u(t, \cdot) : \Omega \to \mathbb{C}$ *to each of the above PDEs is computable in parameterized time polynomial in* $n + \log t + L + \log M$.

Complexity theory becomes subtle when real numbers are involved, and even more so for functional inputs, and the computational cost, in general, cannot be bounded in the output precision parameter n only. While there is a generic and powerful framework of type-2 complexity [7,8] for our work we can use a simpler, parameterized approach depending on the parameters M and L. Here, $M, L \in \mathbb{N}$ are parameters bounding the asymptotic behaviour of the given coefficient sequence that affect the radius of convergence (namely $\geq 1/L$) and computational cost. Adding such parameters as *enrichment* is known to be necessary already for uniform computability of the solution.

The main motivation behind our work is to apply and extend ideas from [16] to an efficient implementation of a solver for analytic partial differential equations (linear systems as a first important step). This makes it necessary to extend Fact 1 to a uniform algorithm that takes a description of the input functions and returns a description of the output functions. We briefly introduce the necessary theoretical concepts from computable analysis in Sect. 2. All our algorithms are based on (partially symbolic) computations with power series. The real or complex valued power series are encoded as exact objects without approximation errors and can be manipulated symbolically.

In Sect. 3 we explain how power series can be used as the basis of an encoding of real analytic functions and how basic mathematical operations can be applied on them. We then use this encoding in Sect. 4 to formalize a uniform version of Fact 1 and prove its correctness. Our algorithm can approximate the solution of the PDEs (1) on some sufficiently small time interval around 0.

To this end we recall, refine and re-analyze the algorithmic idea from [16]: now in dependence of the parameters (M, L). We further show that the size of the time interval where our algorithm provides a solution and the time complexity of the algorithm depend on some natural parameters of the input functions. We also formulate a variation of the algorithm for the simpler case where the coefficients in Eq. (1) are real constants instead of real analytic functions which allows to evaluate on a slightly larger time interval and performs more efficiently in practice.

Subsection 4.2 considers the Heat equation as an example for a PDE that is not covered by the Cauchy-Kovalevskaya Theorem since its solutions are well-known not analytic in time. Here we turn the classical Fourier series approach into a rigorous algorithm. The key is to avoid Riemann integration in the Fourier transformation, since this is well-known infeasible in polynomial time [13, §5.4] unless it holds P = NP (or stronger complexity hypotheses).

Finally, we implement the proposed algorithm in C++ on top of the iRRAM framework for exact real computation [18] and evaluate its performance on the examples of linear Acoustics and Elasticity systems (Sect. 5). To this end, we also add several other new functions to iRRAM such as a simple implementation of automatic differentiation and classes for differential operators. We therefore also consider the implementation itself an important contribution of this work.

2   Recap on Real Bit-Complexity Theory

We follow the computable analysis approach to model exact computation with real numbers. The basic idea is to encode real numbers by functions that give arbitrarily exact finite approximations. More precisely, we use the following definitions.

Definition 5. *a) Computing a real number $x \in \mathbb{R}$ means to compute a total integer function $\varphi \colon \mathbb{N} \to \mathbb{Z}$ such that $|x - 2^{-n} \cdot \varphi(n)| \leq 2^{-n}$ holds for all $n \in \mathbb{N}$. Computing x in polynomial time means to compute $\mathbb{N} \ni n \mapsto \varphi(n) \in \mathbb{Z}$ within a number of steps polynomial in n (rather than in the binary length of n).*

b) Computing a real sequence $\bar{x} = (x_m)_{m \in \mathbb{N}} \colon \mathbb{N} \to \mathbb{R}$ means to compute a total integer function $\psi \colon \mathbb{N} \times \mathbb{N} \to \mathbb{Z}$ (called a realizer) such that $|x_m - 2^{-n} \cdot \psi(m, n)| \leq 2^{-n}$ holds for all $m, n \in \mathbb{N}$. Computing $\bar{x}$ in polynomial time means to compute $\mathbb{N} \times \mathbb{N} \ni (n, m) \mapsto \psi(m, n) \in \mathbb{Z}$ in time polynomial in $n + m$.

c) Computing a (partial) function $f \colon\subseteq \mathbb{R} \to \mathbb{R}$ means to compute a partial integer functional $F \colon\subseteq \mathbb{Z}^{\mathbb{N}} \to \mathbb{Z}^{\mathbb{N}}$ (called a realizer) such that:
(i) For every $x \in \mathrm{dom}(f)$ and every $\varphi \in \mathbb{Z}^{\mathbb{N}}$ satisfying (a), it holds $\varphi \in \mathrm{dom}(F)$; and (ii) in this case $F(\varphi) =: \varphi' \in \mathbb{Z}^{\mathbb{N}}$ satisfies (a) for $x' := f(x)$. Computing f in polynomial time means to compute $(\varphi, n') \mapsto F(\varphi)(n') \in \mathbb{Z}$ in a number of steps bounded polynomially in n' but independently of φ.

d) Computing a (partial) function $g \colon\subseteq (\mathbb{R}^{\mathbb{N}}) \to (\mathbb{R}^{\mathbb{N}})$ means to compute a partial integer functional $G \colon\subseteq \mathbb{Z}^{\mathbb{N} \times \mathbb{N}} \to \mathbb{Z}^{\mathbb{N} \times \mathbb{N}}$ (called a realizer) such that:
(i) For every $\bar{x} \in \mathrm{dom}(g)$ and every $\psi \in \mathbb{Z}^{\mathbb{N} \times \mathbb{N}}$ satisfying (b), it holds $\psi \in \mathrm{dom}(G)$; and (ii) in this case $G(\psi) =: \psi' \in \mathbb{Z}^{\mathbb{N} \times \mathbb{N}}$ satisfies (b) for $\bar{x}' := g(\bar{x})$. Computing g in polynomial time means to compute $(\psi, n', m') \mapsto G(\psi)(m', n') \in \mathbb{Z}$ in a number of steps bounded polynomially in $n' + m'$ but independently of ψ.

Here, argument φ is provided as oracle $n \mapsto \mathrm{bin}(\varphi(n))$; similarly for ψ. Complex data is identified with tuples of reals.

Requiring running time bounded only in terms of the output precision parameter n', but independently of continuous-type arguments like x or $\bar{x}$, is common in Real Complexity [13, Def.2.26]. Such a (not necessarily polynomial) bound exists for any computable function f or g with compact domain. Slightly generalized, sigma-compact domains allow for a *parameterized* notion of complexity [12]:

Definition 6 ([12]). *A function $f : D \subseteq \mathbb{R} \to \mathbb{R}$ is called C-polynomial-time for a function $C : \mathbb{N} \to \mathbb{N}$ w.r.t. to some fixed covering $D = \bigcup_{k \in \mathbb{N}} D_k$ of its domain if f has a computable realizer F in the sense of Definition 5c) and there is a polynomial $p : \mathbb{N} \to \mathbb{N}$ such that whenever $x \in D_k$, the computation of F terminates after at most $p(n' + C(k))$ steps.*

The above definitions extend to mixed partial functions with co/domains Cartesian products comprised of integer/vectors, real vectors and real matrices, and (multi-)sequences of real vectors/matrices.

2.1   Uniform Computation of Operators and Functionals

In this work we are mostly interested in computability and complexity results of operators and functionals, i.e. higher-type mappings that take real-valued functions as argument and return a real-valued function or a real number as value. There are several ways on how to formalize such results. The statement of Fact 1 is *non-uniform* in the sense that it fixes a certain polynomial-time computable PDE and initial condition (=function) and asserts the solution (=function) to be polynomial-time computable. Non-uniform results are most powerful when used negatively, such as stating—for a certain fixed initial condition—the non-computability or hardness of the solution in the sense of computational complexity: This asserts that the problem cannot be solved (efficiently), irregardless of how the argument is encoded or input. Positive results on the other hand—such as polynomial-time computability—are more significant in a uniform setting, where the function argument encoding and means of input is (and has to be) specified. Such an encoding can be made explicit using the framework of *representations* over infinite bit sequences [17] or oracles [8].

Remark 7. Variable-precision numerics suggests encoding a single real number x as a sequence of approximations up to error $1/2^n$. Similarly, sequences of reals $\bar{x}$ are encoded as double sequences of approximations: see Definition 5. The latter applies in particular to the coefficient sequences of analytic functions' power series expansion.

Mathematically, an analytic function can be locally identified with the coefficient sequence of its power series expansion. This identification is in general *not* computable [22, Exercise 6.5.2]; yet evaluation (as one direction of the identification) does become *parameterized polynomial-time* computable when providing, in addition to the coefficient sequence, a *coefficient bound* in the sense of Definition 2: see Fact 9.

Encoding a smooth (but not necessarily analytic) real function $f : [0; 1] \to \mathbb{R}$ on the other hand up to absolute error $1/2^n$ requires recording approximations to exponentially many samples $f(a/2^{\epsilon n})$ for $a = 0, 1, \ldots, 2^{\epsilon n} - 1$ for some $\epsilon >$ 0. Formally speaking, a non-trivial compact subset of a metric function space usually has superpolynomial entropy [11,23]. And a non-local functional (like Riemann integration) depending on most of them thus requires exponential time to even read f up to error $1/2^n$. This obstacle applies to the initial condition in difference scheme approaches to solving PDEs; and to the converse of the aforementioned identification between analytic functions and their power series expansion.

We therefore consider and operate on all analytic function arguments and solution functions in terms of their local power series expansion as multi-sequences of reals; see Sect. 3.

2.2   *Exact Real Computation*: Reliable Numerics, Conveniency

A computational problem involving continuous data may be well-posed, ill-posed, or intermediate. Algorithms processing continuous data similarly roughly classified as stable, unstable, or intermediate. Ill-posed problems cannot be solved by stable or intermediate algorithms; whereas well-posed problems could potentially be solved by stable, intermediate, or even by unstable algorithms: possibly permitting to trade between working precision and number of operations, such as e.g. Runge-Kutta methods of varying order [21]. Focusing on `double` as data type means restricting to stable algorithms only.

To avoid this blind spot, the present work makes use of the *Exact Real Computation* paradigm. Here some object-oriented software library provides an abstract data type for real numbers, vectors, and sequences to operate on exactly, namely without rounding errors: Like Java's `BigInteger`, the finite internal approximation is chosen automatically and adaptively such as to appear to the user program as indistinguishable from the ideal mathematical data type.

More formally, an exact real computation framework is an implementation of the computable reals and basic operations on it. In general, the framework provides an abstract data-type for real numbers and implementations of some basic operations such as addition, subtraction, multiplication and division and it is possible to output arbitrarily exact approximations of real numbers. We also assume that there is an implementation of a limit operation $\lim: \subseteq \mathbb{R}^\omega \to \mathbb{R}$ that takes an efficiently converging sequence $(x_n)_{n \in \mathbb{N}}$ and maps it to its limit. That is, whenever there is some $x \in \mathbb{R}$ such that $|x_n - x| \leq 2^{-n}$ for all $n \in \mathbb{N}$ then $\lim((x_n)_{n \in \mathbb{N}}) = x$.

Many such frameworks already exist for most modern programming languages and there are different ways of how to concretely implement the data-types and operations. In this work, we use the `C++` framework `iRRAM`. `iRRAM` is one of the most efficient exact real computation frameworks and has been shown to be reliable in a large number of applications. `iRRAM` extends `C++` by a class `Real` for error free computations with real numbers. For the user, an object of type `Real` behaves like a real number that can be manipulated without any rounding errors. The framework takes care of all details necessary for the internal finite representation of real numbers. In most cases this internal representation is invisible for the user.

Internally, a real number in iRRAM is represented as an infinite sequence of better and better approximations. More precisely, a real number $x \in \mathbb{R}$ is encoded by a sequence of pairs (d_i, e_i) such that $x \in [d_i - e_i, d_i + e_i]$ and $e_i \to 0$.

An iRRAM program runs several times. Each run is called an *iteration*. In each iteration objects of type Real are replaced by a single member of the sequence, i.e., by a multiple precision number for d and two integers p, z such that $e = z \cdot 2^p$. At some point in the program a certain precision might be needed to make a decision (branch) or the program is supposed to output an approximation. If the precision at this point does not suffice, the whole computation is restarted from the beginning with higher precision.

3   Computing with Power Series

A PDE solver is usually understood to take some description of the right-hand side functions and produce a solution. Previous work (Fact 1) on the other hand supposes the right-hand side to be fixed: a deficiency mended by the present contribution. To this end, we first discuss encoding functional inputs such that they can at least be read in polynomial time.

Functions $f \colon \mathbb{R}^d \to \mathbb{C}$ that are analytic on some connected $D \subseteq \mathbb{R}^d$ are uniquely identified by their d-variate power series around some point in the domain. For simplicity assume $\mathbf{0} \in D$. Then there is a closed polydisc $\Omega_r = \{x \in \mathbb{R}^d \mid \|x\|_\infty \le 1/L\}$ and a power series (a_α) such that

$$f(x) = \sum_{\alpha \in \mathbb{N}^d} a_\alpha x^\alpha, \text{ for all } x \in \Omega_r \tag{6}$$

and f is uniquely determined by the sequence $(a_\alpha)_{\alpha \in \mathbb{N}^d}$. We therefore aim to encode f by its power series coefficient sequence around $\mathbf{0}$. However, any algorithm can only read a finite number of coefficients from the series and thus implementing basic operations like function evaluation requires to estimate the approximation error that occurs when only a finite initial segment of the series is used. Definition 2 captures and formalizes such information: It is well-known [22, Chapter 6.5] that it in general cannot be computed from the coefficient series alone and has to be provided externally.

If $f : D \to \mathbb{C}$ is analytic and Eq. (6) holds, then there exists a coefficient bound (M, L) for the Taylor series of f at any point of its domain. Such a bound can be used to derive an exponentially fast decaying explicit tail estimate

$$\sum_{\substack{\alpha_i \ge N, \\ i=1,\dots,d}} a_\alpha (x)^\alpha \le M \frac{(L \|x\|_\infty)^{dN}}{(1 - L \|x\|_\infty)^d}. \tag{7}$$

Definition 8. *Fix $d \in \mathbb{N}$.*

a) *Denote by $\mathcal{C}^\omega[-1;1]^d$ the space of d-variate real functions f analytic in a neighborhood of $[-1;1]^d$. Abbreviate*

$$\tilde{\mathcal{P}}[-1;1]^d = \{(M,L,a_\alpha) : a_\alpha = \partial^\alpha f(x)/\alpha!\big|_{x=0}$$

$$Taylor\ coefficient\ of\ f \in \mathcal{C}^\omega[-1;1]^d\ at\ origin\ satisfying\ (2)\}$$

b) *Denote by $\mathcal{C}^\omega[0;1)^d$ mod $\mathbf{1}$ the space of d-variate real functions f analytic at each point of the hyper-torus $[0;1)^d$ mod $\mathbf{1}$ (Fig. 1). Abbreviate*

$$\tilde{\mathcal{P}}[0;1)^d\ mod\ \mathbf{1} =$$

$$\left\{\left(M,L,\partial^\alpha f(x)/\alpha!\big|_{x=(2\ell+1)/(2L)} : \ell \in \{0,1,\ldots,L-1\}^d\right) : Taylor\right.$$

$$\left. coefficients\ of\ f \in \mathcal{C}^\omega[0;1)^d\ mod\ 1\ satisfy\ (2)\ at\ each\ x \in [0;1)^d\ mod\ \mathbf{1}\right\}$$

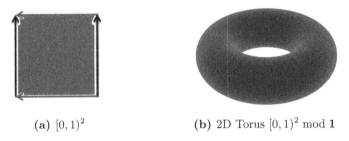

(a) $[0,1)^2$ **(b)** 2D Torus $[0,1)^2$ mod $\mathbf{1}$

Fig. 1. Functions satisfying periodic boundary conditions for all derivatives on the unit (hyper)cube can equivalently be regarded as "living" on the (hyper)torus as a space with no boundary

The connection between the space of analytic functions and the above encoding of power series can be made formal using the framework of representations and can also be used for a parameterized complexity analysis [9,10]). As mentioned in Remark 7, non-local operators on real functions generally cannot avoid incurring exponential bit-cost for information-theoretic reasons. We therefore restrict to the (sigma-)compact subspaces of analytic functions parameterized by (M,L), and operate on their local power series expansions—and evaluate the solution only in the final phase.

Fact 9 *Fix $d \in \mathbb{N}$.*

a) *Consider the following partial function*

$$Eval\colon \tilde{\mathcal{P}}[-1;1]^d \times \mathbb{R}^d \to \mathbb{R}, \quad (M,L,a_\alpha,x) \mapsto \sum_\alpha a_\alpha x^\alpha \in \mathbb{R}$$

that evaluates a power series with coefficient sequence a_α and coefficient bound M,L on arguments $x \in \mathbb{R}^d$ with $\|x\|_\infty \le 1/(2L)$. It can be computed in the sense of Definition 5 (namely evaluated approximately up to guaranteed absolute error $1/2^n$) in time polynomial in $n + L + \log M$.

b) *Similarly, pointwise addition* $+: \tilde{\mathcal{P}}[-1; 1]^d \times \tilde{\mathcal{P}}[-1; 1]^d \to \tilde{\mathcal{P}}[-1; 1]^d$,

$$((M, L, a_\alpha), (N, K, b_\beta)) \mapsto (M + N, \max\{L, K\}, a_\alpha + b_\alpha)$$

is well-defined and computable in parameterized time polynomial in $n + L + K + \log M + \log N$.

c) *Pointwise multiplication* $\cdot: \tilde{\mathcal{P}}[-1; 1]^d \times \tilde{\mathcal{P}}[-1; 1]^d \to \tilde{\mathcal{P}}[-1; 1]^d$,

$$((M, L, a_\alpha), (N, K, b_\beta)) \mapsto ((M + N) \cdot \max\{K, L\}, \max\{K, L\}^2, c_\alpha)$$

is well-defined and computable in parameterized time polynomial in $n+K+L+ \log M + \log N$ *for the convolution* $c_\alpha = \sum_{\beta \leq \alpha} a_\beta \cdot b_{\alpha-\beta}$ *as Taylor coefficient multisequence of the series product.*

d) *Iterated partial derivatives* **Derive**: $\tilde{\mathcal{P}}[-1; 1]^d \times \mathbb{N}^d \to \tilde{\mathcal{P}}[-1; 1]^d$,

$$(M, L, a_\alpha, \boldsymbol{\beta}) \mapsto \left(\frac{(\alpha + \beta)!}{\alpha!} a_{\alpha+\beta}, (3 |\boldsymbol{\beta}| L)^{|\boldsymbol{\beta}|} M, \left\lceil \frac{4}{3} L \right\rceil \right)$$

is well-defined and computable in parameterized time polynomial in $n + L + \log M + |\boldsymbol{\beta}|$.

The proof can e.g. be found in [10]; see also [9, Theorem 16]. Note that the bound "$\|\boldsymbol{x}\|_\infty \leq 1/(2L)$" in (a) could be replaced by $\|\boldsymbol{x}\|_\infty \leq \mathcal{O}(1/L)$, as in this case the r.h.s. of (2) goes to 0 as the number of power series coefficients N approaches ∞.

For $A_\alpha \in \mathcal{P}_d^{m \times m'}$ a matrix-valued multi-sequence and $\boldsymbol{x} \in \mathbb{R}^d$, let us introduce the short-hand notion $\sum_{\alpha \in \mathbb{N}^d} A_\alpha \boldsymbol{x}^\alpha$ for componentwise evaluation of the power series in A_α.

4   Computing Solutions for PDEs

Let us now come back to our original problem of solving partial differential equations. First, we consider the very general problem of analytic PDEs of the form

$$\partial_t \boldsymbol{u}(\boldsymbol{x}, t) = D(\boldsymbol{x}) \boldsymbol{u} \qquad \boldsymbol{u}(\boldsymbol{x}, 0) \equiv \boldsymbol{v}(\boldsymbol{x}) \tag{8}$$

where $\boldsymbol{u} : \mathbb{R}^{d+1} \to \mathbb{R}^{d'}$, $v : \mathbb{R}^d \to \mathbb{R}^{d'}$ and D is a differential operator with coefficients being $d' \times d'$ matrices of d-variate analytic functions using only spatial derivative operators (i.e. no derivatives in t).

In this general case the solution does not need to be analytic again (or even unique). However, if there is an analytic solution $\boldsymbol{u}$ it is not hard to see that the power series is given by

$$\boldsymbol{u}(\boldsymbol{x}, t) = \sum_{k=0}^{\infty} \frac{t^k}{k!} (D^k v)(\boldsymbol{x}). \tag{9}$$

We now consider some special cases of (8) where the solution is indeed analytic.

4.1   Cauchy-Kovalevskaya Type Linear PDEs

Let us first consider linear PDEs with variable coefficients of the form (1). By the Cauchy-Kovalevskaya theorem the PDE has a unique analytic solution around $(\boldsymbol{x}, 0)$. We will show the following theorem.

Theorem 10. *The operator*

$$\texttt{solve}: (\mathcal{P}_d^{m \times m})^d \times \mathcal{P}_d^{m \times 1} \times \mathbb{R}^d \to \mathcal{P}_1^{m \times 1}$$

that maps $(A_\alpha^{(1)}, M_1, L_1), \ldots, (A_\alpha^{(d)}, M_d, L_d), (\boldsymbol{b}_\alpha, M_{d+1}, L_{d+1})$ *and* $\boldsymbol{x} \in \mathbb{R}^d$ *with* $\|\boldsymbol{x}\|_\infty \le \frac{1}{2L}$ *to a vector of (univariate) power series* $(\boldsymbol{c}_k, M_c, L_c) \in \mathcal{P}_1^{m \times 1}$; $L_c = \lceil 4ed(d+1)d'ML \rceil$, $M_c = M_v$ *where* $M = \max M_i$ *and* $L = \max L_i$ *and* $\boldsymbol{u}(\boldsymbol{x}, t) = \sum_{k=0}^\infty \boldsymbol{c}_k t^k$ *is the solution of the PDE (1) (where* f_i, v *are given by the functions defined by the power series in* A_i, b) *is well-defined and computable in time polynomial in* $\log M + L + n$ *for all*

$$|t| \le \frac{1}{4ed(d+1)d'ML}. \tag{10}$$

To prove the theorem we use the following lemma from complex analysis:

Lemma 11. *Let* $f_1, \ldots, f_d : \mathbb{C}^d \to \mathbb{C}^{m \times m}$ *and* $v : \mathbb{C}^d \to \mathbb{C}^m$ *be complex analytic. Assume there are constants* $r, M_f, M_v \in \mathbb{R}$ *and* $j \in \mathbb{N}$ *such that*

$$\|f_i(\xi r)\|_\infty \le M_f (1 - \|\xi\|_\infty)^{-j} \quad \text{and} \quad \|v(\xi r)\|_\infty \le M_v(1 - \|\xi\|_\infty)^{-j}$$

for all $\xi \in \mathbb{C}^d, \|\xi\|_\infty \le 1$ *and* $i = 1, \ldots, d$. *Then*

$$\left\|(f_1 \partial_1 + \cdots + f_d \partial_d)^k v(\xi r)\right\|_\infty \le k! M_v (ed(j+1)m M_f r^{-1})^k (1 - \|\xi\|_\infty)^{-(k+1)j-k}$$

for all $\xi \in \mathbb{C}^d, \|\xi\|_\infty \le 1$.

We will use the following fact:

Fact 12 *[6, Lemma 9.4.4] Let* $v : \mathbb{C}^d \to \mathbb{C}^m$ *be complex analytic and assume there are constants* $M, r \in \mathbb{R}$ *and* $j \in \mathbb{N}$ *such that*

$$\|v(\xi r)\|_\infty \le M (1 - \|\xi\|_\infty)^{-j} \text{ for all } \xi \in \mathbb{C}^d, \ \|\xi\|_\infty < 1.$$

Then
$$\|\partial_i v(\xi r)\|_\infty \le Me(j+1)r^{-1}(1 - \|\xi\|_\infty)^{-(j+1)}$$

for all $i = 1, \ldots, d, \xi \in \mathbb{C}^d, \ \|\xi\|_\infty < 1$.

Proof (Lemma 11). Let $v^{[k]} = (f_1 \partial_1 + \cdots + f_d \partial_d)^k v$. We need to show that

$$\left\|v^{[k]}(\xi r)\right\|_\infty \le k! M_v (ed(j+1)m M_f r^{-1})^k (1 - \|\xi\|_\infty)^{-(k+1)j-k}. \tag{11}$$

The proof is by induction on k. For $k = 0$,

$$\left\|v^{[0]}(\xi r)\right\|_\infty = \|v(\xi r)\|_\infty \leq M_v(1 - \|\xi\|_\infty)^{-j}$$

by the assumption on v. Assume (11) holds. By Fact 12 for $i = 1, \ldots, d$,

$$\left\|\partial_i v^{[k]}(\xi r)\right\|_\infty$$
$$\leq k! M_v (ed(j+1)mM_f r^{-1})^k e\left((k+1)j + k + 1\right) r^{-1}(1 - \|\xi\|_\infty)^{-(k+1)j-k-1}$$
$$= (k+1)! M_v (dmM_f)^k (e(j+1)r^{-1})^{k+1}(1 - \|\xi\|_\infty)^{-(k+1)j-(k+1)}$$

Thus

$$\left\|\sum_{i=1}^d f_i \partial_i v^{[k]}(\xi r)\right\|_\infty \leq \sum_{i=1}^d \left\|f_i \partial_i v^{[k]}(\xi r)\right\|_\infty \leq \sum_{i=1}^d m \|f_i\|_\infty \left\|\partial_i v^{[k]}(\xi r)\right\|_\infty$$
$$\leq dmM_f(k+1)! M_v (dmM_f)^k (e(j+1)r^{-1})^{k+1}(1 - \|\xi\|_\infty)^{-(k+2)j-(k+1)}$$
$$= (k+1)! M_v (ed(j+1)mM_f r^{-1})^{k+1}(1 - \|\xi\|_\infty)^{-(k+2)j-(k+1)}.$$

Proof (Theorem 10). We compute the series $c_k = \frac{1}{k!}(f_1\partial_1 + \cdots + f_d\partial_d)^k(v)(\boldsymbol{x})$. By (9) this is the power series of the solution of the PDEs (1). The series can be computed in the given time bound by applying the operations in Fact 9 (see also [16, Theorem 8]). It remains to show that $(M_v, \lceil 2ed(d+1)mL\rceil)$ is a coefficient bound for c_k.

Let $r := \frac{1}{L}$ and define complex analytic functions $\tilde{f}_i : C^d \to C^{m\times m}$ by $\tilde{f}_i(z) = \sum_{\alpha\in\mathbb{N}^d} A_\alpha^{(i)} z^\alpha$. Then $\left\|\tilde{f}_i^{(j,k)}(\xi r)\right\|_\infty \leq \sum_{\alpha\in\mathbb{N}^d} Mr^{-|\alpha|}(\|\xi\|_\infty r)^{|\alpha|} = M(1 - \|\xi\|_\infty)^{-d}$ for all $\xi \in \mathbb{C}^d, \|\xi\|_\infty \leq 1$. Thus the claim follows by Lemma 11.

It remains to show Theorem 3.

Proof (Theorem 3). For any analytic $f : [-1;1]^d \to \mathbb{R}$ there are $M, L \in \mathbb{N}$ such that $|D^\alpha f| \leq \alpha! ML^{|\alpha|}$ for all $\boldsymbol{x} \in [-1;1]^d$. In particular, (M, L) is a coefficient bound for the power series of f around any point $\boldsymbol{x} \in [-1;1]^d$. We can then encode a function $f \in C^\omega[-1;1]^d$ by a finite sequence of $(4l)^d$ power series centered at equally spaced points in $[-1;1]^d$. For any $\boldsymbol{x} \in [-1;1]^d$ a power series centered at $\boldsymbol{x}_i$ such that $\|\boldsymbol{x} - \boldsymbol{x}_i\|_\infty \leq \frac{1}{2L}$ can be located in time polynomial in $n + l$ and used to apply Theorem 10 and the resulting power series can in turn be used for evaluation of the solution function. Thus Theorem 3 follows by choosing the covering $f \in C_{M,L}^\omega([-1;1])$ if the above inequality holds.

4.2 Polynomial-Time Solution of Analytic Heat Equation

The Heat Equation $u_t = u_{xx}$ is well-known to not be analytic in physical time at $t = 0$. This happens essentially because a smooth initial condition can blow up within finite negative time (see e.g. [5, P. 235]). Nevertheless we present an algorithm for solving the Heat Equation within a number of steps polynomial in the output precision parameter n (and logarithmic in the physical time parameter t).

As usual for complexity considerations, we have to restrict to compact spatial domains: In this case for simplicity the one-dimensional unit interval $\Omega = [0; 1]$. PDEs generally require both initial and boundary conditions for the solution to be unique (in space x at a given time $t > 0$). An analytic solution $u = u(t, x)$ on the other hand is uniquely determined at $t > 0$ by its values on an arbitrarily small open spatial subset $U \ni x$; and locality demands that this restriction $u(t, \cdot)|_U$ in turn depends only on $u(t - \tau, \cdot)|_{U'}$ for sufficiently small $\tau > 0$ and a slightly larger U': hence boundary values cannot be prescribed independently.

This unusual combination of conditions can be accommodated by considering a compact domain with periodic boundary conditions. In our case this means $u(t, 0) = u(t, 1)$ and $u_{x^j}(t, 0) = u_{x^j}(t, 1)$ for all $t \geq 0$ and all $d = 1, 2, \ldots$ It amounts to considering PDEs on a circle in 1D, or on a torus in 2D.

Definition 13. *Consider spatial domain* $\Omega := \big([0; 1) \bmod 1\big)^d = [0; 1)^d \bmod \mathbf{1}$. *Recall from Definition 2c) that a function* $f : \Omega \to \mathbb{C}$ *is analytic if, for some* $L \in \mathbb{N}$ *and for every* $\boldsymbol{x} \in \Omega$,

$$(-1/L; +1/L)^d \ni \boldsymbol{y} \mapsto f(\boldsymbol{x} + \boldsymbol{y} \bmod 1) = \sum_\alpha f_\alpha \cdot \boldsymbol{y}^\alpha$$

is a converging power series, with (complex) local Taylor coefficient sequence $f_\alpha(\boldsymbol{x})$.

a) *For* $\boldsymbol{k} \in \mathbb{Z}^d$, *call* $(t, \boldsymbol{x}) \mapsto \exp(2\pi i\langle \boldsymbol{k}, x\rangle - 4\pi^2|\boldsymbol{k}|^2 t)$ *the* $\boldsymbol{k}$*-th* fundamental solution *of the Heat Equation.*

b) *For* $\boldsymbol{k} \in \mathbb{Z}^d$, *call* $(t, \boldsymbol{x}) \mapsto \exp(2\pi i\langle \boldsymbol{k}, \boldsymbol{x}\rangle - 4\pi^2 i|\boldsymbol{k}|^2 t)$ *the* $\boldsymbol{k}$*-th* fundamental solution *of the Schrödinger Equation.*

c) *To each sequence* $(\hat{f}_{\boldsymbol{k}})$ *of Fourier coefficients associate the formal* Fourier Series

$$f : \Omega \to \mathbb{C}, \quad f(x) = \sum_{\boldsymbol{k}} \hat{f}_{\boldsymbol{k}} \cdot \exp(2\pi i\langle \boldsymbol{k}, \boldsymbol{x}\rangle) \ .$$

Here $\langle \boldsymbol{k}, \boldsymbol{x}\rangle$ *denotes the inner product* $k_1 x_1 + \cdots + k_d x_d$, *and* $|\boldsymbol{k}|^2 = \langle \boldsymbol{k}, \boldsymbol{k}\rangle$.

Since Ω is compact, any analytic function $f : \Omega \to \mathbb{C}$ has a positive radius of convergence $r \geq 1/L > 0$, $L \in \mathbb{N}$. Let $f_j^{(0)}, f_j^{(1)}, \ldots, f_j^{(L-1)} \in \mathbb{C}$ denote the Taylor coefficient sequences of f at $x_0 = 1/(2L)$, $x_1 = 3/(2L)$, $x_2 = 5/(2L)$, ... and $x_{L-1} = (2L-1)/(2L)$. Note that convergence is uniform on the intervals $[x_\ell - 1/(2L); x_\ell + 1/(2L))$ partitioning $[0; 1)$.

We record that every square summable Fourier coefficient sequence (f_k) has a square integrable Fourier series, and vice versa via $\hat{f}_k = \int_0^1 f(x) \cdot \exp(2\pi i k x)\, dx$. Moreover this correspondence is isometric. Let us record some relations between Fourier coefficients and Taylor coefficients of analytic functions:

Lemma 14. *Consider domain* $\Omega := [0; 1) \bmod 1$ *and analytic* $f : \Omega \to \mathbb{C}$, *with radius of convergence* $\geq 1/L$ *(*$L \in \mathbb{N}$*) and Fourier expansion* $f(x) = \sum_k \hat{f}_k \cdot \exp(2\pi i k x)$,

$$\big[-1/(2L); +1/(2L)\big) \ni y \mapsto f\big((2\ell + 1)/(2L) + y\big) = \sum_j f_j^{(\ell)} y^j.$$

For $\ell = 0, 1, \ldots, L-1$ call

$$\widehat{X^j_{\ell\,k}} = \int_{\ell/L}^{(\ell+1)/L} \big(x - (2\ell+1)/(2L)\big)^j \cdot \exp(-2\pi i k x)\, dx$$

$$= \exp\big(-2\pi i k (2\ell+1)/(2L)\big) \cdot \int_{-1/(2L)}^{+1/(2L)} y^j \cdot \exp(-2\pi i k y)\, dy$$

the ℓ-th local monomial coefficients, $j \in \mathbb{N}$, $k \in \mathbb{Z}$. Then

a) *$\big(\sum_{\ell=0}^{L-1} \widehat{X^j_{\ell\,k}}\big)_k$ is the Fourier coefficient sequence to the Sawtooth power function $[\ell/L; (\ell+1)/L) \ni x \mapsto \big(x - (2\ell+1)/(2L)\big)^j$ on $[0;1)$; see Fig. 2. Triangle inequality implies*

$$\big|\widehat{X^j_{\ell\,k}}\big| \leq \int_{-1/(2L)}^{+1/(2L)} |y|^j\, dy = 2^{-j} \cdot L^{-j-1}/(j+1) \ .$$

Moreover, integration by parts yields the recurrence

$$\widehat{X^{j+1}_{\ell}}{}_k = -(2L)^{-j-1} \cdot \exp\big(-2\pi i k (\ell+1)/L\big)/(2\pi i k)$$
$$+ (-2L)^{-j-1} \cdot \exp\big(-2\pi i k \ell/L\big)/(2\pi i k) + \frac{j+1}{2\pi i k} \cdot \widehat{X^j_{\ell\,k}}.$$

Thus $(k, j, \ell) \mapsto \widehat{X^j_{\ell\,k}}$ is computable in time polynomial in $|k| + j + L + n$.

b) *The k-Fourier coefficient of the j-th derivative is $\widehat{f^{(j)}}_k = (2\pi i k)^j \cdot \hat{f}_k$. Therefore $f_j^{(\ell)} = \frac{d^j}{dy^j} f\big((2\ell+1)/(2L) + y\big)\big|_{y=0}/j!$*
$$= \frac{d^j}{dy^j} \sum_{k=-\infty}^{\infty} \hat{f}_k \cdot \exp\big(2\pi i k (2\ell+1)/(2L) + 2\pi i k y\big)\big|_{y=0}/j!$$
$$= \sum_{k=-\infty}^{\infty} \hat{f}_k \cdot (2\pi i k)^j \cdot \exp\big(2\pi i k (2\ell+1)/(2L)\big)/j!.$$

c) *For $x \in \big[\ell/L; (\ell+1)/L\big]$, the d-th derivative satisfies*

$$\big|f^{(d)}(x)\big| = \big|\sum_j f_{j+d}^{(\ell)} \cdot (j+1)\cdots(j+d) \cdot \big(x - (2\ell+1)/(2L)\big)^j\big|$$

$$\leq \sum_j M \cdot L^{j+d} \cdot (j+1)\cdots(j+d) \cdot (2L)^{-j}\big|$$

$$= M \cdot \partial_y^d \sum_j L^j y^j \big|_{y=1/2L} = M \cdot \partial_y^d \tfrac{1}{1-Ly}\big|_{y=1/2L}$$

$$= M \cdot L^d \cdot 2^{d+1} \cdot d!$$

and by Parseval/Rayleigh $\sum_{k=-\infty}^{\infty} \big|\widehat{f^{(d)}}_k\big|^2 = \int_0^1 \big|f^{(d)}(x)\big|^2\, dx \leq M^2 \cdot L^{2d} \cdot 4^{d+1} \cdot d!^2$. Moreover $\widehat{f^{(d+j)}}_k = (2\pi i k)^d \cdot \widehat{f^{(j)}}_k$ implies

$$\big|\widehat{f^{(j)}}_K\big|^2 \leq \sum_{|k|\geq K} \big|\widehat{f^{(j)}}_k\big|^2 = \sum_{|k|\geq K} \big|\widehat{f^{(d+j)}}_k\big|^2/(4\pi^2 k^2)^d$$

$$\leq (4\pi^2 K^2)^{-d} \cdot M^2 \cdot L^{2(d+j)} \cdot 4^{d+j+1} \cdot (d+j)!^2$$

$$\leq 4^{j+1} M^2 L^{2j} (d+j)^{2j} \cdot \big(\tfrac{(d+j)L}{\pi K}\big)^{2d}$$

for every $d \in \mathbb{N}$, and hence

$$\sum_{|k|>K} |\widehat{f^{(j)}}_k| \leq \sum_{|k|>K} 2^{j+1} ML^j (d+j)^j \cdot \left(\tfrac{(d+j)L}{\pi k}\right)^d$$

$$\leq 2^{j+2} KML^j (d+j)^j \cdot \left(\tfrac{(d+j)L}{\pi K}\right)^d \overset{(*)}{\leq} 2^{-n}$$

with (*) for $K := L \cdot (d+j)$ and $d \geq n + 2j \cdot (\log j + \log L) + \log M$ since
$\sum_{k>K} k^{-d} \leq \int_K^\infty y^{-d}\, dy = y^{-d+1}/(1-d)\big|_{y=K}^{y=\infty} = K^{1-d}/(d-1) \leq K/K^d.$

d) $\hat{f}_k = \sum_{\ell=0}^{L-1} \int_{\ell/L}^{(\ell+1)/L} \sum_{j\geq 0} f_j^{(\ell)} \cdot (x - (2\ell+1)/(2L))^j \cdot \exp(2\pi i k x)\, dx ==$
$\sum_{\ell=0}^{L-1} \sum_{j\geq 0} f_j^{(\ell)} \cdot \widehat{X_\ell^j}_k.$

Recall that a smooth function's Fourier Series may be differentiated term-wise.

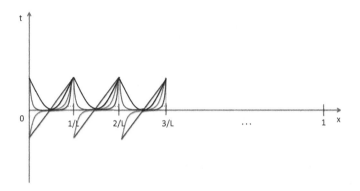

Fig. 2. Sawtooth Power Functions from Lemma 14

Item (b) expresses Taylor coefficients in terms of Fourier coefficients. Conversely, Items (c)+(a) allow to avoid costly Riemann integration when computing the Fourier coefficients of an analytic function [13, §5.4]. Lemma 14 is conveniently stated for $d = 1$ but immediately generalizes to higher dimensions, adding only notational noise.

Proof (Theorem 4). It suffices to present the main idea in the case $d = 1$. Given the spatial Taylor expansion a_j of the initial condition v with parameters M, L, Lemma 14(a)+(c) allow to compute in polynomial time the first polynomially many Fourier coefficients $\hat{v}_k$ of $v = \sum_k \hat{v}_k \cdot \exp(2\pi i k x)$.

a) By linearity of the Heat equation and with its Fundamental solution, it follows
$u(t, x) = \sum_k \widehat{u(t, \cdot)}_k \cdot \exp(2\pi i k x)$ for $\widehat{u(t, \cdot)}_k := \hat{v}_k \cdot \exp(-4\pi^2 k^2 t)$. Since these decay over time $t > 0$, $u(t, \cdot)$ has even larger radius of convergence and thus better computational parameters (M, L) than the initial condition v. And

again, the first polynomially many of these coefficients can be computed in polynomial time; and yield the first polynomially many Taylor coefficients of $u(t, \cdot)$ according to Lemma 14(b).

b) Similarly, $u(t, x) = \sum_k \widehat{u(t, \cdot)}_k \cdot \exp(2\pi i k x)$ for $\widehat{u(t, \cdot)}_k := \hat{v}_k \cdot \exp(-4\pi^2 i k^2 t)$. $\qquad\qquad\square$

5 Implementation

We give a prototypical implementation of the PDE solver in C++[1]. The implementation is based on the iRRAM framework. Our implementation extends iRRAM by classes for analytic functions and power series and solvers for PDEs using these classes. The implementation follows the theoretical part of the paper quite literally. That is, we implemented the operator from Theorem 10 that maps the power series of the right-hand side functions and of the initial value function to the power series of the PDE solution. These power series can be defined explicitly as in the proof of Theorem 3.

However, requiring to define multiple power series around several points in the domain is quite work-intensive and unnecessary in the case where we only deal with combinations of simple standard functions of which we know the derivatives. We therefore follow a more user-friendly approach by also implementing some helper functions that provide efficient ways to compute the power series for some combinations of standard functions based on automatic differentiation.

5.1 Overview of Continuous Data-Types

Let us first give an overview over the most important new continuous data-types that we added to iRRAM. Most of the data-types are implemented in form of C++ class templates with template parameters an integer d for the dimension and a class T for the base type. For the base type we mostly used iRRAM's REAL class for the type but other classes such as COMPLEX should also be possible without any major adaptions.

In the following presentation for conciseness we mostly omit the template parameters. We added the following class templates to iRRAM.

1. Powerseries: A class template for d-variate power series closely following the description in Section 3, i.e. encoding an infinite sequence of power series coefficients together with a coefficient bound. The series itself is encoded as a function mapping a vector of integers to an object of the coefficient type. For efficiency reasons, the coefficients are cached when they are read the first time and read from the cache whenever they are required again instead of reevaluating the coefficient function.

---

[1] The source code for the implementation can be found on https://github.com/holgerthies/irram-pde.

2. `Analytic`: A class template for analytic functions $f : [0,1]^d \to \mathbb{R}$ encoded by coverings of the unit cube by overlapping power series with some fixed radius of convergence.
3. `Cinfinity`: A class template for multivariate smooth functions. It is mostly used as a helper class to quickly generate power series for functions built by combinations of simple standard functions (c.f. 5.2).
4. `Polynomial`: Class for multivariate polynomials (i.e. finite power series) with more efficient evaluation.

These functional classes support standard operations such as arithmetic, function evaluation and computing partial derivatives.

We further implemented some useful class templates for matrices, vectors and multi-indices with some of their standard operations. We denote them by standard mathematical notation instead of their actual name in the source code (e.g. T^d instead of `vector<T,d>` and $\mathbb{N}^d$ instead of `Multiindex<d>`). We use these classes e.g. to define matrix-valued versions of the functional types. We also implemented a class template `DiffOp` for differential operators as in (9) where the coefficients are matrix-valued analytic functions.

5.2 Power Series and Automatic Differentiation

As described in the previous sections, the basic idea behind the PDE solver is to compute the power series of the solution and to provide some additional information that allows to evaluate the series at any point in its domain up to any desired accuracy. In theory, we can work directly with the power series and the coefficients bounds as described in Sect. 3. However, for concrete functions there are often much better algorithms available than just summing up the power series. Also, as we often need power series of some specific functions around different points, inputting the series directly is rather inconvenient.

The idea behind the `Cinfinity` class is that it can be used as a helper class for functions where we have a simple symbolic description of the derivatives (such as polynomials and trigonometric functions) and algebraic manipulations on them and can provide the power series around each point in their domain. Its implementation is similar to (forward mode) automatic differentiation but with a variable order of the power series. That is, an object `f` : `Cinfinity` allows to get any power series coefficient $\frac{1}{\alpha!}D^\alpha f(x)$ for any point x and multi-index α. Concretely, `Cinfinity` provides the methods `set_center`$(c : T^d)$ that updates the center to a new point and `get_derivative`$(\alpha : \mathbb{N}^d)$ that returns the derivative (divided by $\alpha!$) around the center.

The choice of always having a dedicated center is made to prevent unnecessary recomputation of derivatives by caching the coefficients when they are computed the first time, and only resetting the cache when the center is changed. To define a new `Cinfinity` object it suffices to provide a function that for any point x and multiindex α returns the derivative $D^\alpha f(x)$.

Operations on `Cinfinity` objects are implemented as pointer trees: Any k-ary saves pointers to the k input functions and is itself of type `Cinfinity`, i.e. it has to provide operations to set the center and compute derivatives of the result of the operation by using these operations on the input functions.

We implemented arithmetic operations (addition, subtraction, multiplication, division) and their scalar variants as well as composition and partial derivatives. We also implemented some standard functions such as multivariate polynomials and trigonometric functions. A vast amount of functions can therefore already be defined simply by composing these functions. Note that currently most operations are only implemented using straight-forward algorithms but many more sophisticated algorithms exist and could be used for better efficiency in the future.

We also implement a matrix-valued variant of `Cinfinity` that represents functions $f : T^d \to T^{m \times n}$. Basically, the class is just a wrapper around a matrix of `Cinfinity` objects. All functions are expected to have the same center and the class also provides a method `set_center` that sets the center for each function and `get_derivative` that returns an $m \times n$ matrix with elements of type T corresponding to the derivatives of each function.

To work with power series we further implemented a class `Powerseries` that contains the infinite d-variate coefficient series together with a coefficient bound M, r and supports evaluation, arithmetic operations and computing derivatives. It is possible to construct a power series from a `Cinfinity` object by additionally providing a center and valid coefficient bounds. On the other hand, as power series support the evaluation of derivatives in their domain, it is also possible to make a `Cinfinity` object from a `Powerseries`.

5.3 PDE Solving

As in the theoretical section, we consider both the case of Cauchy-Kovalevskaya type linear PDEs and the Heat equation (Schrödinger equation is treated in a similar manner).

1. For the Cauchy-Kovalevskaya type, we followed the theoretical Sect. 4.1 and separated the PDE solving algorithm into two parts. The first part is the computation of the coefficient sequence for the solution of the PDE (8). For this we implemented two different versions of differential operators, one where the coefficients are matrices of `Cinfinity` objects, i.e. variable and one where the coefficients are real matrices, i.e. constant. For the constant version we also implemented multiplication of two differential operators giving a new differential operator in the obvious way.

The algorithm to compute the solution series takes as input a differential operator D, a `Cinfinity` object v for the initial value function and a `vector` x and returns the coefficient of the power series for $u(x, t)$ around $t = 0$. It starts by centering v around x.

In case that D is a differential operator with variable coefficients, the computation is done from right to left, i.e., we start with $v^{[0]} := v$ and then iteratively compute $v^{[k+1]} = \frac{1}{k+1}D(v^{[k]})$. The k-th coefficient of the power series is then given by $v^{[k]}(0)$. In case that D is a differential operator with constant coefficients, the computation can also be done from left to right, i.e., start with

$D^{[0]} = D$ and then iteratively compute $D^{[k+1]} = \frac{1}{k+1} D D^{[k]}$. The k-th coefficient of the power series is then given by $D^{[k]}(v)(0)$.

Remark 15. For the case when $f_j(x) = A_j$ are constant matrices, the time bounds of Theorem 10 can be improved and the computations can be accelerated. Indeed, the coefficient $D^k v$ from Eq. (9) has the form

$$D^k v = \left(\sum_{i=1}^{d} A_i \partial_i \right)^k v = \sum_{|\alpha|=k} \binom{N}{\alpha} \prod_{i=1}^{d} A_i^{\alpha_i} \left(\left(\prod_{i=1}^{d} \partial_i^{\alpha_i} \right) v \right).$$

Thus, computing the power series of the PDE solution is reduced to matrix powering and computing partial derivatives of v. Now assume M_v, r are coefficient bounds for v and there is a constant M_A such that $\|A_i\|_\infty \leq M_A$ for $i = 1, \ldots, d$, where $\|A\|_\infty = \sup_{\|x\|_\infty = 1} \|Ax\|_\infty$ is the operator norm. Then

$$\left\| D^k v(0) \right\|_\infty \leq \sum_{|\alpha|=k} \binom{N}{\alpha} \prod_{i=1}^{d} \|A_i^{\alpha_i}\|_\infty \left(\left\| \left(\prod_{i=1}^{d} \partial_i^{\alpha_i} \right) v(0) \right\|_\infty \right)$$

$$\leq \sum_{|\alpha|=k} \binom{N}{\alpha} M_A^k M_v r^{-k} = M_v \left(\frac{r}{d M_A} \right)^{-k}.$$

It follows that the pair $(M_v, \frac{r}{d M_A})$ is a coefficient bound for the solution.

In both (variable and constant) cases if we are given coefficient bounds for the `Cinfinity` objects in the input, we can then construct a power series object from the series by using the parameters from Sect. 4 as coefficient bounds. To demonstrate that our implementation is feasible we did experiments with such well-known partial differential equations as the Acoustics and Elasticity systems for up to 3 dimensions.[2] For Cauchy-Kovalevskya type PDEs our algorithm could be used to approximate the solutions inside the small time interval (guaranteeing existence) for precisions up to 300 bits.

2. For the Heat equation we implemented the transformation from power series coefficients to Fourier coefficients, computed the Fourier series of the solution and then used Lemma 14 to transform the Fourier series to a power series again. The implementation quite literally follows the theoretical description and we therefore omit the details; we obtain approximations to the solution for any $t > 0$ and $x \in [0, 1]$ for arbitrarily high precisions.

Example 1. As initial value function we used a highly oscillating one: $v(x) = 2^m \sin(2^{m+1} \pi x)$ for different values of m. The function v is given by a covering of the unit interval by 2^m power series and we evaluated the running time and error propagation for various values of m. The running time grows quite quickly with m, and the computation already becomes quite slow for around $m = 7$. On the other hand, this is also where rounding errors become more notable, and where reliability justifies longer running times. For example, for $m = 7$ and small

---

[2] For space reasons, we omit a detailed analysis of our experiments but some more information can be found at the github repository of our implementation.

enough physical time, doing the same calculations using *double* precision is only accurate up to the first 4 decimal digits, and the error is likely to increase for higher values of m.

6 Conclusion

We have developed a guaranteed precision solver of Cauchy problems for Linear Evolutionary systems of PDEs in the case of real analytic initial data (functions at $t = 0$ and matrix coefficients) and bounds on their radii of convergence and upper bounds given as inputs. This solver is based on the rigorous theory of Computable Analysis [22] which allows to treat reals "exactly". We used our theoretical results to implement a solver for analytic linear partial differential equations in the C++ framework iRRAM. Our solver allows to approximate the solution up to any desired output precision. To our best knowledge, our solver is the first implementation of this kind. To this end, we also extended the iRRAM framework by user-friendly classes for continuously differentiable functions, power series, polynomials and matrices of these types.

Acknowledgments. This work was supported by the National Research Foundation of Korea (grant 2017R1E1A1A03071032), by the International Research & Development Program of the Korean Ministry of Science and ICT (grant 2016K1A3A 7A03950702), by the NRF Brain Pool program (grant 2019H1D3A2A02102240) and by JSPS KAKENHI Grant Number JP20K19744.

We thank Filippo Morabito for his lectures about PDEs on manifolds and Pieter Collins and Norbert Müller for helpful discussions on possibilities of implementing differential equations in ERC packages.

References

1. Bournez, O., Graça, D.S., Pouly, A.: Solving analytic differential equations in polynomial time over unbounded domains. In: Murlak, F., Sankowski, P. (eds.) MFCS 2011. LNCS, vol. 6907, pp. 170–181. Springer, Heidelberg (2011). https://doi.org/10.1007/978-3-642-22993-0_18
2. Brattka, V., Hertling, P., Weihrauch, K.: A tutorial on computable analysis. In: Cooper, S.B., Löwe, B., Sorbi, A. (eds.) New Computational Paradigms. Springer, New York (2008). https://doi.org/10.1007/978-0-387-68546-5_18
3. Brauße, F., Korovina, M., Müller, N.T.: Towards using exact real arithmetic for initial value problems. In: Mazzara, M., Voronkov, A. (eds.) PSI 2015. LNCS, vol. 9609, pp. 61–74. Springer, Cham (2016). https://doi.org/10.1007/978-3-319-41579-6_6
4. Collins, P., Graça, D.: Effective computability of solutions of ordinary differential equations the thousand monkeys approach. Electron. Notes Theoret. Comput. Sci. **221**, 103–114 (2008)
5. Evans, L.: Partial Differential Equations. Graduate Studies in Mathematics, vol. 19. American Mathematical Society, Providence (1998)
6. Hörmander, L.: The Analysis of Linear Partial Differential Operators I. Springer, Heidelberg (2003). https://doi.org/10.1007/978-3-642-61497-2

7. Kapron, B.M., Cook, S.A.: A new characterization of type-2 feasibility. SIAM J. Comput. **25**(1), 117–132 (1996)
8. Kawamura, A., Cook, S.: Complexity theory for operators in analysis. In: Proceedings of the 42nd ACM Symposium on Theory of Computing. STOC 2010, pp. 495–502. ACM, New York (2010)
9. Kawamura, A., Müller, N., Rösnick, C., Ziegler, M.: Computational benefit of smoothness: parameterized bit-complexity of numerical operators on analytic functions and Gevrey's hierarchy. J. Complex. **31**(5), 689–714 (2015). https://doi.org/10.1016/j.jco.2015.05.001
10. Kawamura, A., Steinberg, F., Thies, H.: Parameterized complexity for uniform operators on multidimensional analytic functions and ODE solving. In: Moss, L.S., de Queiroz, R., Martinez, M. (eds.) WoLLIC 2018. LNCS, vol. 10944, pp. 223–236. Springer, Heidelberg (2018). https://doi.org/10.1007/978-3-662-57669-4_13
11. Kawamura, A., Steinberg, F., Ziegler, M.: Complexity theory of (functions on) compact metric spaces. In: Proceedings of the 31st Annual Symposium on Logic in Computer Science, LICS, pp. 837–846. ACM (2016)
12. Kawamura, A., Thies, H., Ziegler, M.: Average-case polynomial-time computability of Hamiltonian dynamics. In: 43rd International Symposium on Mathematical Foundations of Computer Science (MFCS 2018). Schloss Dagstuhl-Leibniz-Zentrum fuer Informatik (2018)
13. Ko, K.I.: Complexity Theory of Real Functions. Progress in Theoretical Computer Science. Birkhäuser, Boston (1991)
14. Konečný, M., Duracz, J., Farjudian, A., Taha, W.: Picard method for enclosing odes with uncertain initial values. In: Proceedings of the 11th International Conference on Computability and Complexity in Analysis, 21–24 July 2014, pp. 41–42 (2014)
15. Koswara, I., Pogudin, G., Selivanova, S., Ziegler, M.: Bit-complexity of solving systems of linear evolutionary partial differential equations. In: Santhanam, R., Musatov, D. (eds.) CSR 2021. LNCS, vol. 12730, pp. 223–241. Springer, Cham (2021). https://doi.org/10.1007/978-3-030-79416-3_13
16. Koswara, I., Selivanova, S., Ziegler, M.: Computational complexity of real powering and improved solving linear differential equations. In: van Bevern, R., Kucherov, G. (eds.) CSR 2019. LNCS, vol. 11532, pp. 215–227. Springer, Cham (2019). https://doi.org/10.1007/978-3-030-19955-5_19
17. Kreitz, C., Weihrauch, K.: Theory of representations. Theoret. Comput. Sci. **38**, 35–53 (1985)
18. Müller, N.T.: The iRRAM: exact arithmetic in C++. In: Blanck, J., Brattka, V., Hertling, P. (eds.) CCA 2000. LNCS, vol. 2064, pp. 222–252. Springer, Heidelberg (2001). https://doi.org/10.1007/3-540-45335-0_14
19. Park, S., et al.: Foundation of computer (algebra) analysis systems: semantics, logic, programming, verification. https://arxiv.org/abs/1608.05787 (2020)
20. Plum, M.: Computer-assisted proofs for semilinear elliptic boundary value problems. Japan J. Indust. Appl. Math. **26**(2–3), 419–442 (2009). https://doi.org/10.1007/BF03186542
21. Thies, H.: Complexity theory and practice of integrating lipschitz-continuous functions in exact real arithmetic. Master's thesis, TU Darmstadt, September 2011
22. Weihrauch, K.: Computable Analysis. Springer, Berlin (2000). https://doi.org/10.1007/978-3-642-56999-9
23. Weihrauch, K.: Computational complexity on computable metric spaces. Math. Logic Q. **49**(1), 3–21 (2003)

A New Deterministic Method for Computing Milnor Number of an ICIS

Shinichi Tajima[1] and Katsusuke Nabeshima[2]([⊠])

[1] Graduate School of Science and Technology, Niigata University,
Ikarashi 2-no-cho, 8050 Nishi-ku Niigata, Japan
`tajima@emeritus.niigata-u.ac.jp`
[2] Department of Applied Mathematics, Tokyo University of Science,
1-3, Kagurazaka, Tokyo, Japan
`nabeshima@rs.tus.ac.jp`

Abstract. The Milnor number of an isolated complete intersection singularity (ICIS) is considered in the context of symbolic computation. Based on the classical Lê-Greuel formula, a new method for computing Milnor numbers is introduced. Key ideas of our approach are the use of auxiliary indeterminates and the concept of local cohomology with coefficients in the field of rational functions of auxiliary indeterminates. The resulting algorithm is described and some examples are given for illustration.

Keywords: Milnor number · Lê-Greuel formula · Local cohomology · Isolated complete intersection singularity

1 Introduction

In 1971, H. Hamm [16] studied local topology of an isolated complete intersection singularity (an ICIS) and showed in particular that the Milnor fiber is a nonsingular analytic manifold which is homotopically equivalent to a bouquet of real spheres of middle dimension. The number of spheres is called, as in the case of hypersurfaces [22], the Milnor number of an ICIS. The Milnor number of an ICIS is the most fundamental invariant and it plays important roles in singularity theory.

In 1974, Lê Dũng Tráng published a paper [19], written in Russian in memory of G. N. Tjurina, and gave a formula relevant to Milnor numbers of ICIS's. In 1973, G.-M. Greuel [11] independently derived the same formula in a completely different manner in his study of Gauss-Manin connections. Their formula is called Lê-Greuel formula. Based on this formula, they proposed a method for computing Milnor number of an ICIS which has been considered as the standard method for computation.

This work has been partly supported by JSPS Grant-in-Aid for Scientific Research (C) (18K03320 and 18K03214).

© Springer Nature Switzerland AG 2021
F. Boulier et al. (Eds.): CASC 2021, LNCS 12865, pp. 391–408, 2021.
https://doi.org/10.1007/978-3-030-85165-1_22

Note that, in 1978, G.-M. Greuel and H. A. Hamm [12] gave a formula for computing the Milnor number of quasi homogeneous complete intersections and in 1983 B. Martin and G. Pfister [21], and in 1990 M. Oka [30] gave formulas for computing Newton non-degenerate complete intersections. These closed formulas were generalized in 2007 by C. Bivia-Ausina [3] by utilizing the concept of Buchsbaum-Rim multiplicities, joint reductions and mixed Newton numbers. We refer to [28] for more recent results. Thanks to these investigations, many nice closed formulas are known. We also refer to [5–10] for results relevant to Lê-Greuel formula and ICIS germs.

For Newton degenerate cases for instance, the existence of a closed formula that express the Milnor number of ICIS germs can not be expected. In contrast, the method proposed by K. Saito and Lê-Greuel can be applied to compute the Milnor number even for Newton degenerate cases. Because of this, the method has been considered as the standard method for computation. However, in order to apply the standard method, the given set of defining functions of an ICIS should satisfy certain conditions. In the case, if the given set of defining functions does not satisfy this requirement, one has to find or construct another set of defining functions of an ICIS. In this regard, the standard method is not deterministic.

We consider in the present paper the Milnor number of an ICIS in the context of symbolic computation. We provide a new deterministic method for computing Milnor numbers of an ICIS, in order to complement the standard method. Basic idea of our approach is the use of auxiliary indeterminates for handling generic hyperplanes. We show that local cohomology with auxiliary indeterminates allow us to realize the proposed method as an effective algorithm for computing the Milnor number of an ICIS.

In Sect. 2, we recall the classical Lê-Greuel formula and the standard method of computing Milnor number of an ICIS. In Sect. 3, we recall some basics on local cohomology. In Sect. 4, we recall a result of B. Teissier and present our main tool. In Sect. 5, we present an algorithm for computing Milnor number of an ICIS and give an example for illustration.

All algorithms in this paper have been implemented in the computer algebra system Risa/Asir [29].

2   Lê-Greuel Formula

In this section, we recall Lê-Greuel formula and the standard method for computing Milnor number of an ICIS and we fix some notation. We refer the reader to [20] for some basics on isolated complete intersection singularities

Let X be an open neighbourhood of the origin O in $\mathbb{C}^n$ with a local coordinates system $x = (x_1, x_2, \cdots, x_n)$. Let $\mathcal{O}_X$ be the sheaf on X of holomorphic functions, $\mathcal{O}_{X,O}$ the stalk at O of the sheaf $\mathcal{O}_X$, i.e. the ring of germs at O of holomorphic functions. Let $V_q = \{x \in X \mid f_1(x) = f_2(x) = \cdots = f_q(x) = 0\}$ be a germ of complete intersection with an isolated singularity at the origin O, an ICIS, where $q \leq n$ and $f_1, f_2, \cdots, f_q$ are holomorphic functions defined on X. Notice that the subscript q stands for the codimension of V_q in X.

Let V_{q-1} denote the variety defined to be $V_{q-1} = \{x \in X \mid f_1(x) = f_2(x) = \cdots = f_{q-1}(x) = 0\}$. Let $J(f_1, f_2, \cdots, f_q)$ denote the ideal in $\mathcal{O}_{X,O}$ generated by the maximal minors of the Jacobian matrix $\frac{\partial(f_1, f_2, \cdots, f_q)}{\partial(x_1, x_2, \cdots, x_n)}$. Let $(f_1, f_2, \cdots, f_{q-1})$ be the ideal generated by $f_1, f_2, \cdots, f_{q-1}$ and let I_q denote the ideal $(f_1, f_2, \cdots, f_{q-1}) + J(f_1, f_2, \cdots, f_q)$ in $\mathcal{O}_{X,O}$:

$$I_q = (f_1, f_2, \cdots, f_{q-1}) + J(f_1, f_2, \cdots, f_q).$$

Lê Dũng Tráng [19] and G.-M. Greuel [11] independently obtained the following result.

Theorem 1. *Let $V_q = \{x \in X \mid f_1(x) = f_2(x) = \cdots = f_q(x) = 0\}$ be an ICIS, with $q \geq 2$. Suppose that V_{q-1} is also an ICIS. Then*

$$\mu(V_q) + \mu(V_{q-1}) = \dim_{\mathbb{C}} \left(\frac{\mathcal{O}_{X,O}}{I_q} \right),$$

where, $\mu(V_q)$ and $\mu(V_{q-1})$ are the Milnor number of V_q and of V_{q-1} respectively.

Note that for the case $q = n$, that is the case where the variety V_n is zero-dimensional, the Milnor number $\mu(V_n)$ can be determined by using a formula due to G.-M. Greuel [11, p. 261] as $\mu(V_n) = \delta - 1$, where $\delta = \dim_{\mathbb{C}} \left(\frac{\mathcal{O}_{X,O}}{(f_1, f_2, \cdots, f_n)} \right)$.

Let us also recall the following classical result due to V. Palamodov [31].

Theorem 2. *Let $V_1 = \{x \in X \mid f_1(x) = 0\}$ be a hypersurface with an isolated singularity at the origin O, where f_1 is a holomorphic function defined on X. Let $J(f_1)$ be the ideal in $\mathcal{O}_{X,O}$ generated by $\frac{\partial f_1}{\partial x_1}, \frac{\partial f_1}{\partial x_2}, \cdots, \frac{\partial f_1}{\partial x_n}$. Let $\mu(V_1)$ be the Milnor number of the hypersurface V_1. Then*

$$\mu(V_1) = \dim_{\mathbb{C}} \left(\frac{\mathcal{O}_{X,O}}{J(f_1)} \right).$$

Notice that the above formula can be regarded as a special case of Lê-Greuel formula given in Theorem 1.

Now, for each integer p with $1 \leq p \leq q$, let $V_p = \{x \in X \mid f_1(x) = f_2(x) = \cdots = f_p(x) = 0\}$ and let $I_p = (f_1, f_2, \cdots, f_{p-1}) + J(f_1, f_2, \cdots, f_p)$, the ideal in $\mathcal{O}_{X,O}$ generated by $f_1, f_2, \cdots, f_{p-1}$ and the maximal minors of the Jacobi matrix $\frac{\partial(f_1, f_2, \cdots, f_p)}{\partial(x_1, x_2, \cdots, x_n)}$. Note that for the case $p = 1$ we have $I_1 = J(f_1)$.

We are ready to present the standard method for computing the Milnor number of an ICIS. Note that it is K. Saito who first gave the formula below as a conjecture [4]. Later, two different proofs were given by Lê Dũng Tráng [19] and G.-M. Greuel [11] under the assumption that all $V_p, p = 1, 2, \cdots, q$ are ICIS. In 1984, E. J. N. Looijenger [20] added the refinement and gave the following result.

Theorem 3. *Let* $V_q = \{x \in X \mid f_1(x) = f_2(x) = \cdots = f_q(x) = 0\}$ *be an ICIS, with* $q \geq 2$. *Suppose that, all the ideal* $I_p, p = 1, 2, \cdots, q$ *have finite colength in* $\mathcal{O}_{X,O}$. *Then the following holds.*

$$\mu(V_q) = \sum_{p=1}^{q}(-1)^{(q-p)} \dim_{\mathbb{C}}\left(\frac{\mathcal{O}_{X,O}}{I_p}\right).$$

For the validity of the above result, we refer the reader to [20, page 77].

The standard method given by K. Saito [32] and Lê-Greuel is nice and useful. However it works provided that all the colengths of the ideal $I_p, p = 1, 2, \cdots, q$ are finite. If this requirement is not satisfied, in order to apply the standard method, it is necessary to find another set of defining equations of the given variety V_q. This requires expertise, or some trial and error and it is in general difficult to execute. In this sense, the method is not deterministic.

3   Local Cohomology

In this section, we recall some basics on local cohomology and the fact that colength of an ideal in the local ring can be computed by using local cohomology. We refer the reader to [2,14,15,17] for details.

Let Ω_X^n be the sheaf on X of holomorphic n-forms. where, as in the previous section, X is an open neighbourhood of the origin O in $\mathbb{C}^n$. Let $\mathcal{H}_{\{O\}}^n(\Omega_X^n)$ denote the top local cohomology of Ω_X^n supported at O.

Let I be a $\mathfrak{m}$ primary ideal in $\mathcal{O}_{X,O}$, where $\mathfrak{m}$ is the maximal ideal of $\mathcal{O}_{X,O}$. We define W_I as

$$W_I = \{\omega \in \mathcal{H}_{\{O\}}^n(\Omega_X^n) \mid h(x)\omega = 0, \forall h(x) \in I\}.$$

Then, the complex analytic version of the Grothendieck local duality [13,14,17] says that the pairing

$$\mathcal{O}_{X,O}/I \times W_I \longrightarrow \mathbb{C}$$

induced from the local residue pairing

$$\mathcal{O}_{X,O} \times \mathcal{H}_{\{O\}}^n(\Omega_X^n) \longrightarrow \mathbb{C}$$

is also non-degenerate. Since W_I is dual to $\mathcal{O}_{X,O}/I$ as a vector space, the colength of the ideal I in the local ring $\mathcal{O}_{X,O}$ is equal to the dimension, as a vector space, of W_F. Accordingly, the colength of I can be computed by using W_F.

Let $\mathcal{H}_{[O]}^n(\mathcal{O}_X)$ denote the algebraic local cohomology supported at O defined to be

$$\mathcal{H}_{[O]}^n(\mathcal{O}_X) = \lim_{k \to \infty} \mathrm{Ext}_{\mathcal{O}_X}^n(\mathcal{O}_X/\mathfrak{m}^k, \mathcal{O}_X).$$

We define H_I as

$$H_I = \{\psi \in \mathcal{H}_{[O]}^n(\mathcal{O}_X) \mid h(x)\psi = 0, \forall h \in I\}.$$

Then, since I is assumed to be $\mathfrak{m}$ primary, $W_I = \{\psi dx \mid \psi \in H_I\}$ holds.

Now let $g_1, g_2, \cdots, g_m$ be m polynomials in $K[x] = K[x_1, x_2, \cdots, x_n]$, where $K = \mathbb{Q}$. Let $I = (g_1, g_2, \cdots, g_m)$ be the ideal in the local ring $\mathcal{O}_{X,O}$ generated by $g_1, g_2, \cdots, g_m$. Assume that the ideal I is an $\mathfrak{m}$ primary ideal. Then an algorithm given in [23, 34] can be used to compute a basis of the vector space H_I.

In this paper, we represent an algebraic local cohomology class as a finite sum of the form $\sum c_\lambda \begin{bmatrix} 1 \\ x^\lambda \end{bmatrix}$ where [ ] is the Grothendieck symbol and $c_\lambda \in K$, $\lambda \in \mathbb{Z}^n_{\geq 1}$.

Let fix a term ordering $\succ$ on $\mathbb{Z}^n_{\geq 1}$. For a given algebraic local cohomology class of the form

$$\psi = c_\lambda \begin{bmatrix} 1 \\ x^\lambda \end{bmatrix} + \sum_{\lambda \succ \lambda'} c_{\lambda'} \begin{bmatrix} 1 \\ x^{\lambda'} \end{bmatrix},$$

we call $\begin{bmatrix} 1 \\ x^\lambda \end{bmatrix}$ the *head term*, c_λ the *head coefficient*, $c_\lambda \begin{bmatrix} 1 \\ x^\lambda \end{bmatrix}$ the *head monomial* and $\begin{bmatrix} 1 \\ x^{\lambda'} \end{bmatrix}$ the *lower terms*. We denote the head term by $\mathrm{ht}(\psi)$, the head coefficient by $\mathrm{hc}(\psi)$ and the head monomial by $\mathrm{hm}(\psi)$. Furthermore, we denote the set of terms of ψ as

$$\mathrm{Term}(\psi) = \left\{ \begin{bmatrix} 1 \\ x^\kappa \end{bmatrix} \middle| \, \psi = \sum_{\kappa \in \mathbb{Z}^n_{\geq 1}} c_\kappa \begin{bmatrix} 1 \\ x^\kappa \end{bmatrix}, c_\kappa \neq 0 \right\}$$

and the set of lower terms of ψ as

$$\mathrm{LL}(\psi) = \left\{ \begin{bmatrix} 1 \\ x^\kappa \end{bmatrix} \in \mathrm{Term}(\psi) \, \middle| \, \begin{bmatrix} 1 \\ x^\kappa \end{bmatrix} \neq \mathrm{ht}(\psi) \right\}.$$

For a finite subset $\Psi \subset \mathcal{H}^n_{[O]}(\mathcal{O}_X)$, $\mathrm{ht}(\Psi) = \{\mathrm{ht}(\psi) \mid \psi \in \Psi\}$ and $\mathrm{LL}(\Psi) = \bigcup_{\psi \in \Psi} \mathrm{LL}(\psi)$.

The multiplication by x^β is defined as

$$x^\beta \begin{bmatrix} 1 \\ x^\lambda \end{bmatrix} = \begin{cases} \begin{bmatrix} 1 \\ x^{\lambda - \beta} \end{bmatrix} & \lambda_i > \beta_i, \ i = 1, 2, \cdots, n, \\ 0 & \text{otherwise}, \end{cases}$$

where $\beta = (\beta_1, \cdots, \beta_n) \in \mathbb{Z}^n_{\geq 0}$, $\lambda = (\lambda_1, \cdots, \lambda_n) \in \mathbb{Z}^n_{\geq 1}$. The details for computing algebraic local cohomology classes are in [23, 34].

We give examples to explain our basic idea for computing the Milnor number of an ICIS. The following ICIS is taken from a paper of M. Giusti [10].

Example 1 (W₉ singularity). Let $X = \mathbb{C}^3$ with coordinates (x, y, z). W_9 defined as

$$W_9 = \{(x, y, z) \mid x^2 + yz^2 = y^2 + xz = 0\}$$

is an ICIS. Let $f_1(x, y, z) = x^2 + yz^2$, $f_2(x, y, z) = y^2 + xz$ and $l(x, y, z) = z$.
Set

$$V_2 = W_9, \quad V_3 = \{(x, y, z) \mid f_1(x, y, z) = f_2(x, y, z) = l(x, y, z) = 0\}.$$

Then $J(f_1, f_2, l)$ is generated by $4xy - z^3$, the determinant of the Jacobi matrix

$$\frac{\partial(f_1, f_2, l)}{\partial(x, y, z)} = \begin{pmatrix} \frac{\partial f_1}{\partial x} & \frac{\partial f_1}{\partial y} & \frac{\partial f_1}{\partial z} \\ \frac{\partial f_2}{\partial x} & \frac{\partial f_2}{\partial y} & \frac{\partial f_2}{\partial z} \\ \frac{\partial l}{\partial x} & \frac{\partial l}{\partial y} & \frac{\partial l}{\partial z} \end{pmatrix} = \begin{pmatrix} 2x & z^2 & 2yz \\ z & 2y & x \\ 0 & 0 & 1 \end{pmatrix}.$$

Let I denote the ideal in $\mathcal{O}_{X,O}$ generated by f_1, f_2 and $4xy - z^3$, and let H_I be the set of local cohomology classes annihilated by I:

$$H_I = \{\psi \in \mathcal{H}^3_{[O]}(\mathcal{O}_X) \mid h(x)\psi = 0, \forall h \in I\}.$$

The algorithm mentioned above outputs the following 12 local cohomology classes as a basis of the vector space H_I

$$\begin{bmatrix} 1 \\ xyz \end{bmatrix}, \begin{bmatrix} 1 \\ xyz^2 \end{bmatrix}, \begin{bmatrix} 1 \\ xy^2z \end{bmatrix}, \begin{bmatrix} 1 \\ x^2yz \end{bmatrix}, \begin{bmatrix} 1 \\ xyz^3 \end{bmatrix}, \begin{bmatrix} 1 \\ xy^2z^2 \end{bmatrix}, \begin{bmatrix} 1 \\ x^2yz^2 \end{bmatrix} - \begin{bmatrix} 1 \\ xy^3z \end{bmatrix},$$

$$\begin{bmatrix} 1 \\ xyz^4 \end{bmatrix} + \frac{1}{4}\begin{bmatrix} 1 \\ x^2y^2z \end{bmatrix}, \begin{bmatrix} 1 \\ xy^2z^3 \end{bmatrix} - \begin{bmatrix} 1 \\ x^3yz \end{bmatrix}, \begin{bmatrix} 1 \\ x^2yz^3 \end{bmatrix} - \begin{bmatrix} 1 \\ xy^3z^2 \end{bmatrix},$$

$$\begin{bmatrix} 1 \\ xyz^5 \end{bmatrix} + \frac{1}{4}\begin{bmatrix} 1 \\ x^2y^2z^2 \end{bmatrix} - \frac{1}{4}\begin{bmatrix} 1 \\ xy^4z \end{bmatrix},$$

$$\begin{bmatrix} 1 \\ xyz^6 \end{bmatrix} + \frac{1}{4}\begin{bmatrix} 1 \\ x^2y^2z^3 \end{bmatrix} - \frac{1}{4}\begin{bmatrix} 1 \\ xy^4z^2 \end{bmatrix} - \frac{1}{4}\begin{bmatrix} 1 \\ x^4yz \end{bmatrix}.$$

Since $\dim_{\mathbb{C}}(H_I) = 12$, it follows from Lê-Greuel formula and the refinement due to E. J. N. Looijenger that

$$\mu(V_2) + \mu(V_3) = 12.$$

Let D be the ideal in $\mathcal{O}_{X,O}$ generated by f_1, f_2 and l. Let H_D be the set of local cohomology classes annihilated by D:

$$H_D = \{\psi \in \mathcal{H}^3_{[O]}(\mathcal{O}_X) \mid h(x)\psi = 0, \forall h \in D\}.$$

Then, the algorithm outputs the following 4 local cohomology classes as a basis of H_D:

$$\begin{bmatrix} 1 \\ xyz \end{bmatrix}, \begin{bmatrix} 1 \\ xy^2z \end{bmatrix}, \begin{bmatrix} 1 \\ x^2yz \end{bmatrix}, \begin{bmatrix} 1 \\ x^2y^2z \end{bmatrix}.$$

Therefore $\delta = \dim_{\mathbb{C}}\left(\frac{\mathcal{O}_{X,O}}{D}\right)$ is equal to 4. In fact, it is easy to see that the ideal D is equal to the ideal (x^2, y^2, z) whose colength is equal to 4. Greuel formula presented in the previous section implies $\mu(V_3) = \delta - 1 = 3$. Accordingly we have $\mu(V_2) = 12 - 3 = 9$.

Notice that, in the computation above, if we choose $l' = x$ instead of $l = z$, we fail, because the ideal I' generated by $f_1, f_2, J(f_1, f_2, l')$ is not $\mathfrak{m}$ primary. In fact it is easy to see that the common locus $V(I')$ of the ideal I' contains a line $\{(x, y, z) \mid x = y = 0\}$ passing through the origin.

In order to design deterministic algorithms for computing the Milnor number of an ICIS, one has to avoid such possibilities.

We give another example, which will be examined again in the next section. The next example is also taken from [10].

Example 2 (T_7 singularity). Let $X = \mathbb{C}^3$ with coordinates (x, y, z). T_7 defined as

$$T_7 = \{(x, y, z) \mid x^2 + y^3 + z^3 = yz = 0\}$$

is an ICIS. Let $f_1(x, y, z) = x^2 + y^3 + z^3$, $f_2(x, y, z) = yz$ and $l(x, y, z) = x$.
Set

$$V_2 = T_7, \quad V_3 = \{(x, y, z) \mid f_1(x, y, z) = f_2(x, y, z) = l(x, y, z) = 0\}.$$

Since $\left| \dfrac{\partial(f_1, f_2, l)}{\partial(x, y, z)} \right| = \begin{vmatrix} 2x & 3y^2 & 3z^2 \\ 0 & z & y \\ 1 & 0 & 0 \end{vmatrix} = 3y^3 - 3z^3$, the ideal I defined to be

$I = (f_1, f_2) + J(f_1, f_2, l)$ is given by

$$I = (x^2 + y^3 + z^3, yz, y^3 - z^3).$$

The algorithm mentioned above outputs the following 12 local cohomology classes as a basis of the vector space H_I

$$\begin{bmatrix} 1 \\ xyz \end{bmatrix}, \begin{bmatrix} 1 \\ xyz^2 \end{bmatrix}, \begin{bmatrix} 1 \\ xy^2z \end{bmatrix}, \begin{bmatrix} 1 \\ x^2yz \end{bmatrix}, \begin{bmatrix} 1 \\ xyz^3 \end{bmatrix}, \begin{bmatrix} 1 \\ xy^2z^2 \end{bmatrix}, \begin{bmatrix} 1 \\ xy^3z \end{bmatrix}, \begin{bmatrix} 1 \\ xy^2z^3 \end{bmatrix},$$

$$\begin{bmatrix} 1 \\ xy^3z^2 \end{bmatrix}, \begin{bmatrix} 1 \\ xy^3z^3 \end{bmatrix}, \begin{bmatrix} 1 \\ xyz^4 \end{bmatrix} + \begin{bmatrix} 1 \\ xy^4z \end{bmatrix} - 2\begin{bmatrix} 1 \\ x^3yz \end{bmatrix}.$$

We have $\mu(V_2) + \mu(V_3) = 12$.

Let $D = (x^2 + y^3 + z^3, yz, x)$. Then the algorithm outputs the following 6 local cohomology classes as a basis of the vector space H_D

$$\begin{bmatrix} 1 \\ xyz \end{bmatrix}, \begin{bmatrix} 1 \\ xyz^2 \end{bmatrix}, \begin{bmatrix} 1 \\ xy^2z \end{bmatrix}, \begin{bmatrix} 1 \\ xyz^3 \end{bmatrix}, \begin{bmatrix} 1 \\ xy^3z \end{bmatrix}, \begin{bmatrix} 1 \\ xyz^4 \end{bmatrix} - \begin{bmatrix} 1 \\ xy^4z \end{bmatrix}.$$

From $\delta = \dim_{\mathbb{C}}(H_D) = 6$, we have $\mu(V_3) = 6 - 1 = 5$. Therefore, we have $\mu(T_7) = 12 - 5 = 7$.

4   Genericity

We recall in this section a result of B. Teissier on generic hyperplanes [36, 38] and give our main tool.

Let $V = \{x \in X \mid g_1(x) = g_2(x) = \cdots = g_r(x) = 0\}$ be a germ of complete intersection with an isolated singularity at the origin O with $r < n$.

4.1 Hyperplane Sections

For $\xi = (\xi_1, \xi_2, \cdots, \xi_n) \in \mathbb{C}^n \backslash (0, 0, \cdots, 0)$, let $l_\xi(x) = \xi_1 x_1 + \xi_2 x_2 + \cdots + \xi_n x_n$ and let L_ξ denote the hyperplane $L_\xi = \{x \in \mathbb{C}^n \mid l_\xi(x) = 0\}$.

Let W_ξ denote the hyperplane section of V defined to be $W_\xi = V \cap L_\xi$. Let I_ξ be the ideal in the local ring $\mathcal{O}_{X,O}$ defined to be

$$I_\xi = (g_1, g_2, \cdots, g_r) + J(g_1, g_2, \cdots, g_r, l_\xi),$$

where $J(g_1, g_2, \cdots, g_r, l_\xi)$ is the ideal generated by the maximal minors of the Jacobi matrix $\frac{\partial(g_1, g_2, \cdots, g_r, l_\xi)}{\partial(x_1, x_2, \cdots, x_n)}$. Notice that $\xi = (\xi_1, \xi_2, \cdots, \xi_n)$ are regarded as parameters.

Define a number γ as

$$\gamma = \min_{[\xi] \in \mathbb{P}^{n-1}} \left(\dim_{\mathbb{C}} \left(\frac{\mathcal{O}_{X,O}}{I_\xi} \right) \right),$$

where $[\xi]$ stands for the class in the projective space $\mathbb{P}^{n-1}$ of $\xi = (\xi_1, \xi_2, \cdots, \xi_n) \in \mathbb{C}^n \backslash (0, 0, \cdots, 0)$.

Let

$$U = \left\{ [\xi] \in \mathbb{P}^{n-1} \, \middle| \, \dim_{\mathbb{C}} \left(\frac{\mathcal{O}_{X,O}}{I_\xi} \right) = \gamma \right\}.$$

Then, the result in [36–38] of B. Teissier on polar varieties implies that U is a Zariski open dense subset of $\mathbb{P}^{n-1}$.

Definition 1. *Let $\xi = (\xi_1, \xi_2, \cdots, \xi_n) \in \mathbb{C}^n \backslash (0, 0, \cdots, 0)$.*

*(i) The hyperplane L_ξ satisfies the condition **F** if $\dim_{\mathbb{C}} \left(\dfrac{\mathcal{O}_{X,O}}{I_\xi} \right) < \infty$.*

*(ii) The hyperplane L_ξ satisfies the condition **G** if $\dim_{\mathbb{C}} \left(\dfrac{\mathcal{O}_{X,O}}{I_\xi} \right) = \gamma$.*

Since $W_\xi = \{x \in X \mid g_1(x) = g_2(x) = \cdots = g_r(x) = l_\xi(x) = 0\}$, Lê-Greuel formula implies that if L_ξ satisfies the condition **F**, we have

$$\mu(V) + \mu(W_\xi) = \dim_{\mathbb{C}} \left(\frac{\mathcal{O}_{X,O}}{I_\xi} \right).$$

We say that the hyperplane L_ξ is generic with respect to the variety V, if L_ξ satisfies the condition **G**, and the hyperplane section $V \cap L_\xi$ is also called a generic hyperplane section of V.

Remark 1: Let V be a hypersurface $V = \{x \in X \mid f(x) = 0\}$ with an isolated singularity at the origin. Let $l = x_1$ and let $L = \{x \in X \mid x_1 = 0\}$. Assume that the hyperplane L is generic. The ideal I defined to be $I = (f) + J(f, x_1)$ is equal to $(f, \frac{\partial f}{\partial x_2}, \frac{\partial f}{\partial x_3}, \cdots, \frac{\partial f}{\partial x_n})$. Therefore, for the case $r = 1$, the formula above coincides with the result of Lê Dũng Tráng given in [18] and that of B. Teissier given in [36, 37].

Remark 2: In [27], the authors of the present paper constructed an algorithm to test whether given family of ideals are zero-dimensional or not. Therefore, the set $\{[\xi] \in \mathbb{P}^{n-1} \mid L_\xi$ satisfies the condition $\mathbf{F}\}$ is computable. Furthermore, by combining this algorithm with the algorithm given in [23] for computing parametric local cohomology systems, a method for decomposing the projective space $\mathbb{P}^{n-1}$ according to the dimension of $\dim_{\mathbb{C}}\left(\frac{\mathcal{O}_{X,O}}{I_\xi}\right)$ can be realized as an algorithm. In particular, the set $\{[\xi] \in \mathbb{P}^{n-1} \mid L_\xi$ satisfies the condition $\mathbf{G}\}$ is also computable. See [24] for related results on limiting tangent spaces.

4.2   Auxiliary Indeterminates and Local Cohomology

In [26], in order to address problems that involves generic properties [33,37], the authors of the present paper proposed an approach and implemented an algorithm for computing local cohomology with coefficients in the field of rational functions of auxiliary indeterminates. The method of computing local cohomology classes are completely same as the previous one given in [23,34]. Difference lies in only the coefficient fields of local cohomology classes. The algorithm has been successfully utilized in [25,26,35]. Here we adopt the same approach and use the algorithm mentioned above.

Let $u = \{u_1, u_2, \cdots, u_n\}$ be auxiliary indeterminates and let $K(u)$ be the field of rational functions in u. Let $H^n_{[O]}(K(u)\{x\})$ denote the local cohomology defined to be

$$H^n_{[O]}(K(u)\{x\}) = \lim_{k \to \infty} \mathrm{Ext}^n_{K(u)\{x\}}(K(u)\{x\}/\mathfrak{m}^k, K(u)\{x\}).$$

Let $\ell_u(x) = u_1 x_1 + u_2 x_2 + \cdots + u_n x_n$. Let J_u denote an ideal in $K(u)\{x\}$ generated by the maximal minor of the Jacobi matrix $\frac{\partial(g_1, g_2, \cdots, g_r, \ell_u)}{\partial(x_1, x_2, \cdots, x_n)}$, and let

$$I_u = (g_1, g_2, \cdots, g_r) + J_u.$$

Here, I_u is regarded as an ideal in the local ring $K(u)\{x\}$. Now we consider the set H_{I_u} of local cohomology classes defined to be

$$H_{I_u} = \{\psi \in H^n_{[O]}(K(u)\{x\}) \mid h(x)\psi = 0,\ \forall h \in I_u\}.$$

We have the following.

Lemma 1. *Let* $\dim_{K(u)}(H_{I_u})$ *be the dimension as a vector space over the fields of rational functions of the space* H_{I_u}. *Then, the following holds.*

$$\dim_{K(u)}(H_{I_u}) = \min_{[\xi] \in \mathbb{P}^{n-1}} \left(\dim_{\mathbb{C}} \left(\frac{\mathcal{O}_{X,O}}{I_\xi} \right) \right).$$

Proof. Let $\succ$ be a term ordering on $\mathbb{Z}^n_{\geq 1}$. (Note that coefficients $K(u)$ does not affect the term ordering.) Let Ψ_u be a basis of the vector space H_{I_u} such that, for all $\psi \in \Psi_u$, $\mathrm{hc}(\psi) = 1$, $\mathrm{ht}(\psi) \notin \mathrm{ht}(\Psi_u \backslash \{\psi\})$ and $\mathrm{ht}(\psi) \notin \mathrm{LL}(\Psi_u)$

w.r.t. $\succ$. For $\alpha \in K^n$, let $\sigma_\alpha(\Psi_u)$ denote the set of local cohomology classes in $H^n_{[O]}(K\{x\})$ defined as $\sigma_\alpha(\Psi_u) = \{\sigma_\alpha(\psi_u) \mid \psi_u \in \Psi_u\}$, where σ_α is the map that substitutes u by α. Let Φ_α be a basis of the vector space, over K, of H_{I_α} such that, for all $\varphi \in \Phi_\alpha$, $\mathrm{hc}(\varphi) = 1$, $\mathrm{ht}(\varphi) \notin \mathrm{ht}(\Phi_\alpha \backslash \{\varphi\})$ and $\mathrm{ht}(\varphi) \notin \mathrm{LL}(\Phi_\alpha)$ w.r.t. $\succ$. Recall that the basis Ψ_u is computed over the fields $K(u)$ of rational functions. Accordingly, for *generic* values of $\alpha \in K^n$, $\sigma_\alpha(\Psi_u) = \Phi_\alpha$. Since the set $U = \left\{ [\xi] \in \mathbb{P}^{n-1} \mid \dim_{\mathbb{C}} \left(\frac{\mathcal{O}_{X,O}}{I_\xi} \right) = \gamma \right\}$ is Zariski open and dense, the statement above holds.   □

Remark 3: In the algorithm of computing a basis Ψ_u of H_{I_u}, everything is computed over the field of rational functions. This means, calculation such as $\frac{u_2}{u_2} = 1$ is allowed. Therefore, there is a possibility that, $\sigma_\alpha(\Psi_u)$ is not a basis of the vector space H_{I_α}, for some $\alpha \in K^n$.

We thus arrive at the following criterion.

Theorem 4. *Let* $\alpha = (\alpha_1, \alpha_2, \cdots, \alpha_n) \in K^n$, *and let* L_α *be the hyperplane defined by* $L_\alpha = \{x \in \mathbb{C}^n \mid l_\alpha(x) = 0\}$, *where* $l_\alpha(x) = \alpha_1 x_1 + \alpha_2 x_2 + \cdots + \alpha_n x_n$. *Let* I_α *denote the ideal in the local ring* $K\{x\}$ *defined to be* $I_\alpha = (g_1, g_2, \cdots, g_r) + J(g_1, g_2, \cdots, g_r, l_\alpha)$. *Then, the hyperplane* L_α *is generic with respect to the variety* V, *if and only if the following holds*

$$\dim_K(H_{I_\alpha}) = \dim_{K(u)}(H_{I_u}).$$

Proof. Since $\dim_{K(u)}(H_{I_u}) = \gamma$ holds by Lemma 1, the hyperplane L_α satisfies the condition **G** if and only if $\dim_K(H_{I_\alpha}) = \dim_{K(u)}(H_{I_u})$.   □

The following example is taken from a list given in [10]

Example 3 (T_7 singularity). Let $X = \mathbb{C}^3$ with coordinates (x, y, z). T_7 defined as

$$T_7 = \{(x, y, z) \mid x^2 + y^3 + z^3 = yz = 0\}$$

is an ICIS. Let $f_1(x, y, z) = x^2 + y^3 + z^3$, $f_2(x, y, z) = yz$ and $\ell_u(x, y, z) = x + u_2 y + u_3 z$, where u_2, u_3 are auxiliary indeterminates.

Since $\left| \frac{\partial(f_1, f_2, \ell_u)}{\partial(x, y, z)} \right| = 3y^3 - 3z^3 - 2u_2 xy + 2u_3 xz$, the ideal I_u defined to be $I_u = (f_1, f_2) + J_u$ is given by

$$I_u = (x^2 + y^3 + z^3, yz, 3y^3 - 3z^3 - 2u_2 xy + 2u_3 xz) \subset K(u_2, u_3)\{x, y, z\}.$$

The algorithm mentioned above outputs the following 10 local cohomology classes as a basis Ψ_u, over the field $K(u_2, u_3)$ of the vector space H_{I_u}

$$\begin{bmatrix} 1 \\ xyz \end{bmatrix}, \begin{bmatrix} 1 \\ xyz^2 \end{bmatrix}, \begin{bmatrix} 1 \\ xy^2z \end{bmatrix}, \begin{bmatrix} 1 \\ x^2yz \end{bmatrix}, \begin{bmatrix} 1 \\ xyz^3 \end{bmatrix}, \begin{bmatrix} 1 \\ xy^3z \end{bmatrix},$$

$$u_2 \begin{bmatrix} 1 \\ xy^2z^2 \end{bmatrix} + u_3 \begin{bmatrix} 1 \\ x^2y^2z \end{bmatrix}, u_3 \begin{bmatrix} 1 \\ xyz^4 \end{bmatrix} + \frac{3}{2} \begin{bmatrix} 1 \\ x^2yz^2 \end{bmatrix} - u_3 \begin{bmatrix} 1 \\ x^3yz \end{bmatrix},$$

$$u_3 \begin{bmatrix} 1 \\ xy^4z \end{bmatrix} + \frac{3}{2} \begin{bmatrix} 1 \\ x^2yz^2 \end{bmatrix} - u_3 \begin{bmatrix} 1 \\ x^3yz \end{bmatrix},$$

$$u_2^2 u_3 \begin{bmatrix} 1 \\ xyz^5 \end{bmatrix} + u_2 u_3^2 \begin{bmatrix} 1 \\ xy^5 z \end{bmatrix} + \frac{3}{2} u_2^2 \begin{bmatrix} 1 \\ x^2 yz^3 \end{bmatrix} + \frac{3}{2} u_3^2 \begin{bmatrix} 1 \\ x^2 y^3 z \end{bmatrix}$$

$$- u_2^2 u_3 \begin{bmatrix} 1 \\ x^3 yz^2 \end{bmatrix} - u_2 u_3^2 \begin{bmatrix} 1 \\ x^3 y^2 z \end{bmatrix}.$$

Since $\dim_{K(u_2,u_3)}(H_{I_u}) = 10$, we have $\gamma = 10$. This means, for any generic hyperplane section W of T_7, we have $\mu(T_7) + \mu(W) = 10$.

Let $D_u = (x^2 + y^3 + z^3, yz, x + u_2 y + u_3 z)$. Then the algorithm outputs the following 4 local cohomology classes as a basis of the vector space H_{D_u}.

$$\begin{bmatrix} 1 \\ xyz \end{bmatrix}, \begin{bmatrix} 1 \\ xyz^2 \end{bmatrix} - u_3 \begin{bmatrix} 1 \\ x^2 yz \end{bmatrix}, \begin{bmatrix} 1 \\ xy^2 z \end{bmatrix} - u_2 \begin{bmatrix} 1 \\ x^2 yz \end{bmatrix},$$

$$u_2^2 \begin{bmatrix} 1 \\ xyz^3 \end{bmatrix} - u_3^2 \begin{bmatrix} 1 \\ xy^3 z \end{bmatrix} - u_2^2 u_3 \begin{bmatrix} 1 \\ x^2 yz^2 \end{bmatrix} + u_2 u_3^2 \begin{bmatrix} 1 \\ x^2 y^2 z \end{bmatrix}.$$

Therefore, we have $\mu(T_7) = 10 - (4 - 1) = 7$.

We see that the Milnor number is determined only by the computation of local cohomology with coefficient in the field of rational functions of auxiliary indeterminates. Notice that in this computation, no generic hyperplane is used. It is easy to see, for the case $q = n - 1$ in general, it is not necessary to find generic hyperplane nor generic hyperplane section explicitly to compute the Milnor number $\mu(V_{n-1})$ of V_{n-1}.

Let us compare the computation above with that described in Example 2 in the previous section.

In Example 2, the hyperplane $x = 0$ is chosen. The dimension of H_I for the ideal $I = (x^2 + y^3 + z^3, yz, y^3 - z^3)$ is equal to 12, which is bigger than 10. This means that the hyperplane $x = 0$ that satisfies the condition **F** is not generic. The dimension of H_D for the ideal $D = (x^2 + y^3 + z^3, yz, x)$ is equal to 6, which is also bigger than 4.

We see that, if a generic hyperplane is not selected, this affects the efficiency of the subsequent computations. In other words, it is better to choose in each step, generic hyperplanes to save the cost of computations.

Let us consider a method for finding a generic hyperplane. Let us look at the basis Ψ_u given in Example 3. If we substitute $(1, 0)$ into (u_2, u_3), we obtain 10 local cohomology classes. It seems natural to expect naively that the hyperplane $x + y = 0$ that corresponds to $(1, 0)$ is generic. However, the algorithm described in [34] outputs the following 11 local cohomology classes as a basis of H_I for the ideal $I = (x^2 + y^3 + z^3, yz, 3y^3 - 3z^3 - 2xy) \subset K\{x, y, z\}$

$$\begin{bmatrix} 1 \\ xyz \end{bmatrix}, \begin{bmatrix} 1 \\ xyz^2 \end{bmatrix}, \begin{bmatrix} 1 \\ xy^2 z \end{bmatrix}, \begin{bmatrix} 1 \\ x^2 yz \end{bmatrix}, \begin{bmatrix} 1 \\ xyz^3 \end{bmatrix}, \begin{bmatrix} 1 \\ xy^3 z \end{bmatrix}, \begin{bmatrix} 1 \\ x^2 yz^2 \end{bmatrix}, \begin{bmatrix} 1 \\ x^2 yz^3 \end{bmatrix},$$

$$\begin{bmatrix} 1 \\ xyz^4 \end{bmatrix} - \frac{3}{2} \begin{bmatrix} 1 \\ x^2 y^2 z \end{bmatrix} - \begin{bmatrix} 1 \\ x^3 yz \end{bmatrix}, \begin{bmatrix} 1 \\ xy^4 z \end{bmatrix} + \frac{3}{2} \begin{bmatrix} 1 \\ x^2 y^2 z \end{bmatrix} - \begin{bmatrix} 1 \\ x^3 yz \end{bmatrix},$$

$$\begin{bmatrix} 1 \\ x^2 yz^4 \end{bmatrix} + \frac{3}{2} \begin{bmatrix} 1 \\ xy^5 z \end{bmatrix} + \frac{9}{4} \begin{bmatrix} 1 \\ x^2 y^3 z \end{bmatrix} - \frac{3}{2} \begin{bmatrix} 1 \\ x^3 y^2 z \end{bmatrix} - \begin{bmatrix} 1 \\ x^4 yz \end{bmatrix}.$$

Such a naive guess does not work. Note that if one chooses for instance the hyperplane $x + y + z = 0$, then it turns out by direct computation that the chosen hyperplane is generic. We also have $\dim_K(H_D) = 4$, for the ideal $D = (f_1, f_2, x + y + z)$.

5   Algorithm

Here we give an algorithm for computing a Milnor number of an ICIS and an example.

Let $V_q = \{x \in X | f_1(x) = f_2(x) = \cdots = f_q(x) = 0\}$ be a germ of complete intersection with an isolated singularity at the origin O with $q < n$. Let

$$\ell_1 = u_1 x_1 + u_2 x_2 + \cdots + u_n x_n, \quad u = \{u_1, u_2, \cdots, u_n\},$$

J_1 be the set of all minors of the Jacobian matrix $\frac{\partial(f_1, \cdots, f_q, \ell_1)}{\partial(x_1, \cdots, x_n)}$, and $I_1 = \{f_1, \cdots, f_q\} \cup J_1$, where $u_1, u_2, \cdots, u_n$ are auxiliary indeterminates. Set

$$H_{I_1} = \{\psi \in H_{[O]}^n(K(u)\{x\}) | h\psi = 0, \forall h \in I_1\}.$$

Assume that we have already computed $\gamma_1 = \dim_{K(u)}(H_{I_1})$. Then, by the definition, $l_\alpha = \alpha_1 x_1 + \alpha_2 x_2 + \cdots + \alpha_n x_n$ is generic if and only if $\dim_K(H_{I_\alpha}) = \gamma_1$ where J_α is the set of all minors of the Jacobian matrix $\frac{\partial(f_1, \cdots, f_q, l_\alpha)}{\partial(x_1, \cdots, x_n)}$ and $I_\alpha = \{f_1, \cdots, f_q\} \cup J_\alpha$. Hence, we can easily obtain a generic hyperplane by utilizing random numbers.

Our strategy for getting a generic hyperplane, is the following.

"Take a point $[\alpha] \in \mathbb{P}^{n-1}$, randomly. If $\dim_K(H_{I_\alpha}) = \gamma_1$, then return l_α, if not, repeat the same procedure until we get a generic hyperplane."

Recall that, according to Theorem 4, $U = \{[\alpha] \in \mathbb{P}^{n-1} | \dim_K(H_{I_\alpha}) = \gamma_1\}$ is a Zariski open dense subset of $\mathbb{P}^{n-1}$. Therefore, if a hyperplane is randomly taken, the probability of its genericity is very high. Hence, the strategy will work efficiently. After getting a generic hyperplane l_α in K^n, we can utilize the generic hyperplane in the next step.

Note that as $[\alpha] \in U$, ℓ_1 can be written as

$$\ell_1 = x_1 + u_2 x_2 + \cdots + u_n x_n,$$

namely, we do not need the symbol u_1.

In the next step, we set again $\ell_2 = x_2 + u_3 x_3 + \cdots + u_3 x_3$ and update $u = \{u_3, \cdots, u_n\}$. Let J_2 be the set of all minors of the Jacobian matrix $\frac{\partial(f_1, \cdots, f_q, l_\alpha, \ell_2)}{\partial(x_1, \cdots, x_n)}$ and $I_2 = \{f_1, \cdots, f_q, l_\alpha\} \cup J_2$. Likewise, we can obtain a generic hyperplane of $V_{q+1} = \{x \in X | f_1(x) = f_2(x) = \cdots = f_q(x) = l_\alpha = 0\}$ by utilizing our strategy. (Remark that $\mu(V_q) + \mu(V_{q+1}) = \gamma_1$.) We repeat this procedure $n - q$ times.

Algorithm 1 represents our strategy that computes a generic hyperplane by utilizing random numbers, and is utilized in Algorithm 2.

Algorithm 1

Specification: GENERICITY(I_j, γ_j, u)

Input : $I_j \subset K(u)[x]$, $\gamma_j \in \mathbb{N}$, $u = \{u_{j+1}, \cdots, u_n\}$: auxiliary indeterminates
$(j \leq n - 1)$. (γ_j means the dimension of the vector space H_{I_j}.)

Output: $\alpha = (\alpha_{j+1}, \cdots, \alpha_n) \in K^{n-j}$: for α, $\dim_K(H_{\sigma_\alpha(I)}) = \gamma$ where
$\sigma_\alpha(I) = \{g(\alpha, x) | g(u, x) \in I\}$ (i.e. $x_j + \alpha_{j+1}x_{j+1} + \cdots + \alpha_n x_n = 0$ is a
generic hyperplane w.r.t. V_{q+j}.)

begin
$flag \leftarrow 1$;
while $flag \neq 0$ **do**
$\quad \alpha = (\alpha_{j+1}, \cdots, \alpha_n) \leftarrow$ take random numbers $\alpha_{j+1}, \cdots, \alpha_n$ from K;
$\quad$ **if** $\dim_K(H_{\sigma_\alpha(I)}) = \gamma_j$ **then**   /*$\sigma_\alpha(I) = \{g(\alpha, x) | g(u, x) \in I\}$ */
$\quad\quad$ return α;
$\quad$ **end-if**
end-while
end

Note that when $\dim_K(H_{\sigma_\alpha(I)}) > \gamma$, it is possible to determine whether $\dim_K(H_{\sigma_\alpha(I)}) = \gamma$ or not, without computing a basis of $H_{\sigma_\alpha(I)}$, completely. That is to say, if $\gamma + 1$ algebraic local cohomology classes are obtained in the process of computation, then we can instantly output the fact "$\dim_K(H_{\sigma_\alpha(I)}) \neq \gamma$". We refer to papers [23,34] that give algorithms for computing algebraic local cohomology classes.

The following is the main algorithm for computing the Milnor number of an ICIS.

Algorithm 2

Input : $f_1, f_2, \cdots, f_q \in K[x]$ defines a germ of an ICIS V_q at O in $\mathbb{C}^n$ where
$q \geq 2$ and $q \leq n$.

Output: $\mu : \mu(V_q)$.

begin
$\mu \leftarrow 0$; $L \leftarrow \emptyset$;
for each $j = 1$ to $n - q$ **do**
$\quad \ell_j \leftarrow x_j + \sum_{i=j+1}^{n} u_i x_i$;
$\quad u \leftarrow \{u_{j+1}, \cdots, u_n\}$;
$\quad J_j \leftarrow$ all maximal minors of the Jacobian matrix $\frac{\partial(f_1, \cdots, f_q, l_1, \cdots, l_{j-1}, \ell_j)}{\partial(x_1, \cdots, x_n)}$
$\quad\quad$ (if $j = 1$, then $\frac{\partial(f_1, \cdots, f_q, \ell_1)}{\partial(x_1, \cdots, x_n)}$);
$\quad I_j \leftarrow \{f_1, \cdots, f_q\} \cup L \cup J_j$;
$\quad \gamma_j \leftarrow \dim_{K(u)}(H_{I_j})$;
$\quad (\alpha_{j+1}, \cdots, \alpha_n) \leftarrow$ **GENERICITY**(I_j, γ_j, u);

$l_j \leftarrow$ substitute $(\alpha_{j+1}, \cdots, \alpha_n)$ into u of ℓ_j;
$L \leftarrow L \cup \{l_j\}$;
$\mu \leftarrow \mu + (-1)^{j+1} \gamma_j$;
end-for
$D \leftarrow \{f_1, \cdots, f_q\} \cup L$;   (*1)
$\delta \leftarrow \dim_K(H_D)$;
$\mu \leftarrow \mu + (-1)^{j+1}(\delta - 1)$;
return μ;
end

Remark 4: See (*1). Let $D = \{f_1, \cdots, f_q\} \cup L = \{f_1, \cdots, f_q, l_1, \cdots, l_{n-q}\}$ and $D_u = \{f_1, \cdots, f_1, l_1, \ldots, l_{n-q-1}, \ell_{n-q}\}$. Then, $\delta = \dim_K(H_D) = \dim_{K(u)}(H_{D_u})$. Therefore, we do not need to execute **GENERICITY**$(I_{n-q}, \gamma_{n-q}, u)$. However, in order to keep simple style, we adopt the above. Note that I_j is a set of generators of the ideal (I_j).

Theorem 5. *Algorithm 2 outputs $\mu(V_q)$, correctly.*

Proof. For each i, let J_i be the set of all maximal minors of the Jacobian matrix $\frac{\partial(f_1, \cdots, f_q, l_1, \cdots, l_{i-1}, \ell_i)}{\partial(x_1, \cdots, x_n)}$, $I_j = \{f_1, \cdots, f_q\} \cup \{l_1, \ldots, l_j\} \cup J_j$, $\gamma_j = \dim_{K(u)}(H_{I_j})$ and $V_{q+j} = \{x \in X | f_1(x) = f_2(x) = \cdots = f_q(x) = l_1(x) = \cdots = l_i(x) = 0\}$. Then, by Theorem 1 and Greuel formula, $\gamma_j = \mu(V_{q+j-1}) + \mu(V_{q+j})$ and $\mu(V_{q+(n-q)}) = \mu(V_n) = \delta - 1$. Thus, we have the following simultaneous linear equations

$$\gamma_1 = \mu(V_q) + \mu(V_{q+1}),$$
$$\gamma_2 = \mu(V_{q+1}) + \mu(V_{q+2}),$$
$$\gamma_3 = \mu(V_{q+2}) + \mu(V_{q+3}),$$
$$\vdots$$
$$\gamma_{n-q} = \mu(V_{q+(n-q-1)}) + \mu(V_{q+(n-q)}) = \mu(V_{n-1}) + \mu(V_n) = \mu(V_{n-1}) + (\delta - 1).$$

Hence,

$$\mu(V_q) = \sum_{i=1}^{n-q} (-1)^{i+1} \gamma_i + (-1)^{n-q+2}(\delta - 1).$$

Therefore, Algorithm 2 outputs $\mu(V_q)$, correctly. $\square$

We present an example for illustration. The example is taken from a list given in the paper [39] of C. T. C. Wall. See also [1].

Example 4 (J_9' singularity). Let $X = \mathbb{C}^4$ with coordinates (x, y, z, w). Let $f_1(x, y, z, w) = xy + z^2$, $f_2(x, y, z, w) = xz + y^3 + w^2$ and

$$V_2 = \{(x, y, z, w) \in X \mid f_1(x, y, z, w) = f_2(x, y, z, w) = 0\}.$$

V_2 is an ICIS, known as J_9' singularity.

1: Let us compute the case $i = 1$. Let $\ell_1 = x + u_2 y + u_3 z + u_4 w$, $u = \{u_2, u_3, u_4\}$ where u_2, u_3, u_4 are auxiliary indeterminates. Now,

$$\frac{\partial(f_1, f_2, \ell_1)}{\partial(x, y, z, w)} = \begin{pmatrix} \frac{\partial f_1}{\partial x} & \frac{\partial f_1}{\partial y} & \frac{\partial f_1}{\partial z} & \frac{\partial f_1}{\partial w} \\ \frac{\partial f_2}{\partial x} & \frac{\partial f_2}{\partial y} & \frac{\partial f_2}{\partial z} & \frac{\partial f_2}{\partial w} \\ \frac{\partial \ell_1}{\partial x} & \frac{\partial \ell_1}{\partial y} & \frac{\partial \ell_1}{\partial z} & \frac{\partial \ell_1}{\partial w} \end{pmatrix} = \begin{pmatrix} y & x & 2z & 0 \\ z & 3y^2 & x & 2w \\ 1 & u_2 & u_3 & u_4 \end{pmatrix}.$$

Let J_1 be the set of all maximal minors of the matrix $\dfrac{\partial(f_1, f_2, \ell_1)}{\partial(x, y, z, w)}$, i.e.

$$J_1 = \left\{ \begin{vmatrix} y & x & 2z \\ z & 3y^2 & x \\ 1 & u_2 & u_3 \end{vmatrix}, \begin{vmatrix} y & x & 0 \\ z & 3y^2 & 2w \\ 1 & u_2 & u_4 \end{vmatrix}, \begin{vmatrix} y & 2z & 0 \\ z & x & 2w \\ 1 & u_3 & u_4 \end{vmatrix}, \begin{vmatrix} x & 2z & 0 \\ 3y^2 & x & 2w \\ u_2 & u_3 & u_4 \end{vmatrix} \right\}$$

$$= \{ x^2 - u_2 xy - u_3 xz + 3u_3 y^3 - 6y^2 x + 2u_2 z^2,$$
$$-u_4 xz + 2xw + 3u_4 y^3 - 2u_2 yw, u_4 xy - 2u_3 yw - 2u_4 z^2 + 4zw,$$
$$u_4 x^2 - 2u_3 xw - 6u_4 y^2 z + 4u_2 zw \}.$$

Set $I_1 = \{f_1, f_2\} \cup J_1$. Then, $\gamma_1 = \dim_{K(u)}(H_{I_1}) = 14$.
First, take $(0, 0, 0)$ for (u_2, u_3, u_4). Then, Algorithm 1 detects that the hyperplane $x = 0$ is not generic. In fact, the ideal generated by

$$\{ g(0, 0, 0, x, y, z, w) | g(u_2, u_3, u_4, x, z, y, z) \in I_1 \}$$

is not $\mathfrak{m}$ primary. Second, take $(1, 0, 0)$ for (u_2, u_3, u_4). Then, we find that the hyperplane $x + y = 0$ is generic.
We set $l_1 = x + y$, $L = \{l_1\}$ and

$$V_3 = \{ (x, y, z, w) \in X \mid f_1(x, y, z, w) = f_2(x, y, z, w) = x + y = 0 \}.$$

2: Let us compute the case $i = 2$. Renew u as $\{u_3, u_4\}$ and

$$\frac{\partial(f_1, f_2, l_1, \ell_2)}{\partial(x, y, z, w)} = \begin{pmatrix} \frac{\partial f_1}{\partial x} & \frac{\partial f_1}{\partial y} & \frac{\partial f_1}{\partial z} & \frac{\partial f_1}{\partial w} \\ \frac{\partial f_2}{\partial x} & \frac{\partial f_2}{\partial y} & \frac{\partial f_2}{\partial z} & \frac{\partial f_2}{\partial w} \\ \frac{\partial l_1}{\partial x} & \frac{\partial l_1}{\partial y} & \frac{\partial l_1}{\partial z} & \frac{\partial l_1}{\partial w} \\ \frac{\partial \ell_2}{\partial x} & \frac{\partial \ell_2}{\partial y} & \frac{\partial \ell_2}{\partial z} & \frac{\partial \ell_2}{\partial w} \end{pmatrix} = \begin{pmatrix} y & x & 2z & 0 \\ z & 3y^2 & x & 2w \\ 1 & 1 & 0 & 0 \\ 0 & 1 & u_3 & u_4 \end{pmatrix}.$$

Let $\ell_2 = y + u_3 z + u_4 w$ and

$$J_2 = \left\{ \left| \frac{\partial(f_1, f_2, l_1, \ell_2)}{\partial(x, y, z, w)} \right| \right\}$$
$$= \{ u_4 x^2 + -u_4 xy - 2u_3 xw - 6u_4 y^2 x + 2u_3 yw + 2u_4 z^2 + 4zw \}.$$

Set $I_2 = \{f_1, f_2\} \cup L \cup J_2$. Then, $\gamma_2 = \dim_{K(u)}(H_{I_2}) = 8$.

Let $D = \{f_1, f_2, l_1, \ell_2\}$. Then, we have the following as a basis of H_D.

$$u_3 \begin{bmatrix} 1 \\ xyzw^2 \end{bmatrix} - u_4 \begin{bmatrix} 1 \\ xyz^2w \end{bmatrix}, \begin{bmatrix} 1 \\ xyzw^2 \end{bmatrix} - u_4 \begin{bmatrix} 1 \\ xy^2zw \end{bmatrix} + u_4 \begin{bmatrix} 1 \\ x^2yzw \end{bmatrix},$$

$$(2u_3u_4 - u_4^3) \begin{bmatrix} 1 \\ xyz^3w \end{bmatrix} + u_3^2u_4 \begin{bmatrix} 1 \\ xy^2z^2w \end{bmatrix},$$

$$-(u_4 + u_3^2u_4) \begin{bmatrix} 1 \\ xyzw^3 \end{bmatrix} + (1 - u_3^2) \begin{bmatrix} 1 \\ xyz^2w^2 \end{bmatrix} + (-u_3 + u_3^3 + u_4^2) \begin{bmatrix} 1 \\ xy^2zw^2 \end{bmatrix}$$

$$+(u_3 - u_3^3 - u_4^2) \begin{bmatrix} 1 \\ x^2yzw^2 \end{bmatrix} + u_4 \begin{bmatrix} 1 \\ x^2yz^2w^2 \end{bmatrix} + (2u_3u_4 - u_4^3) \begin{bmatrix} 1 \\ xy^3zw \end{bmatrix}$$

$$+(-2u_3u_4 + u_4^3) \begin{bmatrix} 1 \\ x^2y^2zw \end{bmatrix} + (2u_3u_4 - u_4^2) \begin{bmatrix} 1 \\ x^3yzw \end{bmatrix} + u_3^2u_4 \begin{bmatrix} 1 \\ x^2yzw \end{bmatrix}.$$

Since $\delta = 4$, we arrive at $\mu(V_2) = 14 - 8 + 3 = 9$.

Note that if we take $(0, 1)$ for (u_3, u_4), then Algorithm 1 detects that the hyperplane $y + w = 0$ is not generic. In fact the dimension of the relevant vector space is equal to 9. Next we take $(1, 1)$ for (u_3, u_4). Then, we find that the hyperplane $y + z + w = 0$ is generic. We set $l_2 = y + z + w$, $L = \{l_1, l_2\}$ and

$$V_4 = \{(x, y, z, w) \in X \mid f_1(x, y, z, w) = f_2(x, y, z, w) = x + y = y + z + w = 0\}.$$

Now, we define D as $D = \{f_1, f_2\} \cup L = \{f_1, f_2, l_1, l_2\}$ and compute the dimension of the vector space H_D. We find $\delta = \dim_K(H_D) = 4$. Since $\mu(V_2) = \gamma_1 - \gamma_2 + (\delta - 1)$, we also have $\mu(V_2) = 9$.

References

1. Afzal, D., Afzal, F., Mulback, M., Pfister, G., Yaqub, A.: Unimodal ICIS, a classifier. Studia Scientiarum Math. Hungarica **54**, 374–403 (2017)
2. Altman, A., Kleiman, S.: Introduction to Grothendieck Duality Theory. LNM, vol. 146. Springer, Heidelberg (1970). https://doi.org/10.1007/BFb0060932
3. Bivià-Ausina, C.: Mixed Newton numbers and isolated complete intersection singularities. Proc. London Math. Soc. **94**, 749–771 (2007)
4. Brieskorn, E.: Vue d'ensemble sur les problèmes de monodromie. Astérisque **7**(8), 393–413 (1973)
5. Callejas-Brdregal, R., Morgado, M.F.Z., Saia, M., Seade, J.: The Lê-Greuel formula for functions on analytic spaces. Tohoku Math. J. **68**, 439–456 (2016)
6. Carvalho, R.S., Oréfice-Okamoto, B., Tomazzela, J.N.: μ-constant deformations of functions on an ICIS. J. Singul. **19**, 163–176 (2019)
7. Damon, J.N.: Topological invariants of μ-constant deformations of complete intersection. Quart. J. Math. Oxford **40**, 139–159 (1989)
8. Gaffney, T.: Polar multiplicities and equisingularity of map germs. Topology **32**, 185–223 (1993)
9. Gaffney, T.: Multiplicities and equisingularity of ICIS germs. Invent. Math. **123**, 209–220 (1996)

10. Giusti, M.: Classification des singularités isolées simples d'intersections complètes. In: Singularities Part I, Proceedings of Symposia in Pure Mathematics, vol. 40, pp. 457–494. AMS (1983)

11. Greuel, G.-M.: Der Gauss-Manin-Zusammenhang isolierter Singularitäten von vollständigen Durchschnitten. Math. Ann. **214**, 235–266 (1973)

12. Greuel, G.-M., Hamm, H.A.: Invarianten quasihomogener vollständiger Durchschnitte. Invent. Math. **49**, 67–86 (1978)

13. Griffiths, P., Harris, J.: Principles of Algebraic Geometry. Wiley, Hoboken (1976)

14. Grothendieck, A.: Théorèmes de dualité pour les faisceaux algébriques cohérents. Séminaire Bourbaki **149**, 169–193 (1957)

15. Hartshorne, R.: Local Cohomology. LNM, vol. 41. Springer, Heidelberg (1967). https://doi.org/10.1007/BFb0073971

16. Hamm, H.: Lokale topologische Eigenschaften komplexer Räume. Math. Ann. **191**, 235–252 (1971)

17. Kunz, E.: Residues and Duality for Projective Algebraic Varieties. American Mathematical Society, Providence (2009)

18. Lê D.T.: Calcule du nobmre de cycles évanouissants d'une hypersurface complexe. Ann. Inst. Fourier **23**, 261–270 (1973)

19. Lê D.T.: Calculation of Milnor number of isolated singularity of complete intersection (in Russian). Funktsional. Analiz i ego Prilozhen. **8**, 45–49 (1974)

20. Looijenga, E.J.N.: Isolated Singular Points on Complete Intersections. London Mathematical Society Lecture Note Series, Cambridge, vol. 77 (1984)

21. Martin, B., Pfister, G.: Milnor number of complete intersections and Newton polygons. Math. Nachr. **110**, 159–177 (1983)

22. Milnor, J.: Singular points of complex hypersurfaces. Ann. Math. Stud. **61**, 591–648 (1968)

23. Nabeshima, K., Tajima, S.: Algebraic local cohomology with parameters and parametric standard bases for zero-dimensional ideals. J. Symb. Comput. **82**, 91–122 (2017)

24. Nabeshima, K., Tajima, S.: A new method for computing limiting tangent spaces of isolated hypersurface singularity via algebraic local sohomology. In: Advanced Studies in Pure Mathematics, vol. 78, pp. 331–344 (2018)

25. Nabeshima, K., Tajima, S.: Computing logarithmic vector fields and Bruce-Roberts Milnor numbers via local cohomology classes. Rev. Roumaine Math. Pures Appl. **64**, 521–538 (2019)

26. Nabeshima, K., Tajima, S.: Alternative algorithms for computing generic μ^*-sequences and local Euler obstructions of isolated hypersurface singularities. J. Algebra Appl. **18**(8) (2019). 1959156 (13pages)

27. Nabeshima, K., Tajima, S.: Testing zero-dimensionality of varieties at a point. Math. Comput. Sci. **15**, 317–331 (2021)

28. Nguyen, T.T.: Uniform stable radius and Milnor number for non-degenerate isolated complete intersection singularities. arXiv:1912.10655v2 (2019)

29. Noro, M., Takeshima, T.: Risa/Asir- a computer algebra system. In: Proceedings of International Symposium on Symbolic and Algebraic Computation (ISSAC), pp. 387–396. ACM (1992)

30. Oka, M.: Principal zeta-function of non-degenerate complete intersection singularity. J. Fac. Sci. Univ. Tokyo Sect. IA Math. **37**, 11–32 (1990)

31. Palamodov, V.P.: Multiplicity of holomorphic mappings. Funktsional. Analiz i ego Prilozhen. **1**, 54–65 (1967)

32. Saito, K.: Calcule algébrique de la monodromie. Astérisque **7**(8), 195–211 (1973)

33. Tajima, S.: On polar varieties, logarithmic vector fields and holonomic D-modules. RIMS Kôkyûroku Bessatsu **40**, 41–51 (2013)
34. Tajima, S., Nakamura, Y., Nabeshima, K.: Standard bases and algebraic local cohomology for zero dimensional ideals. In: Advanced Studies in Pure Mathematics, vol. 56, pp. 341–361 (2009)
35. Tajima, S., Shibuta, T., Nabeshima, K.: Computing logarithmic vector fields along an ICIS germ via Matlis duality. In: Boulier, F., England, M., Sadykov, T.M., Vorozhtsov, E.V. (eds.) CASC 2020. LNCS, vol. 12291, pp. 543–562. Springer, Cham (2020). https://doi.org/10.1007/978-3-030-60026-6_32
36. Teissier, B.: Cycles évanescents, sections planes et conditions de Whitney, Singularités, à Cargèse. Astérisque **7**(8), 285–362 (1973)
37. Teissier, B.: Variétés polaires. I. Inventiones Mathematicae, vol. 40, pp. 267–292 (1977)
38. Teissier, B.: Varietes polaires II Multiplicites polaires, sections planes, et conditions de whitney. In: Aroca, J.M., Buchweitz, R., Giusti, M., Merle, M. (eds.) Algebraic Geometry. LNM, vol. 961, pp. 314–491. Springer, Heidelberg (1982). https://doi.org/10.1007/BFb0071291
39. Wall, C.T.C.: Classification of unimodal isolated singularities complete intersections. In: Proceedings of Symposia in Pure Mathematics, vol. 40, Part II, pp. 625–640 (1983)

New Parallelisms of $PG(3,5)$ with Automorphisms of Order 8

Svetlana Topalova[ID] and Stela Zhelezova[✉][ID]

Institute of Mathematics and Informatics, Bulgarian Academy of Sciences,
Sofia, Bulgaria
{svetlana,stela}@math.bas.bg

Abstract. Let $PG(n,q)$ be the n-dimensional projective space over the finite field $\mathbb{F}_q$. A *spread* in $PG(n,q)$ is a set of lines which partition the point set. A partition of the lines of the projective space by spreads is called a *parallelism*. The study of parallelisms is motivated by their numerous relations and applications. We construct 8958 new nonisomorphic parallelisms of $PG(3,5)$. They are invariant under cyclic automorphism groups of order 8. Some of their interesting properties are discussed. We use the system for computational discrete algebra GAP as well as our own MPI-based software written in C++.

Keywords: Finite projective space · Parallelism · System for computational discrete algebra GAP

1 Introduction

Let $PG(n,q)$ be the n-dimensional projective space over the finite field $\mathbb{F}_q$. A spread is a set of lines such that each point is in exactly one of these lines. Two spreads are isomorphic if an automorphism of $PG(n,q)$ maps one to the other. A parallelism is a partition of the set of all lines of the projective space to spreads. Two parallelisms are isomorphic if there is an automorphism of $PG(n,q)$ which maps the spreads of one parallelism to spreads of the other. An automorphism of a parallelisms is an automorphism of $PG(n,q)$ which maps each of its spreads to a spread of the same parallelism.

Background material on projective spaces, spreads, and parallelisms can be found, for instance, in [15] or [24]. Parallelisms are related to translation planes and 2-designs [24], network coding [9], error-correcting codes [13], and cryptography [22].

The authors acknowledge the provided access to the e-infrastructure of the NCHDC – part of the Bulgarian National Roadmap on RIs, with the financial support by the Grant No D01-221/03.12.2018.

© Springer Nature Switzerland AG 2021
F. Boulier et al. (Eds.): CASC 2021, LNCS 12865, pp. 409–419, 2021.
https://doi.org/10.1007/978-3-030-85165-1_23

General constructions of parallelisms are known for $PG(2^n - 1, q)$ [6], for $PG(n, 2)$ [1,30], and for $PG(3, q)$ [8,10,14,17]. All parallelisms of $PG(3, 2)$ and $PG(3, 3)$ are known [3,15]. The classification problem is still open for larger projective spaces. Since solving it in the general case is currently infeasible, many authors have performed restricted searches for parallelisms satisfying certain assumptions. An important approach is based on assuming a non-trivial group of automorphisms. It makes the search more feasible, but excludes objects with trivial or very small automorphism groups. Examples of this approach can be found, for instance, in [4,18,19,21,23]. The present paper also follows this line of research by assuming a cyclic group of order 8. All possibilities for such a group are explored, but besides the automorphism group, additional restrictions on the type of the parallelisms are also assumed.

A spread of $PG(3, q)$ contains q^2+1 lines and a parallelism consists of q^2+q+1 spreads. A set R of $q + 1$ mutually skew lines of $PG(3, q)$ is called a *regulus* if any line which intersects three lines of R intersects all lines of R. Three mutually skew lines determine exactly one regulus. A spread S of $PG(3, q)$ is called *regular* if it contains all the lines of the regulus determined by any triple of lines from S. If all the spreads of a parallelism are regular, the parallelism is *regular* too. If all the spreads of a parallelism are isomorphic to each other, the parallelism is *uniform*.

The number of the points and the planes of $PG(3, q)$ is the same. The dual space of $PG(3, q)$ can be obtained by considering the planes as points and the points as planes. It is defined by the plane-line incidence and is a $PG(3, q)$ too. Each parallelism corresponds to a parallelism of the dual space and is self-dual if it is isomorphic to it (details can be found, for instance, in [4]).

Computer-aided classifications of parallelisms with assumed automorphism groups have been done in projective spaces with relatively small parameters. In $PG(3, 4)$ (the smallest space in which the classification problem is open), all parallelisms invariant under automorphism groups of odd prime orders and some of the parallelisms with automorphisms of order 2 have been classified [5]. The construction of the rest is infeasible by our methods. $PG(3, 5)$ admits parallelisms with automorphisms of prime orders 31, 13, 5, 3 and 2. There are classifications of cyclic parallelisms [19] (with automorphisms of order 31), of parallelisms invariant under groups of orders 13 [26] and 25 [29], and of regular parallelisms with automorphisms of order 3 [25]. In the present paper, we consider the biggest cyclic automorphism groups (they are of order 8) with which parallelisms are possible, but have not been classified.

There are a great number of parallelisms with a cyclic automorphism group of order 8. A small part of them (899) was constructed in [28] to show that all the 21 spreads of $PG(3, 5)$ take part in parallelisms. In the present paper, we use a powerful parallel computer to obtain new parallelisms of $PG(3, 5)$ which are invariant under a cyclic automorphism group of order 8 and for which definite restrictions (different from those in [28]) hold. The construction method is described in Sect. 2, the obtained results are discussed in Sect. 3, and concluding remarks can be found in Sect. 4.

2   Construction Method

2.1   The Projective Space

The projective space $PG(3, 5)$ has 156 points and 806 lines. Each spread of $PG(3, 5)$ contains 26 lines which partition the point set and each parallelism has 31 spreads.

We obtain the points of $PG(3, 5)$ as the 156 vectors (v_1, v_2, v_3, v_4) over $GF(5)$ whose rightmost nonzero element is 1. A lexicographic order is imposed on them and a number is assigned such that $(1, 0, 0, 0)$ is number 1, and $(4, 4, 4, 1)$ number 156. We next find the lines and the hyperplanes.

An invertible matrix $(a_{i,j})_{4\times 4}$ over $GF(5)$ defines an automorphism of the projective space transforming the coefficient vectors of the projective points by the map $v_i' = \sum_j a_{i,j} v_j$. The matrices M_1 and M_2 are generators of the subgroups G_{8_2} and G_{8_6} which we further talk about in the next subsection.

$$M_1 = \begin{pmatrix} 1 & 1 & 2 & 1 \\ 1 & 3 & 3 & 1 \\ 0 & 0 & 3 & 0 \\ 0 & 1 & 0 & 3 \end{pmatrix} \qquad M_2 = \begin{pmatrix} 1 & 3 & 0 & 4 \\ 1 & 4 & 0 & 1 \\ 0 & 4 & 3 & 2 \\ 0 & 3 & 2 & 1 \end{pmatrix}$$

We denote by G the full automorphism group of the projective space, where $G \cong P\Gamma L(4, 5)$ (the projective semilinear group [2]). The number of its elements is $|G| = 2^9 \cdot 3^2 \cdot 5^6 \cdot 13 \cdot 31$. Let H be a subgroup of G. The normalizer $N(H)$ of H in G is defined as $N(H) = \{g \in G \mid gHg^{-1} = H\}$.

2.2   Possible Automorphism Groups

We use GAP [12] to obtain the Sylow 2-subgroup of G. It has $2^9 = 512$ elements. We denote this subgroup by G_{2^9}. Its elements are of orders 2, 4 and 8. We find by GAP that they are in 12 conjugacy classes under G. Table 1 presents some properties of the cyclic group generated by a representative of each of these classes, namely the number of points and lines which it fixes, the order of its normalizer (found by GAP), and the number and length of the line orbits under this group. There are two conjugacy classes of elements of order 8. We denote the corresponding groups by G_{8_2} and G_{8_6} (the indexes 2 and 6 come from the number of fixed points), and we write only G_8 if properties that are the same for the two groups are considered. Each of the cyclic groups of order 8 comprises one collineation of order 2, two of order 4 and four of order 8. In both groups, the element of order 2 is from the first conjugacy class (Table 1) and the elements of order 4 are from the 9th one.

2.3   Spread Orbits Under G_8

There are fixed (of type F_1), short (of type S_2), and long (of type L_8) spread orbits under G_8, where the index is the orbit length.

Table 1. Cyclic groups generated by representatives of the conjugacy classes of elements of order 2, 4, and 8 under G

Conjugacy class	Element order	Fixed points	Fixed lines	Nontrivial line orbits			Normalizer order
				Length 2	Length 4	Length 8	
1	2	12	38	384			115200
2	2	0	26	390			187200
3	2	32	62	372			1488000
4	4	4	6	16	192		512
5	4	0	0	13	195		624
6	4	0	2	18	192		1152
7	4	8	14	24	186		1920
8	4	8	14	12	192		3840
9	4	12	38		192		115200
10	4	32	62		186		1488000
11	8	2	2	18		96	384
12	8	6	2	18		96	5760

Spread Orbits of Type F_1. Since G_8 fixes some lines, the parallelisms must contain fixed spreads containing the fixed lines. In addition to the fixed lines, a fixed spread contains several whole line orbits under G_8. All line orbits of length 2 under G_8 contain points of the fixed lines, so they cannot be involved in a fixed spread together with the fixed lines. Therefore, the fixed spread comprises the two fixed lines l_1 and l_2 and three orbits of length 8 with mutually disjoint lines, namely $\{c_1^i, c_2^i, \ldots, c_8^i\}$, $i = 1, 2, 3$.

$$\boxed{F_1}: \quad \boxed{l_1}\,\boxed{l_2}\,\boxed{c_1^1\ c_2^1\ c_3^1\ c_4^1\ c_5^1\ c_6^1\ c_7^1\ c_8^1}\,\boxed{c_1^2\ c_2^2\ c_3^2\ c_4^2\ c_5^2\ c_6^2\ c_7^2\ c_8^2}\,\boxed{c_1^3\ c_2^3\ c_3^3\ c_4^3\ c_5^3\ c_6^3\ c_7^3\ c_8^3}$$

Spread Orbits of Type S_2. The 18 line orbits of length 2 (short orbits) can be involved in spreads with orbits of length 2. At most six lines from different short orbits do not intersect and can be in one spread. Therefore, a spread with orbit of type S_2 contains six lines from different short orbits ($\{b_1^i, b_2^i\}$, $i = 1, 2, \ldots, 6$) and 5 whole orbits under the subgroup of order 4 that belong to different line orbits under G_{8_2}. This is illustrated below, where $\{c_1^i, c_2^i, \ldots, c_8^i\}$, $i = 1, \ldots, 5$ are five line orbits of length 8, such that $\{c_1^i, c_2^i, c_3^i, c_4^i\}$ and $\{c_5^i, c_6^i, c_7^i, c_8^i\}$ are line orbits under the subgroup of order 4 and the lines included in each orbit of length 4 are mutually skew.

$$\boxed{S_2}: \quad \boxed{b_1^1}\,\boxed{b_1^2}\,\boxed{b_1^3}\,\boxed{b_1^4}\,\boxed{b_1^5}\,\boxed{b_1^6}\,\boxed{c_1^1\ c_2^1\ c_3^1\ c_4^1}\,\boxed{c_1^2\ c_2^2\ c_3^2\ c_4^2}\,\boxed{c_1^3\ c_2^3\ c_3^3\ c_4^3}\,\boxed{c_1^4\ c_2^4\ c_3^4\ c_4^4}\,\boxed{c_1^5\ c_2^5\ c_3^5\ c_4^5}$$
$$\boxed{b_2^1}\,\boxed{b_2^2}\,\boxed{b_2^3}\,\boxed{b_2^4}\,\boxed{b_2^5}\,\boxed{b_2^6}\,\boxed{c_5^1\ c_6^1\ c_7^1\ c_8^1}\,\boxed{c_5^2\ c_6^2\ c_7^2\ c_8^2}\,\boxed{c_5^3\ c_6^3\ c_7^3\ c_8^3}\,\boxed{c_5^4\ c_6^4\ c_7^4\ c_8^4}\,\boxed{c_5^5\ c_6^5\ c_7^5\ c_8^5}$$

Spread Orbits of Type L_8. Spreads with spread orbits of length 8 consist of 26 lines from 26 different line orbits of length 8 under G_8. An L_8 orbit is presented below, where $\{c_1^i, c_2^i, \ldots, c_8^i\}$, $i = 1, \ldots, 26$ are the orbits of length 8.

$$\boxed{L_8} : \quad \begin{array}{|c|c|c|c|} \hline c_1^1 & c_1^2 & \cdots & c_1^{26} \\ \hline c_2^1 & c_2^2 & \cdots & c_2^{26} \\ \hline \multicolumn{4}{c}{\cdots} \\ \hline c_8^1 & c_8^2 & \cdots & c_8^{26} \\ \hline \end{array}$$

Table 2 presents the number of possible spreads with orbits of these types.

Table 2. Possible spreads

Orbit type	G_{8_2}	G_{8_6}
F_1	16	80
S_2	2832	4080
L_8	14227090	14227090

Parallelisms. Each point has to be covered in each spread. Each fixed point under G_8 participates in a fixed line, in 3 line orbits of length 2 and in 3 line orbits of length 8. Therefore, a parallelism invariant under G_8 consists of one spread of type F_1, three spread orbits of type S_2, and three of type L_8.

$$\boxed{P} : \quad \boxed{F_1 \; S_2 \; S_2 \; S_2 \; L_8 \; L_8 \; L_8}$$

We first construct all nonisomorphic partial parallelisms made of a fixed spread and three spread orbits of type S_2, and determine their automorphism groups that belong to the normalizer $N(G_{8_2})$. The results are presented in Table 3.

Table 3. Partial parallelisms with a spread of type F_1 and 3 spread orbits of type S_2

Normalizer automorphisms	8	16	24	32	48	96
Partial parallelisms with G_{8_2}	10279	683	11	9	7	1
Partial parallelisms with G_{8_6}	34235	1118	50	7	35	3

These partial solutions lead to a great number of parallelisms invariant under G_{8_2} or G_{8_6}. Finding all of them in our way is infeasible. That is why we extend only some of the partial solutions.

The nineteen partial parallelisms with G_{8_2} and normalizer automorphism groups of orders 24, 48, and 96 were considered in [28]. In the present work, we extend the 9 partial solutions with G_{8_2} which possess an automorphism group of order 32 and the 95 partial solutions with G_{8_6} which possess an automorphism group of order at least 24.

2.4 Computer Search

Construction of the Parallelisms. We use our own software written for this purpose in C++. Our construction algorithm implies backtrack search. The basic types of backtrack search algorithms for classification of combinatorial structures are described by Kaski and Östergård in [16]. Our approach is based on the algorithm known as *orderly generation* [16] proposed by Faradžev [11] and Read [20]. Orderly generation, however, requires rejection of all the equivalent partial solutions, while we apply a *minimality test for isomorphism* only to some of the partial solutions and to all complete parallelisms that are obtained. This test checks if there exists an element of the normalizer of the predefined group that maps the current partial solution to a lexicographically smaller one. If such an element exists, the partial solution is not extended.

We construct one spread from each orbit (*spread orbit leader*). Thus we find 7 orbit leaders instead of all the 31 spreads. In order to partially check the correctness of the results, all the parallelisms are constructed independently by both authors who apply different software implementations and slightly different algorithms. For finding the partial parallelisms from Table 3 the first author uses backtrack search on the lines of the projective space, and the second on all the possible spread orbit leaders that have been constructed in advance (Table 2). The addition of the next three orbits of length 8 is done by both of us by a search on the lines because of the very big number of possible spreads in this particular case.

The extention of one $F_1S_2S_2S_2$ partial solution (Table 3) would have taken several days on a 3 GHz PC. That is why the computer search was carried out on the high-performance computing system *Avitohol* of the Bulgarian Academy of Sciences (see the Acknowledgements). We used a communication-free MPI based parallel implementation of the backtrack search for parallelisms which proved to be very suitable in this case. It looks like that:

We denote by **prnum** the number of processes, and by **mynum** the number of this process. And let **aa** be a global variable that counts the number of partial solutions of a definite size. Splitting the work among the processes can be done by allowing each process to extend only those partial solutions of the definite size whose number modulo **prnum** equals **mynum**.

It is of major importance to choose a suitable size of the partial solutions after which the job is split into the different processes. On the one hand, we want that the time to obtain these partial solutions will be relatively short, so that the time when all processes do the same job will be as small as possible. On the other hand, we want the number of the partial solutions of the chosen size to be relatively big, so that each process will extend many of them, because in that case, the differences between the running times of the processes will be negligible. We established that it is most efficient to split the job after a partial solution containing a spread of type F_1, four spreads of type S_2 and the first two lines of a spread of type L_8.

We calculate the combinatorial invariants described in [27] for the points, lines, and spreads of each of the newly constructed parallelisms. They comprise an invariant of the whole parallelism. Our software uses them to find the automorphism group of the parallelisms and to test for isomorphism between parallelisms with the same invariants.

3   Properties of the Obtained Parallelisms

All the parallelisms constructed in this paper are available online. They can be downloaded from http://www.moi.math.bas.bg/moiuser/~stela. Since the present work does not aim to find only parallelisms suitable for a definite application, we cannot say which of their properties are most important, and present a summary of those of them which are usually concerned.

Table 4 presents the order of the full automorphism group of the parallelisms invariant under a cyclic group of order 8 that have been constructed in the present work and in [28].

Table 4. Parallelisms invariant under a cyclic automorthism group of order 8

Automorphisms		8	16	24	32	48	96	1200	2400	All
Parallelisms	all	8143	952	610	56	90	6	4	2	9863
	known	630	154	85	16	14	–	4	2	905
	new	7513	798	525	40	76	6	–	–	8958
Selfdual		361	–	24	–	–	–	–	–	385

The parallelisms obtained in [28] are marked as *known*. The six parallelisms with automorphism groups of orders 1200 and 2400 have not been obtained in [28], but are *known* from [29].

Besides the automorphism group, we also study the types of spreads the parallelisms consist of. Some of them have special names. A spread is called

- *Hall spread* if it can be obtained from a regular spread by a replacement of one regulus by its opposite;
- *conical flock spread* if it has q reguli which have exactly one common line;
- *derived conical flock spread* if it can be obtained from a conical flock spread by a replacement of one regulus by its opposite.

There are 21 nonisomorphic spreads in PG(3, 5) [7]. To distinguish them we use invariants based on their relation to the reguli of the projective space. The 21 spreads are partitioned to 20 classes by an invariant made of two numbers - the number of whole reguli in the spread and the number of reguli which share exactly 4 lines (out of all 6 lines) with the spread. For the regular spread of PG(3, 5), these invariants are (130, 0), for the Hall spread (31, 105), for the conical flock spread (5, 200), and for the derived conical flock spread (1, 210). The class containing two nonisomorphic spreads has invariants (0, 104).

The order of the automorphism group, the types of the spreads, and selfduality (or not) partition the constructed parallelisms to 1251 classes. We present here the invariants only of some of them. The rest, however, are available online.

A deficiency one parallelism is a partial parallelism with one spread less than the corresponding parallelism. It is uniquely extendable to a parallelism. Uniform deficiency one parallelisms are of particular interest. Fifty uniform deficiency one parallelisms are constructed in [28] and 4435 in [29]. The latter are made of Hall spreads and there are 12 transitive deficiency one parallelisms among them. We add now 114 new uniform deficiency one parallelisms (Table 5). Part of them are made of (16, 246) spreads which by now were not known to make uniform deficiency one parallelisms.

Table 5. Invariants of parallelisms which yield uniform deficiency one parallelisms

Spreads		Order of the automorphism group								All	Known	New
1	30	8	16	24	32	48	96	1200	2400			
10,192	3,237	8	40	6		8				62	50 [28]	12
10,192	16,246			4						4		4
10,192	31,105	4		6						10		10
130,0	3,237			2						2		2
130,0	16,246			4						4		4
130,0	31,105	16	28	8	8	16	6	4	2	88	6 [29]	82
all		28	68	30	8	24	6	4	2	170		
known			40	2		8		4	2		56	
new		28	28	28	8	16	6					114

The uniform deficiency one parallelisms which admit the richest automorphism groups consist of Hall spreads.

The properties of selfdual parallelisms are of particular interest too. Among the constructed parallelisms with automorphisms of order 8, there are 361 selfdual parallelisms with an automorphism group of order 8, and 24 with an automorphism group of order 24. Their spread types are presented in Table 6.

Table 6. Invariants of selfdual parallelisms with an automorphism group of order 24

F_1	$3 \times S_2$	$3 \times L_8$	All	Known	New
130,0	31, 105	0,72	2		2
130,0	31, 105	0,114	4		4
130,0	31, 105	0,180	2		2
130,0	31, 105	4,102	1		1
130,0	31, 105	130,0	4		4
10,192	31, 105	0,72	2		2
10,192	3, 237	0,114	2		2
10,192	3, 237	1,82	2		2
10,192	3, 237	4,102	1	1 [28]	
10,192	3, 237	130,0	4	2 [28]	2
All			24	3	21

Among the parallelisms constructed in the present work, there are 4888 with exactly one regular spread and 60 with more than one regular spread. The latter are described in Table 7. All of them have an automorphism group of order 8 except the eight ones in bold in Table 7 which have an automorphism group of order 24. The star(*) denotes parallelisms obtained in [28].

Table 7. Invariants of parallelisms with more than one regular spread

130,0	31,105	16,246	10,192	7,150	3,237	1,210	1,82	0,310	0,180	0,104	0,72	num	sd
8		1		6							16	1	
8		1		6						16		4*	2
8		1		6					16			2	
8		1		6	8					8		2	
8		1		6	16							2	
8	4	1					2			16		6	
9				4						16		8	2
9	2			4							16	1	
9	2			4	8					8		2	
9	2			4					16			2	
9	2			4	16							2	
9	6		8								8	4	
9	6									4		6	
9	6					16						2	
24		1		6								4*	
24	4	1					2					4	
25	2			4								4	
25	6											4	

It is not known if a parallelism of PG(3, 5) can admit any number (at most 31) of regular spreads. Up to now parallelisms with 0, 1, 8, 9, 24 and 31 regular spreads have been constructed. The present work shows that there are parallelisms with 25 regular spreads too.

4   Conclusion

The usage of the system for computational discrete algebra GAP [12], the parallel implementation of the search algorithm and the access to the powerful high-performance computing system Avitohol of the Bulgarian Academy of Sciences made it possible to obtain new parallelisms of $PG(3, 5)$. Among them there are parallelisms with properties that had not been observed before, namely, uniform deficiency one parallelisms of a new spread type, and parallelisms with 25 regular spreads. We believe that the present investigation will help future theoretical considerations. The availability of the parallelisms online makes it possible for anyone to use them in relevant applications. The full classification of parallelisms of $PG(3,5)$ which are invariant under a cyclic group of order 8 remains a challenging open problem.

Acknowledgments. The authors are grateful to the anonymous referees for the very careful reading of the paper, and for their adequate remarks and suggestions on the presentation of the material.

References

1. Baker, R.D.: Partitioning the planes of $AG_{2m}(2)$ into 2-designs. Discrete Math. 15, 205–211 (1976) doi: 10.1016/0012-365X(76)90025-X
2. Beth, T.H., Jungnickel, D., Lenz, H.: Design Theory. Cambridge University Press, New York (1993)
3. Betten, A.: The packings of PG(3,3). Des. Codes Cryptogr. 79 (3), 583–595 (2016). doi: 10.1007/s10623-015-0074-6
4. Betten, A., Topalova, S., Zhelezova, S.: Parallelisms of PG(3,4) invariant under cyclic groups of order 4. In: Algebraic Informatics. CAI 2019. Lecture Notes in Computer Science, vol. 11545, Ciric M., Droste M., Pin J.-E. (eds), pp. 88–99, Springer, Cham (2019). https://doi.org/10.1007/978-3-030-21363-3_8
5. Betten, A., Topalova, S., Zhelezova, S.: New uniform subregular parallelisms of PG(3,4) invariant under an automorphism of order 2. Cybern. Inf. Technol. 20(6), 18–27 (2020). doi: 10.2478/cait-2020-0057
6. Beutelspacher, A.: On parallelisms in finite projective spaces. Geom. Dedicata 3 (1), 35–40 (1974) doi: 10.1007/BF00181359
7. Czerwinski, T., Oakden, D.: The translation planes of order twenty-five, J. Combin. Theory Ser. A 59 (2), 193–217 (1992). doi: 10.1007/BF00182289
8. Denniston, R.H.F.: Some packings of projective spaces. Atti Accad. Naz. Lincei Rend. Cl. Sci. Fis. Mat. Natur. 52 (8), 36–40 (1972)
9. Etzion, T., Silberstein, N.: Codes and designs related to lifted MRD codes. IEEE Trans. Inform. Theory 59 (2), 1004–1017 (2013). doi: 10.1109/ISIT.2011.6033969
10. Fuji-Hara, R.: Mutually 2-orthogonal resolutions of finite projective space. Ars Combin. 21, 163–166 (1986)
11. Faradžev, I. A.: Constructive enumeration of combinatorial objects. In: Problèmes Combinatoires et Théorie des Graphes, (Université d'Orsay, 9–13 July 1977). Colloq. Internat. du C.N.R.S., vol. 260, pp. 131–135. CNRS, Paris (1978)
12. GAP - Groups, Algorithms, Programming - A System for Computational Discrete Algebra. http://www.gap-system.org/
13. Gruner, A., Huber, M.: New combinatorial construction techniques for low-density parity-check codes and systematic repeat-accumulate codes. IEEE Trans. Commun. 60 (9), 2387–2395 (2012). doi: 10.1109/TCOMM.2012.070912.110164
14. Johnson, N.L.: Some new classes of finite parallelisms, Note Mat. 20(2), 77–88 (2000). doi: 10.1285/i15900932v20n2p77
15. Johnson, N.L.: Combinatorics of Spreads and Parallelisms. Chapman & Hall Pure and Applied Mathematics. CRC Press, Series (2010)
16. Kaski, P., Östergård, P.: Classification algorithms for codes and designs. Springer, Berlin (2006)
17. Penttila, T., Williams, B.: Regular packings of $PG(3,q)$. European J. Combin. 19 (6), 713–720 (1998)

18. Prince, A.R.: Parallelisms of $PG(3,3)$ invariant under a collineation of order 5. In: Johnson, N.L. (ed.) Mostly Finite Geometries. Lecture Notes in Pure and Applied Mathematics, vol. 190, pp. 383–390. Marcel Dekker, New York (1997)

19. Prince, A.R.: The cyclic parallelisms of $PG(3,5)$. European J. Combin. 19 (5), 613–616 (1998)

20. Read, R.C.: Every one a winner; or, How to avoid isomorphism search when cataloguing combinatorial configurations. Ann. Discrete Math. 2, 107–120 (1978) doi: 10.1016/S0167-5060(08)70325-X

21. Sarmiento, J.: Resolutions of $PG(5,2)$ with point-cyclicautomorphism group. J. Combin. Des. 8 (1), 2–14 (2000). https://doi.org/10.1002/(SICI)1520-6610(2000)8: 1⟨2::AID-JCD2⟩3.0.CO;2-H

22. Stinson, D.R.: Combinatorial Designs: Constructions and Analysis. Springer-Verlag, New York (2004)

23. Stinson, D. R., Vanstone, S. A.: Orthogonal packings in $PG(5,2)$, Aequationes Math. 31 (1), 159–168 (1986) doi: 10.1007/BF02188184

24. Storme, L.: Finite Geometry. In: Colbourn, C., Dinitz, J. (eds.) Handbook of Combinatorial Designs. 2nd edn. Rosen, K. (eds.) Discrete mathematics and Its Applications, pp. 702–729. CRC Press, Boca Raton (2007)

25. Topalova, S., Zhelezova, S.: New regular parallelisms of $PG(3,5)$. J. Combin. Designs 24, 473–482 (2016) doi: 10.1002/jcd.21526

26. Topalova, S., Zhelezova, S.: Types of spreads and duality of the parallelisms of $PG(3,5)$ with automorphisms of order 13. Des. Codes Cryptogr. 87 (2–3), 495–507 (2019) doi: 10.1007/s10623-018-0558-2

27. Topalova, S., Zhelezova, S.: Isomorphism and Invariants of Parallelisms of Projective Spaces. In: Bigatti, A., Carette, J., Davenport, J., Joswig, M., De Wolff, T. (eds.), Mathematical Software – ICMS 2020, Lecture Notes in Computer Science, vol. 12097, pp. 162–172, Cham: Springer (2020). https://doi.org/10.1007/978-3-030-52200-1_16

28. Topalova, S., Zhelezova, S.: Some parallelisms of $PG(3,5)$ involving a definite type of spread. 2020 Algebraic and Combinatorial Coding Theory (ACCT), pp. 135–139 (2020). https://doi.org/10.1109/ACCT51235.2020.9383404

29. Topalova, S., Zhelezova, S.: Parallelisms of $PG(3,5)$ with an automorphism group of order 25, Research Perspectives CRM Barcelona. In: Romero i Sanchez, D. (Ed.) Series: Trends in Mathematics, EUROCOMB (2021, to appear)

30. Zaicev, G., Zinoviev, V., Semakov, N.: Interrelation of preparata and hamming codes and extension of hamming codes to new double-error-correcting codes. In: Proceedings International Symposium on Information Theory, (Armenia, USSR, 1971), pp. 257–263. Budapest, Academiai Kiado (1973)

Optimal Four-Stage Symplectic Integrators for Molecular Dynamics Problems

Evgenii V. Vorozhtsov[1(✉)] and Sergey P. Kiselev[1,2]

[1] Khristianovich Institute of Theoretical and Applied Mechanics of the Siberian Branch of the Russian Academy of Sciences, Novosibirsk 630090, Russia
{vorozh,kiselev}@itam.nsc.ru
[2] Novosibirsk State Technical University, Novosibirsk 630092, Russia

Abstract. The Runge–Kutta–Nyström (RKN) explicit symplectic four-stage schemes for the numerical solution of molecular dynamics problems described by the systems with separable Hamiltonians have been considered. In the case of the zero Vandermonde determinant, 20 schemes are obtained using the Gröbnerbasis technique. Four invertible (symmetric) schemes are also obtained in analytical form. Two of these schemes depend on a parameter whose optimal value is found from the minimum requirement of the leading term of the approximation error. In the general case of nonsymmetric schemes, four new schemes are found using the Nelder–Mead numerical optimization method. Verification of the schemes is carried out on a problem that has an exact solution. It is shown that symplectic four-stage RKN schemes provide more accurate conservation of the total energy balance of the particle system than the schemes of lower orders of accuracy. All studies of the accuracy and stability of the schemes are carried out in an analytical form using the computer algebra system *Mathematica*.

Keywords: Molecular dynamics · Hamilton equations · Symplectic four-stage schemes · Gröbner bases · Stability

1 Introduction

The equations of molecular dynamics (MD) are the ordinary Hamilton differential equations that describe the interaction of material particles. MD equations have an exact analytical solution in a very limited number of cases [9]. Therefore, in the general case, these equations are solved numerically using difference schemes, in which the differential operator is replaced by the difference operator.

When solving Hamilton's equations, it is natural to use difference schemes that preserve the symplectic properties of these equations. Violation of this condition leads to non-conservation of Poincaré invariants and the appearance of non-physical instability in numerical calculations [2,10]. It follows that the difference operator of a numerical scheme must have the properties of a canonical transformation.

© Springer Nature Switzerland AG 2021
F. Boulier et al. (Eds.): CASC 2021, LNCS 12865, pp. 420–441, 2021.
https://doi.org/10.1007/978-3-030-85165-1_24

As is known, explicit difference schemes impose a restriction on the integration step [19, 22]. The advantage of these schemes is the simplicity of their software implementation. In addition, the increased performance of desktop computers allows one to solve many important application tasks using explicit schemes in an acceptable time. Therefore, explicit symplectic integrators are widely used in solving various applied problems in such areas of natural sciences as plasma physics [10], celestial mechanics [5], and solid state mechanics [6].

According to the theory of Hamilton's equations, the law of conservation of the total energy of the particle system [9] must be fulfilled. It is natural to require that the difference scheme also ensures the conservation of the total energy. However, as the practice of calculations shows, the imbalance of the total energy of the system turns out to be more significant for explicit symplectic difference schemes of Runge–Kutta–Nyström (RKN) of low orders of accuracy (second and third). At the same time, it was shown in [19, 22] that the three-stage RKN scheme of the fourth order of accuracy provides a smaller error in energy imbalance than the 2nd and 3rd order schemes. This leads to the conclusion that it is advisable to develop explicit symplectic RKN schemes of higher orders of accuracy.

As a rule, with an increase in the number of stages of the RKN scheme, it becomes possible to obtain an increasing number of real schemes with the same number of stages and with the same order of accuracy. Then there is the question of choosing from this set of schemes such a scheme that would have the highest accuracy while maintaining an acceptable stability robustness. In the theory of ordinary (non-symplectic) Runge–Kutta schemes, such optimal schemes are found from the requirement of the minimum leading term of the approximation error of the scheme [7, 8]. The same approach to the search of optimal RKN schemes was applied for the case of the separable Hamiltonian in [17], and for the more general case of the non-separable Hamiltonian—in [23].

The symplectic integrator of the fourth order of accuracy was first proposed in [3], where a single real RKN scheme was obtained. The same scheme was soon independently found by Neri [13]. The first journal article describing the integrator under consideration is [4], in which two real fourth-order RKN schemes were found in an analytical form without the use of Gröbnerbases. One of these schemes matches the one found earlier in [3, 13]. In [4], a three-stage fourth-order symplectic integrator was also obtained for the first time. All the necessary symbolic calculations were made in [4] using the computer algebra system (CAS) REDUCE. Yoshida's work [24] was published in the same year as [4]. Propagators and commutators were used to obtain approximate solutions to the system of Hamilton equations in [24]. In the special case of the fourth-order accuracy method, one real solution was obtained, which coincided with the solution found earlier in [3, 13].

In [22], explicit symplectic Runge–Kutta–Nyström difference schemes with a number of stages from 1 to 5 were considered using the CAS *Mathematica*. With the use of Gröbnerbases, the schemes with the numbers of stages 2, 3, and 4, were compared in terms of accuracy and stability. For each specific number of stages, the schemes that are the best in terms of accuracy and stability were identified. However, in the case of a four-stage RKN scheme in [22], only one of the six cases of vanishing of the Vandermonde determinant corresponding to this scheme was considered. The present work fills this gap.

The Hamilton equations have the property of reversibility in time. It is desirable that the difference methods of approximate integration of these equations also possess this property. Symmetric four-stage RKN schemes have this property, but they were not handled in [22]. This gap is filled in this paper.

The purpose of this paper is a sufficiently detailed study of four-stage symmetric and nonsymmetric real fourth-order RKN schemes in order to find the optimal real scheme in the considered classes of schemes.

2   Governing Equations

In the method of molecular dynamics, the computation of the motion of N particles is carried out with the aid of the Hamilton equations

$$\frac{dx_{i\alpha}}{dt} = \frac{\partial H}{\partial p_{i\alpha}}, \frac{dp_{i\alpha}}{dt} = -\frac{\partial H}{\partial x_{i\alpha}}, H(x_{i\alpha}, p_{i\alpha}) = \mathcal{K}(p_{i\alpha}) + V(x_{i\alpha}),$$
$$\mathcal{K}(p_{i\alpha}) = \sum_{i=1}^{N} \sum_{\alpha=1}^{3} \frac{p_{i\alpha}^2}{2m_i}, \tag{1}$$

where i is the particle number, α is the number of the coordinate $x_{i\alpha}$ and of the momentum $p_{i\alpha}$, m_i is the particle mass, $\mathcal{K}(p_{i\alpha})$ is the kinetic energy, $V(x_{i\alpha})$ is the potential energy of the interaction of particles, $H(x_{i\alpha}, p_{i\alpha})$ is the Hamiltonian of the system of particles. The solution of system (1) under the given initial conditions $x_{i\alpha}(t=0) = x_{i\alpha}^0$, $p_{i\alpha}(t=0) = p_{i\alpha}^0$ represents a canonical transformation from the initial state to the final state

$$x_{i\alpha} = x_{i\alpha}(x_{i\alpha}^0, p_{i\alpha}^0, t), \quad p_{i\alpha} = p_{i\alpha}(x_{i\alpha}^0, p_{i\alpha}^0, t). \tag{2}$$

Solution (2) of Hamilton equations (1) preserves the phase volume (the Liouville theorem [9]). The condition of the phase volume conservation is [6]

$$G^T J G = J, \quad G = \frac{\partial(x_{i\alpha}, p_{i\alpha})}{\partial(x_{i\alpha}^0, p_{i\alpha}^0)}, \quad J = \left\| \begin{matrix} 0 & I_N \\ -I_N & 0 \end{matrix} \right\|, \tag{3}$$

where G is the Jacobi matrix, J is the symplectic matrix, I_N is the $N \times N$ identity matrix. From (3), it follows the equality to unity of the transformation Jacobian $|G| = 1$. For the following, we rewrite Hamilton equations (1) for the one-dimensional case in the form

$$dx_i/dt = p_i(t)/m, \quad dp_i/dt = f_i(x_i), \tag{4}$$

where $f_i(x_i)$ is the force acting on the ith particle, $f_i(x_i) = -\partial V(x_i)/\partial x_i$, $i = 1, 2, \ldots, N$. In the following, we will omit the subscript i at the discussion of difference schemes for solving the system of ordinary differential equations (4).

3   Four-Stage Symplectic Integrators

The conventional (non-symplectic) explicit difference schemes with a structure similar to Runge–Kutta schemes were proposed for the first time by Nyström in [14]. The K-stage Runge–Kutta–Nyström (RKN) scheme for Hamilton equations (4) has the following form:

$$
\begin{aligned}
x^{(i)} &= x^n + h\alpha_i \frac{p^n}{m} + \frac{h^2}{m} \sum_{j=1}^{K} a_{ij} f(x^{(j)}), \quad i = 1, \ldots, K, \\
x^{n+1} &= x^n + h\frac{p^n}{m} + \frac{h^2}{m} \sum_{j=1}^{K} \beta_j f(x^{(j)}), \quad p^{n+1} = p^n + h \sum_{j=1}^{K} \gamma_j f(x^{(j)}),
\end{aligned}
\tag{5}
$$

where h is the time step, n is the time layer number, $n = 0, 1, 2, \ldots$; $\alpha_i, \beta_i, \gamma_i$, $i = 1, \ldots, K$ are constant parameters, $K \geq 1$.

It is required that the RKN scheme (5) performs a canonical transformation $(x^n, p^n) \to (x^{n+1}, p^{n+1})$ at a passage from the time layer n to the layer $n + 1$. To this end, one must impose in accordance with (3) the following condition on the Jacobi matrix G^{n+1} [9]:

$$
G^{n+1,T} J G^{n+1} = J, \quad G^{n+1} = \frac{\partial(x^{n+1}, p^{n+1})}{\partial(x^n, p^n)}, \quad J = \begin{pmatrix} -0 & -1 \\ -1 & -0 \end{pmatrix},
\tag{6}
$$

where the superscript T denotes the transposition operation, J is the symplectic matrix. Condition (6) gives rise to a class of explicit two-parameter $RKN(\alpha, \gamma)$ schemes for which β_i, a_{ij} in (5) satisfy the conditions [15,20]

$$
\beta_i = \gamma_i(1 - \alpha_i), \quad a_{ij} = \begin{cases} 0, & 1 \leq i \leq j \leq K \\ \gamma_j(\alpha_i - \alpha_j), & 1 \leq j < i \leq K \end{cases}.
\tag{7}
$$

It was noted in [20] that there exist no explicit Runge–Kutta schemes preserving the canonicity of transformation (6).

We now describe a simple technique for determining the accuracy order of any RKN scheme by the example of the RKN scheme for computing the momentum p^{n+1} at the moment of time $t_{n+1} = t_n + h$. Let the value p^n be known. The solution in the next node t_{n+1} is calculated by the formula $p^{n+1} = p^n + \Delta p_{h,n}$. The formula for $\Delta p_{h,n}$ depends on the number of stages K of the RKN method (5) and on $3K$ constants $\alpha_i, \beta_i, \gamma_i$, $i = 1, \ldots, K$. On the other hand, one can easily derive the "exact" formula for the increment Δp by using the expansion of the quantity p^n into the truncated Taylor series:

$$
\Delta p_n = p(t_n + h) - p(t_n) \approx \sum_{j=1}^{N_T} \frac{h^j}{j!} \frac{d^j p(t_n)}{dt^j},
$$

where N_T is a given natural number, $N_T \geq K + 1$. If the difference $\delta p_n = \Delta p_n - \Delta p_{h,n}$ satisfies the relation $\delta p_n / h = O(h^q)$, where $q > 0$, then the RKN scheme has the order of accuracy $O(h^q)$. The maximization of the degree q is done by choosing the parameters $\alpha_i, \beta_i, \gamma_i$ $(i = 1, \ldots, K)$ for a specific K.

It is to be noted that the lengths of intermediate expressions in the derivation of formulas for both ordinary (non-symplectic) and symplectic Runge–Kutta methods increase nonlinearly with the increase in the number of stages of the method. Therefore, it is not surprising that soon after the advent of general-purpose computer algebra systems, the idea of using these systems to derive formulas for multi-stage explicit and implicit Runge–Kutta methods arose. In particular, Sophronius [18] developed a symbolic package in the language of the *Mathematica* system for the derivation and investigation of ordinary (non-symplectic) Runge–Kutta methods using the representations of these methods in the form of Butcher graphs.

It was proposed in [21] to construct generalized explicit Runge–Kutta schemes by decomposing the solution $u(t)$ of the ordinary differential equation $du/dt = f(t, u(t))$ by the Lagrange–Burmann formula. The function $f(t, u)$ was decomposed into a series of powers of two functions of two variables t, u according to the Poincaré formula, which is a generalization of the Lagrange–Burmann formula for the case of a function of two variables. All the necessary symbolic calculations were performed in [21] in CAS MATHEMATICA.

McAndrew [11] proposed using the CAS SAGE to derive nonlinear algebraic equations which must be satisfied by the parameters of the conventional (non-symplectic) Runge–Kutta methods of various orders of accuracy. Fragments of programs in CAS SAGE language are given.

Setting $K = 4$ in (5) and performing symbolic computations according to the algorithm [8], we obtain the expression for δp_n in the form

$$\begin{aligned}
\delta p_n &= hP_1 f(x) + (h^2/2)P_2 u(t) f'(x) + h^3 [P_{31} f(x) f'(x)/m + P_{32} u^2 f''(x)]/6 \\
&+ (h^4 u)/(24m)\{P_{41} \cdot [f'(x)]^2 + 3P_{42} f(x) f''(x) + P_{43} m u^2 f^{(3)}(x)\} \\
&- [h^5/(120m^2)](3P_{51} f^2(x) f''(x) + f(x)(P_{52} \cdot [f'(x)]^2 - 6P_{53} m u^2 f^{(3)}(x) \\
&- m u^2 (5P_{54} f'(x) f''(x) + P_{55} m u^2 f^{(4)}(x))),
\end{aligned} \tag{8}$$

where $u(t)$ is the particle velocity and

$$P_1 = 1 - \sum_{j=1}^{K} \gamma_j, \quad P_2 = 1 - 2\sum_{j=1}^{K} \alpha_j \gamma_j, \quad P_{31} = 1 - 6\sum_{i=1}^{K}\sum_{j=i+1}^{K} \gamma_i \gamma_j (\alpha_i - \alpha_j),$$

$$P_{32} = 1 - 3\sum_{j=1}^{K} \alpha_j^2 \gamma_j, \quad P_{41} = 1 - 24\sum_{i=1}^{K}\sum_{j=i+1}^{K} \gamma_i \gamma_j \alpha_j (\alpha_i - \alpha_j),$$

$$P_{42} = 1 - 8\sum_{i=1}^{K}\sum_{j=i+1}^{K} \gamma_i \gamma_j \alpha_i (\alpha_i - \alpha_j), \quad P_{43} = 1 - 4\sum_{j=1}^{K} \alpha_j^3 \gamma_j,$$

$$P_{51} = 20\sum_{i=1}^{K}\sum_{j=i+1}^{K}\sum_{l=j+1}^{K} \gamma_i \gamma_j \gamma_l (\alpha_i - \alpha_j)(\alpha_i - \alpha_l) - 1, \tag{9}$$

$$P_{52} = 120\sum_{i=1}^{K}\sum_{j=i+1}^{K}\sum_{l=j+1}^{K} \gamma_i \gamma_j \gamma_l (\alpha_i - \alpha_j)(\alpha_j - \alpha_l) - 1,$$

$$P_{53} = 1 - 10\sum_{i=1}^{K}\sum_{j=i+1}^{K} \gamma_i \gamma_j \alpha_i^2 (\alpha_i - \alpha_j), \quad P_{55} = 1 - 5\sum_{j=1}^{K} \alpha_j^4 \gamma_j,$$

$$P_{54} = 12 \sum_{i=1}^{K} \sum_{j=i+1}^{K} \gamma_i \gamma_j \alpha_j^2 (\alpha_i + \alpha_j) - 24 \sum_{i=1}^{K} \sum_{j=i+1}^{K} \gamma_i \gamma_j \alpha_i \alpha_j^2 + 1.$$

The call $\texttt{GroebnerBasis}$[{P1,P2,P31,P32,P41,P42,P43, P51, P52, P53, P54, P55},{a1,a2,a3,a4, g1,g2,g3,g4}] outputs the following result: {1}. By Hilbert's Nullstellensatz [1], if the ideal is {1}, then 12 polynomials $P_1, \ldots, P_{55}$ have no common zero. This involves the conclusion about the absence of the four-stage fifth-order schemes.

3.1   Zero Vandermonde Determinant

The system of equations $P_1 = 0$, $P_2 = 0$, $P_{32} = 0$, $P_{43} = 0$ is linear in γ_i, $i = 1, \ldots, 4$. Its matrix is the Vandermonde 4×4 matrix $\mathbf{V}$ and

$$\text{Det } \mathbf{V} = (\alpha_1 - \alpha_2)(\alpha_1 - \alpha_3)(\alpha_1 - \alpha_4)(\alpha_2 - \alpha_3)(\alpha_2 - \alpha_4)(\alpha_3 - \alpha_4). \quad (10)$$

Below we present the results of consideration of all six special cases of vanishing of this determinant using the technique of Gröbnerbases. In all these cases, the lexicographic ordering of the monomials was used in the calculation of the Gröbnerbasis corresponding to each particular case. It turned out that in each particular case, there is at least one reducible polynomial in the Gröbnerbasis. This allows us to easily find all the free parameters α_j, γ_j, $j = 1, \ldots, 4$, which are the solution of the polynomial system

$$P_1 = 0, \ P_2 = 0, \ P_{31} = 0, \ P_{32} = 0, \ P_{41} = 0, \ P_{42} = 0, \ P_{43} = 0. \quad (11)$$

If there is a real solution to this system, then, according to (8), the four-stage RKN scheme under study has the fourth order of accuracy. It turned out that in six special cases of the vanishing determinant (10), there are 20 real solutions (see below). The problem arises of determining the best fourth-order accuracy method. A well-known method for finding a RKN scheme with the optimal accuracy is a search for the scheme with the smallest value of the leading error term [16,23] in the selected norm. In the case of a four-stage scheme, the leading error term is the term of the order $O(h^5)$, it is available in (8) and depends on five polynomials $P_{51}, P_{52}, P_{53}, P_{54}$, and P_{55}. Knowing the parameters α_j, γ_j, $j = 1, \ldots, 4$, it is not difficult to find the root-mean-square value of the polynomials P_{5k}, $k = 1, \ldots, 5$ and identify the most accurate scheme in the set of real four-stage RKN schemes found.

Let us consider in detail the case when $\alpha_2 = \alpha_1$. Substitute in the polynomials $P_2, P_{31}, P_{32}, P_{41}, P_{42}$, and P_{43} the relation $\alpha_2 = \alpha_1$ and denote the obtained polynomials by $P_{20}, P_{310}, P_{320}, P_{410}, P_{420}$, and P_{430}. The call $\texttt{GroebnerBasis}$[{P1, P20, P310, P320, P410, P420, P430},{a1, a3, a4, g1, g2, g3, g4}] has allowed us to obtain a Gröbnerbasis consisting of the following six polynomials:

$$G_1 = 1728\gamma_4^7 - 5184\gamma_4^6 + 5868\gamma_4^5 - 3510\gamma_4^4 + 1218\gamma_4^3 - 228\gamma_4^2 + 15\gamma_4 + 1, \quad (12)$$
$$G_2 = 537408\gamma_4^6 - 1405440\gamma_4^5 + 1276020\gamma_4^4 - 578046\gamma_4^3$$

$$+ 138720\gamma_4^2 - 11224\gamma_4 + 2398\gamma_3 - 1877, \tag{13}$$
$$G_3 = -537408\gamma_4^6 + 1405440\gamma_4^5 - 1276020\gamma_4^4 + 578046\gamma_4^3$$
$$- 138720\gamma_4^2 + 13622\gamma_4 + 2398\gamma_1 + 2398\gamma_2 - 521, \tag{14}$$
$$G_4 = 7194\alpha_4 + 331776\gamma_4^6 - 965376\gamma_4^5 + 1058688\gamma_4^4 - 626304\gamma_4^3$$
$$+ 218880\gamma_4^2 - 39603\gamma_4 - 3418, \tag{15}$$
$$G_5 = 4796\alpha_3 - 537408\gamma_4^6 + 1405440\gamma_4^5 - 1276020\gamma_4^4 + 578046\gamma_4^3$$
$$- 138720\gamma_4^2 + 16020\gamma_4 - 2919, \tag{16}$$
$$G_6 = 14388\alpha_1 + 489024\gamma_4^6 - 976896\gamma_4^5 + 574884\gamma_4^4 - 237318\gamma_4^3$$
$$+ 49248\gamma_4^2 - 2526\gamma_4 - 3227. \tag{17}$$

The command Factor[G1] has enabled us to find that the polynomial G_1 is reducible: $G_1 = (1 - 3\gamma_4 + 6\gamma_4^2)(-1 - 24\gamma_4 + 48\gamma_4^2)(-1 + 6\gamma_4 - 12\gamma_4^2 + 6\gamma_4^3)$. Seven different roots of the equation $G_1 = 0$ determine seven solutions of the original system. The roots of the equation $1 - 3\gamma_4 + 6\gamma_4^2 = 0$ are complex: $\gamma_4 = (1/12)(3 \pm i\sqrt{15})$. The roots of the equation $-1 - 24\gamma_4 + 48\gamma_4^2 = 0$ are real: $\gamma_4 = (1/12)(3 \pm 2\sqrt{3})$. We find from Eqs. (13)–(17) the values of the remaining parameters of the RKN scheme under study ($z = \sqrt{3}$):

$$\alpha_1 = \tfrac{1}{6}(3 \pm z), \ \alpha_2 = \tfrac{1}{6}(3 \pm z), \ \alpha_3 = \tfrac{1}{6}(3 \mp z), \ \alpha_4 = \tfrac{1}{6}(3 \pm z),$$
$$\gamma_2 = \tfrac{1}{12}(3 \mp 2z - 12\gamma_1), \ \gamma_3 = \tfrac{1}{2}, \ \gamma_4 = \tfrac{1}{12}(3 \pm 2z). \tag{18}$$

One can see from (18) that one parameter, γ_1, remains indefinite. This may be due to the fact that the number of the polynomials in the Gröbnerbasis (12)–(17) is less than the number of parameters $\alpha_1, \alpha_2 = \alpha_1, \alpha_3, \alpha_4, \gamma_j, j = 1, \ldots, 4$.

Consider in more detail a scheme, which is obtained at the use of lower symbols "+" or "−" in (18). We call this scheme the RKN4-1 scheme. Let us calculate the weighted root-mean-square value of five polynomials $P_{5j}, j = 1, \ldots, 5$:

$$P_{5,rms}^{(1)} = \left[\tfrac{1}{5} \sum_{j=1}^{5} (\sigma_j P_{5j})^2 \right]^{1/2}$$
$$= \left\{ \tfrac{1}{5} \left[\left(\sigma_1 \tfrac{7}{72} \right)^2 + \left(\sigma_2 \tfrac{7}{12} \right)^2 + \left(\tfrac{\sigma_3}{36} \right)^2 + \left(\tfrac{\sigma_4}{6} \right)^2 + \left(\tfrac{\sigma_5}{36} \right)^2 \right] \right\}^{1/2} \approx 0.47924.$$

Here $\sigma_1, \ldots, \sigma_5$ are problem-independent factors affecting the polynomials P_{5j} in (8), $\sigma_1 = -3, \sigma_2 = -1, \sigma_3 = 6, \sigma_4 = 5, \sigma_5 = 1$.

Now consider a scheme obtained at the use of the upper symbols "+" or "−" in (18). Let us call this scheme the RKN4-2 scheme. We obtain for it the same weighted root-mean-square value of five polynomials $P_{5j}, j = 1, \ldots, 5$, as in the case of scheme RKN4-1: $P_{5,rms}^{(2)} \approx 0.47924$.

Equation $6\gamma_4^3 - 12\gamma_4^2 + 6\gamma_4 - 1 = 0$ has one real root $\gamma_4 = (1/3)(2 + \tfrac{z^2}{2} + z)$ and two complex conjugate roots, where $z = 2^{1/3}$. We find from Eqs. (12) the values of remaining parameters of the RKN scheme under study (we call it the RKN4-3 scheme):

$$\alpha_1 = \tfrac{1}{12}(4 + 2\zeta + \zeta^2), \ \alpha_2 = \alpha_1, \ \alpha_3 = \tfrac{1}{2}, \ \alpha_4 = \tfrac{1}{12}(8 - 2\zeta - \zeta^2),$$
$$\gamma_2 = \tfrac{1}{6}(4 + 2\zeta + \zeta^2 - 6\gamma_1), \ \gamma_3 = -\tfrac{1}{3}(1 + \zeta)^2, \ \gamma_4 = \tfrac{1}{6}(4 + 2\zeta + \zeta^2). \tag{19}$$

One can see from (19) that one parameter, γ_1, remains indefinite. In the case under consideration,

$$P_{5,rms}^{(3)} = \left[\frac{1}{5}\sum_{j=1}^{5}(\sigma_j P_{5j})^2\right]^{\frac{1}{2}} = \left\{\frac{1}{5}\left[(8.1092\sigma_1)^2 + (2.3780\sigma_2)^2 + (2.0962\sigma_3)^2 + (10.3143\sigma_4)^2 + (0.6386\sigma_5)^2\right]\right\}^{\frac{1}{2}} \approx 26.13695. \tag{20}$$

Note that the numerical values of the functionals $P_{5,rms}^{(k)}$, $k = 1,2,3$, do not depend on the undefined parameter γ_1. The reason for this is that all expressions containing γ_1 in the polynomials P_{5j}, $j = 1,\ldots,5$, are cancelled out. The value of $P_{5,rms}^{(3)} = 26.13695$ is 54.54 times greater than the value of $P_{5,rms}^{(1)}$. Therefore, for calculations using the three considered four-stage schemes, the RKN4-1 and RKN4-2 schemes are preferable.

The remaining five particular cases were also investigated in detail in order to find real four-stage RKN schemes. For the sake of brevity, we do not give the expressions for the polynomials of Gröbnerbases corresponding to the RKN-l schemes ($l = 4,\ldots,20$). These bases are not difficult to obtain using the CAS *Mathematica*. Before giving the analytical formulas for α_j, γ_j, $j = 1,\ldots,4$, we introduce a number of notations:
$z = \sqrt{3}$, $\zeta = 2^{1/3}$, $\varphi_1^{\pm} = \frac{1}{6}(3 \pm z)$, $\varphi_2^{\pm} = \frac{1}{12}(3 \pm 2z)$, $\varphi_3 = \frac{1}{12}(4 + 2\zeta + \zeta^2)$, $\varphi_4 = -\frac{1}{3}(1+\zeta)^2$, $\kappa_{cr}^* = 2\sqrt{2 + \zeta - \zeta^2} \approx 2.586518894520$.

1.° Particular case $\alpha_1 = \alpha_2$.

Scheme RKN4-1	$\alpha_1 = \alpha_2 = \varphi_1^-$, $\alpha_3 = \varphi_1^+$, $\alpha_4 = \varphi_1^-$, $\kappa_{cr} = \kappa_{cr}^*$
	γ_1, $\gamma_2 = \varphi_2^+ - \gamma_1$, $\gamma_3 = \frac{1}{2}$, $\gamma_4 = \varphi_2^-$, $P_{5,rms}^{(1)} = 0.4792$
Scheme RKN4-2	$\alpha_1 = \alpha_2 = \varphi_1^+$, $\alpha_3 = \varphi_1^-$, $\alpha_4 = \varphi_1^+$, $\kappa_{cr} = 2.514918799464$,
	γ_1, $\gamma_2 = \varphi_2^- - \gamma_1$, $\gamma_3 = \frac{1}{2}$, $\gamma_4 = \varphi_2^+$, $P_{5,rms}^{(2)} = 0.4792$
Scheme RKN4-3	$\alpha_1 = \alpha_2 = \varphi_3$, $\alpha_3 = \frac{1}{2}$, $\alpha_4 = 1 - \varphi_3$, $\kappa_{cr} = 1.854382524682$,
	γ_1, $\gamma_2 = 2\varphi_3 - \gamma_1$, $\gamma_3 = \varphi_4$, $\gamma_4 = 2\varphi_3$, $P_{5,rms}^{(3)} = 26.1370$

2.° Particular case $\alpha_1 = \alpha_3$.

Scheme RKN4-4	$\alpha_1 = \varphi_1^+$, $\alpha_2 = \varphi_1^-$, $\alpha_3 = \varphi_1^+$, $\alpha_4 = \varphi_1^+$, $\kappa_{cr} = \kappa_{cr}^*$,
	$\gamma_1 = \varphi_2^-$, $\gamma_2 = \frac{1}{2}$, γ_3, $\gamma_4 = \varphi_2^+ - \gamma_3$, $P_{5,rms}^{(4)} = 0.6013$
Scheme RKN4-5	$\alpha_1 = \varphi_1^+$, $\alpha_2 = \varphi_1^-$, $\alpha_3 = \varphi_1^+$, $\alpha_4 = \varphi_1^-$, $\kappa_{cr} = 2.335025000052$,
	$\gamma_1 = \frac{1}{2} - \gamma_3$, $\gamma_2 = \frac{\varphi_2^+}{2\gamma_3}$, γ_3, $\gamma_4 = \frac{1}{2} - \frac{\varphi_2^+}{2\gamma_3}$, $\quad(21)$
Scheme RKN4-6	$\alpha_1 = \varphi_1^-$, $\alpha_2 = \varphi_1^+$, $\alpha_3 = \varphi_1^-$, $\alpha_4 = \varphi_1^-$, $\kappa_{cr} = \kappa_{cr}^*$,
	$\gamma_1 = \varphi_2^+$, $\gamma_2 = \frac{1}{2}$, $\gamma_3 = \varphi_2^- - \gamma_4$, γ_4, $P_{5,rms}^{(6)} = 0.6013$
Scheme RKN4-7	$\alpha_1 = \varphi_1^-$, $\alpha_2 = \varphi_1^+$, $\alpha_3 = \varphi_1^-$, $\alpha_4 = \varphi_1^+$, $\kappa_{cr} = 2.3658618327942$,
	$\gamma_1 = \frac{\varphi_2^+ - \gamma_4}{1 - 2\gamma_4}$, $\gamma_2 = \frac{1}{2} - \gamma_4$, $\gamma_3 = \frac{\varphi_2^-}{1 - 2\gamma_4}$, γ_4, $\quad(22)$
Scheme RKN4-8	$\alpha_1 = \varphi_1^+$, $\alpha_2 = \varphi_1^-$, $\alpha_3 = \varphi_1^+$, $\alpha_4 = 1$, $\kappa_{cr} = \kappa_{cr}^*$,
	$\gamma_1 = \varphi_2^-$, $\gamma_2 = \frac{1}{2}$, $\gamma_3 = \varphi_2^+$, $\gamma_4 = 0$, $P_{5,rms}^{(8)} = 0.6013$

3.° Particular case $\alpha_1 = \alpha_4$.

Scheme RKN4-9	$\alpha_1 = \varphi_1^+, \ \alpha_2 = \varphi_1^-, \ \alpha_3 = \varphi_1^+, \ \alpha_4 = \varphi_1^+, \ \kappa_{cr} = \kappa_{cr}^*,$
	$\gamma_1 = \varphi_2^-, \ \gamma_2 = \frac{1}{2}, \ \gamma_3 = \varphi_2^+ - \gamma_4, \ \gamma_4, \ P_{5,rms}^{(9)} = 0.6013$
Scheme RKN4-10	$\alpha_1 = \varphi_1^+, \ \alpha_2 = \varphi_1^-, \ \alpha_3 = \varphi_1^-, \ \alpha_4 = \varphi_1^+, \ \kappa_{cr} = \kappa_{cr}^*,$
	$\gamma_1 = \varphi_2^-, \ \gamma_2, \ \gamma_3 = \frac{1}{2} - \gamma_2, \ \gamma_4 = \varphi_2^+, \ P_{5,rms}^{(10)} = 0.4792$
Scheme RKN4-11	$\alpha_1 = \varphi_1^-, \ \alpha_2 = \varphi_1^+, \ \alpha_3 = \varphi_1^+, \ \alpha_4 = \varphi_1^-, \ \kappa_{cr} = \kappa_{cr}^*,$
	$\gamma_1 = \varphi_2^+, \ \gamma_2, \ \gamma_3 = \frac{1}{2} - \gamma_2, \ \gamma_4 = \varphi_2^-, \ P_{5,rms}^{(11)} = 0.4792$
Scheme RKN4-12	$\alpha_1 = \varphi_1^-, \ \alpha_2 = \varphi_1^+, \ \alpha_3 = \varphi_1^-, \ \alpha_4 = \varphi_1^-, \ \kappa_{cr} = \kappa_{cr}^*,$
	$\gamma_1 = \varphi_2^+, \ \gamma_2 = \frac{1}{2}, \ \gamma_3, \ \gamma_4 = \varphi_2^- - \gamma_3, \ P_{5,rms}^{(12)} = 0.6013$

4.° Particular case $\alpha_2 = \alpha_3$.

Scheme RKN4-13	$\alpha_1 = \varphi_1^-, \ \alpha_2 = \varphi_1^+, \ \alpha_3 = \varphi_1^+, \ \alpha_4 = \varphi_1^-, \ \kappa_{cr} = \kappa_{cr}^*,$
	$\gamma_1 = \varphi_2^+, \ \gamma_2, \ \gamma_3 = \frac{1}{2} - \gamma_2, \ \gamma_4 = \varphi_2^-, \ P_{5,rms}^{(13)} = 0.4792$
Scheme RKN4-14	$\alpha_1 = \varphi_1^+, \ \alpha_2 = \varphi_1^-, \ \alpha_3 = \varphi_1^-, \ \alpha_4 = \varphi_1^+, \ \kappa_{cr} = \kappa_{cr}^*,$
	$\gamma_1 = \varphi_2^-, \ \gamma_2, \ \gamma_3 = \frac{1}{2} - \gamma_2, \ \gamma_4 = \varphi_2^+, \ P_{5,rms}^{(14)} = 0.4792$
Scheme RKN4-15	$\alpha_1 = \varphi_3, \ \alpha_2 = \frac{1}{2}, \ \alpha_3 = \frac{1}{2}, \ \alpha_4 = 1 - \varphi_3, \ \kappa_{cr} = 1.573401947435,$
	$\gamma_1 = 2\varphi_3, \ \gamma_2, \ \gamma_3 = \varphi_4 - \gamma_2, \ \gamma_4 = 2\varphi_3, \ P_{5,rms}^{(15)} = 6.3431$

5.° Particular case $\alpha_2 = \alpha_4$.

Scheme RKN4-16	$\alpha_1 = \varphi_1^-, \ \alpha_2 = \varphi_1^+, \ \alpha_3 = \varphi_1^-, \ \alpha_4 = \varphi_1^+, \ \kappa_{cr} = \kappa_{cr}^*,$
	$\gamma_1 = 0, \ \gamma_2 = \varphi_2^-, \ \gamma_3 = \frac{1}{2}, \ \gamma_4 = \varphi_2^+, \ P_{5,rms}^{(16)} = 0.4792$
Scheme RKN4-17	$\alpha_1 = \varphi_1^+, \ \alpha_2 = \varphi_1^-, \ \alpha_3 = \varphi_1^+, \ \alpha_4 = \varphi_1^-, \ \kappa_{cr} = \kappa_{cr}^*,$
	$\gamma_1 = 0, \ \gamma_2 = \varphi_2^+, \ \gamma_3 = \frac{1}{2}, \ \gamma_4 = \varphi_2^-, \ P_{5,rms}^{(17)} = 0.4792$

6.° Particular case $\alpha_3 = \alpha_4$.

Scheme RKN4-18	$\alpha_1 = \varphi_1^+, \ \alpha_2 = \varphi_1^-, \ \alpha_3 = \varphi_1^+, \ \alpha_4 = \varphi_1^+, \ \kappa_{cr} = \kappa_{cr}^*,$
	$\gamma_1 = \varphi_2^-, \ \gamma_2 = \frac{1}{2}, \ \gamma_3, \ \gamma_4 = \varphi_2^+ - \gamma_3, \ P_{5,rms}^{(18)} = 0.6013$
Scheme RKN4-19	$\alpha_1 = \varphi_1^-, \ \alpha_2 = \varphi_1^+, \ \alpha_3 = \varphi_1^-, \ \alpha_4 = \varphi_1^-, \ \kappa_{cr} = 1.560857700727,$
	$\gamma_1 = \varphi_2^+, \ \gamma_2 = \frac{1}{2}, \ \gamma_3, \ \gamma_4 = \varphi_2^- - \gamma_3, \ P_{5,rms}^{(19)} = 0.6013$
Scheme RKN4-20	$\alpha_1 = \varphi_3, \ \alpha_2 = \frac{1}{2}, \ \alpha_3 = 1 - \varphi_3, \ \alpha_4 = 1 - \varphi_3, \ \kappa_{cr} = 1.804401576416,$
	$\gamma_1 = 2\varphi_3, \ \gamma_2 = \varphi_4, \ \gamma_3, \ \gamma_4 = 2\varphi_3 - \gamma_3, \ P_{5,rms}^{(20)} = 11.1448$

Thus, the total number of real schemes is 20. The correctness of each solution was checked by substituting it into the corresponding polynomial system.

In the case of the RKN4-5 scheme, the function $P_{5,rms}^{(5)}$ depends on γ_3:

$$P_{5,rms}^{(5)} = \frac{1}{144\gamma_3\sqrt{5}}\{14992\gamma_3^2 + 36[(84 + 40z)\gamma_3 - \varphi_4]^2 \\ + 9[\varphi_5 + 8\gamma_3(5(3 + 2z)\gamma_3 - 2(9 + 5z)]^2\}^{\frac{1}{2}}, \tag{21}$$

where $\varphi_5 = 5(7 + 4z)$. The γ_3 parameter is undefined (free). Using this, it can be set from the minimum requirement of function (21). This minimum was found analytically by solving an algebraic fourth-degree equation, which is easy to obtain from the equation $d(P_{5,rms}^{(5)})/d\gamma_3 = 0$; this solution γ_3^* is not given here due to its cumbersomeness. The solution in the form of a floating-point machine number is as follows: $\gamma_3^* = 0.452266707470307331$. The same solution is obtained, if one uses the *Mathematica* function NMinimize[...] for minimizing (21); the response is $\gamma_3^* = 0.452266707470307172$, at which $P_{5,rms}^{(5)} \approx 0.3956$.

In the case of the RKN4-7 scheme, the function $P_{5,rms}^{(7)}$ depends on γ_4:

$$P_{5,rms}^{(7)} = \left\{ \frac{1}{5} \left[\frac{937}{1296} + \left(\frac{3 + 5(3 - 2z)\gamma_4}{3} \right)^2 + \left(\frac{7 - 8\gamma_4(3 + 5(3 - 2z)\gamma_4}{24(1 - 2\gamma_4)} \right)^2 \right] \right\}^{\frac{1}{2}}. \quad (22)$$

The minimum of this function is reached at $\gamma_4^* = 1.195384712832130214$, at which $P_{5,rms}^{(7)} \approx 0.3872$.

The value of the functional $P_{5,rms}^{(\nu)}$, $\nu = 1, \ldots, 20$ is presented for all 20 schemes in order to choose a scheme which is the best from the viewpoint of accuracy. It is found that the scheme RKN4-7 with $\gamma_4 = \gamma_4^*$ is the best.

In the above description of the 20 schemes, κ_{cr} is the Courant number which is maximally allowed for preserving the stability of the RKN method; in the case of the above symplectic methods, the stability condition has the form $0 < |\kappa| \le \kappa_{cr}$. The algorithm for calculating κ_{cr} in the analytic form is presented in [22]. The value of κ_{cr} is a function of the parameter γ_3 or γ_4 for schemes, respectively, RKN4-5 and RKN4-7. The corresponding functions $P_{5,rms}^{(5)}$ and $P_{5,rms}^{(7)}$ also depend on these parameters. We used the optimal parameters γ_3^* and γ_4^* at the computation of κ_{cr} for the methods RKN4-5 and RKN4-7. It has turned out that the stability of methods RKN4-19 and RKN4-20 depends on the parameter γ_3; at the same time, the corresponding functions $P_{5,rms}^{(19)}$ and $P_{5,rms}^{(20)}$ are independent of any parameter. The values of κ_{cr} are presented above for methods RKN4-19 and RKN4-20 for the case when $\gamma_3 = \frac{1}{2}$. This value was chosen arbitrarily to show that the stability regions for these two methods are also non-empty.

From the above results, one can see that in the solutions for 16 RKN schemes, one of the four parameters $\gamma_1, \gamma_2, \gamma_3$, and γ_4 is undefined (free). Thus, these 16 schemes are one-parameter families of RKN4 schemes, but the values of the functionals $P_{5,rms}^{(l)}$ do not depend on the free parameter. One can set free parameters in these cases in one of two ways: (i) from the condition for ensuring the maximum size of the stability domain of such schemes; (ii) from the condition for minimizing the functional constructed over polynomials included in the term of order of smallness $O(h^6)$, which is next in order of smallness to the leading error term of order of smallness $O(h^5)$, which is available in formula (8) for δp_n.

3.2   Nonzero Vandermonde Determinant

Symplectic Invertible Schemes. A symplectic method $y_1 = \Phi_h(y_0)$ is called invertible (symmetric), if it is invariant under the permutations $y_0 \Leftrightarrow y_1$ and $h \Leftrightarrow -h$ [7]. It is well known that only the RKN schemes of the even order of approximation can be symmetric [7]. The symmetry requirement imposes the following conditions on the four-stage RKN scheme:

$$\alpha_1 = 1 - \alpha_4, \quad \alpha_2 = 1 - \alpha_3, \quad \gamma_1 = \gamma_4, \quad \gamma_2 = \gamma_3. \tag{23}$$

Under these conditions, the polynomials $P_1, P_2, P_{31}, P_{32}, P_{41}, P_{42}$, and P_{43} simplify significantly:

$$
\begin{aligned}
P_1 &= P_2 = 1 - 2\gamma_3 - 2\gamma_4, \\
P_{31} &= 1 + (6 - 12\alpha_3)\gamma_3{}^2 + 12(1 - 2\alpha_4)\gamma_3\gamma_4 + (6 - 12\alpha_4)\gamma_4{}^2, \\
P_{32} &= 1 + \left(-3 + 6\alpha_3 - 6\alpha_3{}^2\right)\gamma_3 + \left(-3 + 6\alpha_4 - 6\alpha_4{}^2\right)\gamma_4, \\
P_{41} &= 1 + 24(1 - 3\alpha_3 + 2\alpha_3{}^2)\gamma_3{}^2 + 48(-\alpha_3 + \alpha_3{}^2 \\
&\quad + (-1 + \alpha_4)^2)\gamma_3\gamma_4 + 24(1 - 3\alpha_4 + 2\alpha_4{}^2)\gamma_4{}^2, \\
P_{42} &= 1 + 8\alpha_4\gamma_4{}^2 - 16\alpha_3{}^2\gamma_3(\gamma_3 + \gamma_4) - 16\alpha_4{}^2\gamma_4(\gamma_3 + \gamma_4) \\
&\quad + 8\alpha_3\gamma_3(\gamma_3 + 2\gamma_4), \\
P_{43} &= 1 - 4\left(1 - 3\alpha_3 + 3\alpha_3{}^2\right)\gamma_3 - 4\left(1 - 3\alpha_4 + 3\alpha_4{}^2\right)\gamma_4.
\end{aligned}
\tag{24}
$$

The symmetry conditions (23) allow us to reduce the number of required parameters by half. This enables the obtaining of analytical expressions for them. Using the *Mathematica* function Solve[...] four real solutions of system (24) were obtained, two of which do not contain any free parameters, and the remaining two solutions depend on the parameter γ_3. Below are the analytical expressions for the parameters $\alpha_j, \gamma_j, j = 1, \ldots, 4$, corresponding to all four symmetric schemes found. We present also the expressions for the Vandermonde determinant (10) as well as the expressions for the weighted root-mean-square leading term of the approximation error

$$P_{5,sym,rms}^{(l)} = \left[\frac{1}{5}\sum_{j=1}^{5}(\sigma_j P_{5j})^2\right]^{1/2}, l = 1, \ldots, 4.$$

Symmetric symplectic scheme No. 1.
$\alpha_1 = \frac{11+\sqrt{5}}{48}$, $\alpha_3 = \frac{39-\sqrt{5}}{48}$, $\alpha_2 = 1 - \alpha_3$, $\alpha_4 = 1 - \alpha_1$,
$\gamma_1 = \gamma_4 = \frac{1-\sqrt{5}}{4}$, $\gamma_2 = \gamma_3 = \frac{1+\sqrt{5}}{4}$, Det $\mathbf{V}_1 = \frac{11030-2807\sqrt{5}}{47775744} = 0.0000994931$,
$P_{5,sym,rms}^{(1)} = \frac{\sqrt{\frac{4118671904057}{5} - 142849321176\sqrt{5}}}{331776} \approx 2.14045$, $\kappa_{cr} = 2.846896365356$.

Symmetric symplectic scheme No. 2.
$\alpha_1 = \frac{11-\sqrt{5}}{48}$, $\alpha_3 = \frac{39+\sqrt{5}}{48}$, $\alpha_2 = 1 - \alpha_3$, $\alpha_4 = 1 - \alpha_1$,
$\gamma_1 = \gamma_4 = \frac{1+\sqrt{5}}{4}$, $\gamma_2 = \gamma_3 = \frac{1-\sqrt{5}}{4}$, Det $\mathbf{V}_2 = \frac{11030+2807\sqrt{5}}{47775744} = 0.000362247$,
$P_{5,sym,rms}^{(2)} = \frac{\sqrt{\frac{4118671904057}{5} + 142849321176\sqrt{5}}}{331776} \approx 3.2226$, $\kappa_{cr} = 2.979831906188$.

Symmetric symplectic scheme No. 3.

$$\alpha_1 = \frac{1+2\sqrt{2}\xi-16\gamma_3^2+24\gamma_3^3}{6-48\gamma_3^2+48\gamma_3^3}, \quad \alpha_3 = \frac{\sqrt{2}\xi+2\sqrt{2}\xi\gamma_3+6\gamma_3^2+20\gamma_3^3-24\gamma_3^4}{12\gamma_3^2(1+2\gamma_3-4\gamma_3^2)},$$

$$\alpha_2 = 1 - \alpha_3, \ \alpha_4 = 1 - \alpha_1, \ \gamma_1 = \gamma_4 = \tfrac{1}{2} - \gamma_3, \ \gamma_2 = \gamma_3, \ \kappa_{cr} = 2.315290546733.$$

Symmetric symplectic scheme No. 4.

$$\alpha_1 = \frac{1-2\sqrt{2}\xi-16\gamma_3^2+24\gamma_3^3}{6-48\gamma_3^2+48\gamma_3^3}, \quad \alpha_3 = \frac{\sqrt{2}\xi+2\sqrt{2}\xi\gamma_3-6\gamma_3^2-20\gamma_3^3+24\gamma_3^4}{12\gamma_3^2(-1-2\gamma_3+4\gamma_3^2)},$$

$$\alpha_2 = 1 - \alpha_3, \ \alpha_4 = 1 - \alpha_1, \ \gamma_1 = \gamma_4 = \tfrac{1}{2} - \gamma_3, \ \gamma_2 = \gamma_3, \ \kappa_{cr} = 2.553018251497.$$

In the cases of the above symmetric schemes, the stability condition has the form $0 < |\kappa| \le \kappa_{cr}$. In solutions Nos. 3 and 4, $\xi = [\gamma_3^3(2\gamma_3 - 1)(12\gamma_3^2 - 6\gamma_3 + 1)]^{1/2}$. Values $\mathrm{Det}\,\mathbf{V}_3$, $\mathrm{Det}\,\mathbf{V}_4$ and $P^{(3)}_{5,sym,rms}$, $P^{(4)}_{5,sym,rms}$ are very cumbersome functions of the parameter γ_3 and, therefore, are not given.

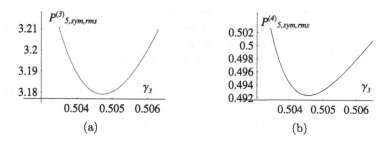

Fig. 1. Graphs of the functions $P^{(3)}_{5,sym,rms}$ (a) and $P^{(4)}_{5,sym,rms}$ (b)

Note that in schemes Nos. 3 and 4, the formulas for α_1 and α_4 contain a polynomial in the denominator: $6 - 48\gamma_3^2 + 48\gamma_3^3 = 6(2\gamma_3 - 1)[\gamma_3 - \tfrac{1}{4}(1 - \sqrt{5})][\gamma_3 - \tfrac{1}{4}(1 + \sqrt{5})]$. Further, in schemes Nos. 3 and 4, the formulas for α_2 and α_3 contain a polynomial in the denominator: $\pm 12\gamma_3^2(4\gamma_3^2 - 2\gamma_3 - 1) = \pm 12\gamma_3^2[\gamma_3 - \tfrac{1}{4}(1 - \sqrt{5})][\gamma_3 - \tfrac{1}{4}(1 + \sqrt{5})]$. The continuous parameter γ_3 that distinguishes schemes can take any value other than 0, $\tfrac{1}{2}$, and $\tfrac{1\pm\sqrt{5}}{4}$. Graphs of the values $\mathrm{Det}\,\mathbf{V}_3$ and $\mathrm{Det}\,\mathbf{V}_4$ were plotted as the functions of the γ_3 parameter. It was found that $\mathrm{Det}\,\mathbf{V}_3 \ne 0$, $\mathrm{Det}\,\mathbf{V}_4 \ne 0$ out of points $\gamma_3 = \tfrac{1}{4}(1 - \sqrt{5})$, 0, $\tfrac{1}{4}(1 + \sqrt{5})$. When the parameter γ_3 tends to the specified points $\mathrm{Det}\,\mathbf{V}_3 \to +\infty$, $\mathrm{Det}\,\mathbf{V}_4 \to +\infty$.

Figure 1 shows the graphs of the quantities $P^{(3)}_{5,sym,rms}$ and $P^{(4)}_{5,sym,rms}$. The points of the minima of these quantities were found with the aid of the *Mathematica* function FindMinimum[...]; let us denote them by $(\gamma_3^{(j)}, P^{(j)}_{5,sym,rms})$, respectively, for methods Nos. 3 and 4. Here $\gamma_3^{(3)} = 0.50472752527437358$, $P^{(3)}_{5,sym,rms} = 3.1792$, $\gamma_3^{(4)} = 0.50454167581559217$, $P^{(4)}_{5,sym,rms} = 0.4924$. From these data, it follows that scheme No. 4 is the best among the obtained four symmetric RKN schemes in terms of the smallness of the leading term of the approximation error. A comparison of the four obtained symmetric schemes with the 20 schemes given in the previous section shows that the symmetric schemes have a slightly lower accuracy than the best non-symmetric schemes in terms of the smallness of the leading term of the approximation error. On the other hand, it turned out that none of the mentioned 20 schemes satisfies the invertibility conditions (23).

Table 1. The values of the parameters of schemes RKN4-la, $l = 1, \ldots, 4$, at Det $\mathbf{V} \neq 0$

Method	α_j	γ_j	$P_{5,\mathrm{rms}}^{(l)}$	κ_{cr}
1a	−0.163552401143382292	0.048726380769174189		
	0.315379254000269726	0.604671155309221442	0.1450	2.601107169201
	0.849651865097469039	0.377059806193216329		
	0.101814165555907346	−0.030457342271611940		
2a	−0.132366908603509081	0.050382034698121490		
	0.554050453573154522	−0.106956632411513153	0.1659	2.853927732257
	0.337015545852672127	0.632484935164970730		
	0.831831238456345323	0.424089662548420954		
3a	0.168126182298635241	0.419065819011724183		
	0.636979619359235749	0.421942016918863572	0.1676	2.855254281741
	0.922878504633673047	0.176843502495841326		
	0.136094487172141509	−0.017851338426429109		
4a	0.073135959738290263	0.179911393946207976		
	0.757772082233232225	−0.041533676753871755	0.1763	2.8424607874720
	0.377483410023031707	0.436525266982659255		
	0.831654913466108980	0.425097015825004532		

Symplectic Nonsymmetric Schemes. To check the availability of the scheme of the order of accuracy $O(h^4)$ at a nonzero Vandermonde determinant we have used the command

GroebnerBasis[{P1, P2, P31, P32, P41, P42, P43}, {a1, a2, a3, a4, g1, g2, g3, g4}],   (25)

where the lexicographic ordering of monomials was used. However, this function did not give the desired result even after six hours of operation of a desktop computer with a variable clock frequency in the range from 3.6 to 4.1 GHz.

One can also use in the function GroebnerBasis[...] the ordering of monomials, which is inverse to the lexicographic one. To this end, one must insert into the call (25) the option MonomialOrder → DegreeReverseLexicographic. As a result, the Gröbnerbasis was obtained, which contained 90 polynomials. However, it has no polynomial that depends on a single variable. In addition, all 90 polynomials turned out to be irreducible over the field of integers. These two circumstances make it impossible to obtain a solution of the considered polynomial system in an analytical form using the obtained basis.

Applied problems of molecular dynamics are nonlinear, so they have to be solved using numerical methods, in particular, RKN methods. To implement these methods programmatically, it is sufficient to set the parameters α_j, γ_j ($j = 1, \ldots, K$) as machine floating-point numbers. The problem of solving a polynomial system that satisfies the specified parameters can be formulated as the problem of numerical minimization of the objective function, which is the sum of the squares of the left-hand sides of the polynomial system to be solved:

$$P(X) = P_1^2 + P_2^2 + P_{31}^2 + P_{32}^2 + P_{41}^2 + P_{42}^2 + P_{43}^2, \tag{26}$$

where $X = (\alpha_1, \alpha_2, \alpha_3, \alpha_4, \gamma_1, \gamma_2, \gamma_3, \gamma_4)$. Let Ω_{8d} be a hypercube with the rib length $2r > 0$ in the eight-dimensional Euclidean space of X-points, $\Omega_{8d} = \{(\alpha_1, \alpha_2, \alpha_3, \alpha_4, \gamma_1, \gamma_2, \gamma_3, \gamma_4) | -r \le \alpha_j \le r, -r \le \gamma_j \le r, \ j = 1, \ldots, 4\}$. We are looking for a solution to the following numerical minimization problem: find $\min_{X \in \Omega_{8d}} P(X)$. We call X^* the approximate solution to the problem of minimizing function (26) in the hypercube Ω_{8d}, if $|P(X^*)| < 10^{-30}$. Then the root-mean-square value of the functions $P_1, \ldots, P_{43}$ satisfies the inequality: $(\frac{P_1^2 + \cdots P_{43}^2}{7})^{0.5} < \frac{10^{-15}}{\sqrt{7}} \approx 0.378 \cdot 10^{-15}$, that is, it has an error at the level of machine rounding errors. Thus, the accuracy of determining the components of the vector X^* is provided, which is quite sufficient for the numerical solution of molecular dynamics problems using RKN schemes.

The minimization problem under consideration was solved numerically using the *Mathematica* function NMinimize[...], which implements the Nelder–Mead method [12]. In order to get several solutions to the minimization problem for the function (26) in a single run of the *Mathematica* program, we used to set several initial X points in the Ω_{7d} domain. The number of these points was set by the program user. The coordinates of the points were set using a pseudo-random number generator available in the *Mathematica* package.

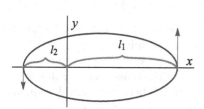

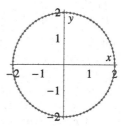

Fig. 2. Initial velocity vectors of particles and the location of the mass center at $m_2 > m_1$

Fig. 3. Circular orbits of particles in the interval $0 < t \le 35.7$: (——)— particle 1, ($\cdot \ \cdot \ \cdot$)—particle 2

When placing 1000 starting points randomly in Ω_{8d}, 164 numerical solutions of the considered polynomial system were obtained. From them, we selected those solutions in which the value of $P_{5,\text{rms}}$ is less than the smallest of the values obtained when considering all particular cases of vanishing of the Vandermonde determinant. The number of such solutions is 21. Of these, we give in Table 1 four solutions in ascending order of the corresponding values of the value $P_{5,\text{rms}}^{(l)}$. One can see that in the general case, it is possible to obtain schemes that have more than twice smaller values of $P_{5,\text{rms}}^{(l)}$ than in cases where Det $\mathbf{V} = 0$.

4   Verification of New Symplectic Integrators

The problem of the motion of a system consisting of two interacting particles (the two-body problem, the Kepler problem) admits a complete analytical solution in the general form [9]. For this reason, it was used in [22] to verify the RKN schemes of different orders of accuracy. The potential energy is given as $U(|r_1 - r_2|) = -Gm_1m_2/|r_1 - r_2|$, where m_1 and m_2 are the masses of particles and G is the gravitational constant, we set $G = 1$. Introduce the notation $p_j = (p_{jx}, p_{jy}) = (m_ju_j, m_jv_j)$, $j = 1, 2$, where u_j and vj are the projections of the particle velocity onto the x- and y-axes. Then the solution of the problem under consideration is reduced to the solution of the following system of ordinary differential equations:

$$\frac{dp_{1x}}{dt} = -\alpha\frac{(x_1-x_2)}{r^3}, \quad \frac{dx_1}{dt} = \frac{p_{1x}}{m_1}, \quad \frac{dp_{1y}}{dt} = -\alpha\frac{(y_1-y_2)}{r^3}, \quad \frac{dy_1}{dt} = \frac{p_{1y}}{m_1},$$
$$\frac{dp_{2x}}{dt} = \alpha\frac{(x_1-x_2)}{r^3}, \quad \frac{dx_2}{dt} = \frac{p_{2x}}{m_2}, \quad \frac{dp_{2y}}{dt} = \alpha\frac{(y_1-y_2)}{r^3}, \quad \frac{dy_2}{dt} = \frac{p_{2y}}{m_2}. \tag{27}$$

Here r is the distance between the both particles, $r = |r_1 - r_2| = \left[(x_1 - x_2)^2 + (y_1 - y_2)^2\right]^{1/2}$, $\alpha = Gm_1m_2$ and it is assumed that $x_1, y_1, x_2, y_2, p_{1x}, p_{1y}, p_{2x}, p_{2y}$ are the functions depending on time t.

The system (27) is solved under the following initial conditions specified at $t = 0$:

$$x_1(0) = l_1, \ y_1(0) = 0, \qquad x_2(0) = -l_2, \ y_2(0) = 0,$$
$$p_{1x}(0) = 0, \ p_{1y}(0) = m_1v_{10}, \ p_{2x}(0) = 0, \quad p_{2y}(0) = -m_2v_{20}, \tag{28}$$

see also Fig. 2. Here l_j is the distance from the coordinate origin to the jth particle, $j = 1, 2$, v_{j0} is the absolute value of the initial velocity of the jth particle in the direction of the y axis, $j = 1, 2$; the value $v_{10} > 0$ is the user-specified quantity. Let r_{mc} be the radius vector of the mass center. Following [1] let us place the coordinate origin in the mass center. Then we obtain the equality: $r_{mc} = (r_1m_1 + r_2m_2)/(m_1 + m_2) = 0$. It follows from here that $m_1l_1 - m_2l_2 = 0$, which implies the relation $l_2 = l_1m_1/m_2$. This means that if the quantities m_1, m_2, l_1 are given, then the value of l_2 is uniquely determined. To ensure that the center of masses remains at rest at $t > 0$ we also impose the condition $m_1v_1 + m_2v_2 = 0$, which implies the relation $m_1v_{10} - m_2v_{20} = 0$. From this it follows that $v_{20} = (m_1/m_2)v_{10}$.

Accounting for (28) we obtain:

$$|E| = |H| = \left|\frac{m_1v_{10}^2 + m_2v_{20}^2}{2} - \frac{\alpha}{l_1 + l_2}\right|. \tag{29}$$

To ensure the finiteness the constants v_{10}, v_{20} and l_1, l_2 must satisfy the inequality $\frac{m_1v_{10}^2 + m_2v_{20}^2}{2} - \frac{\alpha}{l_1+l_2} < 0$. In this case, the motion of each particle at $t > 0$ occurs along its own ellipse. Introduce the vector of the mutual distance between the both points $r = r_2 - r_1$ and place the coordinate origin at the inertia center. This leads to the equality $m_1r_1 + m_2r_2 = 0$. We find from the last two equalities:

$$r_1 = -\frac{m_2}{m_1 + m_2}r, \quad r_2 = \frac{m_1}{m_1 + m_2}r.$$

Table 2. The errors δE_{mean}, $|\delta E|_{mean}$, and $\delta r_{m,\max}$ at $e = 0$ for different RKN methods

K	RKN scheme	Scheme error	δE_{mean}	$|\delta E|_{mean}$	$\delta r_{1,\max}$
1	Verlet	$O(h^2)$	$-1.783e - 14$	$1.783e - 14$	$1.953e - 7$
2	Optimal [22]	$O(h^2)$	$-7.879e - 15$	$7.889e - 15$	$9.605e - 8$
3	RKN34A [22]	$O(h^4)$	$-3.918e - 15$	$4.048e - 15$	$5.684e - 14$
4	RKN4-2	$O(h^4)$	$-3.685e - 15$	$3.805e - 15$	$5.662e - 14$

Table 3. The errors δE_{mean}, $|\delta E|_{mean}$, and $\delta r_{1,\max}$ at $e = 0$ for the fourth-order methods from Table 1

RKN4 scheme	δE_{mean}	$|\delta E|_{mean}$	$\delta r_{1,\max}$
1a	$1.703e - 15$	$3.663e - 15$	$6.706e - 14$
2a	$-3.378e - 15$	$3.462e - 15$	$2.243e - 14$
3a	$-4.781e - 15$	$5.126e - 15$	$3.331e - 14$
4a	$-2.504e - 15$	$2.609e - 15$	$1.954e - 14$

Table 4. Comparison of the accuracy of symplectic symmetric schemes at $e = 0$

Scheme	δE_{mean}	$|\delta E|_{mean}$	$\delta r_{1,\max}$
1	$-4.398e - 15$	$4.453e - 15$	$1.488e - 14$
2	$-3.188e - 15$	$3.267e - 15$	$1.621e - 14$
3	$-2.247e - 15$	$2.341e - 15$	$6.624e - 13$
4	$-5.491e - 15$	$6.046e - 15$	$2.567e - 13$

Let $r = (x(t), y(t))$. Then $x = a(\cos \xi - e), y = a\sqrt{1 - e^2} \sin \xi$. Here a is the ellipse large semiaxis, e is the elliptic orbit eccentricity, $a = \alpha/(2|E|), e = \left[1 + 2EM^2/(m\alpha^2)\right]^{1/2}$, where M is the magnitude of the moment vector, which is directed along a normal to the (x, y) plane; $M = (r_1 \times m_1 v_1) + (r_2 \times m_2 v_2)$. The law of the moment conservation takes place [9]: $M = \text{const } \forall t \geq 0$. We obtain from the initial conditions (28): $M = m_1 l_1 v_{10} + m_2 l_2 v_{20}$.

In order to verify the developed Fortran program, we performed calculations of the two-body problem using all the four-stage RKN schemes discussed in the previous sections. The results presented in Figs. 3, 4 and in Tables 2–7 were obtained at $m_1 = m_2 = 1$. Numerical solution for the coordinates of both particles obtained at $e = 0$ after performing 7140 time steps with a constant step of $h = 0.005$, is shown in Fig. 3. The coordinates of the particles were stored every 80 steps of t. One can see that both particles move in the same circular orbit. Using formula (15, 8) from [9], it is not difficult to find the time period T required for a particle to complete a complete revolution in a circular orbit in the case of zero eccentricity: $T = \pi\sqrt{l_1}$, where l_1 is the radius of the circle along which each particle moves; in our case, $l_1 = 2$. Hence, it is easy to find that during the time $t = 35.7$, each of the two particles made 8 complete revolutions in a circle.

Table 2 presents the computational results for the problem of the motion of two particles along a circular orbit, which were obtained by using the RKN methods with the number of stages from 1 to 4. The quantities δE_{mean} and $|\delta E|_{mean}$ were computed as the arithmetic means of the quantities δE^n and $|\delta E^n|$, where $\delta E^n = (E^n - E_0)/E_0$, $E^n = \frac{(p_{1x}^n)^2+(p_{1y}^n)^2}{2m_1} + \frac{(p_{2x}^n)^2+(p_{2y}^n)^2}{2m_2} - \frac{\alpha}{r^n}$, $E_0 = \frac{m_1 v_{10}^2+m_2 v_{20}^2}{2} - \frac{\alpha}{l_1+l_2}$ according to (29), $r^n = [(x_1^n - x_2^n)^2 + (y_1^n - y_2^n)^2]^{1/2}$. Besides, $\delta r_{m,max}$ is the maximum relative deviation of the magnitude of the radius vector r^n of the mth particle ($m = 1, 2$) from the exact radius $a = 2$ of the circular orbit that is $\delta r_{m,max} = \max_j \left| \sqrt{x_{mj}^2 + y_{mj}^2} - a \right|/a$. It has turned out that at least the first 14 digits of the decimal mantissa of the numbers $\delta r_{1,max}$ and $\delta r_{2,max}$ coincide. Therefore, Table 2 presents only the quantity $\delta r_{1,max}$. From the viewpoint of practical applications, the accuracy of the computation of the coordinates of points (x_m^n, y_m^n) is the most important. One can see in Tables 2 and 3 that the best accuracy of the computation of these coordinates is achieved at the use of the four-stage RKN scheme. It also follows from Tables 2 and 3 that the new scheme RKN4-4a ensures smaller errors in energy δE_{mean}, $|\delta E|_{mean}$ than the method RKN4-2.

Table 5. Comparison of the accuracy of symmetric and non-symmetric schemes at $e = 0$

Scheme	δE_{mean}	$|\delta E|_{mean}$	$\delta r_{1,max}$
RKN4-2	$-3.685e - 15$	$3.805e - 15$	$5.662e - 14$
RKN4-1a	$1.703e - 15$	$3.663e - 15$	$6.706e - 14$
RKN$_{sym}$ No. 4	$-8.156e - 15$	$8.158e - 15$	$2.571e - 13$

Table 4 presents the results of calculating the motion of both particles in a circular orbit using the four symmetric schemes found. One can see from the comparison with Table 3 that the accuracy of these schemes is somewhat worse than in the case of the methods from Table 1. Table 5 compares the accuracy of symmetric scheme No. 4 with the accuracy of some non-symmetric schemes. The much higher accuracy of the RKN4-1a scheme is consistent with the fact that for it, the weighted norm of the leading error term is about 3.4 times less than in the case of the symmetric scheme No. 4.

To consider the case of the motion of each particle along its elliptic orbit let us set in (28) $v_{10} = 0.2$ and $l_1 = 2$. The inequality $4l_1 v_{10}^2 < 1$ is then satisfied, therefore, the eccentricity $e \neq 0$ and $E < 0$. Each particle performs one complete revolution along its elliptic orbit during the period of time [9]

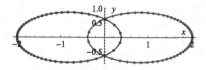

Fig. 4. Elliptic orbits of particle 1 (the right ellipse) and particle 2 (the left ellipse) in the interval $0 < t \leq 164$. Solid lines are the exact ellipses, dotted lines show the numerical solution by the RKN4-2 method

Table 6. Errors δE_{mean}, $|\delta E|_{mean}$, and $\delta y_{1,mean}$ at $v_{10} = 0.2$ for different RKN methods

K	Method	δE_{mean}	$|\delta E|_{mean}$	$\delta y_{1,mean}$
1	Verlet	$2.749e - 7$	$2.749e - 7$	$-3.384e - 5$
2	Optimal [22]	$8.754e - 8$	$8.838e - 8$	$-1.067e - 5$
3	RKN34A [22]	$5.438e - 13$	$6.230e - 13$	$-2.762e - 7$
4	RKN4-2	$6.047e - 13$	$5.753e - 13$	$-2.762e - 7$

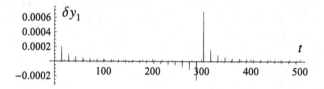

Fig. 5. The error $\delta y_{1,j}$ as a function of t. The RKN4-1a method

Table 7. Errors δE_{mean}, $|\delta E|_{mean}$, and $\delta y_{1,mean}$ at $v_{10} = 0.15$ for different RKN methods

K	Method	δE_{mean}	$|\delta E|_{mean}$	$\delta y_{1,mean}$
1	Verlet	$8.361e - 6$	$8.361e - 6$	$-5.053e - 3$
2	Optimal [22]	$2.954e - 6$	$3.174e - 6$	$-1.581e - 3$
3	RKN34A [22]	$9.686e - 10$	$9.686e - 10$	$-1.630e - 7$
4	RKN4-1a	$1.232e - 9$	$1.232e - 9$	$-1.630e - 7$

Table 8. Errors δE_{mean}, $|\delta E|_{mean}$, and $\delta y_{1,mean}$ at $m_1 = 1$, $m_2 = 5$ and $e = 0$

Method	δE_{mean}	$|\delta E|_{mean}$	$\delta r_{1,max}$
RKN4-2	$2.392e - 15$	$3.150e - 15$	$9.813\,e - 12$
RKN4-1a	$-5.102e - 15$	$5.443e - 15$	$1.278\,e - 11$
RKN$_{sym}$ No. 4	$-1.234e - 15$	$1.589e - 15$	$4.670\,e - 11$

$T = \pi\alpha\sqrt{m/(2|E|^3)}$. Substituting here the values $\alpha = 1$, $m = 1/2$, and $E = v_{10}^2 - 1/(2l_1)$, we obtain $T = 16.3227$. By the physical time $t = 164$, each particle makes 10 complete revolutions along its elliptic orbit. Figure 4 shows the numerical solution for the coordinates of both particles, which was obtained by the method RKN4-2 and by all other considered RKN4 methods at the moment of time $t = 164$ after the execution of 82000 time steps with the step $h = 0.002$. One can see that each particle moves along its elliptic orbit and the locations of particles agree very well with the exact elliptic orbits.

Table 6 presents the values of the relative errors δE_{mean} and $|\delta E|_{mean}$ obtained by numerically solving the problem of the motion of two particles in elliptical orbits according to RKN schemes with the numbers of stages 1, 2, 3, 4.

The value $\delta y_{1,mean}$ was calculated as the arithmetic mean of the values $\delta y_{1j} = y_{1j} - y_{1,ex}$. Here $y_{1,ex}$ is the exact value of the coordinate y at the intersection of the line $x = x_{1j}$ with the ellipse of the first particle (see the right ellipse in Fig. 4). Given the value x from the exact equation for the coordinate $x = -0.5l_1(\cos\xi - e)$ of the ellipse of the first particle the argument $\xi_j = \arccos[e - (2x_{1j}/l_1)]$ is found. After that, the exact value of the y coordinate of the point lying on the ellipse is found by the formula: $y_{1,ex} = -\frac{m_2}{m_1+m_2}b \cdot \text{sign}(y_{1j})\sin\xi_j$, where $b = a\sqrt{1 - e^2}$. The value of $\delta y_{2,mean}$ is calculated similarly using exact formulas for the ellipse of the second particle. It has turned out that the first ten digits of the mantissa of the machine numbers $\delta y_{1,mean}$ and $\delta y_{2,mean}$ coincide, but the signs of these numbers are opposite.

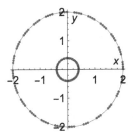

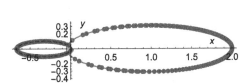

Fig. 6. Circular orbits of particles in the interval $0 < t \leq 35.7$ ($h = 0.005$). The exact orbits: (———)— particle 1, $(- - -)$— particle 2

Fig. 7. Elliptic orbits of particle 1 (the right ellipse) and particle 2 (the left ellipse) in the interval $0 < t \leq 8$ ($h = 10^{-3}$). The exact orbits: (———)— particle 1, $(- - -)$— particle 2. Dotted lines show the numerical solution by the RKN4-2 method

From the condition of zero eccentricity $v_{10} = 0.5/\sqrt{l_1}$, it follows that the eccentricity $e = |4l_1v_{10}^2 - 1|$ increases with decreasing v_{10}. Table 7 shows the relative error values δE_{mean} and $|\delta E|_{mean}$ obtained when $v_{10} = 0.15$, $h = 0.005$. The calculations were carried out up to the time $T = 500$; 10^5 steps were made in time. During this time, each of the two particles made more than 34 complete revolutions in an elliptical orbit. Comparing Table 6 and Table 7 one can see that the relative errors in the implementation of the law of conservation of energy have increased by two to three decimal orders of magnitude compared to the case when $v_{10} = 0.2$. One can specify the following reasons for the decrease in accuracy: first, the calculations were performed until the moment of time $T = 500$, which is three times greater than the time moment $T = 164$. Secondly, the step $h = 0.005$ was used, which is 2.5 times larger than the step with which the calculations were made for Table 6. Third, for $v_{10} = 0.15$, the small semi-axes of the ellipses are smaller than for $v_{10} = 0.2$. This led to an increase in the curvature of the ellipses in the vicinity of the x axis. Figure 5 shows the local error δy_{1j} as a function of time. There is a significant outburst in this quantity at $t \approx 300$. At other time moments, δy_{1j} is much smaller so that the mean value of this quantity is equal only to $-1.630e - 7$ according to Table 7.

Figure 6 shows by dotted lines the numerical results obtained by the RKN4-1a method in the case when $m_1 = 1, m_2 = 5$ and the eccentricity $e = 0$. One can see that the both particles rotate around the same center. The computations were done also for other ratios m_1/m_2. As $m_2 \to m_1$, the inner orbit approaches the orbit produced by particle 1. Figure 7 shows by dotted lines the numerical results obtained by the RKN4-2 method in the case when $m_1 = 1, m_2 = 3$ and the eccentricity $e = 0.9526$. Table 8 presents the values of errors δE_{mean} and $|\delta E|_{mean}$ obtained in the case of different particle masses.

5 Conclusions

We have obtained 20 symplectic four-stage Runge-Kutta-Nyström schemes using Gröbnerbases for all particular cases of vanishing of the Vandermonde determinant. Four invertible (symmetric) four-stage RKN schemes have also been obtained analytically using the CAS *Mathematica* and it is shown that the corresponding Vandermonde determinants are nonzero. Two of these schemes depend on the parameter. Its optimal value is found from the requirement of the minimum of the leading term of the approximation error.

In the general case of non-symmetric four-stage schemes, four new schemes are found using the numerical optimization method. It has turned out that the leading error term of these schemes is less than that of the schemes found in the cases of the zero Vandermonde determinant.

Verification of the schemes has been carried out on the example of a numerical solution of the Kepler problem, which has an exact solution. It is shown that the four-stage schemes provide a higher accuracy of the law of conservation of particle energy than the schemes of lower orders of accuracy. The considered RKN schemes are explicit, which makes it particularly convenient to parallelize the computation by these schemes.

References

1. Adams, A.L., Loustaunau, P.: An Introduction to Gröbner Bases. Graduate Studies in Mathematics, vol. 3. American Mathematical Society, Providence (1996)
2. Feng, K., Qin, M.: Symplectic Geometric Algorithms for Hamiltonian Systems. Hangzhou; Springer-Verlag, Berlin, Heidelberg, Zhejiang Publishing United Group, Zhejiang Science and Technology Publishing House (2010)
3. Forest, E.: Canonical integrators as tracking codes, SSC Central Design Group Technical Report SSC-138 (1987)
4. Forest, E., Ruth, R.D.: Fourth-order symplectic integration. Physica D. 43, 105–117 (1990)
5. Gladman, B., Duncan, M.: Symplectic integrators for long-term integrations in celestial mechanics. Celest. Mech Dyn. Astron. 52, 221–240 (1991)
6. Godunov, S.K., Kiselev, S.P., Kulikov, I.M., Mali, V.I.: Modeling of Shockwave Processes in Elastic-plastic Materials at Different (Atomic, Meso and Thermodynamic) Structural Levels. Institute of Computer Research, Moscow-Izhevsk (2014) [in Russian]
7. Hairer, E., Nørsett, S.P., Wanner, G.: Solving Ordinary Differential Equations I. Nonstiff Problems. Second Edition. Springer-Verlag, Berlin (1993)
8. Krylov, V.I., Bobkov, V.V., Monastyrnyi, P.I.: Computational Methods. Vol. II. Nauka, Moscow (1977) [in Russian]
9. Landau, L.D., Lifshitz, E.M.: Mechanics, third edition. Course of Theoretical Physics. Vol. 1. Elsevier, Amsterdam (1976)
10. Lewis, H., Barnes, D., Melendes, K.: The liouville theorem and accurate plasma simulation. J. Comput. Phys. **69**(2), 267–282 (1987)
11. McAndrew, A.: Developing explicit Runge-Kutta formulas using open-source software. arXiv:1402.3883v1 [math.NA], 17 February 2014
12. Nelder, J.A., Mead, R.: A simplex method for function minimization. Computer J. **7**(4), 308–313 (1965)
13. Neri, F.: Lie algebras and canonical integration. Department of Physics, University of Maryland (1988, preprint)
14. Nyström, E.J.: Ueber die numerische Integration von Differentialgleichungen. Acta Soc. Sci. Fenn. 50 (13), 1–54 (1925)
15. Okunbor, D.I., Skeel, R.D.: Canonical Runge-Kutta-Nyström methods of orders five and six. J. Comput. Appl. Math. **51**, 375–382 (1994)
16. Omelyan, I.P., Mryglod, I.M., Folk, R.: Optimized Forest-Ruth- and Suzuki-like algorithms for integration of motion in many-body systems. arXiv: cond-mat/011058v1 [cond-mat.stat-mech], 29 October 2001
17. Omelyan, I.P., Mryglod, I.M., Folk, R.: Optimized Verlet-like algorithms for molecular dynamics simulations. Phys. Rev. E. **65**, 056706 (2002)
18. Sofroniou, M.: Symbolic derivation of Runge-Kutta methods. J. Symb. Comput. 18 (3), 265–296 (1994)
19. Sofronov, V.N., Shemarulin, V.E.: Classification of explicit three-stage symplectic difference schemes for the numerical solution of natural Hamiltonian systems: A comparative study of the accuracy of high-order schemes on molecular dynamics Problems. Comp. Math. Math. Phys. **56**(4), 541–560 (2016)
20. Surius, Y.B.: On the canonicity of maps generated by Runge-Kutta type methods in the integration of systems $\ddot{x} = -\partial U/\partial x$. Zh. Vychisl. Mat. Mat. Fiz. **29**(2), 202–211 (1989). [in Russian]

21. Vorozhtsov, E.V.: Derivation of explicit difference schemes for ordinary differential equations with the aid of Lagrange-Burmann expansions. In: Computer Algebra in Scientific Computing. CASC 2010. Lecture Notes in Computer Science, vol 6244, p. 250–266. Springer, Berlin, 2010 Gerdt V.P., Koepf W., Mayr E.W., Vorozhtsov E.V. (eds)

22. Vorozhtsov, E.V., Kiselev, S.P.: Comparative study of the accuracy of higher-order difference schemes for molecular dynamics problems using the computer algebra means. In: Computer Algebra in Scientific Computing. CASC 2020. LNCS, vol 12291, p. 600–620. Springer, Cham, 2020 Boulier F., England M., Sadykov T.M., Vorozhtsov E.V. (eds). https://doi.org/10.1007/978-3-030-60026-6_35

23. Wu, Y.-L., Wu, X.: An optimized Forest-Ruth-like algorithm in extended phase space. Int. J. Modern Phys. C **29**(1) (2018). id. 1850006. https://doi.org/10.1142/S0129183118500067

24. Yoshida, H.: Construction of higher order symplectic integrators. Phys. Lett. A 43 (5–7), 262–268 (1990)

On Geometric Property of Fermat–Torricelli Points on Sphere

Zhenbing Zeng$^{(\boxtimes)}$![ORCID], Yu Chen, Xiang Sun, and Yuzheng Wang

Department of Mathematics, Shanghai University, Shanghai 200444, China
zbzeng@shu.edu.cn

Abstract. Given three points on sphere S^2, a point on sphere that maximizes or minimizes the sum of its Euclidean distances to the given points is called Fermat–Torricelli point. It was proved that for $A, B, C \in S^2$ and their Fermat–Torricelli point P, the distance sum $L = PA + PB + PC$ and the edges $a = BC, b = CA, c = AB$ satisfy a polynomial equation $f(L, a, b, c) = 0$ of degree 12. But little is known about the geometric property of Fermat–Torricelli points, even when A, B, C are on very special positions on sphere. In this paper, we will show that for three points A, B, C on a greater circle on sphere, their Fermat–Torricelli points are either on the same greater circle or on one of four special positions (called Zeng Points) determined by A, B, C.

Keywords: Spherical triangle · Fermat–Torricelli points · Euclidean distance · Polynomial equations · Zeng points

1   Introduction

It is well known that given any three points A, B, C in the Euclidean plane, there is a unique point P (called *"Fermat-Torricelli Point"*) so that $PA + PB + PC$, the sum of the distances from P to the given points, is minimal, and if none of the three angles of the triangle ABC are greater than $2\pi/3$, then the optimal point is the isogonal point of ABC, i.e.,

$$\angle APB = \angle BPC = \angle CPA = 2\pi/3,$$

otherwise, P coincides with the obtuse vertex of ABC. Let

$$a = BC, \quad b = CA, \quad c = AB, \quad L = \min\{PA + PB + PC | P \in \mathbb{R}^2\}.$$

Then it is easy to use computer algebra software like Maple to derive a polynomial that connects L, a, b, c as follows

$$(L - b - c)(L - c - a)(L - a - b)(L^8 + k_1 L^6 + k_2 L^4 + k_3 L^2 + k_4) = 0,$$

Supported by National Natural Science Foundation of China Grant Nos. 61772203 and 12071282.

© Springer Nature Switzerland AG 2021
F. Boulier et al. (Eds.): CASC 2021, LNCS 12865, pp. 442–462, 2021.
https://doi.org/10.1007/978-3-030-85165-1_25

where

$$k_1 = -8(a + b + c)^2 + 12(ab + bc + ca),$$
$$k_2 = 16(a + b + c)^4 - 48(a + b + c)^2(ab + bc + ca)$$
$$+ 30(ab + bc + ca)^2,$$
$$k_3 = 64(a + b + c)^3 abc - 40(a + b + c)^2(ab + bc + ca)^2$$
$$+ 28(ab + bc + ca)^3,$$
$$k_4 = 9(ab + bc + ca)^4.$$

In [3], Ghalieh and Hajja studied the Fermat point of spherical triangle. They proved that for any three points A, B, C on the unit sphere S^2, the point $P \in S^2$ that minimizes $d(P, A) + d(P, B) + d(P, C)$ either lies at a vertex of ABC or else satisfies

$$\cos \sphericalangle APB = \cos \sphericalangle BPC = \cos \sphericalangle CPA = -1/2,$$

where the distance $d(X, Y)$ between two points X, Y is defined to be the length of smaller arc on the greater circle passing through the two points, and the spherical angle $\sphericalangle APB$ is defined to be the ordinary angle $\angle XPY$ where XP, YP are the tangents to the arcs AP, BP (respectively). In [4], Guo et al. investigated the Fermat–Torricelli problem of triangles on the sphere under Euclidean metric, namely, to find the optimal point P on the sphere S^2 for three given points $A, B, C \in S^2$, so that the sum of the Euclidean distances $PA + PB + PC$ from that point P to the three vertices is minimal (or maximal). The results can be stated as follows. Let $A, B, C \in S^2$, $a = BC, b = CA, c = AB$, and L be the minimal or maximal of $PA + PB + PC$ over points $P \in S^2$. Then

$$(L - b - c)(L - c - a)(L - a - b)$$
$$\cdot(L^{12} + K_1 L^{10} + K_2 L^8 + K_3 L^6 + K_4 L^4 + K_5 L^2 + K_6) = 0,$$

where $K_1, K_2, \ldots, K_6$ are polynomials of a, b, c. Little is known about geometric properties of Fermat–Torricelli points due to the complexity of symbolic computation involved in this problem, except the following two facts:

- The Fermat–Torricelli point D such that $DA + DB + DC$ is minimal lies in the smaller one of the two spherical caps intersected by S^2 and the plane passing through A, B, C, including the circle determined by A, B, C, and the Fermat–Torricelli point E such that $EA + EB + EC$ is maximal lies in the larger spherical cap, including the circle determined by A, B, C.
- If one of the three angles $\angle CAB, \angle ABC, \angle BCA$ is larger than or equal to $2\pi/3$, then the minimal Fermat–Torricelli point of ABC coincides with one of vertices of ABC.

Curiously to see more geometric properties of the minimal and maximal Fermat–Torricelli points (denoted by D, E hereafter), say, are D, E uniquely determined by A, B, C? when do D, E lie at the circle determined by A, B, C? and what is special about D, E, we have done the following numerical experiments:

(1): Construct Small Squares and Small Cubes to Cover Sphere. Construct a set S_1 that contains small squares of edge length $1/64$ in form

$$[0,0] \times \left[-1 + \frac{m}{64}, -1 + \frac{m+1}{64}\right] \times \left[-1 + \frac{n}{64}, -1 + \frac{n+1}{64}\right]$$

$$(0 \le m \le 63,\ 0 \le n \le 127)$$

to cover the prime meridian $\{(x, y, z) | x = 0, y^2 + z^2 = 1, 0 \le y \le 1, -1 \le z \le 1\}$; construct a set S_2 of squares in form

$$\left[-1 + \frac{k}{64}, -1 + \frac{k+1}{64}\right] \times \left[-1 + \frac{m}{64}, -1 + \frac{m+1}{64}\right] \times [0,0]$$

$$(0 \le k, m \le 127)$$

to cover the whole equator $\{(x, y, z) | x^2 + z^2 = 1, z = 0\}$; construct a set S_3 that contains small cubes of edge length $1/64$ in form

$$\left[\frac{k}{64}, \frac{k+1}{64}\right] \times \left[-1 + \frac{m}{64}, -1 + \frac{m+1}{64}\right] \times \left[-1 + \frac{n}{64}, -1 + \frac{n+1}{64}\right],$$

$$(0 \le k \le 63,\ 0 \le m, n \le 127)$$

to cover the eastern part of the unit sphere

$$\{(x, y, z) | x^2 + y^2 + z^2 = 1, 0 \le x, z \le 1\},$$

and construct a set S_4 of such small cubes that cover the whole sphere. It is verified that S_1 and S_2 contain 254 and 508 small squares, respectively, and S_3 and S_4 contain $38,548$ and $77,096$ small cubes, respectively. It is clear that the intersection of each small square with the unit sphere is an arc (of a greater circle), and the intersection of each cube with the sphere is a curved quadrilateral. Under the stereographic projection, they are mapped to straight line sections (or circular arcs) and curved quadrilaterals on the Euclidean plane. Since rational points are dense in $\mathbb{R}^2$, we are able to take as many as required (here, we take $N = 100$) random rational points in each small line-segment (or circular arc) and curved quadrilateral in the plane. We mapped the selected rational points in $\mathbb{R}^2$ to the squares in S_1, S_2 and cubes in S_3, S_4. Then we have obtained $254 \times N = 25,400$ and $508 \times N = 50,800$ rational points on the prime meridian and the equator, respectively, and $3,854,800$ and $7,709,600$ rational points on the eastern sphere and the whole sphere. Let $r(S_i)$ denote the set of all obtained rational points in S_i ($i = 1, 2, 3, 4$), and $r(X)$ denote the set of rational points in a small square or cube $X \in S_i$ ($i = 1, 2, 3, 4$).

(2): Generate Big Data. Taking $A = (0, 0, 1)$, North Pole of the unit sphere, and for each combination (U, V) where $U \in S_1$, $V \in S_3$, taking randomly a rational point $B \in r(U)$ and a rational point $C \in r(V)$. Then searching rational points D, E from the previously constructed for cubes in S_4, so that

$$D = \arg\min\{XA + XB + XC, X \in r(S_4)\},$$

and
$$E = \arg\min\{YA + YB + YC, Y \in r(S_4)\}.$$

Doing this computation for all $U \in S_1, V \in S_3$ we get a big data set DataSet5 of 5-tuples (A, B, C, D, E), which satisfy that for spherical triangle $A, B, C \in S^2$, D, E, there are the "*approximate*" minimal and maximal Fermat–Torricelli point ABC. It is clear that this data set has $254 \times 38,548 = 9,791,192$ records, and we can generate a new data set by repeating the above computation.

Another big data set DataSet4 can be generated as follows. Taking $A = (-1, 0, 0) \in S^2$, U, V ($U \neq V$) are chosen arbitrarily from set S_2 and rational points B, C randomly from $r(U), r(V)$. Let P be the rational point selected from $r(S_4)$ so that $PA + PB + PC$ is maximal. Doing this computation for all combination $U, V \in S_2$, we obtain a data set of (A, B, C, P) such that for any 4-tuple (A, B, C, P), P is the maximal Fermat–Torricelli point of ABC approximately. It is clear that DataSet4 has $128,271$ records, and the data set can be generated again if required.

(3): Discover Hidden Knowledge Using Statistical Methods. With each item (A, B, C, D, E) in DataSet5, we associate an 11-tuple of rational numbers as follows:

$$\phi : (A, B, C, D, E) \mapsto (a^2, b^2, c^2, d^2, r^2, u^2, v^2, w^2, x^2, y^2, z^2),$$

where $a = BC, b = CA, c = AB, d = DE$, r is the circumradius of ABC, and

$$u = DA, v = DB, w = DC, \quad x = EA, y = EB, z = EC.$$

This transformation maps the DataSet5 into a point set in space $\mathbb{R}^{11}$. Then we apply regression and other statistical methods to find possible connections between the 11 variables. Since our purpose in this paper is mainly to discuss the symbolic algebra computation approach, we will not explain the detail of the statistical methods here. The two things we discovered by analyzing ϕ(DataSet5) that it can be described as follows:

Empirical Formula 1. *Let $A, B, C \in S^2$ and D, E be the minimal and maximal Fermat–Torricelli points of ABC, respectively. If $\angle CAB, \angle ABC$, and $\angle BCA$ are not larger than $2\pi/3$, then $DE \approx 2$.*

Empirical Formula 2. *Let $A, B, C \in S^2$ and D, E be the minimal and maximal Fermat–Torricelli points of ABC, respectively. Then*

$$DA : DB : DC \approx EA : EB : EC.$$

The empirical formulae are obtained by regression on the data set ϕ(DataSet5a), where DataSet5a is the set of (A, B, C, D, E) in DataSet5 that satisfies $\angle CAB$, $\angle ABC$, $\angle BCA$ are not larger than $2\pi/3$. For DataSet4, we used the numerical results to find what is the condition for the maximal Fermat–Torricelli point of three points on the equator to lie also at the equator. Recall that an item $(A, B, C, P) \in$ DataSet4 records a triangle ABC where $A = (0, -1, 0)$, B, C are on the equator, and P is their maximal Fermat–Torricelli point. Construct a map

$$\gamma : \mathtt{DataSet4} \to [0,2] \times [0,2] \times \{\text{dark blue, light red}\}$$

by

$$(A,B,C,P) \mapsto (AB, AC, t), \ t = \begin{cases} \text{dark blue} & \text{if } P \text{ lies at the equator,} \\ \text{light red} & \text{otherwise.} \end{cases}$$

The obtained new data set $\gamma(\mathtt{DataSet4})$ is visualized in Fig. 1.

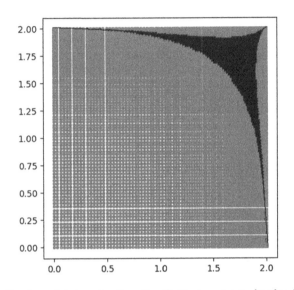

Fig. 1. A visualization of data set $\gamma(\mathtt{DataSet4})$. Each point in $[0,2] \times [0,2]$ represents a triangle on the unit sphere, where $A = (0,-1,0)$ and B, C lie at the equator, with B in the eastern hemisphere and C in the western hemisphere. If the maximal Fermat–Torricelli point P of ABC lies at the equator, the point is marked by dark blue, otherwise it is marked by light red. The horizontal coordinate is $b = AC$ and the vertical coordinate is $c = AB$. (Color figure online)

Inspired by the above numerical computation, we applied the metric equation, the Lagrange multipliers methods, and symbolic algebra computation to derive exact formula $f(a,b,c,d) = 0$ by constructing a system of polynomials

$$f_i(a,b,c,d,u,v,w,x,y,z) = 0 \ (i = 1,2,\cdots,7),$$

that reflect the facts that A, B, C, D, E are on the same unit sphere, $DA + DB + DC$ is minimal, and $EA + EB + EC$ are minimal (we will show this in this paper later), and eliminating u, v, w, x, y, z from $f_1, f_2, \cdots, f_7$. But the elimination was not completed due to the complexity of symbolic computation. For the problem corresponding to $\mathtt{DataSet4}$, by symbolic algebraic computation we proved the following result:

Theorem 1. *Assume that $S^1 \subset S^2$ is the equator of the unit sphere S^2, and $A, B, C \in S^1$, $P \in S^2$ is the point such that $PA + PB + PC$ is maximal. Then either P is on the equator S^1, or P lies in the interior of $S^2 \setminus S^1$ and satisfies*

$$PA^2 : PB^2 : PC^2 = \frac{1}{a^2(4 - a^2)} : \frac{1}{b^2(4 - b^2)} : \frac{1}{c^2(4 - c^2)}, \tag{1}$$

where $a = BC, b = CA, c = AB$.

The problem of finding a polynomial discriminant $G(a, b, c)$ to determine when the maximal Fermat–Torricelli point P of a given equatorial triangle ABC with $a = BC, b = CA, c = AB$ lies at the equator leads to a quantifier elimination problem as follows

$$(L_2 \geq L_1) \, L_2 = x + y + z \wedge L_1 = x' + y' + z'$$
$$\wedge g_1(x, a, b, c) = 0 \wedge g_2(y, a, b, c) = 0 \wedge g_3(z, a, b, z) = 0$$
$$\wedge h_1(x', a, b, c) = 0 \wedge h_2(y', a, b, c) = 0 \wedge h_3(z', a, b, z) = 0,$$

here g_i, h_i are polynomials of degree 4. Again the symbolic computation involved for elimination in this problem is too complicated so we were not able to get the discriminant polynomial.

In this paper, we will present a proof to Theorem 1. The paper is organized as follows: in Sect. 2 we apply metric equations and the Lagrange multiplier method to derive the algebraic representation of the Fermat–Torricelli point, in Sect. 3, we use the Sylvester resultant to do elimination and prove Theorem 1, in Sect. 4, we very briefly discuss the case of maximal-Torricelli point in the equator and present a conjecture related to the condition for the maximal Fermat–Torricelli points of an equatorial triangle lying on the equator.

2 Algebraic Equations Derived for the Fermat–Torricelli Points

Let A, B, C, P be four arbitrary points on the unit sphere. Let $a = BC, b = CA, c = AB$ and $x = PA, y = PB, z = PC$. Then a, b, c, x, y, z satisfy the following polynomial equation written in determinant form:

$$f_{-1} := \begin{vmatrix} 0 & 1 & 1 & 1 & 1 & 1 \\ 1 & 0 & c^2 & b^2 & x^2 & 1 \\ 1 & c^2 & 0 & a^2 & y^2 & 1 \\ 1 & b^2 & a^2 & 0 & z^2 & 1 \\ 1 & x^2 & y^2 & z^2 & 0 & 1 \\ 1 & 1 & 1 & 1 & 1 & 0 \end{vmatrix} = 0. \tag{2}$$

This equation actually reflects the fact that the points A, B, C, P together with the center of the unit sphere O, form a simplex in $\mathbb{R}^4$ of volume 0, as they are embedded in $\mathbb{R}^3$ indeed. The expanded form of f_{-1} has 28 monomials and needs 5 lines to print, so we just show its matrix form by (2). According to Blumenthal's [1] (Lemma 42. 1) and the compactness of the sphere, it is known that if three real numbers x, y, z satisfy equation (2), then there exists a point P on the unit sphere such that $PA = x, PB = y, PC = z$ (Fig. 2).

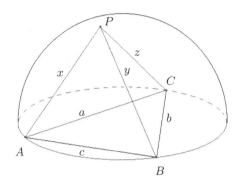

Fig. 2. Points A, B, C lie at the equator of the unit sphere and point P on the hemisphere

Similarly, the assumption that A, B, C are on the equator S^1 can also be written into a polynomial as follows:

$$f_0 := \begin{vmatrix} 0 & 1 & 1 & 1 & 1 \\ 1 & 0 & c^2 & b^2 & 1 \\ 1 & c^2 & 0 & a^2 & 1 \\ 1 & b^2 & a^2 & 0 & 1 \\ 1 & 1 & 1 & 1 & 0 \end{vmatrix}$$
$$= -2a^2b^2c^2 - 2a^4 + 4b^2a^2 + 4c^2a^2 - 2b^4 + 4b^2c^2 - 2c^4 = 0. \quad (3)$$

Computing $\texttt{resultant}(f_{-1}, f_0, a)$ we get a polynomial of b, c, x, y, z as follows:

$$\begin{aligned} f_{1a} = {} & b^4c^2x^2y^2 - b^2c^4x^2z^2 - 2b^4c^2x^2 - 2b^4c^2y^2 + b^4x^4 - 2b^4x^2y^2 \\ & + b^4y^4 + 2b^2c^4x^2 + 2b^2c^4z^2 - 4b^2c^2x^2y^2 + 4b^2c^2x^2z^2 - c^4x^4 \\ & + 2c^4z^2x^2 - c^4z^4 + 4b^4c^2 - 4b^2c^4 + 8b^2c^2y^2 - 8b^2c^2z^2 \\ & - 4b^2x^4 + 8b^2x^2y^2 - 4b^2y^4 + 4c^2x^4 - 8c^2x^2z^2 + 4c^2z^4 = 0. \quad (4) \end{aligned}$$

Therefore, the geometric optimal problem we are discussing, namely, to find a point $P \in S^2$ so that $PA + PB + PC$ is maximal, can be written as

$$\max \quad L = x + y + z, \quad (5)$$
$$\text{s.t.} \quad f_{1a}(b, c, x, y, z) = 0, \quad P \in S_{\geq 0}^2.$$

Here $S_{\geq 0}^2$ denotes the northern hemisphere, i.e., the section of the unit sphere that is north of the equator. According to Lagrange multiplier method, if the optimal point of this problem lies at the interior of the hemisphere, then x, y, z satisfy also the following polynomial equations:

$$f_{2a} := \frac{\partial}{\partial x}(x + y + z + k \cdot f_{1a}(b, c, x, y, z)) = 1 + k\frac{\partial f_{1a}}{\partial x} = 0,$$

$$f_{3a} := \frac{\partial}{\partial y}(x + y + z + k \cdot f_{1a}(b, c, x, y, z)) = 1 + k\frac{\partial f_{1a}}{\partial y} = 0,$$

$$f_{4a} := \frac{\partial}{\partial x}(x + y + z + k \cdot f_{1a}(b, c, x, y, z)) = 1 + k\frac{\partial f_{1a}}{\partial z} = 0.$$

Let

$$f_{5a} := \mathtt{primpart}\left(\frac{\partial f_{1a}}{\partial x} - \frac{\partial f_{1a}}{\partial z}\right), \quad f_{6a} := \mathtt{primpart}\left(\frac{\partial f_{1a}}{\partial y} - \frac{\partial f_{1a}}{\partial z}\right). \quad (6)$$

Then

$$\begin{aligned}
f_{5a} = {}& b^4c^2xy^2 + b^2c^4x^2z - b^2c^4xz^2 - 2b^4c^2x + 2b^4x^3 - 2b^4xy^2 \\
& + 2b^2c^4x - 2b^2c^4z - 4b^2c^2x^2z - 4b^2c^2xy^2 + 4b^2c^2xz^2 \\
& - 2c^4x^3 - 2c^4x^2z + 2c^4xz^2 + 2c^4z^3 + 8b^2c^2z - 8b^2x^3 \\
& + 8y^2xb^2 + 8c^2x^3 + 8c^2x^2z - 8c^2z^2x - 8c^2z^3, \quad (7)
\end{aligned}$$

$$\begin{aligned}
f_{6a} = {}& b^4c^2x^2y + b^2c^4x^2z - 2b^4c^2y - 2b^4x^2y + 2b^4y^3 - 2b^2c^4z \\
& - 4b^2c^2x^2y - 4b^2c^2x^2z - 2c^4x^2z + 2c^4z^3 + 8b^2c^2y \\
& + 8b^2c^2z + 8b^2x^2y - 8b^2y^3 + 8c^2x^2z - 8c^2z^3. \quad (8)
\end{aligned}$$

Therefore, if the optimal solution point P of problem (5) lies at the interior of the hemisphere $S^2_{\geq 0}$, then x, y, z satisfy polynomial equations (4), (7), and (8). We can also eliminate b from polynomial equations $f_{-1}(a, b, c, x, y, z) = 0$, $f_0(a, b, c) = 0$ defined in (2), (3), then construct a polynomial equation system

$$f_{1b}(c, a, x, y, z) = 0, \quad f_{5b}(c, a, x, y, z) = 0, \quad f_{6b}(c, a, x, y, z) = 0, \quad (9)$$

or eliminate c from (2), (3) and construct polynomial equations

$$f_{1c}(c, a, x, y, z) = 0, \quad f_{5c}(c, a, x, y, z) = 0, \quad f_{6c}(c, a, x, y, z) = 0. \quad (10)$$

Clearly, we have the following proposition:

Proposition 1. *Let $A, B, C \in S^2$ be three distinct points lying at the equator of the unit sphere with $a = BC, b = CA, c = AB$, and $P \in S^2_{\geq 0}$ be the point such that $PA + PB + PC$ is maximal. If P does not lie at the equator, then $x = PA, y = PB, z = PC$ satisfy simultaneously the equations*

$$f_{1a} = 0, f_{5a} = 0, f_{6a} = 0, \quad f_{1b} = 0, f_{5b} = 0, f_{6b} = 0, \quad f_{1c} = 0, f_{5c} = 0, f_{6c} = 0$$

defined by (6), (9), and (10).

Using the Sylvester resultant we can eliminate the variable z (or y, or x) from f_{1a}, f_{5a}, f_{6a} as follows:

$$f_{7az} := \texttt{factor}(\texttt{resultant}(f_{1a}, f_{5a}, z))$$
$$= H_{7az}(b, c) \cdot (G_{az}(c, x, y))^4 \cdot F_{7az}(b, c, x, y), \qquad (11)$$
$$f_{8az} := \texttt{factor}(\texttt{resultant}(f_{1a}, f_{6a}, z))$$
$$= H_{8az}(b, c) \cdot (G_{az}(c, x, y))^4 \cdot F_{8az}(b, c, x, y), \qquad (12)$$

here

$$H_{7az}(b, c) = -b^6 c^6 (c - 2)^3 (c + 2)^3 (b - 2)^2 (b + 2)^2, (b^2 - c^2)$$
$$H_{8az}(b, c) = -b^4 c^6 (c - 2)^3 (c + 2)^3 (b - 2)^2 (b + 2)^2 (b^2 - c^2),$$
$$G_{az}(c, x, y) = c^2 x^2 - 2 c^2 - 2 x^2 + 2 y^2,$$

F_{7az} and F_{8az} are irreducible polynomials with 42 and 22 terms, respectively, and

$$\texttt{degree}(F_{7az}, x, y) = 4, \quad \texttt{degree}(F_{7az}, x, y) = 4.$$

Eliminating y from f_{1a}, f_{5a}, f_{6a}, we have

$$f_{7ay} := \texttt{factor}(\texttt{resultant}(f_{1a}, f_{5a}, y)$$
$$= H_{7ay} \cdot G_{ay}^4 \cdot F_{7ay}(b, c, x, z) \qquad (13)$$
$$f_{8ay} := \texttt{factor}(\texttt{resultant}(f_{1a}, f_{5a}, y)$$
$$= H_{8ay} \cdot G_{ay}^4 \cdot F_{8ay}(b, c, x, z), \qquad (14)$$

here

$$H_{7ay} = b^4 c^4 (c - 2)^2 (c + 2)^2 (b - 2)^2 (b + 2)^2,$$
$$H_{8ay} = -b^6 c^4 (c - 2)^2 (c + 2)^2 (b - 2)^3 (b + 2)^3 (b^2 - c^2),$$
$$G_{ay} = b^2 x^2 - 2 b^2 - 2 x^2 + 2 z^2,$$
$$F_{7ay} = \left(b^2 c^4 x z + b^4 x^2 - 4 b^2 c^2 x z - c^4 x^2 - 2 c^4 z x \right.$$
$$\left. - c^4 z^2 - 4 b^2 x^2 + 4 c^2 x^2 + 8 c^2 z x + 4 c^2 z^2 \right)^2$$

and F_{8ay} are irreducible polynomials of degree 4 (taking x, z as variables), with 22 monomials. Eliminating x from f_{1a}, f_{5a}, f_{6a}, we obtain

$$f_{7ax} := \texttt{factor}(\texttt{resultant}(f_{1a}, f_{5a}, y)$$
$$= H_{7ax} \cdot G_{ax}^4 \cdot F_{7ax}(b, c, y, z), \qquad (15)$$
$$f_{8ax} := \texttt{factor}(\texttt{resultant}(f_{1a}, f_{5a}, y)$$
$$= H_{8ax} \cdot G_{ax}^4 \cdot F_{8ax}(b, c, y, z), \qquad (16)$$

here

$$H_{7ax} = -b^6 c^4 (c - 2)^2 (c + 2)^2 (b - 2)^2$$
$$\cdot (b + 2)^2 (b^2 + c^2 - 4) (b - c) (b + c),$$
$$H_{8ax} = b^4 c^4 (c - 2)^2 (c + 2)^2 (b - 2)^2 (b + 2)^2,$$
$$G_{ax} = b^2 y^2 - c^2 z^2 - 2 b^2 + 2 c^2 - 2 y^2 + 2 z^2,$$

F_{7ax} is an irreducible polynomial of degree 4, with 42 monomials, and

$$F_{8ax} = \left(b^4 y^2 - c^4 z^2 - 4\, b^2 y^2 + 4\, c^2 z^2\right)^2$$

Doing the above resultant elimination for systems (f_{1b}, f_{5b}, f_{6b}), we get the following results:

$$f_{7bz} := \mathtt{factor}(\mathtt{resultant}(f_{1b}, f_{5b}, z)) = H_{7bz} G_{bz}^4 F_{7bz}, \tag{17}$$

$$f_{8bz} := \mathtt{factor}(\mathtt{resultant}(f_{1b}, f_{6b}, z)) = H_{8bz} G_{bz}^4 F_{8bz}, \tag{18}$$

$$f_{7by} := \mathtt{factor}(\mathtt{resultant}(f_{1b}, f_{5b}, y)) = H_{7by} G_{by}^4 F_{7by}, \tag{19}$$

$$f_{8by} := \mathtt{factor}(\mathtt{resultant}(f_{1b}, f_{6b}, y)) = H_{8by} G_{by}^4 F_{8by}, \tag{20}$$

$$f_{7bx} := \mathtt{factor}(\mathtt{resultant}(f_{1b}, f_{5b}, x)) = H_{7bx} G_{bx}^4 F_{7bx}, \tag{21}$$

$$f_{8bx} := \mathtt{factor}(\mathtt{resultant}(f_{1b}, f_{6b}, x)) = H_{8bx} G_{bx}^4 F_{8bx}, \tag{22}$$

where $H_{7bz}, \cdots, H_{8bx}$ are polynomials of c, a, $F_{7bz}, \cdots, F_{8bx}$ are trivariate polynomials in x, y, z of degree 4, with coefficients in $\mathbb{Z}(a, c)$, and

$$G_{bz} = c^2 y^2 - 2\, c^2 + 2\, x^2 - 2\, y^2,$$
$$G_{by} = a^2 x^2 - c^2 z^2 - 2\, a^2 + 2\, c^2 - 2\, x^2 + 2\, z^2,$$
$$G_{bx} = a^2 y^2 - 2\, a^2 - 2\, y^2 + 2\, z^2.$$

Doing this for equation system (f_{1c}, f_{5c}, f_{6c}) we have the following results:

$$f_{7cz} := \mathtt{factor}(\mathtt{resultant}(f_{1c}, f_{5c}, z)) = H_{7cz} G_{cz}^4 F_{7cz}, \tag{23}$$

$$f_{8cz} := \mathtt{factor}(\mathtt{resultant}(f_{1c}, f_{6c}, z)) = H_{8cz} G_{cz}^4 F_{8cz}, \tag{24}$$

$$f_{7cy} := \mathtt{factor}(\mathtt{resultant}(f_{1c}, f_{5c}, y)) = H_{7cy} G_{cy}^4 F_{7cy}, \tag{25}$$

$$f_{8cy} := \mathtt{factor}(\mathtt{resultant}(f_{1c}, f_{6c}, y)) = H_{8cy} G_{cy}^4 F_{8cy}, \tag{26}$$

$$f_{7cx} := \mathtt{factor}(\mathtt{resultant}(f_{1c}, f_{5c}, x)) = H_{7cx} G_{cx}^4 F_{7cx}, \tag{27}$$

$$f_{8cx} := \mathtt{factor}(\mathtt{resultant}(f_{1c}, f_{6c}, x)) = H_{8cx} G_{cx}^4 F_{8cx}, \tag{28}$$

where $H_{7cz}, \cdots, H_{8cx}$ are the polynomials of a, b, $F_{7cz}, \cdots, F_{8cx}$ are trivariate polynomials of x, y, z of degree 4, with coefficients in $\mathbb{Z}(a, b)$, and

$$G_{cz} = a^2 x^2 - b^2 y^2 - 2\, a^2 + 2\, b^2 - 2\, x^2 + 2\, y^2,$$
$$G_{cy} = b^2 z^2 - 2\, b^2 + 2\, x^2 - 2\, z^2,$$
$$G_{cx} = a^2 z^2 - 2\, a^2 + 2\, y^2 - 2\, z^2.$$

For saving space we did not print polynomials H_{index}, F_{index} in this paper, as they are well defined by (11) to (28). Let

$$H_1(a, b, c) := (a - 2)(b - 2)(c - 2)(a - b)(b - c)(c - a)$$
$$\cdot (a^2 + b^2 - 4)(b^2 + c^2 - 4)(c^2 + a^2 - 4). \tag{29}$$

Then one can easily observe that

$$H_1(a, b, c) \neq 0 \implies H_{ijk} \neq 0$$

for all $i = 7, 8; j \in \{a, b, c\}$, and $k \in \{x, y, z\}$ when A, B, C are distinct points on the equator of the unit sphere. This immediately leads to the following proposition:

Proposition 2. *Let A, B, C be three points on the equator and P the point on the interior of the hemisphere $S^2_{\geq 0}$ such that $PA + PB + PC$ is maximal. Let $a = BC, b = CA, c = AB, x = \overline{PA}, y = PB, z = PC$, and $H_1(a, b, c)$ be defined by (29). Assume that $H_1(a, b, c) \neq 0$. Then a, b, c, x, y, z satisfy the following equations simultaneously:*

$$G_{az}F_{7az} = 0, \quad G_{az}F_{8az} = 0,$$
$$G_{ay}F_{7ay} = 0, \quad G_{ay}F_{8ay} = 0,$$
$$G_{ax}F_{7ax} = 0, \quad G_{ax}F_{8ax} = 0,$$
$$G_{bz}F_{7bz} = 0, \quad G_{bz}F_{8bz} = 0,$$
$$G_{by}F_{7by} = 0, \quad G_{by}F_{8by} = 0,$$
$$G_{bx}F_{7bx} = 0, \quad G_{bx}F_{8ax} = 0,$$
$$G_{cz}F_{7cz} = 0, \quad G_{cz}F_{8cz} = 0,$$
$$G_{cy}F_{7cy} = 0, \quad G_{cy}F_{8cy} = 0,$$
$$G_{cx}F_{7cx} = 0, \quad G_{cx}F_{8cx} = 0.$$

3   Solving Polynomial Equations with Parametric Coefficients Under Non-degenerate Conditions

In this section, we find solutions of the equation system formed by the 9 polynomials listed in Proposition 1 and the 18 polynomials listed in Proposition 2. For this we first analyze the sub-system

$$\mathrm{GS} := \left\{ \begin{array}{lll} G_{az} = 0, & G_{ay} = 0, & G_{ax} = 0, \\ G_{bz} = 0, & G_{by} = 0, & G_{bx} = 0, \\ G_{cz} = 0, & G_{cy} = 0, & G_{cx} = 0 \end{array} \right\}.$$

Recall that

$$G_{az} = c^2 x^2 - 2c^2 - 2x^2 + 2y^2,$$
$$G_{ay} = b^2 x^2 - 2b^2 - 2x^2 + 2z^2,$$
$$G_{az} = b^2 y^2 - c^2 z^2 - 2b^2 + 2c^2 - 2y^2 + 2z^2,$$

it is clear that we can regard $\mathrm{GS}_a := \{G_{az}, G_{ay}, G_{az}\}$ as a linear equation system of variables x^2, y^2, z^2 with parametric coefficients:

$$\begin{bmatrix} c^2 - 2 & 2 & 0 \\ b^2 - 2 & 0 & 2 \\ 0 & b^2 - 2 & -c^2 + 2 \end{bmatrix} \begin{bmatrix} x^2 \\ y^2 \\ z^2 \end{bmatrix} = \begin{bmatrix} -2c^2 \\ -2b^2 \\ -2b^2 + 2c^2 \end{bmatrix}. \tag{30}$$

Observing that the determinant of the coefficient matrix of (30) is 0, we checked the linear dependence of G_{az}, G_{ay}, G_{ax} and found that

$$(b^2 - 2)G_{az} - (c^2 - 2)G_{ay} - 2G_{ax} = 0,$$

and similarly,

$$(a^2 - 2)G_{bz} - 2G_{by} - (c^2 - 2)G_{bx} = 0,$$
$$-2G_{cz} + (a^2 - 2)G_{cy} - (b^2 - 2)G_{cx} = 0.$$

Therefore, if x, y, z satisfy any two equations in GS_a, then they also satisfy the third equation in that system, and this statement is also true for equation system $GS_b := \{G_{bz}, G_{by}, G_{bz}\}$:

$$\begin{bmatrix} 2 & c^2 - 2 & 0 \\ a^2 - 2 & 0 & -c^2 + 2 \\ 0 & a^2 - 2 & 2 \end{bmatrix} \begin{bmatrix} x^2 \\ y^2 \\ z^2 \end{bmatrix} = \begin{bmatrix} -2\,c^2 \\ -2\,a^2 + 2\,c^2 \\ -2\,a^2 \end{bmatrix}, \tag{31}$$

and $GS_c := \{G_{cz}, G_{cy}, G_{cz}\}$:

$$\begin{bmatrix} a^2 - 2 & -b^2 + 2 & 0 \\ 2 & 0 & b^2 - 2 \\ 0 & 2 & a^2 - 2 \end{bmatrix} \begin{bmatrix} x^2 \\ y^2 \\ z^2 \end{bmatrix} = \begin{bmatrix} -2\,a^2 + 2\,b^2 \\ -2\,b^2 \\ -2\,a^2 \end{bmatrix}. \tag{32}$$

Furthermore, assume that x, y, z satisfy (30), then

$$y^2 = -\frac{1}{2}c^2 x^2 + c^2 + x^2, \quad z^2 = -\frac{1}{2}b^2 x^2 + b^2 + x^2. \tag{33}$$

Substituting them into (31), (32), we obtained

$$G_{bz} = -\frac{1}{2}c^2 \left(x^2 - 2\right)(c - 2)(c + 2),$$

$$G_{by} = \frac{1}{2}\left(x^2 - 2\right)\left(b^2 c^2 + 2\,a^2 - 2\,b^2 - 2\,c^2\right),$$

$$G_{bx} = -\frac{1}{2}\left(x^2 - 2\right)\left(c^2 a^2 - 2\,a^2 + 2\,b^2 - 2\,c^2\right),$$

and

$$G_{cz} = \left(x^2 - 2\right)\left(b^2 c^2 + 2\,a^2 - 2\,b^2 - 2\,c^2\right),$$
$$G_{cy} = -b^2 \left(x^2 - 2\right)(b - 2)(b + 2),$$
$$G_{cx} = -\left(x^2 - 2\right)\left(b^2 a^2 - 2\,a^2 - 2\,b^2 + 2\,c^2\right),$$

respectively. Notice that $x^2 = 2$ and (33) imply that $y^2 = 2, z^2 = 2$. Therefore, if a, b, c satisfy

$$(b - 2)(c - 2)\left(b^2 c^2 + 2\,a^2 - 2\,b^2 - 2\,c^2\right)$$
$$\cdot \left(b^2 a^2 - 2\,a^2 - 2\,b^2 + 2\,c^2\right)\left(c^2 a^2 - 2\,a^2 + 2\,b^2 - 2\,c^2\right) \neq 0,$$

and x, y, z satisfy GS_a and $(x, y, z) \neq (\sqrt{2}, \sqrt{2}, \sqrt{2})$, then all polynomials in GS_b and GS_c are not zero. A similar result is valid for x, y, z that satisfy GS_b and GS_c, since under the following permutation:

$$a \to b \to c \to a, \; x \to y \to z \to x,$$

we have

$$GS_a \longrightarrow GS_b \longrightarrow GS_b \longrightarrow GS_a.$$

Note also that if a, b, c are the lengths of edges of an equatorial triangle ABC, then $f_0 = 0$, where f_0 is defined in (3), then

$$2f_0 - \left((-b^2 + 2) a^2 + 2 b^2 - 2 c^2\right) \left(b^2 a^2 - 2 a^2 - 2 b^2 + 2 c^2\right)$$
$$= b^2 a^2 (b - 2) (b + 2) (a - 2) (a + 2),$$

which means that

$$f_0 = 0 \wedge \left(b^2 a^2 - 2 a^2 - 2 b^2 + 2 c^2 = 0\right) \implies (a - 2)(b - 2) = 0.$$

The above discussion on the solutions of GS_a, GS_b and GS_c can be summarized to the following lemma.

Lemma 1. *Let $N(S)$ be the number of nonzero numbers of a finite set of real numbers. Then, for a, b, c, x, y, z that satisfy $(a - 2)(b - 2)(c - 2) \neq 0$ and $(x, y, z) \neq (\sqrt{2}, \sqrt{2}, \sqrt{3})$, at least two of $GS_a(x, y, z)$, $GS_b(x, y, z)$, $GS_c(x, y, z)$ satisfy $N(S) \geq 2$.* □

In the next lemma, we prove that if $N(GS_j(x, y, z)) = 2$, that is exactly two of $G_{jz}(x, y, z), G_{jy}(x, y, z), G_{jx}(x, y, z)$ are nonzero, then a, b, c must satisfy some extra condition. Here we use j to represent any member of $\{a, b, c\}$.

Lemma 2. *Assume that $j \in \{a, b, c\}$ and x, y, z satisfy the equations listed in Proposition 2, one of $G_{jz}(x, y, z), G_{jy}(x, y, z), G_{jx}(x, y, z)$ equals zero and the other two are nonzero, then a, b, c satisfy*

$$H_1(a, b, c) = (a - 2)(b - 2)(c - 2)(a - b)(b - c)(c - a) = 0.$$
$$\cdot (b^2 + c^2 - 4)(c^2 + a^2 - 4)(a^2 + b^2 - 4) = 0. \tag{34}$$

Proof. According to the symmetry we may assume that $j = a$. We need to consider the following three cases:

1. $G_{az}(x, y, z) = 0, G_{ay}(x, y, z) \neq 0, G_{ax}(x, y, z) \neq 0$;
2. $G_{az}(x, y, z) \neq 0, G_{ay}(x, y, z) = 0, G_{ax}(x, y, z) \neq 0$;
3. $G_{az}(x, y, z) \neq 0, G_{ay}(x, y, z) \neq 0, G_{ax}(x, y, z) = 0$.

In Case 1, we consider the following equation system

$$G_{az} = 0, \quad F_{7ay} = 0, \quad F_{8ay} = 0, \quad F_{7ax} = 0, \quad F_{8ax} = 0.$$

Notice that

$$G_{az} = c^2x^2 - 2c^2 - 2x^2 + 2y^2, F_{8ax} = \left(b^4y^2 - c^4z^2 - 4b^2y^2 + 4c^2z^2\right)^2,$$

we use F_{8ax} to eliminate variable z from $F_{7ay}, F_{8ay}, F_{7ax}$, and then use G_{az} to eliminate y from the obtained polynomials as follows:

$$p_1 := \texttt{factor(resultant}(F_{7ay}, F_{8ax}, z),$$
$$p_2 := \texttt{factor(resultant}(F_{8ay}, F_{8ax}, x),$$
$$p_2 := \texttt{factor(resultant}(F_{7ax}, F_{8ax}, x),$$
$$q_1 := \texttt{factor(resultant}(p_1, G_{az}, y),$$
$$q_2 := \texttt{factor(resultant}(F_2, G_{az}, y),$$
$$q_3 := \texttt{factor(resultant}(F_3, G_{az}, y),$$
$$r_1 := \texttt{factor(resultant}(p_1, p_2, x),$$
$$r_2 := \texttt{factor(resultant}(p_2, p_3, x),$$
$$res := \texttt{primpart(gcd}(r_1, r_2)).$$

The result of the above computation is

$$res = c^{2560}b^{1024}(c^2 - 4)^{768}(b^2 - 4)^{256}(b^2 - c^2)^{256},$$

which implies that $(b-2)(c-2)(b-c) = 0$ in Case 1. A similar computation for Case 2 and Case 3 leads to $(b-2)(c-2)(b^2+c^2-4) = 0$, and the extra factors in (34) are derived by applying the same procedure to $j = b, j = c$. This proves Lemma 2. □

Lemma 1 and Lemma 2 immediately imply the following result.

Corollary 1. *If A, B, C are three points on the equator of the unit sphere, $a = BC, b = CA, c = AB$ satisfy $H_1(a, b, c) \neq 0$, where H_1 is defined by (29), and P is a point in the interior of $S_{\geq 0}^2$ such that $PA + PB + PC$ is maximal, then at least two of $GS_a(x, y, z), GS_b(x, y, z), GS_c(x, y, z)$ satisfy $N(S) = 3$.*

Now we solve the equation system under the assumption that a, b, c satisfy $H_1(a, b, c) \neq 0$. We have the following result.

Lemma 3. *If a, b, c, x, y, z satisfy equations in Proposition 2 and a, b, c satisfies*

$$H_1(a, b, c) \cdot Q(b, c) \cdot Q(c, a) \cdot Q(a, b) \neq 0,$$

where

$$Q(u, v) := -u^6v^4 - u^4v^6 + u^8 + 4u^6v^2 + 9u^4v^4 + 4u^2v^6 + v^8$$
$$-8u^6 - 20u^4v^2 - 20u^2v^4 - 8v^6 + 16u^4 + 16u^2v^2 + 16v^4 \qquad (35)$$

then

$$a\sqrt{4 - a^2}x = b\sqrt{4 - b^2}y = c\sqrt{4 - c^2}z.$$

Proof. According to Corollary 1, without loss of generality we may assume that

$$G_{az} \neq 0, G_{ay} \neq 0, G_{ax} \neq 0, \tag{36}$$

$$G_{bz} \neq 0, G_{by} \neq 0, G_{bx} \neq 0. \tag{37}$$

Firstly, from (36) we get

$$F_{7az} = 0, \ F_{8az} = 0, \quad F_{7ay} = 0, \ F_{8ay} = 0, \quad F_{7ax} = 0, \ F_{8ax} = 0.$$

Computing the following resultants

$$p_1(x) := \texttt{factor1}(\texttt{resultant}(F_{7az}, F_{8az}, y)),$$
$$p_2(y) := \texttt{factor1}(\texttt{resultant}(F_{7az}, F_{8az}, x)),$$
$$p_3(x) := \texttt{factor1}(\texttt{resultant}(F_{7bz}, F_{8bz}, z)),$$
$$p_4(z) := \texttt{factor1}(\texttt{resultant}(F_{7bz}, F_{8bz}, x)),$$
$$p_5(y) := \texttt{factor1}(\texttt{resultant}(F_{7cz}, F_{8cz}, z)),$$
$$p_6(z) := \texttt{factor1}(\texttt{resultant}(F_{7cz}, F_{8cz}, y)),$$

here by `factor1` we denote the computation that factorizes a polynomial and keeps simple factors and takes one factor for each duplicated factor, for example:

$$\texttt{factor1}(a^4 b^4 - 4\, a^4 b^2 - 4\, a^2 b^4 + 16\, b^2 a^2)$$
$$= \texttt{factor1}(a^2 b^2 (a-2)(a+2)(b-2)(b+2))$$
$$= ab(a-2)(a+2)(b-2)(b+2).$$

Then computing the following three greatest common divisors,

$$r_1(x) = \gcd(p_1(x), p_3(x)), r_2(y) = \gcd(p_2(y), p_5(y)), r_3(z) = \gcd(p_4(z), p_6(z)),$$

we obtain three polynomials that can be used to solve x, y, z from a, b, c as follows:

$$\begin{aligned}
r_1(x) = \ & 2b^8 c^6 x^2 - b^8 c^4 x^4 + 2b^6 c^8 x^2 - 2b^6 c^6 x^4 - b^4 c^8 x^4 + b^{10} x^4 - 10 b^8 c^4 x^2 \\
& + 5b^8 c^2 x^4 - 26 b^6 c^6 x^2 + 17 b^6 c^4 x^4 - 10 b^4 c^8 x^2 + 17 b^4 c^6 x^4 + 5b^2 c^8 x^4 \\
& + c^{10} x^4 + 8b^8 c^2 x^2 - 12 b^8 x^4 - 4b^6 c^6 + 88 b^6 c^4 x^2 - 44 b^6 c^2 x^4 \\
& + 88 b^4 c^6 x^2 - 76 b^4 c^4 x^4 + 8b^2 c^8 x^2 - 44 b^2 c^6 x^4 - 12 c^8 x^4 + 16 b^6 c^4 \\
& - 64 b^6 c^2 x^2 + 48 b^6 x^4 + 16 b^4 c^6 - 224 b^4 c^4 x^2 + 112 b^4 c^2 x^4 - 64 b^2 c^6 x^2 \\
& + 112 b^2 c^4 x^4 + 48 c^6 x^4 - 64 b^4 c^4 + 128 b^4 c^2 x^2 - 64 b^4 x^4 + 128 b^2 c^4 x^2 \\
& - 64 b^2 c^2 x^4 - 64 b^4 x^4,
\end{aligned}$$

$$r_2(y) = -b^8c^4y^4 + 2b^6c^8y^2 - b^6c^6y^4 + b^{10}y^4 - 2b^8c^4y^2 + 4b^8c^2y^4 - 12b^6c^6y^2$$
$$+13b^6c^4y^4 - 12b^4c^8y^2 + 8b^4c^6y^4 - 2b^2c^{10}y^2 + b^2c^8y^4 + 8b^8c^2y^2$$
$$-12b^8y^4 - 4b^6c^6 + 32b^6c^4y^2 - 36b^6c^2y^4 + 4b^4c^8 + 64b^4c^6y^2$$
$$-56b^4c^4y^4 + 4b^2c^{10} + 32b^2c^8y^2 - 24b^2c^6y^4 - 4c^{12} + 8c^{10}y^2 - 4c^8y^4$$
$$+16b^6c^4 - 64b^6c^2y^2 + 48b^6y^4 - 96b^4c^4y^2 + 96b^4c^2y^4 - 48b^2c^8$$
$$-96b^2c^6y^2 + 96b^2c^4y^4 + 32c^{10} - 64c^8y^2 + 32c^6y^4 - 64b^4c^4$$
$$+128b^4c^2y^2 - 64b^4y^4 + 128b^2c^6 - 64b^2c^2y^4 - 64c^8 + 128c^6y^2 - 64c^4y^4,$$
$$r_3(z) = -2b^8c^6z^2 + b^6c^6z^4 + b^4c^8z^4 + 2b^{10}c^2z^2 + 12b^8c^4z^2 - b^8c^2z^4 + 12b^6c^6z^2$$
$$-8b^6c^4z^4 + 2b^4c^8z^2 - 13b^4c^6z^4 - 4b^2c^8z^4 - c^{10}z^4 + 4b^{12} - 4b^{10}c^2$$
$$-8b^{10}z^2 - 4b^8c^4 - 32b^8c^2z^2 + 4b^8z^4 + 4b^6c^6 - 64b^6c^4z^2 + 24b^6c^2z^4$$
$$-32b^4c^6z^2 + 56b^4c^4z^4 - 8b^2c^8z^2 + 36b^2c^6z^4 + 12c^8z^4 - 32b^{10} + 48b^8c^2$$
$$+64b^8z^2 + 96b^6c^2z^2 - 32b^6z^4 - 16b^4c^6 + 96b^4c^4z^2 - 96b^4c^2z^4$$
$$+64b^2c^6z^2 - 96b^2c^4z^4 - 48c^6z^4 + 64b^8 - 128b^6c^2 - 128b^6z^2$$
$$+64b^4c^4 + 64b^4z^4 - 128b^2c^4z^2 + 64b^2c^2z^4 + 64c^4z^4.$$

Note that

$$\deg(r_1(x), x) = 4, \quad \deg(r_2(y), y) = 4, \quad \deg(r_3(z), z) = 4$$

and

$$r_1(-x) = r_1(x), \quad r_2(-y) = r_2(y), \quad r_3(-z) = r_3(z).$$

Therefore, we may write $r_1(x), r_2(y), r_3(z)$ in the following forms:

$$r_1(x) = \gcd(p_1(x), p_3(x)) = L_2x^4 + L_1x^2 + L_0, \tag{38}$$
$$r_2(y) = \gcd(p_2(y), p_5(y)) = M_2y^4 + M_1y^2 + M_0, \tag{39}$$
$$r_3(z) = \gcd(p_4(z), p_6(z)) = N_2z^4 + N_1z^2 + N_0, \tag{40}$$

where L_j, M_j, N_j $(j = 0, 1, 2)$ are polynomials of a, b, c. Doing the following computation:

```
M2:=factor(coeff(primpart(r2,y),y 4));
M1:=factor(coeff(primpart(r2,y),y,2));
M0:=factor(coeff(primpart(r2,y),y,0));
N2:=factor(coeff(primpart(r3,z),z 4));
N1:=factor(coeff(primpart(r3,z),z,2));
N0:=factor(coeff(primpart(r3,z),z,0));
```

we immediately see that $M_2 = \mathrm{coeff}(r_2, y, 4)$ and $N_2 = \mathrm{coeff}(r_3, z, 4)$ have a large common divisor, meanwhile, $M_1 = \mathrm{coeff}(r_2, y, 2)$ and $N_1 = \mathrm{coeff}(r_3, z, 2)$ have also a large common divisor, and the constant terms M_0, N_0 have also a large common divisor. Namely, we have

$$\begin{aligned}
\text{M2} = {}& (b-2)(b+2)\big(-b^6c^4 - b^4c^6 + b^8 + 4b^6c^2 + 9b^4c^4 + 4b^2c^6 + c^8 \\
& -8b^6 - 20b^4c^2 - 20b^2c^4 - 8c^6 + 16b^4 + 16b^2c^2 + 16c^4\big),
\end{aligned}$$

$$\begin{aligned}
\text{M1} = {}& -2c^2(c-2)(c+2)(b-2)(b+2) \\
& \cdot \big(-b^4c^4 + b^6 + 2b^4c^2 + 2b^2c^4 + c^6 - 4b^4 - 4c^4\big),
\end{aligned}$$

$$\text{M0} = -4c^4(c-2)(c+2)(b^2 + c^2 - 4)(b-c)^2(b+c)^2,$$

and

$$\begin{aligned}
\text{N2} = {}& -(c-2)(c+2)\big(-b^6c^4 - b^4c^6 + b^8 + 4b^6c^2 + 9b^4c^4 + 4b^2c^6 + c^8 \\
& -8b^6 - 20b^4c^2 - 20b^2c^4 - 8c^6 + 16b^4 + 16b^2c^2 + 16c^4\big),
\end{aligned}$$

$$\begin{aligned}
\text{N1} = {}& 2b^2(c-2)(c+2)(b-2)(b+2) \\
& \cdot \big(-b^4c^4 + b^6 + 2b^4c^2 + 2b^2c^4 + c^6 - 4b^4 - 4c^4\big),
\end{aligned}$$

$$\text{N0} = 4b^4(b-2)(b+2)(b^2 + c^2 - 4)(b-c)^2(b+c)^2.$$

So we may simplify $r_2(y), r_2(z)$ by variable substitution. Taking the following variable substitution:

$$y = \frac{ac}{\sqrt{4-b^2}} y_1, \quad z = \frac{ab}{\sqrt{4-c^2}} z_1, \tag{41}$$

we observe that

$$b^4(b-2)(b+2)r_2 + c^4(c-2)(c+2)r_3 = 0$$

can be decomposed to

$$(y_1^2 - z_1^2)\left(y_1^2 + z_1^2 + \frac{P_1(a,b,c)}{Q_1(a,b,c)}\right) = 0, \tag{42}$$

where $P_1(a,b,c), Q_1(a,b,c)$ are polynomials as follows:

$$P_1 = (c^2 - 4)(b^2 - 4)(-b^4c^4 + b^6 + 2b^4c^2 + 2b^2c^4 + c^6 - 4b^4 - 4c^4),$$

$$\begin{aligned}
Q_1 = a^2 Q(b,c) = {}& a^2\big(-b^6c^4 - b^4c^6 + b^8 + 4b^6c^2 + 9b^4c^4 + 4b^2c^6 + c^8 \\
& -8b^6 - 20b^4c^2 - 20b^2c^4 - 8c^6 + 16b^4 + 16b^2c^2 + 16c^4\big).
\end{aligned}$$

Secondly, doing the above computation for $G_{bz}, G_{by}, G_{bx} \neq 0$ and $F_{ibk} = 0$ ($i = 7, 8$, $k = x, y, z$) in the parallel procedure, we obtain the following decomposition

$$(z_1^2 - x_1^2)\left(z_1^2 + x_1^2 + \frac{P_2(a,b,c)}{Q_2(a,b,c)}\right) = 0, \tag{43}$$

where

$$z = \frac{ab}{\sqrt{4-c^2}} z_1, \quad x = \frac{bc}{\sqrt{4-a^2}} x_1, \tag{44}$$

and

$$P_2(a,b,c) = P_1(b,c,a), \quad Q_2(a,b,c) = Q_1(b,c,a).$$

Finally, from (42) and (43), the original system of equations changed to the following four systems:

$$(Eq_1)\ y_1^2 - z_1^2 = 0,\ z_1^2 - x_1^2 = 0,$$
$$(Eq_2)\ y_1^2 - z_1^2 = 0,\ z_1^2 + x_1^2 + P_2/Q_2 = 0,$$
$$(Eq_3)\ y_1^2 + z_1^2 + P_1/Q_1 = 0 = 0,\ z_1^2 - x_1^2 = 0,$$
$$(Eq_4)\ y_1^2 + z_1^2 + P_1/Q_1 = 0 = 0,\ z_1^2 + x_1^2 + P_2/Q_2 = 0,$$

here

$$x_1 = \frac{\sqrt{4-a^2}}{bc}x,\quad y_1 = \frac{\sqrt{4-b^2}}{ca}y,\quad z_1 = \frac{\sqrt{4-c^2}}{ab}z,$$

as defined by (41) and (44). Now we check that the equation system $Eq_i(i = 2, 3, 4)$ has no real solution under assumption $H_2(a, b, c) \neq 0$, while Eq_1 has two real solutions in general. This is done as follows. For $i = 2, 3, 4$, we get a solution in the following form:

$$y^2 = T(a^2, b^2, c^2)x^2 + U(a^2, b^2, c^2),$$
$$z^2 = V(a^2, b^2, c^2)x^2 + W(a^2, b^2, c^2),$$

where T, U, V, W are fractions of polynomials. Substituting these two results into $f_{-1}(a, b, c, x, y, z) = 0$ defined in (2), we get a polynomial

$$R_i(x, a, b, c) = 0$$

for each $i = 2, 3, 4$, which is also a necessary condition for $P \in S_{\geq 0}^2$ to be an interior maximal Fermat–Torricelli point. It is easy to check that unless

$$H_1(a, b, c) \cdot Q(a, b) \cdot Q(b, c) \cdot Q(c, a) = 0,$$

where $Q(\cdot, \cdot)$ is defined by (35), the system

$$R_i(x, a, b, c) = 0,\quad f_0(a, b, c) = 0,\quad r_1(x, b, c) = 0$$

has no positive solution. Therefore, in general case, the interior maximal Fermat–Torricelli point of equatorial triangle ABC satisfies $Eq_1 = 0$, i.e.,

$$a\sqrt{4-a^2}x = b\sqrt{4-b^2}y = c\sqrt{4-c^2}z. \tag{45}$$

On the other hand, unlike the cases of Eq_j $(j = 2, 3, 4)$, substituting

$$y = \frac{a\sqrt{4-a^2}}{b\sqrt{4-b^2}}x,\quad z = \frac{a\sqrt{4-a^2}}{c\sqrt{4-c^2}}x,$$

into $f_{-1}(a, b, c, x, y, z) = 0$ and eliminating a from the result by resultant with $f_0(a, b, c) = 0$, we obtain a polynomial that has $r_1(x) = r_1(x, b, c)$ (viz, the expression (38)) as its divisor. This indicates that in general case, namely, when a, b, c satisfy

$$H_1(a, b, c)Q(a, b)Q(b, c)Q(c, a) \neq 0,$$

the system Eq_1 will produce a point $P(x, y, z)$ on the hemisphere $S^2_{\geq 0}$ so that $PA + PB + PC$ is possibly local-maximal. This completes the proof of Lemma 3.

$\square$

It is obvious that Corollary 1 and Lemma 3 are sufficient to prove our main result Theorem 1. It is easy to verify that

- in general, the point on the sphere that satisfies (45) does not lie at the equator, and
- when $H_1(a, b, c) \neq 0$, there exist two points P on the hemisphere (hence, four such points on the whole unit sphere) satisfying $x = PA, y = PB, z = PC$ and (45).

To our knowledge, points associated with spherical triangles by condition (45) have not been discussed in literature. Considering their importance in Theorem 1 and the experiment formula in Empirical formula 2, we shall call them *Zeng Points* of ABC for convenience. More generally, for three distinct point A, B, C on the unit sphere (not limited on the equator) with $a = BC, b = CA, c = AB$, we call the point $P \in S^2$ with $x = PA, y = PB, z = PC$ a *Zeng Point*, if

$$a\sqrt{4r^2 - a^2}\, x = b\sqrt{4r^2 - b^2}\, y = c\sqrt{4r^2 - c^2}\, z,$$

where r is the circum-radius of ABC. It is easy to prove that for three points A, B, C that are not lying at a greater circle, there are exactly two Zeng points on the unit sphere.

4   Maximal Fermat–Torricelli Point on the Equator

In this short section, we briefly discuss the computation of the maximal Fermat–Torricelli point on the equator of the unit sphere. Assume A, B, C are points on the equator with $a = BC, b = CA, c = AB$ and P is also a point on the equator with $x = PA, y = PB, z = PC$ as shown in Fig. 3. Then we have $f_0(a, b, c) = 0$ as defined in (3). And in view of Ptolemy Theorem (cf. [2]), P lies at the circle determined by A, B, C and can be represented by

$$g_0 := (ax + by - cz) \cdot (ax - by + cz) \cdot (-ax - by - cz) = 0. \tag{46}$$

Therefore, if $x + y + z$ is maximal over $P \in S^1$, then we have

$$\frac{\partial}{\partial x}(x + y + z + k\, g_0) = 0, \frac{\partial}{\partial y}(x + y + z + k\, g_0) = 0, \frac{\partial}{\partial z}(x + y + z + k\, g_0) = 0. \tag{47}$$

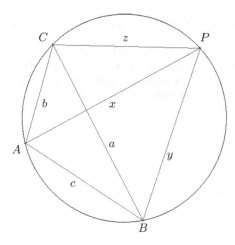

Fig. 3. A, B, C, P are points on the equator of a unit sphere

It is easy to prove that if $x + y + z$ is maximal, then $xyz \neq 0$. So the polynomial equation system formed by (46) and (47) can be decomposed into following equations:

$$Eq_5 : 1/2 \cdot ax = by = cz, \quad Eq_6 : ax = 1/2 \cdot by = cz, \quad Eq_7 : ax = by = 1/2 \cdot cz.$$

Since the circum-radius of PAB is 1, we have the following polynomial equation:

$$g_1 = -2\,c^2x^2y^2 - 2\,c^4 + 4\,c^2x^2 + 4\,c^2y^2 - 2\,x^4 + 4\,x^2y^2 - 2\,y^4 = 0,$$

Therefore, each of Eq_5, Eq_6, Eq_6 leads to a solution in the following form

$$(R_j) : res_j(x) = 0, \quad y = \rho_j \cdot a/b \cdot x, \quad z = \rho_j' \cdot a/c \cdot x,$$

where $res_j(x)$ is a polynomial of degree 4, and $\rho_j, \rho_j' \in \{1/2, 1\}$ for $j = 5, 6, 7$. It is clear that if $P(x, y, z)$ is a maximal Fermat–Torricelli point on the equator, then x, y, z satisfy one of $(R_5), (R_6), (R_7)$.

We conjecture that the equation of the curve that divides blue and red regions in Fig. 1 is one factor of $\texttt{resultant}(r_1(x), res(x), x)$, where $r_1(x)$ is defined by (38), and

$$res(x) = res_5(x) \cdot res_6(x) \cdot res_7(x).$$

References

1. Blumenthal, L.: Theory and Applications of Distance Geometry. Oxford University Press, Oxford (1953)
2. Coxeter, H.S.M., Greitzer, S.L.: Geometry Revisited. Mathematical Association of America, Washington, DC, pp. 42–43 (1967)

3. Ghalieh, K., Hajja, M.: The Fermat point of a spherical triangle. Math. Gaz. **80**(489), 561–564 (1996)
4. Guo, X., Leng, T., Zeng, Z.: The Fermat-Torricelli problem of triangles on the sphere with Euclidean metric: a symbolic solution with maple. In: Gerhard, J., Kotsireas, I. (eds.) MC 2019. CCIS, vol. 1125, pp. 263–278. Springer, Cham (2020). https:// doi.org/10.1007/978-3-030-41258-6_20

Author Index

Printed in the United States
by Baker & Taylor Publisher Services